INDIANA

GEORGE ROBERT CLARK
Miltary Leader — Revolutionary War

Encyclopedia
of the
United States

INDIANA

1976
SOMERSET PUBLISHERS
22929 INDUSTRIAL DRIVE EAST
ST. CLAIR SHORES, MICHIGAN 48080

ENCYCLOPEDIA
OF THE UNITED STATES
— consists of 55 volumes, one for each state,
a volume each for New York City, Washington
D.C., Puerto Rico and U.S. Outlying Territories,
a volume titled The Nation, plus an Index volume.

Copyright © by Somerset Publishers

LC 76-14527

ISBN 0-403-01976-1

Printed in the United States of America

PUBLISHER .... FRANK H. GILLE

MANAGING EDITOR .... INGRID EKLOV JONSSON

ART DIRECTOR .... DOUGLAS E. HOLDAWAY

ART ASSISTANT .... THOMAS GILLE

PRODUCTION SUPERVISION .... DANIEL L. LOY

TYPOGRAPHY .... ALICE LEWANDOSKI

EDITORIAL ASSISTANT .... KATHLEEN FURTAH

ADVISERS

PAMELA ANDERSON
Assistant Director
Indiana Tourism Development
Division

JOY ROTHROCK
Photo Research
Indiana Tourism Development
Division

JAMES GUTHRIE
Former Director
Indiana Bicentennial Commission

JEAN E. SINGLETON
Indiana State Librarian

ACKNOWLEDGEMENTS

MARGARET BONAMY
AAA Travel Department

COLUMBIA CITY
CHAMBER OF COMMERCE

ALF V. EKLOV
JANET EKLOV

CARL HENN, JR.
Indiana State Chamber
of Commerce

PAMELA HESTER
Anderson Chamber
of Commerce

LINDA JESTER
Indiana Tourism
Development Division

LOIS MITTINO
Department of Natural
Resources

VIRGIL O'HAIR

DONALD ORTH
Executive Secretary
U.S. Board on
Geographic Names

SALEM CHAMBER
OF COMMERCE

PATRICIA SASS

VIGO CHAPTER
Daughters of the
American Revolution,
Vincennes

Preface

NOTHING like an encyclopedia of the United States has previously existed. There have been numerous specialized encyclopedias or dictionaries—for example, of American history, of American biography, of American authors—as well as various series covering the geographical regions of the United States. Histories and other specialized studies and federal and state manuals provide only partial views of the nation and the states. The W.P.A. guidebooks from the 1930s, unquestionably were excellent for their time, but they do not offer the structured approach of an encyclopedia. Several states have published volumes with articles on all cities and towns in the state, but these books are not part of a series that is unified in point of view and organization or that places the state in the perspectives of national life.

Encyclopedia of the United States provides a series of volumes that are highly readable as essays on the United States and on its states and its institutions. It is at the same time scholarly and fully referential in the encyclopedic tradition.

We are pleased to present the first volumes in this set on the occasion of the U.S. Bicentennial.

Frank H. Gille
Publisher

Contents

INDIANA: THE HEARTLAND OF AMERICA............ 1
    by Kim Northam

GEOGRAPHICAL CONFIGURATION 27
    by Charles G. Griffo

PREHISTORY AND ARCHAEOLOGY.................. 34
    by Ingrid Eklov Jonsson

HISTORY 43
    by William E. Wilson

PEOPLE AND POPULATION 62
    by Eugene Cadou

NATURAL RESOURCES OF INDIANA................. 75
    by G. Etzel Pearcy

ECONOMY OF INDIANA 91
    by John Lyst

MANAGEMENT OF THE ECONOMY 103
    by Frank Pierce

TRANSPORTATION IN INDIANA 115
    by G. Etzel Pearcy

ADMINISTRATION OF INDIANA 129
    by Lynda R. Hara

ADMINISTRATIVE AGENCIES 141
    by Paul Doherty

INDIANAPOLIS 154
    by Lawrence Connor

THE SOCIAL MILIEU 171
  by Eugene Cadou

BIOGRAPHIES OF FAMOUS HOOSIERS 184
  by Adrianne Carter and Helen Connor

CHRONOLOGY OF INDIANA.........................235
  by Edward A. Leary

CONCISE DICTIONARY 261
  by Ingrid Eklov Jonsson

BIBLIOGRAPHY 499

INDEX... 504

* * *

INTRODUCTION

INDIANA:
The Heartland of America

NO better introduction to the country's heartland can be
found than in Indiana. There blast furnaces and corn-
fields, urban ethnicity and rural homogeneity, tree-covered
hills and unwavering plains, rugged gorges and gentle river
valleys clearly set forth the seemingly contradictory nature of
mid-America. That peculiar juncture of industry and agriculture, with its attendant commerce and transportation networks,
led the Hoosier state in 1937 to adopt as its motto "The
Crossroads of America."

As the hub of the Great Lakes region of the United States,
the 19th state—admitted to the Union in 1816—is bounded on
the north by Lake Michigan, on the east and south by the Ohio
River, and on the southwest by the Wabash River. Its
neighbors include the states of Michigan, Ohio, Kentucky, and
Illinois. Indiana ranks 38th in area with 36,291 square miles
and 11th in population with 5,300,000 people. Its population is
concentrated primarily in the capital city of Indianapolis and
the four major cities of Gary, South Bend, Evansville, and Fort
Wayne.

STATE SYMBOLS

Indianans take their state symbols seriously. The peony, which
blooms throughout the state in May and early June, replaced the
zinnia as the state flower in 1957. The tulip tree, also known as
the yellow poplar, became the state tree in 1931. The Indiana
Historical Bureau reported that this tree was once the "monarch

1

of the great forests which covered most of Indiana in pioneer times," but has since become "comparatively rare." The Historical Bureau added that in 1933 the cardinal, whose "rich and cheery song is heard in Indiana all year round," became the official state bird.

A pioneer woodsman and a buffalo appear on the state seal in a scene which has been used on Indiana seals since territorial days. Hikers can still follow portions of the old buffalo trace and visitors to the south-central part of the state can see preserved in the Hoosier National Forest a sampling of the splendid hardwood stand which attracted the hardy frontiersmen. The format of the state seal has been found on official papers dated as early as 1801.

The state flag, the design of which was adopted in 1917, bears Indiana's colors of blue and gold. The dark blue field provides the background for a golden torch surrounded by 19 stars, one larger than the rest. The torch represents liberty and enlightenment, its rays symbolizing the far-reaching influence of those two concepts. An outer circle of 13 stars stands for the original states, an inner circle of five stars for the five admitted to the Union. The larger, central star is, of course, the 19th state of Indiana.

ORIGIN OF THE NAME "INDIANA"

French trappers and soldiers called the northern portion of the land from which present-day Indiana was carved "Canada," its southern portion "Louisiana." English colonials called the region "Ohio Country." American settlers first called it "Virginia," then the "Northwest Territory," and in 1800 the "Indiana Territory." Eventually, the Indiana Territory formed the states of Illinois, Wisconsin, and parts of Michigan and Minnesota, as well as Indiana.

A myriad of place-names in the Midwest are drawn from the Indian cultures which prevailed prior to the arrival of the first whites late in the 17th century. In fact, the Indian era on that frontier did not end until 1813, when the death of the great Shawnee chief Tecumseh and the resultant defeat of his confederated tribes by federal troops brought about the final cession of Indian lands to the new U.S. government. The Indians were driven westward, their presence in what was to become the state of Indiana—a presence which extended back to prehistoric times—remembered in name only.

ORIGIN OF THE NICKNAME "HOOSIER"

If the name "Indiana" has an obvious derivation, the opposite is true of the state's nickname. The use of the term "Hoosier" to denote a native of Indiana can be documented as early as 1831, but its actual origin remains a mystery.

One theory supposes that when a visitor hailed a pioneer at his door, the settler would respond with "Who's yere?" leading to the appelation of "Hoosier" state. A more facetious explanation was offered by the Hoosier poet James Whitcomb Riley, who claimed that the nickname originated in the pugnacious habits of Indiana's early settlers. "They were enthusiastic and vicious fighters who gouged, scratched, and bit off noses and ears. This was so common that a settler coming into a tavern the morning after a fight and seeing an ear on the floor would touch it with his toe and casually ask: "Whose ear?"

While Riley's yarn is more indicative of his state's penchant for tall tales than it is illustrative of the nickname's origin, others have arrived at a similar conclusion. A popular notion is that Indiana rivermen were so successful in trouncing or "hushing" their adversaries in the brawling that was then common that they became known as "hushers," and eventually as "Hoosiers."

Slightly tamer are the two linguistic theories, the first being that "Hoosier" is derived from *hoosa,* an Indian word for corn. Indiana flatboat men taking corn to New Orleans came to be known as "hoosa men" or "Hoosiers." Unfortunately for this theory, a search of Indian vocabularies has failed to reveal such a word for corn. A second approach noted that "Hoosier" was frequently used in many parts of the South during the 1800s to denote woodsmen or rough hill people. The word was derived from the term "hoozer" which, in the Cumberland dialect of England, referred to a hill dweller or highlander. Immigrants from Cumberland, England, settled in the southern mountains of this country, whose foothills stretch into southern Indiana, and their decendants may have brought the name with them.

Least romantic, but equally plausible is the theory that a contractor named Hoosier preferred to employ laborers from Indiana to work on the Louisville and Portland Canal. They were called "Hoosier's men" and it is possible that from this term all residents of Indiana were eventually called "Hoosiers."

Whatever its origin, "Hoosier" today is a mark of pride for

Indianans, particularly when it is used to refer to the Hoosier hospitality for which the people of the state are known.

CULTURAL HERITAGE

A complete network of interstate highways makes the Hoosier state one of the safest and most convenient in the Union through which to travel. That road system's ubiquity and uncanny ability to homogenize Indiana's remarkably diverse character is, however, a disservice to anyone in pursuit of the colorful cultural heritage and historical roots lodged in that area which constituted the American frontier far longer than did the more popularized Wild West.

The Indiana Divide. The Old National Road (U.S. 40), running just south and parallel to highway I-70, bisects Indiana from the Quaker settlements around the eastern border town of Richmond, through stagecoach-stop towns such as Centerville, Cambridge City, and Knightstown, to Indianapolis and then westward through farming country to Terre Haute, home of such disparate personalities as author Theordore Dreiser, his composer-brother Paul Dresser, socialist leader Eugene Debs, and auto-racing magnate Tony Hulman. Route 40 seems literally to divide Indiana into two cultural areas, the lower half of the state having the flavor of Southern river towns and backwoods hills, the upper portion more Northern in feeling, whether the primary mode of living is industrial or agricultural. Even the indigenous folk music reflects this split personality. Below Route 40, cigar-box fiddles and hand-strung banjos sound a bluegrass note, while above the "Divide" the music is more closely related to that of the northern mountain people, more similar to the old Anglo-Saxon forms.

Northern Indiana. Indiana's diversity is not measured in north-south terms alone. Within both sections of the state there exist differences which add to its nature.

The northwestern corner of the state is regarded by many as an extension of Greater Chicago, Illinois, if not in terms of actual commuter suburbs, then certainly in terms of major industrialization. The region has a distinct personality above and beyond the steel mills of Gary, however. Once past the Burns Harbor Port of Indiana, which is looking toward the future as one of the country's major inland shipping gateways, the Lake Michigan shore reveals unusual sand dunes, their abundant flora and fauna preserved in the Indiana Dunes National Lakeshore and the

Indiana Dunes State Park. The offshore waters offer some of the finest Coho salmon fishing in the country.

Moving south from the huge industrial complex adjacent to Chicago, the remaining northwest section is primarily agricultural, the point of origin of the great plains of the Midwest being claimed by the town of Wolcott. In this region can be seen the pattern of town squares surrounding county courthouses which prevails throughout the Midwest, the state's 90-odd courthouses each possessing a unique personality. Their architecture ranges from staid Germanic proportions in the north to convoluted Baroque designs in the south. Greensburg, just below the "Divide" in the southeast, boasts an aspen tree growing out of its tower.

Northwestern Indiana shares with the northeastern part of the state nearly 1,000 lakes which comprise a natural inland water recreation area. And Indiana's love affair with the automobile is not limited to the drag strips of Terre Haute or the 500-mile auto racing spectacular of Indianapolis. South Bend, best known today as the location of Notre Dame University, was home for the Studebaker Auto Company and Auburn, once vied with Detroit, Michigan, in the bid to become America's motor city. Auburn was the birthplace of the elegant Auburns, Cords, and Duesenbergs whose owners still congregate there in an annual Labor Day car rally.

Northeastern Indiana is home for a large Amish population whose dark carriages and simple lifestyle are in stark contrast to the high living for which Fort Wayne is noted. Once a French outpost inhabited only by trappers and traders, Fort Wayne is now considered Indiana's restaurant capital.

To the south and west of Fort Wayne lies partially reconstructed Fort Ouiatenon, one of the four French frontier settlements in Indiana, and a close neighbor to Lafayette, home of Purdue University. Just outside of Lafayette in 1811, William Henry Harrison defeated the forces of Tecumseh's brother, Tenskwatawa the Shawnee Prophet, in the Battle of Tippecanoe, which is believed by some historians to have been the defeat that ensured the eventual ouster of the Indian from these lands. The battleground is open to the public.

Central Indiana. On either side of the centrally located capital city, moving along the Indiana "Divide," the land is alive with rushing rivers and streams, challenging Hoosiers in one of their latest sports enthusiasms, canoeing. Nor are landlubbers at a loss for outdoor adventure, with hiking trails through the west-central area's boulder-strewn canyons and gorges providing craggy alternatives to the more placid canal and coach towns which entice visitors with bargain-priced antiques and hand-crafted items. The country's largest concentration of covered bridges is also found in central Indiana.

Midway along Route 40 lies Indianapolis, whose fame as an auto-racing capital sometimes overshadows its role as the seat of government for the state. It is the location for outstanding museums including the highly touted Indianapolis Museum of Art, the Museum of Indian Heritage, and the living historical farm at the Conner Prairie Pioneer Settlement and Museum. A vibrant blend of old and new is perceived in Indianapolis' architecture. The dramatic performing arts center, Clowes Hall, states in its massive modernity an excellence similar to that seen in the ponderous brick and masonry facade of the Atheneum, home of the fast-growing Indiana Repertory Theatre. The city's Romanesque Union Station was in the mid-1970s joining the growing number of historical structures adapted to new uses as cultural and commercial centers, while the open-stall City Market, dating back to 1821, formed the hub of an exciting downtown renovation plan. Splashy wall graphics enliven city street, and Victorian turrets continue to grace the cityscape.

Southern Indiana. Crossing Route 40 to the south, the plains and lakes give way to hills and river valleys. The impatience of commerce softens into the slower conduct of daily affairs. The contrast between north and south is apparent even in the types of innovations they generated. In Hammond, the first refrigerator car was successfully used in 1869, and Wabash became the world's first city to be electrically lighted in 1880. Below the "Divide," inventions were more social in nature. One of the earliest experiments in communal living in America took place in 1814 in Harmonie (later New Harmony).

The Wabash River was the earliest focal point in Indiana. As early as 1732 a thriving trading center was operating at Vincennes, a French outpost which drew together a cosmopolitan mixture of Native Americans, European soldiers, trappers, traders, and priests. The Midwest's first Roman Catholic church was established in Vincennes, its bishop's remarkable rare book collection transported from the East coast by pack mule and preserved in the Old Cathedral library there. Vincennes fell under the rule of the British after 1763, when the French lost their claim to that portion of the New World as a result of the French and Indian War. The capture of Vincennes by George Rogers Clark and his men in 1779 was a decisive victory in the movement to bring the Northwest Territory under U.S. jurisdiction.

Vincennes is a history buff's dream, its homes and monuments seeming almost out of place amid the surrounding orchards characteristic of southwestern Indiana. The same holds true for New Harmony, site of the communal Rappite settlement of Harmonie that, in the 1820s under the direction of Robert Owen, was renamed New Harmony and became one of the nation's most ambitious attempts to perfect an intellectual utopia. It is hard to imagine today's tiny town on the Wabash as the location of the first kindergarten, first free public library, first free public school, first women's club, and first geological survey in the United States.

New Harmony is within easy reach of southern Indiana's largest city of Evansville, where the people have a hard time knowing for certain whether they're Kentuckians or Indianans. Evansville is in the "toe" of Indiana, an almost semi-tropical zone compared to the rest of the state. One of the city's more fascinating locations is the Angel Mounds State Memorial. There huge earthen formations erected by a vanished prehistoric Indian people yield artifacts and structural patterns which tease the imagination of archaeologists and visitors alike.

Few people realize that Abraham Lincoln was a Hoosier, his Illinois and Kentucky experiences being far better known. In 1816, however, because of clouded land titles and the growing practice of slavery in Kentucky, the Thomas Lincoln family, including 7-year-old Abe, moved to the Little Pigeon Creek community in south-central Indiana. There they remained until Abraham was 21 years of age. The National Park Service operates the restored Lincoln farm and maintains the Lincoln Boyhood National Memorial. In an almost incongruous juxtaposition, the community adjacent to the Lincoln homestead—Santa Claus, Indiana—operates an amusement park that entertains children of all ages and a post office that does a land office business each December.

The greater part of south-central Indiana is forest and hill

country. The most popular destination is Brown County, where
an artists' colony has for years found stimulation in the log cabins
and brilliant fall foliage for which the county is so famous. A
unique companion to the pioneer flavor of Brown County is the
nearby city of Columbus, where dramatic modern spires and
unusual futuristic architectural shapes dominate the scene. Early
buildings of Eliel and Eero Saarinen, I.M.Pei, Harry Weese, and
others led to the belief that good modern architects in the United
States must have a building in Columbus. A waiting list
comprised of some of the country's most outstanding architects
determines the roll of those seeking the honor of having one of
their structures accepted.

The past still prevails, however, throughout most of southern
Indiana, the southeastern corner having had its heyday during
the steamboat era of the 1850s. Splendid river mansions dot the
river bank, inviting travelers to browse through the quiet
elegance of towns such as Aurora, Madison, and New Albany. At
Vevay, one of the last side-wheel ferries still plied the waters of
the Ohio in 1975. Hydroplane regattas and a solid commercial
barge traffic interrupt on occasion, but the mood of that
now-forgotten way of life cannot be erased.

KIM NORTHAM

* * *

Geographical Configuration

DESCRIPTION OF THE NATURAL LANDSCAPE

Physical Features and Geology

INDIANA has a land area of 36,045 miles. The whole of the state has been glaciated except the south central and southwestern parts. The highest point in the state is in Randolph County, 1,285 feet about sea level, and the lowest is in Point Township, Posey County, at the mouth of the Wabash River, 313 feet. The average elevation is about 700 feet. Indianapolis has an elevation of 718 feet.

Indiana's northern boundary is Lake Michigan and the state of Michigan along 41°50' north latitude. Its southern boundary is the low water mark of the north bank of the Ohio River, the most southerly point being 37°40' north latitude. In longitude it lies between 84°49' to the east, and 88°2' to the west.

About 90 percent of the state lies between 500 and 1,000 feet above sea level. Most of the state's surface slopes toward the west and south. Most of the surface features were formed by the glaciers that covered the greater part of the area during the Ice Age, approximately 1,000,000 years BP (before the present).

Indiana may be divided into three broad physiographic zones. These are the northern lake plain, the central till plain, and the southern hill and lowlands region.

The Northern Lake Plain. This rolling plain covers the northern third of the state. The evidence of glaciation found throughout this region includes swamps and marshes, lakes, and moraines (low ridges or mounds composed of materials deposited by glaciers). In the northwestern section, the swampland has been drained and the land used for truck farming.

Aiso in the northwest, along the shores of Lake Michigan, are the Indiana Dunes, which cover a belt about four miles wide at the western end, and a half mile wide at the eastern end. The Michigan Central Railroad tracks run along the southern boundary of the Dunes area.

In Lake County, to the west, the dunes are low, being for the most part from 5 to 15 feet high, and with the dunes areas alternating with interdunal flats. In the eastern part of Lake County, the dunes increase in height, with the high dunes region continuing eastward through Porter County to the vicinity of Michigan City. The highest dune is Mount Tom in Dunes State Park, Porter County, which is 192 feet high. The dunes proper consist of almost pure sand, and were formerly well wooded.

Since industry encroached upon the dunes and lakefront areas of northwestern Indiana in the early 20th century, conservationists have been struggling to prevent further encroachments and to preserve the natural beauty of the region. A major move for the preservation of the dunes was made in 1972 when the Indiana Dunes National Lakeshore, a preserve surrounding the Indiana Dunes State Park, was established.

Apart from the dunes the northern lake plain has a great variety of habitats, ranging from lakes and rivers, bogs and marshes, dry sand and gravelly places, prairies and remnants of prairies, and mesophytic (moderately moist) forest areas. The line which divides the Lake Plain from the Tipton Till Plain to the south runs roughly westward from Fort Wayne to Huntington, Logansport, and Monticello and on to the state line.

The Tipton Till Plain. This area is bounded on the north by the Lake Plain, and on the south by the southern boundary of the Wisconsin glacial drift. The southern part of this region consists of decidedly irregular territory. Its surface is comparatively level, however, although marked by many terminal moraines. The Tipton Till Plain contains the best agricultural land of Indiana. It has been cleared of most of the woodlands in the relatively brief period of a little more than a century.

The Till Plain is so named for the till, or jumbled earth materials, left behind by the melting edge of the glaciers. Its mainly level surface is broken in places by low hills and shallow valleys.

The Southern Hills and Lowlands Region. This area manifests many surface features including the Illinoian Drift Area, which lies south of the Tipton Till Plain, north of the glacial boundary, and east of the Lower Wabash Valley. The drift area is divided into an eastern and a western lobe. The topography varies from level areas to deeply cut ravines. In Clark, Jefferson, Jennings, and Ripley counties the land is level, poorly drained, and contains acid soil patches known as "flats".

The Prairie. The prairie area of Indiana is small and actually belongs to the eastern limit of the Great Western Prairie. This section is relatively unimportant in the general division of the physiographic zones.

The Lower Wabash Valley. The valley is part of the southern, unglaciated lowlands of Indiana. The Wabash Lowland is a narrow strip of alluvial land along the Wabash River from Vigo County south to the Ohio River and thence north to Little Pigeon Creek in Warrick County. To it belongs the short, alluvial extensions of the White and Patoka rivers. In the lower part of the Wabash Valley is the area known as the "pocket". This relatively low lying area includes Gibson, Posey, Vanderburgh, and Warrick counties. The eastern portion of the unglaciated area of the state is mostly hilly and broken and is divided by the broad valley of the White River.

The area contains numerous scenic knobs, deep valleys, sinkholes, underground rivers, caves, and mineral springs. Marengo and Wyandotte caves in Crawford County are among the most beautiful in the United States, as well as being well-known tourist attractions. The mineral springs at French Lick, West Baden, and Martinsville have an historic past.

South central Indiana is the source of the state's best known mineral resource, oolitic limestone. Extensive layers of the stone, however, underlie most of the southern section of Indiana. Indiana still contains approximately $17 billion of unquarried limestone deposits. The type formation, Salem Limestone, was formed about 300,000,000 years ago from compaction of layers of dead plant and animal matter.

The Crawford Upland. This area contains Indiana's most varied topography. The Upland is extremely rugged and inaccessible. It covers an area of approximately 2,900 square miles. Within this region are low and high hills, sharp and rounded ridges, trench-like valleys, flat-bottomed valleys, rock benches, rolling peneplain remnants, sinkholes, escarpments, canyon-like gorges, and caves. Elevations range from 349 to 980 feet. Alter-

FIGURE 1

Physiographic regions of Indiana based on present topography.

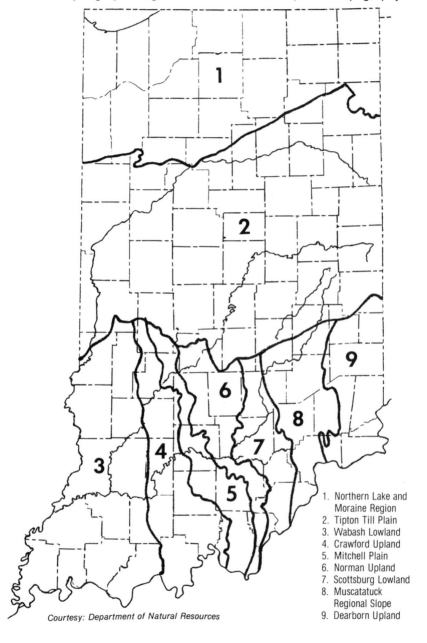

1. Northern Lake and
   Moraine Region
2. Tipton Till Plain
3. Wabash Lowland
4. Crawford Upland
5. Mitchell Plain
6. Norman Upland
7. Scottsburg Lowland
8. Muscatatuck
   Regional Slope
9. Dearborn Upland

Courtesy: Department of Natural Resources

nating non-resistant shales, resistant sandstones, and limestones in the unglaciated section, combined with topographic maturity, have resulted in this scenic maze of land forms. Perry County bordering on the Ohio River, is the most rugged county in Indiana.

The Mitchell Plain. This westward-sloping limestone plain exhibits a well-developed karst (sink- and cave) topography and covers approximately 1,125 square miles. Sinkholes of various sizes are abundant and reach a density of 100 per square mile in some sections. Surface waters drain into subterranean passages and underground rivers through open sinks. Many of the sinks are plugged and form small ponds. The elevation of the plain varies from 600 to 900 feet. Most of Indiana's caves are found on the Mitchell Plain.

The Norman Upland. This elevated section of Indiana encompasses 2,075 square miles of hills and intervening valleys and reaches a maximum width of 40 miles. In Brown County, rugged hills and scenic woodlands make this one of the most scenic and most often visited parts of the state. The maximum elevation of 1,050 feet is at Weedpatch Hill near Nashville. Elsewhere, great local relief is characteristic and uniform dissection by stream action has long been underway. Long, sharp ridges and V-shaped valleys are the result.

The Knobstone Escarpment ("The Knobs") of the Norman Upland is the most prominent relief feature and it extends from southern Jackson County through Harrison County, a distance of 150 miles. In Harrison and Floyd counties, the crest of the escarpment rises 400 to 600 feet above the valley floor. Crests in Clark, Floyd, Scott, and Washington counties reach an altitude of over 1,000 feet.

The Scottsburgh Lowland. Primarily, this lowland is broad, shallow, and of low relief. It is characterized by wide expanses of flat valleys and a notable lack of steep slopes and bluffs. The Lowland covers an area of 950 square miles. Much of the relief is below 600 feet. A deeply dissected upland area of 25 or 30 square miles in Jackson County is known as the "Brownstone Hills", and it represents an upland mass isolated from the Norman Upland by stream erosion. The upper portion of these hills stood above the continental ice sheet during the Illinois Glacial Stage and today rise 300 feet above the surrounding lowland.

The Muscatatuck Regional Slope. The most notable regional slope in Indiana is represented by this area of 1,875 square miles. Its eastern border ranges from 875 to about 1,100 feet in elevation, while the western edge varies from about 500 to 725 feet. Stream valleys of the southern half of the region are canyon-like in character but are never entrenched deeper than 175 feet below the gently inclined plain. In the area of greatest entrenchment, tributary streams have dissected the upland portion. Areas between streams are typically quite flat. Most of the streams passing down the center of the eastern part are comparatively less entrenched.

The Dearborn Upland. About 1,925 square miles of the south-eastern corner of the state makes up this unit. It is an upland composed of drainage basins of the Whitewater River and its tributaries. Elevations range from about 425 feet at the Ohio River to a maximum elevation of 1,100 feet. The streams are short and have a relatively great drop. Local relief is often measured in hundreds of feet; slopes are steep, but bluffs are rare. Long evenly elevated upland tongues lie between the deeply dissected valleys. Terraces of glacial outwash border the White-water River flood plain. In western Dearborn County and eastern Ripley County, a rather extensive upland tract of marked flatness occurs. It rises slightly above the 1,100-foot contour and has not been severely dissected by streams.

Mineral Resources. Indiana is blessed with an abundance of mineral wealth and produces more than 80 percent of the limestone used in the United States. The Salem Limestone has been coveted as an excellent building stone for more than 150 years. It is more porous than other limestones and has a uniform texture and color. It is free from impurities and is easily worked at both the quarry site and at the mill. Although the Salem Limestone outcrops as far north as Owen County and as far south as Washington County, the center for the quarrying industry is in the Bloomington-Bedford area in Monroe and Lawrence counties.

Coal reserves underlie much of southwestern Indiana, and mining of the bituminous variety has long been a major industry. The bulk of Indiana's coal is burned to produce steam for turbine engines in electric power plants. Only about 15 percent is exported to other areas of the country. The coal, in general has a low heat value and does not compare in quality to that of the Appalachian coal fields. Coal recovery is concentrated around Sullivan, Pike, and Gibson counties. Lesser centers are in Clay and Vermillion counties. The Indiana coal fields lie at the western edge of the great Illinois Basin which covers nearly all of central and southern Illinois, parts of western Kentucky, and southwestern Indiana. The coal beds lie in blanket formation and were first mined in 1840. Surface strip mines now number 36 and produced a yield of 782,339 tons in 1974. Many of the strip mines have been made part of Indiana's ambitious land reclamation program designed to return strip mines to their natural state. In 1967, a Hoosier reclamation law was passed which required all coal companies to file reclamation plans with the Department of Natural Resources. Reclaimed lands have been replanted in trees. The largest of these areas is the Greene-Sullivan State Forest, south of Dugger. It contains 6,439 acres of woodland and 100 lakes.

On a lesser scale, Indiana's deposits of oil shale have recently been exploited. The shale is capable of yielding a substance very similar to crude oil. The shale is easily mined in southern Indiana and reaches depths of 110 feet. When refined, it produces kerogens which in turn can be used as oil substitutes. The main drawbacks to full-scale production are the expensive refining process and the lands, containing the shale, which are not zoned for mining.

Other important resources include abundant deposits of peat, clay, sand and gravel, all found throughout the state. Indiana's oil wells are located mainly in the Tri-State area of Illinois, Indiana, and Kentucky. Oil drilling, begun in the 1880's in central Indiana, brought large amounts of natural gas. The supplies of gas, at first thought unlimited, were depleted by the turn of the century.

Geological Formation. All the underlying rock strata found in Indiana are sedimentary, formed in the course of millions of years along the margins and bottoms of the seas. At some time the Precambrian seas covered the Indiana area, and during this earliest time (about 500,000,000 BP), the first sedimentary rocks were deposited upon the original crust. Rocks formed during this time are exposed at no place in the state today, but their presence has been verified through rock samples taken during oil drilling.

Except for this basic layer, all rock strata in Indiana were deposited during the Paleozoic Era (500,000,000 to 200,000,000 years BP), a period of time during which most of the lower orders of plants and animals evolved. The Paleozoic Era is divided into 7 sections of time—the Cambrian, Ordovician, Silurian, Devonian, Mississippian, Pennsylvanian, and Permian periods. These periods are identified by their plant and animal fossil type sections.

Indiana was submerged beneath the seas during the Cambrian, Ordovician, and most of the Silurian periods. Late in the Silurian Period, the continent was uplifted and the great interior seas receded. The land rose slowly—an inch perhaps in a century. The first and sharpest uplift in the Indiana region was the formation of what is now known as the Cincinnati Arch. Pressure from below the Earth's crust slowly forced upwards the layers of rock deposited in the preceding periods. The Cincinnati Arch today extends from Cincinnati to Richmond, and south to Kokomo and Logansport, thence east to Chicago. Most of the arch was formed in the late Silurian and Devonian periods, approximately 350,000,000 to 300,000,000 years BP, but the slow upheaval process continued throughout the Paleozoic Era.

In the Mississippian and Pennsylvanian periods, Indiana was steadily elevated; at the close of the Mississippian, the whole region was above sea level. During the Pennsylvanian Period, about 250,000,000 years BP, Indiana was undoubtedly a lush swamp, populated by amphibian creatures and covered with fern-like plants. It was during this time that most of Indiana's present coal-beds were laid down. The climate steadily became cooler, and by the Permian Period the swamps had dried up.

Paleozoic Formations. In the southeastern corner of the state the surface rocks immediately under the topsoil are of Ordovician Age. Then in order, toward the west, appear belts of Silurian, Devonian, Mississippian, and Pennsylvanian outcrops. A second and smaller Devonian formation to the north indicates the presence in that period of a separate northern basin. Cambrian and Precambrian rocks, though not exposed anywhere in Indiana, underlie these more recent formations. There are no Permian rocks, because Indiana was above sea level during and after this period.

Ordovician rocks were exposed only in the southeastern corner of Indiana, because of the uplift that began at this point to form the Cincinnati Arch. Elsewhere in the state, Ordovician strata was found beneath more recent formations. Next to the Ordovician outcroppings is a belt of Silurian rocks which farther west are overlapped by rocks of succeeding periods. Only in the southwestern part of the state are Pennsylvanian rocks found.

Mesozoic Formations. During the many millions of years between the Permian Period and the Pleistocene Glacial Epoch, Indiana experienced three major cycles of erosion. During the Mesozoic Era (200,000,000 to 70,000,000 years BP), the region was above sea level and no rocks of Triassic, Jurassic or Cretaceous age were formed. At the same time no rocks were formed in Indiana during the Tertiary Period of the Cenozoic Era.

The Pleistocene Glacial Epoch. At the beginning of the Pleistocene or Ice Age (1,000,000,000 BP), Indiana was elevated for the fourth time. The glaciers subsequently advanced and created many of the physical features seen today. During the Ice Age, about 5/6 of the whole region, with the exception of what is now South Central Indiana, was at one time or another under a 2,000 feet thick layer of ice. Geologists say that there were at least three ice invasions into Indiana. The ice at one time extended south of the Ohio River. After each invasion came a warming trend which lasted many thousands of years. The glaciers receded and plants and animals began to flourish.

The most striking effect of the glaciers was the channeling of the Ohio River bed by the melting ice. The glaciers lopped off many hills in the northern part of the state, filled the valleys with the eroded rocks, and smoothed and levelled the entire area. Excellent topsoil was formed from the mixing of the resultant rock flour. Over much of Indiana, the glacial topsoil forms excellent farmland. Glaciers also greatly altered drainage conditions by destroying existing streams and valleys and in turn creating new ones. Water was left in many depressions which formed marshes and lakes. In melting, the glaciers also left extensive deposits of sand and gravel and crated many hills in the north by piling up soil and rocks into morainic deposits.

Drainage and Soils

Naturally, Indiana is divided into three regions. These are the northern lake country, the central agricultural plain, and the southern hill and lowland section. The boundary of the northern region is the Upper Wabash River which flows southwestward across the state to Terre Haute. The northern area, which consists of low plains with little stream action, is broken by many marshes and lakes. The northeastern section has hundreds of small bodies of water. It is characterized by low, morainal hills left by glaciers. Farther west, in Kosciusko County, Lake Wawasee occurs as major drainage basin. It has an extreme length of about six miles.

Northern lake section. In lake country rises the watershed of the St. Lawrence and Mississippi rivers. To the northwest the Kankakee and Iroquois rivers flow across wide expanses of marshy area to finally empty into the Illinois River. The Tippecanoe empties into the Wabash near Lafayette, while the Eel River rises north of Fort Wayne and flows into the Wabash at Logansport. The St. Joseph River of Michigan flows across northern Indiana through South Bend, then northward again into Lake Michigan, having drained a considerable area. The St. Mary's River rises in Ohio and flows northwest to Fort Wayne. It unites there with another stream, also called the St. Joseph, to form the Maumee River. The Maumee in turn, flows northwestward into the St. Lawrence drainage system. The watershed encompasses Adams and Allen counties, northern Indiana's lake country, and part of Lake Michigan.

The central agricultural section. The most important river here is the White River. The West Fork of the White River has its source in Randolph County and flows quietly southwestward across Indiana to confluence with the Wabash River in Gibson County.

through the upper part of the plain and constitute important tributaries of the Wabash River. In eastern Indiana, the twin forks of the Whitewater meet to flow southward into the Ohio River.

The South. The upland-lowland drainage system of the southern part of Indiana is drained by scores of tiny streams and creeks which empty into the Ohio River. The major rivers of the basin are the Wabash and White, which in turn drain 2/3 of the entire state.

Man-made reservoirs. During recent years, a large system of man-made dams and reservoirs have been jointly constructed by the State of Indiana and the U.S. Army Corps of Engineers. They are part of an ambitious program which will substantially increase the state's water supplies and recreational facilities.

The largest of these "lakes" is the Monroe Reservoir, a 10,750-acre body of water that sprawls across southeastern Monroe County. It stretches for 22 miles from the Bloomington vicinity to the Monroe-Lawrence County line north of Bedford. The lake, with 85 miles of shoreline, is Indiana's largest. Fourteen projects are planned which will eventually encompass a flood control system that includes the Upper Mississippi, Ohio, and Wabash rivers.

Soils. Soils are derived from various geological materials. Glacial till, limestone, or wind-blown silt undergo changes as a result of a direct effect of climate. The resulting soil depends on the kind of geologic material, climate, kinds of vegetation, topography of the land, and the length of time the soil has been forming.

Indiana is blessed with a great variety of parent materials needed to form soil. In roughly the northern 5/6 of the state these deposits have resulted from glaciation. The parent materials of the other 1/6 are largely bedrock formations such as limestone and sandstone which are partially covered by windblown silt. Mostly, the soils of Indiana have formed under a growth of hardwood trees. The resulting soils are light colored on slopes and flats and dark colored in depressions. In a small area the soils that have formed under prairie grasses are all dark colored. The young soils of northern Indiana are less acid and have more organic matter than the very old soils of southern Indiana. The depth of free lime varies from about three feet in the young soils of northern Indiana to three to fifteen feet in the south.

Climate

Indiana, mainly the northern half, lies within the sweep of winter cold waves from the west and northwest. In the summer, the state is occasionally visited by hot periods which blanket the middle and northern parts of the great central valleys. Its climate, therefore, is largely continental. There are no large bodies of water, except for Lake Michigan, to influence general climatic conditions which very largely with latitude.

Temperature and precipitation. In the southern half of the state considerable irregularities in topography result in many local variations of temperature and precipitation. On damp, clear nights the numerous ravines and valley bottoms often experience considerably lower temperatures than do the slopes and summits of surrounding hills. The difference in spring and fall results in frost, and even damage from freezing, in the lower areas, while the higher grounds escapes harm.

There is a decrease in mean annual temperature and precipitation from north to south. There is also an occasional period of extreme cold during the winter season, although on a whole, the three winter months are characterized mainly by a mean temperature only slightly below the freezing point. A somewhat greater amount of precipitation occurs in the growing season in Indiana, although precipitation in general is fairly evenly distributed throughout the year. There are occasional droughts of considerable severity. There is seldom, however, a complete crop failure.

Frosts. The last killing frost usually occurs around April 15 in the extreme southern and southwestern counties. The date becomes later to the northward, as late as May 10. In the south there is a large area where the last killing frost occurs between April 20 and 25.

Kankakee Valley and the extreme northeast, but southward the date becomes later rather steadily, occuring around October 20 along the Ohio and Lower Wabash rivers. The influence of Lake Michigan delays killing frosts until about October 15 around the Indiana shores.

Growing season and precipitation. The average growing season is a little more than 190 days in the extreme southern section, decreasing to about 150 days north to the Kankakee Valley and the northeast. Around Lake Michigan the average is 170 days.

The entire state is well-watered. The percentage of annual precipitation received during a growing season increases from 51 in the extreme south to 57 in the extreme north. This is in reverse of the south-to-north decrease in precipitation for the entire year, and it is probably due largely to the greater frequency of the storm movement to northern Indiana during the season when the Sun is north of the Equator.

Snowfall is heavy in the north, again due to the influence of Lake Michigan. An annual snowfall of 50 inches is not uncommon. Southern Indiana receives far less than the north, about 15-16 inches per year. The state's average is 23 inches. Almost all moisture is drawn from the Gulf of Mexico with little being received from the west, north, or south. The average annual temperature is about 52° Fahrenheit. July is the hottest month, with an average around 75°F; January is the coldest month, with an average around 30°F.

Flora and Fauna

Indiana has no clearly defined floral and faunal zones. The climate is nearly uniform, and there is no transition from mountain to lowland or from seacoast to interior. Indigenous plants and animals are distributed fairly evenly throughout the state. The Ohio River area in the south and the lake and marsh regions and the dunes in the north are the most differentiated areas. Most of the plants in these regions, however, can be found elsewhere in the Hoosier state, and even in the whole north central area of the United States. A few plants are restricted to a particular habitat. The persimmon, for instance, is found only in the marshy lowlands of the Ohio River. The black gum tree and the southern cypress are likewise limited to the Ohio's bottomlands.

The marshlands. Years ago, the world "discovered" the northern Indiana swamps (long since cleared and drained) through Hoosier authoress Gene Stratton Porter's novels of the Limberlost. At that time, trees characteristic of the marshy lands were the tamarack and bog willow. Interesting and now rare carnivorous plants abounded; the pitcher plant and the round-leafed sundew could be found in sunny glades of the swamps. The pitcher plant has a deep-purple blossom and cylindrical leaves, or pitchers, which hold water into which unwary insects are lured and absorbed. The round-leaf sundew exudes a sticky fluid onto its leaves which in turn trap insects that are held until the leaves fold over and the insect's body is digested.

Floating pondweeds, bladderwort, and water milfoil are common water plants in the swampy areas. Before the marshes were drained, crops of cranberries and blueberries were raised there. Only peppermint remains as an important product.

The dunelands. This area fosters a wide variety of plant life that is now part of Indiana Dunes State Park. The region has been the focal point of the efforts of conservationists who want to save it from invasion and destruction by industry. The recently developed Indiana Dunes National Lakeshore and an adjoining state preserve cover a total area of 8,700 acres of rare duneland habitats. More than 1,000 species of flowering plants, ferns, and cacti thrive on the sandy slopes and intervening marshlands. White pines and many species of oak are there as well as the jack pine and arctic lichen. Tulip trees, sour gum, and paw paw grow in profusion, and the prickly pear cactus coexists alongside the iris.

Other plant life. Charles C. Deam, former Indiana state forester, lists 134 species of trees in Indiana, 124 of which are native.

Prominent among them are the oak, black maple, beech, sycamore, and the tulip tree, the latter of which is also the state tree. Several species of fruit trees are also common, among them the apple, cherry, pear, and peach tree. A beautiful specimen, the golden raintree was brought from China and first planted in New Harmony. It blooms with large cascades of yellow flowers.

Deam lists 163 species of shrubs including vines. All but one, the Japanese honeysuckle, are native to the state. Summer, fall, and spring bring a profusion of beautiful wild flowers. Common spring arrivals are the lupine, the rue anemone, pussy willows, jack-in-the-pulpit, and violets. Transition into summer brings the ox-eyed daisy, pink clover, and Queen Anne's lace. The colorful fall with its many-hued trees is further accented by the goldenrod, aster, and sunflower.

Animal life. Indiana is rich in mammals, birds, and fish. Deer have increased and many of the smaller animals such as the rabbit, muskrat, raccoon, woodchuck, opposum, mink, and squirrel are hunted. There are plenty of fish in lakes and streams, including the catfish, pike, pickerel, bass, and sunfish. In addition, several species of blind fish inhabit the subterranean waters of Indiana's cave region, although they are becoming rare.

In the north, near Lake Michigan and the dunes, birds from the far north, the plains, and the deep woods, still roost and rest on their migratory routes. Waterfowl and marsh birds are plentiful south of the dune region and to the Kankakee River. Fish duck, teal, the American golden-eyed duck, mallard, great blue heron, American bittern, and the wild goose are probably the most common species found in these areas. Yellow-winged sparrows and the prairie larks have become endangered species.

In the southeastern part of the state, just north of the Ohio River, are found the Cape May warbler, summer redbird, and black-throated blue warbler. They can be seen nesting in the surrounding oak, maple, and gum trees.

Many orchard and meadow birds are found in the heavily farmed central part of the state. These include the field sparrow, yellow warbler, orchard oriole, robin, and meadow swallow. Winter residents include the junco, shore lark, tree sparrow, sapsucker, white snowbird, snowy owl, and several species of waterfowl. During very mild winters, some robins, meadow larks, and woodpeckers remain all season. In all, 48 species of birds are native to Indiana.

Urban and Rural Settlements

Regional population distribution. The 1970 federal census counted 5,193,669 persons living in Indiana. This was an 11.4 percent increase over the 1960 census population of 4,662,498. Indiana ranks 11th in population. The Planning Division of the Indiana Department of Commerce has established 14 state multi-county planning and development regions:

On this basis, Region 8, in the center of the state (**Fig. 2**) has been the most populous area during all of the twentieth century. Census reports show that 21.8 percent of the state's population lives in this area. It is the first and only region with over 1,000,000 population. The zone includes Marion County, with Indianapolis as the focus, the Henricks, Boone, Hamilton, Hancock, Shelby, Johnson, and Morgan counties.

Region 1, in the northwestern corner of Indiana, is the second most populous area with 15.5 percent of the state's population. It includes the industrial areas of Lake, Porter, Laporte, Newton, Jasper, Starke, and Pulaski counties.

Region 12, is the least populated area with only 1.7 percent of the population. The included counties are Jefferson, Ripley, Dearborn, Ohio, and Switzerland.

The population of the northern section of Indiana, which includes regions 1 through 5, is 2,232,920 with 43.0 percent of the total; the population of the central section, regions 6 through 9, is 1,948,365, or 37.5 percent of the total; and the southern section, regions 10 through 14, is 1,012,384, or 19.5 percent of the total.

During the 1960s, the northern section of the state countributed 41.3 percent of the population, the central section 41.8 percent, and the southern section 16.9 percent.

According to the 1970 census, the population of each of Indiana's 92 counties ranged from a high of 793,590 in Marion County to a low of 4,289 in Ohio County. The state's population is somewhat concentrated into a few of the larger counties. The 1970 census shows that 51.0 percent of the state's residents live in the ten largest counties, and 25.8 percent live in only two of the state's largest counties—Marion and Lake. In the 1970 census, 26 counties showed fewer residents than they had in 1900.

Township population. There are 1,008 townships in Indiana, with a varying number in each county. Most of the counties have from 9 to 14 townships. Population of the townships range from 139 for

FIGURE 2
Indiana Planning and Development Regions

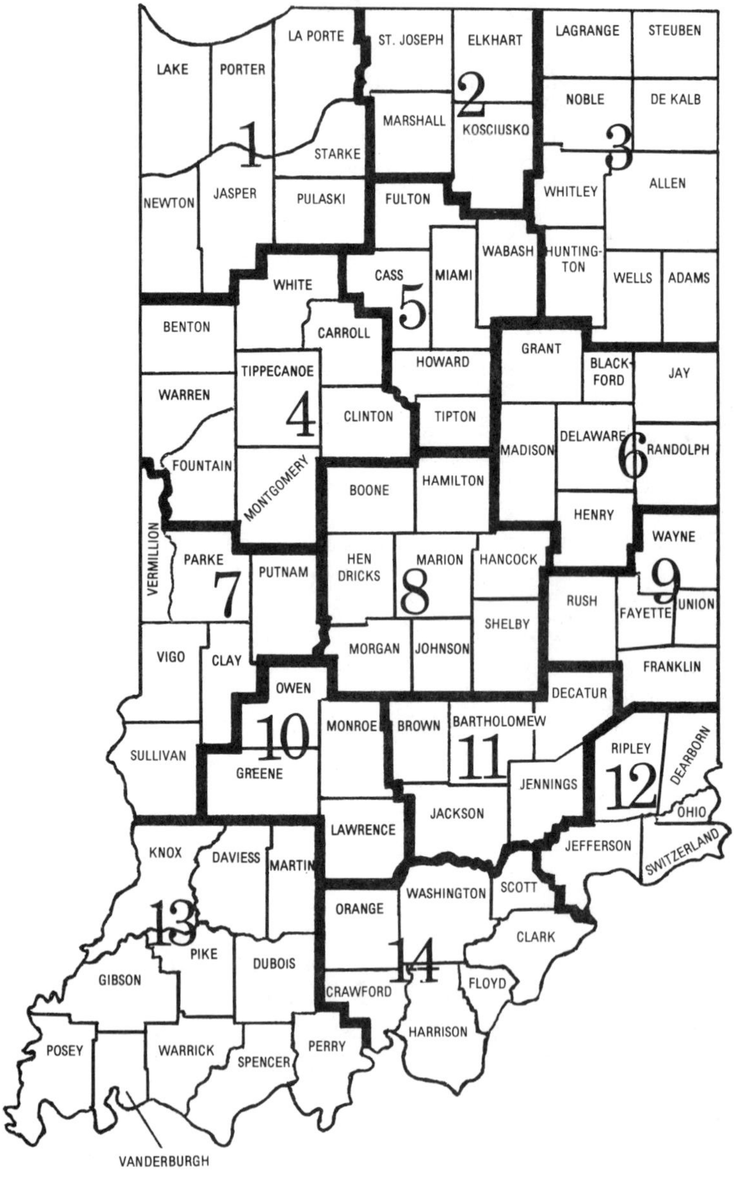

Wabash Township in Gibson County to 273,598 for Center Township in Marion County.

Cities and towns. With 745,739 residents, Indianapolis is the state's largest city as well as being its capital. Fort Wayne is second with a population of 177,671. Following these are Gary (175,415), Evansville (138,764), South Bend (125,580), and Hammond (107,790). The fastest growing city or town in Indiana during the decade from 1960 to 1970 was Carmel in Hamilton County. Its population increased from 1,442 in 1960 to 6,568 in 1970, almost 360 percent. The second fastest growing community during that period was Westville in Laporte County with an increase in population from 789 to 2,615, or 231 percent.

Natural and Ethnic Divisions

Of the persons counted in Indiana during the 1970 census, the sex breakdown was 2,531,170 males and 2,662,499 females. This equals a ratio of 95.1 males to every 100 females, which is also close to the national average. According to race 4,820,324 are white, 357,464 are black, and 15,881 are of other races.

The median age in Indiana is 27.2 years. For whites the median age is 27.6, and for non-whites it is 22.1 years. As an obvious result of the World War II "baby boom", the age group which increased most in proportion to other groups during the 1960s was the 15-24 year olds. This group showed an increase from 628,773 in 1960 to 916,964 in 1970. During that period, the 30-39 year age group slipped numerically in its share of the population, declining form 629,467 persons in 1960 to 573,074 in 1970. The over 50 age groups all increased. An interesting fact is that over 2,381 persons in Indiana are over 100 years old.

Approximately 98 percent of Indiana's residents were born in the United States, and of these, 72 percent in Indiana. Most of the domestic immigrants have come from southern and north central states. Europeans predominate among the foreign-born residents, with persons of Polish descent forming the largest ethnic group in South Bend. Hungarian, Belgian, Italian, and Mexican groups are also strong throughout the state.

A small religious-ethnic group, the Amish, reside in the northeast section of Indiana. Their headquarters are around Middlebury, Nappannee, and Goshen. They conduct a model farm at Amish Acres, near the Mennonites, another religious-ethnic group that also lives in the same vicinity.

FIGURE 3
Counties, Metropolitan Areas, and Selected Places

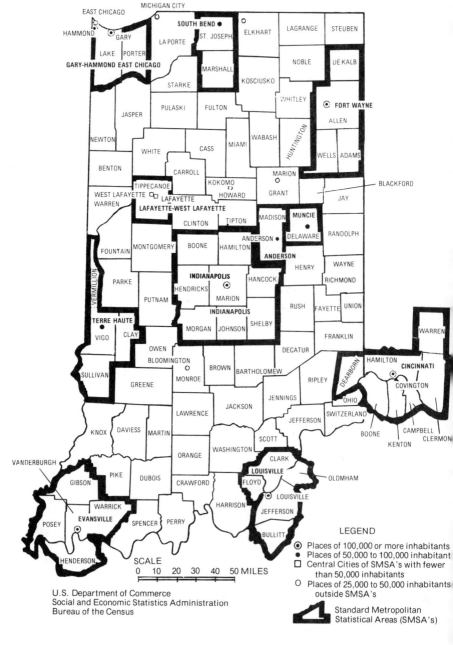

LEGEND

⦿ Places of 100,000 or more inhabitants
● Places of 50,000 to 100,000 inhabitant
☐ Central Cities of SMSA's with fewer than 50,000 inhabitants
○ Places of 25,000 to 50,000 inhabitants outside SMSA's

◤ Standard Metropolitan Statistical Areas (SMSA's)

SCALE
0 10 20 30 40 50 MILES

U.S. Department of Commerce
Social and Economic Statistics Administration
Bureau of the Census

During the 19th century, most of Indiana's black population was rural, but in the 20th century it become urban, with concentrations in the Indianapolis and Gary areas. The black population of Marion and Lake counties constitute 60 percent of the state's total black population.

Summary. Indiana recorded an 11 percent growth during the 1960 to 1970 census periods. This was accounted for entirely by births over deaths. Emigration exceeded immigration by 66,000 persons. Marriage and divorce rates were above the national average.

Most of Indiana's population lives in 42 cities, Populations average between 10,000 and 100,000 persons. The national pattern of moving to the suburbs and out of the cities was prevalent. Fifteen of the state's 92 counties lost population with 10 of these being from the south. More than 70 percent of Indiana's population is Protestant. Catholics, about 15 percent, are located mainly in the urban areas. Jews comprise less than 1 percent of the population and also reside in mainly urban areas.

CHARLES G. GRIFFO

* * *

TABLE 1.
ESTIMATES OF THE POPULATION OF INDIANA COUNTIES: JULY 1, 1972 AND JULY 1, 1973
[State estimates are shown to the nearest thousand, county estimates to the nearest hundred]

County	July 1, 1973 [provisional]	July 1, 1972	April 1, 1970 [census]¹	Change, 1970 to 1973		Components of Change 1970 to 1973²		Net migration	
				Number	Percent	Births	Deaths	Number	Percent
INDIANA	5,316,000	5,286,000	5,195,610	123,000	2.4	301,000	159,000	-21,000	-0.4
Adams	26,800	26,800	26,871	-100	-0.3	1,900	800	-1,100	-4.1.
Allen	289,300	287,900	280,455	8,900	3.2	17,300	7,400	-1,100	-0.4
Bartholomew	59,200	58,300	57,022	2,100	3.7	3,800	1,500	-200	-0.3
Benton	11,200	11,400	11,262	-100	-0.5	600	400	-200	-1.6
Blackford	16,100	16,100	15,888	200	1.3	1,000	600	-200	-1.0
Boone	32,100	31,600	30,870	1,200	3.9	1,600	1,100	700	2.2
Brown	9,300	9,300	9,057	300	2.8	500	300	100	0.8
Carroll	17,700	18,300	17,734	(Z)	-0.1	900	600	-300	-1.9
Cass	40,800	40,700	40,456	300	0.9	2,200	1,500	-400	-0.9
Clark	81,200	79,100	75,876	5,300	7.0	4,500	2,000	2,800	3.7
Clay	24,600	24,400	23,933	700	2.9	1,100	1,100	600	2.7
Clinton	31,300	30,500	30,547	800	2.5	1,800	1,200	200	0.7
Crawford	8,000	8,000	8,033	-100	-0.7	400	400	-100	-1.7
Daviess	26,200	26,700	26,602	-400	-1.6	1,400	1,000	-800	-3.0
Dearborn	30,500	30,200	29,430	1,100	3.6	1,600	1,100	600	1.9
Decat'r	23,400	23,600	22,738	700	2.9	1,400	800	100	0.3
De Kalb	31,200	31,600	30,837	400	1.3	1,900	1,000	-500	-1.7
Delaware	133,300	133,100	129,219	4,100	3.1	7,400	3,500	200	0.1
Debois	31,600	31,600	30,934	700	2.2	1,600	900	-100	-0.2
Elkhart	131,800	129,900	126,529	5,300	4.2	8,100	3,400	600	0.5
Fayette	27,000	26,900	26,216	800	3.2	1,700	900	100	0.3

County									
Franklin	17,700	17,300	16,943	800	4.7	1,000	600	300	2.0
Fulton	17,600	17,700	16,984	600	3.4	900	700	400	2.3
Gibson	30,600	30,700	30,444	200	0.5	1,500	1,200	-100	-0.2
Grant	84,400	84,400	83,955	400	0.5	4,800	2,400	-2,000	-2.3
Greene	28,100	28,200	26,894	1,200	4.6	1,400	1,200	1,100	3.9
Hamilton	61,700	58,400	54,532	7,200	13.1	3,000	1,400	5,600	10.2
Hancock	38,700	36,800	35,096	3,600	10.2	2,100	900	2,400	6.8
Harrison	22,100	21,600	20,423	1,700	8.2	1,100	700	1,200	6.0
Hendricks	58,200	56,100	53,974	4,200	7.8	3,100	1,200	2,300	4.3
Henry	53,500	53,100	52,603	900	1.6	2,900	1,700	-300	-0.6
Howard	86,100	85,100	83,198	2,900	3.5	5,100	2,200	(Z)	(Z)
Huntington	35,400	35,100	34,970	500	1.3	1,900	1,400	(Z)	(Z)
Jackson	33,600	33,200	33,187	500	1.4	1,900	1,100	-400	-1.1
Jasper	22,500	21,400	20,429	2,100	10.3	1,200	600	1,500	7.4
Jay	24,000	24,300	23,575	400	1.8	1,300	900	(Z)	0.1
Jefferson	27,800	27,400	27,006	800	2.9	1,300	900	300	1.2
Jennings	20,300	20,300	19,454	900	4.4	1,200	600	300	1.4
Johnson	66,700	64,400	61,138	5,600	9.1	3,600	1,500	3,500	5.7
Knox	41,500	41,900	41,546	-100	-0.2	1,900	1,800	-300	-0.6
Kosciusko	50,500	49,400	48,127	2,300	4.9	3,100	1,600	900	1.8
Lagrange	22,100	21,600	20,890	1,200	5.7	1,700	500	(Z)	0.2
Lake	549,100	550,200	546,253	2,800	0.5	33,300	15,200	-15,200	-2.8
La Porte	106,200	106,300	105,342	900	0.8	5,900	3,400	-1,600	-1.5
Lawrence	40,700	39,600	38,038	2,600	6.9	2,200	1,400	1,800	4.7
Madison	141,700	141,700	138,522	3,100	2.3	8,200	4,000	-1,100	-0.8
Marion	795,200	796,900	793,769	1,400	0.2	48,200	22,700	-24,100	-3.0
Marshall	36,600	36,800	34,986	1,700	4.7	2,000	1,200	800	2.4
Martin	11,200	11,100	10,069	200	1.8	700	400	-200	-1.5
Miami	39,600	39,900	39,246	300	0.8	2,800	1,200	-1,200	-3.0
Monroe	89,900	89,400	85,221	4,700	5.5	4,400	1,600	1,900	2.2
Montgomery	34,300	34,300	33,930	400	1.1	1,700	1,200	-100	-0.4
Morgan	47,000	45,600	44,176	2,800	6.3	2,700	1,100	1,200	2.8

See footnotes at end of table.

TABLE 1.
ESTIMATES OF THE POPULATION OF INDIANA COUNTIES:
JULY 1, 1972 AND JULY 1, 1973 — Continued

County	July 1, 1973 [provisional]	July 1, 1972	April 1, 1970 [census][1]	Change, 1970 to 1973		Components of change, 1970 to 1973[2]			
				Number	Percent	Births	Deaths	Net migration	
								Number	Percent
Newton	12,600	12,000	11,606	1,000	8.5	600	500	800	7.2
Noble	32,700	32,000	31,382	1,300	4.1	2,000	1,000	300	0.9
Ohio	4,700	4,500	4,289	400	9.9	200	200	400	9.0
Orange	17,400	17,400	16,968	500	2.8	900	700	200	1.2
Owen	13,000	12,700	12,163	800	6.8	700	500	700	5.9
Parke	15,300	15,100	14,628	700	4.6	800	600	500	3.4
Perry	19,100	19,200	19,075	(Z)	(Z)	1,000	600	-400	-2.1
Pike	12,400	12,300	12,281	200	1.3	500	600	200	1.5
Porter	91,700	90,100	87,114	4,600	5.3	5,000	1,900	1,400	1.6
Posey	22,700	22,200	21,740	900	4.4	1,100	700	600	2.5
Pulaski	12,500	12,800	12,534	-100	-0.4	700	500	-200	-1.7
Putnam	27,700	27,600	26,932	800	2.8	1,200	800	400	1.4
Randolph	30,100	29,500	28,915	1,200	4.1	1,700	1,100	600	2.0
Ripley	22,000	21,600	21,138	900	4.1	1,300	800	300	1.4
Rush	20,900	20,900	20,352	500	2.5	1,200	800	100	0.5
St. Joseph	245,000	246,100	245,045	(Z)	(Z)	12,900	7,500	-5,400	-2.2
Scott	17,900	17,400	17,144	700	4.2	1,200	600	100	0.7
Shelby	39,300	38,900	37,797	1,500	4.1	2,200	1,300	600	1.6
Spencer	18,100	17,600	17,134	1,000	5.8	800	600	800	4.6

Starke	20,300	19,900	19,280	1,000	5.1	1,100	800	700	3.6
Steuben	21,500	20,900	20,159	1,400	6.8	1,100	700	900	4.6
Sullivan	19,900	19,900	19,889	(Z)	-0.1	1,000	1,000	(Z)	0.1
Switzerland	6,500	6,400	6,306	200	3.5	300	300	200	3.3
Tippecanoe	113,100	113,000	109,378	3,700	3.4	6,400	2,500	-200	-0.2
Tipton	16,300	16,300	16,650	-400	-2.3	1,000	600	-800	-4.6
Union	6,700	6,700	6,582	200	2.4	400	200	(Z)	0.2
Vanderburgh	168,500	167,800	168,772	-300	-0.2	8,500	6,000	-2,800	-1.7
Vermillion	17,400	17,300	16,793	600	3.6	900	900	600	3.4
Vigo	114,200	115,400	114,528	-300	-0.3	5,800	4,300	-1,800	-1.6
Wabash	35,500	35,500	35,553	(Z)	-0.1	1,800	1,200	-600	-1.8
Warren	8,500	8,500	8,705	-200	-2.8	400	300	-300	-4.0
Warrick	31,700	30,500	27,972	3,800	13.4	1,700	900	2,900	10.5
Washington	19,500	19,500	19,278	(Z)	(Z)	1,100	600	-500	-2.4
Wayne	78,400	79,200	79,109	-700	-0.8	4,400	2,500	-2,500	-3.2
Wells	24,800	24,500	23,821	1,000	4.0	1,400	700	300	1.3
White	21,200	21,200	20,995	200	1.1	1,200	800	-200	-0.8
Whitley	24,700	24,000	23,395	1,300	5.6	1,400	700	600	2.7

(Z) Less than 50 or less than 0.05 percent.
[1]Total does not agree with the sum of the counties due to corrections made to the county populations after release of the official State counts.
[2]Births and deaths are based on reported vital statistics from April 1, 1970, to December 31, 1972, with extrapolations to June 30, 1973.
Net migration is the difference between net change and natural increase.

TABLE 2.
ESTIMATES OF THE POPULATION OF METROPOLITAN AREAS AND THEIR COMPONENT COUNTIES: INDIANA JULY 1, 1972 AND 1973

[SMSA totals rounded independently of county numbers]

Standard metropolitan statistical area and county	July 1, 1973 [provisional]	July 1, 1972	April 1, 1970 [census]	Change, 1970 to 1973		Components of change, 1970 to 1973			
				Number	Percent	Births	Deaths	Net migration Number	Net migration Percent
ANDERSON, IND.	141,700	141,700	138,522	3,100	2.3	8,200	4,000	-1,100	-0.8
Madison	141,700	141,700	138,522	3,100	2.3	8,200	4,000	-1,100	-0.8
CINCINNATI, OHIO-IND.-KY. [Indiana portion]	30,500	30,200	29,430	1,100	3.6	1,600	1,100	600	1.9
Dearborn	30,500	30,200	29,430	1,100	3.6	1,600	1,100	600	1.9
EVANSVILLE, IND.-KY. [Indiana portion]	253,500	251,200	248,928	4,500	1.8	12,800	8,800	600	0.2
Gibson	30,600	30,700	30,444	200	0.5	1,500	1,200	-100	-0.2
Posey	22,700	22,200	21,740	900	4.4	1,100	700	600	2.5
Vanderburgh	168,500	167,800	168,772	-300	-0.2	8,500	6,000	-2,800	-1.7
Warrick	31,700	30,500	27,972	3,800	13.4	1,700	900	2,900	10.5
FORT WAYNE, IND.	372,100	370,800	361,984	10,100	2.8	22,500	10,000	-2,400	-0.7
Adams	26,800	26,800	26,871	-100	-0.3	1,900	800	-1,100	-4.1
Allen	289,300	287,900	280,455	8,900	3.2	17,300	7,400	-1,100	-0.4
De Kalb	31,200	31,600	30,837	400	1.3	1,900	1,000	-500	-1.7
Wells	24,800	24,500	23,821	1,000	4.0	1,400	700	300	1.3
GARY-HAMMOND-EAST CHICAGO, IND.	640,800	640,300	633,367	7,400	1.2	38,200	17,000	-13,800	-2.2
Lake	549,100	550,200	546,253	2,800	0.5	33,200	15,200	-15,200	-2.8
Porter	91,700	90,100	87,114	4,600	5.3	5,000	1,900	1,400	1.6

Area									
INDIANAPOLIS, IND.	1,138,900	1,128,500	1,111,352	27,500	2.5	66,500	31,300	-7,800	-0.7
Boone	32,100	31,600	30,870	1,200	3.9	1,600	1,100	700	2.2
Hamilton	61,700	58,400	54,532	7,200	13.1	3,000	1,400	5,600	10.2
Hancock	38,700	36,800	35,096	3,600	10.2	2,100	900	2,400	6.8
Hendricks	58,200	56,100	53,974	4,200	7.8	3,100	1,200	2,300	4.3
Johnson	66,700	64,400	61,138	5,600	9.1	3,600	1,500	3,500	5.7
Marion	795,200	796,900	793,769	1,400	0.2	48,200	22,700	-24,100	-3.0
Morgan	47,000	45,600	44,176	2,800	6.3	2,700	1,100	1,200	2.8
Shelby	39,300	38,900	37,797	1,500	4.1	2,200	1,300	600	1.6
LAFAYETTE-WEST LAFAYETTE, IND.	113,100	113,000	109,378	3,700	3.4	6,400	2,500	-200	-0.2
Tippecanoe	113,100	113,000	109,378	3,700	3.4	6,400	2,500	-200	-0.2
LOUISVILLE, KY.-IND. [Indiana portion]	138,400	135,100	131,498	6,900	5.2	7,500	3,700	3,100	2.4
Clark	81,200	79,100	75,876	5,300	7.0	4,500	2,000	2,800	3.7
Floyd	57,200	56,000	55,622	1,600	2.9	3,000	1,700	300	0.6
MUNCIE, IND.	133,300	133,100	129,219	4,100	3.1	7,400	3,500	200	0.1
Delaware	133,300	133,100	129,219	4,100	3.1	7,400	3,500	200	0.1
SOUTH BEND, IND.	281,700	282,900	280,031	1,700	0.6	14,900	8,700	-4,500	-1.6
Marshall	36,600	36,800	34,986	1,700	4.7	2,000	1,200	800	2.4
St. Joseph	245,000	246,100	245,045	(Z)	(Z)	12,900	7,500	-5,400	-2.2
TERRE HAUTE, IND.	176,100	176,900	175,143	1,000	0.6	8,900	7,300	-600	-0.3
Clay	24,600	24,400	23,933	700	2.9	1,100	1,100	600	2.7
Sullivan	19,900	19,900	19,859	(Z)	-0.1	1,000	1,000	(Z)	0.1
Vermillion	17,400	17,300	16,793	600	3.6	900	900	600	3.4
Vigo	114,200	115,400	114,528	-300	-0.3	5,800	4,300	-1,800	-1.6

[1] Births and deaths are based on reported vital statistics from April 1, 1970, to December 31, 1972, with extrapolations to June 30, 1973. Net migration is the difference between net change and natural increase.

Prehistory
and Archaeology

SUCCESSIVE groups of Indians lived in Indiana prior to the arrival of the white man in the 17th century. They belonged to many archaeological stages—Paleo-Indian Stage, Archaic Stage, Woodland Stage, and Late Prehistoric Stage—and many cultures—Indian Knoll culture, Adena culture, Hopewell culture, and Mississippi culture.

Paleo-Indian Stage

Indiana remains an anomaly as to the exact time when Paleo-Indians inhabited this area. Radio-carbon dating of sites and classification of fluted arrow and spear points found throughout the state suggest that the region was probably inhabited 20,000 years ago. Little is known about these Paleo-Indians, except that they were probably nomadic hunters of the then plentiful bison, mammoth, and mastodon. The Pleistocene ice sheet was in a recessional stage. As the ice melted, early man followed the animals which lived on the tundra ice fringe. When the animals became extinct, the nomadic hunters moved on and the last traces of them disappeared around 5000 BC. Replacing them were the more sedentary and agricultural people of the Archaic Stage.

Archaic Stage

The earliest inhabitants of the Indian Knoll and Glacial Kame cultures of the Archaic Stage lived in Indiana beginning around

7000 BC. The stage includes hunting and gathering cultures which preceded the introduction and development of agriculture and ceramics. The stage is characterized by full exploitation of the environment. The Indian Knoll culture is named for a site in Kentucky and began about 500 BC. The Glacial Kame culture has been found in northeastern Indiana.

Subsistence activities. Subsistence activities increased as these people became increasingly familiar with local environments. There is evidence of fishing, and taking of shellfish, and of hunting. Archaic peoples also gathered wild plants, nuts, berries, and seeds. Agriculture was unknown, and the dog was the only domesticated animal.

Technology. As changes occurred in subsistence activities, so did changes occur in technology. Artifacts include stone projectile points, knives, scrapers, and bone fishhooks. As time went on atlatl weights, grinding stones, and woodworking tools were added to the inventory. The atlatl, consisting of a wooden shaft tipped with a socketed antler hook, became the principal weapon. It was, in essence, a primitive spear thrower.

Settlement patterns. Villages were placed along river banks on top of refuse shell mounds. Discarded shells of river clams and other garbage was thrown on the floors of the shelters or on the ground outside. Over a period of time, the garbage pile became a huge mound of clam shells, animal and bird bones, and other refuse. The villagers continued to live on top of the mounds in shelters resembling arbors. The shelters were covered with skins and thatching.

Religious and aesthetic activities. Ceremonialism surrounding death and burial is well represented during the Archaic Stage, and the Indian Knoll and Glacial Kame cultures were no exception. Indian Knoll dead were placed in circular burial pits with the skeletons usually flexed. Sometimes red ocher and other offerings were placed in the graves. The inclusion of dog skeletons with those of the humans suggests that the Indian Knoll peoples held this animal in high esteem. Glacial Kame dead were buried in pits and the bodies were usually in a flexed position and accompanied by grave goods. The development of art and aesthetics is evident. Clothing was ornamented with snail-shell beads, and necklaces of shell beads, bone beads, and perforated teeth were worn. The principal articles of clothing were woven breechcloths and skin robes.

Woodland Stage

Adena culture. The Adena culture was in existence from 500 BC until shortly after the beginning of the Christian era in the central Ohio Valley, including Indiana. Adena is the major Ohio Valley representative of the Early Woodland Stage which arose from the Archaic Stage. During the Early Woodland Period, there was a gradual introduction of early domesticated plants, ultimately derived from Mesoamerica. Burial mounds were constructed as monuments and cemeteries for the dead.

Settlement patterns. Most Adena people lived in villages, although a few rock shelters have been found. The houses were generally round and about 25 to 30 feet in diameter, with walls made of paired sapling poles placed in the ground and slanted outward. The most conspicuous architectural features of Adena are large conical burial mounds of earth, usually in groups, although single mounds are not uncommon.

Burial characteristics. The corpse was normally buried in a subfloor pit or on the floor of the mound. The dead were usually either extended or flexed, although disarticulated bundles also occur. Cremations were normal and burials were accompanied by grave goods such as tubular pipes, bracelets, beads, celts, and adzes.

Subsistence activities. Adena peoples depended on hunting, fishing, collecting, and cultivation for their livelihood. Nuts, seeds, wild plants, and berries were gathered and some gourds and squash were apparently raised. Cultivated plants were not a significant part of their diet.

Hopewell Culture

Although southern Ohio was the center of the Hopewell culture, there were subsidiary centers in Indiana, Illinois, Michigan, Pennsylvania, New York, Tennessee, Wisconsin, Iowa, and Kansas. The Hopewell culture was largely responsible for the legend of a "mound builder" race that preceded the Indians in North America. Archaeological investigations, however, have shown this to be a myth. The culture was evidently at its height about 100 AD.

Hopewellian mounds. The large conical burial mounds and the earthwork patterns continue in the Hopewell culture. The earthen mounds are, however, larger than those of Adena time. The mounds show an elaborate cult of the dead, evidenced by rich funerary offerings. Excellent examples of these mounds can be found near the bluffs overlooking the White River in Mounds State Park near Anderson, Indiana. Hopewell mounds tend to be two-stage. The first stage is essentially a low platform prepared to contain a single log tomb or a series of crematory basins. The burials are generally accompanied by tools and elaborate ornaments. The second stage or mantle, is applied so that the final earthwork is a conical mound of earth as much as 100 feet in diameter and from 10 to 70 feet high. Since archaeologists have not extensively explored Hopewell village sites, concentrating instead on mounds, little is known of their subsistence activities.

Aesthetic activities. Hopewell artisans were superior in their craftsmanship. Earspools, head and breast ornaments, bracelets, rings, and panpipes were made of copper. Mica sheets were cut into head dresses, delicate ornaments, and geometric designs. Conch shells were carved into bowls, beads, and gorgets. The craftmen also made stone platform pipes decorated with naturalistic animal and human sculptures.

Much of the Hopewell pottery was standard Woodland—conchoidal in form, with a wide mouth, the surface roughened with cord paddle, and grit-tempered. A small but distinctive percentage—that used in burial ritual—was quite ornate and unique. Common designs were the raptorial duck and bird, along with a variety of geometric and cursive elements.

Late Prehistoric Stage

The Mississippian Period. The Mississipian Period of Indiana was classified into Upper, Middle, and Lower units with the Upper Mississippian culture predominating. Although the period began around AD 500, it seems to have reached its zenith about AD 1400. The Fort Ancient and Tennessee-Cumberland variants (*c.* 1400-1650) of the Upper Mississippian Period are clearly evident in the mound structures along the Ohio River and in the lower Wabash Valley.

Fort Ancient variant. Habitation sites of the Fort Ancient culture near the mounds are large and the great accumulation of debris attests to the sedentary and agricultural nature of the inhabitants. Although these people used burial mounds, shallow earth-and-stone lined graves have been substituted in many instances. The pottery of this group is distinctive, being unpainted to tan, gray, black, or reddish-brown. The jars and vases are characteristically squat and globular with rounded bottoms, broad mouths, and equipped with strap handles. These early artisans were also fond of working in bone. Stone tools were rarely used.

Tennessee-Cumberland variant. The Tennessee-Cumberland variant is primarily developed in Posey, Sullivan, Knox, and Vanderburgh counties in southwestern Indiana. Terraced, flat-topped mounds are characteristic of this culture, which also was sedentary and agricultural.

The houses were built of wattle work and cane and mud combinations. They used copper for both tools and ornaments. Stone, especially flint, was utilized for both tools and weapons. The greatest remnant of this civilization is Fort Azatlan, near Merom on the Wabash River. The site contains a three-sided defensive enclosure measuring 2,450 feet in circumference. Within its confines are 5 mounds and 45 pits.

Conclusive evidence is lacking that these mound builders were the ancestors of the Miami Indians which lived in Indiana in pioneer days. It has definitely been shown, on the other hand, that they are not the ancestors or descendantss of the Aztecs. They were, in point of fact, the first true Indiana Indians.

INDIANS AND EXPLORATIONS

There was considerable movement of Indians in Indiana during the 17th and 18th centuries. The three most important historic tribes were the Miami, Potawatomi, and Delaware. Many lesser tribes such as the Kickapoo, Mascontin, Piankashaw, and Winnebago coexisted with the others but played a minor role in shaping Indiana's history. Limited information is available because the Indians lacked a written language prior to the arrival of the French and English in the 1600s.

The Miami Indians

The Miamis lived mainly in northeastern Indiana in the upper Wabash, Mississinewa, and Saint Joseph river valleys. Their headquarters were at Kekionga (present-day Fort Wayne). The claims of the Miami to aboriginal occupancy were most clearly set forth by a famous leader of the tribe, Little Turtle, but his claims are uncertain as it appears that several other tribes, including the Kickapoo, Potawatomi, and Huron lived there at the same time.

The language of the Miami was Algonquian but varied in dialect from neighboring tribes who also spoke the same tongue.

Subsistence activities. The Miami led a semisedentary life, had fixed villages, but lived away from them on the hunt. Their staple crop was corn, which was supplemented by wild roots, tubers, pumpkins, and beans. They depended largely on hunting and fishing and ate all manner of wild fowl except raven, crow, and loon.

Social structure. The Miami Nation was divided into ten group or gentes, each bearing a designate name such as Turtle, Snow, Moon, or Raccoon. A member could not marry within his own gens but had to take a mate from one of the others. Personal names of members of each gens usually contained a reference to the gens designation. Each Miami village was headed by several officials. Men as well as women could serve as village functionaries. In addition there was a male civil chief, a female civil chief, a male war chief, a female war chief, and several lesser officials. Traditionally, female officials held less power than their male counterparts.

Little Turtle. Perhaps the most influential of all the Miami leaders was Little Turtle. This great war chief was able to keep the nation strong and unified in the ensuing battles which took place in the 1700s between his tribe and the Americans. Until 1794 he was able to keep his lands from falling into enemy possession, but that year he met with disaster at the Battle of Fallen Timbers. Although he fought a savage battle against General "Mad" Anthony Wayne and his soldiers, his defenses were finally weakened and he was forced to withdraw his people from their land. Following a subsequent treaty in 1795, the Miami managed to live for 15 years in relatively peaceful coexistence with the Americans. In the final analysis, they had been reduced to 1,100 in number.

The Delaware Indians

The Delaware Nation lived in the wide valley between the Ohio and White rivers after having been pushed westward in the 1770s by white settlers who claimed their lands. Although written records are sketchy, the tribe managed to keep an account of its wanderings from early times by means of pictographic paintings on sticks. A Moravian mission was established among them in 1801. Its aim of converting them to Christianity failed and the mission was soon abandoned. The Delaware left Indiana in 1818, releasing their lands on the White River to the United States. At that time they numbered about 800 people.

The Potawatomi Indians

The Potawatomi tribe was the largest one in Indiana even though it had been the last one to cross its borders. By 1800 the Potawatomi had numerous settlements in northern Indiana from the Kankakee River all the way East across the state.

Social structure. As with many other tribes, the Potawatomi were divided into gentes. In addition to the gentes they were also divided into two moieties (halves) designated as either Oskush or Kishko. The order of birth of children in a gens predetermined to which moiety each would belong. The eldest child always became part of the Oskush moiety. Traditionally, the Oskush moiety contained the warriors.

Westward Migration of Indians

With the Potawatomi, the migration of Indian groups to Indiana ended. The advance of white settlers brought the usurpation of Indian lands, and most of the Indians had crossed west of the Mississippi by 1838. Only a few scattered Miami remained behind. Today, except for a few musical place names like Kokomo, Maumee, Mississinewa, and Wawasee, rare traces of their vanished life remain.

The French Period

The first white men to enter Indiana were probably French Jesuits who came in hopes of establishing missions and converting the Indians to Christianity. The first white man to actually explore Indiana was Robert Cavalier Sieur De LaSalle who crossed the Saint Joseph-Kankakee portage near South Bend. Two years after his discovery of the portage on December 3, 1679, LaSalle returned to the site to sign a treaty with the Miami Indians. Overly ambitious and demanding, LaSalle was assassinated in 1687 by one of his subordinates.

Early settlement patterns and Indian conflicts. By this time, white infiltration was pretty well established and the first permanent settlement, Ouiatenon (Lafayette), was begun in 1720. Kekionga (Fort Wayne) and Vincennes followed. Vincennes became the largest and most powerful settlement of the French occupancy. Much of its historic past is still preserved today. The quest for furs became the primary goal of the French. The Indians around Kekionga and Vincennes were invited to trade their pelts in exchange for whiskey and tools. Many, because of a large illiteracy rate, were heavily shortchanged or cheated by their so-called white friends. The alliance held in spite of that problem. The Miami Nation was party to the frontier holocaust on June 21, 1752 which grew into the eleven-year French and Indian War, so named because the French and Indians allied themselves against the British who were now beginning to take over Indian lands and the fur trade. The Indians developed a growing dislike for the British, who earlier, unlike the French, had refused to bring gifts to the tribal chiefs. Indian hostility toward the British continued to grow throughout the whole Northwest Territory.

Treaty of Paris. An Indian war instigated by Pontiac, chief of the Ottawa Nation, broke out in 1763. The fury of Indian attacks upon the British were in vain against the powerful enemy garrisons, and on February 10, 1763 the treaty of Paris was signed, ceding all French land holdings to Great Britain. Under the treaty, the British attempted to pacify the Indians and to secure the profitable fur trade. The Indians were subsequently made wards of the British government and were granted all the land located between the Alleghenies and the Mississippi River. This action also served to keep out land-hungry white speculators and homeseekers from the American colonies. Avarice of the colonists for the rich lands of the Ohio Valley and the equal determination of the Indians to hold on to them were prime factors for the Revolutionary War which followed. The Indians, who previously had been enemies of the British, now either supported and fought with them against the Americans or remained neutral.

George Rogers Clark and Indiana's part in the Revolution. Indiana entered the conflict in 1778 when Virginia dispatched young Colonel George Rogers Clark and 200 men on a secret expedition to capture and hold territory which Virginia claimed under its colonial grants. Clark was able to take Fort Sackville at Vincennes in a bloodless strike in July, 1778. A local priest, beloved by the town residents, arranged for the coup when the French militia, who held the fort for the British, turned it over to Clark. Unfortunately, Governor Henry Hamilton, the British commander at Detroit, recaptured Vincennes the following year.

Hearing of this development, Clark returned in February, 1779 with 130 men, made an incredible 18 day journey through 240 miles of drowned, ice-laden swamplands in the dead of winter, and launched an attack on Vincennes. Taken by surprise and having underestimated the size of Clark's army, Hamilton formally surrendered. The flag that Clark subsequently raised was the first American flag ever seen on Indiana soil. Hamilton was sent to Virginia as a prisoner. George Rogers Clark became a hero of the Revolution.

Peaceful beginnings in the Northwest Territory. Warfare continued intermittently until 1783, when under a second Treaty of Paris the Northwest Territory, which included Indiana, was added to the United States. Clarksville (*q.v.*), first American settlement of the Territory, was founded by George Rogers Clark's former soldiers. It was here that Clark himself established his residence and built a saw- and grist-mill. In the next few years townships and towns were planned, laid out, and populated throughout the entire Territory in hopes of an orderly settlement. The former backwoods empire became the "public domain", and in 1787 Congress adopted the ordinance which would provide for a legal government of the Northwest Territory.

INGRID EKLOV JONSSON

* * *

History

TERRITORIAL PERIOD (1787-1816)

AFTER the close of the American Revolution, one of the problems that confronted the new Congress of the United States was the determination of titles to the land northwest of the Ohio River. Virginia, Massachusetts, and Connecticut claimed ownership of this vast territory as extensions of their old colonial boundaries. Individual states, however, were powerless against the British, who remained in illegal possession of strongholds such as Detroit after the Treaty of 1783, and against the Indians, who conducted retalitory raids against the rapidly encroaching white settlers of the region. There was loss of life and property on both sides.

The Ordinance of 1787. In 1784, Virginia yielded its deed to the land, and in 1785 and 1786 Massachusetts and Connecticut gave up their smaller strips of territory. The next year, Congress finally passed the Ordinance of 1787 that created the Northwest Territory. Thus, what is now Indiana, Ohio, Illinois, Michigan, Wisconsin, and part of Minnesota, came under a formally defined government for the first time.

In general, the Ordinance of 1787 adopted the colonial administrative policies of the British Empire. The governorship was an appointive office and the electors of the representative assembly were required to be property owners. Both branches of the government participated in the naming of councillors, but the American governor had wider appointive authority and stronger veto powers than the British administrators of colonial days.

Nevertheless, the Articles of Compact in the Ordinance of 1787 gave the American system a democratic component that the old British system lacked. They allowed for the evolution of the

Northwest Territory into not less than three and not more than five self-governing states as soon as any of these subdivisions had a population of 60,000 inhabitants. These new states could then become members of the Union "on a free and equal footing with the original states in all respects whatever." In addition, the Ordinance provided for trial by jury, the writ of habeas corpus, the setting aside of one-sixteenth of every township for the maintenance of schools, and the prohibition of slavery.

Settlers and the Indians. Arthur St. Clair, a native of Scotland who had served as a general in the Revolution, was named governor of the new territory. His seat of government was at Marietta, Ohio, where New Englanders of the Ohio Company had established their first settlement in 1788. Within one year after passage of the Ordinance, 20,000 men, women, and children came down the Ohio River to establish homes in the river valley. Gen. St. Clair's first priority in his new duties, however, was not surveillance of the immigrants, but the allaying of the fears of the Indians who were alarmed by the sudden invasion of whites into their lands.

St. Clair's efforts were not distinguished by success. A mission into the Wabash country in 1790 by a Vincennes trader, Antoine Gamelin, failed when the Indians claimed the protection and support of the British commander at Detroit and refused his overtures. In the same year, Indian hostility forced Gov. St. Clair to return prematurely to Marietta from a peace-making venture as far west as Kaskaskia, although his secretary, Winthrop Sargent, remained behind and surveyed Knox County. Knox was to be the first or "mother," county of the future state of Indiana, but at that time it sprawled into the present state of Illinois and northward to Canada.

Failing as a peacemaker, St. Clair next tried war, and again failed. He sent Gen. Joseph Harmar north in 1790 to destroy the Miami towns at the headwaters of the Wabash, but most of Harmar's 1,500 men deserted before they reached their destination, and the remainder found the Indian towns abandoned. The venture accomplished nothing more than the burning of five deserted villages and the destruction of the Miami corn crop. Two other excursions, one of them led by Gen. James Wilkinson with Kentucky militia, were equally futile.

These actions were followed by a disaster in November 1791 when St. Clair himself undertood the task of subduing the

Indians. At the headwaters of the Wabash, Chief Little Turtle and a combined force of Miami, Delaware, Shawnee, Ojibwa (Chippewa), Potawatomi, and Ottawa warriors attacked St. Clair's camp. Inflicting the worst defeat on U.S. troops by Indians up to that time, they killed or wounded about 1,000 soldiers and captured some $30,000 worth of supplies and equipment. Gen. St. Clair escaped only because he was not in uniform and supposedly could not be identified by the Indians.

It was not until the federal government sent Gen. Anthony Wayne into the Old Northwest from Pittsburgh in 1793 that the Indians were overcome. Wayne made his first camp at Fort Greenville in Ohio in the fall of that year, and moved on quickly to the site of St. Clair's defeat, naming it Fort Recovery. After wintering there, Wayne established Fort Defiance at the junction of the Auglaize and Miami rivers in the spring of 1794. That August Wayne, with 1,500 U.S. Army troops and 1,600 Kentucky riflemen, defeated Ottawa, Shawnee, and other Indians led by chiefs Blue Jacket, Little Turtle, and Tecumseh at the Battle of Fallen Timbers, near what is now Toledo.

Little Turtle's warriors sought refuge in the British fort at the Maumee rapids, but the British, who had always welcomed them before, would not let them inside the stockade. Betrayed, they scattered and vanished. Therafter, Gen. Wayne established Fort Wayne on the site of the Indian town of Kekionga. This stronghold, which is now Indiana's third largest city, was completed on October 22, 1794.

With the fall of Little Turtle, most of the British military forces and commercial agents retired into Canada. Without British support against the encroachment of white settlers, the Indians agreed to the Treaty of Fort Greenville on August 3, 1795, in which they ceded about 25,000 square miles of what is now eastern and southern Ohio and southeastern Indiana to the U.S. government.

Creation of Indiana Territory. By 1800, there were about 50,000 settlers in the Northwest Territory, most of them in Ohio. The Ohio population was not large enough for the formation of a state under the Ordinance of 1787. It was of sufficient size, however, for William Henry Harrison, the Congressional delegate from the Northwest, to initiate legislation that would separate an Ohio Territory from the Northwest Territory and lead to the admission of the state of Ohio into the Union three years later. This division brought about the creation of Indiana Territory from the remainder of the Northwest in 1800.

Governorship of William Henry Harrison. Indiana Territory encompassed most of modern-day Indiana, all of Illinois, all of Wisconsin, a large part of Michigan, and some of Minnesota. Its capital was Vincennes on the Wabash River, and Harrison was its first governor. He moved to Vincennes on January 10, 1801, and began at once to build a fine brick house for himself and his family. Known as "Grouseland," its architecture is reminiscent of that of the tidewater region of Virginia, and today is a national historic landmark. Michigan Territory was separated from Indiana Territory in 1805 and Illinois Territory in 1809. The latter was composed of the remaining land of the Old Northwest beyond the Wabash River and left Indiana Territory with boundaries very much like those of today.

Since there was no land office at Vincennes when Harrison took up his duties there, he was in full charge of land dealings with settlers during the first four years of his administration. He first untangled the claims of the French *habitants,* who had purchased land from the Indians and then held successive French, English, and American titles. His next and much more complicated task was to extinguish Indian claims to the land while maintaining the peace. Although he was a Virginia aristocrat and only 27 years of age when he became governor of Indiana Territory, Harrison was well prepared for the bold yet subtle and elaborate procedures required of him in his dealings with the Indians. By the time he took up these chores he had already distinguished himself as a captain at the Battle of Fallen Timbers, where he had earned Gen. Wayne's commendation. Afterward, as Wayne's aide-de-camp, he had observed at first hand the maneuvers of an old master at negotiating with the Indians when the Treaty of Greenville was drawn up.

Aided by his secretary, John Gibson, and his three judges, William Clark, Henry Vanderburgh, and John Griffin, Harrison performed his work well, if sometimes ruthlessly. By 1803 he had arranged a treaty with the Indians that opened to white settlement all the land along the Vincennes Trace between Vincennes and Clark's Grant on the Ohio River. Since that date, all land surveys in Indiana have established their origin at a point six miles below the town of Paoli, where the baseline intersects the second principal meridian arbitrarily drawn through the territory. From this point, modern surveyors continue to a number ranges and townships. By 1809, the governor had purchased from the Indians about one-third of the present state for the sum of $10,000 and a small annuity. The survey of that year created what is known in Indiana as the "Ten O'Clock Line," running from Montezuma to Brownstown and so-called because the Indians insisted that it be drawn along the shadow cast by the sun at 10 a.m. on the day that bargain was agreed to.

Tecumseh. The principal obstruction to Harrison's dealings with the Indians was the Shawnee chief, Tecumseh, who had also fought at Fallen Timbers. During the battle Tecumseh's brother was killed, his rifle jammed, and he was forced to retreat, but he refused to accept the Treaty of Greenville. Harrison's equal as a stateman, and eloquent and persuasive Tecumseh went among all the tribes of the Northwest and South, urging them to unite. He was also dramatically effective in his relations with white men. According to one legend, at a conference with Harrison at Grouseland, the governor said, "Your Great White Father offers you a chair." Tecumseh drew himself up and replied, "This man is not my father. The Sun is my father. My mother is the Earth. I shall recline on her bosom," and without loss of dignity, sat down firmly on the ground.

It was because of Tecumseh's denunciation of the "Ten O'Clock Line" that Harrison decided to destroy his opposition by attacking Tippecanoe, the headquarters of the chief's brother, Tenskwatawa, the Shawnee Prophet. Harrison chose a time when Tecumseh was in the South, promoting the cause of Indian federation to the Creek. With 1,000 men the governor marched to Tippecanoe in the autumn of 1811, and there, although he lost 188 killed or wounded troops in a surprise attack at dawn on November 7, he succeeded in killing all but 30 of the 300 or 400 warriors gathered in the town. This victory shattered Tecumseh's pan-Indian movement and drove the Shawnee chief into an alliance with the British in Canada during the War of 1812. Tecumseh died in the Battle of the Thames near Chatham, Ontario, on October 5, 1813.

Jonathan Jennings. Among the white men who most strongly opposed Harrison as governor of Indiana Territory was Jonathan Jennings, a young lawyer from New Jersey who was only 22 years of age when he stepped off a flatboat from Pittsburgh and landed at Jeffersonville in 1806. In the previous year, with the population requirement waived, Indiana had passed into the second grade of territorial government and acquired a legislature despite the objections of Harrison, who foresaw that his powers would be curtailed. By the time Illinois Territory was separated from Indiana in 1809, again in spite of opposition by the governor, Jennings had been elected territorial delegate to the U.S. Congress. An anti-slavery man, he had broken with his former employer, Elihu Stout, the editor of Indiana's first newspaper, the *Indiana Gazette* (later called the *Western Sun*) of Vincennes. Jennings led the "peoples" party in opposition to the "Virginia aristocrats," who were sometimes called "the Vincennes Junta." He won his seat in Congress by defeating Thomas Randolph, a "Virginia aristrocrat," and John Johnson, a Kentuckian who had settled in Knox County. In Congress, Jennings offered numerous bills designed to diminish Harrison's authority and was associated with a movement to remove the governor from office: This latter undertaking was, however, futile.

There were four counties in Indiana Territory in the early 1800s. Dearborn County thrust upward along the present Indiana-Ohio line in a region known as "the Gore." Clark County, another northward-thrusting wedge, lay just west of Dearborn, while Harrison County, still farther to the west, stretched from the Ohio River to the East Fork of the White River. Knox County comprised the remainder of the territory and was the governor's political stronghold. In three successive elections. Jennings again defeated Randolph and two other "Virginia aristocrats." Waller Taylor and Elijah Sparks. By that time the territory had 15 counties and was ready for statehood.

The movement toward statehood. Indeed, Indiana Territory might have become a state earlier than it did if the War of 1812 had not delayed its advancement toward that end. Although Harrison, principal opponent of the movement, resigned his office in 1812 to fight in the war, he was succeeded by his secretary, John Gibson, as acting governor and, later, by another Virginian, Thomas Posey, who held the full title of the office. During the second American conflict with the English, the Indians allied with the British, attacked and almost captured Fort Wayne, and penetrated as far south as what is now Scott County, location of the Pigeon Roost Massacre. During the war, all other concerns temporarily faded in the minds of the white settlers in the territory. In the end, however, the threat of another Indian war convinced the pioneers that a state government would offer them more security than remote Washington could provide. By the end of the war, the movement for statehood had such wide popular support that no territorial official dared openly oppose it.

Congress had already consented to waive the population requirement of 60,000 inhabitants established by the Ordinance of 1787 and to allow submission of an enabling act as soon as the territory had 35,000 white inhabitants. The territorial legislature did not authorize a census until 1814, and another year was to pass before all heads could be counted. Meantime, many new towns were springing up south of the East Fork of the White River—Evansville, Salem, Vernon, and Paoli among them. Others were being laid out farther north, while older settlements such as Jeffersonville, Madison, Brookville, Corydon, and Lawrenceburg were growing rapidly. This population explosion destroyed the grip of the old "Vincennes Junta" on the territory and made statehood inevitable.

The final figure of the census was 63,897 free white settlers. A few black slaves were held illegally in Indiana as late as 1840, but they and the remaining Indians were not counted in the census. As soon as the final tabulations were available, the legislature applied for statehood. Congressman Jennings was chairman of the committee in Washington, D.C., to which the memorial was referred. On January 15, 1816, Jennings introduced a bill for an enabling act, and despite a few last-minute murmurings from some of the old "aristocrats" back home in Indiana, Congress passed the bill in April of that year.

Establishment of the state government. The statehood bill authorized the election of delegates to a constitutional convention on the second Monday of May 1816, and the convening of these delegates in the new territorial capital of Corydon on the second Monday in June. The delegates were to organize a government that would be "republican and not repugnant to the articles of the Ordinance of 1787." There were certain definite provisions in the enabling act. The state of Indiana was to be represented in Washington, D.C., by two senators and one elected member of the House of Representatives until the next general census was taken. Most of the business of the convention, however, was left to the discretion of the delegates. Before they convened, it was already agreed in the territorial legislature's memorial that the new state would "come in free" and that its name would be

Indiana and not Polypotamia, Assenisipia, Pelisipia, or one of the other absurdities conceived for the region by Thomas Jefferson some 30 years earlier.

The 43 elected delegates who met at Corydon on June 10, 1816, were a representative and responsible group. Most were farmers, some were already elected office-holders, about a dozen were preachers, and a slightly smaller number were lawyers. None ever became famous outside the state, but 23 of them later served in the Indiana Senate and 17 in the House, one became a governor, two were elected to the U.S. House of Representatives, two to the U.S. Senate, and three served as state judges. The most familiar names in subsequent Hoosier history of the men at Corydon, aside from the future politicians, were John DePauw, father of businessman and philanthropist Washington C. DePauw, after whom DePauw University was named; John Badollet, friend of Albert Gallatin; and David Maxwell, later a trustee of Indiana University. William Hendricks served as secretary of the convention, although he was not a delegate.

The meeting place of the convention was the county courthouse of Corydon, which served as the Indiana Statehouse until the capitol was moved to Indianapolis in 1824. The weather was hot and most gatherings were held out-of-doors under a "Constitutional Elm." The sessions lasted 18 working days and business was completed on June 29. Most of what the delegates produced was a copy, often verbatim, of the constitutions of Ohio, Kentucky, and Pennsylvania, there being no man of great literary talent among them and no desire to improve upon the language of the founders of earlier states. Article IX, however, was an exception. Under its provisions, Indiana became the first state in the Union to acknowledge and assume responsibility for the education of its citizens. Written by John Badollet, Article IX provided for public libraries as well as public schools, and urged upon the General Assembly "the promotion and improvement of the arts, sciences, commerce, manufactures, and national history." The document drawn up at Corydon was not submitted to popular vote and authorized no amendments, but it did provide for a review by popular referendum every 12 years. The constitution remained in effect unchanged for 35 years.

The labors of the convention were, in the main, a victory of the Jennings party over the Harrison party. In the general election that was held in August 1816, the people of Indiana chose

Jonathan Jennings as their first state governor over Thomas Posey by a vote of 5,211 to 3,934. At the same time, William Hendricks won the seat in the U.S. House of Representatives. Three months later, the General Assembly met and named James Noble and Waller Taylor as the first U.S. senators from the state. Taylor had at one time been a vigorous opponent of Jennings, but the Indiana historian Jacob Piatt Dunn conveniently explained him as an example of "the liberality of the controlling party to the minority." Whatever the reasons for the successes, all these men were a credit to the wisdom of those who chose them.

STATEHOOD TO THE PRESENT

The Pre-Civil War Era

In 1816 the Gibson-Posey county line ran through the center of a village called Harmonie. At the constitutional convention a delegate from Gibson named Frederick Rapp was challenged because, it was said, many of his supporters in Harmonie crossed the street and voted for him illegally. Seated despite the charge, Rapp immediately joined a minority of die-hard obstructionists in voting against the initial enabling motion of the convention, which stated that it was "expedient at this time to proceed to form a Constitution and a State Government." Rapp had been moved by Elihu Stout's argument that statehood would increase taxes. Greater distinction in Indiana history, however, adheres to Frederick Rapp, the adopted son and business manager of the religious leader, George Rapp.

George Rapp. In 1803 George Rapp brought some 800 German immigrants to America and founded a religious community near Pittsburgh, Pennsylvania. In the spring of 1814, he abandoned the prosperous settlement for 25,000 acres on the banks of the Wabash River in Indian Territory. Rapp's followers, known as Rappites, believed that the second coming of Christ was imminent. They were celibates who had no intellectual interests other than learning Bible lessons and religious songs by rote, and were skilled artisans and farmers. In Indiana they prospered again in the town of Harmonie. After 11 years of awaiting the millennium in their new paradise, Rapp sold his town in 1824 to another millennarian and moved back to Pennsylvania.

Robert Owen. This second millennarian was the Welsh social reformer, Robert Owen. He believed that men and women could

achieve eternal happiness for themselves by following his plan
for universal education toward social and economic equality.
Rechristening the town New Harmony, Owen populated it with
scholars, ignoring the need for manual labor. A year after the
purchase, he and a newly acquired partner, the Scottish geologist
and philanthropist William Maclure, dispatched to New Harmony
from Pittsburgh a flatboat so freighted with learned men and
women they they called it the "Boatload of Knowledge."

Among the flatboat's passengers, at least at the outset, were
Owen and Maclure. Others, who stayed aboard throughout the
voyage, were the naturalists Thomas Say and Charles-Alexandre
Lesueur; two teachers from Paris, Guillaume Phiquepal and
Marie Duclos Fretageot; a Philadelphia doctor and his family;
several young women destined to become schoolmistresses; a
flock of children, many of them French, who would be their
pupils; an artist; and Owen's eldest son, Robert Dale Owen, who
would later become a social reformer almost as famous as his
father. Within the next year and a half, experimental schools
were established in New Harmony, books and newspapers were
published, and visitors from Europe and other parts of America
were welcomed to see at first hand the "Community of Equality"
that Robert Owen had advertised in speeches and manifestos.
What they found was a lively group of intellectuals attending
lectures and dances in the old Rappite buildings. But, the mills
and factories were idle, the hogs ran wild in the streets, and the
surrounding fertile fields were sadly neglected.

Owen abandoned his community in less than two and a half
years after he bought it, deeding his property to his children and
delivering two "Farewell Addresses" in May 1827. His four sons
and one daughter and many of his associates and disciples
remained in New Harmony, making a rich contribution to the
cultural and social history of Indiana. Maclure and Madame
Fretageot, for example, worked out a school system that became
a model for future educators. Thomas Say continued his studies
in natural history until his death in New Harmony in 1834, and
the village became a center for geological surveys under the
direction of David Dale Owen. The nation's first woman's club,
the Minerva Society, was organized in Jane Dale Owen
Fauntleroy's home in 1859. Richard Dale Owen became a
professor of natural history at Indiana University and the first
president of Purdue University. Robert Dale Owen was elected to

the U.S. House of Representatives, where he introduced the bill that created the Smithsonian Insitution. In 1850, at Indiana's second constitutional convention, he led the fight for women's rights.

Ironically, George Rapp's religious communal ideology produced material success reflected in the substantial houses and public buildings that continue to delight sightseers in New Harmony. Owen's philosophy, which regarded religion as "superstition" and sought the material comfort of mankind, produced few physical reminders of its existence. It was followed, however, by a spiritual "afterglow" that can be felt in the theatrical performances, artistic activities, and lectures by visiting scholars in modern New Harmony.

Political developments. Soon after Indiana became a state, the influence of the founding fathers disappeared in the growth of the national Whig and Democratic parties and their development of the party caucus. The new political system produced capable governors in James Ray, Noah Noble, David Wallace, Samuel Bigger, James Whitcomb, and Paris Dunning. But the men whom organized politics sent to the U.S. Senate — Robert Hanna, John Tipton, Oliver H. Smith, Albert S. White, Edward A. Hannegan, and Jessie D. Bright — cannot be compared with their colleagues from other states such as Henry Clay, John C. Calhoun, and Daniel Webster.

Andrew Jackson won the Indiana vote in his unsuccessful try as the Democratic candidate for the presidency in 1824, and again carried the state in his successful elections of 1828 and 1832. He introduced the "spoils system" into the state, but his vetoes of bills to improve the Wabash River, the National Road, and the harbor at Michigan City lost the Hoosier vote for his Democratic successor, Martin Van Buren, in 1836. During this election it is said, the Democrats' symbol of a rooster was adopted in Indiana when George Chapman, editor of the *Wabash Enquirer* in Terre Haute and a lukewarm supporter of Van Buren, was urged by a party leader to "Crow, Chapman, crow!".

Four years later, with aging William Henry Harrison as their candidate for president, the Hoosier Whigs finally came into their own. The label of "Virginia aristocrat" was forgotten, and Harrison became suddenly "a man of the people" and a Hoosier. The battle cry of the election was "Tippecanoe and Tyler too." After the votes were counted Indiana claimed the Whig candidates as its first occupant of the White House. The only other Hoosier to live in that mansion was to be Benjamin Harrison, the territorial governor's grandson. Although the second Harrison was a native of Ohio, he was a bona fide resident of Indianapolis, which had been the state's capital since 1824. For some reason, no effort has been made to claim Abraham Lincoln as a Hoosier president, although he lived from 1816 to 1830 between the ages of 7 and 21 in southern Indiana, where his mother is buried. Perhaps the state is more accurately described as the "Mother of Vice Presidents." Of the eight Hoosiers who have been candidates for that office, four—Schuyler Colfax, Thomas A. Hendricks, Charles W. Fairbanks, and Thomas R. Marshall—were elected.

Transport and bankruptcy. Until the mid-19th century, Indianans were largely preoccupied with the development of commerce through improved transportation. Various sections of the state were at odds with each other over priorities in the solutions of this problem. Their rivalry made it obvious that the state needed a single, comprehensive program. As a consequence, the Mammoth Internal Improvement Bill of 1836 appropriated $10,000,000 and enlarged and authorized an existing canal board to develop the Whitewater Canal, the Central Canal, the Wabash and Erie Canal, a railroad from Madison to Crawfordsville via Indianapolis, and a macadamized turnpike from new Albany to Vincennes known as the Paoli Road. The board was also directed to resurvey the route from Jeffersonville to Crawfordsville for the purpose of building either a turnpike or a railroad, to clear the Wabash for steamboat traffic from its mouth to Vincennes, and to survey and make estimates for a canal or railroad to connect the Wabash and Erie Canal near Fort Wayne with Lake Michigan near Michigan City.

Unforunately the bill was overambitious, and within three years the state was bankrupt. The canal board brought to completion only the Whitewater and the Wabash and Erie canals, which were soon supplanted by railroads. It is to the credit of the state, however, that it never fully repudiated its debt and that it also learned from the experience. The second constitutional convention denied the General Assembly the power to incure "any debt, except to meet casual deficits in the revenue, to pay interest on the present state debt, or to repel invasion, or suppress insurrection."

The Mexican War. Another Hoosier preoccupation of this

period was the Mexican War of 1846 to 1848. Although it was sometimes called "the Democrats' War." Hoosier Whigs and Democrats alike supported it loyally. Only 19 days after Gov. Whitcomb issued a call for volunteers on May 22, 1846, Indiana's quota of 3,000 men from a total population of 750,000 was filled. Individuals often undertook the recruiting of their own companies and regiments. Among such patriots was the young Lew Wallce, later the successful author of *Ben Hur.* A Camp Clark on the Ohio River, the men who answered the governor's call elected their own officers. This resulted in the field command being given to political leaders of little or no military experience such as Brig. Gen. Joscph Lane, Col. James H. Lane, Col. James P. Drake, and Col. William A. Bowles.

In civilian life, Bowles was a physician. He had just built a hotel at French Lick Springs, which a half century later Democratic political boss Thomas Taggart would make fashionable and famous. At the Battle of Buena Vista, Dr. Bowles proved so inept in his military role that a blight lingered upon the reputation of Indiana men as soldiers until they redeemed themselves by their generous and valiant record in the Civil War.

The Civil War period. As the Mexican War came to its close, a young lawyer named Oliver P. Morton opened his first office in Centerville, Indiana. Originally a Democrat, by 1860 he had become a member of the new Republican Party and was a candidate for lieutenant governor. Abraham Lincoln carried Indiana that year, and Morton and his running-mate for the governorship, Henry S. Lane, were elected. According to an arrangement Morton had made when he agreed to take second place on the ticket , the General Assembly promptly put Lane in the U.S. Senate and Morton succeeded to the gubernatorial office.

In his first public statement after inauguration, Gov. Morton said he had been elected "to denounce treason and uphold the cause of the Union." This he did for four years, although the danger from copperheads (sympathizers with the Southern cause) in Indiana hardly justified his autocratic rule of the state. For two years he refused to convene the General Assembly and, keeping public funds in a safe in his office, distributed them without legislative sanction while branding critics of his illegal methods as "traitors."

The Confederate raider John Hunt Morgan crossed the Ohio

River at Mauckport with 2,400 veteran calvarymen on July 8, 1863, and penetrated as far as Salem before federal troops could discover their location. Demoralized by their own looting of well-stocked Hoosier stores and rich farmlands, the raiders turned and fled southward again, without having gained the support or aid of Southern sympathizers in Indiana.

One year after the raid, aging Dr. Bowles was a "major general" in the Knights of the Golden Circle, a secret organization sympathetic to the South that envisioned the end of the Civil War through revolution against the Union in the North. Bowles was arrested at French Lick, tried for treason by a military court, and sentenced to be hanged. The U.S. Supreme Court freed him and his co-conspirators, howevr, in its ruling in *ex parte Milligan* on the grounds that military courts have no jurisdiction over civilians in regions were civil courts are functioning.

Of greater glory to Indiana than the witch-hunt for ineffectual copperheads was the activity of the Underground Railroad that ran through the heart of the state for two decades before the Civil War began. The Levi Coffin House in Fountain City, a "station" on the Railroad, is now one of the national historic sites of Indiana. Estimates of the number of runaway slaves sheltered in this "station" range between 2,000 and 10,000, and it was only one of many along the route to Canada and freedom. Support of the Underground Railroad was illegal in its time, but the motives of those who participated were humanitarian, required great courage, and were not self-seeking.

Indiana's loyalty was indeed vital to the war. Fifth largest of the states that remained in the Union, it bordered controversial Kentucky, and its railroads, which ran mostly north and south, were exposed and vulnerable to Confederate attack. Indiana's wheat (16,848,000 bushels in 1860), corn (71,588,000 bushels), and hogs (3,099,000, or twice the human population of the state) were essential to the supplies of the federal army.

After Fort Sumter fell in April 1861, Hoosier Democrats and Republicans rallied to the Union, just as the Whigs and Democrats had done during the Mexican War. Indiana filled its military quota within five days after the first call to arms. When the fighting was finally over in 1865, the state ranked second after Delaware in the percentage of military men who had served in the Union Army. Indiana men and women participated in 308 engagements in the war, including the final action at Palmetto

Ranch, Texas, May 13, 1865. More than 7,200 Hoosiers died in action and almost 17,800 died of disease during the war. The celebrated Nineteenth of Indiana in the "Iron Brigade" lost almost 16 percent of its men to the fighting.

The Post-Civil War Period

Since the Civil War, the story of Indiana has been one of initiative and growth in transportation and industry, of occasional political drama in which it is often difficlut for outsiders to distinguish one political party from another, a phenomenal flowering of literature by Hoosier authors, all-out participation in the two global wars the United States has fought in the 20th century, and at least its full share in the nation's obsession with sports.

Transportation. Most of the state's steam railroad lines were constructed in the pre-Civil War period. They included the famous Monon, which ultimately connected Louisville with Chicago, running diagonally across Indiana and serving, as Hoosier railroad buffs delight in pointing out, a galaxy of universities that included Indiana, Butler, DePauw, Wabash, and Purdue, as well as a state reformatory and a state penitentiary. It was in the post-war period, however, that the great east-west trunk lines were opened. Terre Haute on the Wabash then became one of the major railroad centers of the nation, incidentally producing from its carshops Hoosier Eugene V. Debs, the Socialist Party leader who was five times a candidate for the U.S. presidency, and Indiana author Theodore Dreiser, who as a small boy scavenged for coal for the family stove from the tracks of the E.& T.H.

Indiana's most notable contribution to rail transportation was its preeminence in developing the urban and interurban trolley car. The city of Wabash in 1880 was the scene of one of the first experiments in the country in using electricity for public lighting, and two years later South Bend first tried to move a streetcar with electricity. The initial experiment failed, but in 1885 the city won the distinction of operating the first electrically propelled public electric trolley cars in their streets. The next and inevitable step was to connect them by an interurban trolley system.

Indianapolis became the hub of the network. Centrally situated, the capital opened its Traction Terminal in 1904, and 400 electric trains were entering and leaving that depot by 1910. Four years later, Hoosier "traction lines" had 2,137 miles of main track, with 1,229 cars for passengers, 363 for freight, and 78 for mail and baggage. Of the state's 92 counties, 67 were served by interurban cars.

World War I curtailed this service, and trucks, buses, and private motor cars made inroads upon the trolley business by the 1920s. When the Evansville and Ohio Valley Company converted competely from electricity to gasoline in 1946, the Shore Line for commuters in the Gary-Chicago area became the lone surviving descendant of the once-famous interurban system. Commercial airports were, by that time, mushrooming at the edges of most of the towns and cities in the state, to vie with the new bus lines.

Industry. The city of Gary, now Indiana's second largest, was not established until 1905, when the U.S. Steel Corporation chose the site for the construction of mills in the Midwest. Before that, the site of Gary on the southern end of Lake Michigan had been a wasteland of sand dunes, and Evansville, Fort Wayne, Terre Haute, and South Bend were the principal industrial cities of the state. They produced furniture, flour, carriages, wagons, shoes, farm machinery, beer, and whiskey. In those earlier times, southern Indiana had the advantage of large resources of bituminous coal and easy access to the Ohio River. The development of the Calumet region in the north, however, progressed so rapidly that it took the lead in industry in the 20th century and is now the most densely populated area of the state outside of Indianapolis.

The gasoline engine, which played an important role in ending the era of the interurban trolley car, was almost exclusively a Hoosier product in its beginnings. In 1893, Elwood Haynes assembled the first mechanically successful spark-ignition automobile at Kokomo, Indiana, and on the Fourth of July drove-it a mile and a half out Pumpkin Vine Pike and back at seven miles an hour. For seven years Haynes and the Apperson brothers produced automobiles together in Kokomo; therafter, they operated separately until the mid-1920s. By that time, Indianapolis had become the heart of the automobile industry in the nation as well as the state. Cars were manufactured there until 1937, although long before that year Detroit had taken the ascendancy in the industry with the establishment of the Ford and General Motors companies. Even so, the Marmon, the Stutz, the Duesenberg, the Auburn, the Cole, and the Cord remain classic names in the history of automobile manufacture. In the heyday of Hoosier enterprise in that endeavor, 246 different makes of cars were produced in 56 different Indiana communities.

Sports. The opening of the Indianapolis Motor Speedway in 1909 was a by-product of the Hoosier passion for automobile building. One of the purposes of the annual 500-mile Memorial Day Race was to give car makers and tire manufacturers an opportunity to test their products for improvement. Perhaps because the pari-mutual system of betting is illegal in Indiana, horse racing is less popular than automobile racing. Oxford, Indiana, however, still boasts of being the home of the great racehorse, Dan Patch. Mention of sports in the state must also include the football team of Notre Dame University, where the tradition established by Knute Rockne was very much alive in the 1970s. A Hoosier tribute to baseball was the naming of the bridge over the White River near Petersburg after Gil Hodges, famed first baseman of the Brooklyn Dodgers. Hoosiers continue to take pride in native sons like baseball players Don Lash and Mordecai "Three Finger" Brown.

None of these enthusiasms compares with the hysteria that seized the state every February when the high school basketball tournaments were held. These events come at a time when basketball fans might be expected to have exhausted themselves by three months of cheering the feats of the great teams turned out consistently by Indiana University, Purdue and Notre Dame. But Hoosiers are inexhaustible where basketball is concerned, and probably the most knowledgeable spectators of the game in the world.

Literature. Almost as popular and profitable as basketball is the state's production of best-selling books. Between the turn of the 20th century and World War II, Indiana ranked second only to New York State in this endeavor, producing 213 national bestsellers to New York's 218, while Pennsylvania ranked third with only 125. Before the year 1900 there were many successful writers in and from Indiana, including Edward Eggleston, author of *The Hoosier School-Master* (1871), and Lew Wallace, the creator of *Ben Hur* (1880).

In the late 1890s and early 1900s there was an epidemic of book-writing in the state like none before or since. The best known names of this period are Maurice Thompson (*Alice of Old Vincennes*), Charles Major (*When Knighthood Was in Flower*),

George Barr McCutcheon (*Graustark*), Gene Stratton Porter (*A Girl of the Limberlost*), George Ade (*Fables in Slang*), and James Whitcomb Riley and Booth Tarkington, whose successes are too numerous to mention. Riley and Tarkington were the most typical Hoosier writers of the period, and Theodore Dreiser the most atypical. Since the so-called "Golden Age" of Hoosier writing, other Indiana authors have continued to write in such a wide-ranging diversity of manners and forms that they defy characterization, except as Hoosiers. Among them are Jessamyn West, Kurt Vonnegut, Lloyd Douglas, Joseph Hayes, Rex Stout, Elmer Davis, and Alfred Kinsey, to name only a various assorted few.

Politics. An almost equally diversified collection of political figures appeared on the Hoosier scene in the 20th century. Perhaps the most deplorable was D.C. Stephenson, organizer and leader of the Ku Klux Klan. Three years after his arrival in the state in the 1920s from· Texas, he held such power in Indianapolis that he was able to announce unchallenged and without holding public office, "I am the law in Indiana." But there were also such nationally recognized and respected men as Albert J. Beveridge, Paul V. McNutt, and Wendell L. Willkie. An advocate of American imperialism in the school of Theodore Roosevelt, Beveridge preached his doctrine brilliantly in the U.S. Senate and on the lecture platform in the early years of the 20th century. McNutt, like Oliver P. Morton, was an autocrat in the office of governor in the mid-1930s. With the support of a rubber-stamp legislature he succeeded during his four years in office in converting a large deficit into a surplus of more than $10,000,000 and in modernizing the state's antiquated governmental procedures. Willkie, who had been McNutt's classmate at Indiana University, went further in his quest for the U.S. presidency in the election of 1940, but he was defeated by Franklin D. Roosevelt.

Recent political history in Indiana has been highlighted less by individuals than by reforms in the state government. The Reapportionment Act of 1971 did much to break down voting by party blocs in the General Assembly. The "Two Per Cent Club," inaugurated by Gov. McNutt and requiring party contributions of two percent of salaries by office-holders, had been all but eliminated in both parties by the 1970s. The constitutional amendment of 1972 allowed a governor of the state to run for reelection. Colorful individuals also played a role in state politics, however.

In 1968, Robert F. Kennedy came into Indiana on his "Wabash Cannonball" train to campaign against Eugene J. McCarthy in the Democratic presidential primary. Gov. Roger D. Branigin joined the race and campaigned across the state with these national figures. For a short time that year, Hoosier hysteria almost attained the annual peak reached during the state basketball tournaments. It was all to no avail, however, because none of the contenders won the election.

WILLIAM E. WILSON

* * *

People and Population

THE name of the state of Indiana means "homeland or place of the Indians." For more than 10,000 years it was literally that. Only about 300 years ago did the first known white man set foot within the present borders of the state.

Prehistoric evidence of Indian habitation of the state has been discovered in excavations such as the McKinley Site in Hamilton County, Nowlin Mound in Dearborn County, Angel Mounds near Evansville, and Fort Azatlan near Merom.

When the white man first arrived the Miami and Potawatomi occupied substantial portions of the state, together with the Delaware, Shawnee, and a few members of other Indian tribes. The Miami had come into the state—or perhaps returned to it—from the north during the late 17th and early 18th centuries. They occupied much of northeastern Indiana, including the Upper Wabash and Maumee valleys. The Potawatomi also came from the north somewhat later, principally during the first part of the 18th century. They settled primarily in the central and western sections of northern Indiana. The tribes overlapped somewhat and mingled.

The Delaware came from the east, mainly during the late 18th century. They occupied central and eastern Indiana, especially along the upper reaches of the west fork of the White River.

Other lesser tribes included the Wea, Kickapoo, Wyandot, Shawnee, and Piankashaw. The Indians depended mainly upon hunting, fishing, the gathering of berries, nuts, and fruits, and the cultivation of domestic crops including corn (maize), potatoes, squash, and beans.

Some historians believe it likely that the first white visitor to the region of modern Indiana was the famous Jesuit priest, Jacques Marquette, in 1673. The first white man who with certainty is known to have touched Indiana soil, however, was the explorer, Rene Robert Cavelier sieur de La Salle, in 1679. He crossed the St. Joseph-Kankakee portage near the present site of South Bend. The first French settlers established three small outposts at Miami (Fort Wayne), Ouiatenon (near Lafayette), and Vincennes to guard the Maumee-Wabash route connecting Lake Erie with the Ohio River.

Chief rivals of the French in settling North America, the British followed not far behind. After a series of four colonial wars, the English won a decisive victory in 1763 and took over control of Indiana.

Nearly all the early immigrants to Indiana, after the initial surge of French and British settlers, were native-born Americans. Most came from the Upper South, with Tennessee, Kentucky, Maryland, Virginia, and North Carolina providing substantial numbers. A few came from New England. At first, nearly everyone settled in southern Indiana in close proximity to the Ohio River. Lines of settlements then reached out northward up the Wabash and Whitewater valleys. Many of the early settlers were squatters and sturdy pioneers who cleared the forests of southern Indiana, and established schools, churches and towns.

By 1810, even though Michigan and Illinois had been split off into separate territories, the population of Indiana Territory had jumped to almost 25,000. When Indiana was ready for statehood in 1816, the white population numbered close to 64,000, in excess of the figure necessary for acceptance into the Union.

By 1820, the federal census reported an Indiana population of 147,178. It jumped to 685,866 in 1840 and climbed to 1,350,428 in 1860. The population had multiplied between nine and ten times in four decades.

The people of Indiana have been called Hoosiers since the early 1830s. But the origin of the term is still widely debated and speculated upon. One of the most popular theories is that visitors, upon hailing a pioneer cabin or knocking on its door, usually were greeted with "Who's yere?" and Indiana thus became the "Who's yere?"—or Hoosier—state. A second popular theory is that the brawling rivermen of the state so often trounced or "hushed" their opponents that they were dubbed "Hushers," later corrupted to Hoosiers. James Whitcomb Riley carried the speculation near to the point of absurdity with his tongue-in-cheek explanation that the name grew out of barroom fights in which men would gouge, scratch, and bite off the noses and ears of their opponents. Riley claimed a settler wandering into a tavern after a fight would find an ear on the floor, touch it with his boot toe, and casually ask, "Who's ear?" Historians are more likely to accept a more prosaic theory advanced by Jacob Piatt Dunn, long-time secretary of the Indiana Historical Society. He noted that the world was used to describe woodsmen or rough hill people of the South and traced it back to the term "hoozer," from a dialect in England's Cumberland district. He theorized that descendants of English immigrants brought the name with them when they settled in the hills of southern Indiana.

Indiana's burgeoning population was part of a general westward flow of people into the Mississippi Valley. In addition to the sizeable numbers from the Southern states, settlers came from such Middle Atlantic states as Pennsylvania and New York and also from neighboring Ohio. Immigration from the Middle Atlantic states grew larger than that from the Upper South between 1830 and 1860. Few came from either New England or the Lower South.

There was little foreign immigration to Indiana before 1830. It increased substantially, however, in the 1840s and 1850s. Most of the foreigners coming into the state were either Germans or Irish. According to the 1860 census, Indiana had 118,184 residents of foreign birth—more than twice as many as the 54,426 shown in the 1850 census. Some 56 percent of the foreign-born were natives of German states. About 21 percent were from Ireland and about 8 percent were from England. The foreign-born were distributed in the areas of concentration of population across the state.

The Delaware left Indiana in 1820, clearing. the way for rapid settlement of central Indiana during the ensuing decade. By 1850, the Potawatomi and Miami had been persuaded to depart through various treaties and other moves of the federal government.

Although slavery had never been a legal institution in the

state, free blacks were unwelcome. In 1851, Indiana had only about 11,000 blacks—slightly more than one percent of its population.

Indiana's population was decimated by the Civil War. About 25,000 men—one in every eight the state sent to war—lost their lives from battle wounds, accidents, or disease. Thousands more were maimed. It still ranks as the most costly war to Indiana in terms of human life.

The state population nearly doubled from the 1860 total to the 2,516,000 of 1900. Until World War I, the majority of new Hoosiers continued to come from Ohio, Kentucky, Illinois, Virginia, Pennsylvania, West Virginia, and North Carolina. After the war, immigration from other states in various parts of the country increased as did the outflow of native-born Hoosiers going to other states, especially Ohio, Kentucky, Illinois, Missouri, Kansas, Iowa, Nebraska, Wisconsin, Michigan, California, and Arizona. Since 1890, many other Hoosiers have gone to the great metropolitan centers of the East.

Foreign immigration reached its peak between the Civil War and World War I, then dropped off sharply. Until World War I, the Germans and Irish remained the two leading nationalities among immigrants. Smaller numbers came from Canada, France, England, and Scotland. In the late 19th and early 20th centuries, natives of Poland, Italy, Austria, Hungary, and Russia began to arrive in significant numbers. Others came from Belgium, Wales, Holland, Sweden, and other northern European countries. Foreign immigration virtually was suspended during World War I and was much restricted by quotas established in the post-war period.

The black population of Indiana grew from 11,428 in 1860 to 57,705 in 1900, the majority of the blacks coming from the Lower South, some arriving via the "Underground Railroad" of the Civil War era.

The state's population soared over the 3,000,000 mark in 1930, exceeded 4,000,000, in 1960 and reached 5,193,669 in 1970. In 1970, there were approximately 4,820,000 whites, 357,000 blacks, and 16,000 of other races. There were 351,258 foreign-born in the state. About 18 percent were from Germany, 10 percent from Poland, 9 percent from the United Kingdom, 6 percent from Canada, 5 percent from Mexico, and lesser percentages from other nations.

LINGUISTIC PATTERNS

The "Hoosier twang" is said to be a language all its own, but the overwhelming majority of Indiana residents now speak a rather clean-cut version of American English. It is rare to hear foreign languages spoken in public, other than by visitors from other nations.

It was not always so. The French brought their language with them when they arrived to begin trading with the Indians, and a kind of patois developed for communication between the two groups. The Germans, who accounted for the bulk of the foreign immigration to Indiana, clung tenaciously to their native tongue. Classes were conducted in German at schools established by the immigrants and the language was spoken in the homes and various social and trade societies established by the Germans.

Among later arrivals, the Polish who settled largely in Lake County and in the South Bend area, often continued to speak their native tongue. The Mexicans who followed the tomato harvest continued to speak Spanish.

During World War I, the speaking of German became unpopular and declined substantially. Some terms, however, such as *turnverein, mannerchor, and athenasum* remained and became integrated into the English language.

RELIGIOUS AFFILIATIONS

The Roman Catholics arrived in Indiana first, but the Protestants laid claim to the religious affiliation of the greater numbers of Hoosiers. Roman Catholicism in Indiana dates back even further than 1749 when the first formal Church of St. Francis Xavier was established at Vincennes by the French.

Three of the company of 14 men who came with La Salle to the site where Michigan City now stands in 1679 were Franciscan friars—Hennepin, Ribourdi, and Membre. Father Hennepin—described by Hoosier historian Ross Lockridge as "a very lusty priest, who loved hardship and adventure and had much experience with battles in Europe"—was instrumental in arranging a peace with the Indians in a tense situation.

The French government considered it highly important to establish religious missions along with their forts and trading posts. They were centers of community life in these outposts.

When the English began to move in to contest the French for the furs and hides, they brought Protestantism with them. When the French and Indian Wars ended in 1763 with decisive English victory, it placed Protestantism on the ascendancy.

Most of the early Hoosiers were Methodists, Baptists, or Presbyterians. Also well represented were the Quakers, Disciples of Christ, Episcopalians, Lutherans, United Brethren, and Unitarians.

During the 1800s, "general camp meetings" were popular. They lasted for several days and nights and were usually held in temporary camps. Fervent preaching and testimony were rendered by the light of torches. The religious influence cast by regular church services, as well as the revivals, helped to hold down the drinking, gambling and brawling of the frontiersmen.

The Methodists and some other denominations organized regular circuit and intinerant circuit-riders brought religion to the door of many a pioneer log cabin, calling on the new residents with Bible and hymn book in hand. Log and clapboard churches sprang up in most every community as the population grew.

Many of the state's first schools and universities, which blossomed in the period from 1816 to 1860, were started by churches and religious groups. Although the 1816 state constitution had authorized a public school system, the state was broke from spending too much money building canals, so its actual establishment was delayed until 1851 when a new constitution was ratified. Churches, particularly the Quakers, jumped into the breach and established many excellent schools. Many of the teachers were ministers and priests who taught school as part of their regular duties.

The Quakers were particularly active politically. In October, 1842, Henry Clay visited Indiana and made several speeches. When he finished his speech at Richmond, before some 20,000 Whigs, he was given a petition signed by 2,000 Quakers, asking that he free his slaves. Clay told them that, although he considered the institution of slavery an evil, it was nothing in comparison to what would occur as a greater evil if the slaves suddenly were freed. Clay said he owned 50 slaves, worth about $15,000. Then, he asked the petitioners if they would be willing to raise $15,000 for their support should he free the slaves. Given wide publicity, the incident may have helped to defeat Clay in Indiana and the nation.

The general trend through the years has been one of increasing Protestant domination of the religious picture in Indiana, but with substantial concentrations of Catholic and Jewish worshippers in the major cities.

Judging from recent statistics, Hoosiers as a whole are also considerably less religious than they have been in eras of the past. The volume "Churches and Church Membership in the United States: 1971" by Douglas W. Johnson, Paul R. Picard and Bernard Quinn lists statistics showing that only 45.1 percent of all Hoosiers were adherents of any Christian religion.

Catholics comprised 13.9 percent of the total population. Among the various Protestant groups, the United Methodist church had 8.5 percent, the Christian Church and Church of Christ, 3 percent, the American Baptist Convention 2.9 percent, the United Presbyterian Church 2.4 percent, the Lutheran Missiouri Synod 2.2 percent and all other groups less than 2 percent each.

The Hoosier ratio of those "churched" was 4.5 percent less than the national average of 49.6 per cent of the total population.

But there were some outstanding Hoosier religious leaders. Probably the best known was Henry Ward Beecher, who presided over congregations at Lawrenceburg and Indianapolis.

During the period of from 1880 to 1920, Indiana had many sectarian religious divisions but was also characterized by a sharp decline in the rural church. A survey made in 1911 and quoted by Clifton J. Phillips in "Indiana in Transition" concerned Boone, Daviess, and Marshall counties—chosen as rural areas representative of the central, southern and northern parts of the state. It showed that almost half of the existing congregations were ailing. A disturbing picture of sectarian strife and jealousy emerged, with more separate congregations in each county than the dwindling rural population could support. It also showed heavy reliance upon old-fashioned, fundamentalist gospel which did not give much attention to social and community problems.

Evangelists flourished in the late 1800s. One of them, young Thomas Harrison, was reported to have gained more than 1,200 conversions in a series of revivals at the Roberts Park Methodist Episcopal Church in Indianapolis. Other prominent evangelists included J. Wilbur Chapman, a Presbyterian, and Charles R. Scoville of the Disciples of Christ.

The old-time camp meeting, a remnant of pioneer days, was fast vanishing in the 1880s as larger churches were built and Sunday schools developed, especially in the cities and larger towns. Such centers of summer worship as the Winona Bible Conference, Bethany Assembly and Pine Lake Assembly sprang up to serve as settings for evangelists. The famed Billy Sunday was honored with a tabernacle named for him at Winona Lake, where he often had appeared.

A diamatrically opposed theology was that of a few Protestant liberals who attempted to respond to the challenge of the increasingly urban society. They preached a "social gospel" which had as its goals the lessening of oppression and injustice rather than the religious salvation of individual sinners. Leaders in this group include Gilbert de la Matyr, a Methodist clergyman in Indianapolis who was elected to Congress in 1878; Charles R. Henderson, a Terre Haute pastor who later became a sociology professor; Myron W. Reed, a Presbyterian minister in Indianapolis who later moved to Dever and founded the Interdenominational Broadway Temple, and Worth M. Tippy, Methodist minister who later was one of the founders of the Methodist Foundation for Social Services. But the most effective and influential exponent of the Protestant social gospel in Indiana in this period, Phillips reports, was the Reverend Oscar O. McCulloch, a Congregationalist minister who was pastor of the small and rundown Plymouth Church on Indianapolis' Monument Circle. He recognized the congregation as an "institutional church" with an open membership policy, no creed and a concern for social problems of the city.

A considerable number of holiness sects developed in Indiana, among which the most important was the Church of God. A rather loosely organized fellowship, it stressed the individual's ability to attain full Christian perfection. Chief founder was Daniel S. Warner, who moved to Indiana in 1878. His first church was in Beaver Dam in Kosciusko County. Using itinerant lay preachers and religious tracts, the reformed Church of God spread quickly in the rural villages and small towns of the Midwest. Anderson, Indiana, became the official home for the Church of God movement in the latter part of the 1900 decade.

In a few counties of northern Indiana, there was a fairly sizeable group of German Baptist Brethren who were members of a pietistic sect known popularly as the Dunkards. They shunned worldly things and were recognizable by the long whiskers, broad-brimmed hats plain coats and pants and lack of neckties of the men and by plain dresses, full skirts, three-cornered capes and large, stiff bonnets of the women.

Other sects included the Mennonite and Amish, who were descended from German, Swiss and Dutch pioneers who moved to Indiana from Pennsylvania in the early 19th century and settled primarily in La Grange and Elkhart counties. They split themselves into groups according to the degree of separation from the world practiced by each. The Old Order Amish Mennonites clung to the plain style of costume with hooks and eyes in place of buttons and continued to use the German language for worship services, usually held in private homes. The Mennonites published a large amount of religious literature, disproportionate to their relatively small numbers in Indiana.

A wide variety of Lutheran churches also were supported by the extensive Indiana population of German descent. Fort Wayne was a center of this group, which established Concordia College there, as well as 85 parochial schools throughout the state.

Spiritualism also flourished in Indiana around the turn of the century. The Indiana Association of Spiritualists held its first convention in Anderson in 1888. Spiritualism, however, had been practiced in the state since before the Civil War. Starting in 1892, annual summer assemblies were held at a spiritualist camp-ground near Chesterfield. Christian Science also was introduced in Indiana in 1889 when a study group was formed in Indianapolis. Annie B. Dorland became the first Christian Science Practitioner in the state.

PATTERNS OF RURAL
AND URBAN SETTLEMENT

From beginnings that were almost exclusively rural in nature, Indiana has developed into a nice mix of major urban centers and still-abundant rural population.

The Indians grouped together in some concentrations of population that could, perhaps, pass for very small towns. When the French came, they established three small settlements at Fort Miami where Fort Wayne now stands, at Ouiatenon near the present city of Lafayette and at Vincennes. All were basically forts or stockades for the mutual protection of the settlers.

By the end of 1816 when Indiana acquired statehood, such

small towns as Clarksville, New Albany, Jeffersonville, Madison, Vevay, Charlestown, Brookville, Lawrenceburg, Corydon, Brownstown, Salem, Harmonie, Princeton and Richmond had been established. Most of them were in southern Indiana, predominantly strung along the Ohio River, because it afforded the most feasible means of transportation. Vincennes was the capital until 1813, when considerable agitation resulted in moving it to Corydon, nearer the center of population.

The settlement at Vevay was a Swiss colony where numerous vineyards were planted. Harmonie was settled by thrifty German farmers.

In 1840, the largest town was New Albany and the new capital city of Indianapolis was still in the toddlin' town stage. New Albany had slightly more than 4,000 citizens. By 1850, Madison, New Albany and Indianapolis were vying for population honors with about 8,000 citizens each.

In 1860, more than 90 percent of the people of the state still lived in rural areas. Only a few cities had population in excess of 10,000. Indianapolis, which was now the largest, still had less than 19,000 persons. A majority of the population still lived in the southern half of the state.

Urbanization and the northward sweep of the population were developments that followed in the wake of the Civil War. By 1900, about one-third of the population was urban; and the scales had tipped so that most of the larger cities and the majority of the people were in the northern half of the state.

Because the urban population of Indiana always has been decentralized, the state never has had any one center to dominate its political, cultural and economic life. The urbanites are sprinkled over a number of cities and numerous towns. As a result, Indiana residents have remained closer to the soil and more familiar with farm life than the residents of many other industrialized areas. Many persons who work in the cities have preferred to make their homes in rural areas despite the greater driving distances involved. As a result, the traditional differences between rural and urban communities of the late 19th and early 20th centuries were much modified and partially eliminated during the period following World War I.

Meredith Nicholson, one of a significant number of outstanding men of letters produced by the state, and many of his contemporaries in the era just before our involvement in World War I tended to think of Indiana as a "typical American state." Historian Frederick L. Paxon described Indiana as "a barometer of the American temper."

The fact that the imaginary center of United States population was located then near Columbus, Indiana, helped to reinforce the theory of the average Hoosier's typicality.

Rural population continued to rise slowly—slower than the urban population by far—until 1900; after that, it began an abrupt downward trend. Reaching a high-water mark of 1,653,773 in the 1900 Federal census, it fell off to 1,557,041 in 1910 and to 1,447,535 in 1920. Percentagewise, it slid from a rural population of 80.5 percent of the state's total inhabitants to only 49.4 percent in 1920.

Population growth in the state was distributed most unevenly. Some counties boomed with rapid population expansion while others shrank in number of residents. Three counties lost population in the 1870s, 25 in the 1880s. Between 1900 and 1910, 56 counties lost population and between 1910 and 1920, there were 64 losers. Most of the big losses were in southern Indiana counties. Only three southern Indiana counties made appreciable gains—Knox (Vincennes), Monroe (Bloomington) and Vanderburgh (Evansville).

The big boom in population was in Lake County, which quadrupled in population between 1900 and 1920 as the opening of the U.S. Steel Mills in Gary brought laborers flocking to the "region". Other significant gains were registered by Allen (Fort Wayne), Elkhart, LaPorte and St. Joseph (South Bend) counties. With the notable exception of Evansville, which was close to coal deposits and with good water and rail transportation, the older Ohio River cities withered.

Of the 19 cities which had population between 10,000 and 25,000 in 1920, only three were located in the south—New Albany, Jeffersonville and Vincennes. Only city to reach 1,000,000 population by 1920 was Indianapolis, which passed that mark in the 1890 census and slightly more than doubled in size during the next two decades.

But it did not burgeon into a great metropolis such as Chicago, Detroit and Cleveland in neighboring states. With broad tree-lined streets and its diagonal avenues reaching out from the downtown area, Indianapolis was known as a "city of homes." Nicholson observed that it had more or less become "a city rather against its will.'' By 1920, it had reached 314,194 in population. It also sometimes was scored as ''America's biggest small town'' by out-staters.

Although much of the increase in urban population was drawn from rural areas of the state, especially the southern counties, large-scale migrations from other states and countries also helped to swell the totals. By 1900, some 500,000 Indiana residents had been born outside the state, including more than half of the Negroes and about 20 percent of the native white Americans. In 1920, Indiana had the highest proportion of U.S.-born white population in the entire nation—92.1 percent. The seemingly small number of foreign born was significant because it was heavily concentrated in certain cities. At the height of the European immigration in 1910, a majority of the residents of East Chicago and Whiting, nearly half the citizens of Gary and a quarter of the population of Hammond and South Bend had been born abroad. Most were from eastern and southern Europe, and were unskilled workers and their families. By 1920, the Negro element made up 11 percent of the total population of Indianapolis, at that time one of the highest such ratios in the northern United States.

Growing complexity of urban life in the era of higher industrialization brought with it a demand of better and more efficient administration of municipal government. Government reform followed with the institution of city charters for Indianapolis, Evansville, Fort Wayne, Terre Haute and South Bend.

The latest Federal decennial census, taken in 1970, showed Indiana with a total population of approximately 5,193,000. Of that number, 3,372,000 are classified as urban—about 65 percent—and only 1,821,000—about 35 percent—as rural.

Quite significant is the fact that of the 357,000 Negroes identified in that census, only 8,000 lived in rural areas—about 2 percent. So 98 percent of the Negroes 349,000—lived in the urban areas.

The vast majority of that total—325,000—lived in the 11 metropolitan areas identified by the census as Standard Metropolitan Statistical Areas. They are Indianapolis, Gary-Hammond-East Chicago, South Bend, Fort Wayne, Lafayette, Terre Haute, Muncie, Anderson, Evansville, Cincinnati and Louisville.

Another population trend in Indiana worthy of note is the fact that there are an increasing number of females in comparison with the number of males. In the 1900 census, Indiana showed 104.4 males for every 100 females. By 1950, there were only 99.1 males for every 100 females. As of the 1970 census, there were about 95.1 males for every 100 females. There also are nearly three times as many widowed and divorced women as there are men. The percentage of the total females falling into this class is 16.2 while only 5.8 percent of the total males are included. Nearly 69 percent of all the men are married while only 63 percent of the women are.

Another trend is that the average Hoosier is living longer. In the 1960 census, there were 160,000 Hoosiers over 75. In the 1970 census, there were 195,000 in that category. The number from 70 to 74 years old jumped from 126,000 in 1960 to 132,000 in 1970.

Still another interesting fact emerging from comparison of the 1970 and 1960 census figures is the increasing population growth rate of the Negroes in comparison with the whites. The Negro population was up 32.8 percent during the decade while the white population increased by 9.8 percent.

Indiana undoubtedly has changed more in the last 300 years than in all the milleniums during which the red man stalked the land. But it continues to maintain a rather classic balance between the urban and rural society, between industry and agriculture.

EUGENE CADOU

* * *

Natural Resources
of Indiana

A NY inventory of Indiana's natural resources would reveal a
bountiful land. Environmental advantages have led to a
stirring economic development and the casting of a solid
society symbolic of an American heritage at its best. A limited
number of basic resources are found in great abundance, supplemented by a scattering of others. For example, limestone
suitable for construction purposes is virtually inexhaustible,
while much needed petroleum is in relatively short supply. And
oddly, despite wide-spread sources of nonmetallic minerals, not
a single metal of commercial significance was mined in the
state in the 1970s.

Among the 50 states, Indiana ranks about 25th in the
production of minerals. The state's forests include hardwoods of
high quality, but the production of sawtimber is not great. Even
without mountains, seacoasts, or other spectacular physical
features, the Hoosiers can still boast of scenic beauty and outdoor
recreational features that attract tourists from other states.

Forests, minerals, plentiful water, and wildlife all play major
roles in Indiana, not only from an economic point of view, but
because they also have a dynamic effect on state politics and
contribute to the social well-being of the state's inhabitants.

MINERALS
Coal

Without doubt coal is the most basic natural resource
associated with the economic development of the United States.
Although not known as a "coal state," Indiana has had a
remarkably strong record in the production of this mineral.

Nearly 1,500,000,000 tons of it had been dug out of the ground by the late 20th century. Of the national production of 595,000,000 short tons of coal in 1972, some 26,000,000 or 4.5 percent, came from Indiana mines. This proportion accounted for the state ranking of seventh in the country in coal production during the 1970s. By comparison, West Virginia, the foremost coal-producing state, yielded 24 percent of the nation's total. Without question coal constitutes Indiana's most valuable mineral resource. Its impressive reserves are part of the vast deposits reaching from Ohio to northern Missouri through Indiana and Illinois. Coal beds, for the most part lying near the surface, extend through about 6,500 square miles, or 18 percent of Indiana's total area, and amount to untold billions of tons.

Problems of coal mining. All coal mined is classified as bituminous. Of the total state production, more than 90 percent comes from strip mining. This method, suitable to these vertical dimensions, was first practiced in the area in 1866 at Danville, Illinois. In Indiana the thickness of the coal seams generally ranges from 24 to 57 inches, with some measuring as thick as 82 inches. An overburden varying from 15 to 97 feet in thickness must be removed as part of the mining operation. In the early days this overriding material was removed by horse-drawn plows and hauled away in carts and wheelbarrows.

In the mid-20th century, the operation was much more sophisticated, utilizing elaborate machinery capable of rapidly tearing the earth away from large areas and scooping up the coal. Modern equipment includes power shovels, draglines, front-end loaders, and huge scrapers. Some power shovels have a capacity to lift more than 50 cubic yards at a time. One dragline removing overburden can handle 145 cubic yards, or 215 tons. Most of the coal is transported from the mines by rail and water, with a smaller amount hauled by truck. About one-eighth is converted into electric power near the mine site. In instances where coal is more deeply imbedded in the earth, underground methods are employed. Here the coal seams vary from 71 to 81 inches in thickness, requiring shafts and tunnels and mechanical loading.

Strip mining takes place almost exclusively in the southwestern part of the state, parallel to the lower course of the Wabash River in the rolling or hilly lands between Terre Haute and Evansville. More specifically, almost all of the mines lie in Warrick, Pike, Sullivan, Greene, Vermillion, and Clay counties, with Warrick

County outdistancing all others in production. Coal from underground mines comes from the same general area, with Sullivan County the leading producer.

The problem of strip mining is all the more critical because of the nature of the operation. Initial investments are relatively low since tunnels and shafts are unnecessary and movement of the coal is easily performed. Thus, strip mines, unlike underground mines, can be readily put into operation, and companies can go out of business without losing great investment in installations. For example, during 1972 six new strip mines were opened and ten were abandoned. Control under these circumstances by regulatory methods may often be difficult in the face of slow-moving legislative processes.

Control of strip mining. Areas once subjected to strip mining are rendered useless unless conservation methods are applied to restore the land to productivity. Soil horizons which have taken centuries to develop by the processes of nature disappear or are disrupted to the point where they cannot support crops. Indiana residents place much emphasis on preserving their environment, counter to the success of strip mining enterprises. As a result, attempts were made in the Indiana legislature to abolish, or at least control, this particular industry. Quite understandably, political impasses arose between commercial companies engaged in strip mining and those interests—whether government agencies or environmentalist groups such as the Sierra Club—dedicated to preventing the land from being despoiled.

The first strip mine reclamation program is claimed to have taken place in Indiana, where peach and pear orchards were planted on mined land in 1918. Another solution has been to replace the overburden. The process of reclamation on slopes has involved contouring, which reduces the destructive effects of erosion. By the 1970s, much progress had taken place in lessening the ravages of tearing the earth open. The Indiana Coal Association reported that by June 30, 1971, a total of 156 square miles had been reclaimed. The principal method was that of afforestation: more than 53,000,000 trees were planted on 113 square miles. Other areas were seeded, while still others were converted into lakes. In these reclamation projects 8.5 square miles were incorporated into state forests, 23 square miles converted into recreational areas, and 5 square miles utilized for private homes. These statistics testify to some success by the people of Indiana through decades of effort toward controlling the disposition of their land.

With the advancing importance of petroleum in the mid-20th century, coal industry became down-graded. Indiana was especially hard hit because the quality of its product was only fair at best not measuring up to that of many of the other producing regions in the country. With a world crisis in petroleum and domestic shortages of fuel in the 1970s, however, the coal mining industry took on new life and to an extent returned to its former status as a prime source of energy. Statistics for the mid-1970s were expected to show the upsurge in production.

Production and uses of Indiana coal. Consumption of coal in Indiana in 1972, just before the energy crisis caused by a world-wide shortage of petroleum, approached 60,000,000 tons, or well over twice the figure for production. Of the total consumption, only 44 percent came from mines within the state. Another 40 percent originated in West Virginia and Virginia. Western Kentucky and Illinois also furnished substantial amounts, while smaller quantities were brought in from Pennsylvania, Montana, and Wyoming. Despite the necessity to import coal from out of the state to meet the demand, almost one-quarter of Indiana's production in turn found its way to other states, especially those nearby.

The preponderant amount of Indiana's coal is used for the generation of electrical energy and heat. Although Indiana coal is not of the type to convert into coke for use in the mammoth iron and steel industry, the state stands as the second largest coke producer in the nation after Pennsylvania. During 1972 a total of 13,800,000 tons of coal—all of it shipped in from other states— was carbonated to produce 9,100,000 tons of coke. Nearly 93 percent of the coke production was consumed by the steel industry in producing pig iron and steel.

Natural Gas

In the late 1880s and the 1890s great deposits of natural gas were opened up in a broad area northeast of Indianapolis known as Trenton's Field. Based upon this cheap and seemingly inexhaustible source of energy, numerous industries sprang up in Indianapolis, Muncie, Marion, Anderson, and other cities. By 1902, however, gas lights no longer lit up the sky because judgment had been had and deposits ran out. Some cities, such as Muncie, had developed a sufficient industrial base to survive the collapse. It might be argued that the famous Indianapolis Speedway and its annual 500-mile automobile race originated because of natural gas. The nearby supply of this easy-to-use fuel had attracted a number of industries to the city, including automobile plants. The motor speedway was built for testing and racing cars and continued to operate with fanfare until the annual race became a national tradition.

Natural gas deposits in the 1970s were limited and no longer ranked as a prime resource in the state. Some of the old wells served as storage reservoirs for supplies imported from other states, while other reserves were known to be trapped in association with coal and petroleum formations, requiring more complex and costly methods of extraction. A small production persisted, but was insignificant as compared to the former blazing glory of the late 19th century. Production in the early 1970s reached about 350,000,000 cubic feet, nearly all of it coming from two gas fields. One lies within an area roughly outlined by boundaries forming a triangle with the angles at Muncie, Kokomo, and Marion. The other is located near Connersville in Fayette County. Indiana has belatedly adopted some of the country's most enlightened regulatory measures to control the industry and insure conservation.

Petroleum

Crude petroleum came into production as natural gas declined. Deposits were discovered in the gas fields, but the principal region lies in the southwest in the same general areas as the producing coal mines. Posey, Gibson, Pike, Knox. Vanderburgh, and Green counties had a preponderant proportion of production in the 1970s, although some continued to come from the old natural gas region northeast of Indianapolis. Oil in the southwest counties was discovered between 1940 and 1960, largely accounting for a total of 4,379 individual wells producing in 1972, a little more than three-quarters of one percent of those in the United States. In the late 1960s these wells produced about 11,500,000 barrels per year, but this figure dropped to about 6,000,000 barrels in 1972, or 0.2 percent of the national total.

Most of the production came from the older wells, but exploratory wells were constantly being drilled. In 1971, for example, among the hundreds of wells drilled, 14 new ones were successfully brought in; in 1972 there were 11 new wells. Estimates of proven reserves appear to vary from year to year as geological surveys are made. In 1972 the Bureau of Mines reported 29,000,000 barrels of reserves as compared to an estimated 30,000,000 barrels estimated the year before and 66,000,000 in 1960. Given the rate of production in the 1970s, the state had but a few years to go before underground sources would run dry unless geologists discovered new proven resources.

The demand for petroleum in the state is much greater than the supply. Its refineries were capable of distilling more than 500,000 barrels of crude petroleum per day in the 1970s. As in the case of coal, Indiana industries must look to other states for a substantial proportion of this fuel.

Indiana lies at the heart of a great national network of pipelines that transport crude petroleum, refined oil products, and natural gas. For petroleum, the major lines cross the central part of the state in a west-southwest/east-northeast direction and others focus on the Chicago area, including the industrial cities in northwestern Indiana. Pipelines carrying natural gas form a trellis-like network. The more important lines paralleling a diagonal connecting the southwestern and northeastern extremities of the state.

Non-metallic Minerals

Indiana is favorably endowed with several minerals that extend through vast expanses of its territory. Others are found sparingly in isolated deposits.

Limestone. Probably the most notable nonmetallic resource is limestone, which holds high rank among the state's natural resources both because of its abundance and its many uses. It is considered to be an almost inexhaustible resource. Although the principal deposits are in south-central Indiana, much of the entire southern part of the state is underlain with limestone. Nearly all of the quarries are concentrated in Lawrence, Monroe, Franklin, and Rush counties. Contrary to what might be expected, the preponderant proportion of all limestone quarried is crushed and statistically reported as crushed stone. Of this, nearly two-thirds is used as foundation or paving material in the construction of highways and roads. Other uses are for manufacturing concrete aggregate, portland cement, and ballast.

By weight only some three percent of the limestone produced

in the state comes under the category of building stone, but it is the substance for which Indiana has long been famous. Known as dimension stone, it is quarried for use as building blocks or as slabs to veneer other types of building material. Fine in quality, it is especially good for foundations and walls where a high polish is unnecessary. In addition, as a building stone it is strong, easy to carve, and does not split when cut. It is second only to marble in the designing of architecturally attractive construction, and has dominated the U.S. building stone market for more than a century. In fact, more than 80 percent of the country's production of dimension stone has come from Indiana, most of it from the great quarries in Lawrence and Monroe counties, where Bedford and Bloomington are centers of the industry.

Much of the stone is quarried around the small city of Oolitic, just north of Bedford, so named for the grainy texture of the limestone. In 1920s, when the industry was at its peak, huge blocks of stone were stacked to heights of 50 to 75 feet, awaiting shipment to cutting mills. Because of competition with concrete, glass, and metal in modern building construction, however, the state's building stone works declined in importance in the mid-20th century. On a much smaller scale, sandstone and marl, also found in quantity in Indiana, provide stone for construction purposes.

Sand and gravel. Production of sand and gravel ranks a close second in value to stone among Indiana's mineral resources (excluding coal). Deposits exist throughout the state and are commercially exploited in as many as 80 counties, annual production generally exceeding 20,000,000 tons. Each of six counties—Hamilton, Madison, Marion, St. Joseph, Switzerland, and Tippecanoe—normally produce more than 1,000,000 tons. More than half of the total production goes into road building materials and one-third is used in the building industry. The remainder mainly provides fill material and railroad ballast, or serves as an important ingredient in the manufacture of glass.

Clay, lime, and gypsum. Like those of sand and gravel, deposits of clay and widely scattered over the state. Production takes place in some 20 counties of which Morgan, Clay, Clark, and Parke provide more than two-thirds. Morgan County alone, just southwest of Indianapolis, accounts for 30 percent. Clay may be of innumerable varieties, depending upon its resistance to heat, presence of impurities, and other characteristics. Most of the types found in Indiana are used in the manufacture of building blocks, portland cement, and items such as sewer pipes, drain tiles, conduits, roofing, and ceramics. One type, known as fireclay, is especially adapted to the fabrication of floor and wall tile, terra-cotta, refractories, and some kinds of pottery. Perhaps clay is the most versatile mineral resource found in Indiana, its use ranging from a soil type conducive to vegetative growth to the manufacture of highly decorative glazed tile for fancy architectural design.

Lime, a product not industrially associated with limestone or crushed limestone, has special significance in Indiana industry as a flux in iron and steel-making processes. It is used in oxygen, open hearth, and electric arc furnaces. Small amounts also serve to purify water. Virtually all of the lime produced in the state comes from Lake County in the immediate vicinity of Gary, East Chicago, and other iron- and steel-producing cities. As the fifth largest consumer of lime and only the twelfth largest producer among the states, Indiana must import much of its supplies.

Indiana ranks sixth in the country as a producer of gypsum, most of which occurs in underground mines in Martin County in the southwest. Other deposits, particularly the huge one in La Porte County, had been but little worked by the 1970s. Most of the production of gympsum is used in making wallboard, lath, sheathing, and other items of the building industry. A smaller proportion is converted into land plaster for agricultural use.

Other minerals. A few other minerals are of minor importance. Abrasives are quarried in Orange County for making whetstones. Peat, burned as fuel in early years, is now obtained from bogs in the north as peat moss, used primarily for soil improvement and potting soils. It also provides a substance for packing flowers, and can sustain earthworm culture.

BIOLOGICAL RESOURCES

Forests

When the first settlers filtered over the Appalachians in the early 19th century they found in the Midwest an environment rich in biological resources. Indiana, located in the heart of this pioneer land, was seven-eighths covered with fine stands of timber and inhabited by a variety of wild animals. The broadleafed deciduous forests contained hardwoods such as ash, beech, black walnut, elm, hickory, maple, oak, sycamore, and yellow poplar. Through them roamed deer, bear, elk, wildcats, and timber wolves, not to mention the small fur-bearing animals that had previously attracted French trappers. Early accounts of animals in the region refer to "The Old Buffalo Trail," a route beaten through southern Indiana from Illinois, leading to salt licks in Kentucky. Part of the route is now followed by U.S. Highway 50, that crosses the Wabash River in Vincennes.

Exploitation of the forests. Trees and wild animals offered very little in the way of a livelihood for the breed of settlers who were to become Hoosiers. So the land was cleared of forests to make way for crops, and wood was used for housing and fuel. In the process animals were recklessly killed off or routed. Modern conservationists may look back upon this period as one of environmental devastation, but at the time it was the only logical means of developing the area. With the coming of industry, saw-mills increased so rapidly that by the late 19th century more than 1,000,000 board feet were produced annually. From 1880 until the end of the century, trees were chopped down until the forests approached extinction. Only 1,500,000 acres remained, about 6.5 percent of the original stand when the white man entered the area with his broadax less than a century before.

The seriousness of the situation was realized and in 1898 the Indiana Forestry Association was founded and a forestry management program put into operation. In 1919 this organization was merged with others concerned with resources to form a state Department of Conservation. Many reforms have been effected since, including reforestation and the preservation of existing forest lands.

To make the program as effective as possible, the state was divided into 11 forestry districts, each receiving guidance by specialists in conservation methods. As a result, forests generally now grow more timber each year than is cut. Some inequalities remain, however. For example, the black walnut, one of Indiana's finest woods, has been over cut. Also, trees in some of the present growth may not be of the high quality of the original forests. Finally, statistics show that in some years the removal of sawtimber has exceeded annual growth, reflecting the incomplete control of conservationists.

Contemporary conditions. In the 1970s, forests covered slightly more than 4,000,000 acres, or a little more than one-sixth of the state's total area. The Department of the Interior estimated that of all forest lands in Indiana, about one-half might be classified as sawtimber and another one-third as pole-timber. Seedlings and second growth occupied the remainder. The great majority of all forests are in private hands. Some 70 percent was held by 100,000 farmers in wood lots for lumber, fence posts, fuel, and other products of value in a rural area. In addition, Hoosiers look upon trees as an aesthetic part of any farm, a tradition inherited from their forefathers. The remainder of the privately owned forests belonged to various organizations or individuals, such as sawmill operators and coal companies, or were on estates. Only seven percent of the state's forest lands were government-owned, either national or state.

The U.S. Forest Service manages some 214,000 acres, including a national forest of 137,000 acres in the south-central part of the state southeast of Bloomington. In turn, the Indiana Department of Natural Resources controls the remaining forest in the public domain, having created a number of state forests. Of the total area in the state, only 58,000 acres have been excluded from cutting in an attempt to preserve the small proportion of remaining virgin stands of timber. In the 1970s, some 130 different kinds of trees were scattered throughout the state, of which 30 have been introduced since the early 19th century. More than two-thirds of the forests are in the southern part of the state, partly because the northern region offers better agricultural opportunities.

The extent of Indiana's use of its forestry resources, while locally significant, compares poorly with that of Oregon, one of the more richly endowed states. In 1970 a production of 351,000,000 board feet of sawtimber appeared ridiculously low when measured against the 9,700,000,000 board feet produced in Oregon. The Oregon cut, however, was from coniferous, or softwood, trees as compared to Indiana's choice hardwoods that are especially useful as a high-grade building material and in the manufacture of chairs, desks, and other furniture.

Outdoor Recreation

Natural vegetation accounts for much of a state's scenic beauty, which in itself may be considered a resource. In addition to the satisfaction of aesthetic beauty, an appealing landscape featuring trees and foliage produces revenue as a recreational area. Forest management has included this aspect in its program of seting aside and maintaining state parks with facilities for family fun and relaxation.

Tourism. Indiana lies remote from the many national parks and coastal features in the western and eastern parts of the United States. Therefore an attractive natural environment such as the rolling hills decked with colorful vegetation, the narrow valleys, and the rock-faced cliffs, in the limestone countryside of the southern area, have proved popular for in-state vacations. The scenic beauty in the region promises to widen its appeal and increase tourism in this least industrialized part of the state. Visitors by the thousands come to the area each year to enjoy the the outdoor delights of swimming, fishing, boating, hiking, camping, or just taking it easy under a benevolent Hoosier sun. Facilities for these privileges spring not only from state-sponsorship, but private entrepreneurs as well. All are dependent on a soft and enchanting landscape closely tied to the traditions of the people who have fashioned their "homeland" through multiple generations.

Indiana's state parks. Of the state parks, four are especially noteworthy. Foremost, Brown County State Park has attracted much attention because of its deep gorges and valleys cut by streams and its superb recreational facilities such as bridle paths, hiking trails, and bow-and-arrow hunting grounds. Largest of the parks, it is located near Nashville, and about 45 miles south of Indianapolis. Turkey Run State Park in Parke County, McCormick's Creek State Park near Spencer in Owen County, and Spring Mill State Park near Mitchell in Lawrence County reflect the Indiana countryside at its best. Altogether more than 30 sites have been classified as state parks, memorials, and recreational areas. In addition to specific parks, the southern Indiana landscape offers scenic drives which are appealing to residents of the somewhat monotonous glacial plains of the northern part of the state. Winter sports enliven recreation in the northeast when the myriad of small lakes freeze over from December to March.

The Indiana Dunes. The Indiana Dunes along the shores of Lake Michigan are by far the leading attraction for the nearby metropolitan area of Chicago. Unique in the entire country, the dunes contain one of the most varied plant collections in the world, with species ranging from Arctic bogs to tropical orchids and examples of wetland as well as desert environments. The Indiana Dune State Park was established in 1925, comprising 2,182 acres along the immediate shore front. An ever-expanding industrial complex on the west, however, threatened the natural setting of the park by polluting the air and water and encroaching land use. In 1966, after a long fight by conservationists, the Indiana Dunes National Lakeshore was authorized, adding another 8,720 acres which enveloped the original state park on its land sides.

Wildlife and Fish

The natural habitate for game disappeared as the state underwent economic development through the decades. The situation became so intense that hunting areas available to sportsmen were lost at a rate as high as 200 square miles per year. Encroachment of urban areas into open country and the construction of interstate highways were principal factors in crowding out animal life. North of Indianapolis, for example, huge areas have been engulfed by housing developments. In addition, modern agricultural methods and decreased pasture land have discouraged wildlife. To offset this environmental devastation, the state took constructive measures to provide new habitats. By the mid-1970s, deer, grouse, rabbits, squirrels, and other animals could find refuge. Improvements included the clearing of areas in the forests, the preparation of waterholes, and above all, the encouragement of farmers to increase wildlife on their land.

Restocking the land with vanished and vanishing species of animals has also been effective in making Indiana again a game area. Wild turkeys, deer, and pheasant have proven to be exciting game to hunters. Quail is the most common game bird, while in the north hunters find ducks and geese plentiful. The Fish and Game Division has supervised hunting for the greatest good.

Some 1,000 natural lakes scattered throughout the state, along with man-made lakes, offer opportunity for fishermen. Some of these small bodies of water are on state-owned property where the Fish and Game Division can exercise direct control. A number of fish hatcheries not only provide stock for the lakes and ponds, but serve as a means of selecting the most suitable species of fish for an optimum catch. The most plentiful species attracting sportsmen include bass, catfish, pike, pickerel, and sunfish. The annual purchase of about 750,000 fishing licenses attests to the popularity of sports fishing among Hoosiers and out-of-state fishermen.

Activities of commercial fisheries are limited almost exclusively to the Ohio and Wabash rivers and the Indiana waters of Lake Michigan. Mussel shells from the Wabash River constitute the greatest harvest, but buffalo fish, bullheads, and catfish are the dominant species of fish in the total catch.

Water and Hydroelectric Resources

Indiana has an abundant supply of water. The annual average of precipitation ranges from around 32 inches in the north to 46 inches in the south, with a mean of about 40 inches for state as a whole. Each inch of rain falling within Indiana's boundaries totals more than 632,000,000,000 gallons. A significant proportion sinks into the ground to moisten the soil or is pumped up from wells for domestic use or to water livestock. The remainder, comprising approximately one-third of the total rainfall, known as runoff, drains from the land into rivers and streams. From it an estimated 8,600,000,000 gallons a day is withdrawn for industrial use, mostly for steam electric utilities. Municipalities take about 500,000,000 gallons a day for general use.

As is true throughout the eastern half of the Midwest, precipitation in Indiana from year to year is fairly regular. The maximum generally falls during the warm months when evaporation is highest and the minimum, inlcluding snowfall, when loss by evaporation is low. Nevertheless, there are problems of localized floods and drought which disrupt the agrarian economy. Farmers frequently grumble about the lack of enough rain for a good corn crop, or about an overly wet season which jeopardizes their harvest. Erratic climatic behavior, however, has never approached proportions such as those of the Dust Bowl disasters of the Great Plains to the west. The Ohio, Wabash, and White river systems are all subject to high water and flooding, but only in the southern part of the state, especially along the Ohio, are floods of great magnitude common. Because the boundary between Indiana and Kentucky follows the north bank of the Ohio River, Hoosiers do not necessarily consider it "their" river, as they do the beloved Wabash, which sweeps through most of the length of the state.

The state's river systems. Indiana lies within two contrasting drainage basins. In the northeast drainage is northward, terminating in the Great Lakes and ultimately the Atlantic Ocean. This watershed, even though significant in the state's hydrological pattern, only covers about three percent of Indiana's territory. Virtually all of the remainder of the state drains into the Gulf of Mexico by way of the Ohio and Mississippi rivers. A very small section in northwestern Indiana drains directly into Lake Michigan through a series of creeks and ditches. The divide between the two major watersheds is almost imperceptible. In the days of canals and barge traffic, before the railroad era, continous waterways were opened across this divide. One important link connected the Maumee and Wabash rivers near Fort Wayne, and allowed traffic to pass between Lake Erie and the Mississippi.

Two of the state's principal rivers that drain the more northerly drainage basin over short distances are named St. Joseph. One passes through South Bend and crosses the boundary into Michigan, while the other enters the state from Ohio and joins the St. Mary's in Fort Wayne to form the Maumee.

By comparison, the more southerly drainage basin has several rivers that flow long distances in the state and critically influence its economy. Foremost, the Wabash rises in Ohio and forms a great arc in north-central Indiana before flowing south along the western edge of the state to join the Ohio. Next in importance, the White River rises near the Ohio boundary and passes through Indianapolis before joining the Wabash in the southwest near Princeton. In the northwest the Kankakee River and its tributary, the Iroquois, drain a rich corn-growing area, the water eventually reaching the Mississippi via the Illinois River. Although Kentucky, Ohio, and Pennsylvania have great cities on the middle and upper courses of the Ohio River, Indiana has none.

Hydroelectric potential. It is unfortunate that the absence of any high or sharp relief in this well-watered area limits the number of sites suitable for dams. The highest elevation of 1,285 feet occurs along the Ohio boundary, while the lowest point of 313 feet is located at the juncture of the Wabash and the Ohio rivers. From Lafayette in the north to the mouth of the Wabash, a direct distance of 200 miles, the river drops less than 200 feet.

Such gentle gradients explain in large part the lack of opportunity to install power-generating plants with a strong capacity. In 1972, of Indiana's 61,674,000,000 kilowatt-hours generated, only 385, or 0.625 percent, were classified as hydroelectric, an insignificant proportion. The little produced by running water came largely from the southeastern part of the state along the Ohio River and from the west-central region along the Wabash.

Sub-surface water supplies. An important source of water for homes and farms throughout most of Indiana lies beneath the land surface. Especially in the north, where thick layers of glacial drift were deposited during the Ice Age, ground water is trapped in porous layers known as aquifers. With a thickness averaging about 125 feet in depth, the glacial drift may be trapped by wells to supply water for homes and farms. The glaciers did not reach the south, but glacial outwash from the north was deposited in the southern valleys. Two large areas, one in the southwest and one in the north-central part of the state along the Wabash and White rivers, have unusually fine underground strata which hold copious quantities of ground water easily tapped by drilling wells. These sources especially enhance development of the rural landscape.

Water quality. Indiana has quality as well as quantity in its water resources. In the northern glaciated part of the state the water analyzes favorably, except that it is "hard," a characteristic not good for some purposes but preferred for drinking and cooking. Artesian springs, thought to have had mineral properties of therapeutic value, led to the opening of several spas in the 19th century. The best known and only spa remaining in the late 1970s, French Lick, became an all-year health resort and convention center. In Indiana's early history the spot had been a salt lick for animals and an 18th-century French trading post. In its heyday French Lick was a Midwest version of elite Saratoga Springs, New York, and Bedford Springs, Pennsylvania.

CONSERVATION

Indiana citizens have been deeply concerned about the resurces of their state, and have expressed this concern since the late 19th century. Leaders in the state have acted together with the federal government to bring about many reforms. Inexhaustible resources (falling water) are put to the best possible use; renewable resources (forests and wildlife) are balanced between usage and replacement; and non-renewable resources (minerals) are weighed against reserves and alternate resources.

New problems arose in the 1960s to further challenge the state in its management and control of resources. An increasing population exacted greater demands on the natural wealth. Air and water pollution threatened the state's water resources and interfered with outdoor, recreational facilties. Erosion was another evil that never ceased to plague the state. The benefit of experience and constructive legislation combined to meet these and other problems. In 1965 the Indiana Department of Natural Resources was established, assuming the responsibilities of the former state Department of Conservation. Its tasks are many—forestation, land reclamation, clearing the waters of Lake Michigan, maintenance of game preserves and fish hatcheries, and supervision of state parks. The department also works closely with a number of federal agencies, including the U.S. Forest Service, the Bureau of Mines, the U.S. Army Corps of Engineers, the Federal Water Pollution Control Administration, the Bureau of Sport Fisheries and Wildlife, and the Bureau of Outdoor Recreation.

Given this type of governmental service, together with Hoosier pride in the environment, the future of the state's natural resources seems assured insofar as man and his technical capabilities can cope with the destructive forces of passing time.

G. ETZEL PEARCY

* * *

Economy of
INDIANA

INDIANA is the smallest of the major farm states of the U.S. Although only 38th in total land area, its efficiency in raising plants and animals for income helps rank it consistently among the top ten states in agricultural production. A gross farm income of $3,200,000,000 ranked Indiana as eighth in the nation in cash receipts from farm marketing in 1974.

AGRICULTURE

The state usually is first in the production of popcorn and third in the production of corn, hogs, soybeans, and tomatoes for processing. It ranks twelfth in poultry, fourteenth in dairy cattle, and eighteenth in beef cattle. It is the nation's chief grower of spearmint and peppermint, raised in rich northern lowlands which also yield an abundance of celery, onions, carrots, cabbage, and other small food crops for processing or fresh delivery by truck to the cities of the Great Lakes Region. Commercial growers take pride in their plump strawberries and melons, particularly in the south. Some tobacco is raised near the Ohio River.

Other important crops include wheat, rye, hay, oats, sorghum grain, potatoes, and cucumbers. Apples, peaches, and blueberries are among the state's fruit crops. Milk, eggs, and honey are produced in significant quantity.

Of the 26 states east of the Mississippi River, only the larger states of Iowa and Illinois have more land devoted to agriculture than Indiana, where 106,000 farms averaged 165 acres each in 1974 and totaled approximately 17,500,000 acres. All of the 92 counties support some agricultural activity.

Indiana's north-central midsection is the area of most intense cultivation. There the land is level to a farmer's liking and deep with the mineral-rich loam soils that have allowed the development of corn, hogs, and soybeans as the triple base for an agricultural productivity that is second only to manufacturing as a source of income in Indiana.

The basic agricultural productivity. Corn, hogs, and soybeans account for more than 70 percent of all farm income dollars in a typical year. In 1974 corn accounted for $971,157,000 in cash receipts and soybeans $750,595,000. Corn is largely a crop used to feed meat and dairy animals and poultry, but its industrial uses are many and it continues as an important food source.

Indiana corn goes into meal, mush, and cereal flakes, hominy and whiskey, oil and mayonnaise, starch in all its forms from chewing gum to pudding, and syrups for ice cream, jams, and jellies. It is also creamed, fried, baked, canned, and frozen, but Hoosiers probably most relish it "on the cob."

Soybeans are especially important to Indiana's agricultural export markets and are the prime source of vegetable oil used widely in cooking and edible products. Soybean oil is also used in soap, ink, and paint. Protein-rich soybean meal is a chief livestock feed and important in the manufacture of fire extinguishers and fertilizers, paper coatings and insect sprays, adhesives and drugs.

Hogs have often outnumbered people in Indiana. In 1860 the census recorded an average of ten of the animals for every family. The 37,000 farms which raise hogs reported an inventory of 4,900,000 in 1974. Cash receipts from hogs in that year totalled $608,982,000.

Cattle and poultry. Cattle and calves accounted for cash receipts of $206,422,000 in 1974. Sheep and lambs brought $5,299,000, dairy products $188,747,000, and other livestock exclusive of poultry but including honey, wool, and beeswax, $5,116,000. Total cash receipts from poultry and eggs, including $25,112,000 for turkeys of which Indiana is a leading producer, were $153,963,000.

Poultry pens dot the countryside in Indiana, some with vast automated coops where conveyor belts gather thousands of dozens of eggs a day. In this sphere, modern agriculture reveals itself as big business, drawing its power as much from science and technology as from the blessings of the soil, and as much from capital as from labor.

The economy of Indiana's farms. Hoosier farmers had an investment of an estimated $7,000,000,000, in their land, buildings, and equipment in 1972. The value per farm in the mid-1970s was almost $84,000, or an average of about $500 per acre, more than double the figure for 1960.

In the 1970s, nearly one in three of the young men who took up farming in Indiana went to college. Many others who tilled farmland also hèld jobs in industrial plants, coming home to ride tractors equipped with headlights. In terms of investment per worker, capital in farming outstrips that of industry. Few make a beginning on the rich plains of northern or central Indiana without substantial family or bank assistance.

The number of non-family or hired farm workers declined steadily in the 1960s and 1970s, as did the number of farm owners. There was an average annual employment of 43,000 persons, 130,000 of whom were from farm-owning families in 1973, plus 13,000 hired workers. In 1960, total farm employment was 219,000, with 27,000 of them hired hands. Migrant workers continued to help harvest some crops, including tomatoes.

FORESTRY

One of every six acres in Indiana, or nearly 4,000,000 acres, is forested and 98 percent of that is considered commercial forest land by the U.S. Forest Service. While the farm belt of counties in the central and northern regions is laced with small woodlands, it is the southern third of the state which supports the large stands necessary for a thriving commercial timber industry.

Monroe and Brown counties in the high rolling hill country of south-central Indiana and Perry and Harrison counties on the Ohio River are Indiana's largest commercial forest areas. Together with twelve adjacent counties, they account for half the state's commercial forest trees, chiefly hardwoods.

Hoosiers brag that they have the best walnut wood in the world. Most goes into veneer factories, where the top-quality trees are turned on slicing machines to produce the long continuous sheets of expensive walnut panel facings that are used on bank office walls, fancy hotel bars, and the tops of the great tables in corporation board rooms. Lower grades and smaller diameter trees go into the production of walnut lumber. A substantial portion of the production is used by furniture makers.

While walnut is the most valuable commercial tree, oak and hickory represent the largest commercial varieties. They comprise about 60 percent of the typical saw log production of approximately 235,000,000 board feet annually. In 1974 there were some 350 sawmills in the state, processing a total of about 252,000,000 board feet in a typical year from Indiana, Michigan, Ohio, and Illinois. Indiana is usually a net shipper of logs to Kentucky.

Red and better white oaks often are used to produce the staves for barrels in which whiskey is aged. Oak, hickory, and beech are in strong demand for railroad ties and industrial shipping pallets. Maple, beech, and birch are the state's second largest commerical forest group, and are often used in the furniture factories of southern Indiana. Lowland hardwoods of the elm, ash, and cotton wood varieties are the third major commercial grouping and are most common along the streams and rivers of southwestern Indiana.

FISHING

It is in the southwest, along the Wabash River bordering Illinois, that the state's commercial fishing activities are concentrated. Fishermen there harvest channel catfish, some buffalo, and carp. On Lake Michigan, the Indiana commercial catch includes yellow perch, smelt, and chinook and coho salmon, but typically the total represents less than five percent of the total Great Lakes commercial catch.

MINING AND QUARRYING

Coal. Down in the drowsy slip of southwestern bottomland that is Indiana's big toe, miners, some working in shifts around the clock, extract the coal that is the state's most valuable mineral resource. U.S. Highway 41 runs like a convenient backbone through the middle of the 90-mile-long coal belt from Sullivan south to Evansville. In a typical year, the bituminous or soft coal mined in the 12 counties of the region account for more than half the total value of all minerals produced in the state.

Coal mining enjoyed a rebirth in the early 1970s with national emphasis on the conservation of oil and gas. In 1969 there were 38 active Hoosier mines. By 1975 there were 70 mines that had an annual production of more than 22,000,000 tons of coal. All but one of Indiana's mines in 1975 were strip, or surface, mines. In earlier years there had been more deep mines, and exploration of the mid-1970s anticipated a new era of deep shaft mines once again boring into the coal beds which form a basin under that region of the state and go sloping on southwest into Illinois and Kentucky.

One deep coal mine whose entrance is at Mt. Carmel, Illinois, dips hundreds of feet down and then under the Wabash River into Indiana's Gibson County on the river's eastern shores. These beds in the tri-state area form a major coalfield of the nation. Indiana, which employs 3,500 in its coal industry, ranks seventh among the states in coal production.

Oil. Oil is produced in the same southern quarter of the state. Virtually all of it comes from "stripper" wells, so designated because they produce an average of ten barrels per day or less. Indiana had about 4,250 active stripper wells in 1974 producing at an average rate of three barrels per day. Production methods were about evenly divided between primary pumping of oil and secondary recovery chiefly by flooding the underground rock formations of limestone and sandstone to flush out the oil.

While much of the coal mining operation in Indiana is owned by major energy and oil companies, oil production itself is more typically controlled by independent producers and family enterprises. Gross income from stripper well production in 1973 totaled $23,672,000. Among the 33 states which produce oil, Indiana usually ranks 18th.

Limestone. Indiana is a leading producer of limestone blocks for construction, used on such buildings as the Pentagon in Washington, D.C., and the Empire State Building and Rockefeller Center in New York City, as well as numerous other buildings in the nation. Within the state, the more well-known limestone buildings include the Capitol, the Soldiers and Sailors Monument, and the Scottish Rite Cathedral, all in Indianapolis.

The Indiana limestone industry is centered in the south-central hill country where outcroppings accomodate easy quarry operations. The mills are located chiefly in Monroe and Lawrence counties near the cities of Bloomington and Bedford.

Dimension limestone is a heavy and expensive material to take from the ground. After World War II, it was gradually replaced as a major building material by more easily transportable steel and glass. While some 3,000 persons were employed in the limestone industry in the late 1950s, by the mid-1970s the number was less than 1,000. In 1973 a total almost of 2,337,600 cubic feet of Indiana building limestone was quarried with a value of $3,698,800.

While far less notable, crushed limestone is now more important to the Indiana economy than dimension limestone, and after coal is the second most valuable commercial raw mineral product. It is an important road building material. In 1973 a total of 30,605,000 tons were produced for a value of almost $48,176,000.

Other quarrying products. Sand and gravel accounted for almost $32,000,000 in value with approximately 25,173,900 tons extracted in 1973. Clay and shale production totalled 1,322,400 tons and was valued at $1,522,700 in 1973.

A value of almost $4,165,700 was put on 1973 production of sandstone, gypsum, marl, and whetstone. Of these, gypsum showed the most promising potential for future expansion in the state's economy. Commerical development of gypsum began only in the 1950s, with further important discoveries made in the 1960s. In the mid-1970s, production in large underground mines centered around the town of Shoals. Crushing machines work deep within the mines and the light-colored gypsum rock particles are hauled to the surface on conveyor belts. Gypsum forms the basis of plaster of paris and is used by the building industry in many forms including wallboard and cement. It is also used as filler in such widely diversified products as paint and candy.

Value added to Indiana minerals for the manufacture of cement and clay products and the processing of dimension limestone was put at $92,030,500 in 1973.

Natural gas and peat. Natural gas was once Indiana's most visible commercial underground resource. The ever-burning torches of gas flares lit up night skies for miles in the late 1800s and beckoned new industry to such communities as Gas City, Marion, and Muncie where gas was cheap and seemingly inexhaustible. Gas helped fuel the industrial revolution in Indiana, firing the imaginations of the citizens and the furnaces of the factories. By the 1920s, the factories had lured so many people to the cities that the state's economy was clearly no longer dominated by agriculture, but rather by industry. The gas was soon depleted, however.

In 1973 the value of peat taken from Indiana bogs was far larger than that of natural gas. Peat accounted for a value of $3,386,300, while the natural gas value amounted to only $38,400.

MANUFACTURING

Manufacturing is the mainstay of economic life in Indiana. The state ranks ninth in the U.S. in finished manufacturing value added to raw materials, ninth in the number of employees in manufacturing, and fourth in per capita industrial output.

Indiana's industrial prowess grew first from the strong roots of a farm economy. It has been sustained, however, by virtue of its central location to both raw material sources and markets, abundant fuel and cheap electric power, skilled workers, conservative tax and labor policies, and well-developed systems of roads and railroads. Prior to the scheduled rail reorganization of the mid-1970s, Indiana's 6,571 miles of track represented an exceptionally heavy concentration of one mile of rail for every 5½ square miles of land area.

Industrial products. The twin bases of manufacturing activity are primary metals such as steel and aluminum and consumer goods which include a widely diversified array of products varying from soap to television sets, from telephones to furniture and canning jars.

Among the states Indiana ranks first in the production of mobile homes and recreational vehicles, power transmission equipment, phonograph records, and caskets and other morticians' goods. It is second in the manufacture of truck and bus bodies, motor vehicles parts and accessories, musical instruments and accessories, wooden office furniture, and cut stone and stone products.

In steel production Indiana is third among all states, as it is in the making of pharmaceuticals, wooden household furniture, mattresses and bedsprings, and structural clay products and in the fields of book printing and primary metals as an industrial goods group.

Other important products to the overall economic mix in Indiana include telephones, storage batteries, processed food, television equipment, aircraft engines and engine parts, farm machinery, fabricated metals, and electrical equipment.

Centers of industry. Although manufacturing activity is spread throughout the state, the central and northern tiers of counties are the areas of heaviest concentration. Industrial employment is greatest in Indianapolis and the Calumet River region of Gary, Hammond, and East Chicago.

At the center of a spiderweb of rail and interstate roads, Indianapolis is the hub of a wholesale and distribution network for many major companies. The city is also an important center in the manufacture of electrical machinery, airplane and truck engines, telephones, auto parts, pharmaceuticals and biological products, metal castings, food products including meat, power transmission devices, rubber products, road-building and earth-moving machinery, heating and ventilating equipment, truck bodies, and paper products.

The chief concentration of heavy industry is in the Calumet area, a swamp converted at the turn of the 20th century to a site for the nation's then largest steel mill. In the 1970s it displayed an iron sea of stacks, cranes, soap factories, cement works, refineries, and metalworks. With a half dozen different mills in Lake and Porter counties on Lake Michigan, the region is one of the foremost steel manufacturing complexes in the world. There, Indiana produces a steadily larger annual share of the nation's steel. In 1974 production for the state was 23,000,000 short tons, an amount nearly equal to that of Great Britain.

Other localities of broad industrial activity are Fort Wayne, South Bend, Muncie, and Terre Haute. Important centers for transportation equipment include Columbus, Kokomo, and Richmond. Elkhart is considered the mobile home capital of the nation. Lafayette is noted for the manufacture of pre-assembled houses and basic aluminum, a primary metal also important in southern Indiana's chief industrial city of Evansville.

Employment in industry. The state's manufacturing payroll exceeded $6,000,000,000 in 1971, having doubled in the previous decade. Average annual employment in manufacturing, which made up about 37 percent of the total non-farm employment in Indiana, was put at 755,700 in 1973. Of these, 586,500 were engaged in the manufacture of durable goods, and the rest produced non-durable items. Nearly half of the entire manufacturing work force was employed in three industries — 18 percent in electrical machinery, 15 percent in primary metals, and 14 percent in transportation equipment.

Seven corporations headquartered in Indiana ranked among the nation's 500 largest manufacturing firms in 1974. Five years before there had been ten such firms. The reduction is a partial reflection of the manner in which Indiana's larger companies have continued to move toward consolidation, mergers, and diversified operations. Of *Fortune* magazine's top 500 corporations, more than 240 had facilities of some sort in Indiana in the mid-1970s.

Among Indiana's industrial firsts was the invention in 1862 of the machine gun by Richard Gatling in Indianapolis and the design of the first mechanically successful automobiles by Elwood Haynes at Kokomo in 1893-94. In the brief but heady era that followed Hayne's perfection of the automobile, Indiana was the automobile center of the nation. A total of 246 different kinds of cars were made in 56 Indiana communities at the height of that period, including the Auburn, Cord, Duesenberg, Pierce Arrow, Stutz, and Studebaker. South Bend was the only Indiana city in which automobile manufacture survived competition from the mass production line methods mastered in Detroit, Michigan. Auto production at South Bend, however, also ceased by 1963.

Indiana remains an important producer of a wide assortment of auto parts, trucks, and buses. One of the attractions of such industries has been the plentiful supply of relatively inexpensive electric power.

ENERGY

Electric power in Indiana is almost exclusively generated by private electric utilities which, for the most part, use Indiana coal to fire steam boiler generators. In the mid-1970s, five investor-owned utilities operated 27 major power-generating stations and 8 minor ones including a few small hydroelectric plants for a total generating capacity of 10,143,300 kilowatts. One cooperatively-owned generating station operated with a capacity of 232,000 kilowatts.

The bulk of major generating facilities are located close to the coal fields in southern Indiana, and are most frequently sited on the White, Wabash, or Ohio rivers. Although not in the Indiana power system, one of the country's largest privately-owned power plants is located on the Ohio River at Madison, generating electricity for a federal atomic project in Ohio and 15 private power systems in the Ohio River Valley.

High-voltage transmission lines form the main grid for distributing power to the industrial, commercial, and residential customers of the private utilities. The network of electric coopera- tives and municipally-owned utilities which do not produce electricity buy it from the large investor-owned companies for distribution in their own local service areas. There were more than 40 rural electric cooperatives operating in 90 Indianá counties in the 1970s. The first electric cooperative in the nation was organized in Boone County in 1936.

Indiana's electric utilities are interconnected in power pooling agreements which link them with utilities as far east as the Atlantic coast and with a substantial number of other systems within the Midwest. Energy storage facilties in the state during the mid-1970s included more than 30 underground fields for natural gas and almost 75 petroleum bulk terminals with a total storage capacity of 547,116,000 gallons.

FINANCIAL SERVICES

The wide availability of financial services in Indiana is a vital factor in the prosperity of the state's farms, industries, commercial enterprises, and individual citizens. In 1974, there were more than 400 banking institutions in the state, with total resources of $20,461,017,600. There were almost 300 state chartered banks and more than 100 national banks with almost 750 branches in operation. Two banks, both in Indianapolis, each had assets of $1,000,000,000 or more, and 30 Indiana banks had assets of more than $100,000,000.

Total assets of the state's insured savings and loan associations, the chief source of home mortgage money, were $4,287,000,000 in 1971. Credit unions, one of the fastest growing segments of Indiana's financial structure, had total assets of $523,000,000 at the end of 1971.

Indiana contains an important segment of the national insurance industry, serving as the home office state in 1973 for more than 100 life, property, casualty, and surety companies and more than 60 farm mutual companies. Three Indiana life insurance companies were listed among the 100 largest in assets of U.S. life companies.

Indianapolis is the chief financial center of the state. It is headquarters of several regionally important brokerage and investment baking firms and the primary location of the Indiana branches of national stock and bond brokerages. Indianapolis also contains a bank service branch for the Federal Reserve Bank of Chicago. Other important financial centers include Fort Wayne, South Bend, Evansville, Gary-Hammond-East Chicago, Muncie, and Terre Haute. Lafayette is a center for agricultural trading and financial information.

A thriving real estate brokerage business also contributed to the state's total personal income of $26,091,000,000 in 1973. The per capita personal income for the state was $4,908, as compared with the national average of $4,918. Indiana typically ranks 11th in the nation in total income and 19th in per capita income.

In the 1970s an increasing share of the state's income continued to come from services including those in the fields of health, education, government, and communications. A growing percentage of workers also were dependent on exports.

FOREIGN TRADE

By the 1970s, one in every seven jobs in Indiana was dependent on exports to other countries. Indiana rates among the top ten of the 50 states in the value of its exports. In 1974 it ranked eighth in total exports, being the tenth largest exporter of manufactured goods and the sixth largest exporter of agricultural products.

Export products. The major volume of Indiana manufacturing exports falls into four categories of durable goods led by transportation equipment such as automotive parts, truck bodies, and heavy transmissions. Non-electrical machinery including farm equipment is typically the second leading category, followed by primary metals and electrical machinery. Agricultural chemicals, food products, drugs, and fabricated metal goods make significant contributions to total exports.

The total value of manufactured exports in 1974 was estimated at $2,000,000,000. Of the $1,000,000,000 in estimated agricultural exports that year, the most important cash crops were soybeans, corn, and wheat.

Trade destinations. Canada is Indiana's largest foreign customer for manufactured goods, although total exports to the countries of Western Europe account for approximately the same or slightly more than the dollar volume of Canadian shipments. The balance of the business, roughly 45 percent, is done in Asia, Australia, Oceania, and Africa.

Foreign trade facilities. While truck, rail, and air transport has sustained Indiana's exporting ability, the state has embarked on major port projects on Lake Michigan to the north and on the Ohio River to the south in an effort to further encourage exports with easy access to water-borne freight facilities. Burns Harbor, a deep-water port completed at Portage on Lake Michigan in 1970, is designed to handle 40,000,000 tons of grain, coal, and other bulk cargo annually. It is flanked by two steel mills. Burns Harbor was the first port on the Great Lakes to have its own waste treatment facilities and requires docking ships to discharge sewage into its treatment plant. The long customary dumping of bilge water, thick with oil, scum, and rust, is outlawed. During the summer shipping season, ocean freighters flying foreign flags from all over the world call at Burns Harbor, which gives an otherwise largely landlocked state a link to world shipping via the St. Lawrence Seaway.

Two ports on the Ohio River were in the planning and construction stages during the mid-1970s. They were designed particularly to handle containerized frieght for trans-ocean shipment. The first construction phase of the Southwind Maritime Center at Mount Vernon was completed in 1975. Clark Maritime Center at Jeffersonville was scheduled for completion later in the 1970s.

The Indiana World Trade Center operates at Weir Cook Municipal Airport at Indianapolis, linked in a network of 84 other centers in the United States and 33 other countries. Participating centers, which help world buyers and sellers get together, contribute information to a world data bank and act as brokers for the local goods and services which they list. The center is a joint venture of private firms and public agencies.

JOHN LYST

* * *

Management of
the Economy

INDIANA is both an agricultural and an industrial state. Its farmers are among the most progressive in the country. When Hoosiers talk of jobs and the future of their economy, however, they look to manufacturing for their answers. Young men from the farms of southern Indiana stream to the industrial centers to make their living. Between 1958 and 1972, the factories of the state added more than 150,000 workers to their payrolls — an increase of 28 percent. In the same period, manufacturing employment in the United States as a whole increased by 18 percent.

The men who lead Indiana's industry are determined to keep it growing at as fast a rate as possible. They have a powerful voice in the Indiana State Chamber of Commerce, which speaks for them whenever and wherever the interests of business are at stake. The Chamber was founded in 1914 and reorganized in 1939, its aim being to achieve the best possible economic and governmental climate for business operations and development. It has been particularly active in the fields of legislation, taxation, and personnel and labor relations.

The Chamber worked hard for the enactment of the tax reform legislation of 1973, which was designed to encourage business firms to locate in Indiana. Other legislation which the Chamber has supported includes three acts passed by the General Assembly in 1965 to provide financial assistance for business. These were the Municipal Economic Development Act, the Indiana Economic Development Authority Act, and the Industrial Development Fund Act.

Economic legislation. Under the Municipal Economic Development Act, communities can issue municipal revenue bonds to be used for the construction and leasing of industrial property. This has become a popular device among states to attract industry by supplying it with low-cost loans based on municipal bonds, which are exempt from federal tax. In effect, the city or town raises money through low-interest bonds, and lends the money to a company to establish a plant there. Thus a company wishing to establish itself in Evansville, Indiana, will apply to the Evansville Economic Development Commission. If the Commission approves the proposal, it will recommend to the Evansville Common Council that a bond issue be authorized. The city builds the plant itself and leases it to the company, with an option to purchase it at the end of the term of the lease. The city then mortgages the leased facilities to a trustee, who receives the lease payments from the company. The trustee establishes a bond fund, and pays the owners and holder of the bonds as the principal and interest become due.

Evansville is a thriving industrial community in southwestern Indiana on the Ohio River, in the center of a five-county area where in 1974 some 37,900 workers were employed in manufacturing. In the first year and a half after its Economic Development Commission was formed, it had issued revenue bonds for the benefit of 15 companies—including Ralston Purina, Anchor Industries, Indiana Tube Corporation, Hartford Bakery, and Modern Maid Food Products.

Industrial mortgages are guaranteed by a fund established by the Indiana Economic Development Authority Act. Indiana's fund is similar to those of most other states that use the device. Through it the Indiana Economic Development Authority can guarantee mortgages for commercial business (wholesale or retail), manufacturing, and other enterprises. No project can be insured for more than $1,000,000. The object is to enable companies to secure mortgage financing that would otherwise not be available to them.

The Industrial Development Fund Act established a $3,000,000 revolving loan fund for communities that enable them to borrow up to $200,000 for certain development programs. These programs include the construction, extension, or completion of sewer lines, water lines, sidewalks, streets; the construction of airports; and the leasing or purchase of property. The object is to enable municipalities to provide essential public services to companies that must have them in order to expand or locate in those communities. Without this assistance, a municipality must sell municipal bonds to raise the capital it needs for the extension of public services—a process that may take from six months to one year. Indiana's Industrial Development Fund is intended to provide the necessary capital almost at once, thus helping communities to attract new industry.

Economic overview. "Of *Fortune* magazine's top 500 corporations," declares a pamphlet published by the Indiana Department of Commerce's Industrial Development Division, "241 either directly, or through a subsidiary, operate facilities in the state of Indiana." It goes on to say that of the 50 largest life insurance companies, 42 had offices in Indiana in the 1970s. The Industrial Development Division published a 16-page advertising supplement in *Business Week* setting forth the state's attractions for businessmen. It cited the state's ports, including Burns Harbor on Lake Michigan and two new ports under construction on the Ohio River in the south. It pointed to the state's industrial diversity, with more than 8,000 manufacturers engaged in producing a wide variety of goods. It laid particular emphasis on expanding the state's international trade. A number of state industrial and government leaders have gone on overseas trade missions in recent years, publicizing Indiana's industries in Europe and South America. Thomas B. Hudson, Director of the International Trade Division of the Department of Commerce, said that many foreign businessmen think Indiana is landlocked in the heart of the American prairies. "This is an inaccuracy we are aggressively seeking to correct. Our port on Lake Michigan, Burns Harbor, provides access to all world markets via the St. Lawrence Seaway, and our developing river ports will offer import/export shipments via the Ohio River, a commercial artery that surpasses the Panama Canal in shipping activity."

TAXATION

Hoosiers are great complainers, particularly on the subject of taxes. In the 1960s it was common to see automobiles with license plates proclaiming "Indiana—Land of Taxes." The fact is that Indianans are far from being the highest-taxed people in the United States. According to the Census Bureau, that distinction belongs to New Yorkers. In 1971-72, Indiana placed 29th among the 50 states in terms of state and local taxes per person. Hoosiers paid an average of $444.11 for each man, woman, and child. But that is far from the whole story, since the absolute amount of taxes is not the only standard by which to judge how burdensome they are. The richer people are, the easier they will find it to pay any given amount. Therefore, the Census Bureau also measured state and local taxes in relation to personal income. In these terms, Indiana ranked 36th among the states: taxes amounted to only 11.1 percent of personal income (as against 13.0 percent in Michigan and 12.1 percent in Illinois, two neighboring states).

Federal taxes. For those in Indiana who want to complain about taxes, the place to do so is in Washington, D.C. Like other states, Indiana now receives substantial funds from the federal government. These are used for such purposes as public welfare, highways, administration of unemployment compensation, vocational education, health, and civil defense education. Indiana received more than $388,000,000 in the fiscal year ending in June 1973, or more than one-fifth of the state's budget. As the complainers will tell you, however, Indiana gives more than it receives. For every dollar the state received from the federal government in fiscal 1973, the Indiana taxpayers paid $1.61 to Washington. In fact, Indiana ranked last among the 50 states in the proportion of federal tax funds returned. Whether this was because Hoosiers are better off than most other Americans and therefore ought to contribute more to the common welfare, or because they are less aggressive in seeking help from the federal government, the fact remains that Indiana is one of the pillars of the federal tax structure.

State and local taxes. If the budget-makers in Indianapolis look to the federal government for one-fifth or more of their revenue, they also rely heavily on Indiana's own income tax and retail sales tax. In fiscal 1973 these two taxes accounted for 28 percent and 15 percent, respectively, of the total revenue. Gasoline taxes made up another 15 percent. The remaining 20 percent of state revenue came from motor vehicle licenses and fees, employment security taxes, and taxes on cigarettes, alcoholic beverages, insurance, securities, inheritances, and a variety of other sources.

There is another source of revenue which does not bulk large as far as the state is concerned, but which is important to the municipalities. That is the tax on real property, which is used almost entirely for the support of local governments. The property tax is no more popular in Indiana than elsewhere. In 1973, in a burst of fiscal reform, the Indiana General Assembly overhauled the state's tax structure. One of its chief aims was to reduce the importance of the property tax, which was considered to be a major deterrent to new business in the state. The new legislation reduced property tax payments by 20 percent and declared that in the future property taxes were to go no higher than the 1973 level. The revenues lost in this way were to be made up from other sources. The sales tax (levied on all retail sales except food) was raised from two percent to four percent. Counties were authorized to adopt local income taxes. In effect, the rising costs of schools and local government were to come in the future from income taxes rather than property taxes.

The tax reform was applauded by Indiana businessmen. The State Chamber of Commerce declared, in a report published in August 1975, that "the 1973 Indiana tax program has now reduced the Indiana property tax burden by approximately one-third." The Director of the Industrial Development Division of the Indiana Department of Commerce, a government agency, stated that the purpose of the tax reform was to attract business to Indiana. "In recent years," he said, "Indiana has experienced a lower rate of tax increase than all its neighboring states and the United States as a whole. This is a keen competitive advantage, and we are finding prospective investors and developers most interested."

Income taxes. The most important source of state revenue, the income tax, is levied on both individuals and corporations. In 1974 the individual income tax was a flat rate of two percent on taxable income. The taxpayer figures his taxable income in the same way he does for the federal income tax—by subtracting various adjustments and exemptions from gross income.

To the state and federal income taxes, many Hoosiers must now add a county income tax. In 1973 the legislature authorized counties to impose an income tax to be collected by the state. Employers withhold the tax from their employees' pay just as they do the state and federal income taxes, and the monies are later returned to the counties. The county income tax is imposed at the option of a county council, which may set the rate at 0.5 percent, 0.75 percent, or 1 percent. At the end of 1973, 36 of Indiana's 92 counties had adopted the tax.

Corporations doing business in Indiana are subject to three different state income taxes. A gross income tax is imposed on total receipts from business done in Indiana; this tax was being gradually phased out and is to be eliminated by 1993. An adjusted gross income tax is imposed at a rate of three percent, based on taxable income as defined by the federal Internal Revenue Code, but not allowing deductions for state and local taxes and charitable contributions. Corporations must compute both the gross income tax and the adjusted gross income tax, and pay whichever is higher. With the corporate gross income tax declining, the loss in receipts is to be made up by a supplemental net income tax imposed on the same base as the adjusted gross income tax, at a rate of 2½ percent in 1975 and 3 percent in 1977.

Sales and other taxes. A big revenue raiser is the sales and use tax. In 1974, Indianans paid a sales tax of four cents on the dollar, excepting food. This was the average rate in most other states (ranging from two percent in Oklahoma to six percent in Connecticut;. The tax is also applied to the rental or leasing of property, including lodgings.

The state gasoline tax was eight cents per gallon in 1974. The tax pays 75 percent of the operating expense of the Indiana State Police, and is also used for the construction and maintenance of streets and highways. Vehicle owners also pay an excise tax on their cars and trucks, varying according to age and original price. Fees are also charged for license plates, drivers' licenses, certificates of title, and vehicle registration.

The cigarette tax was only six cents a pack in 1974. This led to a considerable traffic in cigarettes with residents of neighboring states in which taxes were much higher (12 cents in Illinois, 11 cents in Michigan, 15 cents in Ohio). Alcoholic beverages are taxed at the following rates—beer, 9.5 cents per gallon; wine, 45 cents per gallon; spirits, $2.28 per gallon.

Insurance companies headquartered in Indiana must pay a tax on their net receipts from premiums. Insurance companies headquartered outside the state must pay a tax on their gross receipts from fire insurance policies sold in the state.

Owners of "intangibles"—mortgages, notes, stocks, bonds, commercial paper, etc.—are required to pay an annual tax of ¼ of one percent of the value of their holdings. The stocks of corporations located in Indiana, however, are not taxed when held by Indiana residents.

Indiana employers, like those in other states, pay an employment security tax on the wages of their employees. The funds are used to pay unemployment compensation to workers who are laid off. An employer who is able to avoid heavy layoffs may eventually reduce his state tax rate to 0.08 of 1 percent. In past years the average tax rate paid by Indiana employers is said to have been lower than in most other industrial states. In 1972, according to the Chamber of Commerce, the average rate in Indiana was estimated to be 1.0 percent as compared with a national average of 1.8 percent.

There are also the usual licenses and fees for barbers, doctors, beauticians, dentists, private detectives, librarians, insurance brokers, hunters, fishermen, and other persons engaged in activities that are regulated by the state.

Where the taxes go. Half of the state dollar was funnelled down to local governmental units in fiscal 1973, including $437,000,000 for schools, $131,000,000 for local streets and highways, and $233,000,000 for public welfare. Looked at another way, the state spent 38.1 percent of its budget on education, including state educational institutions as well as aid to local schools. State highways took up 13.9 percent of the budget dollar, benevolent and correctional institutions got 6.0 percent, 3.7 percent went for unemployment compensation, 1.7 percent was spent on natural resources and the activities of the Department of Commerce, and 11.8 percent was devoted to "miscellaneous"— the judiciary, state retirement funds, public welfare, public safety, public health, and the costs of state administration. Total disbursements were $1,703,851,534, not including certain activities paid for with non-tax funds.

UNIONS

Organized labor has a long history in Indiana. Eugene V. Debs of Terre Haute organized the first industry-wide union in 1893—the American Railway Union—and led it in the famous Pullman Car Company strike. He afterward ran for president of the United States five times as the candidate of the Socialist Party. The capital city of Indianapolis once housed the headquarters of the United Mine Workers, Carpenters, Teamsters, Barbers, Bookbinders, Bricklayers, Masons and Plasterers, Laundry Workers, Stone Cutters, and Typographers unions. With labor's rise to political power, most of these unions moved their headquarters to Washington, D.C.

Labor activity in Indiana is now very much like that on the national level. The state AFL-CIO is a federation of unions within the state, most of which belong to national unions affiliated with the national AFL-CIO. But it does not include all of organized labor. The Autoworkers, Teamsters, Mine Workers, and some other unions are not affiliated with either the national or the state AFL-CIO. A U.S. Department of Labor study made in 1968 found 129 national unions in Indiana, of which 102 were affiliated with the AFL-CIO. In that year the unions had 653,000 members, representing 36.3 percent of the employees in nonagricultural establishments. There were also some local unions, not affiliated with nationals, that had 11,000 members.

In recent years the battle between management and labor has been relatively still. Business circles like to point out to industrialists elsewhere that labor-management relations have been better than in neighboring states, with less time lost in labor disputes. The struggle, of course, goes on. According to the State Chamber of Commerce, any company that thinks it is too small to be of interest to union organizers is wrong. It says, "The sheer facts are that the union organizer's favorite target in Indiana is the establishment with less than 60 employees." During the eight months from August 1974 to March 1975, union organizers got the National Labor Relations Board to hold 158 elections in Indiana plants, and more than three-quarters of those elections (on the question of union recognition) were in units with fewer than 60 employees. The Chamber adds some practical advice for nonunion employers: "The best preventive medicine is a sound, well-administered personnel program buttressed with well-conceived and realistic personnel policies that have been 'explained' to employees."

In the past, the status of unions has been bitterly contested in Indiana. In 1957 the state legislature passed a "right-to-work" law forbidding various union security measures and particularly the union shop (under which workers are required to join a union within a specified time after they begin employment). Indiana was the only industrial state to pass a right-to-work law. After the Democrats won control of the General Assembly in the 1964 election, however, one of their first acts was to repeal it.

ECONOMIC POLICIES

If any of Indiana's policymakers were asked about the state's economy, their reply would almost certainly include the word "develop." A few years ago the Division of Planning in the State Department of Commerce issued a modest statement of the policies it thought Indiana should follow. (1) Development of the Indiana economy should be encouraged at a greater rate than those of the nation and the East North Central region. (2) Those dynamic forces affecting the Indiana economy should be enhanced (especially the encouragement of foreign trade and the development of the transportation system). (3) The economic status of all Hoosiers should be improved. (4) The quality of Indiana's labor force should be developed. (5) The Indiana economy should diversify to guard against severe negative effects during periods of recession. (6) Agricultural development and productivity should be maximized. (7) Tourism and recreation industries should be developed to their greatest potential.

PROBLEMS AND PROSPECTS

What happens in Indiana's economy depends very much on what is happening in the national economy as a whole. The swings of the business cycle register more strongly in Indiana than in most other states. The reason is that Indiana's economy is more concentrated on the manufacture of durable goods—such as electrical machinery, primary metals, and transportation equipment—than is the national economy, and the demand for these goods fluctuates more than does the demand for most other goods.

Indiana recession. A U.S. Department of Commerce study published in 1973 noted that when business is on the upswing nationally, the personal income of nonfarm workers increases faster in Indiana than elsewhere (except in the neighboring industrial state of Michigan). During recessions, the personal income of nonfarm workers is much harder hit in Indiana than elsewhere (except, again, in Michigan).

The pattern was repeated in the recession of the mid-1970s. In March 1975, unemployment in Indiana reached a level of 9.3 percent, compared with the national average of 8.7 percent.

Employment in the manufacture of durable goods had dropped sharply, that in nondurable goods less sharply, and employment in nonmanufacturing jobs had fallen very little.

The effects of the recession were felt more heavily in some metropolitan areas than in others. The heavy industrial areas of Gary-Hammond-East Chicago in the northwest, Fort Wayne in the northeast, and Muncie in the east-central area were hardest hit. Employment in the Gary area declined by more than 11 percent in nondurables, more than 9 percent in steel and fabricating, more than 4 percent in wholesale and retail trade, and about 3 percent in government service. In Fort Wayne unemployment ran at a rate of 10.5 percent in March 1975. Much of the joblessness in that area was accounted for by layoffs in Fort Wayne's truck manufacturing companies. In the Muncie area, unemployment shot up from 4.7 percent in October 1974 to 11.2 percent in March 1975. Recovery in all three of these industrial areas was expected to lag behind the national pattern because of the relatively poor outlook for the capital goods and automotive industries generally.

Industrial pollution. Anyone who travels along Interstate 90, the tollway that cuts across northern Indiana through Gary, will see one of the problems of modern civilization looming before him. From the blast furnaces and chimneys of Gary rises a sulfurous miasma that casts a pall over the sky for dozens of miles. On particularly bad days the sky takes on a yellowish tinge as far away as Waukegan, 50 miles to the north. In January 1953 an official of the Environmental Protection Agency (EPA) described the air in Northwest Indiana as the "dirtiest in the Midwest." He said the EPA was preparing legal cases against at least 20 firms in Lake and Porter counties, primarily in steel, oil, power, and other heavy industries in the Gary area. In the months that followed, pollution became a political issue. Representatives of the offending companies declared that they had been working on pollution for years, but that it would be impossible to meet the standards set forth by the EPA without financial assistance. Gary's political leaders finally managed to win approval of a bond issue to help finance the companies' antipollution effort, but only after overcoming the resistance of some local citizens' groups who maintained that the U.S. Steel Corporation needed no assistance from Gary.

Socio-economic problems in Gary. Gary is a young city, but it has been caught up in many of the problems that beset older and larger cities in the United States. Its "inner city" is reminiscent of Chicago or Los Angeles. A reporter for the *Chicago Tribune* wrote on February 11, 1973: "In the last decade, shoppers have turned away from downtown stores, housing in the center city has fallen into disrepair or been abandoned, and recreation and the arts have scattered. The inner city of Gary has suffered despite growth and prosperity in the metropolitan area that surrounds it." This was true despite the fact that in the proceding five years Gary had received $150,000,000 in federal funds — a sum amounting to $3,260 for every household in the city.

Gary began in 1906 as a steel town, supplying living quarters for the workers in the new Gary Works of the U.S. Steel Corporation. By 1973 it had grown to a population of 175,415, within a metropolitan area of 546,253 persons. The Gary Works is still the town's largest employer, providing 22,000 jobs. After World War II it became the destination of thousands of blacks from the South, and by 1973 the blacks comprised about 62 percent of the population. As blacks moved in, whites moved out to the suburbs. Along with them went the professional offices, hotels, clubs, theaters, and auditoriums. Gary became one of the first two cities in the United States to have a black mayor. But, as the black politicians were quick to point out, "We may have political control, but the whites still run the economy." Only one-third of Gary's residents held white-collar jobs in the mid-1970s. Half of the labor force was employed in factories, two-thirds of them worked in steel before the recession of 1974-75.

But the picture is not one of decay. As some businesses have moved out of downtown Gary, others have moved in. One important recent trend in Gary is the acquisition of trucking terminals and industries that make use of trucks. Placed at the intersection of four interstate highways, and at the center of an expanding industrial complex, Gary is not declining, but only changing. In the years between 1967 and 1971, retail sales in Gary increased by 26.5 percent. During that same period, retail sales in Chicago increased by only 7.5 percent.

From a long-run point of view, Gary's problems, and those of Indiana, may be said to be problems of growth. Those who look ahead view the prospects for Indiana with optimism. A group of planners in the State Department of Commerce recently tried to project what Indiana's economy would be like in the year 2000. They estimated that the labor force would grow by more than 40 percent in comparison with 1970, and that output per man-hour would grow by 165 percent. The total flow of goods and services would more than treble, and personal income per capita would more than double. A more conservative projection made by the same group saw per capita income increasing by roughly 50 percent between 1966 and 1990.

Regional differences. There are some fairly conspicuous regional differences within the state. The people of the northern, industrial area of Indiana have higher incomes on the average than those of the southern, rural area. These regional differences are expected to diminish between 1975 and 1990, but the order of precedence will remain the same—that is, the richest area (Indianapolis) will still be the richest in 1990, and the poorest (Bloomington) will still be the poorest, or least rich.

The prognosticators, of course, are not infallible. They could easily be wrong. A new industry yet undreamt of could spring up somewhere in the rural regions and turn all of the planners' assumptions upside down.

The authorities in Indianapolis take the view that progress must include all the people of the state, not just those who happen to live in regions favored by nature or by past development. If the rural areas are to share in economic growth, special efforts will have to be made to attract industry to them. Southern Indiana's small farms and rugged terrain are not favorable from the standpoint of modern agriculture, and there has been a migration of young people out of farming. Those who remain on the farms tend to look to off-farm employment for a large part of their income—when they are able to find jobs. In 1970, more than half of all farmers in Indiana had jobs off the farm, but more in northern Indiana than in southern Indiana.

At least some of the authorities in Indianapolis believe that the best way to help the rural areas and smaller communities is to push the development of larger communities. They maintain that the industrial towns have the conditions for future growth and hence the ability to absorb immigrants and commuters from the villages and smaller towns. Consequently, they favor the concentration of future development efforts on a smaller number of communities than in the past, with the hope of obtaining more results for the money invested.

FRANK PIERCE

Transportation
in INDIANA

TWO strong factors have led to the development of a high-density traffic pattern in Indiana. First, because of an environment favoring economic growth, the area has become important in both agriculture and industry. This combination requires adequate transport facilities, not only for development, but for survival as well. Second, the location of the state places it in the heart of America. Indiana reaches from Lake Michigan, which borders the north-central states, to the Ohio River, the northern boundary of the traditional "South." Thus, the state is a transitional area between two great blocks of productive territory which give strength and diversity to the national economy. Perpendicular to this north-south axis, the state lies between the highly industrialized East and the more open spaces of the agricultural West, representing another transitory position.

Restricted size perhaps detracts from the overall importance of Indiana — smallest of the Midwestern states — in many economic fields. In terms of economic activity and production per square mile, however, it often ranks well above the national average. The bustling movement of people and goods on land, on water, or in the air explains the affluence of Hoosier society.

HISTORIC DEVELOPMENT

The story of Indiana's evolution from a wilderness to its current status in technical achievement has hinged upon an ever-changing sequence of transportation systems. From the days of the American Revolution, when the first settlers straggled over the

Appalachians from the Atlantic coastal plain into the forested land of Indiana, to the achievement of statehood in 1816 required one generation. Another generation saw the formation of settlement patterns and communities linked together by roads and waterways, while state politicians were talking of the railroads to come. Early settlers had moved out of their log cabins into better homes and began the flow of wheat, corn, and pork to. the marketplace. A third generation of Hoosiers brought to the state many of its recognizable features—large farm houses, small thriving cities, and a crisscrossing pattern of transportation routes. It was a period of progress seriously marred only by the tragedy of the Civil War.

Succeeding generations have added many refinements to the basic settlement patterns and interconnecting lines of transport. During these exciting decades a few noteworthy trends may be isolated from the maze of historical detail. The direction of growth in the state was not only from east to west, as the early settlers drove ever onward toward opportunities offered by new lands, but also from south to north. The first Hoosiers arrived from the East coast through North Carolina and Kentucky. Caravans brought settlers to Kentucky, from which a spillover formed the initial nucleus of settlement along the northern bank of the Ohio River. A second trend has been that of great diversity in transportation in and through Indiana. Historians speak of the Road Building Era, the Canal Era, and the Railroad Era. All of these periods are readily discernible, but never did one actually displace another. Stagecoaches continued to rattle over the rough roads at the same time that small, flat-bottomed steamers chugged their way along both natural and artificial waterways. Transport policy favoring one or another form of travel was frequently a controversial issue in the state legislature. Diversity and flexibility in transportation facilities dating from this early interest is still reflected in today's overall network. Each major type of transport system can be traced through two centuries to help account for the modern partern.

Road Building

Prior to white settlement in Indiana the only roads were Indian trails, called "traces" by the settlers, some of which were forerunners of major highways. One junction of these early trails at the present site of Fort Wayne later became a key point along the route of the famous Wabash and Erie Canal. Another junction, located where Fall Creek emptied into the White River, is now in the city of Indianapolis, about midway between the State Capitol Building and the Indianapolis Speedway. Another of the first roads in what was to become Indiana extended through the state between Louisville, Kentucky, and St. Louis, Missouri, one stretch sometimes known as the Paoli Turnpike (now U.S. Highway 150).

The National Road. Without doubt the National Road was the most outstanding element in the historical advance of ground transportation to and through Indiana. First called the Cumberland Turnpike, or Cumberland Road, it was begun in Maryland in 1808. Predating the great Lincoln Highway, it served as a main street from the East in the first monumental surge of the westward movement. Progress was not rapid, however, for only in 1825 were surveys run to extend the National Road through Ohio, Indiana, and Illinois. After 1827 it carried heavy traffic farther and farther to the west as construction advanced. Over it streamed stagecoaches, Conestoga freight wagons, and pack trains of mules and horses.

Specifications of the roadway called for a 30-foot strip of broken stone with a gravel surface, to be flanked by 25 feet of right-of-way on either side. No grade was to be greater than four percent, an easy requirement on the relatively flat terrain of the Midwest.

By mid-century, the road had been built across Indiana, passing through Vandalia, central Illinois, on the route to connect the Atlantic coastal plain with the Mississippi River at St. Louis. Before its completion, however, the tremendous enthusiasm for roads had slackened in favor of canals. Beyond Terre Haute the route amounted to no more than a dirt trail across the Illinois prairies. Three-quarters of a century were to pass before this western extension again assumed national importance as part of a major transcontinental highway known as U.S. 40.

The Michigan Road. Second only to the National Road among Indiana's historic turnpikes was the Michigan Road, perpendicular to the east-west artery and crossing it at Indianapolis. Constructed during the same period as the National Road, it connected Lake Michigan and the Michigan settlements with the Ohio Valley. Beyond that it blazed the trail for settlement in the state and was an imporant factor in increasing the population in the north.

Early travel conditions. Travel over even the better roads during the first half of the 19th century was difficult and slow. A combination of poorly suspended vehicles and rutty surfaces taxed the most sturdy of travelers. Stagecoaches ran as much as 16 hours a day, stopping for meals and overnight lodging at inns strung along the way. The rate of progress could be as slow as two or three miles per hour, and only the most skilled drivers could attain and hold a speed of ten miles per hour.

The Canal Era

Deep indentations along the Atlantic coast, a myriad of rivers, the Great Lakes, and extensive stretches of terrain with low gradients all encouraged a waterway system over much of the northeastern part of the United States. Indiana was relatively well placed to participate in a canal-building program. The Ohio River on the south, Lake Michigan on the north, and the Wabash River flowing for several hundred miles from north-northeast to south-southeast gave the state a prominent role and a broad regional network linking eastern and northern waters with those flowing through the Mississippi River system to the Gulf of Mexico. It was little wonder that imaginative minds of the day saw boat traffic extending from eastern ports such as New York City and Baltimore to Cincinnati, Ohio; St. Louis; New Orleans, Louisiana; and other new cities to the West. Where there were no estuaries, rivers, or lakes to carry water craft, canals would be dug.

The Wabash and Erie Canal. Early in the pioneer period Indiana was reached by means of waterways along part of the route. Many of those migrating westward made their way overland to Pittsburgh, Pennsylvania, to reach the headwaters of the Ohio River, from where they could proceed by flat-bottom boats to Cincinnati, Louisville, or Evansville. Rapids, such as those at Cincinnati, slowed but did not block traffic. Another route followed the Hudson River and Erie Canal to Lake Erie and filtered traffic southward on Ohio tributaries of the lake. This latter situation was to give rise to construction of the Wabash and Erie Canal, 467 miles in length and the longest ever operated in the United States.

The geography of northeastern Indiana and northwestern Ohio was a crucial factor in providing a connection between the drainage basin of the St. Lawrence River and that of the

Mississippi. The water divide between the two was very low, allowing the construction of a connecting canal. On the east it tapped the Maumee River at Fort Wayne, which flowed into Lake Erie. No more than seven miles to the west flowed the Wabash, its waters destined to reach the Ohio River, and eventually the Mississippi.

In contrast to favorable geographic factors, the canal was built amid a political climate which at times was most unfavorable. Progress was slowed by opposition in both the Indiana and Ohio legislatures. A principal reason for discord between the two states was Ohio's reluctance to see traffic flow westward into Indiana, when it could be directed southward into the Ohio River and never leave the state.

Work on the Ohio portion of the canal system began in 1825 and was scheduled to be carried on by Indiana as part of a cooperative effort. After much delay, Indiana in 1828 decided to continue the project, but only after the federal government had given the state a substantial tract of land in the interest of providing a national transportation facility. Not until 1835 was the first segment of the Wabash Canal, a 30-mile stretch from Fort Wayne to Huntington, completed and opened to traffic. Progress continued as Logansport was reached in 1838 and Lafayette in western Indiana in 1843. An additional ten years was required before the canal was completed to Evansville.

Failure of the canal system. At the outset, traffic in the canal across northern Indiana was heavy and the venture seemed successful. The state expressed its satisfaction by approving and planning other stretches of artificial waterways, but none on so grandiose a scale as the Wabash and Erie Canal. Despite heavy receipts through tolls, the Wabash Canal nevertheless suffered financial reverses, and the costs of maintenance and operation could not be met. The Panic of 1837 added to a financial crisis, and the new canals and other transportation plans to be sponsored by the state were discontinued. Private companies carried on some of the projects, but most were abandoned. The Wabash and Erie Canal was an exception; it continued to receive state support until its completion. Its usefulness faded, however, when canals in general were replaced by a newer and faster method of transportation—the railroad.

The Indiana legislature became as enraptured with railroads as it had previously been with roads and canals. Rights were given to railway lines that paralleled the canals, actually creating unfair competition when the speed and flexibility of the two types of transportation were compared. But even the locomotive, whistling its way through Indiana, did not sound the death knell of water transport in the state. It is interesting to note that the Ohio River, with locks and improved navigational facilities, carried more low cost cargo in the 1970s than ever before, the total surpassing that of the Panama Canal.

The Railroad Era

A railroad from the Indiana town of Madison located on the Ohio River about midway between Cincinnati and Louisville, to Indianapolis was the pacemaker for the state's rail system. Construction on the line began in 1836, although there had been fanfare in the state in favor of railroads for ten years. In fact, one Indiana governor had wanted to give priority to railroads over canals long before the change was actually made. He supported a plan for a rail line connecting the Great Lakes with the Ohio River, mostly through Indiana, which in 1830 was a revolutionary concept.

The early railways. Many years were to elapse before the first train from Madison puffed into Indianapolis in 1847. Trains, however, had operated over part of the route as construction proceeded from 1838. Evidently the fervor for railways increased, for more than 30 railway charters were granted before the Madison-Indianapolis Railroad was actually started. Most of the planning came to naught because the private companies which undertood the enterprises suffered from a lack of capital. In all, only one and one-quarter miles of track on the Lawrenceburg and Indianapolis line was laid, a rather ridiculous exhibition after so much effort and planning for a facility so sorely needed in the state. For example, a line chartered in 1832 to connect Cincinnati and St. Louis via Indianapolis failed to receive enough financial support until the project was revived by the state of Indiana in 1848.

Immediately after the completion of the Madison-Indianapolis line in 1847, the Railroad Era was inaugurated on a tremendous scale. The first union station in the United States was built in Indianapolis in 1853. By 1854 railway construction was taking place in many parts of the state to the detriment of the canal system. Also in 1854, the Monon Railroad connecting Michigan

City with New Albany across the Ohio River from Louisville, was completed, creating a line that ran north and south through the entire state. In 1857 it was possible to travel continuously from the Atlantic coast to the Mississippi River.

Travel time on the early railway lines, while revolutionary for the period, appears incredibly slow today. For example, in the early 1850s it was possible to take a train from Indianapolis to Lafayette, but the 63-mile journey lasted four hours. The 117-mile ride to Cincinnati from the Indiana capital took nine hours. Rail travel in this period had not been integrated from railroad to railroad because the gauges varied from six feet to the later standard guage at 4 feet 8½ inches.

Post-Civil War expansion. During the 1850s, railroad mileage increased remarkably, as it did following the Civil War. This growth continued until World War I, when track mileage not only ceased to increase, but started to decline. During the great Railroad Era, the new lines opened up numerous communities and brought prosperity to farmers, marking a period of development that incorporated more changes in a few years than had taken place during the proceding three-quarters of a century. Greater contact was made with the more industrially advanced East, which controlled more capital, bought quantities of agricultural goods, and needed outlets for an increasing volume of manufactured goods.

THE MODERN ERA

The transportation pattern of the 1970s continued to reflect the same fundamental factors of location and economic activity which led to its development. The prime changes have been those of speed and increased capacity. It may be noted, however, that before the turn of the 20th century, some trains streaking across the level Indiana land attained speeds up to 120 miles per hour. Also, there is undoubtedly a greater degree of synchronization between one type of transportation and another than was true in the days of surging growth.

Roads

An examination of a road map of Indiana reveals two distinctive route patterns which do not clash, but are enmeshed one into the other. Most obvious is the crisscrossing of north-south and east-west roads to form a trellis design.

Noticeable also are two foci on which many roads converge — one at Indianapolis in the geographic center of the state, and the other in the extreme northwest corner near the colossal magnet of Chicago, Ilinois.

Origin of the road pattern. The trellis pattern applies quite rigidly in the northern part of the state, but is somewhat askew in the south, where hilly land may in places disrupt the geometric design of the/route structure. Also, the locations of Cincinnati near the southeastern corner of Indiana, Louisville near the extreme south center, and Evansville in the southwest have to a degree deflected the north-south orientation of some roads. The trellis design of the preponderant number of roads in Indiana, particularly those of secondary and tertiary importance, rests first upon the lack of sharp relief over most of the area and second upon the Ordinance of 1785. This decree referred to the township and range system whereby the land was surveyed in tracts of 36 square miles, each tract divided into sections of one square mile. Along each side of each section ran a road, many of which became county, state, and national highways. Indiana's 92 counties are largely based upon blocks of townships, and the county seats tend to be lined up with reference to the road pattern. The level land of Indiana was particularly adapted to this survey and most of the roads thus reflect a practice dating back nearly two centuries.

Some 20 highways lead into Indianapolis, a number greater than that of any other U.S. city. They range from national routes to major cities such as Cincinnati, Louisvile, St. Louis, and Chicago, to county roads tapping various county seats and small commercial centers ringing the capital city. The pattern of city streets in Indianapolis is in some ways similar to the road pattern of the state as a whole. East-west streets intersect north-south streets at right angles, while avenues from all directions coverge on the city center near the Capitol building.

Greater Chicago, part of which lies in Indiana, draws eastern traffic crossing the northern part of the state, some of it swinging south from Michigan to round the southern end of Lake Michigan. The Indiana Toll Road runs through the northernmost part of the state and has aptly been labeled the "Main Street of the Midwest."

State highways in the 1970s. Indiana has an estimated total of 90,000 miles of roads including those maintained by the counties and cities. Statistically the state ranks fifth in the country in highway mileage in relation to area, or about two and one-half miles of roadway for each square mile of territory. Of the total mileage of roads about 95 percent is paved, comparing favorably with 75 percent for the United States as a whole.

Until the early 1960s the principal highways were national routes, such as U.S. 50, which crosses the state latitudinally from Vincennes to Lawrenceburg and U.S. 31, which runs longitudinally from South Bend to Jeffersonville via Indianapolis. The new 41,000-mile limited-access international highway system carries a substantial proportion of the nation's through traffic. Since their inception in the 1960s, these superhighways have included approximately 1,100 miles within Indiana.

Traffic counts show that five of the new interstate routes carry a flow of 5,000 or more vehicles a day. These routes are No. 70, from Gary to Louisville via Indianapolis; No. 65, from Terre Haute to Richmond via Indianapolis; No. 69, from Indianapolis to a juncture with east-west routes in northern Indiana via Fort Wayne; No. 74, from Indianapolis to Cincinnati; and No. 60/90, which runs across the northern part of the state connecting Chicago with eastern cities. It can be noted that like other U.S. highways, interstate routes have been given even numbers to designate east-west orientation, and odd numbers to designate north-south direction.

Over Indiana's highways run some 3,200,000 vehicles, or roughly 600 for each 1,000 persons. The great majority of vehicles registered are privately-owned or fleet-operated passenger automobiles, but large numbers of buses serve virtually every community in the state. Greyhound and Continental Trailways each normally operate from three to five daily schedules over major routes, while numerous smaller companies handle most of the local traffic. In addition, Indianapolis is an important trucking center with headquarters for several major moving companies.

The Indianapolis Motor Speedway, featuring the "Indy 500" as the world's greatest auto racing event, has added to the state's concern with roads and automobiles. As in southeastern Michigan, the level land of northern Indiana served as an excellent proving ground for motor cars. Several of the early automobile manufacturing companies such as Studebaker concentrated there. In response to this interest, the Indianapolis Speedway was constructed and the first race held in 1911.

Although auto manufacturing no longer plays a primary role in the state, the industry remains a tradition which figures strongly in such cities as Elkhart, Fort Wayne, and Indianapolis.

Railroads

The railroad pattern in Indiana differs markedly from that of the highways. Foremost, there is far less crisscrossing of routes. The major routes of the state either focus on Indianapolis or converge on Chicago through northwesternmost Indiana. Cincinnati and Louisville also constitute foci of lines which traverse the state. Most of the railway lines in the state are oriented east and west as part of transcontinental systems. Chicago and St. Louis have been gateways between the eastern and western United States, and all lines which operate between them and the east coast pass through Indiana. Some lines are oriented north and south through the state, especially those operating between Chicago and either Cincinnati or Louisville. Traffic to Florida, for example, uses these lines.

In 1972, a total of 6,405 miles of railroad track was reported. In addition, more than 5,000 miles of multiple track along main lines, together with sidings and yard trackage, were also reported. Since passenger traffic on American railroads has been drastically reduced since World War II, the 25 railroads serving the state are devoted almost exclusively to carrying freight. The principal routes are limited principally to traffic between important cities — Chicago to Cincinnati via Indianapolis; across the state between St. Louis and eastern cities via Indianapolis; and across northern Indiana between Chicago and Detroit, Cleveland, Pittsburgh, New York City, Philadelphia, and Washington, D.C. Despite the inroads made by trucks on long-distance hauls freight carried by the railroads is impressive. For example, Indianapolis alone handles 540 carloads each day.

Decline of passenger service. The decline of passenger traffic by rail has had drastic effects on the railways. As late as 1936, large segments of the population travelled by train. The Union Station in Indianapolis teemed with arriving and departing trains and crowds of passengers. Through the station seven mainline trains on the Pennsylvania Railroad ran each way each day between New York City or Washington, D.C. and St. Louis, The Big Four Division of the New York Century also ran six trains each day over the same general route. Added to that, five New

York Central schedules passed through Indianapolis en route between Chicago and Cincinnati. A number of famous trains sped through northern Indiana, en route to and from Chicago, including the New York Central's 20th Century Limited, the Pennsylvania Railroad's Broadway Limited, and the Baltimore and Ohio's Capitol Limited.

Within the Indiana of 1936, also, some train schedules showed surprising frequency. Two lines in the Indiana railroad system connected Indianapolis with Fort Wayne, one passing through Anderson and Muncie and the other through Kokomo, Peru, and Wabash. Over these routes ran 27 trains each way each day. On the other side of the state, the Chicago, Indianapolis, and Louisville Railroad served local traffic through numerous cities. One line extended from Michigan City to Evansville and the other from Chicago to Louisville. The two lines crossed at the little city of Monon, for which the railroad received its popular name. One of its schedules was especially favored by college students, with stops at Lafayette (Purdue University), Crawfordsville (Wabash College), Greencastle (De Pauw University), and Bloomington (Indiana University).

At the beginning of the 1970s passenger traffic by rail in the United States was all but defunct, except for commuter trains and a few scattered lines. Then it was that the National Railroad Passenger Corporation, sponsored by the federal government and popularly known as AMTRAK, began operation of a nationwide rail network under a single direction.

AMTRAK. By 1975, five AMTRAK lines crossed Indiana and served eight of the state's cities. Though this passenger train network was a mere skeleton of that of former days, revived interest has kept passenger rail travel alive and promised to develop further. One of the AMTRAK routes, the National Limited, goes through Terre Haute, Indianapolis, and Richmond en route from St. Louis to New York City. The James Whitcomb Riley stops at Peru and Muncie en route from Chicago to Washington, D.C., while the Mountaineer continues to Norfolk, Virginia. A third routing carries the Floridian from Chicago to Miami, with stops in Logansport and Indianapolis. Between Chicago and New York City, the Broadway Limited schedules stops at South Bend and Fort Wayne. The route from Chicago to Detroit, however, does not stop in Indiana. Over all of the routes with stops in Indiana cities, there is only one scheduled run each way each day. Thus, only four trains a day pass through the Union Terminal in Indianapolis.

Interurban lines. At one time, interurban railways carried passengers to cities throughout Indiana. The Interurban Terminal in Indianapolis, built in 1904, was the largest in the United States. Its fate was worse than that of the railroads, for it went completely out of business. The only interurban line operating in the state in the mid-1970s was the South Shore Line running eastward from Chicago through Indiana's densely populated strip along the Lake Michigan shoreline.

Airlines

While railroads have declined in importance, air transportation has come to the fore. As an air network developed in the United States, major lines carried passengers over greater distances from one large city to another. Smaller regional lines sprang up to handle much of the short distance travel. Cities in Indiana, however, were too closely spaced to justify a regional system of routes centering at Indianapolis. Consequently mainline carriers—especially Trans World Airlines (TWA), American Airlines developed the early services. In the mid-1970s, major airlines and regional companies centered outside the state such as Allegheny Airlines, Ozark Airlines, and North Central Airlines provided all scheduled air service to Indiana cities other than commuter flights.

The first semblance of an air network over the United States appeared in 1926, sparse though it was. Within ten years, air travel had become a widely accepted means of travel with routes crisscrossing each other in large cities. In 1936 three major companies scheduled stops in Indianapolis—one flight a day on American Airline's Chicago-Indianapolis-Cincinnati-Washington, D.C.-New York route; two flights a day on Eastern's Chicago-Indianapolis-Louisville segment of the route to Miami; and three flights a day on TWA's transcontinental route. They were named Grand Canyon, Sun Pacer, and Sky Hawk, respectively. A dozen planes landed and took off in the Indianapolis airport daily, each one carrying no more than 21 passengers.

In 1974 Indiana reported the departure of 54,994 scheduled aircraft on which 1,249,207 passengers enplaned. Indianapolis accounted for more than half of the total. In fact, the capital city is rated as an Air Traffic Hub, medium category, along with such cities as Milwaukee, Wisconsin; Jacksonville, Florida; Birmingham, Alabama; San Antonio, Texas; and Louisville. In respect to numbers of passengers handled, the city ranked thirty-second in the county. Evansville was the only other city among the top 100, ranking one-hundredth.

In total Indiana had close to 200 airports in the 1970s, of which more than half handle freight and charter passenger service. Twelve had scheduled commercial service, although half of them were limited to commuter flights. From Indianapolis six airlines had 100 departures per day, destined to cities in the Southwest and throughout the Midwestern, Southern, and Eastern states. As a more specific example, Allegheny, Delta, and American airlines together had nine flights daily from Indianapolis to Chicago. Bloomington, Evansville, Fort Wayne, Lafayette, and South Bend also had trunk line service. Because many of the airliners on these flights carry 100 or more passengers at a time, the growth of airline traffic can be considered phenomenal.

As an example of commuter services, Kokomo has four daily flights to Chicago, three to Lafayette, and one to Elkhart. There are also helicopter flights between Gary and Chicago.

Waterways

Water transportation continues to be important in Indiana, although it is largely limited to the short shoreline along Lake Michigan and the Ohio River along the southern border. In the north, the state's largest port in Indiana Harbor in East Chicago, just across the Illinois state boundary. The area, known as the Calumet Region, also has two other ports a few miles to the east, one at Buffington and the other at Gary. Still further eastward is the site of the state's newest harbor facility, the Burns Waterway Harbor located near the Indiana Dunes State Park.

These northern harbors play a dual role in fostering industry and commerce in the state. Gary and its environs constitute one of the nation's greatest iron and steel centers. Lake freighters bring coal, iron ore, and limestone to the city's furnaces, capitalizing on the relatively lower costs for hauling bulky goods. Since the opening of the St. Lawrence Seaway, Indiana has handled ocean-going vessels capable of going to any port in the world. This advantage has strengthened the industrialization of northern Indiana and lessened its dependence on Chicago and Atlantic seaboard ports.

Along the Ohio River the relatively rapid current has been tamed, permitting vessels to use it over a water route system which also includes the Mississippi River. Although the Indiana-Kentucky boundary follows the right, or north, bank of the river, both states share it in terms of water traffic. For example, both Evansville and Mount Vernon are Indiana river ports.

These various waterways are seldom highlighted along with the roads, railroads, and airlines of the state because they rarely carry passengers. Nevertheless, they figure prominently in a few specialized segments of the state economy.

G. ETZEL PEARCY

✳ ✳ ✳

Administration of
INDIANA

THE administration of Indiana is similar to that of other states, but there are some marked differences. The state's first constitution, regarded as a liberal document for its time, was drawn up in mid-1816 and became effective with Indiana's admission to the Union, without being submitted to or ratified by the voters. Indiana's present constitution, adopted in 1851, is the seventh oldest among the 50 states. It was drafted by a convention that began its deliberations on October 7, 1850, and adjourned on February 10, 1851. The constitution was ratified in 1851, by a vote of 113,230 to 27,638, and became effective on November 1, 1851.

INDIANA'S CONSTITUTION

The present constitution, drafted under Democratic influence, reflects Jacksonian concepts of democracy. It called for more frequent elections, increased the number of elective offices, prohibited a state debt except for certain emergencies, substituted biennial for annual sessions of the General Assembly, and limited regular sessions to 61 days.

The Indiana constitution begins with a preamble and contains 16 Articles ranging from a bill of rights (Article one) to miscellaneous subjects and amendments (Articles 15 and 16). It also defines the three branches of government, the distribution of power, the educational structure, boundaries, and the state militia.

Branches of government. The constitution provides for

executive, legislative, and judicial branches of government. The General Assembly, consisting of a Senate and a House of Representatives, is the law-making body. The executive department consists of the governor, the lieutenant governor, and the administrative branch — the secretary of state, treasurer, auditor of state, and a system of county officers. The judicial branch deals with the administration of justice and the upholding of the laws. It works through a system of courts running from the Supreme Court of the state to the town court. The judicial article was revised by an amendment adopted by the voters in November 1970 and took effect on January 1, 1972.

The state constitution requires that the legislature must reapportion itself according to population every six years. This law was ignored, however, from 1923 to 1963, during which time the rural areas acquired an influence far out of proportion to their declining populations. Under pressure from the U.S. Supreme Court, the state finally achieved reapportionment based on the "one man, one vote" principle in 1965.

Education. Article VIII, on education, provided for a school fund from various sources, and this, in time, has led to the present school system in Indiana. It also provides for the election of a state superintendent of public instruction.

The amendment process. The constitution has been amended less than 40 times in the 124 years since its adoption. Article 16 spells out the rather lengthy amendment process. "Any amendment or amendments to this constitution, may be proposed in either branch of the General Assembly," and if agreed to by a majority of the members of both branches, then the question shall be referred to the next legislature. If, in turn, the majority of that body should be in favor of the proposed amendment, it shall be submitted to the voters of the state, and if they approve it, the addition becomes part of the constitution.

The first amendment, adopted in 1873, dealt with the state's financial obligations to the Wabash and Erie Canal project. Seven amendments were adopted in 1881, relating to the right of suffrage and to elections, to the legislative system, to fees and salaries, to the judicial power, and to political and municipal corporations. Amendments in the 1970s provided that the governor could immediately succeed himself, provided for the joint election of governor and lieutenant governor, and revised Article 12 on the militia.

STRUCTURE OF STATE GOVERNMENT

The state government is divided into three branches, providing for checks and balances, under the constitution. They are the executive, legislative, and judicial branches.

Executive branches. The executive branch consists of the governor and lieutenant governor and administrative officers including the secretary of state, auditor of state, treasurer of state, attorney general, and superintendent of public instruction.

The governor is elected for a four-year term and, until 1972, could not immediately succeed himself. As a result, this influence on the General Assembly was generally weak during the second half of his administration. The voters, however, approved a constitutional amendment in 1972 which allows a governor to serve two consecutive four-year terms in any 12-year period.

The governor is responsible for signing legislative measures into law, overseeing the National Guard, and operating more than 80 departments, divisions, and other agencies. He also appoints some members of the boards of trustees of state colleges and universities. The governor's authority is wielded largely through his statutory power to appoint and remove the heads of nearly all departments, commissions, and governing boards of institutions. Some 12,000 jobs are unprotected by civil service and subject to the spoils system.

As of 1974, the governor and lieutenant governor run jointly for election—a vote cast for one is a vote cast for the other. Both must be at least 30 years old and have been a citizen of the United States and a resident of Indiana during the five years preceding the election. Prior to 1974, the governor and lieutenant governor ran independently of one another. In 1960, a Democrat was elected governor and a Republican was elected lieutenant governor.

The lieutenant governor, elected to a four-year term, serves as president of the Senate, director of the Department of Commerce, and commissioner of agriculture. He assumes the governor's office when the governor is no longer able to serve. As president of the Senate, the lieutenant governor may join in debate and cast the deciding vote in the case of a tie.

The secretary of state is also elected to a four-year term. He oversees official state documents, regulates corporate securities, and issues charters for incorporation.

The auditor of state is elected for four years and is the bookkeeper of state funds. The treasurer, also elected for four years, receives and disburses all state money. The attorney general serves as the state's legal counsel, checking the constitutionality of all laws passed by the legislature. He is elected to a four-year term. The superintendent of public instruction oversees the operation of the state's public schools. He is elected to a two-year term. A 1972 constitutional amendment, however, provides that the legislature may enact another method of selection.

Legislative branch. The bicameral General Assembly is composed of 50 senators, serving four-year terms, and 100 representatives, serving for two years. The assembleymen must be U.S. citizens and residents of Indiana for two years and of their county or district for one year. Senators must be at least 25 and representatives at least 21 years of age.

In 1970 the voters approved annual meetings of the legislature. Until then the legislature met biennially, with sessions beginning on the first Thursday after the first Monday in January of odd-numbered years. Regular sessions are limited during odd-numbered years and to 30 days during even-numbered years. Regular sessions may not extend beyond April 30 of the year in which they are convened. Two-thirds of the members must be present to make a quorum, and an actual majority of the members of each house is required to pass legislation. The governor has veto power over legislation, but the veto can be overridden by a simple majority of the two houses.

The General Assembly has the power to enact all types of laws not specifically prohibited by the state or federal constitutions.

Bills may originate in either house and may be amended or rejected in the other. Revenue-raising bills, however, must originate in the House of Representatives. An administrative body, the Legislative Council, conducts studies for the legislature, drafts bills, does research, and fills printing needs.

Senators and representatives are privileged from arrest, except in cases of treason, felony, and breach of the peace, during the session of the General Assembly, and in going to and returning from the session. They cannot be subject to any civil process either during a session or in the 15 days preceding a session. Either house may punish its members for disorderly behavior, and may, with a two-thirds majority, expel a member.

The lieutenant governor serves as president of the senate, and the leader of the majority party presides as president pro tempore in the absence of the lieutenant governor. The presiding officer of the house is the speaker, who is elected by the other house members.

LOCAL GOVERNMENT

Four principal types of local government are found in Indiana. They are the county, township, town, and civil town. There are also cities, towns, and school towns concerned with the operation of the school system; these may be independent or may overlap other political units.

County government. Indiana has 92 counties, widely varying in size and population. Counties were originally established to provide a local government unit to enforce laws and carry out services of the legislature.

Counties are governed by a three-member Board of County Commissioners that is responsible for the administration of all county business. The commissioners' authority is fixed by the constitution and by acts of the General Assembly. They run for office from the district in which they reside, but their election is determined on the basis of the countrywide vote. Terms are for four years, on a staggered basis.

Financial powers of the counties are in the hands of a seven-member County Council, which acts as a check on the Board of County Commissioners. Terms are for four years. A council member is elected from each of four designated council districts within the county, and three are elected from the county at large. The council has the exclusive power to fix the rate of taxation in the county and to borrow money for county purposes. Other functions include the transfer and approval of funds and the payment of county salaries and expenses.

The constitution provides for the election, at the time of a general election, of a clerk of the circuit court, an auditor, a recorder, a treasurer, a sheriff, a coroner, and a surveyor in each county. They serve four-year terms and may not serve more than two terms within 12 years. All county officers must reside in the county for at least one year preceding the election.

The auditor is the general bookkeeper and record-keeper for the county and secretary of the Board of County Commissioners. The treasurer collects local and state taxes and fees, and disburses county funds. In some counties he also serves as treasurer ex-officio of the county board of education and treasurer to the board of hospital trustees. He is also authorized to serve as ex-officio city treasurer in many cities, a service for which he receives additional compensation.

The clerk of the circuit court, commonly called the county clerk, attends sessions of circuit and county courts, issues licenses and collects fees, records wills and probate records, and exercises control of voter registration in the county. The surveyor surveys, keeps records, and supervises all civil engineering work in the county including ditch construction and maintenance.

The county sheriff is in charge of the county jail, acts as officer of the county courts, serves warrants and subpoenas, holds forclosure sales, attends sessions of the County Council and the Board of County Commissioners, and serves processes for the County Board of Review. He appoints his own deputies and matrons, but appointment of his chief deputy is subject to the approval of the county commissioners.

The coroner determines the manner of a person's death when circumstances are not explainable and in cases where violence or casualty are involved. He obtains assistance of the police in such cases, has the power to order an autopsy and to employ a physician to make the autopsy, and files a report with the local health officer and the clerk of the circuit court. He may also act as a peace officer and is the only county officer who may arrest the sheriff. The coronor may also name deputies and clerical assistance subject to the approval of the county commissioners.

City government. Indiana's cities are governed by a mayor and a common council, generally called a city council, who are elected to four-year terms in odd-numbered years. Candidates are nominated in city primaries and must be registered voters and residents of the city for one year. The number of councilmen vary according to the classification of the city.

The mayor is the executive head of the city government. He reports to the common council on finances, executes and supervises enforcement of city ordinances, appoints or fills vacancies in administrative boards, appoints the heads and employees of various city departments, and is empowered to suspend or remove all appointees from office, including those of his predecessor. His veto may be overridden by a two-thirds vote of the common council.

The common council is the city's legislative body, meeting at least once a month. It may be called into special session by the mayor and its meetings are open to the public. The city clerk is clerk of the council. The council enacts all city ordinances, reviews the city budget, establishes tax rates, and fixes salaries.

Towns and townships. Indiana's incorporated towns are governed by a Board of Town Trustees, the members of which are elected to four-year terms in odd-numbered years when county, state, and national elections are not being held. Other elected officials include a clerk-treasurer and judges of the town court. All other officers, including the town marshal, are appointed by the Board of Town Trustees.

Townships, greatly reduced in importance in recent years, function primarily in matters of social welfare. Under specific conditions, townships may consolidate with adjoining townships or join a city for planning and zoning purposes. The Board of County Commissioners may abolish a township upon petition of a majority of the freeholders in the townships affected.

THE POLITICAL PROCESS

Indiana through the years has been a "swing" state politically. Republicans have served as governors, 19 times, while Democrats have held the office 18 times. Three governors were Whigs, one was a Jeffersonian Republican, and one was an indepedendent. Indiana has sent two Jeffersonian Democrats, three Democratic Republicans, two Whigs, 19 Democrats, one Union, and 13 Republicans to the U.S. Senate. The state is the birthplace of three political parties—the Greenbacks in 1874; Social Democrats in 1898; and the Socialists in 1901.

The political party system. Indiana depends on party conventions to choose candidates for the U.S. Senate, governor, state administrative offices, and delegates to national conventions. Presidential candidates and candidates for the U.S. House of Representatives, the General Assembly, and county, township, and city offices are chosen in primary elections.

The primary is a party election. Indiana has a closed primary—in order to vote a person must declare his party preference and vote for the candidates of that party only. A voter may change party affiliation, but is subject to challenge. If challenged, the voter must sign an affadvit stating his intention to vote in the next general election for a majority of the candidates of the party whose ballot was requested. Primary expenses are paid from public funds. Parties administer the primaries, but they in turn are under the supervision of state government officials.

Each major party's state nominating convention must be held within 60 days after the primary. A convention is composed of about 2,000 delegates elected in the state primaries. Conduct of state conventions is established by law. A state party chairman, however, may decide whether the delegates will vote for all contested offices at the same time or select one at a time beginning with the least important one. To prevent permanent deadlock of a nominating convention, the rules provide that after several ballots have been taken and no candidate has received a majority, the candidates with the lowest vote totals in subsequent balloting are automatically removed from the running.

Voters express their preference for their party's presidential candidate through Indiana's presidential preference primary. They vote for the presidential candidate of their choice during the same primary election held for candidates of state offices.

Under Indiana law, delegates to the national party conventions are required to vote for the winning candidate on the first ballot. Delegates representing congressional districts must vote for the winning candidate from their district. Delegates representing the entire state must vote for the winning candidate in the state-wide vote. After the first ballot, however, delegates are no longer bound by the results of the primaries.

Election boards. The state election board is composed of the governor, who acts as ex-officio chairman; two members appointed by the governor; and the director of public printing, who serves as clerk. The appointed members must be from each of the two major political parties and are nominated in writing by their respective party chairmen. The county election board in each county is vested with the sole and exclusive power of conducting all elections in cities and towns. The board is composed of the clerk of the circuit court and two members from the two major political parties who are appointed by the clerk. One of the board members is elected chairman and the clerk of the circuit court serves as secretary. Precinct election boards are established in each precinct of a city or town holding an election. The precinct board is composed of an inspector and two judges who are appointed by the County Election Board. The other election officials in each precinct are: two clerks, two assistant clerks (if deemed necessary), two sheriffs, one challenger, and one poll-book holder for each political party participating in the election. Where two officers are selected for the same office, each must be of a different political party.

State parties. The precinct committeemen form the broad base of Indiana's political party organizational pyramid. Committeemen are elected in each of the state's precincts in the state primary election. The elected committeemen appoint a vice-committeemen who, under party rules, must be of the opposite sex.

Shortly after the primary, the precinct committeemen and vice-committeemen in each county meet at the county seat and elect a county chairman and vice chairman, secretary, and treasurer. The county chairmen and vice chairmen in each of the state's congressional districts then meet and elect a district chairman and vice chairman. These district leaders constitute the state central committee.

The state central committee elects a state party chairman and other officers and names a national committeeman and a national committeewoman to represent the state in the party's national convention.

City committees are established by the county committee preceding city elections and function until after the election when the committee expires. Its unused funds are returned to the county committee. Ward, township, and town committees are also appointed by, and are responsible to, the county committee.

THE JUDICIAL SYSTEM

The Indiana constitution provides for the establishment of a Supreme Court, a Court of Appeals, circuit courts, and such other courts as the General Assembly might deem necessary. The entire judicial system established by the constitution was revised by an amendment adopted by the voters in November 1970. The amendment took effect on January 1, 1972.

The Supreme Court. The Supreme Court consists of a chief justice and four associate justices. The chief justice is selected by the judicial nominating commission from the members of the Supreme Court and retains the office for five years. He may be reappointed in the same manner, however. A member of the court may resign the office of chief justice without resigning from the court. During a vacancy, whether caused by illness, absence, death, incapacity, or resignation, all powers and duties of the chief justice fall upon the justice who has been on the bench for the longest period. The chief justice must prepare and submit to the General Assembly regular reports on the condition of the courts.

The Supreme Court has no original jurisdiction except in the admission of attorneys to the practice of law, the discipline or disbarment of those admitted, the unauthorized practice of law, the removal and retirement of justices and judges, the supervision of the exercise of jurisdiction by other courts of the state, and the issuance of writs necessary or appropriate in aid of its jurisdiction.

Lower court decisions imposing the death sentence, life imprisonment, or imprisonment for more than ten years may be appealed directly to the Supreme Court. The court also has, in all appeals of criminal cases, the power to review all questions of law and to review and revise the sentence imposed. The court's jurisdiction also includes cases in which a trial court judgment has declared all or part of a law unconstitutional, as well as petitions to transfer from the Court of Appeals. A decision of the state's Supreme Court may be appealed to the U.S. Supreme Court.

Court of Appeals. The Court of Appeals consists of three judges from each of three geographic districts in the state. The legislature has the power to determine the number of districts and their locations. The Court of Appeals has no original jurisdiction except that it may review decisions of administrative agencies. It exercises appellate jurisdiction in all other cases.

Selection and tenure. A vacancy on the Supreme Court or the Court of Appeals is filled by the governor, without regard to political affiliation, from a list of three nominees prepared by the judicial nominating commission. If the governor fails to make an appointment within 60 days, the chief justice of the Supreme Court makes the appointment from the same list.

To be eligible for nomination a person must be a citizen of the United States, must reside within the state's geographic districts, must have been admitted to the practice of law in Indiana's courts for not less than ten years, or must have served as a judge of a circuit, superior, or criminal court of Indiana for not less than five years.

Following appointment, a justice of the Supreme Court or a judge of the Court of Appeals serves on the bench for two years. Subject to approval or rejection by the electorate, in the next general election, he then continues to serve in ten-year terms. Supreme Court justices are approved or rejected by the state's entire electorate; Court of Appeals' judges are approved or rejected by the voters within the geographic district in which he serves. The General Assembly establishes manadatory retirement ages for the courts.

The Judicial Nominating Commission. The constitution provides for a commission to nominate persons to the Supreme Court and the Court of Appeals. In addition, the commission also defines the judicial qualifications for the Supreme Court and the Court of Appeals.

The Judicial Nominating Commission consists of seven persons, one of whom is the chief justice of the Supreme Court or a justice designated by the chief justice. Three members are attorneys elected by members of the bar, and the governor appoints three citizens who are not attorneys to serve on the commission. Commission members, under the constitution, may not hold an office in a political party or organization. Also, no member except the chief justice or his designee may hold a salaried public office. Commission members are not elegible for appointment to judicial office while on the commission and for three years thereafter.

Clerk, reporter, and public defender. The clerk of the Supreme Court and the Court of Appeals was a constitutional office until January 1, 1972. The General Assembly provided that this office is elective in the same manner as the governor and other state officials. The clerk serves as an administrative officer of the Supreme Court and the Court of Appeals.

The reporter is elected in the same manner as the clerk. The primary duty of the reporter is to publish and distribute the bound volume of the official reports of the Supreme Court and the Court of Appeals.

The public defender provides legal representation for any inmate of an Indiana penal institution who claims he is unlawfully imprisoned, but is without sufficient funds to employ counsel. The public defender, who must be an attorney with at least three years of practice in Indiana, is appointed by the Supreme Court.

Prosecuting attorneys. The constitution provides for the election of a prosecuting attorney in each judicial circuit of the state. The prosecuting attorney must have been admitted to the bar prior to his election. He serves for four years.

LYNDA R. HARA

* * *

Administrative
Agencies

ADMINISTRATIVE agencies of Indiana grew slowly through the 19th and early 20th centuries with a few exceptions. The Great Depression of 1930s created a substantial increase in the number of agencies and employees in state and local government. A second surge, with emphasis on education and social services, occurred in the 1960s. By 1975 the total number of state employees in agencies directly responsible to the governor exceeded 25,000, and the state budget reached the level of $3,000,000,000 a year.

The structure of state government retained major executive power for the governor, but grew increasingly complex. A legislative committee found that by 1975 there were 240 agencies reporting to the governor. Urban government generally also grew more complex. The limited consolidation of Indianapolis and Marion County in 1969, known as Uni-Gov, howver, provided more central control.

In 1961, a Department of Administration was created with a commissioner reporting directly to the governor and selected by him. The department has control of non-educational state public works of most types, as well as general services, data processing, purchase, property management and personnel matters for most departments. In addition, the State Budget Agency, consisting of the governor and his appointed budget director, has extensive discretionary power over the allotment of state funds. The agency's staff, working with a bipartisan committee of legislators, prepares for the governor budget proposals for each yearly legislative session.

Public Education

The education system of Indiana has evolved from early constitutional and legislative decisions which reflected the cultural values of the times. A state university was contemplated but not achieved in the first land grant for the planned capital of Indianapolis, created in 1821. The 1851 Constitution, the state's second, charged the General Assembly to provide by law "for a general and uniform system of common schools, wherein tuition shall be without charge, and equally open to all." Compliance was halting, however, and it was not until the 1880s that this obligation was interpreted as requiring high schools as well as elementary schools. Systems of 12 grades began in major cities in the 1860s.

Similar language in the original state constitution had also been ignored, and the 1850 census showed Indiana to have the highest illiteracy rate in the North. In 1852 provision was made for a state property tax in aid of public schools, to be supervised by township trustees. The same year the first state superintendent of public instruction was elected, with power over the certification of teachers and approval of textbooks.

Until the 1870s public schools were allowed to exclude blacks. Segregation of schools by race was allowed by law until 1949, when it was banned by the legislature.

Public school system. State financial support of pre-college public schools has varied from about 20 to about 40 percent of operating costs in recent decades, with local property taxes furnishing the vast bulk of the remainder. Starting in the mid-1960s, federal aid has had a growing impact on state educational programs.

The enrollment in grades 1 through 12 of the public schools reached slightly more than 1,200,000 before the decline in the birthrate of the 1970s. The largest systems were those of Indianapolis, Fort Wayne and Gary. Indianapolis reached an enrollment of 109,000 before the 1970s.

The state superintendent's office has extensive influence under the policy control powers of the State Board of Education. The board has commissions composed of its members that regulate general education, textbook selection, and teacher certification. Educators predominate in the membership, which is appointed by the governor. The superintendent is an ex officio member of all three commissions. He was elected by partisan ballot until the constitutional amendment of 1972, which provided that the legislature may establish some other method of choosing the superintendent. The term now is for two years.

Since the 1960s, teachers have been required to commence work on and receive masters' degrees within stated periods or lose their licenses. Incentives for hiring teachers with advanced degrees or other graduate training were written into the formula for state financial support to local scool systems. Minimum salaries are mandated by state law. Standards for school curriculum, transportation, safety and inspection, and building plans are provided by law or by board rules.

Legislation intended to force the consolidation of small, declining or underfunded school systems took effect in the 1950s, introducing more than a decade of controversy.

The number of systems was cut from 970 in 1957 to 497 in 1964. The consolidation made it possible to offer broader curriculums to students in less populous areas, thereby improving the equality of opportunity. There remained, however, substantial problems of disparity in the spending power among school systems. The legislature for several years had given some weight to the property tax resources of each system in its school aid formula, and in 1975 moved further toward the concept of equalizing the support available to each student, according to indicated needs.

Indiana Vocational and Technical College. The 1970 census showed for the first time an average educational attainment for the state population aged 19 or older of more than 12 grades. A significant element in the educational advance, apart from increased college and graduate-level study, was the creation in the 1960s of Indiana Vocational and Technical College. A state-wide system of regional programs that are flexible and career oriented, the college features low tuition. Federal manpower training and other programs furnish financial aid to the students. Two-year associate degrees are offered in some programs, but the system is not a junior college in the accepted understanding of the term.

The college is operated by a board of trustees appointed by the governor, and is not answerable to the state superintendent or the Board of Education.

State Universities

Indiana has five state institutions of higher education. They are operated by boards of trustees and are dependent upon the legislature for most of their operating and capital funds not obtained from student fees.

Although the universities have retained a substantial amount of autonomy, the legislature in 1969 established a State Commission for Higher Education. The commission has authority over budget submissions to the legislature and the right of acceptance or rejection of any new graduate degree programs proposed by the institutions.

The 1816 Constitution instructed the legislature to provide for "a state university, wherein tuition shall be gratis and equally open to all," but that language was left out of the 1851 document. There was, in fact, great controversy about whether the state should dedicate any assets to higher education, when there was no substantial system of free public common schools. The Indiana House of Representatives in 1852 adopted a resolution stating that income from Indiana University property be given to the common school fund.

Indiana University. The struggling state university began as a county seminary chartered by the legislature in 1820 and renamed Indiana College in 1827, and Indiana University in 1838. The first academic degrees were conferred in 1841, and there were only seven graduates in the class of 1852. The legislature did not provide operating funds for the university until 1867, and the law and medical departments were disbanded before 1880. It was not until the university presidency of David Starr Jordan in 1885 that the university began to specialize and to offer the wide curriculum appropriate to a major university.

By 1974 Indiana University had more than 70,000 students, enrolled on its nine campuses. Its School of Music was among several of the departments to achieve particular prominence on a world scale. Indiana University was the home of the Institute for Sex Research that supported the pioneer work on human sexuality of Dr. Alfred Kinsey and others.

Indiana State University. The State Normal School at Terre Haute, which was to become Indiana State University, opened in 1870 after the 1865 legislature authorized a school to be established in a city which offered the largest donation of $50,000 or more.

The school broadened its curriculum greatly in the 1950s and 1960s, reached an enrollment of 13,000, and became the dominant institution and physical feature of the community by the 1970s. A regional campus at Evansville enrolled more than 2,500. Indiana State University offers schools of education, graduate studies, arts and sciences, nursing, business, physical education, and technology.

Purdue University. Under the terms of the national Morrill land grant act, the legislature in 1869 enacted a bill for the establishment of a state agricultural and mechanical arts college. Purdue University opened in 1874 in Tippecanoe County. It faced the same grave financial difficulty that Indiana University had encountered of small appropriations from the legislature during the early years. Abram C. . Shortridge, who had been an Indianapolis school superintendent, was the second president of the university and the first to conduct actual operations of the school.

The university attained great prestige with its engineering, agriculture, and indistrial management programs, among others. By 1974 it had 28,000 full-time students.

Ball State University. Ball State University at Muncie is a descendant of Eastern Indiana Normal University, which was founded in 1898 and given state support in 1918. The Ball brothers, priminent in industry, donated the campus to the state. Until 1929 the school was a division of Indiana State Normal School (now Indiana State University). University status was granted by the legislature in 1965.

The university offers undergraduate programs in 80 fields and graduate programs in 11. Enrollment is more than 15,000 full-time students.

Vincenes University. Vincennes University at Vincennes is the oldest of the state institutions of higher learning. It was founded in 1801, but lacked clear standing as part of the public system supported by regular operating appropriations from the legislature until the 1960s. The first Indiana territorial General Assembly incorporated the school in 1806, but it furnished only local public school instruction until 1873. Knox County has provided tax funds to the university since 1931, and the state later adopted a policy of providing double the county funds.

Health and Welfare

The oldest and most central element of state agency action in the field of health and welfare is the State Board of Health, dating from 1881. The Department of Public Welfare was created in 1936 and the Department of Mental Health consolidated programs of previously independent benevolent institutions, such as the mental hospitals, in the late 1950s.

State Board of Health. Responsibilities of the State Board of Health include collecting and storing vital records, regulating air, food, water, drugs, and public buildings for cleanliness and safety (often through staff assistance to appointed boards); and detecting, reporting, preventing, and controlling communicable diseases. The Board also provides laboratory services, conducts maternal and child care programs, gives service to relieve chronic diseases and those of the aging; licenses hospitals and assures the improvement of hospitals and other health care facilities; and provides public health education. Local boards of health are established in each county and in some cities, with the State Board providing technical assistance.

In the 1970s, the State Board employed 900 persons, about half of whom were professionally trained. The board is responsible for residential schools for the blind, the deaf, and the orphans of military personnel from Indiana. The board also supervises matters of weights and measures.

Public Welfare. The Department of Public Welfare administers the law in regard to aid to families with dependent children and food stamps. It has also expanded a program of comprehensive services while withdrawing in favor of the federal administration from its former duties involving assistance to the aged, blind, and disabled. The state department has administrative responsibilities in the Medicare and Medicaid programs, and has a child welfare services division.

Mental Health. The Department of Mental Health was created as an independent agency in 1961. It supervises treatment, centered on professional psychiatric care, at 11 state mental health institutions, and plans and helps develop units in a growing system of community mental health and retardation centers. It also examines and treats criminal sexual offenders and psychotic prisoners. The department has research, public education, and alcohol and drug abuse programs.

Indiana's spending for mental health increased dramatically after 1955. By the mid-1970s the system had reached the landmark point at which the number of employees equalled the number of patients in mental hospitals. Both staff expansion and increased emphasis on care outside the institutions were reflected in the trend. Since the 1950s extensive capital additions and renovations have been made at mental hospitals in Indianapolis, Evansville, Logansport, Madison, New Castle, and Richmond, and new hospitals were built at Westville and Indianapolis. The department started a system of grants-in-aid for local community programs furnishing services to the mentally ill and the retarded.

Other agencies. Other state agencies are also concerned with health and welfare. The Administrative Building Council approves plans for all public or multi-unit residential buildings; while the Division of Labor enforces occupational safety, wage and hour, and other labor restrictions. There are also the Commission on Aging and the Aged; the Arts Commission; the Athletic Commission; the State Scholarship Commission, Licensing agencies regulate physicians, health care facilities, barbers, and beauticians.

Hospitals. Until the mid-19th century, hospitals were viewed by the public as breeding places for pestilence, and the institutions received no governmental support. In 1859 the Indiana legislature authorized township trustees to provide medical care for the poor. Indianapolis City Hospital was authorized in 1856 as a military hospital; it opened as a general hospital for charity cases in 1866. The 612-bed institution operated in the mid-1970s as the Marion County General Hospital. There are public hospitals in most of the state's major cities, and county general hospitals are common in the rural areas.

Housing

State government in Indiana never has taken a direct role in the provision of housing for the general public. Efforts in the legislature in the 1960s and early 1970s to provide a state housing authority were rebuffed. In fact, from the 1940s until 1965, local government was forbidden by law to participate in federally-assisted public housing programs. Principal elements behind this attitude were probably a conservative bent among lawmakers and an "open space" psychology in a state where high density housing was almost unknown and where home ownership was the norm. Distruct of the federal government was also involved.

Public housing had been built directly by federal agencies at Indianapolis and Gary during the 1930s and 1940s. The capital city had a housing authority which took over responsibility for the major project there—Lockefield Gardens. Since the late 1940s a redevelopment commission has cleared the slums and blighted areas of Indianapolis and opened them for new private development including housing. An active city public housing program began in the late 1960s and had more than 2,800 units by 1975.

Protective Agencies

The Department of Correction, Bureau of Motor Vehicles, and state police are the three prominent agencies among those of the state which have protective roles.

Department of Correction. The correction department took its present form in the 1960s, with a single executive and a board appointed by the governor. The centralized organization involves adult and juvenile divisions. Institutions under its control include the State Prison at Michigan City, the State Reformatory at Pendleton, State Farm at Putnamville, Women's Prison at Indianapolis, the Youth Center and the Boys' School at Plainfield, and the Girls' School at Clermont. There also is a Youth Rehabilitation Facility consisting of a group of camps. Divisions of Probation and Adult Parole provide counseling, practical assistance, surveillance, and control of persons convicted of felonies and paroled, or to those placed on probation. The department in 1975 had about 4,800 prisoners.

A work-release program was initiated in 1967. It allows prisoners thought to have good rehabilitation potential to leave the institutions or pre-release centers to work at jobs in cities during designated hours. Prison factories and vocational-training programs produce vehicle license plates, furniture, bricks, metal products, brooms, foundry products, shelter houses, highway signs, repaired equipment, and other goods and services.

Some of the correction institutions have four-year high schools on their premises, and provide for college study by mail. While spending for the correctional system has increased markedly, the subject remained a matter of critical concern for state officials. Higher crime rates and convictions reversed the trend of reduced prison populations of the late 1960s and early 1970s. Tense conditions produced by overcrowding, aged facilities, and a growth of political militancy among prisoners were met with a heightened public concern that the criminal justice system had failed to protect society. A 1974 federal court decision required the state administration to make further concessions to prisoners' rights after a riot in the State Prison. Gov. Otis R. Bowen installed two ombudsmen in the department to whom prisoners could directly report their grievances.

Misdemeanants under Indiana law may serve terms of one year or less at the State Farm or in county jails. The jails vary widely in quality and size, some of the smaller ones being nearly empty most of the year. Litigation also has improved conditions for prisoners in local jails, notably at the Marion County Jail in Indianapolis.

Bureau of Motor Vehicles. With more than 450 employees the Bureau of Motor Vehicles is responsible for the licensing of drivers and maintenance of a discipline system of "points" that produces suspension of licenses for repeated offenses. The Bureau also registers and titles vehicles, administers a vehicle excise tax, provides information on stolen vehicles to the police; and disposes of abandoned cars. The commissioner of motor vehicles is charged with the licensing of commercial driver-training schools and of driving instructors.

In a particularly piquant example of the Indiana view of the prerogatives of major political parties, the local branches for issuance of driver's licenses, license plates, and titles are fiefdoms of the political party to which the governor in office adheres. The motor vehicles commissioner appoints the manager (with informal but real approval from political party heads), and the manager retains each year the "branch fees" attached to the issuance of documents. The sum may amount to $100,000 a year in some cases, although office expenses must be paid from the money. The system works to extort a political contribution from each driver or vehicle owner, regardless of his attitude toward the party doing the collecting.

State police. Indiana was the 12th state to organize a state police department, having done so in 1921. The first department was composed of 16 deputies, under the secretary of state, whose only power was to enforce the Motor Vehicle Certificate of Title Act. In 1925 the department was given the power to enforce some traffic laws, but full police authority was not granted until 1933. The department was set up on a bipartisan basis in 1935, and a state-wide police radio system was inaugurated the same year.

In 1975 the department with more than 1,500 employees, was under the jurisdiction of the governor, a six-member police board, and a superintendent. The board members were appointed by the governor to four-year terms. The superintendent was also appointed by the governor, and served at the governor's pleasure.

The department is composed of eight divisions, including the Bureau of Criminal Identification and Investigation and departments of motor carrier inspection, public relations, records and communications, traffic, and training and personnel. The state is divided into 11 districts and the department maintains 13 posts. Each post serves from five to nine counties, and patrols toll roads and interstate highways. Between 20 and 50 men, including commanding officers and detectives, are assigned to each post. Troopers are selected on a competitive basis following the successful compoletion of an eight-week training course held at Indiana University.

The trooper has two major duties—enforcing laws and rendering services. He also patrols roads, arrests persons, and conducts investigations. Some of the services performed include the dissemination of information, administration of first aid, delivery of emergency messages, and return of recovered lost or stolen property. The department licenses private detectives and handguns.

Armed forces. The Indiana National Guard is composed of the Army National Guard and the Air National Guard. The governor serves as commander-in-chief of the National Guard. The adjutant general, who is appointed by the governor and serves at his pleasure, administers the National Guard program.

The National Guard is subject to call by the U.S. president and by the governor in time of disaster (natural or man-made). Members are paid by the federal government unless they are called up by the governor. They always use federal equipment.

In 1975 Indiana's Army National Guard was the second largest in the nation, with an actual strength of 11,700. Authorized strength was 10,450. The 38th Infantry Division, a tri-state division, was the major component of the army guard. Personnel were located throughout the state in approximately 70 communities in 68 National Guard armories.

The Air National Guard had an actual strength of 1,900 in 1975 and an authorized strength of 1,985. It is based at Baer Field in Ft. Wayne and Hulman Field in Terre Haute. Both branches utilize Camp Atterbury, an outdoor training site near Edinburgh.

The state guard reserve is composed of about 500 volunteers whose purpose is to man the armories if the National Guard is called up to federal duty. The volunteers provide their own uniforms.

The U.S. Department of Defense lists a number of Army, Navy, and Air Force installations in Indiana including two Air Force bases—Bakalar at Columbus and Bunker Hill at Bunker Hill. There are also several manufacturing and storage facilities in the state. A finance center, Fort Benjamin Harrison, is reportedly the largest administrative unit outside the Pentagon.

Civil defense. Indiana maintains a small civil defense organization under an executive director appointed by the governor. It maintains a state plan for relief and recovery in wartime or during natural or other disasters. It furnishes assistance and guidance to local community disaster-relief programs in co-ordination with the federal government and other states.

Financial agencies. The Department of Financial Institutions supervises, examines, and licenses the banks, trust companies, savings and loan institutions, credit unions and other financial organizations formed under Indiana state laws. It is responsible for protecting the intcrests of depositors, borrowers, shareholders, and consumers. A six-member bipartisan board and the director are appointed by the governor.

The Department of Insurance operates under a commissioner named by the governor. It supervises all insurance companies and sales, and licenses bail bondsmen and "runners" under a special law.

Safety. The Department of Traffic Safety and Vehicle Inspection was formed in 1969 by the union of three agencies. It administers an annual vehicle inspection program and a general program of traffic safety. The department assists local communities in seeking funds under the national traffic safety program.

The Aeronautics Commission of Indiana certifies sites and designs for public and private airports in the state. It provides engineering advice and assistance in the obtainment of federal aid for airport development.

Alcoholic beverages. The Alcoholic Beverage Commission is a four-member bipartisan group appointed by the governor. Its staff enforces state law and regulations on the consumption and sale at all levels of alcoholic beverages. State excise police with 11 branch offices report violations, and a prosecutor and judge recommend disposition to the commission. The commission for more than a decade was involved in a mandatory minimum percentage price mark-up scheme on whiskey and wine. The practice was found by a federal judge in 1974 to be horizontal price fixing, in and therefore violation of federal law.

Civil rights. The Indiana Civil Rights Commission, established in 1961, enforces state law against discrimination in employment and public accommodations on the basis of race, religion, national origin, or sex. It uses an approach of negotiation, but may seek injunctive relief from the courts in cases of continuing violations. The commission delegates some investigative power to local government anti-discrimination agencies. It has had substantial impact on housing desegretation.

Public Service Commission. The Public Service Commission is charged with the deermination of routes, schedules, rates, debts, and the like for public utilities including intrastate railroad and bus lines; water, gas, and electric services; urban bus and rail services; and contract and common carrier motor truck services. The Commission is composed of three members, no more than two of whom may belong to the same political party. The members are appointed by the governor. A public counselor's office, independent of the commission, can assure an adversary proceeding in matters of commanding importance.

Other state agencies. Other agencies with protective functions in state government include the Architects Registration Board, Boiler and Pressure Vessel Inspection Board, Criminal Justice Planning Agency, State Election Board, Law Enforcement

Training Board, and Public Defender. The State Board of Tax Commissioners controls the local use of property taxes. There is also a Television and Radio Service Examiners Board.

Local agencies. Local protection is furnished by county sheriffs' road patrols, city police, and town marshals. Size of such uniformed forces varies, the largest being the more than 1,000-member Indianapolis Police Department. Other notable protective agencies include the local fire departments, with volunteer departments predominating in rural areas and small towns. There also are city building codes and inspection systems, weights and measures divisions, and city departments of transportation or public works.

The state adopted basic principles of zoning in the 1920s, and by the 1950s the major cities had metropolitan planning agencies. The agencies of Indianapolis-Marion County and other major metropolitan areas controlled land use county-wide or beyond urban limits. While some insulation against political pressures was built into the systems, basic control over comprehensive plans, re-zonings, and variances of use was kept in the hands of elected officials.

A fiscal crisis faced many of the urban areas in the mid-1970s because of a combination of increasing liabilities for rising and fire pensions and state limitations upon property tax levies and rates which furnished the funds. Further, while bargaining rights had been extended to organizations of public employees generally, none were extended in the case of policemen and firemen. Their militancy was rising, and informal, non-binding negotiations did in fact become the rule in the larger cities.

PAUL DOHERTY

Indianapolis

CREATED out of swamp and forest on the banks of the White River in 1821, Indianapolis has become a major regional trade and manufacturing center. Centrally located within the state, it became the 12th largest city in the United States when it boldly adopted a metropolitan form of government in 1970.

Indianapolis is a city of contrasts. It has given the United States one president and three vice-presidents; bank robber John Dillinger; the conservative John Birch Society and liberal author Kurt Vonnegut, Jr.; the Indianapolis Symphony Orchestra and basketball star Oscar "Big O" Robertson. It boasts of a magnificent Museum of Art, but its downtown streets are deserted during the nights and weekends because of a lack of nightlife. The city contains a Carmelite monastery and the Indiana Women's Prison. Once headquarters for most of the major labor unions, it also was once controlled by the Ku Klux Klan. A city of fierce political fighting, Indianapolis is flat and landlocked, wealthy, somewhat bland and provincial, and considered a nice place to raise a family. The city spent the first decades of the 20th century tending to itself, opening its gates once a year to welcome visitors to the greatest spectacle in car racing, the annual Indianapolis 500.

About 1960, a decision was made to change the city's image and bring it forth from its shell. By the 1970s the dramatically changed skyline of the downtown area was rimmed with an interstate belt that attracted shopping centers and motels and hurried the exodus of its residents to the suburbs. Professional sports were introduced, conventions attracted, magnificent structures for cultivating the arts and culture constructed, and the long-standing policy of disdaining dollars from the federal government reversed.

HISTORY

The city's location on both banks of the West Fork of the White River was chosen as the site for the state's capital because of its central position—despite the fact that in the early 19th century the land was covered with forest and supported only about a dozen settlers who traded with the Indians. The seat of government was moved to Indianapolis in 1824 from Corydon, a few miles north of the Ohio River. When the legislature met in Indianapolis for the first time the following year, there were 600 settlers. As cities go, Indianapolis is a youngster—but an active one. The swamps and diseases that rose from them to plague the early settlers were conquered; the forests were leveled and farms were created. Indianapolis got its name by simply adding the Greek word for city (polis) to the name of the state. In 1836 Indianapolis was incorporated as a town and in 1847 became a city.

The city plan. Alexander Ralston, a gentle Scot who had helped an imaginative Frenchman, Pierre Charles L'Enfant, to plan Washington, D.C., was commissioned to lay out Indianapolis. He employed a simplified Washington plan, creating a circle with four diagonal streets emanating from it, and then using a grid system of nine north-south and nine east-west streets. He had the foresight to make the streets wide boulevards; Washington Street, the main east-west street, was made 30 feet wider than the others in anticipation of the National Road reaching the city.

At the center of the city circle was a little knoll which Ralston circled with an 80-foot wide street. This hill is still the center of the city, from which the downtown area fans out in four directions. The original plans called for a governor's mansion to occupy the knoll, but the chief executives' wives objected to the lack of privacy. For awhile it was a park, and then was fenced off for grazing cows. It wasn't until 1901, when the Soldiers and Sailors Monument was completed, that the heart of Indianapolis received its permanent character. The monument, an ornate structure with fountains and statuary including a statue of Miss Liberty atop a 284-foot shaft, is the focal point of the city. Intermittently criticized by visiting journalists for its ostentation,

Monument Circle nonetheless is revered by its citizens. It is the site of parades and rallies, streakers and evangelists. During the Christmas season the monument is adorned with colored lights and turned into the world's largest Christmas tree.

Economic growth. The founding legislators envisioned the White River as the source of the city's growth as a trade center, but the river has never been navigable. It was the railroad that most influenced the growth of the city into a major trade and manufacturing center. Water power was introduced in 1839 when the canal—part of a statewide network of canals that never was completed—was built. Woolen, grist, and paper mills then sprang up. By 1860 more than 100 manufacturing firms were located in Indianapolis, most of them owned by a group of wealthy, close-knit families—a situation that continued until after World War II when many of the industries were merged with the nation's major corporations. A ready access to coal and the proximity of farmers accelerated the city's growth.

THE CONTEMPORARY CITY

Environment. Indianapolis enjoys moderate temperatures, with a winter average of 31° F and a summer average of 73° F. The mean annual precipitation is 39 inches.

Residents who do not drive automobiles—and there are not many—rely on the Metro Bus System for travel. The city purchased it from private investors in 1974 after they threatened to abandon the operation because of financial difficulties. Efforts were then made to upgrade the system and attract riders, but it likely will take a gasoline shortage to make it effective.

Demography. The city's population was roughly 850,000 in the mid-1970s. The 1970 census showed that 82.7 percent of population was white, 17 percent was black, and the small remainder was of other races. Of those professing religious affiliation, more than 70 percent were Protestant, 20 percent were Roman Catholic, and the rest were adherents to Judaism and other religions or sects.

Ethnic groups. The old ethnic neighborhoods, which retained their identity through the Great Depression and World War II, began breaking up when postwar affluence gave the children and grandchildren of immigrants an opportunity to move into homes far removed from those of their parents. Early Italians settled on the Southside near the produce markets, where they sold fresh fruits and vegetables to the city's grocers. Many of the Italians still maintain stalls in the City Market, an ancient structure located across Market Street from the City-County Building, the towering glass structure that houses local government offices. The Market, with its colorful and aromatic displays of shiny fruit, bread and meats, cheese and fish, fresh flowers and spices, long ago would have been torn down had it not been for a covenant that mandated the city to maintain it. One of the city's treasures, it was undergoing major renovation in the mid-1970s, sponsored by Lilly Endowment Inc.

German influence was especially strong in Indianapolis, bringing industriousness to the city and a penchant for culture, athletic fitness, and making money. Anti-German feelings ran so high during World War I, however, that teaching German in the schools was abandoned, Das Deutsche Haus was renamed the Athenaeum, the Turnverein became the Indianapolis Athletic Club, and the Maennerchor was renamed the Academy of Music. In the mid-1970s there were nearly 20 German groups in Indianapolis; 11 members of the Federation of German Societies operated German Park and the Indianapolis Saenger-Chor gave annual spring and fall concerts.

The Irish came to the city in great numbers. They were assimilated, as were many of the Eastern European immigrants who settled on the industrial Westside. Estonians, Latvians, and Syrians, however, diligently try to hold on to their customs. There is a Hispano-American Center and the Brittania Club is active. The International Center coordinates international cultural services in the city.

The Northside. The Northside always has been home to the wealthy. Indeed, North Meridian Street, north of 38th Street, long has been considered one of the finest residential streets in America. An avenue of large brick mansions set well back from the street, it give testimony to the wealth that produced them half a century ago. Residents have managed to maintain the beauty of the street and were instrumental in inducing the state to relocate the Governor's Mansion four blocks north of its location in the 4300 block of North Meridian Street.

A nice view of what Indianapolis looked like when Booth Tarkington was describing "the Establishment" at the turn of the 20th century may be found along a half-mile stretch of North

Delaware Street, one mile north of the downtown district. The three-story home of Benjamin Harrison, who served as president of the United States from 1889 to 1893, is preserved as a National Historic Landmark. The propylaeum, an ornate Victorian mansion, is nearby and has been the home of one of the oldest women's cultural clubs in the city since 1923. Meredith Nicholson's Georgian home is a few houses south of 16th Street. Still a private residence, it was lighted during the holidays as "The House of a Thousand Candles" in honor of his popular novel of that name. "The Little Wedding Cake House," built as a wedding present in 1873, was rescued and restored by Eli Lilly and given to the Indianapolis Episcopal Diocese. The small, white house with a rich array of gingerbread was renamed Kemper House for the first Episcopal bishop in Indiana.

Lockerbie Square. In the 1970s Indianapolis was making an effort to renovate a nearby area called Lockerbie Square. Its principal attraction is the home of the famed Hoosier poet James Whitcomb Riley, the dapper bon vivant whose poetry was so loved that 35,000 mourners passed by his bier when he died in 1916. The Victorian home is a National Historic Landmark.

Urban transition. Noted as a city of homeowners, Indianapolis has not developed any particular architectural style, but thousands of one-story ranch homes—many fronted with Indiana limestone—were erected following world War II. The city's growth all but destroyed the ornate residences that once fanned north from Monument Circle. The Northsiders were able to move farther north to avoid encroaching slums. The old neighborhoods of middle-class housing were rapidly occupied by poor blacks who, in turn, continued to move north in an ever-widening fan. Left behind was a familiar American phenomon of a growing wasteland of abandoned and boarded-up frame houses standing among hundreds of vacant lots.

Indianapolis' growth has not been impeded by suburban communities. As the city moved outward, it absorbed small communities such as Irvington, once the home of Butler University and an intellectual center, and Woodruff Place, an attractive walled community about one mile east of the downtown area. The creation of James O. Woodruff, a native of New York, Woodruff Place is more than 100 years old. It features gracious two- and three-story homes overlooking grassy esplanades adorned with statuary. It was the setting for Booth Tarkington's

The Maganificent Ambersons. Because it is on the National Register of Historic Landmarks, homeowners in Woodruff Place are allowed to receive federal financial assistance in restoring their properties.

Architecture. Indianapolis has a few architectural treasures. The Central Library is considered one of the finest examples of Doric architecture in the world. An unusual Tudor Gothic structure is the Scottish Rite Cathedral. Christ Church Cathedral, the city's oldest, is a gray stone gem on Monument Circle whose neat little lawn is the site of a Strawberry Festival each June. St. John's Catholic Church, once the Cathedral for the Indianapolis Roman Catholic Archdiocese, has been restored to serve the visiting conventioners at the new Indiana Convention-Exposition Center across Capitol Avenue.

Indianapolis treasures its few open spaces downtown, principally University Square, which is part of a five-block showcase area. At one end is the beautiful Federal Courts Building, at the other the Central Library. Also in the stretch is the World War Memorial, a massive monument to the victims of World War I; both the state and international Headquarters of the American Legion; and a paved block with an obelisk set in a fountain, which is part of the War Memorial. The Scottish Rite Cathedral faces the paved square on one side, and the new Federal Building is situated on the opposite side.

Renovation of the downtown area. Government has led the way in the rebirth of the downtown area. There is the City-County Building, a new Marion County Jail, the Education Center, the Post Office, the State Office Building, a convention center, and Market Square Arena, a 17,500-seat sports arena. Plans for additional government structures were being made in the mid-1970s.

The business community has also invested in the rebuilding of the downtown district. A glittering array of glass structures of clear, blue, and gold hues, the most spectacular being the Indiana National Bank tower of 37 stories, have been erected. American Fletcher National Bank, which vies with the Indiana National Bank as the state's largest, has planned a new headquarters on the convention center mall. Next to the mall, Merchants National Bank was erecting in the 1970s a complex that included a 535-room Regency Hyatt Hotel. The 87-year-old Union Station, considered the finest example of Romansque

Revival architecture in the United States, is to be converted into a collection of shops, pubs, and restaurants in a Victorian setting.

There is hardly a block in the downtown area that has not undergone some major change since the 1950s. The city, however, continues to struggle with its image as a somewhat staid town. A state law banning the sale of alcohol on Sundays was amended to allow establishments earning $100,000 a year in food sales to sell liquor on Sundays. The city hopes that the change, along with the sports arena, convention center, and new hotels will turn its image around and put some pedestrian traffic on the streets after office hours.

ECONOMY

Indianapolis is economically healthy. In a 1974 study by the Council of Municipal Performance, Indianapolis and Houston were rated the first among cities in the United States with the healthiest economies. Among cities of 500,000 or more population, the city in 1973 boasted of the second highest median per capita family income of $9,313, seven percent above the national average. The economic boom has been dramatic; personal income in the Indianapolis metropolitan area (Indianapolis and seven contiguous counties) in 1973 totaled $5,400,000,-000 — double that of 1963 — according to the U.S. Department of Commerce. In 1950, 8.3 percent of all employees were in the service industries, and by 1973, the percentage had jumped to 14.1 percent. Government workers comprised 9.7 percent of the work force in 1950; they were 16.3 percent in 1973. In the same period manufacturing dropped from 33.5 percent of the work force to 28.4 percent.

Manufacturers. Indianapolis primarily is a trade and manufacturing center. More than 1,100 firms in the eight-county metropolitan area manufacture more than 1,200 products. The main ones are pharmaceuticals, transportation equipment, communication and electronic equipment, and rubber and paper products.

The largest and most prestigious manufacturing firm in Indianapolis is Eli Lilly & Co., whose 25,000 employees (7,500 of whom work in Indianapolis) produce a major amount of the world's pharmaceuticals. In the 1970s the firm was undergoing a $150,000,000 expansion program. Lilly Endowment, established by the Lilly family, has assets of $1,003,500,000, making it the second largest foundation in the nation. The endowment has been a major source of many of the cultural, educational, and health improvements in the city.

Indianapolis produces automobile parts and truck engines and bodies in huge amounts. At one time it was the major producer of automobiles in the United States, turning out as many as 65 different cars. Indianapolis' reign in the auto industry ended in 1937, however, largely because local industries refused to pay the wages demanded. It still is proud of the quality cars once produced, including the Stutz, Duesenberg, and Marmon.

Trade and transport. The city is a major trade center of corn and grain. At one time Indianapolis liked to call itself the "Crossroads of the World," a title it still can defend. Seven interstate highways, more than any other city, funnel into Indianapolis. Another nine federal highways bring traffic to the city. In addition to an interstate belt (I-465) that rings the fringe of the city, Indianapolis was completing an inner loop circling the downtown area in the 1970s.

Indianapolis is a leading truck, rail, and airline center. Weir Cook Municipal Airport, which handles about 110 scheduled airline flights a day, is located on the western edge of the city. It has undergone steady expansion since the 1950s.

Research. More than 7,500 scientists and engineers are engaged in research both in industry and at universities. In recent years Indianapolis has been able to lure scientists with three new organizations. They are the Indianapolis Center for Advanced Research at Indiana University-Purdue University at Indianapolis, the Holcomb Research Institute at Butler University that deals with the biological sciences, and the Regenstrief Institute for Health Care that is operated by the Indiana University School of Medicine.

Financial services. Indianapolis is a large insurance center. One of the most unusual insurance headquarters is located in three 11-story glass buildings shaped like modern pyramids in College Park, a development unveiled by College Park Life Insurance Company in 1972. The city has six banking institutions, two of which have more than $1,000,000,000 on deposit each. The six banks operate 115 branches. There are also ten savings and loan associations that operate 30 branch offices.

Labor unions. Socialist leader Eugene V. Debs spent a great deal of time in Indianapolis in his efforts to lead the first industry-wide union, the American Railway Union, in its battle with railroad management in the 1890s. The Socialist Party of America on March 6, 1900, nominated Debs as its presidential candidate in Indianapolis — site of the party's first convention.

Most of the country's labor unions are now located in Washington, D.C., to be near the seat of power. Many of them moved there from Indianapolis, including the Carpenters, Teamsters, Laundry Workers, Stonecutters, Bookbinders, and Bricklayers unions. John L. Lewis established the United Mine Workers Union in Indianapolis, and the city was home at one time for Samuel Gompers and William Green, both of whom became presidents of the American Federation of Labor. Big Bill Hutchenson of the Carpenters Union and Dan Tobin of the Teamsters also lived in Indianapolis.

GOVERNMENT AND POLITICS

Uni-Gov. In 1970 Indianapolis adopted a modified form of metropolitan government popularly known as Uni-Gov. Under the System, the administration has jurisdiction throughout all of Marion County, except for four small communities. They are Beech Grove (population 14,651), which was established in the early 20th century when the New York Central repair shops opened there) Speedway (14,253), which developed after the Indianapolis Motor Speedway was built in 1909; Lawrence (20,260), located near Fort Benjamin Harrison, which employs 9,000 soldiers and civilians at the U.S. Army's Finance Center and other military offices; and Southport (2,505), a small community on the Southside. Each of the four towns has its own government, but their residents may vote for the mayor of Indianapolis.

Uni-Gov does not completely integrate city and county functions — schools and fire and police departments adhere to pre-Uni-Gov boundaries. It does, however, reorganize and consolidate 40 former city and county governmental units into the six major departments of public works, metropolitan development, parks and recreation, transportation, public safety, and administration. The system operates under a mayor and a 29-member city-county council.

Uni-Gov enlarged the city from an area of 82 square miles with 520,000 residents to 388 square miles and 792,229 residents. Overnight, Indianapolis became the 12th largest city in the

United States, even though much of its territory is used to cultivate corn and other farm products.

The new system has eliminated a lot of overlapping government operations and has enabled the city to obtain a record number of federal grants. Many blacks and poor—and to some extent Democrats—saw the reorganization as an attempt by the Republicans to control the city, but there have been no serious efforts to repeal the law which created it.

Political life. Much like the rest of the state, Indianapolis is fiercely political and has a rich political heritage. Three U.S. vice-presidents—Thomas A. Hendricks, Thomas R. Marshall, and Charles W. Fairbanks—lived in the city. Indianapolis gave birth to the ultraconservative, anti-Communist John Birch Society on Dec. 9, 1958, when 11 men from as many states drew up the society's first charter. Robert H. Welch, a former candy manufacturer from Boston, was elected president. There was no fanfare connected with the group's formation.

It was a far different beginning than that of another right-wing organization which flourished in the city 30 years earlier. The Ku Klux Klan in the 1920s staged parades and conducted rallies to attract new members. The Klan's target was not Communists, but blacks, Jews, and Roman Catholics. Its self-proclaimed leader was D.C. Stephenson, who declared, "I am the law in Indiana." His home in Irvington was a showcase and he loved to live extravagantly. A super-salesman of hate. Stephenson and the Klan dominated the Indianapolis city hall, school board, and police department. The Klan's power waned after Stephenson was convicted of murdering a 28-year-old woman in 1925, but its influence lingered until the 1930s.

Generally, the party in power—Democrat or Republican—has tended to maintain a conservative profile, reflecting the views of the majority of Indianapolis residents. The mayor with the greatest success in obtaining federal grants for the city has been a Republican, Richard G. Lugar. A Rhodes scholar and young businessman, Lugar employed a brilliant mind and articulate tongue to become mayor in 1968 at the age of 35. During his two terms he was elected president of the National League of Cities, capitalizing on the slogan, "President Nixon's favorite mayor," until the Watergate scandal of the early 1970s. By the time Lugar attempted to gain a U.S. Senate seat in 1974, the slogan was no longer an asset and a scandal in the Indianapolis Police

Department had been exposed by the *Indianapolis Star*. As a result, Democrat Birch Bayh, Jr., was returned to the Senate for a third term.

PUBLIC SERVICES

Police and fire services. The police department—controlled by the Ku Klux Klan in the 1920s—has been periodically tainted with scandal, most recently in 1974. As a result, the entire high command of the 1,100-member department was replaced. Under Uni-Gov, the department's jurisdiction remained limited to the old city limits. The 400-member Marion County Police Department, under an elected sheriff, oversees the rest of the county.

The Indianapolis Fire Department of more than 800 men always has maintained a high standard of operation. Its jurisdiction, too, is limited to the old city boundaries. Volunteer fire departments protect residents in the eight townships outside the old boundaries. Beech Grove and Speedway also maintain their own departments.

Utilities. Indianapolis is served by four utilities. The Indianapolis Water Company is one of the largest investor-owned water utilities in the United States. Its primary sources of water are the White River and Fall Creek, each supplemented by 7,000,000-gallon reservoirs. Additional supplies from the Eagle Creek Reservoir were planned in the 1970s. The city has not had to restrict water usage, although water usage rose to 34,800,000,-000 gallons in 1972—up 29 percent in one decade. The water utility also owns the canal that winds through part of the city.

Citizens Gas & Coke Utility operated by the city as a public charitable trust since 1935, serves 200,000 customers in the city. To protect them, Citizens Gas in 1974 adopted a quota system for accepting new business. Indianapolis Power & Light Company supplies virtually all of the power in the Indianapolis area. More than $561,000,000 has been invested in the company's system and $441,000,000 has been budgeted for expansion through 1977.

Indianapolis is one of the nation's leading compmunications centers because of Indiana Bell Telephone Company's long-distance center located there. Indiana Bell serves 313,765 customers in Indianapolis.

Health facilities. Health and hospital services in Indianapolis are outstanding. About 25 percent of the state's medical and hospital personnel work in the city. Indianapolis has 17 major hospitals with a total bed capacity of 7,100. Three new hospitals—St. Vincent, Indiana University, and Westview Osteopathic—opened in the 1970s and many of the others have undergone extensive expansion. Methodist Hospital, with a bed capacity of 1,150, is the sixth largest private hospital in the country. Methodist also operates two health clinics and a drug abuse center in the inner city.

Marion County Health and Hospital Corporation a government agency, operates public health services and runs the vast Marion County General Hospital, although Indiana University had plans in the 1970s to take over its operation. The Indiana University Medical Center operates four hospitals including the famed Riley Hospital for Children.

EDUCATIONAL INSTITUTIONS

Educational opportunities abound in Indianapolis. The city has two major universities—Indiana University-Purdue University at Indianapolis (IUPUI) and Butler University—and other institutions of higher learning.

Major Universities. IUPUI was formed in 1969 by combining the Indiana and Purdue regional campuses on the western edge of downtown Indianapolis, adjacent to the sprawling Indiana University Medical Center. The move dramatically altered the face of the area, clearing out some of the worst slums in the city. IUPUI had almost 18,300 students in the mid-1970s; more than 900 were enrolled in the medical school, making it the largest in the United States. IUPUI also offers schools of dentistry, nursing, law, physical education, social services, arts, engineering and technology, and liberal arts and sciences. The law school is the largest in Indiana.

Butler University in 1974 had 2,200 day and 2,100 night students. Opened in 1855, it is situated on an attractive Northside campus and boasts of a beautiful, 12-year-old library designed by famed architect Minoru Yamasaki, the new Holcomb Institute, and Holcomb Planetarium, which is equipped with a 39-inch telescope. Butler's basketball team plays a major schedule each season in Hinkle Fieldhouse—a cavernous structure that was built when Butler University was national basketball champion in 1929. It was renamed in 1965 for Paul D. "Tony" Hinkle, who coached three sports at the university for 45 years before retiring in 1969.

Other institutions of higher learning. Marian College and Indiana Central University are also located in Indianapolis. Marion College, opened in 1937 and operated by the Sisters of St. Francis, is a Roman Catholic institution with an enrollment in the 1970s of 600 day students and 250 part-time students. Indiana Central University is operated by the United Methodist Church. It opened in 1902 and had 1,200 day students and 1,500 night students, in the 1970s. In addition, Christian Theological Seminary, affiliated with the Disciples of Christ, has its national headquarters in Indianapolis. St. Maur's Theological Seminary, a Roman Catholic institution, is also located in the city. Indianapolis is the national headquarters of 14 college fraternities and sororities.

Elementary and high schools. In the 1970s the city had 102 elementary schools and 11 public high schools with an enrollment of almost 87,600. In addition, each of the townships outside the old city limits operated their own elementary and high schools. The Indianapolis Roman Catholic Archdiocese, with 43 parishes in Indianapolis, operated 34 elementary schools with an enrollment of almost 11,300 pupils, and five diocesan high schools were attended by 3,000 pupils. Five other private Roman Catholic high schools were attended by almost 2,000 children. The city has several private schools run by the Lutheran, Episcopal, Baptist, and Jewish faiths, as well as some non-denominational schools.

The Indianapolis public school system has waged a long court battle over the issue of integration. The suburban school systems joined the battle to prevent the busing of black pupils to their schools.

Libraries. An excellent library system is offered Indianapolis residents. Central Library, which opened an addition in 1975, had 21 branches throughout the city with almost 1,192,200 volumes. The material offered gets heavy use. In 1974, more than 3,580,700 books, pamphlets, and films were borrowed.

CULTURAL LIFE

Indianapolis at the turn of the 20th century was known as a literary center. At the time, the city also boasted of fine bars, hotels, elegant restaurants, theaters, and scores of private clubs.

Known as the city's golden era, it produced such authors as Booth Tarkington, two-time Pulitzer Price winner who wrote about the weatlhy; James Whitcomb Riley, who produced volumes of Hoosier homespun poetry; Meredith Nicholson; Charles Major; and Lew Wallace, author of *Ben Hur.* The city has continued to produce well-known authors including the incisive and humorous Kurt Vonnegut, Jr., Dan Wakefield, John Bartlow Martin, Tristram Coffin, Joseph Hayes, and Jeannette Covert Nolan.

Cultural Institutions. Two magnificent new structures offer a rich variety of cultural activity. Clowes Hall, with a breathtaking interior, opened on the Butler University campus in 1963. It is home for the renowned Indianapolis Symphony Orchestra and also offers opera, ballet, concerts, and productions by Butler University students. The Indianapolis Museum of Art is the city's jewel, built overlooking the White River and the canal on the lavish estate of the late J.K. Lilly of the pharmaceutical family. The museum houses many famous original works of American and European artists. It has a library, auditorium, outdoor pavilion for concerts, and a theater that serves as home for the 50-year-old Booth Tarkington Civic Theatre. Oldfields, Lilly's beautiful French chateau mansion, is maintained as a museum through which more than 600,000 visitors passed in 1974.

During the summer months, Broadway musicals are performed in Starlight Musical productions in the Butler Theatron, an unusual outdoor theater built in one end of Butler University's football stadium. More than two dozen professional and amateur drama centers are located in Indianapolis, including the innovative Christian Theological Seminary Repertory Theater and the Indiana Repertory Theater, which stages its productions in the fine old German clubhouse, the Athenaeum. Butler University's Romantic Music Festival attracts thousands of serious music lovers each spring with programs of long-forgotten classics of 19th century composers.

For those who prefer museums, Indianapolis offers the State Museum located in the 66-year-old Neo-Classic City Hall with its Doric facade, left vacant for 12 years when city offices moved to the City-County Building. The Children's Museum was nearly completed in 1975, replacing smaller quarters on the site. The museum will offer outstanding exhibits of natural science, history, art, and travel. Also available is the State Library and

Historical Building, the Museum of Indian Heritage, and the Indianapolis Zoo, one of the nation's newest, located in Washington Park. The beautifully restored Morris-Butler House is representative of upper-middle class Hoosier life in the mid-Victorian days of 1875

Just north of the city is Conner Prairie Farm, where the city's first settler, William Conner, established a farm and trading post. Through the help of Eli Lilly and Earlham College, the settlement with its original farm and trading post and nearly two dozen buildings was developed as the "Sturbridge Village of the Midwest." Persons dressed in authentic period costumes conduct guided tours.

The Indianapolis Motor Speedway. The city's claim to fame is the Indianapolis Motor Speedway, where the annual 500-Mile Race has been run since 1911. The huge plant features a 2½-mile oval, inside of which is a 9-hole golf course and a new museum for old race cars. A motel and another 18-hold golf course are located outside the track. Visitors may ride around the track by bus.

The Speedway was built by four Indianapolis industrialists principally as a place to test the performance of new cars. Its guiding genius, Carl Fisher—the same man who later built Miami Beach out of a swamp—turned the Speedway into a grand spectacle each May. The track was sold in 1927 for $700,000 to Eddie V. Rickenbacker, the famed World War I aviator, who in turn sold it in 1946 to Anton "Tony" Hulman, a Terre Haute millionaire. Hulman has since practically rebuilt the entire complex.

The drama begins in early May when the big cars arrive for practice races. On opening day of the qualification trials (held on two successive weekends), more than 250,000 fans arrive to witness the decision of the pole position. While the Speedway never announces attendance figures, crowds of more than 300,000 are on hand for the Memorial Day race, the richest in the world. When Ray Harroun won the first race in 1911, the total purse was $27,550. In 1974 the purse had grown to $1,015,686. The winner, Johnny Rutherford, took home $245,031.

Indianapolis hums inside and outside the track during May, mainly because of the activities planned by the "500" Festival organization. A wide range of activities are provided, from art contests for both children and adults to bridge and gin rummy tournaments. Other attractions include the Mayor's Breakfast, when 1,700 persons gather to officially open the month, and the Queen's coronation ball and parade just prior to the race. Upwards of 400,000 line the streets for the parade, an extravaganza that receives national television coverage.

Communications media, The city has two daily newspapers, the *Indianapolis Star* and the *Indianapolis News.* Both are owned by Eugene C. Pulliam, an independent publisher who was born on May 3, 1889, in a dugout in Grant County, Kansas, 54 miles from the nearest railroad. Pulliam has purchased 46 papers in his career, owning 23 at one time. He bought the *Star* in 1944 and the *News* in 1948. The newspapers were merged, but editorially continued to be competitive. By the 1970s, the *Star* had a daily circulation of 218,100 and a Sunday circulation of 359,300. The *News,* which publishes six days a week, had a circulation of 161,800. Editorially conservative, both newspapers are run by Pulliam's son, Eugene S. Pulliam.

Indianapolis also has 20 weekly newspapers, including the black community's *Recorder,* the Roman Catholic *Criterion,* and the *Jewish Post* and *Opinion.* The *Macedonian Tribune,* which has readers worldwide, is published in the city. Bobbs-Merrill Co. Inc., a long established book publishing firm, is located in Indianapolis, as is the Curtis Publishing Company, which produces the *Saturday Evening Post, Holiday,* and several children's and trade magazines.

Four commercial television stations, three of which are affiliated with the major networks, broadcast in Indianapolis. The one public station is financed largely by local philanthrophy. A non-profit religiously-oriented television station also operates. There are eight commercial radio stations on AM frequencies and six commercial and five educational stations on FM frequencies.

Recreational facilities. In the 1970s, the Indianapolis Parks and Recreation Department supervised more than 220 parks on 9,350 acres, 10 municipal golf courses, 109 tennis courts, 68 softball diamonds, 23 football fields, and 17 major swimming pools. The new 4,900-acre Eagle Creek Park was developed in connection with the 1,300-acre Eagle Creek Reservoir, which was opened in 1970 as a flood control and recreation project. The park is an unspoiled nature preserve which had been owned and maintained by the Lilly family since the turn of the 20th century. With 200 deer roaming on its grounds, it is the largest municipally-owned park in the United States within city limits.

The 17,500-seat Market Square Arena, which opened in downtown Indianapolis in 1974, is the home of the Indiana Pacers, three-time champions of the American Basketball Association, and the Indianapolis Racers of the World Hockey Association. Each summer Indianapolis hosts the National Clay Courts tennis tournament and the National Drag Races. The Hoosier Hundred sprint-car automobile race, sanctioned by the U.S. Auto Club, is run at the sprawling Indiana State Fairgrounds each September a few days after the State Fair. The Indianapolis Indians of the American Baseball Association, a Cincinnati Reds farm Club, play before sparse crowds at Bush Stadium, and the Indy Caps team of the Midwest Football League plays scheduled games in late summer and early fall. The headquarters of the American Athletic Union is in the city. If a resident's taste for sports is a bit more European, Indianapolis offers bocce, rugby, soccer, cricket, and polo on the grounds of Fort Benjamin Harrison.

The Indianapolis-Scarborough Peace Games provide additional evidence that the city has joined the outside world. Each summer the two cities (Scarborough is a suburb of Toronto, Ontario) field about 1,000 young athletes for an Olympic-style competition, alternating the sites every other year. The four days of competition are held after each city has engaged in a long process of elimination trials to choose the top athletes in a dozen or more sports.

LAWRENCE CONNOR

* * *

The Social Milieu

IT is ironic that such a conservative state as Indiana could be the site of both a classic experiment in communal living that failed and a lamentable example of organized bigotry that succeeded, all too well. Perhaps these two radical developments in opposite directions are the exceptions that go to prove how conservative is the average Hoosier in his politics and his life style.

The first was New Harmony (the spelling was changed from Harmonie). The latter was the Ku Klux Klan. Although they don't agree at all with the philosophy behind it, most Hoosiers are proud of the fact the state hatched the New Harmony experiment. But they would rather forget the era in which the Klan rode high, wide and ugly over the Hoosier landscape.

Harmonie was established in Posey County by the Harmonie Society, also known as the Rappites because they were led by Father George Rapp. It actually was the scene of two famous experiments in socialization, though the latter is far better known.

It had its origin in 1814 and 1815, just before Indiana's ascension to statehood of 1816. It blossomed as a balanced community of almost a thousand persons, a major population center in the young Indiana Territory.

All of its inhabitants were middle-class Germans from a single old-world city, Wurttemberg. They had been grouped into a compact band there by Father Rapp, who preached a type of religion based on primitive Christian brotherhood and common ownership of property, which was not approved by the established Protestant church of Germany.

The civil authorities in Germany weren't very happy with him

171

so Father Rapp brought his followers to America in 1804 to enjoy the same freedom of worship which the Pilgrims had sought earlier. They first established a settlement in Butler County, Pennsylvania, which also was known as Harmonie. It was some 25 miles from Pittsburgh, near the Ohio River. The community grew for 10 years, at which time they decided to find a better location farther west, in a warmer climate and with a navigable stream. In February, 1814, Father Rapp took two of his associates and made an exploratory trip down the Ohio River. They then came up the Wabash River to the present site of New Harmony. They liked it and ultimately chose it as their new home.

They bought about 30,000 acres of land bordering the Wabash and started preparations to move the Harmonie Society there. Father Rapp also found time to write the first of many songs that were to be written about the Wabash, a thing called Wabash Lied, written in German.

In June of 1814, the first group of about 100 men came by flatboat and platted the town. During the next 12 months, the rest of the population followed, also by flatboat. By June of 1815, they had established a well-integrated community with skilled workers who could produce all the goods and services needed by the town.

Four fundamental tenets bound the group together. They were: community living, uniform religious devotion, (including belief in the rapid approach of the Millennium), celibacy and endless toil and self-denial. Their motto was:

"We endure and suffer, labor and toil, sow and reap, with and for each other."

Speaking only German, they had minimal association with their English-speaking Hoosier neighbors.

The celibacy was supposed to be absolute. There were to be no marriages and men and women already married were to live as brothers and sisters, rather than as man and wife. They saw no need for reproduction in view of the fact they believed the world was about to come to an end. They wished to devote their remaining time on Earth to preparing for transition to the here-after.

They must have adhered remarkably well to this concept because there is no record of either any marriage or any birth in Harmonie on the Wabash.

Since they were not occupied with child birth or rearing, the women were free to be as productive as the men, economically speaking. They did most of the factory work, sheep shearing and worked in the fields during planting and harvest time.

Father Rapp was prophet, minister and king in their eyes and his leadership never was questioned. One probably reason is that he was a giant physically.

He published a book entitled "Thought on the destiny of man" at Harmonie in 1824. In it, he expressed his view of the union of work and worship: "pure enjoyment of that brotherly union, where the true principles of religion and the prudent regulation of industry and economy, by their unified influence, produce a heaven on Earth—a true Harmony."

The Rappites built two outstanding churches, the first a two-story frame building with a high steeple which contained a huge clock and a big bell. The latter tolled the hours and could be heard for seven miles. In 1822, they built a brick church in the form of a Maltese Cross in the same block. The plan for it had come to Father Rapp three times in a dream and it was a majestic temple indeed for those times.

Father Rapp constructed a Millennial Arch, or Rose Door, for one of the four wing entrances to the latter church. It is now preserved in the west entrance to the New Harmony school building, which stands on the same ground where the great church stood.

Father Rapp preached twice every Sunday and one or more times during the week and everyone in the community attended. The people worked during all their waking hours and Harmonie evolved into a garden spot in the wilderness. The people cultivated many grains, fruits and other crops suited to the soil and climate. This included a considerable amount of cotton and flax. They also raised all kinds of domestic animals and manufactured their own products. An adopted son, Frederick (Reichert) Rapp was Father Rapp's lieutanant. He directed the business affairs of Harmonie and was its principal contact with the outside world. He supervised a manufacturing center that covered an entire city block and included a sawmill, a cotton mill, an oil mill, a linen mill, a brick yard, a brewery and a distillery and several small shops. They also operated a large grist-mill at the dam in the Wabash some two miles below the town. They also hunted and trapped along the Wabash and sold several hundred skins each year, also using many in the manufacture of their own wearing apparel.

Producing nearly everything they needed for themselves, they also had a vast surplus, which they sold by flatboat shipments to Louisville, St. Louis and New Orleans, as well as Vincennes, Terre Haute and Shawneetown. Their goods were of top quality and commanded the highest prices in the market-place. With little use for money, they invested much of it in uncoined silver and are believed to have accumulated at least a million dollars' worth of it. The community became a charming pioneer village of log, frame and brick homes. In addition to the two churches, they built four large, brick community houses in which their men lived and a large combination fort and granary of five floors, in which their silver treasure was protected.

There was no discord in the community. They practiced the "Harmonious-Spirit", which prevented any quarreling. The first rule was not to speak the last word. They cherished Father Rapp's slogan, "Let not the sun go down upon your wrath." Keeping the peace was no problem and the town needed no police force. They had common wash houses and ovens and common piggery, goose pasture and sheepfold. All shared equally in their common possessions. They cultivated all kinds of flowers. They had a labyrinth or maze of flowering plants symbolizing the mystic ways of life, which has been restored by the state. Music was the chief recreation of the community and it was mostly attuned to friendship and religion. Practically every inhabitant could play one or more instruments and all could sing.

Although they were more or less a state within a state, the community still was in harmony with the government of Indiana. Frederick Rapp was an influential member of the Constitutional Convention at Corydon and also of the state commission that chose the site of Indianapolis as the new state capital.

After 10 years of flourishing prosperity, Harmonie was sold outright in 1824. The buyer was Robert Dale Owen of New Lanark, Scotland. The total price was only $190,000, certainly a bargain even in those days. There was never any official explanation of the sale but historians believe Father Rapp thought life was becoming too easy and comfortable for his people and wanted to again go through the hard work of establishing a new settlement among wilderness conditions. So, they went back to Pennsylvania, this time to the upper Ohio River in Beaver County, where they established Economy (later known as Ambridge.) They left gradually on their new steamboat, the

William Penn, and all were gone by May of 1825. It was their last move. Foredoomed to extinction by their well-kept vow of celibacy, they also failed to get the anticipated Millennium, so just gradually faded away through attrition.

Owen, a Welshman who had spent most of his life in Scotland had been a reformer in the cotton mills of New Lanark, in an era where woman and child labor was common and hours were incredibly long and pay unbelievably low. Owen reformed the community by providing schools, libraries and gymnasiums, while reducing hours and increasing wages. It made him famous throughout Europe as an industrial reformer.

At 54, Owen decided to lend his knowledge and talents to reformation of the world and determined to start in America. He hit upon building on the foundation already so well established by the Rappites at Harmonie and spent 80 percent of his entire fortune to buy the community.

Owen was welcomed joyfully by America and he was invited to explain his plan to Congress, which he addressed on two different occasions. He said his purpose was "to commence a new empire of peace and good will to men" in the little community he had just bought.

Owen issued an invitation to the "industrious and well disposed of all creeds" to come to his community. It drew a quick response and by late 1825, there were more than a thousand people in the newly named town of New Harmony. Many undoubtedly came to get free houses.

A Community of Equality was formed under a written constitution which established a pure democracy on the basis of liberty, equality and fraternity with equal opportunity for all. The community was organized into six working departments with regular duties assigned to each member. All were to share alike in duties and benefits without personal profit to any — true community socialization. Owen was to furnish all the financial backing to begin with.

Even the most cultured men and women had to take their turn at such menial tasks as milking the cows and working in the fields.

They hoped to spread this form of reformation around the world from New Harmony. It was to be "an adventure in happiness." There were weekly dances, concerts, dramas and forums.

"The end of government is to make the governed and the governors happy," said Owen.

He found a timely ally in William Maclure, a wealthy Scotsman of 63 who invested $150,000 in New Harmony, primarily to promote the schools.

Owen and Maclure assembled a brilliant company of educators, scientists, musicians and artists, about 43 of them, and brought them down the Ohio and up the Wabash—the famous "Boatload of Knowledge". New Harmony quickly became a center of educational activity. Schools were established for children from 2 years old to upper high school age. (The new community did not adopt the Rappites' celibacy vows.)

Children were taught to "earn while they learn" and did much part-time work in gardens and shops. Teachers came from England, Scotland, France, Holland, Switzerland and other parts of the United States to participate in the experiment.

New Harmony will be remembered by the women's movement as the first place on Earth where women received recognition as equal partners in both home and community life. Frances Wright, a well educated British woman, founded the Female Social Society in New Harmony and was an early leader in the humane attempt to abolish slavery.

It soon became apparent that, laudable as it might be, Owen's experiment simply was not going to work. The factories, homes, fences, fields, flower gardens began to look neglected and unkempt. The town obviously was not functioning properly as a community under the policy of equality. Although many were willing to do whatever was assigned to them, they simply lacked the knowledge or ability to perform many of the tasks. Others saw in Owen's plan an opportunity to get something for nothing and were not pulling their own weight.

It was obvious the principle of economic equality must be abandoned in regard to assignment of tasks. So, it was decided that each person should do what he did best, specifically the type of work he had previously done in life. Realizing all this, Owen dissolved the Community of Equality as an organization in 1828. Maclure's schools, however, kept alive the spirit of the idealistic plan for developing a better world. Educators who were more than fifty years ahead of their time developed teaching forms which spread to most of the world. Firsts credited to New Harmony included: first infant school in America, first public school kindergarten anywhere, first trade and industrial school as part of a public school system and most enlightened and humane system of school government.

Ku Klux Klan

Whereas the spirit of brotherhood and equality reached a high peak in the Harmonie and New Harmony experiments, social conscience sank to an all-time low in Indiana during the era of the Ku Klux Klan which followed in the wake of World War I.

The Klan reached its peak—or more accurately its nadir—during the administration of Governor Ed Jackson, a Republican. The part it played in Hoosier government during the first half of the 1920s will probably never be known fully, but its influence undoubtedly was tremendous.

David Curtis Stephenson was the Grand Dragon, the highest official of the Klan in Indiana. He was reputed to have bragged, "I am the law in Indiana."

Judging from the words of one Hoosier historical writer, he probably was entirely correct. This man wrote:

"Stephenson captured the Republican machine, forced two senators...to adopt a friendly attitude toward the Klan, and elected his candidate for Governor, Ed Jackson. But he desired to be more than a boss: he wished to stand in the limelight as senator and perhaps some day as president."

An entirely sinister organization the Klan had been organized in the South after the Civil War as an instrument to keep the Negroes in a state of terror. Members wore great, flowing white robes and covered their heads with pillow-cases with holes cut in them for their eyes. It disappeared after a few years in the Reconstruction Era South.

But it reappeared with a vengeance after World War I. This time it had as its theme intolerance of religion, of race and of the foreign born. Self-righteously, it claimed its mission to be to uphold the home, womanly virtue, Americanism and law and order. Actually, it waged war on Negroes, Catholics, Jews, Bolsheviks, bootleggers, pacifists, evolutionists, foreigners—and anyone it considered immoral.

Meetings and ritual were secret. White-hooded figures paraded through the streets of many a Hoosier city and fiery crosses were burned almost nightly to strike terror into the heart of the Klan's numerous enemies.

The strength of the Klan was amazing for, as eminent historian Ross Lockridge points out in his "The Story of Indiana," the Klan "stood for the things that are un-American and against the things for which America has always prided herself. The spirit of neighborliness, the desire to help one another, and a mutual respect for the opinions of the other fellow have always been strong features of Hoosier character. For a year or two, it appeared that Indiana had renounced this right. Then events occurred which quickly discredited the Klan.

In April, 1925, Stephenson was charged with murder in the death of an Indiana Statehouse secretary whom he had taken on a train ride for purposes which would not star ' the light of investigation. His sensational trial brought forth in.,ormation about lurid debauchery which hardly fit the pattern of conduct of morality, religion and "true Americanism" which the Klan proclaimed as among its tenets. Stephenson was convicted and sentenced to life imprisonment. His followers, who had reached an estimated 100,000 persons, were disillusioned. The Klan empire began to come apart. Thomas H. Adams of the *Vincennes Commercial* demanded an investigation of political corruption and the connections between the Klan and the Indiana Republican state organization.

Members of the Republican Editorial Association obtained evidence which led to the calling of a grand jury in Indianapolis. Mayor John L. Duvall of the Hoosier capital city was the first to feel its sting. He was sentenced to 30 days in prison and fined $1,000. Six Indianapolis city council members were punished for receiving bribes to vote against impeachment of the mayor.

In September, 1927, Governor Jackson was indicted for violation of the corrupt practices act by offering Governor Warren T. McCray, his predecessor, a bribe of $10,000 to appoint a "suitable person" as Marion County (Indianapolis) prosecutor.

Stephenson was brought from prison to appear as chief witness at the trial. He at first refused to testify, intimating that he feared for his life, but the following day, he admitted making the offer and holding conferences with Jackson on the subject. But Jackson was aquitted on a legal technicality.

Both the *Indianapolis Times* and *The Indianapolis News* called immediately for Jackson's resignation. "Governor Jackson emerges from the court wholly unvindicated," said *The News,* "Mr. Jackson should retire, and at once, from the governorship...He should spare Indiana the humiliation of having him at the head of its government." *The Times* was even more blunt: "Get out Ed Jackson...If he has the slightest regard for the honor of the state which paid him the highest tribute in its power by electing him Governor, he will resign before night." But Jackson served out his term and by frugality and efficiency, managed to pay off a debt of $3 million which the state owed when he took office.

Lamentably, the Klan received considerable support from many Protestant ministers. But it should also be reported that a majority of both Protestants and Republicans refused to join it.

The colorful extremes of New Harmony and the Ku Klux Klan only serve to illustrate by contrast the relative orderly development of the Hoosier social environment. From the log cabin to the high-rise apartment, the average Hoosier has traditionally been conservative in his conduct, dress and political ideas.

Although he has his roots planted deeply in the soil, the average Hoosier has undergone a slow but definite transition through the years to become something of a cosmopolite.

Indiana's transtition from a frontier state to an industrial commonwealth began to accelerate during the 1850s. But the factory system was still in its infancy and the value of manufactured goods still was much less than that of agricultural products. It was a decade of peace and prosperity, interrupted only briefly by the panic of 1857, and the Hoosier standard of living increased sharply. General diffusion of wealth provided a sound base for cultural and industrial advancements to come.

Farming was romanticized and agriculture was viewed as the most honorable of occupations. County fairs and agricultural societies proliferated and the state fair was born, and a state board of agriculture established. Railroad mileage increased ten-fold in the decade. Communication also improved greatly, paced by the coming of the telegraph. The majority of Hoosier trade still was with the states of the South. Roads were terrible. Plank roads proved impractical.

Far reaching political changes also occurred during the decade. A new state constitution was adopted in 1851, showing something of the Hoosier conservative philosophy of the times. A rather remarkable document, it has severe restrictions against state indebtedness, prohibits local and special legislation, and emphasizes common schools.

During the 1850s, a state supported system of elementary schools finally became a reality. County seminaries were abolished and a few public high schools began to appear, although private and church schools still manitained almost total dominance in the secondary field. Some racial tensions did develop with the coming of the initial substantial waves of German and Irish immigrants, which caused concern and nativist sentiment among the home-born Hoosiers.

The Civil War during the 1860s decade has a far-reaching impact on Hoosier society. Issues of the war tended to divide the people into groups, although Indiana as a state cast its lot with the Union and sent many more volunteers than its quota to join the Boys in Blue.

Peace Democrats, opposed to force, thought the Union could be preserved by making concessions to the South. Another element was the constitutional union men. They wished to preserve the union and supported the war, but opposed the tarriff and banking acts of the national administration. A few War Democrats supported the state and national administrations and joined the Republicans in forming the Union party.

The family dislocations were extremely serious as Indiana sent some 200,000 to the colors. There also were considerable readjustment problems when the hardened fighting men attempted at war's end four years after its beginning to turn themselves back into gentle farmers and factory workers.

A fundamental problem during the reconstruction period in Indiana was elimination of war prejudices and the resumption of normal thinking. At low ebb during the war years, the Democratic party gradually gathered strength, due partially to a growing weariness with the war issues the Republicans kept talking about, and gained control of the legislature in 1870 and elected a governor two years later. It also was something of a reaction against radical reconstruction policies.

It was an era of wild and wooly politics. During a visit by President Andrew Johnson, a riot erupted between Democrats who were trying to hold a torchlight parade on Monument Circle and Republicans, who were trying to stop them. Shots were fired. Several persons were wounded, one (a Republican) fatally.

Negro suffrage came in the wake of the Civil War, and it served to give impetus to the move for women's suffrage. A resolution to amend the state constitution to extend voting rights to women was introduced in the 1865 Indiana General Assembly but tabled. The Indiana Women's Suffrage Convention of 1869 heartily endorsed Congressman George W. Julian's proposed amendment to the U.S. Constitution to prohibit the denial of the right to vote because of sex, the Sixteenth Amendment.

One member of the Indiana General Assembly said in debate that woman's suffrage would "revolutionize society, array the sexes against each other for a different role than men—and made it plain that role did not include casting of ballot.

Despite this and other rebuffs, the suffragists persisted. Many of the same women also were active in another movement which gathered strength about the same time, the temperance crusade. It led to passage by the 1873 legislature of the Baxter bill, which provided an application for permission to sell liquor could be granted only if a majority of voters in any ward, town or township signed a petition. This was a form of what came later to be known as local-option.

Women also began a crusade of "moral suasion" in which they visited liquor stores and saloons and offered prayers for the proprietors, while also calling on them to give up their business and trying to get them to sign a pledge to do so. Temperance was a major issue in the city elections of 1874.

The Democrats won control of the legislature in 1875 and put through a new liquor law, which replaced the Baxter law with a provision giving the county commissioners authority to license persons selling liquor.

Full suffrage for Hoosier women did not come until 1921 when a special election ratified an amendment to the state constitution.

The free-and-easy divorce laws which had made the state a mecca for dissident couples were tightened in 1873 to require a bona fide residence of two years' duration and also to forbid persons getting divorces to remarry again for two years. Divorce grounds also were tightly restricted.

Examples of lynchings continued to be numerous in post-war Indiana. In 1867, two men who had been charged with slaying an old woman in a robbery attempt were taken from the Jackson County Jail by a mob and hanged. Later the same year, another mob broke into the Johnson County Jail and hanged a man charged with murder during a robbery.

A "vigilance committee" at Seymour stopped a train carrying several members of a gang who had stagged a daring railroad robbery. The prisoners were carried off, made to confess and hanged. The committee then published a proclamation saying "We will swing by the neck, until'they be dead, every thieving character we can lay our hands on, without inquiring whether we have the persons who committed that particular crime or not." That December, the group broke into the New Albany Jail, seized and hanged four more men accused of taking part in the same robbery. In his message to the legislature in 1860, Governor Baker reported more than a dozen prisoners had been taken from authorities and hanged during the last two years. He asked the legislature to make it a felony to join such a lynch mob but the assembly failed to act. In 1871, a mob stormed the Clark County Jail at Charlestown, carried off three Negroes and hanged them. They had been arrested on flimsy evidence in connection with the slaying of a white family. The grand jury even had failed to return an indictment against them. Baker then threatened to call upon the Federal government for help in quelling job. But no such action was taken and frequent mob violence continued.

One of the sorriest chapters in Hoosier mob violence happened in 1878 in Mount Vernon in Posey County. A mob overpowered guards at the jail and took custody of five Negroes who had been arrested for the horrible crime of forcing their way into a house of white prostitutes. One prisoner was butchered on the spot. The other four were marched to the town square and hanged.

The sad fact wat that local officials seldom requested state or Federal assistance and made little effort to prevent the carrying out of mob law. Identity of mob leaders was usually well known but no efforts were made to prosecute them. The legislature failed to do anything to cope with the situation.

World War I sent thousands of Hoosier men away to a foreign war for the first time and disrupted family life and caused numerous readjustment problems. Just about the time the state was recovering from that—and from the Klan area mentioned here previously—the Great Depression came and brought with it the bank failure, soup kitchens, apple and pencil sellers and salary cuts and layoffs which brought dark days to Indiana.

Governor Paul V. McNutt, a handsome white-haired product of American Legion politics, did a good job of coping with the depression, at least as well as a state government could, and the state rode out the storm.

World War II made its predecessor look something like the proverbial Sunday picnic and was very costly to the state in terms of life and injury, to say nothing of the disruptive affect on the typical Hoosier family.

As Hoosiers moved into the era of the atom bomb, the old many-gabled house with bay windows, cupolas and porches had given way to the slim, clean lines of the 1940s, which featured ranch houses, split levels and contemporary homes. Often pre-cut or prefabricated, the new homes contained more glass, aluminum, steel and plastic. Frequently, they were mobile homes.

And the Hoosier citizen, particularly those in the major cities, had taken on a sophistication which made him a far cry from his great grandfather who lived in a log cabin a hundred years before.

EUGENE CADOU

* * *

Biographies of
Famous Hoosiers

ADE, GEORGE (b. February 9, 1866 Kentland, Indiana—d. May 16, 1944, Kentland, Indiana.)

Ade graduated from Purdue University in 1887 and worked for three years for a Lafayette, Indiana newspaper. In 1890, he moved to Chicago where he became a successful reporter for the Chicago *Morning News* (later the *News Record* ND *The Record*). Ade used his daily column "Stories of the Street and of the Town" to write the vignettes about everyday people and incidents that helped to make him popular. In 1896, a collection of tales about one of these characters was published in a book entitled *Artie.* Two similar collections followed: *Pink Marsh* (1897) and *Doc' Horne* (1899).

Ade hit upon the idea of modern fables about everyday people in 1898 while looking for something new and interesting to offer his newspaper readers. The first of his "fables in slang", "The Blond Girl Who Married the Bucket Shop Man" was a hugh success. This and the subsequent fables that made up his best selling books, *Fables in Slang* (1900), *More Fables* (1900) and *Forty Modern Fables* (1901) all had certain elements in common: picturesque colloquialisms, irregular capitalizations and satirical humor.

In 1900 Ade left the *Record* to try his hand at writing plays. His career as a playwright got off to a very good start with the popular musical comedy, *The Sultan of Sulu* (1902). A string of successful farces followed, including *The County Chairman* (1903), *The College Widow* (1904), *Just Out of College* (1905) and *Father and the Boy* (1908).

Ade also wrote motion picture scripts including *Our Leading Citizen* and *Woman Proof* at the age of 77.

In June, 1943 at the age of 77, Ade suffered a cerebral hemorrage. He died about one year later.

Sources:
Herzberg, *The Reader's Encyclopedia of American Literature*
New York Times May 17, 1944
DAB

BAYH, BIRCH EVANS JR. (b. January 22, 1928, Terre Haute, Indiana-) U.S. Senator and politician.

Bayh still owns and manages the Shirkieville, Indiana farm where he once lived with his grandfather. Bayh temporarily abandoned his rural environment in 1946 to serve a two year term in the U.S. Army, and later to spend four years at Purdue University where he earned a B.S. degree in Agriculture in 1951. Soon after graduating, he married the former Marvella Hern and returned to his first interest of farming. Bayh gradually became involved in politics and in 1954 he began an eight-year stay in the Indiana House of Representatives where he served as the Democratic Minority Leader in 1957 and 1961 and as Speaker of the House in 1959. During this time, he also attended law school at Indiana University. In 1962, two years after he received his law degree, he ran a successful race against Homer Capehart for the U.S. Senate. Bayh was able to maintain his seat in the two successive elections, defeating William Ruckelshaus in 1968 and Richard Lugar in 1974.

Following the assassination of President Kennedy, Bayh as chairman (1963) of the U.S. Senate Judicary Subcommittee, introduced the amendment on presidential disability. This legislation, which became the 25th Amendment in 1967, allowed for the filling of a Vice-Presiddential vacancy through the approval of a presidential choice by a majority vote in both houses of Congress.

Bayh was also influential in the writing and passage of the 26th Amendment which gave the vote to 18-year olds. His strong support of civil rights was also instrumental in winning Senate approval of the Equal Rights Amendment which, if ratified, will prohibit discrimination based on sex.

Bayh is also known for his opposition to two Nixon Supreme Court nominees. Bayh's successful campaign against the two would be appointees—W. Clement Haynsworth and G. Harrold

Carswell was a result of a thorough screening of the men's ethical conduct, which Bayh felt did not life up to the needed standards.

In 1972, Bayh ran a well-supported campaign for the Democratic presidential nomination, but withdrew when his wife became ill. He is still viewed by many as a viable candidate for the 1976 presidential election.

Sources:
Biogrpahical Directory of the American Congress
Biography News September, 1974
Ralph Nader Congress Project, Citizens Look at Congress

BOONE, SQUIRE (b. Oct. 5, 1744—August 1815) was an early explorer of what are now the states of Indiana, Kentucky, and Virginia.

Squire Boone was the tenth of eleven children and the brother of the famous explorer and frontiersman, Daniel Boone. Born near Reading, Pennsylvania, he received little formal education, and was trained at the age of 16 to be a gunsmith. Most of his life, however, was spent investigating unexplored territory and fighting Indians in the process.

The first of a series of exploratory trips began in the mid-1760s, when Boone accompanied his brother, Daniel, to central Kentucky and Florida. In 1775, he helped to carve out the Wilderness Road to Richmond, Kentucky, and assisted Daniel in building Fort Boonesborough near the Kentucky River in the central part of the future state. The following year, Squire Boone moved his family to Boonesborough, where they remained until he established Squire Boone's Station near the present city of Shelbyville, Kentucky, in 1779. When Kentucky Territory became a county of Virginia, Boone undertook a brief political career, and was elected to the Virginia House of Delegates as the Jefferson County representative in 1781.

From 1787 to 1791, Boone explored land in Louisiana and Florida, and made an unsuccessful attempt to start another settlement in Mississippi. Upon returning to Kentucky, he discovered that fraudulent claims had resulted in the loss of most of his land in that state. This, in addition to a brief imprisonment for unpaid debts, caused him to migrate to Harrison County, Indiana, in the early 1800s. There he built Boone Mill on Buck Creek near the famous Squire Boone Caverns that he had discovered in 1790. About 1813, Boone was instrumental in the building of the first Baptist church in Indiana, Old Goshen Church of Laconia.

Boone died at the age of 71' and was buried near the site of his mill. His remains were later moved to Kentucky.

BORMAN, FRANK (b. March 14, 1928-   ) was a U.S. astronaut who made two flights of major importance into outer space.

Born into a well-known family of Gary, Indiana, Borman was taken to Arizona for his health when he was six years of age. He graduated from the U.S. Military Academy at West Point, ranking in the first ten of his class, in 1950. Choosing the Air Force as his career, he underwent pilot training and served in the Philippines (1951-56). He earned a master's degree in aeronautical engineering in 1957 and subsequently was an instructor at West Point and the Aero-Space Research Pilot School at Edward Air Force Base, California.

Borman joined the astroanut team of the U.S. space program in 1962. He was the command pilot of the 14-day Gemini 7 flight of December 1965 which orbited the Earth long enough to prove that a flight to the Moon was possible. Gemini 7 also made the first rendezvous in space with another craft, Gemini 6.

In December 1968 Borman again commanded a space flight. He and two colleagues in the Apollo spacecraft left the Earth's orbit and became the first men to travel to the Moon. Orbiting 70 miles from the Moon, they took photographs and transmitted television pictures of the lunar surface.

Borman became the deputy director of flight-crew operations for the National Aeronautics and Space Administration (ˌA) after the Apollo 8 flight. Leaving the space program, he joined a commercial airline in 1970.

BOWEN, OTIS R. (b. February 2, 1918-   ) is a physician and state political leader who was elected governor of Indiana in 1973. During his long career in the state legislature, he was credited with helping to give the House of Representatives a more business-like tone and a higher place in public esteem.

Born on a farm near Rochester, Indiana, Bowen was graduated from Indiana University in 1939 and its school of medicine in 1942. He served in the Army Medical Corps in the South Pacific (1943-46), returning to practice at Bremen.

Bowen exhibits a liberal attitude toward humanitarian issues. He was active in the community—Boy Scouts, medical groups, recreation, the Farm Bureau, the American Legion—while practicing medicine at Bremen. He began his political career as a Republican township chairman. He served as the coroner of Marshall County (1952-56) and as a member of the Indiana House of Representatives (1957-58, 1961-72). Bowen was the minority leader (1965-66) and the speaker (1967-72) of the House before his election as governor in 1973.

Bowen's most cherished accomplishment as governor was a restructuring of the tax system that lowered property taxes, although sales, individual income, and business income taxes rose.

CARMICHAEL, HOAGLAND HOWARD "HOAGY" (b. Nov. 22, 1899-   ) is a songwriter, actor, singer, and composer of such popular songs as "Stardust" and "Georgia on my Mind."

Born in Bloomington, Indiana, Carmichael learned to play the piano from his mother, a ragtime pianist. He organized his first band, The Collegians, in 1923 while attending the University of Indiana law school in Bloomington. It was also during this period that he wrote and recorded some of his first songs for Gennet Studios in Richmond, Indiana. After receiving his law degree in 1926, Carmichael held several law-related positions in New York, Florida, and Indiana. He joined the Jean Goldette Band for about three months in the late 1920s before leaving to organize his own group in Indianapolis. The assembly broke up after an unsuccessful attempt to become established in Hollywood, and Carmichael moved to New York City, where he became a music arranger.

Carmichael's most famous work, "Stardust," was published in 1931. It signalled the start of a long list of hits such as "Rockin' Chair," "Two Sleepy People," "I Get Along Without You Very Well," and "In the Cool, Cool, Cool of the Evening." In addition to songwriting, Carmichael also appeared in several movies including *To Have and Have Not* (1944) and *The Best Years of Our Lives* (1946). During the 1950s and 1960s, he became a popular television and radio personality. He has also written several books—*The Stardust Road* (1946), *Washboard Blues* (1947), and *Sometimes I Wonder* (1965).

CHAPMAN, JOHN (b. c. 1775—d. March 11, 1847) Pioneer, popularly known as Johnny Appleseed.

Chapman is believed to have been born either in Boston or Springfield, Massachusetts. His first recorded appearance in the Midwest was in the early 1800s near Steubenville. Chapman was reportedly transporting a cargo of decaying apples from Pennsylvania down the Ohio River. About 1810, Chapman took up residence in the area of Ashland County, Ohio which he apparently used as a base to tend his widely scattered apple orchards.

Chapman has also been described as a religious man who would read the Bible to anyone who would listen as a medicine man who spread the seeds of such "healing" herbs as catnip and hoarhound. Chapman's concern for his fellow settlers is evidenced by a hasty night trip about 1812 to Mt. Vernon, Ohio to summon troops to protect Mansfield from British-instigated Indian attacks.

Chapman moved to northern Indiana about 1838 where he continued planting apple orchards. During a trip to one of his orchards, Chapman contacted the pneumonia that led to his death in a cabin in Allen County, Indiana.

Sources:
DAB

CLARK, GEORGE ROGERS (b. Nov. 19, 1752—d. Feb. 13, 1818) was a U.S. military leader famous for capture of British territory in what is now Illinois and Indiana during the American Revolution.

Clark was born in Charlottesville, Virginia. He received some formal education during his youth, but his first occupation as a surveyor was largely self-taught. His initial military experience was as a militia captain in Lord Dunmore's War against the Shawnee Indians in 1774. Early the next year, he went to Kentucky as a surveyor for the Ohio Company and became the leader of the settlers' defense against the British and the Indians. Clark's strategy was to conquer the British forts in Illinois territory from which the Indians received supplies. Kaskaskia and Cahokia were captured by Clark and his men in 1778. Envoys sent to the settlement of Fort Sackville (Vincennes, Indiana) on the Wabash River persuaded the French inhabitants to switch their allegiance from Britain to Virginia. Fort Sackville returned into British hands the following December, but was recaptured by Clark in February 1779. A lack of supplies and reinforcements prevented Clark from carrying out a planned march against the British headquarters in Fort Detroit.

From 1780, when Clark established Fort Jefferson, until the end of the war, Clark was active in a series of campaigns to protect the land he had won from attempted takeovers by the British and the Indians. Because of his efforts, most of the territory of what was known as the Old Northwest was awarded to the United States in the Treaty of Paris of 1783. As a reward for their services, in 1781 the state of Virginia awarded Clark and his men a 150,000-acre tract of land known as Clark's Grant.

In 1784 Clark accepted a position as an Indian commissioner of the Northwest Territory. This led him to establish a garrison at Vincennes to combat Indians. In order to maintain his army, he impressed privately-owned merchandise. Unfortunately, both the state of Virginia and the U.S. government refused to pay for the goods, resulting in legal judgments against Clark which were used by his enemies to prevent him from obtaining further government appointments. Desperate and deeply in debt, he sold a large part of the land he was entitled to under Clark's Grant and accepted commissions in the French army in 1793 and 1798. He resigned the last commission at the insistance of the U.S. government and took refuge in St. Louis, returning to Louisville in 1799.

In 1803 Clark settled in Clarksville, Indiana, the town that was founded on Clark's Grant. There he ran a grist mill and served on the commission to appropriate land on Clark's Grant to veterans of his Illinois regiment. Ill health and the amputation of his right leg forced him in 1809 to move to his sister's home near Louisville, where he remained until his death.

DEBS, EUGENE VICTOR (b. Nov. 5, 1855—d. Oct. 20, 1926) was a labor leader who ran for the U.S. presidency on the Socialist Party ticket five times between 1900 and 1920.

Debs was one of a large family born to immigrant parents in Terre Haute, Indiana. His world was peopled with workers who labored long grinding hours for little pay. Mostly self-educated after grammar school, Debs' heroes were Thomas Paine, Patrick Henry, and John Brown. The book that most impressed him in boyhood was Victor Hugo's *Les Miserables*.

At the age of 14, Debs worked in the railway yards, scraping paint off old railway cars. He soon became a locomotive fireman, earning $1 a day. After studying bookkeeping, he obtained a job as a ledger clerk in a wholesale grocery establishment.

Debs helped to organize a lodge of the Brotherhood of Locomotive Firemen in 1875, and became the organization's secretary-treasurer in 1880. He put the union on a sound financial basis while simultaneously holding the positions of city clerk of Terre Haute (1879-83) and representative in the Indiana Legislature (1885).

Although Debs initially opposed labor strikes, he soon decided that they were a necessary weapon. It was his belief that the only hope of the working man was in the organization of labor by industry, rather than by craft or trade.

Debs helped to organize the American Railway Union and became its president in 1893. The following year the union conducted a successful strike against the Great Northern Railroad for higher wages. Debs helped to direct the bitter Chicago Pullman Car Company strike that same year. As a result of the strike, he and other union leaders were jailed for six months on a contempt of court conviction. A later federal investigation could find no evidence that Debs or the other union leaders had participated in or advised intimidation or violence. After his release from the Illinois jail in 1895, he was greeted by 100,000 persons at Chicago as he went through that city on his way home to Terre Haute.

A confirmed socialist thereafter, Debs was a founder of the Socialist Party in the United States. As the party's presidential candidate in the election of 1900 he won 96,000 votes, and in 1904 he received 402,000 votes.

While working as an editor for a Socialist weekly and as a lecturer, Debs helped found the Industrial Workers of the World (IWW) in 1905. As the Socialist Party presidential candidate, he polled 420,000 votes in 1908, 901,000 (amounting to almost six percent of the total) in 1912, and 900,000 votes in 1920.

Debs' final candidacy for the presidency occurred while the Socialist leader was in prison. He had been convicted of sedition under the provisions of the 1917 Espionage Act because of his views against World War I. Pres. Harding released Debs from jail in 1921, but did not restore his U.S. citizenship, which had been revoked because of his conviction.

Debs hailed the Russian October Revolution, but soon

condemned the resulting Communist Party because it did not adhere to his belief that socialism should be achieved through the democratic methods of debate and consent. Debs continued to lecture and work as a contributor and editor of periodicals until his death in Elmhurst, Illinois. His writings include *Unionism and Socialism* (1904) and *Walls and Bars* (1927).

DOUGLAS, LLOYD CASSEL (b. Aug. 27, 1877—d. Feb. 13, 1951) was a clergyman and author of several popular religious novels including *The Robe* and *The Big Fisherman.*

Douglas was born in Columbia City, Indiana. He earned his bachelor of arts degree from Wittenberg College in 1900. Three years later, he received a master's degree from his alma mater and a bachelor of divinity degree from Hamma Divinity School in Springfield, Ohio. Also in the same year, he was ordained in the Lutheran ministry and assigned to the pastorship of Zion Church in North Manchester, Indiana, where he remained until 1905. Between 1905 and 1911 he held the ministry of a church in Lanchester, Ohio, and another in Washington, D.C. He returned to the Midwest in 1911 and became director of religious work at the University of Illinois. A series of pastorships in Michigan, Ohio, Los Angeles, and Montreal, Canada, ended when he retired in the late 1920s to devote more time to lecturing and writing.

In all, Douglas wrote more than ten novels. A few were derived from his religious essays, while others were written to dramatize Christian faith and morals. His first novel, *The Magnificent Obsession* (1929), was written when Douglas was more than 50 years old. The book became a huge success and was followed by two other equally popular novels—*The Robe* (1942) and *The Big Fisherman* (1948). Other works include *Precious Jeopardy* (1933), *Green Light* (1935), *White Banners* (1936), *Disputed Passage* (1939), and *Invitation to Live* (1940). His autobiography, *Time to Remember,* was published in 1951, the year of his death in Los Angeles, California. A sequel *The Shape of Sunday,* was written by his daughter and published in 1952.

DRESSER, PAUL (b. April 21, 1857—d. Jan. 30, 1906) was an actor and composer of popular songs. He wrote the music for the Indiana state song, "On the Banks of the Wabash," for which his brother, Theodore Dreiser, wrote the words.

Dresser was born in Terre Haute. He left home at the age of 16 to join a medicine show. Shortly afterward, he changed his last name and toured in vaudeville as a singer, monologist, and comedian. He also toured with the Billy Rice Minstrels as an end man.

Dresser wrote his first song, "Wide Wings," around 1875. After becoming established as a songwriter, he helped organize the music publishing firm of Howley, Haviland, and Dresser in 1901. He started his own publishing company a few years before his death in New York City in 1906. His compositions include "The Letter that Never Came" (1886), "The Blue and the Gray" (1890), "Just Tell Them That You Saw Me" (1903), and "My Gal Sal" (1903).

FISHER, CARL GRAHAM (b. January 12, 1874, Greensburg, Indiana—d. July 15, 1939, Miami, Florida).

Promoter and developer of Miami Beach, the Indianapolis Speedway, and Lincoln Highway, the country's first coast to coast motorway. Fisher spent part of his youth as a bicycle and automobile racing star. In 1904 he organized the Prest-O-Lite Company to supply carbide gas headlights for late model automobiles.

The idea of the "Indy 500" originated during a trip to Europe in 1905 when Fisher witnessed the defeat of the U.S. entry to the James Gordon Bennet Cup Races. The need for a place for U.S. car drivers to test drive racing cars was immediately apparent to Fisher who successfully completed the track in 1909.

Fisher is best known as the promoter who developed Miami Beach. He acquired a large part of the land in 1912 and preceded to build the hotels, boulevards, recreation areas, and stores that helped to make Miami Beach one of the world's leading resort areas.

Fisher was also a major promoter of the Lincoln Highway, the first motorway from New York to California and thus indirectly influenced the trend to long-distance automobile travel in the United States. Fisher took his crusade for marked and paved roads to the masses using the slogan "See America First." To accomplish his goal, Fisher organized the Lincoln Highway Association which eventually raised ten million dollars to build the highway which was not completed until the government took over the task in the early 1920s.

A more successful undertaking for Fisher was the Dixie Highway, which was the country's first north/south motor road.

Sources:
New York Times Obituary
Joe McCarthy, "The Lincoln Highway"

GRISSOM, VIRGIL IVAN "GUS" (b. April 3, 1926—d. Jan. 27, 1967) was the second American astronaut to enter space and the first to maneuver an in-flight space capsule.

Grissom was born in Mitchell, Indiana. He earned his nickname "Gus" after joining the U.S. Army Air Corps pilot-training program in 1944. He left the Corps in 1945 and shortly afterward entered Purdue University, from which he received his bachelor of science degree in engineering in 1950. He then reenlisted in the Air Force and flew more than 100 missions in the Korean War. When the war ended, he remained in the Air Force first as an instructor in the pilot-training program, and later as a test pilot. On April 9, 1959, the National Aeronautics and Space Administration (NASA) announced that Grissom was one of seven men chosen to be astroaut trainees for the U.S. space program. On July 17, 1961, NASA disclosed that Grissom was to become the second American to enter space in a flight similar to the one undertaken by Alan B. Shepard, Jr., in May of that year. Grissom's flight took place on July 21, 1961, in the Liberty Bell 7 space capsule. The suborbital flight lasted 16 minutes, covering a distance of 302 miles and reaching an altitude of 118 miles.

Project Mercury was followed by Project Gemini, which was designed to perfect the docking and rendezvous maneuvers essential to the success of the Project Apollo lunar flights. Grissom's contribution to Project Gemini began with the early design and construction stages of the Gemini 3 spacecraft and included a four-hour space journey in the vehicle on March 23, 1965. During the flight, Grissom (accompanied by John W. Young) successfully piloted the first flight maneuvers by a space capsule under human control.

Grissom, together with Edward H. White and Roger B. Chaffe, died on Jan. 27, 1967. The first casualties of the U.S. space program occurred during a simulation of what was to be the first flight of the Apollo mission, when a fire broke out in the test capsule while it was grounded at Cape Canaveral (now Cape Kennedy), Florida.

HALLECK, CHARLES A. (b. Aug. 22, 1900-   ) is a lawyer and politician who served in the U.S. House of Representatives longer than any Hoosier before him.

Halleck was born in DeMotte, Indiana, to Abraham (a lawyer) and Lura Luce Halleck. He was a Phi Beta Kappa graduate of Indiana University and its law school. The year he completed his schooling (1924), he was elected county prosecutor, a post that he held until he was first elected to the U.S. Congress in 1932.

An expert at winning elections — his northern Indiana district returned him to Congress from 1932 until he announced in 1968 he would retire at term's end — he could make his magic work for others as well. Serving as Congressional campaign chairman in 1946, he helped the national Republican Party regain control of Congress for the first time in 15 years.

Halleck was believed to have come close to his party's vice-presidential nomination on two occasions, but he never managed to grasp it. He was credited with a key role in obtaining the 1940 Republican presidential nomination for Hoosier Wendell L. Willkie.

As majority leader of the 80th and 83rd Congresses and minority leader of the 86th and 88th Congresses, his legislative prowess was an aid to both Republican and Democratic presidents. He described himself as a political "gut fighter," but the description is belied by his ability to make friends in the opposition party, as well as his own.

In all probability it was his gravelly voice on the "Ev and Charlie" television program with Sen. Everett M. Dirksen of Illinois that drew him the most national attention.

HARRISON, BENJAMIN (b. August 20, 1833, North Bend, Ohio — d. March 13, 1901, Indianapolis, Indiana) Twenty-third President of the United States.

Harrison, the grandson of former U.S. President, William Henry Harrison, graduated from Miami University in Oxford, Ohio in 1852 and read law for two years at a Cincinnati based law office. In 1854, he moved to Indianapolis where he started a law practice and became involved with the Indiana Republican Party. He was subsequently appointed to several governmental offices including city attorney (1857) and reporter of the Indiana Supreme Court (1860 and 1864).

During the Civil War, he organized the 70th Indiana Infantry and was appointed its colonel in 1862. Two years of relatively quiet duty in Kentucky was followed by heated action alongside General Sherman at the Atlanta campaign (1864). The next year, Harrison left the army a breveted brigadier general, whereupon he immediately resumed his law career.

He was thrust into the national spotlight in 1876 when he made an unsuccessful bid for the governorship of Indiana. His prestige and viability mounted with his appointment by President Hayes to the Mississippi River Commission in 1876 and his chairmanship of the Indiana delegation to the Republican National Convention in 1880. The following year, he was elected to represent Indiana in the U.S. Senate, serving in this position until 1887 when his bid for relelection was defeated.

In 1888, Harrison secured the Republican nomination to oppose President Grover Cleveland in the upcoming election. In the November contest, Cleveland won the popular vote by a margin of 100,000 votes; but Harrison received 233 electoral votes, 65 more than his opponent, making Harrison the 23rd President of the United States.

The most notable events of the Harrison administration were the McKinley Tariff Act (1890); the Sherman Silver Purchase Act (1890); and the Sherman Anti-Trust Law (1890) and the Conference of 1889-90 which formed the Pan-American Union.

Under Harrison, the Union grew by six states — North Dakota, South Dakota, Montana, Washington, Idaho, and Wyoming. In addition, Oklahoma was opened for public settlement. An attempt to annex Hawaii was defeated by the anti-Imperalist. Harrison also gave the country its first "billion dollar Congress."

Public reaction to the higher tariffs enacted by the McKinley Act helped to wipe out the Republican majority in ·1890 congressional elections and contributed to Harrison's defeat in the presidential election two years later.

Harrison eventually returned to his home in Indianapolis and resumed a highly successful law practice. In one of his better known cases (1898-99) he served as senior counsel to Venezuela in its arbitration with Great Britain over a boundary dispute. Many of Harrison's aricles and speeches were published in *This Country of Ours* (1897) and *Views of an Ex-President* (1901).

Sources:
Morgan, *Our Presidents*
Armbruster, *The Presidents of the U.S.*
DAB

HARRISON, WILLIAM HENRY (b. Feb. 9, 1773—d. April 4, 1841) was a military hero who became the first territorial governor of Indiana and the ninth president of the United States.

Harrison was the third son of Benjamin Harrison, a prominent politician and one of the original signers of the Declaration of Independence. He was born at Berkeley Plantation, Charles City County, Virginia, and educated at Hampden-Sydney College in Virginia (1787-90) and the University of Pennsylvania (1790-91) where he studied medicine. Immediately after leaving school, he joined the army and served as an aide-de-camp under Gen. Anthony Wayne in 1783.

Harrison resigned from the army in 1798 and was appointed to the position of secretary of the Northwest Territory. He served in this capacity for one year before he was elected the territory's first delegate to the U.S. Congress. His work on the act which created Indiana Territory led to his appointment on May 12, 1800, the first territorial governor of Indiana, an office he held for 12 years.

During the first four years of Harrison's term, the inhabitants of Indiana Territory were subject to the Ordinance of 1787, which provided for a non-representative type of government. Harrison used this enormous power to alter existing tax laws, change the court system, and permit a form of slavery. In 1805, he allowed the territory to pass into a semi-representative stage of government, which actually did very little to alter his sovereign type of leadership. The creation of Illinois Territory by an Act of Congress on Feb. 3, 1809, greatly reduced the size of Indiana Territory and resulted in an increase of the anti-Harrison representation in the territorial assembly. The 1810 legislature reflected this opposition by repealing the laws permitting slavery, nullifying the requirement of land ownership in order to vote, and persuading the U.S. Congress to strip Harrison of much of his power. This marked the beginnings of a true democracy in Indiana.

As Superintendent of Indian Affairs, Harrison negotiated treaties that turned over millions of acres of land in what is now Indiana and Illinois to the U.S. Opposition to these treaties by the famous Shawnee leader, Tecumseh, and his brother, Tenskwatawa, the Shawnee Prophet, was unsuccessful. Harrison defeated the Indian forces in the Battle of Tippecanoe on Nov. 7, 1811.

With the outbreak of the War of 1812, Harrison was

commissioned major general in the Kentucky militia and brigadier general in the regular army. In October 1813, he overwhelmed Gen. Proctor of the British forces and Tecumseh in the Battle of the Thames. His victory broke the British hold on the Northwest Territory and, with the death of Tecumseh in the battle, marked the end of Indian resistance to White settlement in the area. In 1816 and 1825, Harrison was elected to the U.S. Congress by the state of Ohio. He served as the U.S. minister to Colombia in 1828 and, upon returning to the U.S. in 1829, he settled on his farm in North Bend, near Cincinnati, Ohio, where he was active as the clerk of the county court and president of the County Agricultural Society.

Harrison's first attempt to gain the U.S. presidency came with his unsuccessful Whig candidacy in 1836. He was renominated by the party in 1840 and, together with John Tyler, ran against Pres. Van Buren. Harrison ran as a people's candidate and a military hero, incorporating his victory at Tippecanoe into the famous slogan "Tippecanoe and Tyler Too." Harrison won the election, receiving 234 electoral votes to Van Buren's 60. He was inaugurated in Washington, D.C., on March 4, 1841, at the age of 68, making him the oldest president to take office. One month later he developed a fatal case of pneumonia, and became the first president to die in office.

HATCHER, RICHARD GORDON (b. July 10, 1933, Michigan City, Indiana—) lawyer who became the first black mayor of Gary, Indiana.

Hatcher grew up in the slum area of Michigan City known as The Patch. Funds raised through summer employment, his church, and a track scholarship allowed him, in the fall of 1951, to enter Indiana University where he majored in government and economics. The following summer, Hatcher organized Michigan City's first civil rights sit-in against a restaurant that had once employed him as a dishwasher.

Soon after receiving his B.A. in 1956, Hatcher entered Valpariso University Law School from which he obtained his L.L.B. in 1959. Hatcher set up his first law practice in East Chicago Heights, Indiana but was most politicaly active in Gary where he led civil rights demonstrations and helped to end de facto segregation in the school system. In 1961, he was appointed deputy prosecutor of the Criminal Court of Lake County but resigned two years later to make a successful bid for a seat on the Gary City Council.

At this time, the city of Gary was controlled by a powerful democratic machine that received most of its support from organizd crime and corruption and thus did very little to provide the average citizen with a workable, efficient government. It was against this background that Hatcher decided to run for mayor in 1967.

Hatcher won the Democratic primary despite a lack of monetary and moral support. However he was not endorsed by the Democratic machine which had decided to back the Republican candidate, Joseph Radigan. This same group was also responsible for an unsuccessful attempt to sway the election by adding 5,000 ghost voters to the voter registration rolls.

Despite such foul play, Hatcher won the election and became the first black mayor in Gary's history. His popularity carried him through the next mayoral election of November, 1971 at which time he defeated the Republican candidate, Theodore Nering by a margin of three to one. Hatcher's efforts to eliminate government corruption and provide better housing, employment and services to the people of Gary won badly needed federal funds which have been very useful to the city in its battle against urban blight.

Sources:
Curren Biography, 1972
Drotning and South, *Up From the Ghetto*

HAYNES, ELWOOD (b. October 14, 1857 Portland, Indiana — d. April 13, 1925 Kokomo, Indiana) inventor and metallurgist who designed one of the first successful U.S. automobiles.

Haynes studied at Worcester Polytechnic Institute (1881) and Johns Hopkins University before becoming a science teacher in Portland, Indiana. He subsequently became the manager of the Portland Natural Gas and Oil Company (1886-1890) and a field superintendent for the Indiana Natural Oil and Gas Company (1890-1901). During the mid 1890s Haynes (with the help of two machinists—Elmer Edgar Apperson) designed and built one of the first American automobiles. The car was tested near Kokomo, Indiana on July 4, 1894 and is now on exhibit at the Smithsonian Institution in Washington, D.C.

In 1898 Haynes established and became president of the

Haynes-Apperson Automobile Company, a position he held until his death in 1925.

Other contributions by Haynes to the U.S. automobile industry include the rotary valve gas engine (1903) and the use of aluminum in the construction of the automobile engine.

Haynes was also a successful metallurgist, discovering tungsten chrome steel in 1881 followed by an alloy of cobalt and chromium in 1900. His greatest contribution to this field came in 1911 for his discovery of Stellite, or "stainless steel" which he patented in 1919.

Sources:
New York Times April 14, 1925
Usher, *Indiana Scientist*

LIEBER, RICHARD (b. Sept. 5, 1869—April 5, 1944) was a conservationist and architect of the Indiana state park system.

Lieber was born in St. Johann Saarbrucken, Germany, and was educated at the Municipal Lyceum and Royal Lyceum in Dusseldorf. He emigrated to the U.S. in 1891 and became a naturalized citizen in 1901. From 1892 to 1900, Lieber worked for two newspapers, the *Indianapolis Journal* and the *Indianapolis Tribune*. He was later employed by an Indianapolis-based importer (1905-18).

Lieber accepted his first conservation-related position in 1912, when he became chairman of the board of governors for the Fourth National Conservation Congress. He became chairman of the Indiana State Park Commission (1915-19) and chairman of the Indiana Board of Forestry (1917-19). In 1919, the Indiana Department of Conservation was formed by the consolidation of all state conservation agencies. Lieber became the new department's first director and remained so until his resignation in 1933.

In addition to his efforts to develop state parks in Indiana, Lieber worked with the National Conference on State Parks, the American Planning and Civic Association, and the National Park Service. His literary contribution to the field of conservation includes numerous official reports and one book, *America's Natural Wealth: A Story of the Use and Abuse of our Natural Resources* (1942). His work in building and administering the Indiana park system was officially recognized in 1932, when a monument was erected in his honor at Turkey Run State Park.

LITTLE TURTLE (b. 1752—d. July 14, 1812) was a chief of the Miami Indians of Indiana who, in 1786, organized the Indian confederacy that defeated Gen. Joseph Harmar in 1790 and Gen. Arthur St. Clair in 1791. His victory in a 1790 battle with French soldiers who had attacked his village served to destroy the prestige of the French in the Northwest Territory.

Little Turtle's tribe settled in Indiana about 1763 after having inhabited several different regions. The Miami under the leadership of Little Turtle long resisted the movement of white settlers to their area. Through various treaties from 1795 to 1854, however, they ceded their Ohio and Indiana land claims and moved west to the Mississippi. Little Turtle served as the spokesman of the Miami at the signing of many of these treaties, including the 1795 Treaty of Greenville. Little Turtle spent his last years counseling peace with the white man, travelling to Philadelphia to meet Pres. Washington in 1797. He died at Fort Wayne.

MC NUTT, PAUL V(ORIES) (b. July 19, 1891—d. March 24, 1955) was the 34th governor of Indiana and a politician of great sagacity and national stature.

McNutt was born in Franklin, Indiana, the son of a prominent lawyer. A Phi Beta Kappa, he was graduated from Indiana University in 1913 and Harvard Law School in 1916. He began his law practice in his father's office in Martinsville, and became an assistant professor of law at Indiana University in 1917. Within one year he joined the U.S. Army, and at the end of World War I returned to Indiana University as a professor of law. In 1925, again at Indiana University, he became one of the nation's youngest deans of a law school.

McNutt's rise in politics was based on his position with the American Legion. He became state commander in 1927 and national commander in 1928-29. He was director of the American Legion Publication Corporation from 1928 to 1931. From these posts he gained the political power to be elected governor of Indiana in 1933.

A man with the gift of accepting the sound ideas of others and making them work, McNutt guided Indiana through the Great Depression. He imposed strict economic measures throughout the administration, but did not reduce the budget of the school system.

Because he was the first Democratic governor in 16 years, McNutt had little party organization to support him. He reorganized the state's 169 departments and agencies into eight, giving him complete control as well as a more reasonable budget. The party was not only without power, but without financial resources. One solution was the issuance of liquor franchises, following the repeal of Prohibition, to those willing to contribute to the party's funds.

McNutt's most publicized innovation — and one the Republicans quickly adopted when they returned to power — was the establishment of the "Two Per Cent Club." Not an actual club, it was a system of collection of two percent of the salaries of all state employees for the coffers of the party in power. The practice was not changed until 1974.

It is generally believed that McNutt was given a series of federal posts after his governorship because his political power made him a possible presidential rival of Franklin D. Roosevelt. His posts included those of U.S. high commissioner (1937-39, 1945-46) and ambassador (1946-47) to the Philippines, head of the Federal Security Agency (1939-45), director of Defense, Health and Welfare Services (1941-43), and chairman of the War Manpower Commission (1942-45). McNutt served as chairman of the board of the Philippine-American Life Insurance Company after 1948 and practiced law in New York City and Washington, D.C.

NICHOLSON, MEREDITH (b. Dec. 9, 1866—d. Dec. 20, 1947) was a writer of best-selling novels and an essayist of distinction whose fondness for Indiana shone through his works.

Born at Crawfordsville, Nicholson spent most of his life in Indianapolis. After nine years in the public schools, he spurned further formal education to the regret of his mother, a nurse for the South during the Civil War. His father had fought with Indiana troops for the North.

Nicholson held a variety of jobs before he became involved in newspaper journalism. His writing career was established in 1900 with the publication of *The Hoosiers,* a book of essays about many aspects of Indiana life and lore, including the mysterious origin of the Hoosier sobriquet. His novels, fashioned into the literary mold of the day, were smoothly written in a highly readable style. Publication of *The Main Chance* (1903) and *Zelda*

Dameron (1904) brought him national reknown. His *The House of a Thousand Candles* (1905) drew warm notices in France.

Nicholson, a Jeffersonian .Democrat, held deep beliefs in democracy, in self-government, and in tolerance. For years he worked and wrote for the Democratic Party. He was named U.S. minister to Paraguay (1933-34), Venezuela (1935-38), and Nicaragua (1938-41).

After his foray into diplomacy, Nicholson returned to Indianapolis, where he had been a great friend of the poet James Whitcomb Riley. Nicholson's *The Poet* (1914) is a fictionalized biography of Riley. Heeding his mother's advice about education, he taught himself Latin, Greek, French, and Italian. Nicholson was awarded several honorary degrees, honorary membership in Phi Beta Kappa, and membership in the American Academy of Arts and Letters.

PORTER, COLE (b. June 9, 1892—d. Oct. 15, 1964) was a composer who wrote songs for more than 30 musical comedies including *Kiss Me Kate* and *Can Can.*

Porter was born in Peru, Indiana. He received considerable musical training during his childhood in a wealthy farm environment. While he studied for a bachelor of arts degree at Yale University (1909-13), he wrote music and lyrics for programs sponsored by his fraternity and the Yale Dramatic Association. He attended Harvard Law School for one semester during 1914, and then entered the university's graduate music school (1915-16). During this time he wrote *See America First* (1916). his first Broadway musical comedy and his most dismal failure.

Porter then went to North Africa to entertain the French Foreign Legion. He served in the French army during World War I and had a brief period of study with the French composer, Vincent d'Indy. After returning to New York City, he wrote the scores and lyrics for two mildly successful Broadway musicals, *Hitchy-koo* (1919) and *Greenwich Village Follies* (1924). An unproductive period ended in 1927 when Porter wrote the score for the musical *Paris* (1928), for which he composed one of his most popular tunes. "Let's Do It Again." Porter's reputation as one of the most talented lyricist of his time was further enhanced by his composition of scores for a string of successful musicals such as *Fifty Million Frenchmen* (1929), *The Gay Divorcee* (1932), *Anything Goes* (1934), and *Jubilee* (1935). From these and some of his other musicals came the songs most associated with the Porter name—"Night and Day," "Just One of Those Things," "You're the Top," "I Get a Kick Out of You," "Begin the Beguine," "Anything Goes," and "In the Still of the Night."

In 1937, Porter was severely crippled in an accident while horseback riding. He continued his highly prolific career, however, with productions such as *DuBarry Was a Lady* (1939; and *Kiss Me Kate* (1948), which some critics consider to be his best work. His last two musicals—*Can Can* (1953) and *Silk Stockings* (1955)—also enjoyed high levels of success. Ill health and the amputation of his right leg in 1958 led him to a self-imposed confinement which lasted until his death in Santa Monica, California.

PORTER, GENE (VA) STRATTON (b. August 17, 1863, Wabash County, Indiana—d. December 6, 1924) novelist and naturalist.

Geneva Stratton was born on a farm in Wabash County, Indiana, the twelfth child of a Methodist minister. In October, 1874, Geneva and her family moved to Wabash, Indiana where she received most of her formal education. Two years after her marriage to Charles D. Porter in 1866, the couple moved to Geneva, Indiana where Gene spent a great deal of her time in Limberlost Swamp where she took nature photographs for *Recreation* magazine.

Her first literary work, "Laddie, the Princess and the Pie" was published in *Metropolitan* magazine in 1901. She later returned to writing novels which, in some cases were geared strictly toward her interest in nature. In other cases, her novels combined the elements of romance, adventure and sentimentality. Such works include: *Laddie* (1913), *Freckles* (1904), *A Girl of the Limberlost* (1909), *The Song of the Cardinal* (1902), *The Harvester* (1911), *Birds of the Limberlost* (1914) and *Moths of the Limberlost* (1912).

After World War I Porter and her family moved to California where she wrote editorials for *McCalls* Magazine and organized a company to make movies based on her novels.

By the time of her death in an automobile accident in 1924, Porter's books had sold more than ten million copies. Her biography, *The Lady of the Limberlost* (1928) was written posthumously by her daughter, Jeanette Porter Meehan.

PYLE, ERNEST TAYLOR "ERNIE" (b. Aug. 3, 1900—d. April 18, 1945) was one of the most well-known U.S. war correspondents during World War II. .

Pyle was born near Dana, Indiana. He left Indiana University in his senior year in 1923 for a job on a LaPorte, Indiana, newspaper. Within months he was recruited by the Scripps-Howard newspaper chain and worked as a reporter and copy reader for the Washington, D.C., *Daily News.* After two years on New York City newspapers, he returned to the *Daily News* as telegraph editor. He wrote a well-received aviation column, and reluctantly served as managing editor.

In 1935 Pyle received an assignment as a roving reporter from Scripps-Howard. Drawing national attention, he roamed across the country and abroad, writing a daily column about whatever he chose. At the height of his fame, his column was printed in 366 daily and 310 weekly newspapers. Whenever the occasion allowed, Pyle would detour through Indiana to visit his mother, father, and aunt, Mary Bales.

Pyle covered World War II from the viewpoint of the foot soldiers, slogging it out with them in North Africa, Sicily, Italy, and France. He was awarded the Pulitzer Prize in 1944. He covered the war on Iwo Jima and Okinawa and was killed by Japanese machine-gun fire on Ie Shima, a small island off the tip of Okinawa.

RALSTON, SAMUEL MOFFETT (b. Dec. 1, 1857—d. Oct. 14, 1925) was the 28th governor of Indiana, and a United States senator. During his tenure as governor, the state debt was paid and the state park system was established.

Ralston was born in Tuscarawas County, Ohio, but soon moved to a farm in Indiana. The property was lost in the panic of 1873 and his father turned to mining. As a youth, Ralston farmed, mined, and assisted a butcher. He graduated from Central Indiana Normal College in Danville in 1884 and then read law for one year at Spencer. Ralston was admitted to the bar in 1886, and established his practice in Lebanon.

At first Ralston was unable to attain public office. In 1908, when a deadlock for the gubernatorial nomination occurred, he withdrew in favor of the future U.S. vice president, Thomas R. Marshall.

Ralston secured the governorship for one term (1913-17) in the next election, however. He was elected to the U.S. Senate in 1922, and died in office. At the national Democratic Party convention of 1924, he had received 196½ votes for the presidential nomination, but withdrew despite urging to the contrary from his fellow Indianans.

Big in spirit—he is recalled as earnest, modest, and courageous—he was also large in physique, more than six feet in height and 300 pounds in weight. He was a believer in the principles of Thomas Jefferson, and his important legal cases centered on equity and constitutionality of the laws.

RILEY, JAMES WHITCOMB (b. October 7, 1849, Greenville, Indiana—d. July 22, 1916, Indianapolis, Indiana.)

Writer whose dialect poems about the lives of the country people of Indiana earned him the reputation of "The Hoosier Poet." Riley left school at the age of 16 to travel around Indiana painting signs and advertisements on houses, barns, and fences. Further travels as a musician in a medicine show ended when he returned to Greenville, Indiana where he joined the staff of the Greenville *Times*. Riley later became the local editor of the Anderson *Democrat*. He was forced to resign from this position as a result of the so called "Leonainei hoax" in which Riley, wishing to prove the instant popularity awarded a poem assumed to be written by an established writer, wrote a poem in the style of Edgar Allen Poe. The poem was published in a rival paper under the pretense of a newly discovered work of "a genius known to fame". The poem caused quite a stir among prominent literary critics until the true identity of the author was revealed.

From 1877 to 1885, Riley was affiliated with the Indianapolis *Journal* from whom he wrote the folksy poems in Hoosier dialect which were to make him famous. Riley published his poems under the pen name of Benjamin F. Johnson of Boone whom the readers were led to believe was an area farmer. During this time, Riley wrote one of his most famous works—"When Frost is on the Punkin'".

Riley's collection of poems *The Old Swimmin' Hole and 'Leven More Poems* (1883) sold more than half a million copies and was

Sources:
Herzberg, *The Readers' Encyclopedia of American Literature*
Kunitz and Haycroft, *American Authors 1600-1900*
McGraw Hill, *Encyclopaedia of World Biography*

followed by 40 more books in which he created such literary characters as "Little Orphan Annie," "The Raggedy Man," and "Nine Little Goblins."

ROCKNE, KNUTE KENNETH (March 4, 1888-March 31, 1931) was a football coach who, with an alchemy all his own, molded the nation into a vast fan club for the University of Notre Dame football teams.

Rockne was born in Voss, Norway, and emigrated with his family to Chicago, Illinois, when he was five years of age. After high school he worked for four years in the post office to earn enough money to attend the University of Notre Dame in South Bend, Indiana, where he became a football and track star. Rockne was graduated in 1914 and returned to the university as a teacher of chemistry and an assistant football coach. He was head football coach from 1918 until his death in an airplane crash in Kansas.

Rockne taught summer football schools across the country at the height of his career. He accepted numerous after-dinner speaking invitations and was the author of many articles on sports. A stickler for details, which he often carried out himself, he nonetheless had time to talk kindly with parents whose sons had not won a coveted position on Rockne's team. For the boys who played for him, he pricked with wit any ballooning football ego. He understood the players, and they responded enthusiastically.

As a strategist, Coach Rockne had no peer. He brought new concepts to the game including the forward pass, the Notre Dame shift, and the substitution of entire teams during a game. Even while he lived, legends grew about him. He coached such famous players as George Gipp and the Four Horsemen. His 13-year record was 105 victories, 12 defeats, and 5 ties, with 5 undefeated seasons.

Newspapers across the country carried column after column about Rockne when he died. Damon Runyon said: "The entire world of sport will mourn his passing. And the nation generally must deplore the death of a man who was one of its greatest men makers and one of its finest influences for good."

SKELTON, RICHARD BERNARD "RED" (b. July 18, 1913-   ) is a famous U.S. comedian.

Skelton was born in Vincennes, Indiana, two months after the death of his father, a circus clown. The indigence of his family caused him to seek employment at an early age and to later leave school while a seventh grade student. His debut as an entertainer came at the age of ten, when he toured with the "Doc" R.E. Lewis Medicine Show. This was followed by tours with a tent show, a minstrel group, a showboat act, and the Hagenbeck and Wallace Circus that had also employed Skelton's father. When 17 years of age, he married Edna Stilwell, who became his partner, scriptwriter, and agent. The couple toured the U.S. and Canada as a vaudeville team during the 1930s, achieving varying degrees of success.

Skelton made his first radio and Broadway guest appearances in 1937. The following year, while entertaining at the White House during Pres. Franklin D. Roosevelt's campaign against infantile paralysis, he met the screen actor Mickey Rooney, who arranged Skelton's first appearance in motion pictures. His career blossomed during the 1940s, when he received numerous motion picture and radio assignments and became a popular entertainer among World War II servicemen. Skelton made more than 30 movies before turning his attention to television during the early 1950s. His biggest success, the *Red Skelton Show,* was broadcast for 18 years. The changing taste of television viewers made an attempt to establish a second program a failure. Skelton retired from show business in 1972, greatly disillusioned by what he considered unfair treatment from television network executives.

STEELE, THEODORE CLEMENT (b. Sept. 22, 1847—d. July 24, 1926) was an accomplished portraitist and still-life artist and founder of the Indiana School of Art.

Steele was born in Owen County, Indiana, and educated at Waveland Collegiate Institute, Waveland, Indiana (1859-68). While a student at the Institute, he taught drawing to his fellow classmates and eventually became popular for his exceptional portait painting abilities.

In 1872 Steele moved to Indianapolis, where he earned a living painting portraits. His reputation in the city as an outstanding artist precipitated the formation of a citizens' group intent upon raising the necessary funds to permit Steele to study abroad. As a result of the efforts of this group, he was able to enter the Royal Academy of Munich in 1880 to study under Gyula Benczur and

Ludwig von Lofftz. Steele returned to Indianapolis in 1885 and established the Indiana School of Art four years later. In 1890 he published *The Steele Portfolio,* a volume of photogravure prints of portraits, still lifes, and landscapes. His awards and honors include an honorable mention at the Paris Exposition of 1900 and a 1910 Fine Arts Corporation prize. "Gordon Hill," "Oaks at Vernon," "Portrait of Rev. N.A. Hyde," "Whitewater Valley," and "Landscape" are some of his better known paintings.

TARKINGTON, (NEWTON) BOOTH (b. July 29, 1869—d. May 19, 1946) was an author and dramatist whose portrayal of life in the Midwest pleased the nation over a remarkably long period.

Tarkington was born in Indianapolis to an affluent family. Educated at Phillips Exeter Academy, Purdue University, and Princeton University, he earned a questionable reputation in the staid Indianapolis of the 1890s for writing all night. Otherwise, he was the gentleman about town that novels of the era so often depicted.

Tarkington spent much time abroad, and in New York City and Maine, but kept strong ties and a home in Indiana. A sentimental realist, he portrayed Midwestern America as it was, and people happily recognized themselves in his works. His first published work, *The Gentleman from Indiana* was serialized in *McClure's* magazine in 1899.

Tarkington gradually evolved his own brand of realism, with emphasis on character and humor. His light touch was most evident in his studies of adolescents, such as *Penrod* (1914) and *Seventeen* (1916). He was twice awarded the Pulitzer Prize for fiction. The prize-winning novels were *The Magnificent Ambersons,* a socio-economic study of a "better" family on the decline, and *Alice Adams,* character study of a girl faced with impossible odds in courting competition. Tarkington also collaborated with Henry Leon Wilson, Julian Street, and E.G. Sutherland on a number of successful comedies for the stage.

Tarkington found his material everywhere, including the Indiana General Assembly, in which he spent one term (1902-03) as a Republican delegate. Despite an utter inability to speak in public, he disagreed with the governor and learned the workings of politics. This paralysis on the public platform led him in later years to refuse honorary degrees rather than be forced to appear on the dais to receive them.

Tarkington died in the Indianapolis he had seen change from a peaceful rural town to a bustling, dirty city. Even his severest critics admitted that he saw with a critical eye, and wrote with insight and sympathy.

TECUMSEH (b. 1768—d. Oct. 5, 1813) was a Shawnee chief who organized an Indian confederation in the early 1800s in an unsuccessful attempt to prevent white expansion into the Ohio Valley.

Tecumseh was born in the village of Piqua near present-day Springfield, Ohio. He was the fifth child of the Shawnee chief, Puckeshinwa, who died as a result of Indian-white hostilities when Tecumseh was six years old. He was later adopted by Chief Blackfish who, with Tecumseh's older brothers was responsible for most of his early training as a warrior and a hunter.

About 1787, Tecumseh and a band of Shawnee led by his brother, Cheeseekan, went south to join the Cherokee in their fight against the white settlers. Upon the death of his brother, Tecumseh assumed the leadership of the band, and remained in the South for three years. Soon after his return to the Northwest Territory, he became a scout for the Shawnee chief, Blue Jacket, assisting him in his defeat of Gen. Arthur St. Clair in 1791 and in the Battle of Fallen Timbers of 1794, in which Blue Jacket and Little Turtle were defeated by Gen. Anthony Wayne.

The idea of a league of Indians was first presented at an Indian council held at Greenville in 1807, when Tecumseh strongly denounced the treaties that gave the settlers claim to land north of the Ohio River. Tecumseh believed in the community principle of land ownership, asserting that no one tribe had the right to sign treaties that gave away the land. Tecumseh and his brother, Tenkswatawa, the Shawnee Prophet, began organizing the Indians with the objectives of regaining the land that had been taken and preventing the further signing of treaties such as those that had recently turned nearly half of the present state of Indiana over to the U.S. government.

The confederacy was still in the organizing stages when it suffered irreparable damage with the defeat of Tenskwatawa in the Battle of Tippecanoe in 1811. The battle was ill-planned and unsanctioned by Tecumseh, who was away trying to gain the support of southern Indian tribes. The subsequent weakening of the confederacy caused Tecumseh to side with the British in the

War of 1812 with the hopes that the combined efforts of the British and Indians could defeat the Americans.

Tecumseh died in 1813 in the Battle of the Thames near present-day Chatham, Ontario. His death caused the collapse of the confederacy and signalled the end of Indian resistance to white settlement in the Northwest Territory.

VONNEGUT, KURT, JR. (b. Nov. 11, 1922-   ) is a novelist and playwright whose works are popular among U.S. college students. His novels seem inherently a criticism of society, although he denies that they contain any great truths.

Vonnegut was born in Indianapolis and graduated from Shortridge High School. His studies at Cornell University (1940-42) were interrupted by the outbreak of World War II. Vonnegut served in the U.S. Army, was captured by the Germans, and survived the bombing of Dresden, Germany, in February 1945.

While studying at the University of Chicago (1945-47), Vonnegut worked as a newsman and corporation publicist. He began his career as a freelance writer in 1950. Recognition of his works came in the 1960s, and he has since held positions with the University of Iowa (1965-67) and Harvard University (1970).

Vonnegut's novels include *Player Piano* (1952), *Sirens of Titan* (1959), *Mother Night* (1961), *Cat's Cradle* (1963), *God Bless You, Mr. Rosewater* (1965), *Slaughterhouse Five, or The Children's Crusade* (1969), and *Breakfast of Champions* (1973). He has also written *Welcome to the Monkey House* (1968), a collection of short stories, and *Happy Birthday, Wanda June* (1970), a play. He received the literature award of the National Institute of Arts and Letters in 1970.

The popularity of Vonnegut's books among college students in the 1960s surprised the author. He believes that perhaps they shared his concept of the importance of our planet. Vonnegut claims that he became a writer because he kept out of the clutches of English teachers. His 'crazy ideas about socialism and pacifism,'' however, were acquired in the public schools of his native Indianapolis.

Slaughterhouse Five is the result of his presence as a prisoner-of-war in Dresden during the Allied firebombing that killed 135,000. Bits and pieces of that experience are seen by critics in his earlier works, as well.

WALLACE, LEWIS (b. April 10, 1837—d. Feb. 14, 1905) was a Civil War military leader and author of popular novels including *Ben Hur: A Tale of the Christ.*

Wallace was born in Brookville, Indiana. He preferred adventure to study and as a result received a minimum of formal education. His father's election to the Indiana governorship in 1837 necessitated a move to Indianapolis, where Wallace studied law in his father's law office. Upon the outbreak of the Mexican War in 1846, Wallace organized an army of volunteers. He returned to Indianapolis after the war and was admitted to the bar in 1849. He then established a law practice and served two terms (1850 and 1852) as the prosecuting attorney of Covington, Indiana. In 1853, Wallace moved to Crawfordsville and three years later was elected to the Indiana Senate, where he advocated a change in divorce laws and the popular election of U.S. senators.

The onset of the Civil War brought Wallace the appointment of adjutant general of the state militia and, soon afterwards, of colonel of a volunteer regiment. He played a decisive role in the fighting at Harper's Ferry and Romney. His part in the capture of Fort Donelson led to his promotion to major-general on March 21, 1862. The following year, he prevented the capture of Cincinnati and was awarded the command of the Middle Division and the 8th Army Corps in Baltimore, Maryland. Commanding 4,800 men, he helped defend Washington, D.C., against a force of 28,000 men under Gen. Jubal A. Early in July 1864. Before leaving the army in November 1865, Wallace served on the court martial panels that tried the men implicated in the assassination of Pres. Abraham Lincoln and that tried Henry Wirz, commander of the Confederate prison camp at Andersonville, Georgia.

In 1866 Wallace spent several months in Mexico assisting Benito Juarez in his fight against Maximilian and the French. He returned to Crawfordsville, where he established a law practice and ran an unsuccessful campaign for a Republican seat in the U.S. Congress. In 1878 Wallace assumed the governorship of New Mexico, and held the post until Pres. Garfield appointed him to a four-year term as minister to Turkey in 1881.

Wallace is best known for his novels, the most famous of which, *Ben Hur,* was published in 1880. Other works include *The Fair God* (1873), *The Life of Benjamin Harrison* (1888), *The Boyhood of Christ* (1888), and *The Prince of India* (1893). Wallace died in Crawfordsville. *Lew Wallace: An Autobiography* (1906) was completed posthumously by his wife.

WAYNE, ANTHONY (b. Jan. 1, 1745—d. Dec. 15, 1796) was an American Revolutionary War general whose victory at the Battle of Fallen Timbers ended Indian resistance to white settlement in the Ohio Valley.

Wayne was born on the family farm of Waynesborough, near present-day Paoli, Pennsylvania, and attended an academy in Philadelphia (1761-63). His training as a land surveyor helped him secure a position in a surveying expedition of Nova Scotia in 1765. He returned to Pennsylvania in 1766 and was eventually elected to several public offices. During the pre-Revolutionary War period, he was aided in the formulation of formal protest resolutions against the British and the organization of a regional army.

On Jan. 3, 1776, Wayne was commissioned colonel of the 4th Pennsylvania Battalion of the Continental Army. His regiment was sent to assist Gen. Benedict Arnold in his retreat from Canada. Wayne then assumed command of Fort Ticonderoga and remained there until February 1777, when he was promoted to brigadier general and ordered to join George Washington's army at Morristown, New Jersey. His participation in the Battle of Brandywine (September 1777) was followed by a dramatic defeat at Paoli, for which he was charged and later cleared of negligence. He resumed his military duties in the battles of Germantown (October 1777) and Monmouth (June 1778).

In 1779, the army was reorganized and Wayne was put in charge of a light infantry brigade. Leading these troops, he captured Stony Point (July 16, 1779), the northernmost British fort on the Hudson River, and prevented Benedict Arnold from turning West Point over to the British (September 1780). Another notable victory came the next year with the defeat of Cornwallis in Green Spring, Virginia. After the British surrender at Yorktown, Virginia, in October 1781, Wayne was assigned to aid Gen. Nathanael Green in disarming the British, Loyalists, and Creek Indians in Georgia. A defeat by Wayne of the Indians in May 1782 resulted in successful treaty negotiations with the Creek and Cherokee.

Wayne retired from the army in 1783 and embarked upon a political career. He held a series of offices including one in the

Pennsylvania Council of Censors (1783) and another in the Pennsylvania General Assembly (1784-85). In 1785 he moved to Georgia, where he made an unsuccessful attempt to farm a rice planation given to him by the state for his military service. From 1791 to 1792 he served in the Georgia House of Representatives, but was forced to vacate his seat because of charges of election irregularities.

The unsuccessful campaigns of Gen. Joseph Harmar and Gen. Arthur St. Clair against the Indians of the Northwest Territory brought about another reorganization of the army in 1792. Wayne was commissioned commander-in-chief of the forces and during the next two years he produced a well-trained force of 1,000 men. His march from Pennsylvania to the Northwest Territory was marked by the establishment of Forts Washington, Greenville, and Defiance, which were used to train the soldiers in the basics of Indian warfare.

The inevitable clash between "Mad Anthony" and the Indians came on Aug. 20, 1794, when Wayne attacked and defeated the Indian forces at the Battle of Fallen Timbers, near the present-day city of Toledo, Ohio. Wayne's victory, combined with the Jay Treaty with England which withdrew British support from the Indians, made the defeated tribes more willing to negotiate peace. The result was the 1795 Treaty of Greenville, by which the Indians ceded land in the present states of Ohio, Indiana, Illinois, and Michigan to the U.S. government. In August 1796, Wayne took command of the British fort in Detroit. He died at Presque Isle (now Erie), Pennsylvania, during the withdrawal of his troops from the fort.

WRIGHT, WILBUR (b. April 16, 1867—d. May 30, 1912) was an engineer and inventor who, together with his younger brother Orville, built the world's first successful powered airplane.

Wright, born in Millville, Indiana, was the third of five surviving children of Milton Wright, a bishop of the United Brethren in Christ church. As young boys, Wilbur and Orville (b. Aug. 19, 1871, in Dayton, Ohio) earned money by selling home-crafted mechanical toys. They also published the *West Side News,* a weekly newspaper edited by Wilbur and printed on a press of Orville's design. About 1892 they opened the Wright Cycle Company where they sold, repaired, and later manufac-tured bicycles.

The written works and subsequent death in 1896 of the German aeronaut, Gustav Lilienthal, inspired the brothers to begin experimenting in the area of aeronautics. In 1899, Wilbur built and tested the first product of their efforts—a biplane kite with a wing spread of five feet and three-axis control. The results of this and similar experiments made it possible for Wilbur and Orville to construct a much-improved glider, which they tested in September 1900 at Kill Devil Hills near Kitty Hawk, North Carolina. In 1902 and 1903, they made nearly 1,000 manned glider flights at Kitty Hawk. This eventually led to the development of a glider with a complete system of control, improved wing design, and greater stability. In 1903, a four-cylinder, twelve horsepower motor was mounted on one such glider and tested at Kitty Hawk by Wilbur and Orville on Dec. 17 of that year. The world's first powered flight was made by Orville, who remained in flight for 12 seconds. The fourth and final flight was made by Wilbur, who remained in flight for 59 seconds and covered 852 feet. An improved model was flown on Oct. 5, 1905, at Huffman Field in Dayton, covering a total of 24 miles, and on May 22, 1906, Wilbur and Orville received a patent for the world's first airplane.

European governments were the first to show interest in the Wrights' invention. Consequently, Wilbur spent part of 1908 and 1909 making demonstration flights in England, France, and Italy.

The U.S. Army awarded them a contract for the world's first military plane in 1909, and The Wright Company was organized to commercially manufacture the Wright airplane. The brothers were occupied in improving their planes and training pilots to fly them when Wilbur contracted typhoid fever and died in Dayton.

ADRIANNE CARTER

HELEN CONNOR

* * *

Helen Connor

Frank Borman

218

Helen Connor

Otis R. Bowen

Helen Connor

Charles C. Deam

Helen Connor

Eugene V. Debs

Helen Connor

Theodore Dreiser

222

Helen Connor

Charles A. Halleck

Caleb Mills

Paul McNutt

Helen Connor

Meredith Nicholson

Helen Connor

James Oliver

Helen Connor

Robert Owen

228

Helen Connor

Samuel Ralston

Knute Rockne (*ca.* 1930)

Helen Connor   James Whitcomb Riley

Helen Connor

Booth Tarkington

Helen Connor

Rawson Vaile

Kurt Vonnegut

234

Helen Connor

Harvey W. Wiley

Chronology of
INDIANA

20,000 BC—Probable arrival of early man to Indiana.

19,000 BC—Paleo-Indians were probably nomadic hunters.

7,000 BC—Indian Knoll and Glacial Kame cultures develop and their members become the first sedentary inhabitants of Indiana.

500 BC—Adena mound builders come to Indiana. Gradual introduction of domesticated plants takes place.

AD 100—Hopewell culture reached its zenith. Mounds reached their largest and most elaborate stage.

AD 500—The Mississippian Period of cultural development began. Ceramics, house construction, and agricultural methods were well developed.

1400—The first true "Indiana Indians" of the Tennessee-Cumberland and Fort Ancient variants infiltrated southern Indiana.

1609—The northwest country granted to Virginia by charter.

1671—France took possession of the "West" at Sault Sainte Marie.

1679—Exploring party headed by Robert Cavelier Sieur De La Salle crosses St. Joseph-Kankakee portage near South Bend sometime in December. He becomes first known white man to explore Indiana soil.

1681—LaSalle meets with Miami Indians in Oak Tree Council and negotiates treaty against Iroquois.

1720—French build Fort Ouiatenon near present Lafayette to guard the Maumee-Wabash route.

1722—French build Fort Miami on present site of Fort Wayne.

1732—French build their largest fort, Vincennes, on present site of Vincennes.

1749—Beginning of extant records in Vincennes Roman Catholic Church, first church in Indiana.

1760—Montreal surrenders to British in French and Indian War and all of New France, including forts in Indiana, pass into hands of British.

1763—French and Indian War ends with Treaty of Paris, Feb. 10. France cedes to Great Britain all of her territory east of Mississippi.

Pontiac's Rebellion, May 7-Nov. 28. Among forts taken by Indians are Miami, May 27 and Ouiatenon, June 1.

1763—Royal Proclamation, Oct. 7, forbids settlement west of the Appalachian watershed. Land is reserved for Indians and licensed fur traders.

1774—Quebec Act extends Canada's boundaries to the Ohio River.

1775—American Revolution begins with battles of Lexington and Concord.

1777—Col. Henry Hamilton, governor of Detroit, dispatches Northwest Indians and British soldiers to destroy Kentucky outposts and settlements.

1778—Kentuckian George Rogers Clark, armed with authority of State of Virginia, assembles a force of 200 men and captures forts at Kaskaskia in southern Illinois· and Vincennes. The latter fort is recaptured by British under Hamilton, Dec. 17.

1779—Clark musters his forces and after an incredible march across flooded lands in dead of winter, recaptures Vincennes and sends Hamilton to Virginia as a prisoner.

1780—Virginia legislature presents 150,000 acres of Indiana land to Clark and his soldiers in Indiana.

1781—Don Pierro, Spanish commander of St. Louis, captures British post of St. Joseph, laying basis for Spanish claim to territory northwest of the Ohio River.

1783—Official end of Revolutionary War.

1784—Former soldiers of Clark begin construction of Clarksville, the first authorized settlement in Northwest Territory. Virginia formally ceded its western lands to the U.S.

1785—Congress adopted plan for the orderly settlement of the Northwest Territory. Townships were to be six miles square, divided into 36 sections with each 16th section reserved for the support of common schools. The minimum purchase of land was 640 acres at no less than $1 per acre.

1787—Congress adopted the Ordinance of 1787 that provided for government of the Northwest Territory and allowed for the ultimate attainment of statehood. Slavery was excluded from the territory.

1788—Arthur St. Clair, first governor of the Northwest Territory, arrived at the capital of Marietta, Ohio.

1790—Knox County, embracing all of Indiana and parts of Ohio, Michigan, Illinois, and Wisconsin, was organized by Winthrop Sargent, secretary to the governor of the Northwest Territory.

Northwest Indians, smarting under the peace treaty of 1783, launched a series of fierce raids led by Chief Little Turtle. Gen. Joseph Harmar marched against the Indians, but suffered two overwhelming defeats.

Gen. Charles Scott and 800 men destroyed Indian villages of Ouiatenon, near present-day Lafayette, and Kethippecanunk, at the mouth of the Tippecanoe River, June 1-3.

Col. James Wilkinson destroyed the Eel River village near present-day Logansport in August.

1791—Gov. St. Clair, acting on orders from Congress, marched against Little Turtle in November, but was overwhelmingly defeated in a surprise attack on his headquarters near the headwater of the Wabash.

1792—Gen. Anthony Wayne, Revolutionary War veteran, was appointed by Pres. Washington to lead a special force of 5,000 troops against the Indians. Wayne spent the next two years drilling and equipping his army and urging the Indians to accept a peace treaty.

1794—Gen. Wayne defeated the Indian forces in the Battle of Fallen Timbers, near present-day Toledo, Ohio, on August 20. Wayne's decisive victory marked the end of Indian power in the area and of the Miami confederacy.

Fort Wayne was built at the headwaters of the Maumee River on the site of the Indian town of Kekionga and French post of Miamis.

1795—Gen. Wayne and the Indians signed the treaty of Fort Greenville on August 3. Under its provisions, the Indians ceded the greater part of Ohio and a slice of southeastern Indiana to the U.S.

1798—A Baptist church, said to be the first Protestant church in Indiana, was organized at Owen's Creek, Knox County.

1800—Congress on May 7 divided the Northwest Territory into the Ohio and Indiana territories. The Harrison Land Law provided for the sale of half sections of 320 acres to be sold for small down payments made in four annual installments.

1801—William Henry Harrison assumed his duties as the first governor of Indiana Territory at the capital of Vincennes. Clark County was created from part of Knox County. The town of Lawrenceburg, Carlyle, and Vevay were founded.

1802—Harrison concluded the first of a series of treaties with the Indians. Within the next eight years, the Indians would give up their claims to the southern third of the state.

1802—Swiss colonists settled at Vevay in future Switzerland County and established the first permanent vineyard community in the U.S. Jeffersonville was founded.

1804—Elihu Stout published Indiana Territory's first newspaper, the weekly *Indiana Gazette,* in Vincennes. When the plant burned down two years later, he rebuilt it and published under the name of *Western Sun.*

With the population totalling more than 5,000, Indiana Territory became eligible to elect a legislature.

1805—First territorial election was held and first sessions of territorial legislature met at Vincennes.

Michigan Territory was organized from part of Indiana

Territory. Towns of Richmond, Madison, and Mount Vernon were founded.

1806—Vincennes University, the first state insitution of higher learning in Indiana, was incorporated by the territorial legislature. First circulating library was established at Vincennes.

1807—Territorial laws were published.

1808—Harrison County, named for William Henry Harrison, became the first county to be organized by the territorial legislature on Oct. 11. Corydon, the future state capital, was platted.

1809—Illinois Territory was detached from Indiana Territory on February 9.

Charleston and Brookville were founded.

First Masonic lodge was organized at Vincennes.

Treaty of Fort Wayne was ratified, enabling Gov. Harrison to purchase 3,000,000 acres of land for $10,000 and a small annuity.

1810—Tecumseh, a chief of the Shawnee, held two meetings with Gov. Harrison at Vincennes and demanded the return of Indian lands.

1811—Gov. Harrison and the Indians clashed at the Battle of Tippecanoe. Although Harrison's victory was not clear cut, it marked the fall of the Indian army east of the Mississippi River and ended Tecumseh's dream of an Indian confederacy.

1812—War of 1812 began in the area with the attack on Fort Dearborn (now Chicago) and the fall of Detroit. The Indians, allied with the British, failed to capture Fort Wayne or Fort Harrison. Col. John B. Campbell destroyed the Miami forces on the Mississinewa. Twenty inhabitants of Pigeon Roost in present day Scott County were massacred by Indians.

1813—Territorial capital was moved from Vincennes to Corydon. John Posey became governor, succeeding acting-governor John Gibson, who had been appointed upon Harrison's resignation to command troops in the War of 1812.

1814—Banks were chartered at Vincennes and Madison.

A German cooperative society, the Harmonits or Rappites, led by George Rapp established a communal colony on 24,000 acres in Posey County.

Rising Sun and Salem were founded.

Census figures revealed a free white population of 63,897 in the territory.

1815—Indiana submitted the memorial for statehood, asking authority to hold a constitutional convention in 1816.

Bloomington and Orleans were founded.

1816—Pres. Madison signed the enabling act creating the state of Indiana on April 19. Delegates met at Corydon and drew up the first state constitution, June 10-29. Jonathan Jennings was named the first state governor in the elections of August 5. The first General Assembly met at Corydon and named James Noble and Waller Taylor as U.S. Senators and William Hendricks as the U.S. Representative for Indiana.

Indiana was formally admitted to the Union at the 19th state on December 11.

Family of Abraham Lincoln moved to Little Pigeon Creek in Spencer County.

Terre Haute was founded.

1817—First medical society in the state was organized by Vincennes physicians.

1818—Indians met with U.S. Commissioners at St. Mary's, Ohio, and signed the "New Purchase" treaty, which opened the middle third of the state of Indiana to white settlement.

1819—Jacob Whetzel cut a 60-mile trace from Laurel to the bluffs of the White River, thereby establishing the first east-west route in central Indiana.

1820—Legislature-appointed commissioners chose the site at the juncture of the White River and Fall Creek as the location of the new state capital.

1821—Legislature accepted recommendations of the commissioners and named the proposed capital, Indianapolis. Sale of lots in the city began on October 9.

1823—Alexis Coquillard established a fur trading post at the present site of South Bend. Noblesville, Crawfordsville, and Anderson were founded.

1824—U.S. mail delivery by stagecoach began operating between Vincennes and Louisville on April 10.

Indiana Seminary opened at Bloomington with ten students.

1825—State capital was moved to Indianapolis.

Robert Owen bought New Harmony from Frederick Rapp on January 2, and launched a new Utopian experiment in communal living. Lafayette and Muncie were founded.

General Assembly established the Indiana State Library.

1826—Treaty was negotiated with the Potawatomi Indians, securing land for the northern section of the Michigan Road from Lake Michigan to the Ohio River.

"Boatload of Knowledge" arrived with the new settlers at New Harmony. Owen's experiment produced the first kindergarten, first night school, first trade school, and first dramatic club in the state.

Treaty of Wabash was signed in which the Indians ceded most of their lands lying north and west of the Wabash River to the U.S.

1827—Survey of the National Road across Indiana was completed.

Congress granted land to Indiana for construction of the Wabash and Erie Canal.

Presbyterians established Hanover College, the first denominational college in Indiana.

1828—Stagecoach route was opened between Madison and Indianapolis.

Williamsport was founded.

First state Democratic convention was held in Indianapolis.

1829—Indiana Colonization Society was founded at Indianapolis for the purpose of sending blacks to Liberia.

Thornton, Gosport and Logansport were founded.

1830—Construction was underway on both the National and Michigan roads.

La Porte was founded.

Cholera epidemics that lasted throughout the decade took thousands of lives all over the state.

Lincoln family moved from Indiana to Illinois.

Indiana Historical Society was organized at Indianapolis.

1831—Marion was founded.

First known route of the Underground Railroad began operation at Cabin Creek, Randolph County.

1832—Three hundred troops mobilized at Indianapolis and marched off to the Black Hawk War, but arrived too late.

Wabash College was founded at Crawfordsville.

Michigan City was founded.

1834—Legislature chartered the second state bank with its ten branches supervised from a central office in the capital.

Plymouth and Shelbyville were founded.

Frances Slocum, the Quaker girl taken by the Indians in 1773 from her home in Pennsylvania was found living with her Miami family near Peru.

State's first railroad was founded as a short line in Shelbyville, the car pulled by horse.

Bishop Gabriel Brute arrived in Vincennes to organize the Indiana Roman Catholic diocese.

1835—First capitol building was completed at Indianapolis:

1836—Legislature passed the Mammoth Internal Improvement Bill, appropriating $10,000,000 for the construction of canals, railroads, and highways. Irish and German workmen were imported to build the canals. Construction of the railroad from Madison to Indianapolis was begun.

LaGrange was founded.

1837—Cannelton, where the first coal was mined for river steamers, was founded.

Indiana Asbury College (now DePauw University) was opened at Greencastle.

Indiana Baptist Mannual Labor Institute (now Franklin College) was opened at Franklin.

1838—Last of the Potawatomi Indians in northern Indiana were forced to leave the state under military escort in a "Trail of Death."

Indiana Seminary was restablished by legislative action as Indiana University.

1839—Work was abruptly halted on all internal improvement projects when the state found itself virtually bankrupt and in debt for $14,000,000. Investigation disclosed mismanagement and chicanery. To provide operating funds, the legislature issued scrip.

Lutherans founded Concordia College in Fort Wayne.

Henry Ward Beecher became pastor of the Second Presbyterian Church in Indianapolis.

Gov. David Wallace proclaimed the state's first and official Thanksgiving.

1840—William Henry Harrison, former governor of Indiana Territory and hero of the Battle of Tippecanoe, was elected U.S. President.

St.-Mary-of-the-Woods College opened at Terre Haute.

Census ennumerated Indiana's population at 685,866.

New Albany, with a population of 4,000, became the state's largest city.

1842—University of Notre Dame was founded at South Bend and chartered two years later.

First medical school in the state was established at LaPorte.

Sullivan was founded.

1843—Wabash and Erie Canal was formally opened at Fort Wayne on July 4.

1844—Madison and Indianapolis railroad reached Columbus.

Kokomo was founded.

1846—Mexican War began on May 11. During two years of war, Indiana contributed five regiments, a total of 5,000 men of whom 542 were killed in action.

Caleb Mills began his campaign for the establishment of a free system of public schools and wrote the first in a series of "messages" urging action.

1847—The Madison and Indianapolis railroad, begun eight years earlier reached Indianapolis on October 1.

Indianapolis was chartered as a city, elected its first mayor, and voted a school system.

State School for the Blind and State Hospital for the insane were constructed.

Quakers established a coeducational boarding school in Richmond that attained collegiate status as Earlham College in 1859.

1848—State-wide craze for the construction of plank roads began. During the following two years, part of the National and Michigan roads were planed, and many planked roads became toll roads.

1850—Constitutional convention met in Masonic Hall, Indianapolis, from October 7 to February 10, 1851.

State School for the Deaf established.

Population of the state numbered 988,416.

1851—Electorate ratified new state constitution, 113,230 voting for and 27,638 voting against it in August.

State Board of Agriculture was established.

Central Canal at Indianapolis was sold to a private firm.

Sarah Bolton achieved national fame with her poem, "Paddle Your Own Canoe."

1852—Tax-supported state public school system was established by law.

Liberalized banking law led to the establishment of many "wildcat" banks, a flood of worthless or devalued money, and serious economic problems.

Studebaker Brothers arrived in South Bend and began to develop the future Studebaker Corporation.

First Indiana State Fair was held in Indianapolis in October.

1853—Nation's first Union Station was opened in Indianapolis on September 30.

Wabash and Erie Canal, the world's largest, was completed but was already obsoleted because of competition from the railroads.

1854—General Assembly, over the governor's veto, approved the renewal of the charter of the Second Bank of Indiana. A scandal ensued when the bank was sold to a group of private investors.

State-wide prohibition law went into effect on July 1, but the Supreme Court struck down the measure in August.

First large coal mine opened in Sullivan County.

Indianapolis became the hub of eight railroads. Monon Railroad, connecting New Albany and Michigan City, was completed.

1855—Northwestern Christian University (now Butler University) opened in Indianapolis on November 1. It was one of the first colleges in the U.S. to admit students "without regard to sex, race or color."

Legislative Act, reminiscent of New England's "blue laws," imposed fines for quarreling, fishing, hunting, mail deliveries, or working on Sunday.

Eugene V. Debs, labor leader and Socialist, was born in Terre Haute.

1856—Oliver P. Morton was nominated for governor by the People's Party, forerunner of the Republican Party, but was unsuccessful in the fall election.

1857—St. Meinrad Seminary was opened in Spencer County.

Anti-slavery newspapers published in the state included the *Free Soil Democrat, Western Presage,* and *Indiana America* at Indianapolis. *Freie Press* was the first of a number of German language anti-slavery newspapers.

Fleeing slaves escaped to Canada on three routes of the Underground Railroad that ran through Indiana. Most of the "conductors" or "stationmasters" on the Railroad were Quakers.

1858—Indiana Academy of Science was organized in Indianapolis.

1859—Minerva Club, the first women's club in the U.S. with a constitution and by-laws, was organized at New Harmony.

First air-delivered mail was carried by balloon from Lafayette to Crawfordsville.

1860—Indiana delegates to the Republican convention at Chicago played a key role in Abraham Lincoln's nomination. In the fall elections, Lincoln carried the state and the Republicans and Harry S. Lane and Oliver P. Morton were elected governor and lieutenant governor, respectively.

Population of the state numbered 1,350,428.

1861—In keeping with pre-election bargain, Gov. Lane was named U.S. senator. He resigned as governor after three days in office and was succeeded as governor by Oliver P. Morton.

Morton condemned the secession of the Southern states as an "unlawful and revolutionary" act.

Lincoln, enroute to his inauguration, stopped in Indianapolis on February 11-12, and conferred with Morton.

Morton offered 10,000 men for the Union Army as news reached Indianapolis of the surrender of Fort Sumter. Indiana filled its quota of 5,000 men and the state fair grounds were converted into a military camp. Indianapolis became an important war center and eventually was ringed by 24 camps.

1862—Camp Morton became a prisoner-of-war camp when the first captured Confederate soldiers arrived on February 22. Dr. Richard Gatling of Indianapolis invented the first rapid-fire gun. First military execution of the war was carried out at Camp Burnside, Indianapolis, when a deserter was put to death by a firing squad. System of bounties was instituted by towns and cities to spur recruitment for the Union Army.

Soldiers Home, with accomodations for 1,800 persons, was

established at Indianapolis, in the area of Union Station. State Sanitary Commission was established.

Democrats captured control of both houses of the state General Assembly.

1863—Divided legislature was marked by acrimonious debate. The Republicans bolted and the Democrats adjourned, confident of a special session to act on appropriations. Gov. Morton took over the state government and ran it singlehandedly for the next two years. Democrats called him a "tyrant" and "usurper."

Many newspaper offices were wrecked, suppressed, or threatened by the U.S. Army. Union Leagues and Union Clubs were formed to meet the "menace" of the secret organization sympathetic to the South, the Knights of the Golden Circle.

Soldiers broke up a Democratic meeting in Indianapolis on May 20, stopped a train at Union Station and searched for weapons in an incident satirically called the "Battle of Pogue's Run."

Gen. John Hunt Morgan and 2,500 rebel cavalrymen invaded southern Indiana in July. As Indiana troops mobilized, Morgan and his men escaped into Ohio.

1864—Gov. Morton was re-elected in October.

Leaders of the Knights of the Golden Circle were arrested, many of them prominent men in their communities. Three of them were convicted of treason and sentenced to be hanged by a military court. They were later freed by the U.S. Supreme Court decision, *ex parte Milligan.*

First mule-drawn streetcars appeared on Indianapolis streets in June.

1865—Civil War was ended. The body of assassinated Pres. Lincoln laid in state in the capitol building in Indianapolis.

Thirteenth amendment to the U.S. constitution was adopted.

Legislation enabled blacks to testify in court.

Petroleum was discovered at Terre Haute.

1866—First national convention of the Grand Army of the Republic was held at Indianapolis.

1867—Indiana adopted the 14th Amendment to the U.S. Constitution.

State Soldiers' and Sailors' Orphans Home was established.

Indiana University became coeducational and state funds were appropriated for the first time for the university's support.

1868—James Oliver of South Bend invented the chilled-steel plow.

1869—John Holliday began publication of the Indianapolis *News.*

Purdue University was founded by John Purdue at Lafayette.

Hammond was founded.

Indiana adopted the 15th Amendment to the U.S. Constitution.

State Department of Geology was established.

Legislature enacted law requiring school trustees to organize separate schools for black children where their numbers were large enough to justify such a school.

1870—Indiana State Teachers College was opened at Terre Haute.

Population of the state numbered 1,680,637. Census revealed that amost eight percent of the population, mostly adults, could not read or write—a higher illiteracy rate than in the other Northern states.

1871—Novelist, Theodore Dreiser, was born at Terre Haute.

Edward Eggleston's *The Hoosier Schoolmaster* was published, marking the beginning of Indiana's "Golden Age of Literature."

1873—Grange Movement of agricultural fraternal organizations swept the state. By the end of the year, 650 Grange programs were organized; by 1875, there were nearly 3,000 in the state.

Office of County Superintendent of Schools was created.

Women's Prison was established at Indianapolis.

First beltline railroad in the U.S. was built around Indianapolis.

1874—Rose Polytechnic Institute (now Rose-Hulman Institute of Technology) was founded at Terre Haute by industrialist Chauncey Rose.

1876—Greenback Party held a convention in Indianapolis.

1878—Ancient Order of United Workmen was reported to have 37 lodges in Indiana. The Knights of Labor, a secret organization, was also organizing.

Plans were underway for a new state capitol building, which would cost $2,000,000 and take ten years to complete.

1879—Legislation was enacted providing for mine inspection and safety.

Legislation to aid mentally retarded persons was enacted for the first time in the state.

1880—Lew Wallace's famous novel, *Ben Hur*, was published.

Population of the state numbered 1,978,301.

Of the 77 labor unions in Indiana, the Knights of Labor were the most numerous group.

1881—American Federation of Labor was organized at Terre Haute.

State Board of Health was established.

1882—South Bend tested the first electric streetcars; they were not successfully operated, however, until three years later.

1883—Art Association of Indianapolis founded by May Wright Sewall.

James Whitcomb Riley published *The Old Swimmin' Hole and 'Leven More Poems.*

Bowen-Merrill, forerunner of the Bobbs-Merrill Company, Inc., published a second edition of Riley poems, thereby launching the successful book publishing firm.

1886—A 3,500-square mile natural gas field was discovered at Eaton near Muncie. Within three years, 500 wells were sunk and production reached 2,000,000 cubic feet per day.

1888—Benjamin Harrison, Indianapolis railroad lawyer and grandson of William Henry Harrison, was elected U.S. president.

Ball Brothers began the manufacture of their Mason jars for home canning and preserving.

1889—First oil well in Indiana was drilled near Keystone in Wells County.

Standard Oil built the world's largest oil refinery at Whiting.

Australian ballot was adopted.

Electric streetcars began operation in Lafayette.

1890—United Mine Workers were organized with headquarters in Indianapolis.

Population of the state numbered 2,192,404.

1893—Eugene V. Debs organized the American Railway Union, the first industrial union in U.S. labor history.

Inland Steel Mills were moved to the Calumet region.

First interurban electric cars were run between Marion and Gas City.

Elwood Haynes successfully tested the one cylinder horseless carriage on Pumpkin Vine Pike near Kokomo.

1894—Debs leads the Pullman strike at Chicago and was imprisoned for contempt of court.

1895—Streetcar operators went out on strike as Indianapolis changed from mule cars to electric cars.

First State Federation of Labor was organized.

1897—First compulsory school attendance law was enacted.

Legislation was enacted requiring the inspection of manufacturing plants for sanitation and safety.

United Mine Workers called a strike of coal miners.

1898—Indiana regiments joined in fighting the Spanish-American

War. One Indiana battery and one company reached Cuba as the war ended. First interurban car line between Anderson and Alexander began regular service.

Haynes formed a company to manufacture automobiles in Kokomo.

Eugene V. Debs founded the Social Democratic Party.

1899—Booth Tarkington's novel, *The Gentleman from Indiana,* was published.

Charles Black started the manufacture of automobiles at Indianapolis.

1900—Debs was nominated for U.S. president at the national convention of the Social Democratic Party held in Indianapolis.

Meredith Nicholson's novel, *The Hoosiers,* was published.

Population of the state numbered 2,516,462.

1901—Compulsory education law was amended, requiring children from 7 to 16 years of age to attend classes during the school year.

First Socialist Party national convention was held in Indianapolis and nominated Debs for U.S. president.

Golden age of automobile manufacture began in Indiana. By the mid-1930s, more than 256 makes of cars and trucks were made in the state, when Indianapolis wsas the leader and first capital of the auto industry.

1902—George Ade's *Fables in Slang* began to appear.

Soldiers and Sailors Monument was formally dedicated in Indianapolis on May 15.

1904—Largest interurban terminal in the U.S. was opened at Indianapolis.

Debs polled 402,312 votes for U.S. president.

Frank McKinney "Kin" Hubbard produced his first "Abe Martin" cartoon in the Indianapolis *News.*

1905—Gary was founded.

U.S. Steel Corporation built its largest plant in the Calumet region.

Lew Wallace died at Crawfordsville.

1906—Fort Benjamin Harrison was constructed.

1907—High schools were brought into the state public school system.

Indiana passed a pioneering Pure Food and Drug Act.

Indiana University School of Medicine was established.

1980—Interurban cars operated in 72 of the state's 92 counties over 2,300 miles of track.

1910—Population of the state was numbered at 2,700,876.

1911—First 500-mile race was held at the Indianapolis Motor Speedway.

Legislation was enacted making employers responsible for industrial safety.

1914—State Workmen's Compensation Act went into operation.

1915—Indiana Historical Bureau was established.

Little Theater Society was organized at Indianapolis with George Ade as its first president.

1916—First primary election was held in the state.

Indiana marked its centennial year with parades, pageants, and ceremonies and launched the first phase of a park and conservation program.

James Whitcomb Riley died at Indianapolis.

1917-18—State established a conscription program for soldiers for World War I while the U.S. Congress debated the draft. Industry and agriculture mobilized for war.

Liberty aircraft engines were built at Allison and Indianapolis. Alexander D. Arch of South Bend became the first American to fire an artillery round on the European front. During the war, 130,670 Indiana men and women served in the armed forces. The death toll was 3,354 men and 15 women (nurses).

State-wide prohibition law was voted in, effective April 2, 1918, following a court decision on its validity.

Ball Brothers of Muncie purchased the Muncie Normal Institute and turned it over to the state. It was renamed

Ball State Teachers College in 1918 and Ball State University in 1965.

1919—Thousands in Indiana were affected by nation-wide coal and steel strikes.

Newly-organized American Legion selected Indianapolis for its national headquarters.

1920—General Assembly authorized construction of a five-block War Memorial (including the American Legion headquarters) in downtown Indianapolis.

Debs, serving a prison sentence for opposing the war, polled 915,302 votes for U.S. president.

Albert J. Beveridge, turn-of-the-century apostle of American imperialism, won the Pulitzer Prize for his *Live of John Marshall.*

Population of the state numbered 2,930,390.

1920—Carl Fisher, president of the Indianapolis Motor Speedway, created Miami Beach and became one of Florida's outstanding promoters. Genett Records of Richmond produced perhaps the first jazz record, King Oliver's Creole Jazz Band.

Hoagy Carmichael, a law student at Indiana University, wrote "Stardust" and became famous as a musician, songwriter, and movie star. Noble Sissle, an orchestra leader in Indianapolis, produced Broadway shows. Dance marathons proliferated. Indiana was one of the three states in which the Ku Klux Klan took secret control of the government.

1921—Pres. Harding freed Debs on December 23.

Francis Hamilton began his radio broadcasting station, 9ZJ, from a garage in Indianapolis on December 31.

1922—David Curtis Stephenson was appointed Grand Dragon of the Ku Klux Klan for Indiana and began his climb to power in Hoosier political and economic life.

Purdue University started radio broadcasts in April.

1925—Stephenson was arrested and charged with murder. His trial resulted in a startling expose of the corrupt role the

Ku Klux Klan played in Indiana politics. Several officials, including the mayor of Indianapolis, were sentenced to jail.

Theodore Dreiser's *An American Tragedy* was published.

1926—J. Arthur MacLean excavated an Indian mound on Albee farm in Sullivan County, the first scientific archaeological excavation in the state.

Eugene V. Debs died on October 20.

1927—Charles A. Linbergh was given a tumultous welcome on his visit to Indianapolis, where, several months later, he set up TAT-Maddux Transcontinental Airline, a coast-to-coast transport service using planes and trains.

Indianapolis Motor Speedway was sold to Capt. Eddie V. Rickenbacker.

1928—Indianapolis *Times* won the Pulitzer Prize for its campaign against the Ku Klux Klan.

Beveridge's two-volume *Life of Abraham Lincoln* was published posthumously.

1929—The five circuses of the American Circus Company, headquartered for many years at Peru, were purchased by Ringling Bros. & Barnum & Bailey Circus and, within the next few years, were moved out of Indiana.

1930—Population of the state numbered 3,238,503.

1932—Indiana began to feel the effects of the Great Depression. Dozens of banks failed, businesses and industries suspended operations, thousands were unemployed and farm prices dropped.

Paul V. McNutt, a Democrat, was elected governor of Indiana, gaining national attention by running ahead of presidential candidate F.D. Roosevelt in Indiana.

1933-37—McNutt administration, favored with near-record Democratic majorities in the General Assembly, gave the U.S. a preview of the New Deal. The administration reorganized the state government and enacted the first gross income and intangibles tax, a model banking law, unemployment compensation, and pensions for the blind, aged, and dependent. A State Welfare Department was established in 1936. McNutt also built one of the state's most powerful political machines and inaugurated the "Two Per Cent Club," in which state employees paid two percent of their earnings into the Democratic Party treasury.

1933—John Dillinger, a native of Mooresville, became the nation's most wanted criminal after his dramatic escape from jail and a series of bank robberies. He was gunned down by FBI men in Chicago during July 1934.

1935—Public Utility Holding Company Act struck a virtual death blow to consolidated interurban car lines, which were already in financial difficulty.

1937—Gov. Clifford Townsend inaugurated the "Indiana Plan" of adjusting labor disputes by contract.

Ohio River flood waters submerged entire towns and cities in southern Indiana. Scores died, thousands were made homeless, and damage was estimated at $500,000,000.

Marian College was founded at Indianapolis by the Sisters of the Third Order of St. Francis.

1940—Wendell L. Willkie of Elwood was nominated for U.S. president by the Republican Party. Although he carried the state of Indiana, he was defeated by F.D. Roosevelt and Democrat Henry F. Schricker was elected state governor.

Population of the state numbered 3,427,796.

1941—Indiana, preparing for World War II, became "Toolmaker to the Nation."

Last of the interurban car lines closed in September.

1942-45—Hoosiers sent off 388,000 men and women to war, 10,000 of whom died in camps and battlefields all over the world. Allison Division of General Motors in Indianapolis produced 70,000 aircraft engines. Hundreds of other Indiana plants turned out products for a war whose logistics were staggering.

1942—A Republican General Assembly enacted legislation restricting and limiting the powers of the governor, but the Indiana Supreme Court, in a far reaching decision, declared the acts null and void.

1948—Gov. Schricker was reelected governor, the only man elected twice under the constitution of 1851 barring consecutive terms.

1949—Two television stations, WTTV Bloomington, and WFBM (now WRTV) Indianapolis, went on the air. WFBM's inaugural programs included the last G.A.R. national convention and the first and only live broadcast of the 500-mile automobile race.

Indiana schools were integrated under legislative act. It was announced that most of Indiana's "little red school houses" had been consolidated.

1950—D.C. Stephenson, former Ku Klux Klan Grand Dragon, was freed on March 17 after serving 25 years of a life term.

Many communities including Indianapolis began replacing trolley cars with buses or trackless trolleys.

New $2,500,000 American Legion headquarters building was dedicated at Indianapolis.

1952—First patients were admitted to the newly-completed Veterans Administration Hospital.

Most cities and towns announced Civil Defense Plans.

1953—Indiana Motor Vehicles Dept. announced new "point system" for erring motorists.

Army Finance Center at Fort Benjamin Harrison was dedicated.

Many new shopping centers, including that of Glendale in Indianapolis, were announced to be under construction.

State voted a bonus for World War II veterans.

Bell Telephone Company employees went on strike.

Polio vaccine was first used "commercially" in Marion County and it was announced taht the counties would issue shots free to all first and second grade students.

1956—Indiana Toll Road, an east-west highway in northern Indiana, was opened to traffic.
Izler Solomon was chosen as the permanent conductor of the Indianapolis Symphony Orchestra, replacing Fabian Sevitzy, conductor from 1930.

East side of Indianapolis was virtually paralyzed by high water.

1958—Highway programs were expanded, a new 13-story State Office building was started, and the gross income tax and motor fuel tax were increased.

Democrats elected a U.S. senator, R. Vance Hartke, for the first time in 20 years.

Convictions and indictments on bribery and conspiracy charges were reported as the state pushed its investigation into state highway scandals that were first uncovered in 1957.

John Birch Society was organized at Indianapolis and named Robert Welch as president.

1959—Rampaging Wabash River, hurling ice floes before it, forced the evacuation of thousands from their homes in Peru and Wabash, smashed a levee at Terre Haute, and threatened extinction of Georgetown, Cass County.

Republicans fought off a Democratic attempt to repeal the state's "right to work" law.

1960—Northwest Orient Airlines prop-jet crashed at Tell City, killing all 63 persons aboard.

Two persons were killed and scores injured as a spectator-filled, makeshift scaffold collapsed during a pace lap of the 500-Mile Race in Indianapolis.

New convictions were announced in the highway scandal.

1961—New Indiana Port Commission selected Burns Ditch for a proposed deep-water port on Lake Michigan.

Explosion at Viking Mine near Terre Haute killed 22 coal miners.

1962—Birch Bayh, Jr., of Terre Haute defeated three-term Sen. Homer Capehart in an off-year election.

Bethlehem Steel announced plans to build an integrated steel mill in Porter County, thereby boosting the state's plan for a deep-water port on Lake Michigan at Burns Ditch.

Sherwood H. Egbert, president of Studebaker, was arrested after a picket line scuffle at the South Bend plant.

1963—Exploding tank of propane gas under a section of the seats at the State Fairgrounds Coliseum killed 73 persons and injured nearly 400 adults and children watching the finale of an ice show.

An explosion at the Home Packing Co. of Terre Haute claimed the lives of 17.

Legislature enacted the state's first sales tax.

1964—Attendance records at the Indiana State Fairgrounds Coliseum were broken by the English music group, the Beatles.

1965—Tornadoes swept the northern part of the state on Palm Sunday, killing 140 in the state's worst natural disaster. Property damage was estimated in the billions of dollars.

Indianapolis *Times* suspends publication on October 11.

1966—Indiana celebrated its 150 years of statehood with a year-long and state-wide Sesquicentennial program.

Severe drought destroyed the corn and soybean crops in 39 central and western counties.

1967—Virgil "Gus" Grissom, a native of Mitchell and Purdue University graduate, and two fellow astronauts—Roger B. Chaffee, a Purdue graduate, and Edward White II, who grew up in FortWayne—perished in a Jan. 27 flash fire on Apollo I during a simulated countdown at Cape Kennedy. Grissom was the first astronaut in history to journey twice into outer space in 1961 and 1965.

1967—Richard Hatcher became the first black mayor of Gary.

Claude R. Wickard, secretary of agriculture in the Roosevelt administration and a native of Carroll County, was killed instantly in a car-truck crash near Delphi.

Dr. Joseph C. Muhler, research professor of basic sciences at Indiana University and a native of Fort Wayne, was awarded the Navy's highest civilian award, the Distinguished Service Award, for his development of stannous flouride as a tooth decay preventive agent.

A.J. Foyt became fourth three-time winner of the Indianapolis 500-Mile Race.

Racial unrest broke out in several Indiana cities. Widespread rumors in Indianapolis of a pending race riot proved unfounded and Mayor John J. Barton appointed a 60-member task force to study race problems in the city. Racial unrest in South Bend resulted in three nights of disorder.

An important railroad era ended as a Monon passenger train made its final run from Louisville to Chicago.

1967—Indiana Civil Liberties Union lost another round in a 13-year battle to use the Indiana War Memorial. The Memorial Commission refused use of the building as veterans groups continued to protest.

Indiana State Museum opened at Indianapolis in the former city hall.

1968—Gov. Roger D. Branigin joined in the Democratic presidential primary race for U.S. president.

Louis Russell, a black industrial arts teacher in Indianapolis, underwent heart transplant surgery at Medical College of Richmond, Va. Upon his death on Nov. 27, 1974, he was the longest lived heart transplant patient.

1969—Mid-air collision between Indianapolis-bound Alleghany airlanes jet and a small private plane over Shelbyville resulted in the loss of 83 lives.

Legislature approved the consolidation of Indianapolis and Marion County into a single administrative unit ("Uni-Gov") effective Jan. 1, 1970. Indianapolis, as result, became the nation's 11th largest city.

1971—Reapportionment Act broke down party bloc voting in the General Assembly. "Two Per Cent Club" virtually disbanded in both political parties.

1972—State sales tax was increased to four percent as Gov. Otis Bowen backed a property tax reduction by 20 percent.

1973—Lt. Governor R. Dorr swims to safety after Brazilian airliner crashes and sinks in Quandahara Bay, Rio de Janeiro.

1974—U.S. Senator Birch Bayh wins re-election to 3rd term defeating Republican challenger Richard G. Lugar by a narrow margin.

1976—After announcing candidacy for Democratic nomination for President of the U.S., Senator Birch Bayh withdraws after poor showing in early primaries.

EDWARD A. LEARY

Concise Dictionary

INTRODUCTION

NOT since the ambitious WPA projects of the 1930s has an in-depth state guide been written. This Indiana volume, in addition to providing highly readable and scholarly essays devoted to the state as a whole, contains the concise dictionary of every important political, historical, and geographical unit of the state.

The main body of the volume deals with the state on a general level, the concise dictionary tries to deal with it on a more specific one. The A through Z format simplifies the reader's task, whether it be one of research or one of simple curiosity. The concise dictionary attempts to help familiarize the reader with the more intimate facets that have helped shape Indiana's destiny. A state, after all, is a composite of all its parts. Each entry lists important information such as location, physical and natural characteristics, history, points of interest, and economic data. The concise dictionary can double as a reference guide and a tour guide. Places of interest to the tourist contain data on camping and recreational facilities and offers cross-references to other nearby attractions. Indiana, especially southern Indiana, is a land of bountiful scenic wonders and is a showplace of history.

Subjects covered in the essay section of the volume are handled in a more in-depth, specific manner in the concise dictionary. Hopefully, the reader's task, whatever it may be, can be simplified. It is also the intended aim of the concise dictionary entries to relate to the rest of the book as a whole. By combining topical accessibility (main body essays), alphabetical accessibility (concise dictionary entries), and a wealth of photographs, the Indiana volume will serve both as an educational instrument and as a handy reference guide where subjects can be readily "looked up".

INGRID EKLOV JONSSON

ACTON, town (pop. 650), Marion County, central Indiana, zip 46259, within the Indianapolis Metropolitan Area. The town is basically a rural community specializing in the cultivation of corn hybrids and feeds and the manufacture of poultry loaders.

ADAMS, county (pop. 26,871), E Indiana, area 345 sq. mi., bounded on the E by the Ohio state line, and drained by the Wabash and St. Mary's rivers and Longlois Creek. Adams County is primarily agricultural, but has some diversified industry, such as food processing. Decatur is the county seat.

ADVANCE, town (pop. 561), Boone County, central Indiana, zip 46102, 16 mi. ESE of Crawfordsville, in a grain and livestock area.

AKRON, town (pop. 946), Fulton County, N Indiana, zip 46910. 45 mi. SSE of South Bend, in a grain and livestock area.

ALBANY, city (pop. 2,293), Delaware County, central Indiana, zip 47320, 12 mi. NE of Muncie. Located in an agricultural region noted for feed grains and livestock, Albany is a manufacturing center and producer of dyes, lumber, wire products, and sheet metal.

ALBION, resort town (pop. 1,498), seat of Noble County, NE Indiana, zip 46701, 26 mi. NNW of Fort Wayne. The "Old Jail" museum, built in 1875, is sponsored by the Noble County Historical Society. Although the tourist trade dominates the economy, the production of furniture, lumber, tiles, and dairy products is also important. Nearby is Chain O'Lakes State Park (q.v.), comprised of a string of nine natural, connecting lakes.

ALEXANDRIA, city (pop. 5,097), Madison County, E central Indiana, zip 46001, on Pipe Creek, 40 mi. NE of Indianapolis. Alexandria's main industry is the production of rock wool; the Johns-Manville Company plant was the first rock-wool insulation factory in the world. Argillaceous limestone, essential to the manufacture of rock wool, is taken out of local quarries. Gloves, asbestos, and magnesium products are also manufactured.

ALFORDSVILLE, town (pop. 105), Daviess County, SW Indiana, zip 47511, 7 mi. S of Loogootee, in an agricultural and lumbering area.

ALLEN, county (pop. 280,455), NE Indiana, area 671 sq. mi. It is bounded on the east by Ohio, and drained by the Maumee, St. Joseph, and St. Mary's rivers. Formed in 1823, it was named for John Allen. Allen County is noted for stock raising, farming, and dairying. Fort Wayne is the county seat.

ALTONA, town (pop. 269), DeKalb County. NE Indiana, zip 46738, 19 mi. N of Fort Wayne. The town is in a predominantly agricultural region, noted for the production of grain and livestock.

AMBIA, town (pop. 300), Benton County, W Indiana zip 47917, about 18 mi. SW of Fowler. In an agricultural area noted for its corn cultivation, the town is a producer of fertilizer and grain feed.

AMBOY, town (pop. 473), Miami County, N central Indiana, zip 46911, 13 mi. SE of Peru in a primarily agricultural region.

AMISHVILLE, Amish community, Adams County, NE Indiana, 5 mi. SE of Berne. The unincorporated community of "Plain People," so-called because of their religious beliefs, contains no automobiles, motors, plumbing, or other modern conveniences. For transportation the population uses horse-drawn buggies or sleighs in winter.

AMO, town (pop. 422), Hendricks County, central Indiana, zip 46103. On Mill Creek, it lies 25 mi. WSW of Indianapolis in a primarily agricultural region.

ANDERSON, industrial city (pop. 70,787), seat of Madison County, E central Indiana, zip 46000, 34 mi. NE of Indianapolis.
  Picturesquely located in the low hills along the White River, Anderson lies on the site of an old Delaware Indian village. Chief Anderson, for whom the city is named, lived in a double log cabin located at present Eight and Central avenues. In 1801, Moravian missionaries arrived at the village in hopes of

converting the Indians to Christianity. Their efforts failed, and they returned to their headquarters in 1806. The first white settler, William Conner, owned much of the land around the present site and sold it to John Berry, who platted the town in 1823. In 1827, the town, then known as Andersontown, became the county seat. Growth was initially slow, but increased rapidly when it was announced that a canal from Logansport to Indianapolis, which would pass through Andersontown, was planned. An influx of workers almost doubled the population in one year. Bankruptcy hit Indiana in 1838, however, and the canal project was abandoned. Andersontown began to deteriorate, but its economy was saved when the first railroad station was established in 1852. Andersontown became Anderson; incorporation to city status came in 1865.

In 1887, natural gas was discovered, bringing fame and prosperity to Anderson. Shortly the city became known as the "Queen City of the Gas Belt." "Old Vesuvius," one of the largest producing wells in the country, was piped into the White River and lighted to burn night and day for the benefit of visitors, who would see it roaring skyward from the water. The gas boom brought much industry into the area. Almost 40 factories, as well as financial institutions and publishing companies, were established because of the promise of the seemingly endless supply of gas. The gas did diminish, however, and by 1917 the boom was over. Anderson settled into a less frenetic pace. Later developments were largely based on the automobile industry. The car factories are gone, but production of automobile equipment continues to play a large role. Two subsidiaries of General Motors—Delco-Remy and Guide Lamp—are located in Anderson. Other manufactures include files and rasps, fire trucks, corrugated boxes, copper wire, and packaging machinery. Anderson is also an important grain and livestock distribution center.

Anderson College (1917), affiliated with the Church of God, is a coeducational liberal arts college. On campus is a large collection of artifacts from the Holy Land. Nearby is Mounds State Park (q.v.), a scenic archaeological site along the White River that contains a cluster of prehistoric Indian mounds.

ANDREWS, town (pop. 1,207), Huntington Countyt, central Indiana, zip 46701, 6 mi. WSW of Huntington. Andrews is the birthplace of Ellwood Patterson Cubberley, the well-known educator who presented Stanford University with a building to house a school of education in 1938. The local economy is based on agriculture.

ANGEL MOUNDS STATE MEMORIAL, state memorial in Vanderburgh County, SW Indiana, just E of Evansville. The mounds are named after the Angel family, on whose property they are located. Angel Mounds is the largest group of prehistoric Indian mounds in Indiana, covering 100 acres. Excavation began in 1939 under the leadership of Glenn A. Black, an archaeologist and anthropologist from Indianapolis. The mounds are conical in shape. They were built by prehistoric Indians of the Mississippi culture (AD 500- AD 1650) as burial places or as elevations for temples and palaces.

Since the early diggings, the Angel Mounds have yielded nearly 2,000,000 artifacts, which prove that about 1,000 people inhabited the area between 1400 and 1600. Evidence shows that a wooden stockade enclosed the settlement, which contained houses, a town square, and temples. A series of archaeological studies sponsored by the Indiana Historical Society and Indiana University was underway in the 1970s. A visitor center funded by the Lilly Foundation includes a museum which houses a large collection of artifacts including stone implements, pottery, jewelry, and effigies.

ANGOLA, resort city (pop. 5,117), seat of Steuben County, NE Indiana, zip 46703, 40 mi. N of Fort Wayne.

The city, at an altitude of 1,055 ft. is a quiet college town located in a scenic, hilly region of woods and lakes. There is some manufacturing (feed, brick, tiles, automobile parts), but Angola depends largely on the tourist trade both in summer and winter.

Tri-State College (1884) is located in the town. A four-year institution, it offers programs in engineering, business administration, computer technology, and the arts and sciences. The average enrollment is 1,500. Nearby are Crooked and Silver lakes and Pokagon State Park (*q. v.*).

ARCADIA, town (pop. 1,338), Hamilton County, central Indiana, zip 46030, 29 mi. N of Indianapolis. The town's economy is based on agriculture.

ARGOS, town (pop. 1,393), Marshall County, N Indiana, zip 46501, 30 mi. S of South Bend. Argos began as a stagecoach stop and flourished as a regional dairy farming center. The town has a fish hatchery and a lumber mill. Nearby is scenic Lake Maxinkuckee.

ARLINGTON, town (pop. 500), W central Rush County, E Indiana, zip 46104, 25 mi. SE of Indianapolis in a primarily agricultural area. Of note is the Beckner-Nelson House, built in Classic Italian style in 1853.

ASHLEY, town (pop. 721), on the DeKalb-Steuben county line, NE Indiana, zip 46705, 33 mi. N of Fort Wayne. The economy is based on agriculture and some manufacturing. Products include canned goods and cement.

ATLANTA, town (pop. 620), Hamilton County, central Indiana, zip 46031, 32 mi. N of Indianapolis in a primarily agricultural region.

ATTICA, city (pop. 4,262), Fountain County, W Indiana, zip 47918, on the Wabash River, 21 mi. WSW of Lafayette. The city originally was the site of a Potawatomi village, and contained the home of Chief Topenbee, who signed the Treaty of Greenville in 1795. Here, Tecumseh gathered tribal chiefs to form an alliance to fight the advance of white settlers; the site is marked on Perry Street. Attica was officially founded in 1825 and grew rapidly with the coming of the Wabash and Erie Canal. Incorporation came came in 1866.

The magnificent scenery of the gorges and escarpments dissected by the Wabash River has earned Attica the name of "Gem City." It inspired the state song written by Paul Dresser and his brother Theodore Dreiser, "On the Banks of the Wabash."

Attica is an agricultural and industrial trading center; manufactures include cement products, steel castings, canned goods, and railroad equipment. Bear Creek Canyon and a natural arch are nearby.

ATWOOD, town (pop. 250), Kosciusko County, N central Indiana, zip 46502, 7 mi. W of Warsaw in an agricultural area.

The town is a manufacturing center for copper and aluminum bits and fracture equipment.

AUBURN, city (pop. 7,337), seat of DeKalb County, NE Indiana, zip 46706, 21 mi. N of Fort Wayne in a gently rolling prairie region shaped by glacial drift. Settled in 1836, Auburn was the home of early American automobiles. The Auburn and the Cord were manufactured there, and on the Saturday before Labor Day, the city holds its annual Auburn-Cord-Duesenburg rally. The event attracts owners of more than 100 of the classic cars.

Auburn is a trading center for livestock, dairy products, automobile parts, rubber specialties, lumber, and stationery. In town is the DeKalb Memorial Hospital, which was financed entirely by contributions from private sources.

AURORA, city (pop. 4,293), Dearborn County, SE Indiana, zip 47007, on the Ohio River, 22 mi. WSW of Cincinnati, Ohio.

Founded in 1819, the city was named for the Roman goddess of dawn. Houseboats are plentiful along the river and rustic houses cling precariously to the hillsides. The city was hard-hit by the flood of 1937, which raised the water level to a height of more than 80 ft. and ruined the homes of 3,000 inhabitants. Industry includes a few lumber mills and a furniture factory. Mainly agricultural, Aurora is a center for livestock and tobacco.

AUSTIN, village (pop. 4,902), Scott County, SE Indiana, zip 47102, 32 mi. N of New Albany. Sometimes called the "canning center of Indiana," Austin markets millions of dollars worth of canned goods each year. Morgan Packing Company and the American Can Company have plants there. The town was platted in 1853.

AVILLA, town (pop. 881), Noble County, NE Indiana, zip 46710, 21 mi. NNW of Fort Wayne in a primarily agricultural region.

AVOCA, village (pop. 300), Lawrence County, S central Indiana, zip 47420, 4 mi. NW of Bedford. Bluegill, redear, sunfish, crappies, and bass are bred annually at the Avoca State Fish Hatchery. The fish are used to stock Indiana's rivers and lakes. Cold Water Spring supplies water for the hatchery pools.

BAINBRIDGE, town (pop. 703), Putnam County, W central Indiana, zip 46105, 35 mi. W of Indianapolis in a scenic, wooded valley devoted mainly to agriculture.

BARGERSVILLE, town (pop. 873), Johnson County, central Indiana, zip 46106, 17 mi. S of Indianapolis in an agricultural area noted for feed grains and livestock. Manufactures include lumber, dyes, and special machinery.

BARTHOLOMEW, county (pop. 57,022), S central Indiana, area 402 sq. mi. Founded in 1821 by Gen. Joseph Bartholomew and Gen. John Tipton, the county is drained by the White River and its tributaries and is in a primarily agricultural region. Columbus is the county seat.

BASS LAKE, town (pop. 300), Starke County, NW Indiana, 6 mi. S of Knox. It is a popular fishing resort near Bass Lake State Beach (*q. v.*).

BASS LAKE HATCHERY, state fishery in Starke County, NW Indiana, on the shores of Bass Lake. The hatchery is the largest and most productive of its kind in Indiana.

BASS LAKE STATE BEACH, Starke County, NW Indiana, on the shores of Bass Lake and 5 mi. S of Knox. Bass Lake, Indiana's fourth largest natural lake, was named for its former abundance of black and silver bass. It is a popular resort and, although the bass have been depleted, it remains an abundant fishing ground for bluegills, yellow perch, and wall-eyed pike.

BATESVILLE, city (pop. 3,799), Ripley County, SE Indiana, 40 mi. SSW of Richmond. The large German population is employed primarily in one of the city's six furniture factories. Other products include hospital equipment, tiles, and mirrors.

BATTLE GROUND town (pop. 818), Tippecanoe County, W central Indiana, zip 47920, 7 mi. N of Lafayette. On Nov. 7, 1811, Battle Ground was the scene of the Battle of Tippecanoe, where Gen. William Henry Harrison defeated the Indians led by Tenskwatawa, the Shawnee Prophet, brother of Tecumseh. A 100 foot shaft marks the battle site. Other markers show exactly where officers fell in battle. National fame came to Harrison as a result of the victory, and 30 years later he was elected to the U.S. presidency on the slogan "Tippecanoe and Tyler Too." Today, most of the town's population is involved in small business and agriculture.

BECK'S MILLS, site of a water-powered mill built in 1865, Washington County, S Indiana, 9 mi. S of Salem. The mill is one of the few in Indiana which have survived with their water wheels intact. The water source is a dammed cave spring above the mill. The original mill site was developed in 1808 by George Beck, a prospector along the Buffalo Trace.

BEDFORD, city (pop. 13,087), seat of Lawrence County, S Indiana, zip 47421, 22 mi. S of Bloomington.

Bedford was platted in 1825 and by the 1850s had become the state's leading limestone quarrying center. The beautiful limestone, with excellent cleavage and carving properties, has been used in many famous buildings throughout the U.S., including the Empire State Building in New York City. Indiana supplies 80 percent of the nation's limestone, much of which is cut in the quarries of the Indiana Limestone Corporation. Each block averages 4 ft. thick by 10 ft. wide by 50-120 ft. long. There are three major stone mills with an average employment of 5,000 workers. The production of grain and fruit also plays a major role in Bedford's economy.

Bedford is the seat of Hoosier National Forest. The Lawrence County Historical Museum houses a fine collection of Indiana limestone, Indian artifacts, and Civil War memorabilia.

BEECH GROVE, city (pop. 13,468), Marion County, central Indiana, zip 46107, SE of Indianapolis. Located on the Tipton Till Plain, the city was named for the many beech and maple trees that thrive on the unassorted glacial soils. Beech Grove was founded in 1900 and incorporated as a town in 1906 and as a city in 1935. Mainly residential, the city has extensive railroad shops. It is the seat of Indiana Central College (1902).

BELLEVILLE, town (pop. 400), Hendricks County, 5 mi. W of Plainfield in an agricultural and tourist area.

BENJAMIN HARRISON MEMORIAL HOME, Indianapolis,

Marion County, Indiana. The home was built by Harrison in 1872, 18 years after his arrival in Indianapolis to practice law. It remained his home until his death in 1901, except for the years he resided in Washington, D.C., as a U.S. senator (1881-87) and the 23rd president of the U.S. (1889-93). The home has been restored as a national shrine and contains a collection of clothes worn by Harrison's first wife, Caroline Lavinia Scott, and some of the original furniture.

BENTON, county (pop. 11,262), W Indiana, area 409 sq. mi., bounded on the W by the Illinois state line. Benton was organized in 1840 and was named for Thomas H. Benton. The county is drained by Sugar and Pine creeks and is a primarily agricultural region. The county has several canneries and poultry hatcheries. Fowler is the county seat.

BENTONVILLE, town (pop. 85), Fayette County, E central Indiana, zip 47322, 13 mi. NW of Connersville in an agricultural area noted for the production of livestock and feed grains.

BERNE, town (pop. 2,988), Adams County, E Indiana, zip 46711, 31 mi. SSE of Fort Wayne.
Settled in 1840 by Swiss immigrants from Alsace-Lorraine, Berne has become known for its large Amish population and for its authentic Amish farm, "Amishville," which is a popular tourist attraction. The largest Mennonite church in the U.S. is located there, and Amish and Mennonite farmers work side by side on the surrounding farmlands using only horse-drawn plows. Little of the Amish lilfestyle has changed since the 1840s. Their religion dictates that they must live frugally and have no automobiles or other modern conveniences. All of their clothes are plain and home-made. The men are bearded and wear black hats, and the women wear shawls and bonnets. There are four large furniture plants in the town. Other products include dairy foods and work clothes. The Mennonite Book Concern (1893) is the largest publisher and distributor for the Mennonite faith in the U.S. and Canada.

BEVERLY SHORES, town (pop. 946), Porter County, NW Indiana, zip 46301, in a resort, farming, and industrial area. In the 1920s, the town was part of a giant land speculation scheme in which 8,000 acres of land were acquired along Lake Michigan. Lots were bought and sold on a grand scale and savings were invested, only to be lost during the Great Depression. Prior to this time, Beverly Shores was a center for cranberry and blueberry farming. Tourism aided the economy and the town became a summer resort for Chicagoans. Three-quarters of the town has become part of the Indiana Dunes National Lakeshore and the rest is to be included in future park expansion.

Of note are the several vintage houses brought by barge in 1933 from the Chicago Century of Progress complex. They include the House of Tomorrow, Old North Church, and Paul Revere House. The town is surrounded by quiet marsh- and dunelands, and is an ideal focus for nature studies and hiking.

BICKNELL, city (pop. 3,717), Knox County, SW Indiana, zip 47512, 13 mi. NE of Vincennes. The town was founded in 1875 after the opening of the first bituminous coal mine in Indiana. Mining is still important, although other industries have begun to predominate. Leading products include lumber, women's clothing, and mobile homes. A mine rescue station is also located in the city.

BIDDLE'S ISLAND, island in the Wabash River at Logansport, N central Indiana. On the island is the home of Judge Horace Biddle (1811-1900), jurist, writer, illustrator, and painter. In the yard of the mansion is the grave of No'Kamena, a Miami chieftain. The judge permitted the burial of the chief on this spot because it was his original home site.

BIG BLUE RIVER, central Indiana, rises in Henry County and flows for 75 mi. SW past New Castle and Shelbyville to the East Fork of the White River at Edinburg.

BIRDSEYE, town (pop. 404), Dubois County, SW Indiana, zip 47513, 14 mi. ESE of Jasper. It is an important agricultural and bituminous coal-mining center.

BLACKFORD, county (pop. 15,888), E Indiana, area 167 sq. mi. Formed in 1838, it was named for Judge Isaac Blackford, the noted pioneer jurist. The county is drained by the Salamonie

River and Lick Creek. Mining and agriculture are the main economic activities. Hartford City is the county seat.

BLOOMFIELD, town (pop. 2,565), seat of Greene County, SW Indiana, zip 47424, approximately 40 mi. SE of Terre Haute. The land around Bloomfield was originally donated by Peter Van Slyke, a settler. The town grew as a manufacturing center specializing in furniture, metal products, and silos.

BLOOMINGDALE, town (pop. 391), Parke County, W Indiana, zip 473832, 28 mi. NNE of Terre Haute. A marker for a stop on the Underground Railway is just north of town. The economy is based on agriculture and coal-mining. In town is the beautiful Friends Church (1865) which has many historic pictures and record books on display.

BLOOMINGTON, city (pop. 42,890), seat of Monroe County, S central Indiana, zip 47401, 45 mi. SSW of Indianapolis in an industrial, farming, and quarrying area. Bloomington was founded in 1818 and two years later became the seat of Indiana University, the second oldest state university W of the Alleghenies. The beautiful campus encompasses 1,850 acres and boasts the Daily Art Collection and the Thomas Hart Benton murals.

Bloomington owes its initial growth to the development of the stone industry. It is a center for oolitic limestone quarrying and has more than 30 quarries and stone mills, some of which are open to the public. Other industries include the manufacture of screw machine items, beverages, printed circuits, iron, metal, refrigerators, elevators, plastics, molds, and escalators.

The city is a popular stop-over for tourists who come to visit the nearby state parks, six of which are located within 25 miles of Bloomington. They include Spring Mill and Brown County state parks (*q. v.*), and Lake Monroe, the state's largest lake.

BLUE RIVER, S Indiana, rises in Washington County and flows about 50 mi. SW and S past Salem to the Ohio River near Leavenworth.

BLUFFTON, city (8,297), seat of Wells County, E Indiana, zip 46714, on the Wabash River and 24 mi. S of Fort Wayne.

Bluffton was settled in 1829 and incorporated in 1858. The city is built on the bluffs overlooking the Wabash River and contains several century-old houses. Of note are a tulipwood log cabin (1855) preserved in its original state and the courthouse (1889), which has a Richardson Romansque architecture. Bluffton manufactures pianos, windmills, and machinery, and has some limestone quarrying.

The city contains a large arboretum and the Wells County Historical Museum. Southwest of Bluffton, peat bogs are preserved as a rare reminder of the marshlands immortalized by Gene Stratton Porter in her novel *A Girl of the Limberlost.* Porter was Indiana's most widely-read authoress from 1893 to 1913. Ouabache State Recreational Area is nearby.

BOGGSTOWN, town (pop. 286), Shelby County, central Indiana, zip 46110, 9 mi. NW of Shelbyville in an agricultural and manufacturing area.

BOONE, county (pop. 30,870), central Indiana, area 427 sq. mi., drained by Sugar and Raccoon creeks and the Eel River. Boone County was formed in 1830 and named in honor of Daniel Boone, the famous pioneer and Indian fighter. It is situated on a ridge of what was once known as the dividing swamps between the White and Wabash rivers. The area was the headquarters of the Eel River tribe of the Miami Indians. The Indians left the area in 1835, three years after Lebanon became the county seat. Agriculture is the mainstate of the economy, although manufacturing (metal containers, heating equipment) plays a large role in some areas.

BOONE GROVE, town (pop. 200), Porter County, NW Indiana, zip 46302, 10 mi. SW of Valparaiso in an agricultural area noted for livestock and feed grains.

BOONE'S POND STATE FISHING AREA, S Boone County, central Indiana, 5 mi. NE of Indianapolis. The 28-acre lake has facilities for fishing and boating.

BOONVILLE, city (pop. 5,736), seat of Warrick County, SW Indiana, zip 47601, 18 mi. ENE of Evansville. Platted in 1818, the city was named for Ratliff Boon, cousin of the frontiersman

Daniel Boone, who became one of Indiana's governors. His one-story cabin is well-preserved on First Street. Abraham Lincoln, in his early years as a lawyer, used to walk to Boonville to listen to courtroom oratory. The townspeople enjoyed a relatively quiet existence until the coming of the railroad in 1880. Manufacturing plants sprang up, and Boonville became a center for tocacco-growing, flour-milling, and the production of bricks and tiles.

Scales Lake State Forest, a reclaimed strip-mining region with an artificial lake, is two miles from town.

BORDEN, town (pop. 426), Clark County, S Indiana, zip 47106, 22 mi. NW of Jeffersonville in a farming and lumbering area. Borden is a manufacturing center for wooden cabinets, office furniture, dyes, jigs and fixtures.

BOSTON, town (pop. 210), Wayne County, E Indiana, zip 47324, near the Ohio border and 7 mi. S of Richmond.

BOSWELL, town (pop. 998), Benton County, W Indiana, zip 47921, 26 mi. WNW of Lafayette. The town is a popular truck stop.

BOURBON, town (pop. 1,606), Marshall County, N Indiana, zip 46504, 26 mi. SSW of South Bend in an agricultural area noted for livestock, feed grains, and poultry. There is some manufacturing, including the production of iron castings, truck caps, roofing materials, heater wire, and automatic screw machine products. In town is a monument of the Old Town Pump, first source of a water supply for the townspeople.

BOWLING GREEN, town (pop. 235), Clay County, W central Indiana, zip 47833, 15 mi. SE of Brazil in an agricultural and lumbering area. The town has a sawmill.

BRAZIL, city (pop. 8,163), seat of Clay County, W Indiana, zip 47834, on Birch Creek, 16 mi. ENE of Terre Haute. The city was named for the country of Brazil by William Stewart. It became a leader in interurban transportation in 1893, when one of the first electric interurban coaches was put into operation between Brazil and Harmony. Brazil is a mining and livestock center, but is best known for its building brick, tile, and block coal. The area has ten clay plants and several huge strip mines of bituminous coal.

BREMEN, town (pop. 3,487), Marshall County, N Indiana, zip 46806, 15 mi. SSE of South Bend. It is a center for the mint-growing belt and has a spearmint and peppermint extraction plant. Manufactures include feed, flour, building materials, and clothes.

BRIDGEPORT, town (pop. 700), Marion County, central Indiana, zip 46231, 9 mi. W of Indianapolis in an agricultural and farming area. Major manufactures include the production of aircraft components and assemblies.

BRIDGETON, town (pop. 350), SE Parke County, SW Indiana, zip 47836, on Raccoon Creek. Of note is the covered bridge, built in 1868 and typical of the 36 covered bridges that remain in Parke County.

BRIMFIELD, town (pop. 253), Noble County, NE Indiana, zip 46720, 6 mi. N of Albion in an agricultural area noted for feed grains and livestock. The town is a manufacturer of electro-harnesses for refrigerator units.

BRINGHURST, town (pop. 275), Carroll County, N Indiana, zip 46913, 11 mi. SE of Delphi in an agricultural area noted for feed grains and sweet corn. Kirk's Popcorn Company manufactures popcorn machines and bags, boxes, and oils for popcorn.

BRISTOL, town (pop. 1,100), Elkhart County, N Indiana, zip 46507, on the Saint Joseph River, 9 mi. ENE of Elkhart. Bristol is a manufacturer of canned vegetables and electrical pumps. East of town is the Bonneyville Mill, one of Indiana's oldest continuously operating mills.

BRISTOW, town (pop. 100), Perry County, S Indiana, zip 47515, 20 mi. N of Cannelton in a bituminous coal-mining and farming area.

BROADVIEW, village (pop. 2,362), Monroe County, central

Indiana, just S of Bloomington in a limestone quarrying and agricultural area.

BRONSON CAVE, Lawrence County, S Indiana, near Mitchell. Bronson Cave is one of many in a system of interconnecting caverns within Spring Mill State Park (*q.v.*). It is especially dangerous for spelunkers because water flows into it rather than out of it. Boat trips are on occasion taken through the cave.

BROOK, town (pop. 919), Newton County, NW indiana, zip 47922, 40 mi. NW of Lafayette in an agricultural area. Brook is the home of the Hess Manufacturing Company, which makes cosmetics. Beginning as a one-man operation, the company grew to a daily production of 20,000 packages. The historical Hazeldon Home of author and playwright George Ade has been restored. Ade became known in the early 20th century for his *Fables in Slang.*

BROOKLYN, town (pop. 911), Morgan County, central Indiana, zip 46111, on the Whitelick River, 20 mi. SW of Indianapolis. A covered bridge spans the Whitelick River near Brooklyn. Two tile and brick plants are supplied with raw materials from vast deposits of fire clay at the south edge of town.

Lake Jewell, formed from a drained and dammed swamp, is located at Bethany Park. In the park is Gold Creek, the scene of a minor gold rush in the 1900s. Analysis of the creek's water indicated that the spot had enormous gold resources. About 3,000,000 shares of stock were sold, but after the gold pans were found to yield only 25 cents worth of gold per day, the enterprise was quickly abandoned.

BROOKSTON, town (pop. 1,232), White County, NW central Indiana, zip 47923, 13 mi. N of Lafayette in an agricultural area noted for livestock and feed grains. There is some industry including the manufacture of industrial batteries, paper boxes, dyes, and farm supplies.

BROOKVILLE, town (pop. 2,864), seat of Franklin County, SE Indiana, zip 47012, on the Whitewater River and 21 mi. SSW of Richmond. Brookville was platted in 1808 by Jesse Brooks Thomas and Amos Butler; it was named for Thomas' mother, whose maiden name was Brooks. Amos Butler has been called the "father of social work in Indiana." Brookville contains many of the original houses built by the Quakers in the 1790s. It is also the home of four Indiana governors and four men who were to become governors of other states. Lew Wallace, author of *Ben Hur,* was born there. Commercially, Brookville is a trading center for grain, tobacco, furniture, and fiber boxes.

Nearby is the Whitewater Canal, which still offers boat rides reminiscent of the days when canal and river boat traffic was at its peak. (*See* Whitewater Canal State Memorial.)

Three mi. S of Brookville is the Little Cedar Grove Baptist Church (1811), the oldest church in Indiana still standing on its original foundation. A series of earthquakes in 1811 reminded the pioneers of their religious responsibilities, and they began work on their church. Although carpenters were hired, much of the labor was donated by the parishioners themselves. The original timbers are still in place, as are the bricks which were kneaded by oxen. The church was rededicated in 1955 to the faith and spirit of early pioneers in this part of the country.

BROOKVILLE RESERVOIR, Union and Franklin counties, E Indiana, at the northern edge of Brookville. The Brookville Reservoir was developed jointly by the state of Indiana and the U.S. Army Corps of Engineers and covers an area of 16,445 acres. Both Mounds State Park and White Water State Park (*q.q.v.*) are near its eastern shore. Recreational facilities are available for hiking, picnicking, fishing, camping, boating, hunting, and swimming.

BROWN, county (pop. 9,057), S central Indiana, area 324 sq. mi. Founded in 1836, it was named for Gen. Jacob Brown, a hero of the War of 1812. It is known as the "most picturesque county in the Midwest," with its rugged hills and rustic, century-old cabins that are scattered throughout the area. Brown County is drained by Salt Creek and is mainly agricultural in character. Nashville is the county seat.

BROWN COUNTY STATE PARK, 15,428-acre state park in Brown County, S Indiana, 2 mi. S of Nashville. Largest of the state's parks, it has scenic vistas of lakes and wooded hills. Inside the boundaries are a game preserve and an 80-foot observation tower. From the tower is a magnificent view of Weed Patch Hill (alt. 1,167 feet; *q.v.*), highest point in southern Indiana.

The park has been called a "sampler" from which the tourist can get a taste of all that Brown County has to offer in its breath-taking vistas of hills, woods, rivers, and lakes. The park is traversed by 27 miles of blacktop roads, along which there are 15 lookouts providing magnificent scenic panoramas. The park also provides horseback riding, an archery range, fishing, wildlife and floral exhibits, nature trails, and camping. Under construction in the mid-1970s was the 110-site horsemen's campground in the Greenhorn Valley sections of the park. Indiana's oldest covered bridge, the Ramp Bridge (1838), spans the North Fork of Salt Creek at the north entrance to the park.

BROWNSBURG, village (pop. 5,186), Hendricks County, central Indiana, zip 46112, 14 mi. WNW of Indianapolis. The economy is based on agriculture, and the town has a vegetable canning plant.

BROWNSTOWN, town (pop. 2,376), seat of Jackson County, S Indiana, zip 47220, near the East Fork of the White River, 24 mi. E of Bedford. The town was platted in 1816 and is picturesquely located among the low hills of southern Indiana. A land survey in 1809 was conducted to obtain 3,000,000 acres of land from the Indians. Brownstown lies along the historic "Ten O'Clock Line," so called because the Indians insisted that the land border be drawn where the sun cast its shadow at 10 A.M. on the day the cession treaty was signed. Nearby is Jackson State Forest and Skyline Drive which winds its way through some of the most breathtaking areas of Indiana's hill and valley country.

Commercially, Brownstown is a trading center for agricultural products and for silverware, brick, lumber, and canned goods.

BROWNSTOWN STATE FISHING AREA, Jackson County, S Indiana, 3 mi. W of Brownstown. The 11-acre lake has a boat-launching ramp and excellent fishing facilities.

BRUCEVILLE, village (pop. 627), Knox County, SW Indiana, zip 47516, 8 mi. NE of Vincennes in an agricultural area noted for feed grains and livestock. The town was platted in 1811 and was named for its founder, Maj. William Bruce. It prospered as a mining town for a short while after the first mine was sunk in 1914. Following a mine disaster in 1923, the operations were shut down, and the village has remained a peaceful farming community.

Abraham Lincoln once spoke at the Bruce House in behalf of Henry Clay, Whig candidate for the presidency.

BRYANT, town (pop. 320), Jay County, E Indiana, zip 47326, 34 mi. NE of Muncie in an area noted for the production of limestone and feed grains.

BUCK CREEK, village (pop. 276), Tippecanoe County, N Indiana, zip 47924, 11 mi. NE of Lafayette in a farming area. Buck Creek is a trade center for grain, feeds, fertilizer, and seeds.

BUFFALO TRACE, ancient buffalo path and later settlers' trail across S Indiana, from Ohio Falls, Kentucky to Vincennes, Indiana. The route was often travelled by Gen. William Henry Harrison, Col. Francis Vigo, and Gen. John Gibson.

BUNKER HILL, village (pop. 956), Knox County, SW Indiana, zip 46914, just S of Vincennes in a coal-mining and agricultural region.

BURKET, town (pop. 210), Kosciusko County, N Indiana, zip 46508, 40 mi. SSE of South Bend in a farming area.

BURLINGTON, town (pop. 685), Carroll County, NW central Indiana, zip 46915, 24 mi. SE of Delphi in a gently rolling, agricultural area. The town was founded in 1832 and long served as a stagecoach stop. It was named for Chief Burlington of the Wyandotte Indians, who lived in the vicinity for many years. Industries include the manufacturing of bricks, pet food, concrete blocks, and hog sausage.

BURNETTSVILLE, town (pop. 510), White County, NW central Indiana, zip 47926, 12 mi. W of Logansport. Burnettsville is a center for custom-blended fertilizers, herbicides, and insecticides and has the distinction of being the seat of the first normal school in Indiana (1852). The old school building is now used for storage.

BURNEY, town (pop. 250), Decatur County, SE Indiana, zip 47222, 10 mi. SW of Greensburg in an agricultural area noted for feed grains and livestock.

BURNS HARBOR, town (pop. 1,284), Porter County, NW Indiana, zip 46368, in the Calumet Industrial District. Incorporated as a town in 1967, Burns Harbor is the newest community in Porter County. The Bethlehem plant, which opened in 1964, employs a large portion of the population and is one of the most modern steel-making facilities in the U.S. The plant houses the largest blast furnace in the Western Hemisphere.

BUSH CREEK STATE FISH AND WILDLIFE AREA, Jennings County, SE Indiana, 1 mi. N of Butlerville. Public access is provided at the wildlife area, which contains a 180-acre lake. Boating and fishing are available.

BUTLER, town (pop. 2,394), DeKalb County, NE Indiana, zip 46721, 29 mi. NNE of Fort Wayne. Butler's economy is based on small businesses that specialize in such diversified products as leather jackets, windmills, pumps, and condensed milk. It is also an agricultural trading center.

BUTLERVILLE, town (pop. 350), Jennings County, S Indiana, zip 47223, 13 mi. W of Versailles. Just E of town is the Jefferson Proving Ground. Between North Vernon and Butlerville is the Quaker cemetery, which contains the grave of former U.S. president Richard Nixon's great-grandfather, Joshua Milhouse. Nearby is Bush Creek State Fish and Wildlife Area, a popular recreation area which has a 180-acre lake.

CAMBRIDGE CITY, town (pop. 2,481), Wayne County, E Indiana, zip 47327, 15 mi. W of Richmond. Located on the banks of the Whitewater River, Cambridge City retains many fine homes from the early 1800s. It was the home of Gen. Solomon

Meredith, leader of the Iron Brigade that fought in the Battle of Gettysburg. The town serves a large grain and livestock area, and is a manufacturer of metal products, chairs, pottery, and feed.

CAMBY, town (pop. 200), Marion County, central Indiana, zip 46113, 7 mi. from Indianapolis in a farming and manufacturing area. Camby is a manufacturing center for electronic coils and windings.

CAMDEN, town (pop. 577), Carroll County, N Indiana, zip 46917, 8 mi. E of Delphi in an agricultural area noted for grains, feeds, and poultry. Camden is a trade center for fertilizer, coal, salt, and eggs.

CAMPBELLSBURG, town (pop. 678), Washington County, S Indiana, zip 47108, 20 mi. SE of Bedford. Located in the scenic unglaciated hills of southern Indiana, the town is the gateway to the Cave River Valley. A park, enclosing a major portion of the valley, has its headquarters in a restored 150-year-old cabin that sits on the site of once prosperous Hammer's Mill. A river winds its way through the deep canyon into River Cave.

Campbellsburg serves a large agricultural area, but depends in large measure on the tourist trade. A popular event is the annual Strawberry Festival which attracts visitors from all over Indiana.

CANNELBURG, town (pop. 149), Daviess County, SW Indiana, zip 47519, 28 mi. E of Vincennes in a primarily agricultural area.

CANNELTON, city (pop. 2,280), seat of Perry County, S Indiana, zip 47520, on the Ohio River, 50 mi. E of Evansville. Founded in 1837, the city was named for the nearby deposits of cannel coal (coal with a fine texture and large amounts of volatile matter). During the mining days, Cannelton was one of the most important Ohio River ports, but its economy dwindled as the coal supply was exhausted. Today the city depends mainly upon sandstone quarrying and on the manufacture of cotton cloth, furniture, toys, and caskets. The city gives an impression of great age, and as such is an attraction to tourists. Rough-hewn century-old buildings mingle with the new.

Cannelton Cotton Mill (1849), a factory with twin towers, was once Indiana's largest industry, housing 10,800 spindles and 372 looms.

East of Cannelton is Lafayette Springs, which contains a shallow cave with an active spring. Gen. Lafayette landed there after his steamboat "Mechanic" capsized and was lost along with all its baggage and $8,000 worth of gold. Off Hwy. 166 is the Electra Memorial, which marks the site where a plane went down in 1960, killing 63 people.

CARBON, town (pop. 344), Clay County, W Indiana, zip 47837, 19 mi. NE of Terre Haute in a coal-mining area.

CARLISLE, town (pop. 714), Sullivan County, SW Indiana, zip 47838, 21 mi. NNE of Vincennes. One of the oldest towns in Indiana, it was settled in 1803 and platted in 1812 by Samuel Ledgerwood. It was an important coal-mining center until its deposits were exhausted. Today the town is a producer of lumber, canned goods, and liniment.

In Carlisle is the Treaty Elm, an old elm tree under which a treaty was negotiated to acquire additional lands.

CARLOS, village (pop. 100), Randolph County, E central Indiana, zip 47329, 12 mi. SW of Winchester. Carlos is a trade center for butter, flour, and feed, and is a manufacturer of casket shells, dolls, and stampings.

CARMEL, city (pop. 6,568), Hamilton County, central Indiana, zip 46032, 10 mi. N of Indianapolis in an agricultural area noted for feed grains and livestock. Carmel is a manufacturing center for ready-mix concrete, elevators, safety belts, dental equipment, automatic screw machine products, and electric cords. The town also has two newspapers and a typesetting plant.

CARROLL, county (pop. 17,734), N. central Indiana, area 374 sq. mi., drained by the Tippecanoe River and Wildcat and Deer creeks. Carroll County was organized in 1828 and named for Charles Carroll, at the time the only surviving signer of the Declaration of Independence. In the past, Shawnee and Miami Indians claimed the area as their own, and many Indian relics can still be found. Prehistoric Indian mounds are also located in the NW sector of the county. Delphi became the county seat in May,1828. Carroll County's economic progress was enhanced in the 1800s by the trade facilities provided by the Wabash and Erie Canal. Today it is a leader in agricultural products, meat and poultry packing, lumber milling, and plumbing fixture fittings.

CARTHAGE, town (pop. 946), Rush County, E central Indiana, zip 46115, 32 mi. E of Indianapolis. It is a marketing center for the paper industry and an agricultural center for livestock, poultry, and grain.

CASS, county (pop. 40,456), N central Indiana, area 415 sq. mi., drained by the Eel River and Deer Creek. The county was organized in 1829 and named for Lewis Cass, governor of Michigan Territory (1813-31) and the 1848 Democratic presidential candidate. Cass County is noted for livestock, grain, fruit, poultry, truck and dairy products, plant nurseries, and timber. Manufactures include electrical wire assemblies, wire springs, rubber and plastic products, and machinery. Logansport is the county seat.

CASTLETON, town (pop. 267), Marion County, central Indiana, zip 46250, 12 mi. NE of Indianapolis in an agricultural and manufacturing area. Castleton manufactures cabinets, clutches, couplings, and leather apparel.

CAYUGA, town (pop. 1,090), Vermillion County, W Indiana, zip 47928, near the Wabash River and 34 mi. N of Terre Haute in a coal-mining and agricultural region.

CEDAR LAKE, town (pop. 7,589), Lake County, NW Indiana, zip 46303, 7 mi. SW of Crown Point. Cedar Lake became a popular resort for the wealthy in the 1890s. The Monon Railroad was instrumental in its development, carrying trainloads of Chicagoans to the community, which sits on the edge of a forest-rimmed lake. The boom days ended in 1929 with the beginning of the Great Depression. The cottages remain, but many of them are dilapidated.

Cedar Lake still attracts thousands every weekend. They can

enjoy the lake's excellent bathing, boating, and fishing facilities. The Moody Bible Institute holds sacred music concerts every Saturday during July and August on the site of Old Monon Park. Of note to visitors is the Indian Mound Cemetery which has tombstones of early settlers and an old Indian burial ground. Industry is light, including only the manufacture of violin strings and ironwork.

CEDAR GROVE, town (pop. 248), Franklin County, SE Indiana, zip 47016, 6 mi. SE of Brookville in an agricultural area noted for feed grains and livestock.

CENTERPOINT, town (pop. 275), Clay County, W Indiana, zip 47840, 18 mi. ESE of Terre Haute in an agricultural and bituminous coal-mining region. Dietz Lake, a popular recreational spot, is nearby.

CENTERVILLE, town (pop. 2,380), Wayne County, E Indiana, zip 47330, 6 mi. W of Richmond. Centerville is well-known for its fine old homes. Arches and fancy architecture abound on Main Street. The George W. Julian House (1846) is built in Georgian style and was later remodeled in the Italian Renaissance and Greek Revival styles. Julian was a radical leader of the Indiana Congress (1849-51). The Salisbury Courthouse (1811) is the oldest standing log courthouse in Indiana. The town is a marketing center for livestock and dairy farmers, and is a manufacturer of furniture and canned goods.

CHAIN O'LAKES STATE PARK, Noble County, NE Indiana, 5 mi. SE of Albion. The park, so named because of its many interconnecting lakes, ecompasses 2,731 acres of woods and water. Recreational facilities are available for bathing, boating, fishing, picnicking, horseback riding, hiking, and camping.

CHALMERS, town (pop. 544), White County, NW central Indiana, zip 47929, 17 mi. N of Lafayette in an agricultural area.

CHANDLER, village (pop. 2,032), Warrick County, SW Indiana, zip 47610, 13 mi. ENE of Evansville in an agricultural and bituminous coal-mining region. The Wabash and Erie Canal passed through Chandler; the canal bed can still be seen west of the town.

CHARLESTOWN, town (pop. 5,890), Clark County, SE Indiana, zip 47111, 15 mi. NE of New Albany. Charlestown was platted in 1808 and was the county seat from 1811 to 1878. A gradual economic decline ended in 1940, when E.I. duPont de Nemours and Company built a powder plant at the edge of town. The subsequent arrival of the Goodyear Tire and Rubber Company brought an influx of people into Charlestown and resulted in the biggest boom in its history. Although industry has taken over, much of the historic past has been preserved. The first Methodist Church in Indiana was moved to Charlestown and other century-old buildings remain. Near the church is the grave of Jonathan Jennings (1784-1834), first governor of Indiana. Old Tunnel Mill (1820) operated until 1854; its giant wheel and foundation are preserved in a picnic area.

On military property atop a 180-ft. ridge between Fourteen Mile Creek and the Ohio River lie Indian earthworks thought to have been built by the Mound Builders of the Mississippian culture.

CHARLOTTESVILLE, town (pop. 400), Hancock County, central Indiana, zip 46117, 29 mi. E of Indianapolis in a farming and dairy area. The town is a producer of steel pipe, farm supplies, and liquid fertilizers.

CHESTERFIELD, town (pop. 3,001), Madison County, central Indiana, zip 46017, 39 mi. NE of Indianapolis. It was named for an Indian trader called McChester, who had a cabin near Mill Creek. Several settlers arrived and built three mills, one of which was a carding mill that brought some measure of prosperity to the town. Chesterfield was organized in 1830, but was not incorporated until 1858. In 1890, the State Spiritualist Association built a camp and a 500-seat auditorium nearby. Every August, thousands of visitors arrive for the meeting of the Spiritualist faith.

CHESTERTON, town (pop. 6,177), Porter County, NW Indiana, zip 46304, 15 mi. E of Gary. Chesterton is a center for poultry, fruit, and dairy products, and is a manufacturer of printer's supplies. North of Chesterton is a series of giant sand dunes created by centuries of beach erosion along the shore of Lake Michigan.

CHRISNEY, town (pop. 550), Spencer County, SW Indiana, zip 47611, 30 mi. E of Evansville is a mainly agricultural area. Chrisney City Lake, in the town, is a popular fishing and boating spot for the local populace.

CHURUBUSCO, town (pop. 15,428), Whitley County, NE Indiana, zip 46723, 15 mi. NW of Fort Wayne. Named for the Mexican town of Churubusco, it is a farming community and a shipping point for vegetables. Blue Lake, a 239-acre recreational site, is located 3 mi. NW of the town.

CICERO, town (pop. 1,378), Hamilton County, central Indiana, zip 46034, 27 mi. NNE of Indianapolis. Named for a Delaware Indian chief, it is a headquarters for the Seventh-Day Adventists who have a camp nearby. The town is a center for agricultural products.

CLARK, county (pop. 75,876), SE Indiana, area 384 sq. mi., bounded SE by the Ohio River and drained by Silver Creek. Clark County was founded in 1801 and named for George Rogers Clark, a Revolutionary War hero. The county is mainly agricultural in character, but has some manufacturing at Charlestown, Clarksville, and Jeffersonville (*q.q.v.*).

CLARKSBURG, town (pop. 300), Decatur County, SE Indiana, zip 47225, 12 mi. NE of Greensburg in an agricultural area noted for feed grains and livestock.

CLARKS HILL, town (pop. 741), Tippecanoe County, W central Indiana, zip 47930, 15 mi. SSE of Lafayette. The town economy is based on agriculture and farming.

CLARK STATE FOREST, Scott and Clark counties, SE Indiana, near Henryville in the scenic "Hoosier Hills." Clark State Forest covers an area of 22,871 acres and contains several lakes which are stocked with game fish. The forest contains facilities for camping, picnicking, boating, fishing, hiking, and horseback riding.

Clark State Forest is the oldest and one of the largest state forests in Indiana. Much of the land was once part of Clark's Grant, given to George Rogers Clark in the Virginia Cession of

Claims to the Northwest Territory after the Revolutionary War. Virgin stands of maple and beech are abundant and the many rocky, fern-clad ravines make the area attractive to visitors.

CLARKSVILLE, town (pop. 13,806), Clark County, SE Indiana, zip 47130, just E of New Albany. Clarksville was founded in 1783 by George Rogers Clark. Located on the Ohio River, the original settlement overlooked Corn Island, on which Clark established his first military outpost. After creating the town, however, he did not develop it, and it soon fell into decay. Since Clarks' death in 1818, Clarksville has merged with the Louisville, Kentucky, metropolitan area and has benefitted from its industrial economy. The Colgate-Palmolive plant lies along the river and has the world's second largest clock on its roof. In town is the Howard Steamboat Museum, which has memorabilia of the Howard Shipyards (1834-1941) that built some of the most famous steamboats.

CLAY, county (pop. 23,933), W Indiana, area 364 sq. mi., drained by the Eel River and Birch Creek. Clay County was organized in April 1825 and named for Henry Clay, the famous statesman. In the 1800s Clay County ranked as the largest producer of coal in the state, but the supply was largely exhausted. Mining is still carried out in some areas. Leading industries are clay products and brick manufacturing. Agriculture (livestock, feed grains) is the economic mainstay. Brazil is the county seat.

CLAY CITY, town (pop. 900), Clay County, W Indiana, zip 47841, 22 mi. SE of Terre Haute. Clay City was founded in 1873 and was incorporated in 1888. Manufacturing began with the building of a pottery plant; the old works still remain and are popular with visitors. Pottery is still produced, but other industries which manufacture concrete products and preserves have emerged. Coal mines and clay pits are nearby.

CLAYPOOL, town (pop. 468), Kosciusko County, N. Indiana, zip 46510, 45 mi. SSE of South Bend. Located in the northern lake and moraine region, it is a center for feed grains and livestock in one of the best agricultural areas of the state.

CLAYTON, town (pop. 736), Hendricks County, central Indiana, zip 46118, 22 mi. WSW of Indianapolis. It is a center for flour, timber, fruit, and grain.

CLEAR CREEK, village (pop. 250), Monroe County, S Indiana, zip 47426, 4 mi. S of Bloomington in an agricultural and limestone quarrying area. Concrete products are manufactured in the village.

CLERMONT, town (pop. 1,058), Marion County, central Indiana, zip 46119. Clermont was platted in 1849. The oldest remaining log cabin in Marion County is outside of town. The cabin was built in 1821, and is dedicated to the pioneers of the county. Historical memorabilia are on display. Most of the population is employed in Indianapolis, and the remainder relies on mining and agriculture.

CLIFFORD, town (pop. 275), Bartholomew County, S central Indiana, zip 47226, 37 mi. SSE of Indianapolis. Clifford is in an agricultural area. Crops include corn, wheat, and soybeans.

CLIFTY FALLS STATE PARK, Jefferson County, SE Indiana, 1 mi. W of Madison. The park, situated on a high wooded plateau, is one of the most beautiful in Indiana. Encompassing 1,200 acres of hills and woods, Clifty Falls offers a striking view of the Ohio River from a point 400 ft. above the shoreline. Scenic waterfalls along Clifty Creek and Little Clifty Creek and a deep, boulder-strewn canyon are popular attractions for thousands of tourists who visit the park annually. In 1974 a tornado damaged the forest and guest facilities near the park's southern end.

CLINTON, county (pop. 30,547), central Indiana, area 407 sq. mi., drained by Sugar and Wildcat creeks. The county was organized in 1830 and named after DeWitt Clinton, early governor of New York. Frankfort became the county seat the following year, when the first court was held in the new log courthouse. The land is generally rolling and the numerous streams afford good drainage, making the entire region conducive to farming and livestock raising. Many areas have large deposits of excellent clay which is used in the manufacture of bricks, tiles, and pottery. Leading industries are food processing and the manufacture of electronic components and plumbing fixtures.

CLINTON, city (pop. 5,340), Vermillion County, W Indiana, zip 47842, on the Wabash River, 14 mi. N of Terre Haute. Clinton was platted in 1829 after the discovery of large coal deposits in the area. It was named for DeWitt Clinton, a governor of New York. Early in its existence, Clinton was an important river port and packing center. Coal mining is still the leading activity, but the manufacture of flour, meat products, and overalls is also important.

CLOVERDALE, town (pop. 870), Putnam County, W central Indiana, zip 46120, 33 mi. E of Terre Haute in a hog-raising and general farming area. Cloverdale is located close to Lieber State Park (*q. v.*) and Cataract Lake.

COAL CITY, town (pop. 235), Owen County, central Indiana, 20 mi. W of Spencer in an agricultural and mining area.

COATESVILLE, town (pop. 453), Hendricks County, central Indiana, zip 46121, 28 mi. WSW of Indianapolis in a primary agricultural area specializing in dairy, grain, and livestock farming. A large area of beech-maple forest growth has been a natural asset for the town's thriving timber business.

COLFAX, town (pop. 633), Clinton County, central Indiana, zip 46035, 19 mi. SSE of Lafayette in a feed grain and livestock area. There is some furniture manufacture and mining of bituminous coal.

COLLEGEVILLE, village (pop. 1,400), Jasper County, NW Indiana, zip 47978, on the Iroquois River, 45 mi. S of Gary in a dairy and livestock region. The village is the seat of St. Joseph's College, a junior college for men founded in 1891.

COLUMBIA CITY, city (pop. 4,911), seat of Whitley County, NE Indiana, zip 46725, 20 mi. WNW of Fort Wayne. Columbia City is distinguished for its many famous residents. Thomas Riley Marshall (1854-1925), U.S. vice-president under Woodrow Wilson and governor of Indiana (1909-13), once practiced law there. He is well-known for his adage: "What this country really needs is a good five-cent cigar." His home has been preserved as a museum by the Whitley County Historical Society. The city was also the home of Maj. Gen. Merritt W. Ireland, surgeon-general of the U.S. Army (1918-23). Lloyd C. Douglas, author of *The Magnificent Obsession* and *The Robe,* was born in Columbia City in 1877.

The Miami Indian chief Little Turtle, who was one of the signers of the Treaty of Greenville (1795), had his village on the Eel River near the site of Columbia City.

The city has diversified manufacturing, producing clothes, flour, condiments, automotive parts, and woolen goods. Whitley County Hospital and a school for retarded children are located in the city.

COLUMBIA, town (pop. 70), Fayette County, E Indiana, about 8 mi. E of Rushville in an agricultural area noted for wheat and corn production. One mile north of town is the 654-acre Mary Gray Bird Sanctuary, which harbors more than 60 species of birds.

COLUMBUS, city (pop. 27,141), seat of Bartholomew County, S central Indiana, zip 47210, on the White River, 40 mi. SSE of Indianpolis. The site was first settled in 1820 by Gen. John Tipton, John Lindsay, and Luke Bonesteel, who built cabins along the White River. The following year, Tipton donated 30 acres of his property for the county seat with the understanding that the town be named for him. The county commissioners, however, named the town Columbus. Tipton left hastily and settled in northern Indiana.

Economic progress was initially slow because the town was located in a swampy area where malaria killed many of the residents. It was many years before health conditions were corrected.

Often called the "Athens of the Prairie," Columbus has some of the most outstanding architecture in the country. An ambitious project began in the 1930s, when Eliel Saarinen, the Finnish architect, was commissioned to design a church. Since then, 40 additional buildings have been designed by such world famous architects as Eero Saarinen, Eliel's son; John Carl Warnecke; Harry Weese; I.M. Pei; and Kevin Roche. The

Columbus Chamber of Commerce operates daily tours of the buildings. The First Christian Church, designed by Eliel Saarinen, is an outstanding example of Fundamentalist arcnitecture; its 166-ft. chimes tower can be seen for miles. The North Christian Church is an hexagonal structure that tapers to a spire topped by a golden cross. Other outstanding examples are the Irwin Union Bank, the Cleo Rogers Memorial Library, the post office, and the Cummins Engine Factory.

Large numbers of parks and landscaped areas are scattered throughout the city's business district. Irwin's Sunken Gardens are contained in three-quarters of a city square and harbor hundreds of flowers and have some rare historical items. The gardens' sundial was made in England in 1699, the fountains came from Vienna, and the coping of the rock wall is from a ruined Italian city, once buried in lava. At the west end of Third Street is Tipton Knoll, one of the largest prehistoric Indian mounds in the state; a house occupies the site. Nearby are several developed fishing sites, including Azabia, Grouse Ridge, Lowell Bridge, and Millrace.

Columbus has a dual farming and industrial economy that helped the city survive the Great Depression. The Cummins Diesel Engine Company is the world's largest producer of diesel engines for locomotives, boats, trucks, and cars. Other manufactures include metal products, furniture, clothing, cement products, and canned goods.

Columbus has the dubious honor of being the home of the Reeves Octoauto. Invented in the early 1900s, its four additional wheels were said to act as "a shock absorber beyond the dreams of the neurotic." This oddity was later reduced to the Sextoauto, but it was hastily abandoned for its impracticality.

CONNER PRAIRIE, Hamilton County, central Indiana, 4 mi. S of Noblesville. A restored pioneer settlement, Conner Prairie contains the brick mansion and farm buildings of William Conner, a Hoosier fur-trader and businessman who settled there in 1823. Other log buildings are on the grounds and the settlement has been called "a living museum area of Indiana's earliest days."

CONNERSVILLE, city (pop. 17,604), seat of Fayette County, E Indiana, zip 47331, on the Whitewater River, 55 mi. E of

Indianapolis. Connersville was a fur trading post in 1808, run by John Connor, a white man who had been raised by the Delaware Indians. He founded Connersville in 1813, and became its first sheriff. He was one of the nine men to select Indianapolis as the state capital.

Connersville has been called "Little Detroit" because it formerly manufactured ten classic automobiles, among them the McFarlan, Kelsey, Auburn, and Cord. Today, the automobile industry is gone, but automobile parts are still manufactured. Other products include machine-shop equipment, refrigerators, air conditioners, and metal and enamel items.

A major tourist attraction is the office of the Whitewater Canal Company and the "Elmhurst" mansion, which was built in 1831.

CONVERSE, town (pop. 1,163), Miami County, N central Indiana, zip 46919, 10 mi. W of Marion. A center for livestock and grain, it is also a manufacturer of canned goods, mops, and milk-bottle caps.

CORTLAND, village (pop. 170), Jackson County, S Indiana, zip 47228, 10 mi. NE of Brownstown in an agricultural area. The village is a trade center and shipping point for eggs, chickens, feeds, and fertilizer.

CORUNNA, town (pop. 359), DeKalb County, NE Indiana, zip 46730, 26 mi. N of Fort Wayne. Located in the northern moraine region, the town is in a primary agricultural area producing feed grains and livestock.

CORYDON, town (pop. 2,719), Harrison County, S Indiana, zip 47112, 17 mi. WSW of New Albany. Corydon was founded by William Henry Harrison in 1808. When Indiana Territory was established in 1813 Corydon was named the territorial capital. Under the "Constitution Elm," the 44 Indiana delegates met in 1816 to draft Indiana's first constitution and name Corydon as the first state capital. The huge tree once stood 50 ft. tall and measured 5 ft. in diameter. By 1925, however, it was totally dead, and its trunk was later surrounded by a sandstone memorial. Corydon remained the state capital until 1825, when the government was moved to Indianapolis. The Battle of Corydon (July 8, 1863) was the only battle of the Civil War to take place in Indiana. Confederate raiders occupied the town for a short time while holding the home guard captive.

Corydon is a center for lumber and grain, dairy, and poultry farming. The town has some stone quarries and natural gas reservoirs. Much of its prosperity, however, is due to the tourist trade. Not only is the town attractive in itself, but it is centrally located to several popular sight-seeing attractions—Wyandotte Cave, Squire Boone Caverns, the Hayswood Nature Reserve, and the Zimmerman Art Glass Factory. The Harrison County Fair is held annually in Corydon, and features harness racing and agricultural exhibits. (*See* also Squire Boone Caverns; Corydon Capitol State Memorial.)

CORYDON CAPITOL STATE MEMORIAL, Corydon, Harrison County, Indiana, on Old Capitol Avenue. Completed in 1812 at a cost of $3,000, the blue limestone building originally served as a courthouse for Harrison County's territorial assembly. Corydon became the territorial capital when Vincennes relinquished its seat in 1813. Corydon became the first state capital in 1816 and the building served as the capitol until 1825. The capitol was restored in 1929, and houses memorabilia of Indiana's history.

COVINGTON, city (pop. 2,641), seat of Franklin County, W Indiana, zip 47932, 50 mi. N of Terre Haute. Covington was laid out in 1826 along the east bank of the Wabash River. Beautiful scenery is part of the town; many streams flow through magnificent, deep gorges into the Wabash River. In town is the house of Edward A. Hannegan (1807-1859), U.S. senator and minister to Prussia. He coined the phrase "Fifty-Four Forty or Fight" during the Northwest Boundary dispute. Lew Wallace, author of *Ben Hur,* once lived in Covington; his house remains on Eighth and Crockett streets. The town is a center for agriculture (farm produce, fruit) and the coal-mining industry. Sand and gravel pits are nearby.

CRANDALL, town (pop. 188), Harrison County, S Indiana, zip 47114, on Indian Creek, 14 mi. W of Albany. Crandall is on the sandy Mitchell Plain which has virgin stands of beech and maple. Much of the landscape is given over to grazing.

Agriculture and the raising of cattle, hogs, and pigs are the main activities.

CRAWFORD, county (pop. 8,033), S Indiana, area 312 sq. mi., bounded on the S by the Ohio River and drained by the Blue and Little Blue rivers. Crawford County was founded in 1818 and named for Col. William Crawford, the land agent of Gen. George Washington, who was captured by Indians and burned at the stake in 1782. English is the county seat.

The county is very picturesque, being almost totally covered by rugged hills and scenic forests. Rich in natural resources, Crawford County is a leading producer of livestock, feed grains, tobacco, timber, and limestone. Manufactures include concrete blocks, lime, cement, wagon parts, and canned goods. Within the county are two of the Midwest's finest caves—Wyandotte and Marengo.

CRAWFORDSVILLE, city (pop. 13,842), seat of Montgomery County, W central Indiana, zip 47933, 27 mi. S of Lafayette. Crawfordsville, the "Athens of Indiana," was platted in 1822 and named for William Crawford, a land agent who was killed by Indians in 1782.

Several nationally famous authors made their homes in Crawfordsville, among them Lew Wallace, Maurice Thompson, and Meredith Nicholson. The Lew Wallace Study, a tower-like structure, is centrally located on a beautifully landscaped three and one-half acre site. *Ben Hur* was Wallace's most famous novel, and the Ben Hur Museum, now part of a park, contains many mementoes of the author's life as a writer, soldier, and painter. Crawfordsville is the seat of Wabash College (1832), a nonsectarian liberal arts college for men.

The city is a commercial center for agricultural products, farm implements, fences, caskets, bricks, conduits, and nails. The Milligan Park Gold Course is in town. Shades State Park (*q.v.*), a 2,900-acre tract of semi-virgin oak and hickory forest, is nearby. The annual Sugar Creek Canoe Race begins at Darlington, passes through Crawfordsville, and finishes at Shades State Park.

CRAWFORD UPLAND, wooded hill region of S Indiana which contains some of the most spectacular scenery in the state. It stretches from Parke County to the Ohio River, trending generally N to S, and is intersected by hills, sharp ridges, knolls, valleys, wall-like bluffs, gorges, natural bridges, caves, and waterfalls. Its best-known features are Wyandotte and Marengo caves and Jug Rock and the Pinnacle (natural pillars of rock) near Shoals (*q.v.*) in Martin County.

Geologically, the upland is part of the Cincinnati Arch which was formed during the Silurian and Devonian periods in a time of great upheaval. The region is generally unglaciated and is underlain by sandstones, shales, clays, limestones, and thin coals. The area has traditionally been noted for bituminous coal mining and limestone quarrying. The Crawford Upland is drained by the White River and its tributaries.

CROMWELL, town (pop. 475), Noble County, NE Indiana, zip 46732, 33 mi. NW of Fort Wayne in a mainly agricultural area (soybeans, corn, wheat, livestock).

CROSLEY FISH AND WILDLIFE AREA, Jennings County, SE Indiana, 4 mi. S of North Vernon. Fishing is provided in Otter Creek, which flows through the 4,042-acre wildlife area. There are facilities for hiking, picknicking, fishing, camping, hunting, and boating.

CROTHERSVILLE, town (pop. 1,663), Jackson County, S Indiana, zip 47226, 28 mi. S of Columbus in an agricultural area.

CROWN POINT, residential city (pop. 10,931), seat of Lake County, NW Indiana, zip 46307, 12 mi. S of Gary. Crown Point was founded in 1832 by Solon Robinson, a settler who came from Connecticut and later left the town to become the agricultural editor for the New York *Tribune.* An historical marker is located on the site of his log cabin. Lake County jail is famous for one of its nortorious boarders, John Dillinger, who escaped from the prison only to be killed in Chicago, Illinois, by federal agents.

Crown Point is a manufacturing center in its own right, and has refused to become incorporated in the metropolitan areas of Gary and Hammond. It is a producer of monuments, signs, leather goods, and grinders.

CULVER, town (pop. 1,783), Marshall County, N Indiana, zip 46511, on Lake Maxinkuckee, 32 mi. SSW of South Bend. Culver is the seat of the Culver Military Academy (1894), which is beautifully situated on the shores of the lake. Cadets of the world-famous Black Horse Troop are trained there. The academy is oriented toward a four-year military program with an optional two-year junior college course. Opposite the academy is the Culver Bird Sanctuary. Culver is a trade center for livestock, dairy products, and apples.

CYNTHIANA, town (pop. 793), Posey County, SW Indiana, zip 47612, 17 mi. NNW of Evansville in an agricultural region.

DALE, town (pop. 1,113), Spencer County, SW Indiana, zip 47523, 36 mi. ENE of Evansville. Named for the philanthropist, industrialist, and social reformer Robert Dale Owen, the town is a center for the production of lumber, cheese, and canned foods. Near the sawmill is the O.V. Brown Home, which contains historical memorabilia of pioneer days.

DALEVILLE, town (pop. 1,730), Madison County E central Indiana, zip 47334, just S of Anderson. Daleville was platted in 1838 when plans to build a canal and dam were announced. The canal project was dropped, but the arrival of the railroad in 1852 helped to temporarily boost the economy. The Trenton oil and gas field is in the vicinity, but the main source of income is small private business and agriculture (corn, soybeans, wheat, livestock).

DANA, town (pop. 720), Vermillion County, W Indiana, zip 47847, 24 mi. NNW of Terre Haute near the Illinois border. Dana is an agricultural community and contains the largest round barn in the state. Ernie Pyle, the nationally known World War II correspondent, was born there in 1900. In the 1970s there were plans to move his house to the Ernie Pyle Rest Park, which contains a covered bridge built in 1876.

DANVILLE, town (pop. 3,771), seat of Hendricks County, central Indiana, zip 46122, 20 mi. W of Indianapolis. The town was founded in 1824 and named for Daniel Clark, a local justice of the peace.

In 1878, Central Normal College was relocated from Ladoga to Danville in a unique and direct manner. When a group of Danville citizens failed to purchase the college, they "kidnapped" it. At the break of dawn on May 10, 1878, they hauled the students, library, and laboratory equipment away in their carriages and drays, and were well on their way before Ladoga realized what had happened. The relocated institution in Danville continued to operate as Central Normal College until 1946, when the trustees relinquished control to the board of newly-renamed Canterbury College. Canterbury College encountered financial difficulty in 1951 and, despite attempts by the town to raise the necessary funds, it closed its doors that year.

Danville is a trading center for flour, oil dispensers, and cement blocks. It has often been called "Gable Town" because many of the small businesses are located in old buildings that have gabled roofs. The mainstay of the economy is farming (livestock, feed grains).

DARLINGTON, town (pop. 802), Montgomery County, W central Indiana, zip 47940, 9 mi. NE of Crawfordsville in an agricultural area. Of note is the Darlington Covered Bridge, spanning Sugar Creek, which is a favorite spot for fishermen.

DAVIESS, county (pop. 26,602), SW Indiana, area 430 sq.mi., bounded on the S by the East Fork and on the W by the West Fork of the White River. It is drained by the tributaries of the White River. Daviess County was organized in 1817 and named for Joseph Hamilton Daviess, a lawyer who was killed in the Battle of Tippecanoe (Nov. 7, 1811). Washington has remained the county seat since the county's formation.

The Wabash and Erie Canal, which runs the full length of the county, was later supplanted by a railroad. The railroad was built along the towpaths of the canal in order to save money and has been called on occasion the "Crooked Wonder of the World." Daviess County is rich in natural resources. Perhaps its greatest asset is coal, but farming, nursery plantations, and oil and gas wells are also important. Principal industries are the manufacture of air conditioners and air conditioner parts.

DEAM LAKE STATE RECREATION AREA, Clark County, SE

Indiana, 6 mi. E of Borden in the scenic "Hoosier Hills." Deam Lake is located within Clark State Forest. It covers 200 acres and has a maximum depth of 35 feet. The state recreation area has 1,000 acres of beech and maple forest and has excellent facilities for camping, picnicking, fishing, boating, and swimming.

DEARBORN, county (pop. 29,430), SE Indiana, area 306 sq.mi., bounded on the E by the Ohio line and on the SE by Kentucky. It is drained by the Whitewater River and Laughery Creek.

The county was organized in 1803 and named for Gen. Henry Dearborn, secretary of war of the U.S. Lawrenceburg is the county seat. The county is filled with archaeological remains, some of which are believed to be more thn 2,000 years old. It is basically an agricultural area given over to livestock, tobacco, and truck farming. There is some manufacturing; the leading industries produce distilled liquors and glass containers.

DECATUR, city (pop. 8,445), seat of Adams County, E Indiana, zip 46733, 21 mi. SSE of Fort Wayne. Located on the St. Mary's River, the town was settled in 1837 and named for Stephen Decatur, a U.S. naval hero. The city is an industrial center (motors, castings, wood and cement products) and a shipping point for soybeans, cheese, and beet sugar. A monument to Gene Stratton Porter—authoress of *A Girl of the Limberlost,* who lived in the city for three years—is in the courthouse yard. The Peace Monument, the first war memorial in the U.S. dedicated to peace, is also in the yard.

DECATUR, county (pop. 22,738), SE central Indiana, area 370 sq.mi., drained by Flatrock, Duck, Clifty, and Sand creeks. The county was organized in 1821 and was named for Stephen Decatur. Shortly thereafter Greensburg became the county seat. The county is especially adapted to agriculture and has a large grain, tobacco, and livestock market. Some of the finest limestone quarries are located there, as are several oil and gas wells.

DECKER, town (pop. 268), Knox County, SW Indiana, zip 47524, on the White River, 11 mi. S of Vincennes. It is in an agricultural area that produces grains (especially wheat) and livestock.

DEKALB, county (pop. 30,837), NE Indiana, area 366 sq.mi., bounded on the E by the Ohio line. It is drained by the St. Joseph River and Cedar and Fish creeks. The county was organized in 1837 and named for Baron DeKalb, a German nobleman who fought in the American Revolution. Auburn became the county seat the same year.

DeKalb is a leading agricultural county, and most of the land is under some form of cultivation or pasture. Livestock, truck, poultry, soybeans, corn, wheat, oats, and dairy items are the leading agricultural products. There is diversified manufacturing in some of the larger cities such as Auburn, Butler, and Garrett; products include automobile parts, hand tools, rubber parts, and castings.

DELAWARE, county (pop. 129,219) E Indiana, area 396 sq.mi., drained by the Mississinewa River, the West Fork of the White River, and Kilbuck, Bell, and Buck creeks. The county was organized in 1827 and named for the Delaware Indians. Muncie became the county seat and developed into a leading industrial center for the county. The land is mostly level or gently undulating, and most of the soils are well adapted to the cultivation of corn, feed grains, soybeans, and tomatoes. The raising of livestock (especially hogs) is also prevalent. Major industries produce automobile parts, glass containers, packaged meats, canned goods, steel wire, iron castings, and transformers. Delaware County is located within the Trenton oil and gas field and was part of the great natural gas boom of 1887.

DELPHI, town (pop. 2,582), seat of Carroll County, NW central Indiana, zip 46923, on Deer Creek, 17 mi. NE of Lafayette. Delphi was named by Samuel Milroy, a member of the state constitutional convention; it was laid out in 1828. A bustling port during the heyday of the Wabash and Erie Canal, it is now an agricultural and farming community. Manufactures include decoys, food products, and automobile bodies. The Carroll County Historical Society operates the Historical Museum, which is in the courthouse. The Carroll County Country Club and a nine-hole golf course are in town.

DEMOTTE, town (pop. 1,697), Jasper County, NW Indiana, zip 46310, about 28 mi. SW of Valparaiso in an agricultural area.

DENVER, town (pop. 566), Miami County, N central Indiana, zip 46926, on the Eel River, 8 mi. N of Peru in an agricultural area. A farming community, it specializes in poultry, fruit, and dairy products.

DEPUTY, village (pop. 250), Jefferson County, S Indiana, zip 47230, 19 mi. NW of Madison in a farming and lumbering area. The village is a trade center for lumber, pallets, and wood products.

DERBY, village (pop. 60), Perry County, S Indiana, zip 47525, 18 mi. NE of Cannelton in a mining and quarrying area. The village has one stone quarry which produces crushed stone and agricultural limestone and riprap.

DEVIL'S BACKBONE, natural ridge in the hills of Lawrence County, S Indiana. The view from the high, narrow summit takes in a breathtaking panorama from both sides.

DILLSBORO, town (pop. 840), Dearborn County, SE Indiana, zip 47018, 32 mi. SE of Greensburg in an agricultural region. The town is the seat of Dillsboro Sanatorium, a 100-room hotel in which patients suffering from arthritis, rheumatism, and nervous disorders are treated with medicinal waters. Two miles west of town is Lake Dilldear, a favorite resort and fishing spot.

DUBLIN, town (pop. 1,021), Wayne County, E Indiana, zip 47335, 17 mi. W of Richmond. The first women's suffrage group in Indiana was formed by Amanda Way in Dublin in 1851. Their resulting petition, which was recorded at the Indiana General Assembly, was filed away as being "inexpedient at this time."

Dublin is a peaceful rural community which relies heavily on feed grain cultivation and livestock farming. The Maples, a tavern in town, is an historic building of homemade brick which dates back to 1825. It was one of the most popular inns along the National Road in the early 19th century.

DUBOIS, town (pop. 520), Dubois County, S Indiana, zip 47527, 9 mi. NE of Jasper in an agricultural and lumbering area. The town is a manufacturing center for furniture, custom cabinets, and poultry products.

DUBOIS, county (pop. 30,934), SW Indiana, area 433 sq.mi., bounded partially by the East Fork of the White River and drained by the Patoka River and Huntley, Little Pigeon, and Pokeberry creeks. It was organized in 1817 and named for Toussaint Dubois, a French soldier who had charge of the spies and guards in the Battle of Tippecanoe (Nov. 7, 1811). Jasper was selected as the second and permanent county seat because of its central location.

Dubois County is noted for its large number of manufacturing plants which produce wooden office, school, and household furniture. It is also the fourth ranking county in the U.S. for the production of turkeys. Bituminous coal mining, lumbering, and stone quarrying aid the economy.

DUGGER, town (pop. 1,062), Sullivan County. SW Indiana, zip 47848, 8 mi. E of Sullivan is an agricultural area dotted with small lakes. The town has a stone crushing plant. Several popular fishing spots are at nearby Briarwood, County Line, Dugger Boat, and Hi-Pit lakes.

DUNE ACRES, (pop. 301), Porter County, NW Indiana, 6 mi. N of Chesterton on Lake Michigan. Dune Acres is a select community of summer homes and rambling estates nestled between steel mills and Porter Beach. Headquartered there is the Richardson Wildlife Foundation. Cowles Bog, a remnant of an ancient marshland, is an excellent outdoor study area of marsh, bog, and transitional swamplands. Centuries-old matted moss floats there on an underground lake.

DUNKIRK, city (pop. 3,465), on the border of Jay and Blackford counties, E Indiana, zip 47336, 16 mi. NNE of Muncie. Dunkirk is an agricultural and manufacturing (brick, tile, glass) community.

DUNLAP, village (pop. 2,000), Elkhart County, N Indiana, 4 mi. SE of Elkhart in an agricultural area. Most of the residents commute to Elkhart for their jobs. Nearby is the Kunderd Gladiolus Farm, a 175-acre tract used for the commercial cultivation of gladioli.

DUNREITH, town (pop. 200), Henry County, E central Indiana, zip 47337, 16 mi. E of Greenfield in an agricultural area noted for feed grains and livestock. The town is a manufacturing center for sanitary well seals.

DUPONT, town (pop. 357), Jefferson County, S Indiana, zip 47231, 14 mi. NW of Madison in an agricultural area.

DYER, town (pop. 4,906), Lake County, NW Indiana, zip 46311, 10 mi. S of Hammond in an agricultural region. Dyer is the site of State Line House (1838), a tavern which has been used as a hostelry since the early 1800s.

EARLHAM, unincorporated community, Wayne County, E Indiana, zip 47374, adjacent to Richmond. The community is the site of Earlham College, founded by Quakers in 1847 and chartered in 1859. The college includes Indiana's first natural history collection and the first astronomical observatory (1861) in the state.

EARL PARK, town (pop. 478), Benton County, W Indiana, zip 47942, 34 mi. NW of Lafayette in an agricultural area (feed grains, livestock). Towering old maple trees have been preserved throughout the town. Parish Grove, near the western edge of town, is named for Chief Parish, a Kickapoo Indian who fell to his death from one of the trees.

EAST CHICAGO, city (pop. 46,982), Lake County, NW Indiana, zip 46312, SSE of Chicago, on Lake Michigan.
   East Chicago was founded in 1888 and incorporated as a town in 1889, at which time its population numbered about 1,300. With the ever-increasing demand for steel in the early 1900s, the city found its niche. Its strategic location at the lower end of Lake Michigan made it a perfect site for a harbor and industrial complex. In 1901, the Block Brothers built a small steel mill in the bleak dunes region north of town. A harbor needed to obtain ore shipments was then constructed, and the industrial revolution in East Chicago began. By 1928, the first mill had expanded to 100 times its original size. Affiliated industries began to pour into the city, among them Inland Steel and Youngstown Sheet and Tube Company, which today are among

the largest in the steel industry. The Indiana Harbor, connected to the Grand Calumet River by a three-mile ship canal, is the state's largest port.

East Chicago is part of the Calumet district, one of the largest industrial complexes in the country. It is included in the Chicago-Gary-Hammond-East Chicago standard metropolitan statistical area. Among other diversified industries are oil refineries, meat-packing plants, railroad repair shops, chemical plants, automobile factories, hardware shops, and a tank and valve factory. East Chicago contains Washington Park, with the only zoo in the Calumet district. The city is the seat of the Calumet Extension Center of Indiana University.

EAST GARY, town (pop. 9,858), Lake County, NW Indiana, zip 46405, a SE suburb of Gary. East Gary is part of the Calumet district, one of the largest industrial complexes in the country. Its main industrial products include surgical instruments, food products, and cement blocks.

EATON, town (pop. 1,594), Delaware County, E Indiana, zip 47338, on the Mississinewa River, 11 mi. N of Muncie. Eaton was the major location of the natural gas boom in Delaware County. In 1876, while boring for coal near the town, miners struck a natural gas pocket. The hole was plugged and forgotten until 1887, when the demand for natural gas began to rise in Indiana's cities. Eaton, located well within the Trenton gas field, was remembered. The old hole was uncapped, and a well was sunk. The roar from the escaping gas was heard and the burning flame seen in Muncie. The gas boom in both Delaware and neighboring Madison counties brought many industries into the area.

Manufacturing is still important in Eaton, the major products being paper, canned goods, and glass jars. Natural beech and maple vegetation and productive soils have made Eaton a center for livestock grazing and feed grains, especially oats and corn.

ECKERTY, town (pop. 150), Crawford County, S Indiana, zip 47116, 9 mi. W of English in a limestone quarrying and agricultural area. Eckerty is a producer of crushed stone, sand, and lumber.

ECONOMY, town (pop. 285), Wayne County, E Indiana, zip 47339, 15 mi. NW of Richmond. The area in and around Economy was originally settled in the early 1800s by Quakers who farmed the land around the Whitewater River. Agriculture is still the leading activity in Economy. Cattle and hogs, feed grains, and soybeans are the main farm products.

EDGERTON, village (pop. 125), Allen County, N Indiana, zip 46797, in an agricultural area noted for feed grains and livestock. Edgerton is a trade center for grain, feed, seeds, and fertilizer.

EDGEWOOD, town (pop. 2,326), Madison County, E central Indiana, zip 46000, just W of Anderson. Edgewood is a restricted suburb of Anderson, and most of the population is composed of executives and employees who commute to manufacturing plants in the neighboring city.

EDINBURG, town (pop. 4,906), on the border of Johnson and Bartholomew counties, S central Indiana, zip 46124, 31 mi. SSE of Indianapolis. Endinburg is a manufacturing and agricultural community (livestock, wood products, canned goods) and has a large veneer mill. The Roth Museum has memorabilia of Edinburg's pioneer days. Nearby is the Atterbury State Fish and Game Area, a conservation and recreational site.

EDWARDSPORT, village (pop. 482), Knox County, SW Indiana, zip 47528, 17 mi. ENE of Vincennes. The village is located on the West Fork of the White River and was previously a leading port for flatboats. Edwardsport is centrally located in a region rich in natural resources. Within easy reach are fertile farmlands and deposits of oil, natural gas, and bituminous coal. The electric power plant in town, which also serves the surrounding area, is supplied with coal from near-by strip mines.

EEL RIVER, W central and SW Indiana, rises in Boone County and flows generally SW past Greencastle to SW central Clay County, then SE to join the West Fork of the White River at Worthington. The 110-mile long river was once the site of Potawatomi and Delaware Indian villages. It was named the

Shakamak (meaning "snakefish" or "eel") by the Delaware. It still abounds with eels.

ELBERFELD, town (pop. 834), Warrick County, SW Indiana, zip 47613, 14 mi. NNE of Evansville in a primarily agricultural area.

ELIZABETH, town (pop. 195), zip 47117, Harrison County, S Indiana, 14 mi. SW of New Albany in an agricultural area.

ELIZABETHTOWN, town (pop. 519), Bartholomew County, S central Indiana, zip 47232, 8 mi. SE of Columbus in an agricultural area.

ELK CREEK STATE FISH AND GAME AREA, Washington County, S Indiana, 15 mi. NE of Salem. The state property covers 421 acres and has a boat launching ramp and excellent fishing.

ELKHART, city (pop. 43,152), Elkhart County, N Indiana, zip 46514, at the confluence of the Elkhart and Saint Joseph's rivers, 15 mi. E of South Bend. The city was named by the Indians for an island in the Elkhart River, the shape of which resembled an elk's heart. Among the first settlers was a Baptist missionary who adopted the name in 1822. The site was a popular one with the Indians and lay at the junction of some of their trails.

Elkhart was platted in 1832, whereupon its population grew rapidly. After the arrival of the first railroad company in 1850, the growth of the town was closely linked with railroad development, especially that of the New York Central system. Incorporation came in 1877, and industrialization continued at a rapid rate.

Elkhart is the world center for the manufacture of mobile homes. Miles Laboratories began in Elkhart as a small drug business in the late 19th century and grew to be one of the largest such concerns in the world. In 1875, Charles G. Conn, a small-town band instrument craftsman, set up shop in Elkhart after he had successfully invented a soft rubber mouthpiece for cornets. Today, Elkhart is the world leader in the manufacture of band instruments. In all, the city had more than 550 industrial plants in the mid-1970s. Other manufactured products include electronic components, construction machinery, fishing tackle, and rubber goods.

Elkhart was the boyhood home of noted journalist and short story writer Ambrose Bierce. His house has been reconstructed in town. The Elkhart Institute of Technology is also located there. Recreational facilities are found at nearby Heaton and Simonton lakes.

ELKHART, county (pop. 126,529), N Indiana, area 468 sq.mi., bounded on the N by the Elkhart and St. Joseph rivers. The county was formed in January 1830 and Goshen was platted and chosen as the county seat in 1831. Elkhart County is one of Indiana's leading industrial areas and is a center for the manufacture of mobile homes, automobile parts, fabricated metals, pharmaceuticals, furniture, and electronic components. It is also a leading agricultural area given over to dairying, livestock, soybeans, corn, wheat, oats, potatoes, hay, mint, and onions.

ELKHART RIVER, N Indiana, rises in Elkhart County and flows about 50 mi. NW to SE across the county to Goshen. It is the site of the Elkhart County River Preserve and the Elkhart River Hydroelectric Canals which supply power for local industries.

ELLETTSVILLE, town (pop. 1,627), Monroe County, S central Indina, zip 47429, 6 mi. NW of Bloomington. A mining town, it has produced some of the finest limestone stonework in the country. The town was named for Edward Ellets, an early resident. The Matthews Mansion (1865), in French Mansard style, has four carved heads above its entrance which are said to depict the builder's children. Bizarre stone carvings are displayed in a park at the rear.

ELNORA, town (pop. 873), Daviess County, SW Indiana, zip 47529, 28 mi. ENE of Vincennes in an agricultural area. There is some industry (concrete products, flour, packed poultry).

ELWOOD, city (pop. 11,196), Madison County, E central Indiana, zip 46036, 15 mi. NW of Anderson. The town was platted in 1853 along the S bank of Duck Creek. The settlement was first known as Duck Creek, then as Quincy, and finally was named Elwood in 1869. Incorporation followed in 1872. Elwood began to prosper in 1887 with the discovery of natural gas, and became the second largest town in the county. Among the many industries that were fostered by the gas boom were the American Sheet and Tinplate Company, Pittsburgh Plate Glass and Window Glass, foundries, machine shops, and saw mils. Like so many other towns in the county, Elwood's prosperity dwindled with the gas supply, and the population decreased. Elwood settled down to a more peaceful existence, and farming began to take precedence over industry.

The city is now a center for agriculture, especially tomatoes, and is a manufacturer of canned goods, mobile homes, and glassware. Wendell L. Willkie, the Republican presidential candidate of 1940, was born in the town in 1892. His father, Herman F. Willkie, was principal of the high school. A memorial park contains a granite monument to the famous politician.

ENGLISH, town (pop. 664), seat of Crawford County, S Indiana, zip 47118, 36 mi. W of New Albany. English was founded in 1839 and named for William Hayden English, a vice presidential candidate in 1880. It did not begin to prosper until it became the county seat in 1893. Wilderness surrounds the town, which is picturesquely situated in a deep, wooded valley. Timber and lumbering are the leading industries, followed by agriculture and railroad repair shops.

ETNA GREEN, town (pop. 516), Kosciusko County, N Indiana, zip 46524, 30 mi. SSE of South Bend. It is a small shipping and trading center for agricultural products.

EVANSVILLE, city (pop. 138,764), seat of Vanderburgh County, SW Indiana, zip 47708, on the Ohio River, 145 mi. SSW of Indianapolis.

The site on which Evansville is located was once occupied by a prehistoric Indian village. The inhabitants lived there for 200 years, abandoned it for unknown reasons, and today the site, known as Angel Mounds, is one of the finest archaeological localities in the Ohio Valley (*see* Angel Mounds State Memorial).

The Evansville area remained untouched by white men until

March 27, 1812, when Col. Hugh McGary built his cabin on a bend of the Ohio River. Realizing the natural potential of the area, McGary purchased 200 acres from the Vincennes Land Office. He started a ferry service, and more settlers filtered into the vicinity. In 1814, the growing village became the seat of newly-formed Warrick County. McGary later sold 130 acres of his holdings to Col. Robert M. Evans and James W. Jones, who replatted the village and named it Evansville. In 1818, Evansville became the seat of Vanderburgh County, which was formed when Warrick County was split into three sections. Incorporation to town status came the following year, and McGary was named president of the first board of trustees. The population then numbered 101.

An influx of new settlers began in 1824 when salt was discovered beneath the town. New jobs were created for mining the salt, but it was subsequently found to be brackish and unsuitable for preserving purposes. The town began to decay; there were no industries, not even a mill, and an epidemic of milk sickness took its toll on the population. In 1832, four disastrous spring floods inundated Evansville, cutting it off from river trade and temporarily making the town an island. In that summer, 391 people died from cholera. The town again began to grow with the announcement in 1834 that it was to become the southern terminus for the Wabash and Erie Canal. Sawmills were erected on Pigeon Creek to supply timber to shipbuilding and fuel for steamboats. Industry began to flourish, and on Jan. 27, 1847, Evansville was incorporated as a city. The first mayor, James G. Jones, was a son of the earliest proprietors. The riverfront was improved and a fire department was added.

By 1850 Evansville boasted a cabinet shop, sawmill, pottery works, tobacco plant, foundries, and an iron casting factory. By 1853 river traffic business was booming. Down the Ohio River had come such famous steamboats as the "Robert Fulton," "Robert E. Lee," and "Eclipse." Although the canal project was abandoned in 1860, it had brought business into the city. By 1880 Evansville was the greatest hardwood market center in the U.S. and by 1895 had become the future manufacturing capital of the nation.

River traffic was limited to freight shipments, which declined appreciably after the coming of the railroad in 1853. By

1900, more than 300 iron, steel, and furniture manufacturing businesses flourished there, as did two of the nation's largest cotton mills. Periods of economic recession were followed by periods of growth. Vast coal deposits and oil fields were discovered in the vicinity, which provided new sources of energy for industries. The city is located in the center of the Illinois Oil Basin, and annually produces 65,000,000 barrels of crude oil.

By the 1970s, Evansville stood alone as the major industrial, transportation, and trade center of southern Indiana. Whirlpool Corporation was the largest single employer, followed closely by Arkla Air Conditioning, Burch Plow, Alcoa, Mead Johnson and Company, and Coca-Cola Bottling. There was total of about 450 industries, and manufactures included agricultural implements, bathroom fixtures, soft drinks, canvas products, casters and furniture hardware, furniture, clothing, road excavation equipment, paint, plastics, uniforms, and sheet metal products. Agriculture forms a solid economic foundation, as the soils around Evansville are ideally suited for feed grains, melons, apples, peaches, potatoes, and small fruits.

Evansville combines the old with the new. A community center was completed in 1972, and a civic center which includes an auditorium, convention center, and government buildings was completed in 1969. Evansville remains as the second largest convention center in Indiana. Many of the old 19th century mansions from the riverboat days have been restored. Admirable examples are the Morgan Manor (1853) in Georgian style; the Sonntag-Bayard-Kiechle House (1863) owned by Samuel Bayard, founder of the city's library system; the Rudd-Miller House (1865); the Viele-Koch House (1854) of French Imperial style which had a ballroom papered in gold leaf; the courthouse (1888), one of the finest examples of Baroque-Dresden style in the U.S.; and the post office (1876).

The people of Evansville are devoted to cultural activities. The city has an excellent museum of arts and sciences, a philharmonic orchestra, and six fine arts theatres. The press and media were represented in the 1970s by three newspapers, four television stations, and six radio stations. Mesker Zoo in Mesker Park is one of the most modern zoos in the country and the largest in Indiana. There are no cages around the animals; their areas are surrounded by hidden moats giving the illusion of a natural, in-the-wild setting. More than 1,000 animals are housed there.

Evansville has excellent educational facilities. It is the seat of the University of Evansville (1854), a private, coeducational, four-year college with an average enrollment of 5,500 students. Indiana State University, a branch of the Terre Haute institution, opened its doors to 2,700 students in 1965. Other vocational institutions include Indiana Vocational Technical College (1968), ITT Business and Technical Institute, Lain Technical Institute, and Lockyear College of Business.

The city's economy includes the tourist trade. Evansville attractions, southern Indiana's scenic beauty, Angel Mounds, the Lincoln Heritage Trail, the New Harmony State Memorial, and Burdette Park have made it a primary visitor's center throughout the year. Water recreation can be found at Lost Lake, 7 mi. SW. of the city.

FAIRFAX STATE RECREATION AREA, Monroe County S central Indiana, approximately 16 mi. S of Bloomington. It is actually one of two recreational facilities that encompass 22,500 acres on the Monroe Dam and Reservoir, which was dedicated in 1965. Fairfax, the southern unit, offers swimming, picnicking, boating, camping, fishing, and hunting.

FAIRLAND, town (pop. 1,150), Shelby County, central Indiana, zip 46126, 7 mi. NW of Shelbyville in an industrial and agricultural area. The town is a trade center for fertilizer, lumber products, and farm machinery. It has several industries, among them the production of concrete, trailer skirts, lathe specialities, and precision machinery.

FAIRMOUNT, town (pop. 3,427), Grant County, central Indiana, zip 46928, 10 mi. S of Marion. Basically a farming community, it is also a center for the Wesleyan and Methodist state conferences. The population is comprised largely of Quakers, whose simple frame churches are scattered throughout the town.

FAIRVIEW PARK, town (pop. 1,067), Vermillion County, W Indiana, zip 47808, 17 mi. N of Terre Haute in an agricultural and coal-mining region.

FARMERSBURG, town (pop. 962), Sullivan County, SW Indiana, zip 47850, 15 mi. S of Terre Houte. Named for its large concentration of farmers, the town was settled in 1854 and incorporated in 1871. Natural resources are plentiful in the area, and Farmersburg has become a small center for the production of oil and natural gas, lumber, and coal.

FARMLAND, town (pop. 1,262), Randolph County, E Indiana, zip 47340, 13 mi. E of Muncie. A trading and agricultural community, it also manufactures auto cranes and canned goods.

FAYETTE, county (pop. 26,216), E Indiana, area 215 sq.mi., drained by the Whitewater River. The county was organized in 1818 and named for the Marquis de Lafayette. Connersville became the county seat. Much of the county is composed of drained bottom lands which are highly suitable for the cultivation of feed grains. Manufactures include refrigerators, hardware, porcelained panels, and industrial blowers.

FERDINAND, town (pop. 1,432), Dubois County, SW Indiana, zip 47532, 45 mi. ENE of Evansville. The town is almost entirely composed of the descendants of German settlers who continue to speak a unique mixture of German and English. Agriculture is important and some manufacturing has developed in town. A furniture factory, whose products reflect Old World craftsmanship, and a foundry employ a large portion of the population. Stone quarries are nearby.

Ferdinand is the seat of the Immaculate Conception Convent and Girls' Academy (1859), the buildings of which resemble a medieval castle. The church has an imposing 37-ft. dome topped by a gold cross. The Ferdinand Railroad Company, which began operations in 1909, is one of the shortest, self-supporting railroads in the U.S. It runs for a mere 7 mi. between Ferdinand and Huntingburg.

Recreational facilities (boating, camping, swimming) can be found 6 mi. E of Ferdinand at the 87,000-acre Ferdinand State Forest.

FERDINAND STATE FOREST, Dubois County, S Indiana, 2 mi. N of Rochester. The forest encompasses 7,875 acres of beech and maple woods and contains the Ferdinand State Fish

Hatchery, which stocks lakes in the state with game fish. Water recreation is available on a 4,200-acre lake, and there are excellent facilities for camping.

FILLMORE, town (pop. 550), Putnam County, central Indiana, zip 46126, 6 mi. NE of Greencastle in an agricultural area noted for feed grains and livestock. The town has a sawmill and a limestone quarry which produces crushed stone and agricultural limestone.

FISHERS, town (pop. 628), Hamilton County, central Indiana, zip 46038, 15 mi. NE of Indianapolis in an agricultural area. The town is also known as Fishers Station.

FLAT ROCK, town (pop. 250), Shelby County, central Indiana, zip 47234, 12 mi. S of Shelbyville in an agricultural and industrial area. Flat Rock is a manufacturer of crushed limestone and food-processing equipment.

FLORA, town (pop. 1,877), Carroll County, W central Indiana, zip 46929, 22 mi. ENE of Lafayette in an agricultural region. Poultry, condensed milk, lumber, and cement are among the leading products.

FLOYD, county (pop. 26,216), S Indiana, area 149 sq.mi., bounded on the S by the Ohio River and drained by its small tributaries. The county was organized in 1819 and named for Col. John Floyd, a member of a Virginia family that had been ambushed by Indians across the Ohio River from the county. New Albany became the county seat in 1819.

Floyd County is a hilly region which is best suited for stock raising, dairying, lumbering, and fruit orchards. There is also some manufacturing (wood products, men's apparel, foods) in the larger towns. A scenic range of hills known as The Knobs runs the entire length of the county from N to S, making the entire region a popular summer vacation spot.

FLOYDS KNOBS, town (pop. 300), Floyd County, S Indiana, zip 47119, 4 mi. NW of New Albany. The town is a center for strawberry-growing and is located in a valley surrounded by high, scenic hills known as The Knobs. It was founded in 1815 when James Moore from New York State built a gristmill on the site. The present name was adopted in 1843 in honor of Col. Davis Floyd of nearby Jeffersonville, who was a member of the first General Assembly of Indiana Territory.

Floyds Knobs is a manufacturing center for wooden furniture, cabinets, welded items, and conveyors.

FOREST, town (pop. 400), Clinton County, N Indiana, zip 46039, 13 mi. NE of Frankfort in an agricultural area noted for livestock and feed grains. Forest is a trade center for feeds, grain, fertilizer, and seeds.

FORT BRANCH, town (pop. 2,535), Gibson County, SW Indiana, zip 47533, 19 mi. N of Evansville. The town is located on the site of a fort built in 1811. There is a 5-ft. monument depicting the history of the fort as a defense against Indian attack. Agriculture and the manufacture of concrete blocks are the leading activities.

FORTVILLE, town (pop. 2,460), Hancock County, central Indiana, zip 46040, 20 mi. NE of Indianapolis. The town was platted by Cephas Fort in 1849. It has an agricultural and manufacturing economy; products include chemicals and automobile parts. Nearby is Fort Benjamin Harrison, a U.S. Army post established in 1903.

FORT WAYNE, city (pop. 177,671), seat of Allen County, NE Indiana, zip 46802, at the confluence of the St. Marys and St. Joseph rivers, forming the Maumee. Fort Wayne is the state's third largest city and is located approximately 105 mi. NE of Indianapolis in a rich farming and dairying region. In the 1600s and 1700s the site was a meeting place for two powerful Indian tribes—the Miami and the Potawatomi—who called it Kekionga.

Fort Miami, the first fortified outpost, was built by the French in 1682 where the aqueduct now stands. The settlement was under the jurisdiction of the governor of Louisiana, who managed a large section of that part of the country. As a result of the French and Indian Wars, the fort was surrendered to the English in 1760. Until the close of the American Revolution, the site at the rivers' confluence was a lawless settlement known as

Miami Town. It remained a stronghold for the surrounding Indian tribes, who resisted settlement of the area by the white man. Chief Little Turtle of the Miami became famous for his valiant efforts of resistance against white soldiers. Little Turtle was finally defeated in 1794 by Gen. "Mad Anthony" Wayne in the Battle of Fallen Timbers at Maumee, Ohio. The Americans erected a fort at Miami Town in Wayne's honor, giving the city its present name.

The settlement flourished as a peaceful fur-trading center after the end of the Indian fighting in the War of 1812. The fur trade remained the principal enterprise of the town for many years. Fort Wayne incorporated as a town in 1829, and acquired city status in 1840.

Fort Wayne's industrial growth was stimulated by the building of the Wabash and Erie Canal. The Canal teemed with ladened boats and a business district of sizeable proportions sprang up around it. The real boom, however, did not start until the coming of the railroads, the first of which arrived in 1854. The next five years saw the arrival of other railroad companies and the building of huge railroad repair shops which came to do the largest business of its kind in the U.S. Diversified manufacturing was introduced into Fort Wayne following the Civil War. The lumber business was outstanding until the hardwood forests of the region were exhausted. Branch industries included the production of wagon wheels, organs, and pianos.

The city had been lighted with gas in 1855, but modernization brought electric lighting. Fort Wayne claims to be the originator of night baseball games. On a balmy Saturday night in June 1883, League Park was lighted with 17 low-intensity arc lights for the game which was witnessed by 2,000 spectators.

Fort Wayne contains the grave of John Chapman, better known as Johnny Appleseed, who was a plant nurseryman, preacher, and herb doctor. He came to the area in the 1800s after wandering for thousands of miles distributing and planting appleseeds and sprouts. He was 70 years old when he died near Fort Wayne in 1845. His grave site overlooks Memorial Coliseum.

Fort Wayne today is a modern industrial and manufacturing center. The gasoline tank and pump industry originated there, and the city has two of the nation's largest manufacturers of these products. Other manufactures include electrical appliances, mining equipment, truck bodies, tools, paint, paper, clothing, and processed food. The International Harvester Company, one of the largest in the nation, gives tours through the axle and transmission machine division, forge and die shops, and heat treating department.

Fort Wayne is the seat of several institutions of higher learning, among them Concordia College (1839), a four-year liberal arts school; Indiana Institute of Technology (1930); St. Francis College (1890); St. Benedict's College; Fort Wayne Bible School; and the Fort Wayne School of Fine Arts.

The Lincoln Library and Museum, regarded as the best museum for research on the subject in the United States, is operated by the Lincoln National Life Foundation and contains more than 10,000 items of Lincoln memorabilia including books, paintings, original photographs, and autographs. Cultural institutions are an important part of Fort Wayne. Of note are the Allen County-Fort Wayne Historical Society Museum, the Jack D. Diehm Museum of Natural History, the Fort Wayne Art Institure, the Festival Music Theatre, and the Fort Wayne Civic Theatre. The city has three parks which provide recreational facilities for horseback riding, hiking, picnicking, and tennis. Of note is Franke Park, which contains a large bird sanctuary and a children's zoo. Other points of interest include the Cathedral of the Immaculate Conception, with its beautiful Bavarian stained glass windows and carved wood altar, and the old hotel from which William Jennings Byran spoke in 1898 during his campaign for the presidency.

FOUNTAIN, county (pop. 18,257), W Indiana, area 397 sq.mi., bounded on the W and N by the Wabash River and drained by Coal Creek. The county was organized in December 1825 and Covington was named the county seat a few months later. The county was named for Maj. Fountain of Kentucky, who was killed in the Battle of Maumee (1790) near Fort Wayne.

Fountain County has a diversified agricultural, industrial, and mining economy with most of the manufacturing taking place in Attica, Covington, and Veedersburg. Major manufactures include steel castings, electronic components, and storage batteries.

FOUNTAIN CITY, town (pop. 852), Wayne County, E Indiana, zip 47341, 10 mi. N of Richmond. Originally known as Newport, its name was changed in 1834 when a subterranean lake was discovered under the town. Pipes driven into the ground caused an immediate rise in the water level, and gave the town its name.

Fountain City became famous for its role as the "grand central station" of the "freedom train" for runaway slaves. The so-called Underground Railroad was run by Levi Coffin, a Quaker, who helped 2,000 slaves escape to Canada in the years 1827 to 1847. His house still stands in good condition on North Main Street. Levi Coffin and the rest of the large Quaker population were ardent Abolitionists, and they gave many slaves work until they could be sent north or to Canada. Today, Fountain City is a quiet farming community, and descendants of fugitive slaves still live there.

FOWLER, town (pop. 2,643), seat of Benton County, W Indiana, zip 47944, 27 mi. NW of Lafayette. Fowler was laid out in 1871 at an attractive site covered with virgin forest. Remnants of this forest can still be seen in the stately old trees that line downtown sidewalks. The town was named for Moses Fowler, who contributed money for the courthouse. Fowler is a center for corn, soybeans, grain, livestock, and poultry. Just outside of town is the Benton County Country Club.

FOWLERTON, town (pop. 337), Grant County, E central Indiana, zip 46930, 18 mi. NNW of Muncie in an agricultural region noted for feed grains and livestock. The town is a producer of catsup.

FRANCES SLOCUM STATE FOREST, Wabash County, N Indiana, 17 mi. SW of Wabash. Located on the east side of the Mississinewa River, it is one of the best state forests developed for recreational purposes. It encompasses 1,089 acres of woods and water and has expanded its facilities to meet the need for new campgrounds and picnic areas. Excellent fishing, swimming, and horseback riding are available. The grave of Frances Slocum, for whom the forest is named, is across the river. A white woman, she lived with the Miami Indians after they captured her at the age of five.

FRANCESVILLE, town (pop. 1,015), Pulaski County, NW Indiana, zip 47946, 40 mi. N of Lafayette. It is a center for flour and machine shop production, and is a shipping point for milk and grain.

FRANCISCO, town (pop. 621), Gibson County, SW Indiana, zip 47534, 7 mi. ESE of Princeton in a region rich in natural resources (fertile soils, oil, natural gas, bituminous coal). The town was named for a Spanish worker on the Wabash and Erie Canal.

FRANKFORT, city (pop. 14,956), seat of Clinton County, central Indiana, zip 46041, 40 mi. NNW of Indianapolis. Frankfort was platted in 1830. It was named for Frankfurt-am-Main, Germany, which was the home of the grandfather of the Pence brothers who owned the land around the present site. The first court session was held in 1831 at the log courthouse.

Frankfort is a modern commercial and shipping center. It is stategically located in an apple-growing district and is a leading distributor of the fruit. Manufactures include enameled sheet metal, clothing, and brass fittings. Railroad repair shops and an oil refinery are in the city. Frankfort was once the home of the world's largest handle factory.

The Goodwin Funeral Home Museum has a large collection of classic cars and Lincoln memorabilia, as well as pioneer artifacts. Just west of town is the Peter-Paul Candy Factory, which offers tours to visitors. North of Frankfort is the country club, which features an 18-hole golf course.

FRANKLIN, city (pop. 11,477), seat of Johnson County, central Indiana, zip 46131, 20 mi. SSE of Indianapolis. Founded in 1822, it features a stone-brick courthouse built in 1883. History pervades the town, making it a popular tourist attraction. There are monuments honoring heroes of the Revolutionary, Civil, Spanish-American, and World wars. The Methodist Home, the Indiana Masonic Home, a museum of local pioneer history, and the original log cabin (1834) from which Franklin College grew, are all there. Franklin was the home of two distinguished citizens, Paul V. McNutt, the 34th governor of Indiana, and William M. Chase, noted 19th-century painter.

Franklin College, east of the courthouse, began as the

Indiana Baptist Manual Labor Institute in 1834. It became the first coeducational college in the state after a financial crisis in 1842. Basically a liberal arts college, its 8-acre campus features a library, gymnasium, dormitories, science hall, and auditorium. Franklin is a trading center and leading manufacturer for automobile parts, household appliances, furniture, lumber, glue, paint, canned goods, and flour.

FRANKLIN, county (pop. 16,943), SE Indiana, area 394 sq.mi., bounded on the E by Ohio and drained by the Whitewater River and its East Fork. The county was organized in February 1811 and named in honor of Benjamin Franklin. Shortly, thereafter, Brookville became the county seat. The topography is generally rolling; the best agricultural areas are found in the bottomlands of the Whitewater River. Tobacco and feed grains are cultivated there and the higher elevations have been turned over to pasture for livestock and dairy animals.

FRANKTON, town (pop. 1,796), Madison County, E central Indiana, zip 46044, on Pipe Creek, 10 mi. NNW of Anderson. The town was founded in the 1830s by Jacob Sigler, an early settler who blazed a trail across the first 80 acres of the present site. The original sawmill is still standing. Development was aided by the Panhandle Railroad. The glassworks and rolling mill were located next to the tracks and were able to easily distribute their products. In 1866, however, the railroad bridge over Pipe Creek collapsed, plunging a freight train into the water. The Frankton railroad station remains as a landmark. Frankton is now a thriving agricultural community. Most of the population commutes to work in the General Motors plant in Anderson.

FREDERICKSBURG, town (pop. 207), Washington County, S Indiana, zip 47120, 21 mi. SW of Salem on the Blue River in a lumbering and agricultural area. Fredericksburg was first settled in 1805 along an ancient buffalo trace. Salt licks can still be found in the vicinity. The Lick Creek Friends Church (1815) was one of the first Quaker churches in the area. Annually the town hosts the Olde Blue River Festival, a popular local event.

FREELANDVILLE, town (pop. 720), Knox County, S Indiana, zip 47535, 20 mi. N of Vincennes in an agricultural and lumbering area. Freelandville is a producer of chickens, fertilizer, seed corn, crushed rock, and lime.

FREEMAN RESERVOIR, Carroll County, N Indiana, just S of Monticello. The 2,800-acre lake has excellent boating, swimming, and black bass and silver bass fishing. It is also known as Lake Freeman.

FREETOWN, town (pop. 450), Jackson County, S Indiana, zip 47235, 10 mi. NW of Brownstown in an agricultural area noted for feed grains and livestock. It is a trade center for pet food, seeds, and fertilizer.

FREMONT, town (pop. 1,043), Steuben County, NE Indiana, zip 46737, 45 mi. N of Fort Wayne. An agricultural community, it also has a lumber mill. Nearby is 53-acre Walter's Lake, which has recreational facilities.

FRENCH LICK, town (pop. 2,059), Orange County, S Indiana, zip 47432, 45 mi. WNW of New Albany. Founded in 1811, its name was derived from an animal salt lick within the confines of the pioneer settlement, which had a French trading post. The town is a popular resort, its appeal based on the French Lick-Sheraton Hotel (formerly French Lick Springs Hotel) and its medicinal springs. Thomas Taggart, former U.S. senator, was one of the many owners of the rambling hotel. It was built in 1840 by Dr. William A. Bowles, who realized the commercial value of the mineral-laden springs. Just north of the hotel are the three artesian springs—Pluto, Proserpine, and Bowles—which are enclosed in a marble and tile bathhouse. Golfing, tennis, horseback riding, and trap shooting are offered on the 1,700-acre grounds. Once a gambling casino, the hotel was frequently visited by wealthy Eastern families including the Vanderbilts, Morgans, and Whitneys.

French Lick is located in a region rich in natural resources. Supporting industries include bituminous coal mining, quarrying, lumbering, and fruit farming.

FULTON, town (pop. 372), Fulton County, N Indiana, zip 46931, 15 mi. NNE of Logansport in an agricultural area. South of Fulton is Fletcher Lake, a popular local resort.

FULTON, county (pop. 16,984), N Indiana, area 367 sq.mi., drained by the Tippecanoe River. The county was organized in February 1836 and named for Robert Fulton, inventor of the steamboat. Four months later Rochester was selected as the county seat. The land of the county is level to undulating and is dotted with numerous lakes. Lake Manitou has been dammed to encompass 775 acres. The county is primarily agricultural in character (truck, poultry, livestock, soybeans), with minor manufacturing carried on at Rochester and Akron. The primary industry is the production of men's apparel.

GALENA, town (pop. 350), Floyd County, SE Indiana, approximately 10 mi. NW of Louisville, Kentucky. Located at an altitude of 840 ft., Galena was once a popular Indian camping and hunting ground. Numerous streams and salt springs were located along the ancient buffalo trail. Galena was platted in 1836 and has many fine century-old homes. The town had hopes of becoming a great city because of its location on the Paoli Turnpike, Indiana's firs toll road (1840). The New Albany-Paoli Toll House, used until 1913, still stands just east of town. Livestock and some truck farming are the mainstay of Galena's economy.

GALVESTON, town (pop. 1,284), Cass County, N central Indiana, zip 46932, 8 mi. NW of Kokomo in an agricultural area based on livestock farming and feed grains. There is also a cheese-making plant in town.

GARRETT, city (pop. 4,715), DeKalb County, NE Indiana, zip 46738, 20 mi. N of Fort Wayne. Garrett was once a division point for the Baltimore & Ohio Railroad. It is now primarily a farming community and shipping point for livestock, grain, and soybeans. The railroad shops manufacture air hoses and lubricators.

GARY, city (pop. 175,415), Lake County, extreme NW Indiana, zip 46401, at the south end of Lake Michigan, 25 mi. SE of Chicago, Illinois. The second largest city in Indiana, Gary was founded in 1906 in a previously desolate, uninhabited region of the Indiana dune country. The tract had been purchased by the U.S. Steel Corporation in 1905, which intended to found a city centered between the iron regions of the Northwest and the coal mines of the East and Northeast.

Named for Judge Elbert H. Gary, the city was practically born overnight. The steel mill site was elevated 15 ft. by pumping material from Lake Michigan through pipes and spreading it over the surrounding swamplands. A whole river was diverted to a new location, and three railroad rights-of-way were repositioned. Early inhabitants were mostly rugged steel workers who lived in shacks spread out along a single street surrounded by white sand dunes.

The Gary Land Company took over the camp and platted the new city. U.S. Steel bought an adjacent 7,000 acres of land and zoned it according to city regulations. A water system was laid, streets and sidewalks were paved, and electrical facilities were provided. To soften the bleak atmosphere, an ambitious landscaping project ensued, which resulted in tree-lined streets and **Marquette Park**, a landscaped tract of land along the shores of Lake Michigan. The park was subsequently dedicated to the Jesuit missionary Père Jacques Marquette.

Gary has become the hub of the Calumet industrial district. Together with Hammond, Burns Harbor, East Chicago, and Whiting, it mushroomed into one of the nation's most important steel-producing areas. Although U.S. Steel is the leading steel producer, subsidiary industries have developed and flourished. These include Republic Steel, Standard Steel Spring Company, and Pittsburgh Screw and Bolt Corporation. Eighty percent of the nation's industrial output is produced in the Calumet district. Other smaller industries produce cement, chemicals, automobile accessories, clothing, and metal products. Gary's steel works boast ingots with an 8,000,000 net ton capacity, coke plants, 12 blast furnaces, 50 open-hearth furnaces, and rolling, rail, plate, wheel, and axle mills. Unfortunately, industrial pollution has taken its toll in Gary. The Grand Calumet and Little Calumet rivers, both of which have port facilities, are heavily polluted. A thick, orange mist—a product of chemical and industrial wastes from the steel mills—can be seen frequently over the city.

Recreational facilities can be found at various Lake Michigan beaches and at South Gleason Park, an 18-hole golf course in the city.

GAS CITY, city (pop. 5,742), Grant County, E central Indiana, zip 46933, 5 mi. SSE of Marion. Gas City owes its existence to the natural gas boom of 1887, which affected many of the settlements in E central Indiana. Business boomed until 1891, when the gas suply was exhausted. A relic of the gas boom, and still the leading industry in town, is the Owens-Illinois Glass Company plant. Other manufactures include barrels and concrete products. Agriculture plays an important role in the town's economy. Large numbers of dairy, livestock, grain, and poultry farms border the town. Recreational facilities can be found at nearby Lake Galacia, a 17-acre lake especially popular for ice-fishing.

GASTON, town (pop. 928), Delaware County, E central Indiana, zip 47342, 12 mi. NNW of Muncie in an agricultural area. There is a cannery in town.

GENE STRATTON PORTER STATE MEMORIAL, Noble County, NE Indiana, near Rome City. The estate in Wildflower Woods was the last Indiana home of Hoosier authoress Gene Stratton Porter, who wrote such noted books as *A Girl of the Limberlost* and *Freckles* in the early 1900s. The estate is maintained by the Indiana Department of Conservation. The red cedar log house was named "Limberlost Cabin" for Porter's earlier home at Geneva (*q.v.*).

GENEVA, town (pop. 1,100), zip 46740, Adams County, E Indiana, 35 mi. NE of Muncie. Geneva was the home of Gene Stratton Porter from 1886 to 1913. The famous authoress wrote novels including *A Girl of the Limberlost,* which was inspired by the Limberlost Swamp (now drained), and *Freckles* while living there. The 14-room cabin is preserved as a state memorial in town.

Geneva is an agricultural community with farming generally concentrated on feed grains and livestock. Just north of town is a large Amish colony. Recreational facilities can be found at nearby Rainbow Lake and the Wabash Valley Golf Club. (*See* also Limberlost State Memorial.)

GENTRYVILLE, town (pop. 281), Spencer County, SW Indiana, zip 47537, 32 mi. ENE of Evansville. The town was named for

James Gentry, an early merchant who employed young Abraham Lincoln. In 1830, Lincoln and his father moved from Gentryville to Illinois. Lincoln was once an overnight guest in the Col. William Jones Home (1834), preserved intact.

Farming is the mainstay of Gentryville's economy. Soybeans, corn, wheat, and tobacco are the leading agricultural products.

GEORGE ROGERS CLARK NATIONAL HISTORIC PARK AND MEMORIAL, Knox County, S Indiana, at Vincennes. The memorial, which is circular in form, 90 ft. in diameter, and 82 ft. high, commemorates the winning of the Old Northwest and the achievements of George Rogers Clark in the American Revolution. The park also contains the first capitol of Indiana Territory (1800-13). The Clark Memorial consists of 16 Doric columns, each 39 ft. high and more than 6 ft. in diameter. The interior contains a bronze statue of Clark and 7 murals by Ezra Winter depicting scenes in the history of the Northwest Territory.

GEORGETOWN, town (pop. 1,273), Floyd County, S Indiana, zip 47122, 8 mi. W of New Albany in an agricultural region with predominant beech-maple forest that is ideal for cattle grazing. Just east of town is Georgetown Reservior, a nine-acre lake that offers public fishing. The town is a manufacturing center for metal detectors for the lumber and veneer industry, and has a meat-processing plant.

GIBSON, county (pop. 30,444), SW Indiana, area 498 sq.mi., bounded on the W by the Wabash River and on the N by the White River. It is drained by the Patoka and Black rivers and Pigeon Creek. Gibson County was formed in April 1813 and named for Gen. John Gibson, secretary of the territory from 1801 to 1816. Princeton has been the county seat since the county was formed. Gibson County is known for its cantaloupe, watermelon, peaches, and potatoes. There are also numerous bituminous coal mines and oil and natural gas wells.

GLENDALE STATE FISH AND WILDLIFE AREA, Daviess County, SW Indiana, 12 mi. SE of Washington in a scenic, hilly area. Water recreation is available on a 1,400-acre lake which has a maximum depth of 40 feet. There are excellent facilities for camping, boating, fishing, and hunting.

GLENWOOD, town (pop. 452), on the border of Rush and Fayette counties, E Indiana, zip 47343, 8 mi. W of Connersville. It is located in an argicultural area given over to livestock and feed grains.

GOLDSMITH, village (pop. est. 235), Tipton County, central Indiana, zip 46045, 6 mi. W of Tipton in an agricultural area noted for livestock and feed grains. The town is a trade center for poultry feeds.

GOODLAND, town (pop. 1,176), Newton County, NW Indiana, zip 47948, 32 mi. NW of Lafayette in an agricultural and dairying area. There is some stone quarrying nearby. The town is a manufacturing center for electric coils and transformers, coil assemblies, dry-mix and liquid fertilizer, and feeds.

GOSHEN, city (pop. 17,171), seat of Elkhart County, N Indiana, zip 46526, on the Elkhart River, 24 mi. ESE of South Bend. Goshen is an agricultural community with Mennonite and Amish influences. The city was settled around 1830 and incorporated in 1868. Goshen College, a Mennonite institution, evolved from the Elkhart Academy in 1894. It became a four-year, coeducational college in 1909.

Goshen is the principal trading center for the Mennonites of Elkhart County. Manufactures include steel products, hydraulic presses, batteries, wood products, radios, phonographs, rubber products, and refrigerators. Recreational facilities can be found at nearby Fish and Wolf lakes.

GOSPORT, town (pop. 692), Owen County, SW central Indiana, zip 47433, on the West Fork of the White River, 40 mi. SW of Indianapolis. Gosport was platted in 1829 on the site of the "Ten O'Clock Line," an imaginary boundary established in a land cession treaty between William Henry Harrison and the Indians at Fort Wayne in 1809. The boundary was so-called because the Indians insisted that it be drawn where the sun cast its shadow at 10 A.M.

Gosport began as a leading shipping point for the flatboat

trade on the White River. With the decline of the river trade, the importance of Gosport waned. The city retains a residential character and is a center for agricultural and cement products. Gosport contains Indiana's only remaining brick train barn and depot, built in the 1850s.

GRABILL, town (pop. 570), Allen County, NE Indiana, zip 46741, 13 mi. NE of Fort Wayne in an agricultural area noted for cattle, calves, truck crops, and soybeans. Nearby is Cedarville Lake, which is a popular local recreational site.

GRANDVIEW, town (pop. 696), Spencer County, SW Indiana, zip 47615, on the Ohio River, 33 mi. E of Evansville. The town is named for its picturesque location atop a bluff overlooking the river. The view is unobstructed for five miles in either direction. Grandview is in an agricultural area noted for livestock, soybeans, corn, and tobacco.

GRANGER, town (pop. 125), St. Joseph County, NW Indiana, zip 46530, 10 mi. NE of South Bend in an industrial and agricultural area noted for livestock and feed grains. The town is a manufacturing suburb of South Bend producing trailers, motor homes, septic tanks, pre-cast dry-wells, steel dies, rafters, trusses, silk-screen products, and specialty machinery.

GRANT, county (pop. 83,955), E Indiana, area 421 sq.mi., drained by the Mississinewa River. Grant County was organized in April 1831 and named for Capt. Samuel Grant and Moses Grant, both of whom were killed in an Indian battle in 1789. Marion is the county seat.

The county is both agricultural and industrial in character. It played a large role in the natural gas boom of 1887 because of its location within the Trenton natural gas field. Leading industries produce automobile parts, cathode ray tubes, lighting and wiring equipment, glass containers, iron castings, paperboard, tablets, and envelopes.

GREENCASTLE, city (pop. 8,852), seat of Putnam County, W central Indiana, zip 46135, near the Eel River, 40 mi. WSW of Indianapolis. The town was laid out in 1822. It grew up around De Pauw University (1837), a four-year nonsectarian institution which includes a college of liberal arts and a school of music. On campus is the restored First Methodist Church of Indiana, which was built in Charlestown in 1807.

Greencastle is a center for livestock, lumber, cement, and crushed rock. Among some of the larger industries is an International Business Machine plant. Recreational facilities can be found at the city park and at nearby Mansfield, Cataract, and Edgewood lakes. The area is attractive to visitors because of its ever-changing scenery of wooded hills, limestone bluffs, prairies, and rolling farmlands.

GREENDALE, town (pop. 3,783), Dearborn County, SE Indiana, zip 47025, near the Ohio River, just N of Lawrenceburg. Greendale's only major industry is whiskey distilling. The aroma of the fermenting mash permeates the town. The first whiskey still was built in 1809. The industry shut down during Prohibition, but after 15 years of inactivity the equipment was bought, reactivated, and modernized. The industry has grown to become Greendale's major economic asset. Visitors are treated to a tour of either the James Walsh & Company Distillery or the Joseph E. Seagram plant.

GREENE, county (pop. 26,894), SW Indiana, area 549 sq.mi., drained by the White River and Indian, Doans, Plummer, Richland, and Beech creeks. The county was formed in February 1821 and was named for Gen. Nathaniel Greene, a hero of the American Revolution. Bloomfield is the county seat (1821). Bituminous coal mining is a leading activity, along with agriculture and fruit farming.

GREENE-SULLIVAN STATE FOREST, Green and Sullivan counties, SW Indiana, 7 mi. S of Dugger. The forest encompasses 4,692 acres of bluestem prairie and oak-hickory forest and has excellent facilities for camping, picnicking, hiking, boating, swimming, and horseback riding. The 1,000 acre lake has a ten-mile shoreline and a maximum depth of 15 feet.

GREENFIELD, city (pop. 9,986), seat of Hancock County, central Indiana, zip 46140, 21 mi. E of Indinapolis. The city is the birthplace of James Whitcomb Riley, the famous Hoosier poet. Brandywine Creek, along whose banks the city was settled in 1828, inspired many of his poems. "Old Swimmin' Hole," "L¹ttle Orphan Annie," and "The Raggedy Man" are among the many poems Riley wrote in the Riley Homestead (1850), now a museum. James Whitcomb Riley Memorial Park, at the eastern edge of town, preserves the "old swimming hole." Also in the park is the County Log Jail, which still contains the original cell and houses many pioneer artifacts. A statue of the poet stands in front of the courthouse.

Greenfield is in a noted agricultural area (livestock, grain, vegetables), and is a shipping point for tomatoes. Manufactures include underwear and canned goods. Nearby is the Eli Lilly Company Biological Laboratories, which keeps experimental animals used in pharmaceutical research.

Recreational facilities are found at nearby Sugar Creek Park.

GREENSBORO, town (pop. 225), Henry County, E central Indiana, zip 47344, 6 mi. SW of New Castle in an agricultural region noted for feed grains and livestock.

GREENSBURG, city (pop. 8,620), seat of Decatur County, SE central Indiana, zip 47240, 45 mi. SSE of Indianapolis. The city was founded by Col. Thomas Hendricks. Of note is the Courthouse Tower Tree, an aspen which grows out of the concrete block roof of the county courthouse 110 ft. above the ground. Carl G. Fisher, founder of the Indianapolis Speedway and developer of Miami Beach, Florida, was born in Greensburg in 1874. The city is on the 9-mile excursion route of the 1936 Baldwin steam locomotive sponsored by the Indiana Railway Museum.

Greensburg is in an agricultural area noted for tobacco and is at the southern edge of the Trenton oil and natural gas field. Manufactures include food products, wire fences, hardware, and brooms.

GREENSBURG RESERVOIR STATE FISHING AREA, on the Greensburg Reservoir, Decatur County, SE central Indiana, adjacent to Greensburg. The state lands cover 36 acres and have facilities for boat launching and fishing.

GREENS FORK, town (pop. 444), Wayne County, E Indiana, zip 47345, on a fork of the Whitewater River, 9 mi. NW of

Richmond in an area noted for cattle, hogs, oats, soybeans, wheat, and corn.

GREENTOWN, town (pop. 1,870), Howard County, central Indiana, zip 46936, 9 mi. E of Kokomo. Founded in 1848, the settlement was named for Chief Green, a Miami Indian. Greentown grew up along Wildcat Creek and developed into a farming community. The Greentown Glass Museum has a vast collection of glassware recovered from the Indiana Tumbler and Goblet Company, which was destroyed by fire in 1903. The glassware has become a nation-wide collector's item.

GREENVILLE, town (pop. 611), Floyd County, S Indiana, zip 47124, 11 mi. NW of New Albany. Settled in 1807 and platted in 1816, Greenville is Floyd County's second oldest town. It began as a stagecoach stop, and later grew up along the old Paoli Turnpike. Its location in a region of white-oak timber aided Greenville's expansion as a manufacturing center for barrels, wine kegs, and wooden clocks. The principal activity is now livestock and grain farming.

GREENWOOD, town (pop. 11,408), Johnson County, central Indiana, zip 46142, 12 mi. S of Indianapolis. It is a manufacturing and agricultural shipping point for household appliances, canned goods, automobile parts, and livestock remedies. South of town is the Presbyterian Westminister Village.

GRIFFIN, town (pop. 178), Posey County, SW Indiana, zip 47616, 25 mi. NW of Evansville in an agricultural area noted for livestock, soybeans, wheat, and corn. Oil deposits are nearby. Big Bayou and the Black River provide recreational facilities.

GRIFFITH, town (pop. 18,168), Lake County, NW Indiana, zip 46319, 8 mi. SW of Gary. Settled in 1891, it was incorporated in 1904. It is a commercial center for castings, paper products, and photographic supplies.

GROUSELAND, Knox County, S Indiana, in Vincennes. It was the home of William Henry Harrison, governor of Indiana Territory (1800-12). In 1801, Harrison purchased 300 acres of cleared land and built the spacious house during 1803 and 1804. Surrounded by a grove of walnut trees, Grouseland was the first brick building in Vincennes. The stone for the foundation was brought from the nearby Wabash River. Some of the original floors remain.

After 1812, Grouseland passed into other hands, and was once used as a storage place for grain. In 1909 the building was saved from destruction by the Francis Vigo Chapter of the Daughters of the American Revolution, which continues to maintain it. Of note is the Council Chamber, or parlor, in which Harrison signed treaties with the Shawnee Indians.

HAGERSTOWN, town (pop. 2,059), Wayne County, E Indiana, zip 47346, on the Whitewater River, 16 mi. WNW of Richmond. An agricultural trading center, it is also a manufacturer of machinery, piston rings, and fertilizer.

HAMILTON, town (pop. 537), NE Indiana, zip 46742, 34 mi. NNE of Fort Wayne. The town was founded in 1836 as Enterprise. Located on Hamilton Lake, the site was originally chosen for its hydropower potential. A water-driven mill and a sawmill constitute the major industries. Lake Hamilton is a popular tourist spot, providing good fishing and swimming. Spring Hills Golf Course is located there.

HAMILTON, county (pop. 54,532), N central Indiana, area 401 sq.mi., drained by the White River. The topography is generally level and the soils are fertile, making the county a leading agricultural producer of feed grains and livestock. Hamilton County was organized in April 1823 and was named for the patriot and statesman Alexander Hamilton. Noblesville is the county seat. North of the county seat is Strawtown, the approximate location of the earliest crossroad trail in central Indiana and also the site of the Indian mounds of the White River. Hamilton County's leading industry is the manufacture of rubber products.

HAMLET, town (pop. 688), Starke County, NW Indiana, zip 46532, 27 mi. SW of South Bend. Hamlet was platted in 1863 and named for its founder, John Hamlet. It grew up at the junction of the Pennsylvania and New York Central railroads.

and is a shipping point for farm produce. The town has an 18-hole golf course.

HAMMOND, city (pop. 107,790), Lake County, NW Indiana, zip 46320, just W of Gary. Hammond is the oldest city of the Calumet industrial complex. It was originally named Hohman for its first settler, Ernest Hohman, a Prussian tailor who escaped the cholera epidemic of 1851 in Chicago and settled in the sand dunes and swamps of the area. He then built the Hohman Inn, the site of which is now occupied by the American Steel Foundries. George Hammond, a Detroit butcher, later located his slaughterhouse across from the inn. From 1869 onward, his business thrived, employing up to 1,500 workers at one time. Much of the meat was shipped to Europe, and Hammond perfected the method of shipping beef in refrigerated railroad cars. Hammond died in 1886 and his business was bought for $6,000,000.

In 1882 the first railroads came to the town. As a result, it was incorporated as a city in 1884. The real economic boom came at the turn of the century, when the steel industry began to establish plants there and in other Calumet area cities. Hammond has become the commercial center for the area and today is Indiana's sixth largest city. Diversified manufactures include cold-rolled steel, castings, dairy produdts, tile roofing, railway supplies, corn syrup, car wheels, forgings, candy, chains, books, petroleum products, surgical instruments, clothing, and soap.

Hammond is a city of many firsts. It was the home of the nation's first professional football team and of the inventor of the first automatic potato digger. Alvah Roebuck, the co-founder of Sears & Roebuck, was from Hammond.

There are many city parks, among them Lake Front, Dowling, Riverside, and Wolf Lake. Most visitors tend to prefer the natural beauty of nearby Indiana Dunes State Park, a rugged wilderness of sand dunes, swamps, and lakeshore.

HANNA, town (pop. 500), La Porte County, N Indiana, zip 47126, 10 mi. S of La Porte in an industrial and farming area. The town is a manufacturer of agricultural chemicals, fertilizers, and feeds.

HANCOCK, county (pop. 35,096), E central Indiana, area 305 sq.mi., drained by the Big Blue River and Sugar and Brandywine creeks. The county was formed in March 1828 and named for John Hancock, a signer of the Declaration of Independence. Greenfield has been the seat of government since the county's inception. The land is level and the soils fertile and ideally suited to the cultivation of feed grains and the raising of hogs and cattle. There is some manufacturing and canning at Greenfield and Fortville.

HANOVER, town (pop. 3,018), Jefferson County, SE Indiana, zip 47243, 5 mi. WSW of Madison. The town is the seat of Hanover College (1827), Indiana's oldest private four-year college. The campus sits atop a bluff overlooking the Ohio River, but the buildings were destroyed by a tornado that struck Hanover in 1974. The town is a farming community and an agricultural center for feed grains and livestock. To the east is the largest privately-owned power plant in the world.

HARDINSBURG, town (pop. 263), Washington County, S Indiana, zip 47125, 28 mi. WNW of New Albany in an agricultural region noted for livestock and feed grains. Hardinsburg's only industry is the Schmidt Cabinet Company.

HARDY LAKE STATE RECREATION AREA, Scott County, S Indiana, 10 mi. NE of Austin. Hardy Lake covers 1,902 acres and has facilities for hiking, picnicking, fishing, camping, boat launching, hunting, and swimming.

HARLAN, town (pop. 500), Allen County, NE Indiana, zip 46743, 16 mi. NE of Fort Wayne in an agricultural area noted for livestock, corn, and other feed grains. Industries produce pre-hung doors, custom-built cabinets, plastics, and wood products.

HARMONIE STATE RECREATION AREA, Posey County, S Indiana, near New Harmony, on the Wabash River. The state lands cover 3,192 acres of elm, ash, and southern floodplain forest and have water recreation on the river. Other facilities include campgrounds and picnic areas.

HARRISON, county (pop. 20,423), S Indiana, area 479 sq.mi., bordered on the S by the Ohio River and drained by the Ohio and Blue rivers and Indian Creek. The county was organized in December 1808 and named for William Henry Harrison.

Rich in history, Harrison County is one of the oldest in the state. Corydon is the county seat and contains the state's first capitol building. The topography is diversified. Much of the land is broken by hills, woods, and streams. The Knobs, a series of wooded ridges, border the eastern section of the county. The whole area is rich in natural resources, and lumber milling, limestone quarrying, and natural gas extraction supplement the county's basic agricultural economy. Tobacco is a leading commodity.

Several large caves and underground streams are located in Harrison County. Among the most noted cave systems are the Squire Boone Caverns, which were explored by Daniel Boone's brother.

HARRISON-CRAWFORD STATE FOREST, Harrison County, S Indiana, 10 mi. SW of Corydon. The state lands cover 22,489 acres of southern floodplain forest. A popular tourist area, it is noted for its fine hills and valleys spread out along the Ohio River. Recreational facilities include campgrounds, hiking trails along the rocky bluffs and ledges, picnicking areas, boating and fishing areas, and horseback riding trails.

HARTFORD CITY, city (pop. 8,207), seat of Blackford County, E Indiana, zip 47348, 18 mi. N of Muncie. Settled in 1832 and platted in 1839, the city was named for Hart's Ford, a crossing at Lick Creek which was the property of David Hart. Hartford City is an agricultural and manufacturing (glass, school supplies, hardware) community. Its location in a region rich in natural resources (fertile soil, natural gas, petroleum) has made the city a leading trade center. The first two gas wells in Blackford County were located there. Recreational facilities are at nearby Lake Mohee and Lake Placid. There is also a golf course 2 miles east of town.

HARTSVILLE, town (pop. 434), Bartholomew County, S central Indiana, zip 47244, 12 mi. ENE of Columbus in an agricultural area noted for livestock and feed grains. It was the original home of Hartsville College (1850), which was destroyed by fire in 1898. A park marks the site.

HAUBSTADT, town (pop. 1,171), Gibson County, SW Indiana, zip 47539, 17 mi. N of Evansville in an area noted for cantaloupe, watermelon, peaches, sweet potatoes, and feed grains.

HAZELTON, town (pop. 416), Gibson County, SW Indiana, zip 47540, on the White River, 9 mi. N of Princeton. The town was founded in 1807 by Jarvis Hazelton, a local hunter. Located in the midst of the cantaloupe belt of the Midwest, Hazelton is a leading shipping point for the melons. There is also a tomato cannery in the town, which is also known as Hazelton.

HEBRON, town (pop. 1,624), Porter County, NW Indiana, zip 46341, 13 mi. SW of Valparaiso in an agricultural area noted for livestock and feed grains.

HELMER, village (pop. 110), Steuben County, NE Indiana, zip 46744, 16 mi. SW of Angola. Helmer is near Pokagon State Park (*q. v.*), a popular summer and winter playground. Manufactures include feeds, seeds, insecticides, and fertilizers.

HELMSBURG, town (pop. 180), Brown County, S Indiana, zip 47435, 6 mi. NW of Nashville in a scenic section of the Hoosier Hills. Industries include the production of lumber and household and industrial brooms and mops.

HELTONVILLE, town (pop. 400), Lawrence County, S Indiana, zip 47436, 8 mi. NE of Bedford in an agricultural and limestone quarrying area. The town is a trade center for limestone products, cabinets, and lumber.

HEMLOCK, town (pop. 125), Howard County, central Indiana, zip 46937, 9 mi. SE of Kokomo in a farming and dairying region. The town is a farm trade center for grains and fertilizers.

HENDRICKS, county (pop. 53,974), central Indiana, area 417 sq.mi., drained by the Eel and Whitelick rivers and Mill Creek. The land surface is rolling, and the extremely fertile soils are conducive to agriculture and stock raising. Hendricks County was formed in December 1823 and named for William Hendricks, then governor of Indiana. Danville was selected as the county seat.

HENRY, county (pop. 52,603), E Indiana, area 400 sq.mi., drained by the Blue River and Fall Creek. The county was formed in June 1822 and named for Patrick Henry, patriot and orator during the American Revolution. Newcastle is the county seat.

The topography is gently undulating with a large percentage of the land given over to stock-raising and feed-grain cultivation. It is also an industrial leader; major manufactures include automobile parts, piston rings, castings, steel, canned goods, vinyl folding doors, and brake linings. Henry County was the setting for the novel *Rain Tree County.*

HENRYVILLE, town (pop. 600), Clark County, SE Indiana, zip 47126, 14 mi. N of Jeffersonville in a timber and farming area. Henryville is a manufacturer of furniture parts and hardwood lumber products.

HIGHLAND, town (pop. 24,947), Lake County, NW Indiana, zip 46322, 7 mi. SW of Gary. A Dutch settlement, it was founded in 1850 in the midst of a truck-farming region. Little commercial activity is evident, and most of the population is employed in the Calumet district cities of Gary and Hammond.

HILLSBORO, town (pop. 505), Fountain County, W Indiana, zip 47949, 15 mi. WNW of Crawfordsville. Rough countryside and infertile clay soils have made farming unfavorable, but the town has used the clay, which is of excellent quality, for the manufacture of tile and bricks. Bituminous coal mining is the only other major industry.

HINDOSTAN FALLS STATE FISHING AREA, Martin County, S Indiana, 6 mi. S of Loogootee. The area covers 134 acres and has facilities for fishing, camping, and boat launching. The falls are located on the White River and contain the scenic bluffs of Beaver Bend.

Amish family, Amishville.

Angel Mounds State Memorial, a 14th century
prehistoric Indian settlement, Evansville.

336

Anderson Chamber of Commerce

Nicholson File Company, one of the
main industries in Anderson.

Ingrid Eklov Jonsson

Soldiers and Pioneers Monument, Bedford.

Benjamin Harrison's home (1872), Indianapolis.

Limestone quarry near Bedford from which was taken the stone used for the Empire State Building in New York City.

Amish schoolhouse, Berne.

City of Bluffton, located on the banks of the Wabash River.

Indiana Department of Commerce
Conner Prairie, a restored pioneer settlement near Noblesville.

Indiana Department of Commerce
Annual ''Little Italy Festival'', Clinton.

Ingrid Eklov Jonsson

North Christian Church, Columbus.

Ingrid Eklov Jonsson

Whitley County·jail, Columbia City.

First state capital building (1813)
of Indiana, Corydon.

Whitley County Courthouse, Columbia City.

Ingrid Eklov Jonsson

Soldiers Monument outside Carroll County Courthouse, Delphi.

Wabash College (1832), Crawfordsville.

Washington Elementary School (1894), one
of the many historic buildings in Elwood.

Furnace at the Inland Steel Company, East Chicago,
capable of producing 2.2 million tons of steel per year.   345

346

Ingrid Eklov Jonsson

Allen County Courthouse, Fort Wayne.

347

Indiana Department of Commerce
Johnny Appleseed's gravesite, Fort Wayne.

Indiana Department of Commerce
The George Rogers Clark Memorial, Vincennes.

Pharmaceutical research laboratories of the Eli Lilly Company, Greenfield.

Grouseland (1803-1804), home of William Henry Harrison, Indiana's territorial governor from 1800 to 1812. The home, in Vincennes, is maintained by the Daughters of the American Revolution.

Ingrid Eklov Jonsson

The Moravian Church (1874), Hope.

Ingrid Eklov Jonsson

Interior of Grouseland, Vincennes.

The Huntington Grain Company, one of
Huntington County's large farm co-ops.

A gravel pit near Huntington, attests to the
area's mining and agricultural economy.

The first capitol (1800) of Indiana Territory, Vincennes.

Dune and marsh landscape in Indiana Dunes State
Park at the south end of Lake Michigan.

Ingrid Eklov Jonsson

Elihu Stout's print shop, home of *The Western Sun,*
Indiana Territory's first newspaper, Vincennes.

Indiana Department of Commerce

352   The Indiana State Capitol (1878), Indianapolis.

Soldiers and Sailors Monument in Monument Circle, Indianapolis.

Central Public Library, Indianapolis.

353

354   State Office Building, Indianapolis.

Indianapolis Museum of Art

Museum of Art, Indianapolis.

Ingrid Eklov Jonsson

Dubois County Courthouse, Jasper. 355

Ingrid Eklov Jonsson

Covered bridge in Highland Park, Kokomo.

Ingrid Eklov Jonsson

Delco Electronics plant in Kokomo.

HOAGLAND, town (pop. 500), Allen County, NE Indiana, zip 46745, 12 mi. SE of Fort Wayne in an agricultural and dairying area. The town is a trade center for sheet-metal products, grains, seeds, fertilizers, twine, and plating products.

HOBART, city (pop. 21,485), Lake County, NW Indiana, zip 46342, 7 mi. SE of Gary. The city was platted in 1849 and named for a brother of its founder, George Eavleo. Hobart was incorporated in 1921. The city is a trading center for clay products and packed meat. Clay pits are nearby. The Indian Ridge Lake Country Club is located 1 mi. S of the city.

HOLLAND, town (pop. 662), Dubois County, SW Indiana, zip 47541, 36 mi. NE of Evansville. Located in the Wabash Lowland, the surrounding fertile soils have aided its development as an agricultural center (soybeans, corn). In 1969, a large Dutch windmill was built in the American Legion Memorial Park. Recreational facilities can be found at Holland Lake No. 1 and Holland Lake No. 2, both at the N edge of town.

HOLTON, town (pop. 800), Ripley County, S Indiana, zip 47023, 7 mi. W of Versailles and Versailles State Park (*q.v.*). The Jefferson Proving Grounds are just N of town. Holton is producer of liquid-mix fertilizers, grain bins, and sawmill products.

HOME CORNER, village (pop. 900), Grant County, NE central Indiana, zip 46952, a suburb of Marion. Home Corner, like many of the cities of central Indiana, grew up during the natural gas boom of 1887. It is a quiet farming community in an area noted for livestock and feed grains.

HOOSIER NATIONAL FOREST, S Indiana, covering 172,000 acres and affording some of the most breathtaking scenery in the state, particularly in the spring and autumn. Within the forest are several recreation areas including Buzzard Roost Overlook, German Ridge, Saddle Lake, and Hardin Ridge. An area called the Pioneer Mothers' Memorial Forest has been set aside near Paoli for ecological studies of its virgin timbers. Much of the surface is hilly and encompasses the Crawford and Norman uplands, which are divided NW to SE by the Mitchell

Plain. The sandy soils are covered by dense stands of climax forest which include beech, maple, oak, and hickory. Much commercial lumbering is carried on in the towns of Paoli, West Baden Springs, Nashville, and Bedford. Squirrel, turkey, deer, grouse, and fox hunting are popular. Recreational facilities provide for camping, picnicking, hiking, boating, fishing, and swimming. Hoosier National Forest also encompasses Brown County State Park and the Monroe Dam and Reservoir (*q.q.v.*).

HOPE, town (pop. 1,603), Bartholomew County, S central Indina, zip 47246, 39 mi. SSE of Indianapolis. The town was founded in 1830 by Moravians, members of a religious sect from Bohemia. The Moravian church, built in 1874, has been preserved and stands near the original cemetery with its unusual horizontal tombstones. Hope is an agricultural center for truck and fruit farming and has a lumber mill. A popular local recreational spot is Shaefer's Beach, 3 mi. SE of the town.

HOVEY LAKE, Posey County, SE Indiana, 10 mi. S of Mount Vernon, in the Hovey Lake State Fish and Game Area. The lake has a maximum depth of only 4 ft. but covers 1,400 acres, making it the largest lake south of Indianapolis. Great numbers of cypress stands surround the shoreline and the encompassing area is a natural bird sanctuary for herons, cormorants, and wild ducks.

HOVEY LAKE STATE FISH AND GAME AREA, Posey County, SW Indiana, 10 mi. S of Mount Vernon. The state lands encompass 4.400 acres of woods and water and have excellent facilities for fishing, picknicking, camping, and hunting. In the area are large stands of virgin oak, cottonwood, maple, wild pecan, red birch, and cypress. It is a bird sanctuary and flyway for herons, wild ducks, and cormorants.

HOWARD, county (pop. 83,198), N central Indiana, area 293 sq.mi., drained by the Wildcat River and its tributaries. The county was organized in May 1844 and named for Tilghman A. Howard, noted Indiana statesman of the 1800s. It is an agricultural county given over to corn, oats, soybeans, and other feed grains, as well as to stock raising. Kokomo, the county seat, is also the leading manufacturer. Industries include the manufacture of automobile radios and transmissions, magazine printing, and food processing.

HOWE, town (pop. 650), Lagrange County, NE Indiana, zip 46746, 6 mi. N of Lagrange in an agricultural area noted for livestock and feed grains. Howe is a manufacturer of travel equipment, mobile homes, feeds, seeds, fertilizers, metal stampings, and dairy products.

HUDSON, town (pop. 464), Steuben County, NE Indiana, zip 46747, 32 mi. N of Fort Wayne in a potato and onion-growing area.

HUNTERTOWN, town (pop. 775), Allen County, NE Indiana, zip 46748, 10 mi. N of Fort Wayne in an agricultural and dairying region. The town is a manufacturer of lumber, feed, custom electrical and electronic control panels and systems, and winding equipment parts.

HUNTINGBURG, city (pop. 4,794), Dubois County, SW Indiana, zip 47542, 40 mi. NE of Evansville. Founded in the 1840s by German immigrants, the town's economy is based on the clay deposits of the area, which are among the finest in the U.S. The Uhl Pottery Works is noted for its 60-gallon clay jars which weigh 400 lbs. each. Other manufactures in Huntingburg include electronic eqiupment, furniture, and wood products. The Peter Morgan Greenhouses have taken prizes at the National Flower Show for the American Beauty rose. Recreational facilities are at nearby Huntingburg Lake and the Huntingburg Country Club. Every Labor Day, the Huntingburg Airport is the scene of a spectacular air show.

HUNTINGTON, city (pop. 16,217), seat of Huntington County, NE central Indiana, zip 46750, on the Little River, 24 mi. SW of Fort Wayne. Originally called Wepecheange ("place of flints"), the town was renamed in 1831 for Samuel Huntington, a member of the first Continental Congress. Numerous treaties with the Indians were signed there. Francis La Fontaine, a Miami Indian chief, is buried at the Mount Calvary Cemetery north of Huntington; his house (1833) has been reconstructed.

Huntington was also the home of John R. Kissinger, a soldier who submitted to the yellow fever tests conducted by Dr. Walter Reed in 1900. He contracted the disease and never fully recovered.

The Little River was an important waterway for the Maumee-Wabash Portage. Buildings constructed over the river have been preserved as unique landmarks. The Huntington Reservoir, a 900-acre man-made lake, is located within the Little Turtle State Recreation Area. The reservoir was developed by Indiana and the U.S. Army Corps of Engineers.

Huntington is a manufacturing and farm trade center. Products include rubber goods, furniture, cranes, radios, phonographs, machinery, furnaces, paint, and disinfectants. There are also some limestone quarries. *Our Sunday Visitor,* the Roman Catholic newspaper with the largest circulation in the U.S. is published there, as are the Catholic magazines *Living Light* and *Priest Magazine.* The city is the seat of Huntington College (1897), a liberal arts institution.

HUNTINGTON, county (pop. 34,970), NE central Indiana, area 369 sq.mi., drained by the Wabash, Salamonie, and Little rivers and by Longlois Creek. The county was formed in December 1834 and named for Samuel Huntington, a Connecticut delegate to the Continental Congress and a signer of the Declaration of Independence. Huntington is the county seat.

The soils are fertile and ideally suited for growing fruit, grains, and soybeans and raising stock. Diversified manufacturing supplements the economy; leading industries produce electronic components, canned goods, dairy products, brake linings, and fabricated metals. There is also some limestone quarrying and lumbering.

The 900-acre Huntington Reservoir and a large section of the Salamonie Reservoir lie within Huntington County. Both were jointly developed for recreational and water supply purposes by Indiana and the U.S. Army Corps of Engineers.

HUNTSVILLE, town (pop. 300), Madison County, E central Indiana, 7 mi. from Anderson. The town was founded in 1830 and named for Eliazer Hunt. The first Madison County fair was held in Huntsville in 1839, but because of poor attendance and lack of interest, the fair headquarters were moved to Anderson.

There are some small businesses, but Huntsville remains essentially an agricultural community (livestock, feed grains).

HYMERA, town (pop. 907), Sullivan County, SW Indiana, zip 47855, 21 mi. SSE of Terre Haute. The town was platted in 1870 after the discovery of rich bituminous coal deposits. It was originally named Pittsburgh. When it was discovered that there already was a Pittsburgh, Indiana, the town was renamed High Mary, after the postmaster's tall daughter. This name was later shortened to Hymera. Coal mining is still the leading industry, followed by grain and livestock farming. Nearby is Shakamak State Park (*q.v.*), a popular tourist attraction.

IDAVILLE, town (pop. 600), White County, NW Indiana, zip 47950, 5 mi. E of Monticello in an agricultural area noted for livestock and feed grains. The town is a manufacturing center for pallets, furniture, tank car culverts, and feeds.

INDIANA DUNES STATE PARK, south end of Lake Michigan in Lake County, Indiana. Comprising 2,182 acres, the park was created in 1925. It is a magnificent blend of shifting sand, pearly beaches, and luxuriant, almost tropical forest. Some of the dunes are "dead," or non-shifting, whereas others are "live" and shifting, such as the giant dune, Mount Tom, which reaches a height of 192 feet. Binding plants, such as grasses and vines, keep many of the dunes from migrating. The Big Blowout, a semi-circular dune which looks like an explosion crater, was actually formed by wind erosion.

In 1972, the Indiana Dunes National Lakeshore was established. It surrounds the state park, which has remained a separate entity.

INDIANA TERRITORY STATE MEMORIAL, Knox County, S Indiana, at Vincennes. It includes the first capitol of the Indiana Territory (1800) and a reconstruction of Elihu Stout's print shop, home of the first newspaper in the territory. The memorial is located in Harrison Park across from Vincennes University. The old capitol, restored in 1919, consists of a simple two-storied frame building with a stoop porch and small paned windows. Original furniture is placed throughout, including the oddly-shaped walnut desk upon which were signed the laws for the

Indiana Territory. The first territorial legislature met there in 1805.

INGALLS, town (pop. 888), Madison County, E central Indiana, zip 46048, 24 mi. NE of Indianapolis. The town was founded in 1893 and named for M.E. Ingalls, president of the Big Four Railroad Company. Essentially a farming community (livestock, feed grains), Ingalls benefited on a lesser scale than many of the Madison County towns from the natural gas boom of 1887. As a direct result of the boom, however, a glass factory and zinc works were established there. Ingalls incorporated in 1896, but never achieved the economic status that its founders had envisioned.

IRELAND, town (pop. 340), Dubois County, S Indiana, zip 47545, 4 mi. NW of Jasper in an agricultural and timbering region. The town is a trade center for logs, sample cases, cabinets, vanities, and poultry.

IROQUOIS RIVER, in Indiana, flows generally NE to SW for 50 mi. across the NW corner of the state to empty into the Illinois River.

JACKSON, county (pop. 33,187), S Indiana, area 520 sq.mi., drained by the East Fork of the White River and tributaries of the Muscatatuck River. The county was organized in 1816 and named in honor of Gen. Andrew Jackson, hero of the Battle of New Orleans. Brownstown is the county seat.

Jackson County is one of the most scenic counties in Indiana. A range of hills passes through it from NE to SW. The NW corner contains another set of hills, or knobs. Breathtaking panoramas can be viewed along Skyline Drive in the Jackson-Washington State Forest. The intervening bottomlands occupy half of the county and are extremely fertile. Grain, livestock, truck and poultry are the leading agricultural products. Diversified manufacturing (automobile parts, shoes, shirts, plastic products) is evident in the larger towns.

JACKSON-WASHINGTON STATE FOREST, Jackson and Washington counties, S Indiana, just S of Brownstown. The forest consists of a north and south unit and encompasses an area totaling 15,181 acres. There are excellent facilities for hiking, picnicking, camping, fishing, hunting, and horseback riding. The forested hills and valleys within the area are unexcelled for beauty. Knob Lake, covering 10 acres, has been stocked with fish.

JAMES, LAKE, Steuben County, NE Indiana, near Agola. Located within the boundaries of Pokagon State Park (*q. v.*), Lake James covers 900 acres and has a maximum depth of 94 ft. It is Indiana's third largest natural lake. It is picturesquely surrounded by low hills and woods and has long been a popular lake for sailing and swimming by enthusiasts from Indiana, Michigan, and Illinois.

JAMESTOWN, town (pop. 938), Boone County, central Indiana, zip 46147, 17 mi. SE of Crawfordsville in an agricultural area noted for livestock and feed grains. Once a busy stagecoach stop, Jamestown is now a quiet farming community with a lumber mill.

JASONVILLE, city (pop. 2,335), Greene County, SW Indiana, zip 47438, 24 mi. SSE of Terre Haute in an agricultural area noted for grain and fruit. Manufactures include rubber goods and cold-storage lockers. Recreational facilities are at nearby Lake Lenape and Shakamak State Park (*q. v.*).

JASPER, city (pop. 8,641), seat of Dubois County, SW Indiana, zip 47546, on the Patoka River, 45 mi. NE of Evansville. Jasper was settled in 1828, largely by German immigrants, and until World War II German was the primary language of the townspeople. Colloquial speech, known as "Jasper Dutch," is still prevalent. The city is a farming (strawberries, grain) and manufacturing (desks, canned goods, wood products, pianos, gloves) center. Many of the buildings date from the late 1800s and exhibit a unique German stepped-gable architecture. A fine example is the Gramelspacher-Gutzweiler House (1849). Southeast of town is Emlow's Mill (1866), built to replace the mill to which Abraham Linconi brought his grain.

The Jasper Summer Theatre presents popular Broadway plays every June, July, and August. Other recreational facilities are at Beaver Dam Lake, Jasper Country Club, and the Jasper Municipal Golf Course.

JASPER, county (pop. 20,429), NW Indiana, area 562 sq.mi., bounded on the N by the Kankakee River and drained by the Iroquois River. The county was formed in 1838 and named for Sgt. Jasper from South Carolina. The original seat was at Parish Grove, selected because it was near the center of population and because it was one of the few high and dry spots in the region. The honor was ceded to Rensselaer in 1839, and it remains the county seat. Much of the history of the county is vague because two fires (1843, 1864) almost totally destroyed the records for that period.

The county's main economic activities are agriculture and stock raising, with almost no industry except lumber milling.

JASPER-PULASKI FISH AND WILDLIFE AREA, Jasper and Pulaski counties, N Indiana, 6 mi. N of Medaryville. The state lands cover 7,585 acres and have facilities for hiking, picnicking, camping, and hunting. The game-breeding station is noted for its pheasant. A bird sanctuary offers refuge for thousands of waterfowl in spring and fall.

JAY, county (pop. 23,575), E Indiana, area 386 sq.mi., bounded on the E by Ohio and drained by the Salamonie River. The county was organized in March 1836 and named for John Jay, patriot and statesman. Portland is the county seat.

Originally, Jay County was a leading producer of hardwood timber. After the forests were depleted, agriculture (livestock, grain, poultry, soybeans, truck) became dominant in the economy. Diversified manufacturing is carried out in the larger towns such as Portland and Dunkirk. Leading industries produce glassware, canned and processed foods, work clothes, and automobile parts.

JEFFERSON, county (pop. 27,006), SE Indiana, area 366 sq.mi., bounded partly on the S by the Ohio River and drained by Big Creek. The county was formed in February 1811 and named for Pres. Thomas Jefferson. Madison is the county seat.

A notable feature of Jefferson county is its varied topography. The western area is gently rolling, the center is a wooded plateau, and the southern and eastern region is traversed by the Ohio River and consists of a series of uninterrupted hills and valleys which are everywhere interspersed with high bluffs and d?ep ravines. Wheat and corn are grown on the fertile alluvial soils. Fruit and tobacco—successfully introduced in the late 1800s—have become two of the county's leading exports. Limestone quarrying and some manufacturing supplement the agricultural economy.

Jefferson County encompasses Clifty Falls State Park (*q.v.*), a 1,200-acre park which offers a striking view of the Ohio River. The county hosts the annual Madison Regatta and Governor's Cup Race, a hydroplane spectacular which is held on the Ohio River during the Fourth of July weekend.

JEFFERSONVILLE, city (pop. 20,008), seat of Clark County, SE Indiana, zip 47130, just E of New Albany, on the Ohio River. The city was platted in 1802 by William Henry Harrison, who named it for Thomas Jefferson, the original planner.

The Howard Shipyards, once the city's major industry, were active from 1834 to 1931. The famous "Robert E. Lee" steamboat was rebuilt there in 1870 after a race with the "Natchez" from New Orleans to St. Louis. Some of the first large boats to ply the Yukon River during the gold rush of 1898 were built at the shipyards.

Jeffersonville was severely damaged in 1937 by a flood that inundated 95 percent of the city. The city is now a farming and manufacturing community. Products include wood items, machinery, canned goods, soap, clothing, and animal oils. It is the location of a state prison and a U.S. Army quartermaster depot. American Commercial Line, Inc., one of the world's largest river transport companies, has a terminal there. Every year Jeffersonville sponsors the Steamboat 1800 Festival on the riverfront. On the Ohio River is the John Fitzgerald Kennedy Memorial Bridge, which connects the city with Louisville. Kentucky.

JENNINGS, County (pop. 19,454), SE Indiana, area 377 sq.mi., drained by Vernon, Graham, and Sand creeks. The county was organized in February 1817 and named for Jonathan Jennings, first state governor of Indiana. Vernon was selected as the county seat shortly thereafter.

Jennings County is located in a bituminous coal, limestone, and agricultural (livestock, feed grains, tobacco) area. Some manufacturing is carried out in Vernon. Fabricated metal production is the main industry.

JOHNSON, county (pop. 61,138), central Indiana, area 315 sq.mi., drained by the West Fork and tributaries of the East Fork of the White River. The county was organized in May 1823 and named for John Johnson, one of the first judges on the Indiana Supreme Court. Franklin is the county seat.

The land surface is level and covered with glacial drift. It has been called the greatest corn-producing county in the world, although other feed grains and vegetables are grown in great abundance. Manufacturing is diversified and generally centered in Franklin, Greenwood, and Edinburg. The major industries produce automobile parts, processed food, and plastics.

JONESBORO, town (pop. 2,466), Grant County, E central Indiana, zip 46938, on the Mississinewa River, 6 mi. S of Marion. Jonesboro was named for Obadiah Jones, one of its founders, who platted the town in 1837. Jonesboro is a farming and manufacturing trade center for feed, electric wire, and cable.

JONESVILLE, town (pop. 202), Bartholomew County, S central Indiana, zip 46938, 10 mi. S of Columbus in an agricultural area dedicated to cattle, poultry, and feed-grain farming.

JUDSON, town (pop. 35), Parke County, W Indiana, zip 47856, 28 mi. NNE of Terre Haute in an agricultural and coal-mining region.

JUG ROCK, Martin County, S Indiana, in Jug Rock Park, 5 mi. N of Shoals. Jug Rock, a natural stone pillar, is 60 ft. high and 15 ft. in diameter. Resembling a huge jug, it is formed of variegated rock strata in which hikers and picnickers have carved their initials. Also within the park is The Pinnacle, another stone formation.

KANKAKEE RIVER, rises near South Bend, Indiana, and flows SW into Illinois. The Kankakee is approximately 135 mi. long and drains a major portion of Indiana's cornbelt. It is dredged along amost its total length to provide drainage for the flat terrain. The Iroquois River is its major tributary. The Kankakee daily carries 1,300,000,000 gallons of water out of Indiana.

KANKAKEE STATE RECREATION AREA, Starke County, NW Indiana, west of Knox. The recreation area, which encompasses 2,200 acres of state land, centers on the Kankakee River and is noted for its fishing and wildlife refuge. Recreational facilities include a primitive campground and fishing, boating, and picnic areas.

KEMPTON, town (pop. 469), Tipton County, central Indiana, zip 46049, 14 mi. SSE of Kokomo in an agricultural area noted for cash grains and vegetables.

KENDALLVILLE, city (pop. 6,838), Noble County, NE Indiana, zip 46755, on the Elkhart River, 27 mi. NNW of Fort Wayne. Kendallville was founded in 1833 by David Bundle, who opened a prosperous tavern at the site. The tavern is still standing on Gold Street. The settlement grew slowly until the coming of the railroad in 1857. Progress followed, and Kendallville became the state's leading shipping point for onions. It is also a center for livestock, dairy products, and soybeans; manufactures include refrigerators, pumps, brushes, and artificial bait. The Mulholland Museum contains pioneer relics and Indian artifacts.

Recreational facilities are at nearby Bixler, Cree, Round, and Wible lakes.

KENNARD, town (pop. 518), Henry County, E central Indiana, zip 47351, 8 mi. W of New Castle in an agricultural area noted for livestock and feed grains.

KENTLAND, town (pop. 1,864), seat of Newton County, NW Indiana, zip 47951, 38 mi. NW of Lafayette. Kentland was settled in 1860 and is the birthplace of George Ade, famous Hoosier author, humorist, and playwright. His home stands opposite the county courthouse. The town is basically a farming community and has a large whole-milk cheese-making plant.

KEWANNA, town (pop. 614), Fulton County, N Indiana, zip 46939, 20 mi. N of Logansport in an agricultural region noted for livestock and feed grains. Bruce Lake is nearby.

KIMMELL, town (pop. 350), Wells County, NE Indiana, zip 46759, 12 mi. S of Bluffton in an agricultural and dairying area. The town is a trade center for grain, feeds, seed, fertilizer, popcorn, and hybrid seed corn.

KINGMAN, town (pop. 530), Fountain County, W Indiana, zip 47952, 21 mi. WSW of Crawfordsville in a region of fertile soils ideally suited for farming and cattle grazing. There is some bituminous coal mining.

KINGSBURY, town (pop. 314), La Porte County, NW Indiana, zip 46343, 6 mi. S of La Porte. The town is a shipping point for grain, onions, and peppermint.

KINGSBURY STATE FISH AND WILDLIFE AREA, La Porte County, NW Indiana, 5 mi. S of La Porte. It covers 4,498 acres and has facilities for hiking, picnicking, fishing, camping, boating, and hunting.

KINGSFORD HEIGHTS, village (pop. 1,200), La Porte County, NW Indiana, zip 46346, 10 mi. S of La Porte in a livestock and feed grain area.

KIRKLIN, town (pop. 736), Clinton County, central Indiana, zip 46050, near Sugar Creek, 10 mi. SE of Frankfort. Kirklin was founded in 1832 on the Michigan Road, which is now the Main Street of town. Nathan Kirklin, for whom the town was named, built a thriving tavern after the first settlers arrived. Today, farming is predominant, and the fertile soils are ideally suited for feed grains (corn, oats, soybeans) and livestock.

KNIGHTSTOWN, town (pop. 2,456), Henry County, E central Indiana, zip 46148, on the Big Blue River, 34 mi. E of Indianapolis. Knightstown was founded in 1825 and named for John Knight, the government engineer in charge of construction of the National Road through the town. Knightstown is an agricultural and manufacturing center for the area. Manufactures include car bodies, furniture, and fences. It is the site of the Indiana Soldiers' and Sailors' Children's Home, which offers vocational training. Fort Montgomery is a resort 2 mi. N of town.

KNIGHTSVILLE, town (pop. 788), Clay County, W Indiana, zip 47857, just NE of Brazil in an agricultural area noted for feed grains and livestock. There is some bituminous coal mining.

KNOBS, THE, Floyd County, S Indiana, near New Albany. The Knobs are a range of hills that rise 200 ft. above sea level and are covered with dense woods. The scenery is unsurpassed anywhere in the state. The ancient hills have been worn down by stream erosion over the centuries until they have become rounded or "knobby."

KNOX, town (pop. 3,519), seat of Starke County, NW Indiana, zip 46534, on the Yellow River, 33 mi. SW of South Bend. Basically a farming community, Knox has a large population of Scandinavian, Slavic, and Italian immigrants who raise mint and onions. Knox has become a leading shipping center for their produce. Manufacturing (electrical appliances, clothing) is also important.

Nearby is Bass Lake, Indiana's largest lake. The Lightning Dude Ranch is a popular resort which offers rodeos, trail rides, and horse shows.

KNOX, county (pop. 41,546), SW Indiana, area 516 sq.mi., bounded on the W by the Wabash River, the E by the West Fork of the White River, and the S by the White River. It is drained by the Deshee River and Maria Creek. Knox County is known as the "Mother of Indiana Counties," having been surveyed before the territorial government was established. The county was officially organized on June 30, 1790, by Winthrop Sargent, secretary of the Northwest Territory. It was named for Gen. Henry Knox, the first secretary of war of the U.S. Vincennes, the only county seat, attracts thousands of visitors to its multitude of historic shrines (George Rogers Clark Memorial; the first territorial capitol; Grouseland; Elihu Stout's print shop).

Knox County encompasses some of the richest land in Indiana. It is famous for the "Decker" cantaloupe and is a center for the production of livestock, fruit, feed grains, and coal. Principal industries produce wire springs, structural steel, glass, and glass products.

KOKOMO, city (pop. 44,042), seat of Howard County, central Indiana, zip 46901, on Wildcat Creek, 50 mi. N of Indianapolis. Kokomo was platted in 1844 and named for Chief Kokomo, a renowned Miami Indian leader. A monument to him is in the Pioneer Cemetery.

As did many other cities in central Indiana, Kokomo experienced rapid growth during the natural gas boom of 1887. Businesses flourished as glass factories, steel works, and furnace factories were erected. Perhaps Kokomo's greatest claim to fame came in 1893, when the Hoosier inventor Elwood Haynes (1857-1925) tested the first clutch-driven, electric-ignition automobile. He ran it successfully on Pumpkin Vine Pike. Haynes' home has been restored and is now a public museum which houses memorabilia of his life, including early Haynes automobiles.

Today, Kokomo is a thriving industrial city. Both General Motors and Chrysler have plants there, and numerous other businesses produce tools, ceramics, cutlery, canned goods, clothing, playground equipment, and cosmetics. A branch of Indiana University opened there in 1965.

Highland Park on Deffenbaugh Street has two superlative exhibits. "Old Ben," a taxidermically preserved steer, is reported to have weighed 4,470 lbs. and was 16 ft. 8 in. long and 6 ft. 4 in. high. The hollow stump of a sycamore tree, 59 ft. in circumference, has held 12 people and a telephone booth comfortably. Kokomo is the site of the Greentown Glass Museum, noted for its "chocolate ware" and "holly amber" glass last manufactured in 1903. The Howard County Historical Museum has a collection of Lincoln, Indian, and Civil War artifacts. Recreational facilities are at the two city golf courses and Kokomo Reservoir No. 2, 4½ mi. E of the city.

KOSCIUSKO, county (pop. 48,127), N Indiana, area 540 sq.mi., drained by the Tippecanoe and Eel rivers and by Turkey Creek. The county was formed in June 1837 and was named for Gen. Thaddeus Kosciusko, a Polish soldier, patriot, and aide-de-camp to Gen. George Washington. Warsaw is the county seat.

One of the state's largest counties, Kosciusko is also in the center of Indiana's lake region. More than 100 sparkling lakes afford a summer playground to thousands of visitors who come there annually to enjoy the bathing, boating, and fishing.

Kosciusko is an agricultural county. It is a center for livestock, poultry, truck, dairy products, soybeans, and timber. Diversified manufacturing produces automobile parts, boats, mobile homes, iron castings, movie screens, and books.

KOUTS, town (pop. 1,388), Porter County, NW Indiana, zip 46347, 11 mi. S of Valparaiso in an agricultural region noted for livestock and feed grains.

LACONIA, town (pop. 64), Harrison County, S Indiana, zip 47135, 23 mi. SW of New Albany. The town is a farming community in an area noted for cattle and hogs. Of note is the Kintner-Withers Plantation House (1837), built in Classic Revival style and containing a large private collection of Civil War antiques.

LA CROSSE, town (pop. 696), La Porte County, NW Indiana, zip 46348, 30 mi. SE of Gary in a region noted for livestock and feed grains.

LADOGA, town (pop. 1,099), Montgomery County, W central Indiana, zip 47954, on Raccoon Creek, 11 mi. SSE of Crawfordsville. Ladoga was the seat of Central Normal College which, on May 10, 1878, was virtually "kidnapped" and taken to Danville, 22 mi. away. The town is now a quiet farming community and a trade center for livestock, soybeans, and corn.

LAFAYETTE, city (pop. 44,955), seat of Tippecanoe County, W central Indiana, zip 47901, on the Wabash River, 60 mi. NW of Indianapolis. Lafayette was founded and named in 1825 by William Digby for the Marquis de LaFayette, who served as a general under George Washington in the American Revolution.

For many years, Lafayette was a leading river port. Produce was brought in by wagons from the surrounding area and in turn was shipped to other markets via steamboats on the Wabash River or the canal boats of the Wabash and Erie Canal. Modern Lafayette is the manufacturing center of Tippecanoe County. Agriculture and coal mining vie with the production of rubber, paper, gears, tools, drugs, soap, safes, plumbing supplies, and automotive products.

Historical sites abound in and around Lafayette. Fort

Ouiatenon, 4 mi. NE of the city, was built by the French in 1717 to guard the Maumee-Wabash route and to establish a fur trading post with the Indians. It was the first guarded post established by the white man in Indiana. The fort was destroyed in 1791, but a blockhouse replica marks the site. The Tippecanoe Battlefield, 7 mi. N of Lafayette, is preserved in memory of those soldiers who died in the battle fought between Tenskwatawa, the Shawanee Prophet, and Gen. William Henry Harrison in 1811 (*see* Tippecanoe Battlefield State Memorial). Prophet's Town, established in 1808 by Tecumseh, Tenskwatawa's brother, was located 3 mi. downstream on the Tippecanoe River. The Tippecanoe County Historical Museum (1852) has relics of the battle, as well as pioneer artifacts from Fort Ouiatenon and the local countryside.

West Lafayette, sister city to Lafayette, is the seat of Purdue University (1869), one of the first land-grant colleges. Recreational facilities can be found at the city's Columbian Park, which includes a zoo, and at nearby Hoon and Marsh lakes.

LA FONTAINE, town (pop. 793), Wabash County, NE central Indiana, zip 469490, near the Mississinewa River, 8 mi. NNW of Marion in an area noted for livestock and feed grains.

LAGRANGE, town (pop. 2,053), seat of Lagrange County, NE Indiana, zip 46761, on the Pigeon River, 28 mi. E of Elkhart. The original settlement was founded in 1835, platted in 1836, and named for the Marquis de LaFayette's residence near Paris, France.

Lagrange became the county seat in 1844 and developed into a leading dairying center surrounded by fertile farmland. There are several poultry hatcheries in town. Some of the many small lakes in the area are remnants of previously drained swamplands. The Mongo Reservoir and Royer Lake have been developed into recreational sites, and the Pigeon River State Fish and Game Area is a popular sportsman's attraction.

LAGRANGE, county (pop. 20,890), NE Indiana, area 381 sq.mi., bounded N by Michigan and drained by the Pigeon and Little Elkhart rivers. The county was organized in April 1832 and the town of Lagrange became the county seat in 1844. Both were named for the home of the Marquis de LaFayette near Paris, France.

Lagrange is basically an agricultural county (dairying, soybeans, feed grains, stock raising, poultry). One of the largest Amish settlements in the U.S. is located in the western part of the county between Topeka and Shipshewana.

LAGRO, town (pop. 552), Wabash County, NE central Indiana, zip 46941, on the Wabash River, 5 mi. ENE of Wabash. The town was named for Les Gros, an Indian chief. It developed during the canal boat era, and the bed of the Wabash and Eerie Canal can still be seen running along Main Street.

Lagro is a center for rock-wool products. The Salamonie River State Forest is 3 mi. from town. It encompasses the Lost Bridge State Recreation Area (Salamonie Reservoir), which contains a 2,855-acre lake noted for its beaches and fishing.

LAKE, county (pop. 546,253), NW Indiana, area 513 sq.mi., bounded on the N by Lake Michigan (for which it is named), W by Illinois, and S by the Kankakee River. The county is traversed by the Grand Calumet and Little Calumet rivers. Lake County was formed in February 1837 and Crown Point was made the county seat.

Prior to 1899, the whole northern tier of Lake County was a desolate wasteland of sand dunes, marshes, and scattered farms. With the construction of the U.S. Steel Company mill at Gary in 1905, however, Lake County mushroomed into the leading industrial county of the state. The Calumet district, ''American's Ruhr Valley,'' embraces the cities of Gary-Hammond-Whiting-East Chicago, and is one of the world's greatest industrial centers. It is a leading producer of steel, oil, petrochemicals, cement, soap, and related products.

Southward is a farm belt where the soils were relcaimed from the mosquito and muskrat-infested Kankakee Marshes. The fertile bottomlands now yield wheat, corn, oats, vegetables, and soybeans. Livestock and horses are prominent features of the county's diversified economy.

Lake County has, for a long period of time, been an anomaly to the Hoosier state. It is more often than not identified with its sister counties in northern Illinois. Proposals to deed Lake County to Chicago have been presented to numerous legislative sessions.

LAKETON, town (pop. 500), Wabash County, N Indiana, zip 46943, 12 mi. N of Wabash in an agricultural area noted for livestock and feed grains. The town is a manufacturing center for rubber and plastic molds and petroleum products.

LAKE VILLAGE, town (pop. est. 650), Newton County, N Indiana, zip 46349, 26 mi. N of Kentland in an agricultural area noted for livestock and feed grains.

LAKEVILLE, town (pop. 712), St. Joseph County, N Indiana, zip 46536, 11 mi. S of South Bend. Lakeville was named for the group of nearby lakes, and has become a popular summer resort and trading center. Pleasant and Riddle lakes provide good fishing and boating facilities.

LANESVILLE, town (pop. 586), Harrison County, S Indiana, zip 47136, 10 mi. WSW of New Albany. The town was settled in 1792 and platted in 1817. It was named for Gen. Lane, a government surveyor and early settler in the area. It developed originally as a stagecoach stop between Corydon and New Albany, and is now a trading center for livestock and feed grains.

J.F.D. LANIER STATE MEMORIAL, Madison, Jefferson County, S Indiana. The stately mansion was built in 1844 for James F. D. Lanier, a banker and financier whose loans helped Indiana avert bankruptcy during the late 19th century. The house was designed by the famous architect Francis Costigan; it contains the original furnishings.

LAOTTO, town (pop. 300), Noble County, N Indiana, zip 46763, 13 mi. N of Fort Wayne in an agricultural and dairying area. Laotto is a manufacturing center for truck equipment, fertilizer, LP gas tank trailers, tools, dies, and molds.

LAPAZ, town (pop. 604), Marshall County, N Indiana, zip 46537, 16 mi. S of South Bend in an agricultural area noted for livestock and feed grains. It is also known as La Paz.

LAPEL, town (pop. 1,725), Madison County, E central Indiana, zip 46051, 26 mi. NE of Indianapolis. Platted by David Conrad in

1876, it was named for the shape of the plat map, which resembled a coat lapel. The town is basically an agricultural community, but contains the Brockway Glass Company, which was founded during the natural gas boom of 1887. The company employs almost 550 people. Small businesses thrive in town. The limestone quarry, which is geologically part of an ancient reef, has yielded many fine fossil samples.

LA PORTE, city (pop. 22,140), seat of La Porte County, NW Indiana, zip 46350, on Pine Lake, 33 mi. E of Gary. The city was founded in 1830 at the time the Michigan Road was built. It was named La Porte (French for "door" or "gate") because of its location at the point where Indiana's original forests met the open prairie. La Porte became a trading center between central and southern Indiana, the Indiana lake region, Illinois, and Michigan.

Diversity is evident in La Porte's manufactures, which include farm implements, rubber products, radiators, furniture, metal doors, baby carriages, and automobile equipment. One of the finest historical museums in Indiana is located in the basement of the county courthouse. A pioneer log cabin, which contains pioneer relics including an 1833 Kentucky squirrel rifle, is in the museum. Other displays include the Edward Vail collection of native birds and a coin collection. Winter recreation is available at Ski Valley, 5 mi. W of town.

LA PORTE, county (pop. 105,342), N Indiana, area 607 sq.mi., bounded on the NW by Lake Michigan, N by Michigan, and S by the Kankakee River. The county was organized in January 1832. The city of La Porte has been the seat since the county was formed.

Fruit growing is a big business in La Porte County. Small lakes are interspersed with rolling hills that are covered with orchards and vineyards. Much of the rest of the county is farmland drained from the Kankakee Marshes and ideally suited to feed grains.

La Porte County is also a leading manufacturing center. Its main industries produce farm and industrial machinery, railroad cars, truck trailers, furniture, fabricated metals, appliances, and electronic equipment.

LARWILL, town (pop. 324), Whitley County, NE Indiana, 26 mi. WNW of Fort Wayne in an agricultural area noted for livestock and feed grains. Larwill, Robinson, and Troy Cedar lakes are popular resort spots.

LASALLE FISH AND WILDLIFE AREA, Newton County, N Indiana, near Lake Village. The wildlife area covers 3,551 acres and has a 500-acre lake with facilities for water recreation. There are also a campground, picnic area, and boat-launching ramp.

LAUREL, town (pop. 753), Franklin County, SE Indiana, zip 47024, 10 mi. SSE of Connersville in an agricultural area noted for livestock and feed grains. The town was founded in 1836 by James Conwell who named it for Laurel, Delaware. Historical buildings can be seen throughout the town, including the one-cell stone jail and the Methodist Church (1846). Nearby is an old remnant of the Whitewater Canal, which now contains a feeder dam. At the north edge of town and rising 150 ft. above it is Laurel Hill, a prehistoric Indian mound. The view from its summit has been described as "one of the loveliest in Indiana."

LAWRENCE, town (pop. 16,646), Marion County, central Indiana, zip 46226, on the West Fork of the White River, just NE of Indianapolis. Lawrence is a quiet residential community; most of its inhabitants are employed in Indianapolis.

LAWRENCE, county (pop. 38,038), S Indiana, area 459 sq.mi., drained by the East Fork of the White River and by Salt Creek. The county was formed in March 1818 and named for Capt. James Lawrence. Bedford became the county seat in 1825.

Out of Lawrence County has come some of the finest building limestone in the world. The quarries at Bedford and Oolitic have been the main suppliers. Other industrial products include cement and nonferrous castings. Fruit and grain are the leading agricultural products.

LAWRENCEBURG, city (pop. 4,636), seat of Dearborn County, SE Indiana, zip 47025, 50 mi. S of Richmond. Lawrenceburg was founded in 1801 by Capt. Samuel Vance and became a prosperous Ohio River port. Gambler's Row, an early vice district, was known from Pittsburgh to New Orleans. A flood destroyed much of the city in 1937, leaving 6,000 people homeless. Industries began to flourish after the flood, and today Lawrenceburg has some of the nation's largest distilleries. Other manufactures include feed, machinery, lumber, shoes, and pharmaceuticals.

LEAVENWORTH, town (pop. 330), Crawford County, S Indiana, zip 47137, near the Ohio River, 29 mi. W of New Albany. The town was founded in 1818 on the banks of the Ohio River, but a flood in 1937 swept most of it away. The new town, dedicated on Dec. 15, 1938, was located atop a bluff overlooking the river. Remnants of the old site can still be seen. Leavenworth remains a farming community in an area noted for feed grains and livestock.

LEBANON, city (pop. 9,766), seat of Boone County, central Indiana, zip 46052, 25 mi. NW of Indianapolis. Lebanon was founded in 1832 and named for the surrounding forest, the trees of which were likened to the Biblical cedars of Lebanon. Agriculture and manufacturing (farm equipment, bus bodies, concrete products, tools, condensed milk) are the mainstays of the economy.

Of particular note is the county courthouse, dedicated July 4, 1912, which is built of granite and Bedford limestone. The 8 huge pillars at the north and south entrances are the largest one-piece limestone columns in the world. Each column is 3 stories high and weighs 50 tons. Lebanon was the home of Samuel M. Ralston (1857-1925), an Indiana governor and U.S. senator.

Cool Lake Park and golf course are 7 mi. N of town.

LEESBURG, town (pop. 561), Kosciusko County, N Indiana, zip 46538, 31 mi. SE of South Bend in an agricultural area noted for livestock and feed grains. James and Tippecanoe lakes and Indian Hills Golf Course provide recreational facilities for the surrounding area.

LEITERS FORD, town (pop. 250), Fulton County, N Indiana, zip 46945, 11 mi. NW of Rochester in an agricultural area noted for feed grains and livestock. Leiters Ford has a gravel and sand pit and a fertilizer plant.

LEO, town (pop. 600), Allen County, NE Indiana, zip 46765, 11 mi. NE of Fort Wayne in an agricultural and dairying area. Leo is a manufacturing center for bulletin boards, steel, and garage and patio doors.

LEWISVILLE, town (pop. 530), Henry County, E Indiana, zip 47352, near Flatrock Creek, 9 mi. S of New Castle in an agricultural area noted for livestock and feed grains.

LEXINGTON, town (pop. 350), Scott County, S Indiana, zip 47138, 10 mi. SE of Scottsburg in a lumber and farming area. Lexington is a manufacturing center for tools, dies, jigs, and wood products.

LIBERTY, town (pop. 1,831), seat of Union County, E Indiana, zip 47353, 13 mi. S of Richmond. A quiet farming community, it dates back to 1822. The town is a shipping center for livestock, dairy products, paint, and agricultural implements. Liberty was once a stop on the Underground Railway, the "freedom train" for runaway slaves. Gen. Ambrose Burnside, a Civil War leader credited with originating the "sideburns" hairstyle, was born there. Nearby is Whitewater State Park, which is dedicated to those men who served in World War II.

LIBERTY MILLS, town (pop. 300), Wabash County, N Indiana, zip 46946, 18 mi. N of Wabash in an agricultural and dairying area. Wabash is a trade center for grain and feeds and is a manufacturer of screens and knives.

LIGONIER, city (pop. 3,034), Noble County, NE Indiana, zip 46767, on the Elkhart River, 37 mi. SE of South Bend. It is a peaceful farming and trade center whose products include dairy items, furniture, refrigerators, work clothes, bedding, and flour. Nearby Diamond Lake is a popular recreational area.

LIMBERLOST STATE MEMORIAL, Geneva, Adams County, E Indiana. The memorial contains the original two-story 14-room "Limberlost Cabin" designed and occupied from 1893 to 1913 by Gene Stratton Porter, Indiana's most famous authoress. At the log cabin, which is surrounded by lattice work, she began writing her best-known novels, *Freckles* and *A Girl of the*

Limberlost. Limberlost Swamp, which inspired her books, has since been drained.

LINCOLN BOYHOOD NATIONAL MEMORIAL, Spencer County, S Indiana, just S of Lincoln City. The memorial is dedicated to Abraham Lincoln and his mother, Nancy Hanks Lincoln. Established in 1932, it encompasses 1,731 acres of wooded hills and forests of which Lincoln State Park is also a part. In this area Lincoln spent his boyhood years from the ages 7 to 21 before moving to Illinois.

The memorial contains the site of the family's log cabin and grave of Lincoln's mother, who died of the "milk-sick" in 1818. (The "milk-sick" was an epidemic caused by cows eating white snake-root, which poisoned their milk.) Included at the site are Abraham Lincoln Hall, which houses a chapel; Nancy Hanks Lincoln Hall; a museum; and a Living Historical Farm. The visitor's center is a wrap-around structure that winds behind the sculptured panels of the memorial halls.

LINCOLN HERITAGE TRAIL, a three-state network of highways in Kentucky, Indiana, and Illinois that traces the migration route of Abraham Lincoln from his birthplace in Kentucky to his final resting place in Illinois. Along the entire route are restored shrines and numerous memorials and markers depicting events in the president's life. The Indiana sector includes the Lincoln Boyhood National Memorial Park, Lincoln Pioneer Village, and Lincoln State Park.

LINCOLN STATE PARK, Spencer County, S Indiana, just S of Lincoln City. The park, one of Indiana's tributes to Abraham Lincoln, encompasses 1,731 acres of beautiful, natural woodlands. It was established in 1932; an additional 114 acres were dedicated in 1963. There is a large artificial lake which offers excellent swimming and fishing. A modern campground, picnic area, and observation tower are also situated there.

LINDEN, town (pop. 713), Montgomery County, W Indiana, zip 47955, 17 mi. S of Lafayette in an agricultural area noted for livestock and feed grains.

LINTON, city (pop. 5,450) Greene County, SW Indiana, zip

47441, 32 mi. SSE of Terre Haute. Located in one of Indiana's richest coal fields, Linton grew up in the 1830s as a mining town with a varied ethnic population. The earliest German and English populations intermingled with Scots, Poles, Hungarians, and French. Near Linton, a 6-ft. lacquered coal marker designates the nation's center of population in 1930.

Good fishing facilities an be found at nearby Downing, Stephen's, and Wampler lakes, and at the Linton Conservation Ponds.

LITTLE YORK, town (pop. 191), Washington County, S Indiana, zip 47139, 29 mi. N of New Albany in an agricultural area noted for cattle, hogs, vegetables, and feed grains.

LIVONIA, town (pop. 120), Washington County, S Indiana, 31 mi. NW of New Albany in an agricultural region noted for livestock and feed grains. Several Amish farms are in the vicinity.

LIZTON, town (pop. 397), Hendricks County, central Indiana, zip 46149, 22 mi. WNW of Indianapolis, The 1851 settlement was located in a swampy lowland which has since been drained and converted to fertile farmland. Corn, hogs, and cattle figure prominently in Lizton's economy.

LOGANSPORT, city (pop. 19,255), seat of Cass County, N central Indiana, zip 46947, at the confluence of the Eel and Wabash rivers, 36 mi. NE of Lafayette. In 1828, land in the vicinity of the present city was purchased from the Potawatomi and Miami Indians by the U.S. government. Logansport sprang up almost overnight as stores were erected to serve the Indians. The settlement was dedicated the same year and named for James Logan, a nephew of Tecumseh, who was killed fighting for the U.S. in the War of 1812. Logansport flourished as a leading trade center for more than 100 years and by 1860 was reputed to be one of the Midwest's most prominent railroad centers.

Modern Logansport is an industrial city. Batteries, missile components, cement, dishes, radiators, and fishing tackle are a few of the city's diversified manufactures. Nearby is the Logansport State Hospital for the mentally ill.

The Cass County Historical Museum contains pioneer objects and Civil War memorabilia. The ancestral home of the Miami Indians, known as "Olde Towne," is 6 mi. E of the city. France Park, 4 mi. W of town, provides camping and recreational facilities. Twin Hills Lake is also a popular recreational site.

LOST RIVER, S Indiana, rises near Orleans and flows generally NE to SW across Orange County to empty into the White River in Martin County. The river is a "disappearing stream"—that is, in various places along its course it disappears into the surrounding limestone bedrock, which is everywhere traversed by cave systems and sinkholes. The entire Lost River system occupies 352 sq.mi. in sections of Washington, Orange, Lawrence, and Martin counties.

The first 15 mi. of the river's course appears like that of a normal stream. Its middle course is marked by sudden disappearances into and reappearances from underground caverns. At Tolliver Swallowhole, the river at times takes trees, mud, and parts of farmer's fields underground with it. The stream is also a habitat for blind fish and crayfish.

LONG BEACH, town (pop. 2,740), La Porte County, NW Indiana, on Lake Michigan, 4 mi. NE of Michigan City. Long Beach caters mainly to the tourists who annually visit the sand dune country surrounding the town. The region is known as the summer playground of Indiana.

LOOGOOTEE, city (pop. 2,953), Martin County, SW Indiana, zip 47553, near the East Fork of the White River, 14 mi. E of Washington. Located in a ruggedly beautiful section of Indiana, the city is rich in natural resources. Fertile farmland, stands of timber, bituminous coal deposits, and oil and natural gas pockets all contribute to Loogootee's prosperity. The main manufactures include clothing, veneer, and tile products.

LOSANTVILLE, town (pop. 212), Randolph County, central Indiana, zip 47354, 20 mi. SE of Winchester. The town is a manufacturer of tools, dies, special machinery, casket shells, and farm supplies.

LOST BRIDGE STATE RECREATION AREA, near Lagro,

Wabash County, NE central Indiana. Lost Bridge, under development in the 1970s, comprises 12,000 acres of woods and water in the Salamonie River State Forest. Salamonie Lake is the main attraction. It covers 2,855 acres and offers excellent camping, swimming, fishing, and boating. Bridle paths and nature trails have been blazed through the surrounding forest.

LOWELL, town (pop. 3,839), Lake County, NW Indiana, zip 46356, 22 mi. S of Gary. Lowell was founded in 1849 on the Kankakee marshes. Fertile farmlands have made it a commercial center for dairy products and nursery stock. The leading manufacture is brushes. The Crown Point-Lowell Race Course was popular in the early 1900s. George Ade, noted Hoosier humorist, once said of it: "The race course runs through the center of town, and the speed maniacs from the city help make life more interesting and uncertain in the sylvan retreat."

LYDICK, village (pop. 650), St. Joseph County, N Indiana, 7 mi. WNW of South Bend in an agricultural area noted for livestock and feed grains.

LYNN, town (pop. 1,360), Randolph County, E Indiana, zip 47355, 16 mi. N of Richmond. A quiet livestock and farming center, it was founded in 1847. Rugged beauty surrounds the town; to the E is the highest point in Indiana, rising to 1,240 ft.

LYNNVILLE, town (pop. 556), Warrick County, SW Indiana, zip 47619, 22 mi. NE of Evansville in an area noted for livestock and feed grains. Lynnville Park is a popular resort and visitor's attraction.

LYONS, town (pop. 702), Greene County, SW Indiana, zip 47443, 32 mi. NE of Vincennes in an area noted for livestock and feed grains. Mining of bituminous coal is a major activity. An annual handicraft and agricultural fair is held in September.

MACY, town (pop. 273), Miami County, N Indiana, zip 46951, 15 mi. N of Peru in an agricultural area noted for livestock and feed grains. Macy is a manufacturing center for farm post-buildings and lumber products.

MADISON, city (pop. 13,081), seat of Jefferson County, SE Indiana, zip 47250, on the Ohio River, 40 mi. NNE of New Albany. The area around Madison was first settled in 1805, and the city was founded four years later. Advantageously situated on the banks of the Ohio River, it quickly mushroomed into a leading river port.

Madison is one of Indiana's oldest and most beautiful cities. Many pre-Civil War homes have been preserved along the riverfront and the many narrow sidestreets. Among the finest examples of 19th-century architecture are the Paul House (1809), oldest brick building in Madison; the Schofield Mansion (1817), the James F.D. Lanier Home (1844), an elaborate building complete with a cupola, a portico with 30-ft. pillars, and a three-story spiral staircase; and the Shrewsbury House (1846). On the west edge of town is the 1835 railroad which climbs 400 ft. in one mile, the steepest non-cog railroad in the world. Historic Madison, Inc., is a non-profit organization founded in 1960 for the purpose of preserving the old homes and landmarks in and around the city.

Madison is a leading tobacco market and a manufacturer of wood products and packed meats. The river is still important. Heavily laden barges carry oil, steel, coal, iron, sulphur and other commodities. The Delta Queen, one of the last remaining passenger-carrying stern-wheelers, makes a regular stop at Madison. The annual Governor's Cup hydroplane race is held there annually on the Ohio River. Entertainers Frank Sinatra, Dean Martin, and Shirley MacLaine caused much excitement in 1958, when the motion picture *Some Came Running* was filmed in the city.

Nearby is Clifty Falls State Park (*q.v.*), one of the most scenic tourist attractions in Indiana. Hanover College, now at Hanover, was temporarily located at Madison in 1844. The campus consists of 400 wooded acres overlooking the Ohio River Valley.

MADISON, county (pop. 138,451), E central Indiana, area 453 sq.mi., drained by the West Fork of the White River and by Pipe, Kilbuck, Fall, Duck, and Lick creeks. The county was formed in July 1823 and named for James Madison, fourth president of the U.S. Anderson is the county seat.

Madison county began to develop with the building of the

Central Canal, which connected with the Wabash and Erie Canal. After the canal-building boom ended, the entire county declined until the arrival of the railroads in 1851. Business increased after trade and transportation routes were improved, and natural gas was discovered on a farm near Alexandria in 1887. The subsequent industrial boom was unequalled in the history of the county. Many factories sprang up almost overnight. First were the glass factories, attracted by the cheap source of fuel, in almost every town in the county. Even after the gas supply was depleted, the industrial momentum continued.

Madison today is one of the leading industrial counties in the state. Major industries produce electrical wire assemblies, headlights, fabricated metals, canned goods, packaged meats, processed food, glass products, ceramic tile, insulation, and industrial machinery. Agriculture (hogs, cattle, corn, tomatoes, soybeans, poultry) is also important. There is some oil refining and limestone quarrying. The county contains Mounds State Park (*q.v.*) which contains the mounds and relics of an ancient Indian culture.

MARENGO, town (pop. 1,350), Crawford County, S Indiana, zip 47140, on a fork of the Blue River, 30 mi. WNW of New Albany. The town is a quarrying center and has a tomato cannery and lumbermill. It is probably best noted for Marengo Cave, which is a popular tourist attraction. Spectacular stalagtite and stalagmite formations have been discovered in the limestone cave, which has been open to the public since 1883. The cave reaches a depth of 286 ft., has two mi. of explored passageways, and keeps a constant temperature of 54° F all year round. An oddity is the group of chime formations which, when struck, emit various musical tones.

MARION, city (pop. 39,607), seat of Grant County, E central Indiana, zip 46952, on the Mississinewa River, 30 mi. NNW of Muncie. Marion was laid out in 1831 and named for Gen. Francis Marion, a cavalry officer in the American Revolution. The Battle of Mississinewa (1812) was fought 4 mi. NW of town on the Francis Slocum Trail. Marion remained a peaceful farming community until 1887, when natural gas was discovered beneath the city. As in other E central Indiana towns, industry mushroomed with the discovery and Marion became known as the "Queen City of the gas belt." Glass factories, paper mills, iron works, and rolling mills sprang up almost overnight.

Marion has maintained the momentum ever since. It is a leading southern Indiana industrial center. Its diversified manufactures include trucks, glass, paper, oil-well machinery, radios, railroad equipment, furniture, and food products.

Marion College (1920), a liberal arts and sciences school, is located there. The average enrollment is 700 students. Matter Park, 3½ mi. N of town, has the Octogenarian Museum, which contains a fine display of pioneer relics and Indian artifacts.

MARION, county (pop. 792,299), central Indiana, area 392 sq.mi., drained by the West Fork of the White River and Eagle Fall and Buck creeks. The county's topography is diversified, ranging from a nearly level plain to rolling hills. The County was created in December 1821 and named for Gen. Francis Marion, a cavalry officer in the American Revolution. Indianapolis, already the state capital, was selected as the county seat.

Marion County is an important commercial, market, and manufacturing area. Farming (wheat, corn, truck, soybeans) and stock raising (cattle, hogs) go hand in hand with heavy industry. Major manufactures include automobile parts, aircraft parts, television receivers, telephones, electronic components, packaged meats, processed foods, metal work, industrial machinery, drugs, and chemical products.

MARKLE, town (pop. 963), on the border of Huntington and Wells counties, NE central Indiana, zip 46770, on the Wabash River, 9 mi. SE of Huntington in an agricultural area noted for livestock and feed grains.

MARKLEVILLE, town (pop. 457), Madison County, E central Indiana, zip 46056, 32 mi. ENE of Indianapolis. The town was platted in 1852 by John Markle, for whom it was named. Near the town in 1824, 9 Indians were murdered by white men. Fearful of a revenge attack, the settlers tried, found guilty, and hanged the white men. It was the first case in U.S. in which a white man was executed for killing an Indian. Markleville is an agricultural community and center for livestock and feed grains.

It is also a trade center for tools, dies, and extruded aluminum products.

MARSHALL, town (pop. 365), Parke County, W Indiana, zip 47859, 30 mi. NNE of Terre Haute, in an agricultural area noted for livestock and feed grains. There are also some bituminous coal mines.

MARSHALL, county (pop. 34,986), N Indiana, area 392 sq.mi., drained by the Yellow and Tippecanoe rivers. The surface of the land is composed of glacial till. Numerous lakes are located within the county, among them Maxinkuckee, which is one of the most beautiful lakes in the state. Much swampland has been drained; the fertile soils are excellent for the cultivation of corn, wheat, oats, mint, and hay. Marshall County was formed in April 1836 and named for John Marshall, chief justice, of the U.S. Supreme Court. Plymouth is the county seat. The county is a leading producer of mobile homes and boats.

MARTIN, county (pop. 10,969), SW Indiana, area 345 sq.mi., drained by Lost River and the East Fork of the White River. The county is very picturesque, its many steep hills having been eroded and sculptured into strange, natural stone formations. The region is generally unsuitable for cultivation; the White River bottomlands, however, have been given over to hay, corn, and wheat. Bituminous coal, natural gas, oil, and timber supplement the economy. Gypsum and clay products are manufactured at Shoals and Loogootee. The county was formed in 1820 and named for Maj. John T. Martin of Kentucky. Shoals is the county seat. The Pinnacle, Hindostan Falls, Jug Rock, and McBride's Bluff are all scenic natural features of the county.

MARTIN STATE FOREST, Martin County, S Indiana, 2 mi. E of Shoals. The forest covers 6,000 acres and has a 15-acre lake with a maximum depth of 15 ft. The lake is available for public fishing, boating, and swimming. There are also facilities for camping, picnicking, and hiking. The forest, located in scenic hill country, contains thousands of pine trees that were planted by the State of Indiana. Within the forest is a 100-ft. high firetower.

MARTINSVILLE, city (pop. 9,723), seat of Morgan County, central Indiana, zip 46151, on the West Fork of the White River, 28 mi. SSW of Indianapolis. The city was founded in 1822 and flourished as a health spa because of the large number of artesian springs discovered while prospectors were drilling for natural gas. The curative properties of the waters are believed to be beneficial in the treatment of arthritis, rheumatism, and similar ailments. Martinsville is also a commercial trade center for wood products, furniture, bricks, flour, canned goods, and timber. Two former Indiana governors, Paul V. McNutt (1933-37) and Emmet Branch (1924-25), grew up there; their homes have been restored.

The world's largest collection of phonographs is housed in a museum at the edge of town. Spruce Hill Farm, a zoo, is 4 mi. S.

The Diamond Mineral Spring Resort and Grassy Fork Fish Hatchery, the world's largest producer of goldfish, are popular visitor's attractions. Many good recreational facilities are near Martinsville, including Dalton, Dillman, Jines, and Paradise lakes.

MATTHEWS, town (pop. 728), Grant County, E central Indiana, zip 46957, 14 mi. SSE of Marion. Matthews grew up in the 1830s around a gristmill, sawmill, blacksmith shop, and general store. It has changed little since those days. The only other addition to its business district is a small canning factory.

MAUCKPORT, town (pop. 119), Harrison County, SE Indiana, zip 47142, on the Ohio River, 27 mi. SW of New Albany in an agricultural area noted for livestock and feed grains.

MAUMEE RIVER, formed by the confluence of the St. Joseph and St. Mary's rivers at Fort Wayne. It flows NE for 130 mi. and enters Lake Erie at Maumee Bay, just NE of Toledo, Ohio.

MAXINKUCKEE, LAKE, Marshall County, N of Indiana, just S of Culver. The lake, encompassing 1,800 acres, is one of the most scenic in the state. On its shores is the Culver Military Academy, whose sailboats can often be seen on its waters.

MAXWELL, town (pop. 280), Hancock County, central Indiana, zip 46154, 5 mi. N of Greenfield in a manufacturing and farming area. Maxwell is a trade center for fertilizers, steel grain bins, and concrete products.

MAYS, town (pop. 200), Rush County, E central Indiana, zip 46155, 10 mi. N of Rushville in a farming area noted for livestock and feed grains. Mays is a manufacturing center for kitchen cabinets, fertilizer , plating products, and machine shop products.

McCORDSVILLE, town (pop. 350), Hancock County, central zip 46055, 13 mi. NE of Indianapolis in an agricultural area noted for livestock and feed grains. The town is a producer of tools, dies, special machinery, metal products, and expandable foam moldings.

McCORMICK'S CREEK STATE PARK, Owen County, W Indiana, 3 mi. E of Spencer. The 1,833-acre park, which is centered around McCormick's Creek, was the first of Indiana's state parks acquired in 1916. The creek joins the White River at the border of the park; it has cut a 100-ft. deep canyon through the limestone. Foot trails, bridle paths, and roads wind through the thick pine and beech forests which are interrputed at various points by cool, deep ravines and gullies. Of note is Wolf Cave, a small, natural limestone cavern which was hollowed out by the stream's rushing waters centuries ago.

An abandoned quarry within the park provided building stone for the State Capitol in Indianapolis. Recreational facilities include a modern campground, picnic areas, playgrounds, bicycle paths, and a swimming pool. A visitor's center, which has a nature display, is located near the pool. The Canyon Inn offers year-round accommodations and dining.

MEDARYVILLE, town (pop. 732), Pulaski County, NW Indiana, zip 47957, on Big Monon Creek, 45 mi. N of Lafayette. Medaryville is a commercial trade center for tile, bricks, and cheese, and is located in an area noted for cattle and hogs. The Jasper-Pulaski Fish and Game Area is 5 mi. NW of town.

MEDORA, town (pop. 788), Jackson County, S Indiana, zip 47260, 18 mi. E of Bedford in an agricultural region noted for livestock and feed grains. East of town is the longest covered bridge in Indiana, built in 1875 and measuring 434 ft.

MELLOTT, town (pop. 325), Fountain County, W Indiana, zip 47958, 17 mi. NW of Crawfordsville in an agricultural area noted for livestock and feed grains.

MENTONE, town (pop. 830), Kosciusko County, N Indiana, zip 46539, 12 mi. SW of Warsaw in an agricultural and dairying area. The town is a manufacturing center for hospital equipment, ice-vending equipment, woodworking machinery, farm products, grains, and metal machining products.

MEROM, town (pop. 305), Sullivan County, SW Indiana, zip 47861, on the Wabash River, 26 mi. N of Vincennes in a fertile agricultural region (feed grains, livestock). The town was once a popular Chautauqua site, attracting 50,000 people annually. Noted speakers included William Jennings Bryan and "Billy" Sunday. To the north are Indian mounds and village sites, but they are obscured because of extensive cultivation. Numerous skeletons and artifacts dating back to the Stone Age have been unearthed.

Of note is the former Merom Institute (1859), now a conference center, which has one of the country's tallest wooden spiral staircases.

MERRILLVILLE, town (pop. 26,000), Lake County, NW Indiana, zip 46410, adjacent to Crown Point in an agricultural and tourism area. The town was once the crossroads of 16 Indian trails and the site of an Indian village. A historical marker denotes the location of the Great Sauk Trail.

Merrillville is an important trade and manufacturing center. Industries include ornamental iron works, plastic and steel fabricating, and drapery manufacturing.

MEXICO, town (pop. 800), Miami County, N Indiana, zip 46958, 5 mi. NW of Peru in an agricultural area noted for livestock and feed grains. Manufacturing includes grain milling and the production of compasses for cars, boats, and airplanes. Mexico was once an important stagecoach stop between Indianapolis and Michigan City.

MIAMI STATE RECREATION AREA, Miami County, E central Indiana, 7 mi. E of Peru. One of two facilities located on the Mississinewa Dam and Reservoir, it encompasses 14,000 acres and includes 3,210-acre Mississinewa Lake. Public recreational facilities are managed by the Indiana Department of Conservation and include areas for boating, fishing, swimming, water-skiing, picnicking, and camping.

MICHIGAN CITY, city (pop. 39,369), La Porte County, NW Indiana, zip 46360, on Lake Michigan, 5 mi. ENE of Gary. The city was founded at the mouth of Trail Creek in 1832 as the northern terminus of the old Michigan Road. Although it is a manufacturing center (oil refining, wire, building material, clothing), Michigan City is probably best known for its recreational advantages. Called "Indiana's summer playground," it is located in the middle of southern Lake Michigan's dune country. Michigan City has vast expanses of beach area and also one of the finest yacht harbors on the Great Lakes. Two lighthouses that mark the shore are contained within Washington Park, the city's amusement park, zoo, and marina. Nearby are the international Friendship Gardens, a "perpetual flower show" which attracts thousands of visitors annually. Flowers and plants from many nations are cultivated there.

Indiana Dunes State Park (*q.v.*), is 11 mi. W of town. Every year the Canterbury Summer Playhouse and the Dunes Summer Theatre put on popular plays and musicals. At the western edge of Michigan City is the Indiana State Prison.

MICHIGAN, LAKE, third largest of the Great Lakes, measuring 307 mi. long, 118 mi. wide, 923 ft. deep, and 22,400 sq. mi. in area. The lake lies at an altitude of 580 ft. above sea level and is bordered S by Indiana, E and N by Michigan, and W by Illinois and Wisconsin. Lake Michigan derives its name from the Algonkian Indian term *michigami* ("large body of water"). It was first explored by white men in 1634. The lake was formed in the Pleistocene Epoch by glacial scouring of the relatively weak, underlying sedimentary rocks to form a lowland which subsequently filled with water.

The Indiana Dunes National Lakeshore was dedicated in 1972 to preserve a part of the hundreds of miles of rugged sand dunes and marshes and the wealth of flora and fauna which exist at the southern boundary of the lake. The Indiana dunelands also were formed during the last glacial advance 75,000 years ago which left a curved belt of hilly land known as the Valparaiso Moraine at the southern shores of Lake Michigan. Abandoned shorelines, from which the dunes developed, attest to the lake's higher level in glacial times. Around 1000 BC the present level was reached, and the dunes came into existence. In Indiana, the lake is an important seaway for the Calumet industrial district and has deep harbors at Michigan City and Gary.

MICHIGANTOWN, town (pop. 457), Clinton County, central Indiana, zip 46057, 8 mi. ENE of Frankfort in an agricultural area (livestock, feed grains), Founded in 1830, the town was named for the Old Michigan Road, on which it was a stagecoach stop. When the road declined, so did Michigantown, and it is now a quiet farming community.

MIDDLEBURY, town (pop. 1,055), Elkhart County, N Indiana, zip 46540, on the Little Elkhart River, 14 mi. E of Elkhart in an agricultural area noted for dairy farms. The town is a commercial trade center and specializes in nursery stock and dairy products. Recreational facilities are at nearby Hunter Lake.

MIDDLETOWN, town (pop. 2,046), Henry County, E central Indiana, zip 47356, on Fall Creek, 8 mi. ESE of Anderson in an agricultural area (livestock, feed grains). The town has a cannery.

MILAN, town (pop. 1,260), Ripley County, SE Indiana, zip 47031, 42 mi. ESE of Shelbyville in an agricultural area (livestock, feed grains).

MILFORD, town (pop. 1,267), Decatur County, SE central Indiana, zip 46542, 7 mi. W of Greensburg in an agricultural area noted for livestock and feed grains.

MILLERSBURG, town (pop. 618), Elkhart County, N Indiana, zip 46543, 17 mi. SE of Elkhart in an agricultural area (livestock, feed grains).

MILLHOUSEN, town (pop. 252), Decatur County, SE central Indiana, zip 47261, 29 mi. SE of Shelbyville in an agricultural region (livestock, feed grains).

MILLTOWN, town (pop. 829), on the boundary of Crawford and Harrison counties, S Indiana, zip 47145, on the Blue River, 25 mi. WNW of New Albany. The economy is based on the quarrying and processing of limestone. The quarrying is done in underground mines, and the resulting huge caverns are popular attractions for rock and fossil collectors.

MILROY, town (pop. 696), Rush County, central Indiana, zip 46156, 8 mi. S of Rushville in a manufacturing and farming area. Milroy produces trim stampings, plastic products, stone and cement products, school supplies, canned goods, and agricultural products.

MILTON, town (pop. 694), Wayne County, E Indiana, zip 47357, on the Whitewater River, 14 mi. W of Richmond in an agricultural area (livestock, feed grains).

MISHAWAKA, city (pop. 35,517), St. Joseph County, N Indiana, zip 46544, on the St. Joseph River, just E of South Bend. Mishawaka was founded in 1832 and named for the daughter of Chief Elkhart of the Shawnee, who lived in the vicinity before 1800. Mishawaka is mainly an industrial suburb of South Bend. Its diversified manufactures include clothing, furniture, rubber goods, industrial machinery, bedding, trunks, and food products. An ethnic community of Flemish-Dutch citizens resides in the southwestern part of the city. Most of the 6,000 Belgians arrived there after World War I. They work in the city and in South Bend and are noted for their meticulously-kept vegetable and flower gardens.

Mishawaka is the seat of Bethel College, a four-year, fully-accredited liberal arts college with an average enrollment of 500 students. The Mishawaka Children's Museum contains outstanding exhibits of Alaska, pioneer life, and science. The St. Joseph River and Merrifield Park offer excellent recreational facilities.

MISSISSINEWA DAM AND RESERVOIR, Miami County, E central Indiana, 7 mi. SE of Peru. The facility was developed jointly by the State of Indiana and the U.S. Army Corps of Engineers. It encompasses the 3,210-acre Mississinewa Lake with 59 mi. of shoreline and two state recreation areas—Miami and Red Bridge. The land area totals 14,000 acres and includes facilities for camping, swimming, fishing, picnicking, hunting, and boating. Four boat launching ramps are situated around the lake.

MISSISSINEWA RIVER, rises in Darke County, Ohio, and flows W into Indiana, NW past Marion, and empties into the Wabash River at Peru. Approximately 100 mi. long, the river is dammed 7 mi. SW of Peru to form 3,210-acre Mississinewa Lake, a popular recreational facility.

MITCHELL, city (pop. 4,092), Lawrence County, S Indiana, zip 47446, 9 mi. S of Bedford. Mitchell was a community as early as 1813, but it was not until the 1850s, when the Monon Railroad extended its services to Lawrence County, that the city was platted. The Baltimore and Ohio Railroad followed in 1856, at which time Mitchell began to flourish as an important manufacturing and shipping center for limestone, agricultural products, cement, clothing, and lime.

Mitchell was the childhood home of Virgil "Gus" Grissom, the American astronaut who died at Cape Canaveral in 1967. A memorial to him has been erected at nearby Spring Mill State Park (*q.v.*). A persimmon festival is annually held in town in conjunction with a candlelight tour of the authentic pioneer village in the state park.

MODOC, town (pop. 275), Randolph County, E Indiana, zip 47358, 16 mi. SE of Muncie in an agricultural area (livestock, feed grains).

MONON, town (pop. 1,548), White County, NW central Indiana, zip 47959, on Little Monon Creek, 29 mi. WNW of Logansport. The town was incorporated in 1879 and named for the stream which flows through town. "Monon" is derived from the Indian word *monon* ("swift running water"). The town became the division point for the Monon Railroad, which took its name from the town. Railroad repair shops are in Monon, which is an important shipping and manufacturing center for corn, oats, soybeans, dairy products, and crushed stone.

Monon was the home of William Girard, a Union soldier who became the first casualty from Indiana to die in the Civil War. The G.A.R. post is dedicated to his memory.

MONROE, county (pop. 84,849), S central Indiana, area 386 sq.mi., drained by the West Fork of the White River, and by Salt, Beanblossom, and Clear creeks. The county was formed in April 1818 and named in honor of James Monroe, fifth president of the U.S. Bloomington is the county seat and home of Indiana University (1824). The economy is based on farming, stock raising, dairying, limestone quarrying, and some manufacturing. Leading industries produce electronic components, television receivers, and processed food.

The Monroe Reservoir, largest body of water in Indiana (10,750 acres), is located almost wholly within the county.

MONROE, town (pop. 622), Adams County, E Indiana, zip 46772, 25 mi. SSE of Fort Wayne in an agricultural area noted for (livestock, feed gains). Monroe is a manufacturer of rat and mouse bait, mobile homes, fertilizer, and sprinkler systems.

MONROE CITY, town (pop. 603), Knox County, SW Indiana, zip 47557, 10 mi. SE of Vincennes in an agricultural area noted for feed grains and livestock. Bituminous coal mines are nearby.

MONROE DAM AND RESERVOIR, Monroe County, S central Indiana, 6 mi. S of Bloomington. The reservoir, which was under development in the 1970s, was jointly established by the state of Indiana and the U.S. Army Corps of Engineers. The central focus is 10,750-acre Lake Monroe. The Monroe facility, Paynetown State Recreation Area, and Fairfax State Recreation Area together comprise 22,500 acres of recreational lands. Boat ramps are situated around the lake, which has excellent fishing and swimming. Other facilities include a modern campground and picnic sites.

MONROEVILLE, town (pop. 1,353), Allen County, NE Indiana, zip 46773, 16 mi. ESE of Fort Wayne near the Ohio border. It is in an agricultural area noted for livestock and feed grains.

MONROVIA, town (pop. 600), Morgan County, central Indiana, zip 46157, 12 mi. NW of Martinsville. Monrovia is a manufacturer of precision tools and dies, agricultural fertilizers, and chemicals.

MONTEREY, town (pop. 268), Pulaski County, NW Indiana, zip 46960, on the Tippecanoe River, 38 mi. SSW of South Bend in an agricultural area (livestock, feed grains).

MONTEZUMA, town (pop. 1,192), Parke County, W Indiana, zip 47862, on the Wabash River, 22 mi. N of Terre Haute. A large Indian village once occupied the site. The area remained uninhabited by white men until Samuel Hill built his two-story log cabin there in 1821. Montezuma, named for the Aztec emperor of Mexico, grew up around Sam Hill's cabin. The town remained quiet until 1848, when the Wabash and Erie Canal was completed. Montezuma was platted the following year, flourished for a while as a river and canal port, but declined when the canal project was abandoned in the 1860s.

Today, Montezuma is a peaceful farming community which also depends heavily upon coal mining, fishing, and the manufacture of clay products. The town participates in the annual autumn Parke County Covered Bridge Festival, the proceeds of which go toward preservation of the county's 36 covered bridges. Reeder Park on the Wabash River is a popular picnicking site.

MONTGOMERY, county (pop. 33,930), W central Indiana, area 507 sq.mi., drained by Sugar and Raccoon creeks. The county was formed in March 1823 and named for Gen. Richard Montgomery. Crawfordsville is the county seat. The land is composed of some of the most fertile soils in the state. Aside from its great agricultural and livestock resources, Montgomery County also has a vast supply of shale deposits and is a leader in the manufacture of bricks. Other industries include book printing and the production of fabricated metals.

MONTGOMERY, town (pop. 411), Daviess County, SW Indiana, zip 47558, 26 mi. E of Vincennes in an agricultural area (livestock, feed grains). There are several bituminous coal mines in the vicinity. Montgomery was built up around St. Peter's Church (1818) in hopes that it would eventually become the site of a great Catholic university. Plans were abandoned when construction of the University of Notre Dame began at South Bend in 1842. Ruritan Park contains a recreational facility, including a 26-acre lake.

MONTICELLO, city (pop. 4,869), seat of White County, NW central Indiana, zip 47960, on the Tippecanoe River, 21 mi. W of Logansport. The city was founded in 1834 on a high bluff overlooking the river. Its location between Freeman and Shafer lakes has rendered it a popular vacation spot. Fishing, boating, and swimming are excellent on all waters and it is said that "Noah unloaded the original pair of black bass into the Tippecanoe River at this point."

Monticello is also an important manufacturing center. It has a thread mill, a printing plant, and a hydroelectric power station. Products include flour, packed meat, and furniture. Of note is the suspension bridge, Indiana's largest, which spans a section of Shafer Lake. Indiana Beach, "Indiana's Atlantic City," is on the lakes and includes three beaches, ski shows, dancing, horseback riding, excursion boat rides, and an amusement park.

MONTPELIER, town (pop. 2,093), Blackford County, E Indiana, zip 47359, on the Salamonie River, 27 mi. NNE of Muncie. The town was platted in 1836 by Abel Baldwin, who named it for the capital of Vermont, his home state. Incorporation came one year later. Nearby, Francois Godfroy, a Frenchman, had operated a trading post for the Miami Indians. The Godfroy Reserve, part of his landholdings, can be seen in NE Blackford County. The area is noted for dairy farms, livestock, soy beans, and feed grains. Montpelier, like many other E central Indiana towns, benefited from the natural gas boom of 1887. Manufacturing products, directly related to the gas discovery, include crude oil, chemical supplies, and glass.

MOORELAND, town (pop. 495), Henry County, E Indiana, zip 47360, 8 mi. NE of New Castle. It was named for Philip Moore, an early settler. The main business in town is a grain elevator. The vicinity is noted for livestock and feed grains.

MOORES HILL, town (pop. 616), Dearborn County, SE Indiana, zip 47032, 12 mi. W of Aurora. Located at an altitude of 917 ft., Moores Hill is on the highest point in Dearborn County. A Methodist college was built there in 1854, but it burned down in 1915. The college was removed to Evansville in 1919, and was subsequently renamed. Moores Hill remains a quiet agricultural community.

MOORESVILLE, town (pop. 5,800), Morgan County, central Indiana, zip 46158, on the Whitelick River, 16 mi. SW of Indianapolis. The town was settled in 1824 and became a noted agricultural and commercial center for dairy products, fruit, flour, burial vaults, and engine bearings. Mooresville was the home of Paul Hadley, a Hoosier artist who designed the official state flag in 1971. The original flag can be seen at the Children's Museum in Indianapolis. John Dillinger, notorious gangster of the 1930s, made his childhood home in Mooresville.

Nearby is the Goethe Link Observatory, subsidized by Indiana University. During the summer months, the observatory is a popular visitor's attraction because of its weekly lectures and viewings.

MORGAN, county (pop. 44,176), central Indiana, area 406 sq.mi., drained by the West Fork of the White River, Whitelick River, and Camp Creek. The county was organized in February 1822 and named for Gen. Daniel Morgan. Martinsville has been the seat since the county's inception.

Morgan County is in a rich agricultural area (hogs, grain, fruit, poultry), and there is manufacturing in Martinsville and Mooresville (food processing, lumbering, brick, tile). The Grassy Fork Fish Hatchery, largest producer of goldfish in the world, is located at Martinsville.

MORGAN-MONROE STATE FOREST, Morgan and Monroe counties, S Indiana, 8 mi. S of Martinsville. The state lands encompass 25,000 acres of primarily beech-maple forest and have facilities for camping, picnicking, hiking, boating, fishing, and riding. There are 6 artificial lakes in the park, with water recreation available on a 20-acre lake.

In 1929 a destructive forest fire annihilated much of the virgin stands of walnut, oak, hickory, and maple. Successful reforestation has helped to reclaim much of the land since that time. Cascade Park, within the confines of the forest, has scenic cliffs, deep ravines, and small waterfalls.

MORGANTOWN, town (pop. 1,134), Morgan County, central Indiana, zip 46160, near Camp Creek, 28 mi. S of Indianapolis. Morgantown is a farming community and a manufacturer of furniture.

MORNINGSIDE, village (pop. 1,700), Delaware County, E central Indiana, near Muncie in an agricultural area (cattle, hogs, pigs, feed grains). The village is in the midst of the Trenton oil and natural gas field.

MOROCCO, town (pop. 1,285), Newton County, NW Indiana, zip 47963, 48 mi. S of Hammond. The town was once known as Beaver Prairie because its streams and Beaver Lake teemed with beaver. Willow Slough is a remnant of Beaver Lake, which once encompassed 10,000 acres. The lake was drained and the resulting fertile soils were planted in grain and soybeans. Willow Slough has been designated a State Fish and Game Area, and nearby J.C. Murphy Lake (1,700 acres) has excellent camping, swimming, and fishing facilities.

MORRISTOWN, town (pop. 838), Shelby County, central Indiana, zip 46161, on the Big Blue River, 26 mi. ESE of Indianapolis. For years, Morristown's only industry was a canned goods plant. With a readily available supply of natural gas, however, Morristown since 1968 has managed to boost its economy by bringing in three new industries. Located there are the International Packing Company, a producer of rubber goods; Indiana Steel Products, a manufacturer of leaf springs for heavy trucks; and the Nabisco soybean processing plant. As a result, new banks, schools, and subdivisions have been built.

Of note is the Kopper Kettle Restaurant (1923), which was originally a grain elevator (1849). The elevator became obsolete in 1958 when the Junction Railroad, which served the town, was abandoned. Recreational facilities can be found at nearby Gordon's Lake.

MOUNDS STATE PARK, Madison County, E central Indiana, 4 mi. N of Anderson. The 254-acre state park, situated on a bluff overlooking the White River, contains an enigmatic cluster of earthworks believed to have been constructed by prehistoric moundbuilders belonging to a branch of the Hopewell Culture of Woodland Indians, who lived in this area from 500 BC to 500 AD. Among the several mounds, the largest measures 1,200 ft. around and is 9 ft. high. The park provides numerous hiking trails and bridle paths, as well as playgrounds and limited camping facilities.

MOUNT AYR, town (pop. 194), Newton County, NW Indiana, zip 47964, 7 mi. W of Rensselaer in an agricultural area (livestock, feed grains.)

MOUNT SUMMIT, town (pop. 345), Henry County, E Indiana, zip 47361, 13 mi. S of Muncie. Mount Summit, at 1,088 ft. altitude, was named for its location at one of the "loftier" elevations in Henry County. The town is a farming community (livestock, feed grains).

MOUNT VERNON, city (pop. 6,770), seat of Posey County, SW Indiana, zip 47620, on the Ohio River, 18 mi. W of Evansville. The city was founded in 1805 by Andrew McFadden and was known as McFadden's Landing until 1816. Indiana's southernmost city, Mount Vernon is an important agricultural trade center for the surrounding area. Products include flour, corn, canned goods, and cheese.

Reminders of the river boat era can be seen in several early buildings. The courthouse dates from 1876. On the courthouse square is the Soldiers and Sailors Monument (1908), designed by Hoosier architect Rudolph Schwartz. South of town is the Hovey Lake State Game Preserve noted for its variety of wildlife and the stands of bald cypress that grow in the shallow waters of Lake Hovey.

MULBERRY, village (pop. 1,075), Clinton County, central Indiana, zip 46058, 10 mi. NW of Frankfort in an agricultural area noted for livestock and feed grains.

MUNCIE, city (pop. 69,080), seat of Delaware County, E Indiana, zip 47302, on the West Fork of the White River, 50 mi. NE of Indianapolis. White settlers first came to the area in 1818, after the local Indians ceded their lands to the U.S. in the Treaty of St. Mary's. A 672-acre tract was bought and platted as Munseytown in 1827. The name was derived from the Munsee tribe of the Delaware Indians which had previously occupied the site. Munseytown was changed to Muncie in 1845, was incorporated as a town in 1847 and as a city in 1865.

In 1887, Muncie was part of the great natural gas boom that affected many towns in central Indiana. Wells were drilled, natural gas was struck, and the seemingly endless supply brought in speculators and industries almost overnight. Glass works, iron mills, and pulp and rubber factories, which all depended on the fossil fuel, boomed and thousands of workers poured into the newly-formed manufacturing city. The lure of fabulous job offers brought in so many new people that housing projects could not keep up with the pace. As a result, ramshackle shanties were erected by the newcomers in Avondale, the only unplatted section within the city limits. "Shedtown" remained for years until the shacks were replaced by modern cottages.

Reports ran rampant that the gas supply was inexhaustible. Fires at the wells were kept burning night and day, but the gas supply dwindled in 1890. Some of the industries left the city, but the groundwork for an industrial city had been laid, and most of the businesses remained. They found other means to power their equipment and in the 1970s, more than 100 plants were located in Muncie. Notable among them are the Ball Brothers plant, which manufactures glass canning jars; Warner Gear Division; Delco Battery; a Chevrolet plant; Indiana Steel and Wire Company; and a Westinghouse Electric transformer plant. Other manufactures include electric equipment, castings, cutlery, furniture, bedding, sporting goods, and dairy products.

In 1924, Muncie became the national focus of attention when two sociologists, Robert and Helen Merrell Lynd, conducted a research study on the psychological and sociological trends of the city. Their findings were published in two well-known books *Middletown* (1929) and *Middletown in Transition* (1937). Their study was aimed at reflecting the life in an average American city.

Muncie is the seat of Ball State University (1918), a four-year, fully-accredited teacher's college which was almost wholly subsidized by funds donated by the Ball brothers. The 538-acre campus contains the Ball State Gallery, Emens Auditorium, Christy Woods (arboretum and gardens), and a 5-telescope planetarium and observatory. Average enrollment is 17,500 students.

Muncie contains a replica of the statue "Appeal to the Great Spirit," designed by Cyrus Dallin. The original stands in front of Boston's Museum of Fine Arts. The statue is a life-size image of an Indian on his pony, and it is located on the original campsite of the Munsee tribe.

Excellent recreational facilities can be found at McCullough and Heekin parks, and at Prairie Creek Reservoir (1,215 acres), 6 mi. SE of the city. Muncie also has two golf courses. Annual events include the Delaware County Fair and the National and Hoosier Cup hydroplane and speedboat races on the Prairie Creek Reservoir.

MUNSTER, town (pop. 16,514), Lake County, extreme NW Indiana, zip 46321, on the Illinois border, 4 mi. S of Hammond. Located in an agricultural area noted for livestock and feed grains, Munster is a shipping point for garden produce and nursery stock.

MUSCATATUCK STATE PARK, Jennings County S Indiana, 1 mi. from North Vernon. The park covers 205 acres and contains the ruins of Vinegar Mill (1830s). The park offers rugged scenery and is a popular rendezvous for hikers and nature lovers. Fishing is available on adjacent Muscatatuck River; the Muscatatuck Fish Management Headquarters are within the park. There are also areas for camping and picnicking.

NAPOLEON, town (pop. 282), Ripley County, E central Indiana, zip 47034, 12 mi. NW of Versailles in a farming and lumbering area. The town is noted for crushed stone and stone products, lumber, portable farm buildings, feeders, and casket hardware.

NAPPANEE, city (pop. 4,159), Elkhart County, N Indiana, zip 46550, 21 mi. SE of South Bend in an agricultural area noted for mint, onions, and grain. The town was platted in 1874 along the tracks of the Baltimore & Ohio Railroad. It has become a railroad shipping center for furniture (its principal industrial product), canned goods, and flour. There is a large Amish farming population in and around Nappanee. Their horse-drawn carriages are a common sight in town.

NASHVILLE, town (pop. 527), seat of Brown County, central Indiana, zip 47448, 40 mi. S of Indianapolis. Turn-of-the-century homes are located everywhere in Nashville, which is nestled among wooded hills. Some of the most beautiful scenery in the Midwest can be found there, and as a result, the town has become a haven for painters, photographers, and tourists. Log cabins built in the 19th century have been restored and turned into studios for members of the famous Brown County Artists' Colony. The Brown County Art Gallery has a fine display of Hooiser art.

Next to the county courthouse is an old log jail (1837) with walls 5 ft. thick. The jail contains an excellent collection of Indian artifacts. Nashville is a tourist attraction in every season. In the spring, visitors come to view the scenery enhanced by blooming redbud and dogwood trees. Autumn foliage brings others who come to buy berries, nuts, maple syrup, and apple butter. Nearby are Brown County State Park and the Hoosier National and Yellowood state forests, all of which have excellent recreational facilities.

NEW ALBANY, city (pop. 38,402), seat of Floyd County, S Indiana, zip 47150, on the Ohio River, opposite Louisville, Kentucky. New Albany was founded in 1813 on an 86½ acre tract nestled at the foot of the Knobstone Escarpment. From its inception, the city depended upon the river for its prosperity and flourished as a port-of-call for ferries operating between Indiana and Kentucky and steamboats running from Pittsburgh to New Orleans. Seven shipyards operated between 1830 and 1860, and such famous steamboats as the "Eclipse" and the "Robert E. Lee" were built there.

After the prosperous riverboat era, New Albany continued to grow as a commercial center. Until 1887, it was a leader in glass manufacturing, but the natural gas boom removed the industry to the eastern part of the state. Climatic conditions and natural resources favored the location of a hardwood veneer plant in New Albany. Today, the city is one of the largest plywood manufacturing centers in the U.S. Other principal manufactures are furniture, prefabricated houses, machine tools, clothing, fertilizer, and automobile parts.

Many of the historic buildings of the riverboat era have been preserved. Notable examples are the 27-room Culbertson Mansion (1868), with its cantilever staircase; Sloan House (1853), which resembles a riverboat; and the Scribner House (1814), home of the first settlers in New Albany. Many scenic parks line the riverfront, and the view from the Knobs is breathtaking.

North of the city is Indiana University Southeast (1941), a branch of Indiana University at Bloomington. Annual events include the 4-H Fair in July and the Harvest Homecoming in October. New Albany was selected as an All-American City in 1969.

NEW AUGUSTA, town (pop. 225), Marion County, central Indiana, zip 46268, 11 mi. N of Indianapolis in an agricultural area. The town is a trade center for shade trees, plants, fertilizers, and various industrial products.

NEWBERRY, town (pop. 295), Greene County, SW Indiana, zip 47449, on the West Fork of the White River, 32 mi. ENE of Vincennes in an area noted for feed grains, livestock, and bituminous coal mining.

NEWBURGH, town (pop. 2,302), Warrick County, SW Indiana, zip 47630, on the Ohio River, 9 mi. E of Evansville. Settled in 1803, the town flourished as a river port. The modern economy is based on manufacturing and agriculture (tobacco, flour). On the riverfront can be seen the old Ohio Dam #47 and the locks.

NEW CARLISLE, town (pop. 1,434), St. Joseph County, zip 46552, N Indiana, 12 mi. W of South Bend in an agricultural area noted (livestock, feed grains). Of note is the Augustine Homestead built in 1834 by carpenter Henry Brown. Its squared logs are believed to have been hauled from distant sawmills. The house is built in Greek Revival style.

NEW CASTLE, city (pop. 21,215), seat of Henry County, E Indiana, zip 47362, on the Big Blue River, 18 mi. S of Muncie. The city was founded in 1820 and platted in 1836. A monument to Wilbur Wright, a propeller mounted on a stone base, is near New Castle, outside of which the pioneer aviator once lived. The city was an early pioneer automobile manufacturing center, producing such classic cars as the Maxwell, Lawter, and Universal.

New Castle is a trade and distribution center for livestock, grain, and poultry. Manufactures include automobile parts, machinery, steel products, furniture, and clothing. New Castle is the seat of the Henry County Historical Museum (1870), which has a fine display of pioneer, Civil War, and Wilbur Wright memorabilia. Recreational facilities can be found at Henry County Memorial and Baker parks.

NEW CHICAGO, town (pop. 2,231), Lake County, NW Indiana, zip 46342, just SE of Gary in an agricultural area noted for livestock and feed grains. New Chicago is located on the old council grounds of the Potawatomi Indians. It is best known for the electric buggy, invented there by the U.S. Electric Carriage Company.

NEW HARMONY, town (pop. 971), Posey County, SW Indiana, zip 47631, on the Wabash River, 22 mi. WNW of Evansville. Originally known as Harmonie, the town was founded in 1814 by members of the Rappite Society for the purpose of establishing a colony based on communal living. The Rappites, a religious group under the leadership of George Rapp, had emigrated from Wurttemberg, Germany, to Pennsylvania before settling along the Wabash River. They cleared 25,000 acres of forest and swampland and converted it into farms. Their town of 200 homes and 2 churches became the showplace for the surrounding countryside. The Rappites sold the town in 1825 to Robert Owen, a Welsh philanthropist and social reformer who renamed the settlement New Harmony. Owen intended to establish a society of social and economic equality based on a system of universal education. The program failed, however, because of his frequent absences and the rivalries among his followers.

New Harmony developed into one of the first scientific centers in the U.S. Sir Charles Lyell, the noted Scottish geologist, and James Audubon, the ornithologist, visited there. The Laboratory Building, built by David Dale Owen, the first U.S. geologist, became the headquarters for the U.S. Geological Survey. Much scientific research was carried on there between 1824 and 1856.

The Workingmen's Institute, Library, and Museum (1838) is still in use today. It was founded by William Maclure, who was a pioneer in establishing traveling libraries.

For the past century New Harmony has remained a farm trading center for the surrounding countryside, but the town thrives well on the tourists who are attracted by the many historic landmarks. A state memorial commission was established in 1935 to restore the sturdy Rappite buildings. Notable examples are the Rappite Community House (1816); the Old Rappite Fort Granary, built as a defense against "marauding neighbors"; the Rapp-Maclure Mansion (1814); the Colonial Dames Harmonist Museum House, a restored Rappite family dwelling; and the Barrett-Gate House (1814), the oldest house in New Harmony. The city's beauty is further enhanced by thousands of "gate trees" that were imported from China and Korea in 1825. The round-topped trees have long sprays of yellow flowers which bloom in June and shed their blossoms in a golden rain. The Rappite Cemetery, a 3-acre tract, contains the unmarked graves of 230 Rappites.

The Restored Labryinth, made of boxwood hedges, has only one exit leading to the Temple, a summer house. The Roofless Church, erected in memory of New Harmony settlers, is a rectangular structure enclosed by brick walls but without a roof. In the center of the church is a large bronze sculpture, "Descent of the Holy Spirit," by Jacques Lipschitz. Paul Tillich Park contains the remains of the world-famous theologian, and is a noted visitor's attraction.

NEW HAVEN, town (pop. 5,728), Allen County, NE Indiana, zip 46774, on the Maumee River, 6 mi. E of Fort Wayne. The town was named for New Haven, Connecticut, and owes its existence to the Wabash and Erie Canal. A suburb of Fort

Wayne, its manufactures include showcases, cement vaults, and wood products. The Havenurst Golf Course is NE of town.

NEW MARKET, town (pop. 640), Montgomery County, W central Indiana, zip 47965, 6 mi. S of Crawfordsville in an agricultural area (livestock, feed grains).

NEW MIDDLETOWN, town (pop. 133), Harrison County, S Indiana, zip 47160, 15 mi. SW of New Albany in an agricultural area (feed grains, livestock).

NEW PALESTINE, town (pop. 863), Hancock County, central Indiana, zip 46163, on Sugar Creek, 15 mi. ESE of Indianapolis in an agricultural area (feed grains, cattle, horses, hogs, sheep).

NEW PARIS, town (pop. 1,080), Elkhart County, N Indiana zip 46553, 6 mi. S of Goshen. The town produces popcorn, publications, sheet metal, feed and dairy products, cabinets, recreational vehicles, plastic-laminated products, sporting equipment, and specialized welded products.

NEW POINT, town (pop. 381), Decatur County, SE central Indiana, zip 47263, 29 mi. ESE of Shelbyville. New Point began as a limestone quarrying center, but its economy declined after the industry was moved to Bloomington and Bedford. Today, farming constitutes the main sources of income.

NEWPORT, town (pop. 708), seat of Vermillion County, W Indiana, zip 47966, near the confluence of the Little Vermillion and Wabash rivers, 30 mi. N of Terre Haute. The Newport courthouse burned down twice (1844,1866), but all the county records were saved. Cannel coal mining is an important activity, and the area around Newport is noted for its fruit orchards and Shetland ponies.

NEW RICHMOND, town (pop. 381), Montgomery County, W central Indiana, zip 47967, 18 mi. SSW of Lafayette in an agricultural area (livestock, feed grains). The inexhaustible supply of shale around the town has provided a base for the manufacture of bricks and tile.

NEW ROSS, town (pop. 318), Montgomery County, W central Indiana, zip 47968, near Raccoon Creek, 12 mi. ESE of Crawfordsville in an agricultural area (livestock, feed grains).

NEW SALISBURY, town (pop. 350), Harrison County, S Indiana, zip 47161, 17 mi. NW of Louisville, Kentucky, in a lumbering and agricultural area. The town is a manufacturing center for dog and cat foods, furniture, cabinets, and agricultural products.

NEWTON, county (pop. 11,606), NW Indiana, area 413 sq.mi. bounded on the W by the Illinois and on the N by the Kankakee River. It is drained by the Kankakee and Iroquois rivers. The last county to be organized in Indiana, it was formed in December 1859 and named for Sgt. John Newton. Kentland is the county seat.

Newton County is very fertile and a leading producer of grain and seeds which are shipped to nearby markets. Manufacturing (electronic and appliance parts, cheese, cosmetics) is carried out in the larger towns. A fine road-building limestone is quarried near Kentland. The quarry is unique because its strata stand on edge rather than lying horizontally, apparently the result of volcanic upheaval. George Ade, famous turn-of-the-century author, humorist, and playwright, made his home in Newton County.

NEWTOWN, town (pop. 286), Fountain County, W Indiana, zip 47969, 18 mi. NW of Crawfordsville in an agricultural area (feed grains, livestock).

NOBLE, county (pop. 31,382), NE Indiana, area 412 sq.mi., drained by the Elkhart River. The county was formed in 1836 and named for Noah Noble, governor of Indiana (1831-37). Albion is the county seat. The county was part of the Underground Railroad that aided runaway slaves on their northward flight to freedom.

Numerous small lakes have made Noble County a popular resort area. Chain O'Lakes State Park (*q.v.*) is probably the most popular attraction. Agriculture (livestock, poultry, fruit, grain, soybeans, truck) and manufacturing (food processing, refrigeration, machinery, electrical wire assemblies, iron castings, plastic products, candy) aid the county's prosperity.

OAKLAND CITY, town (pop. 3,289), Gibson County, SW Indiana, zip 47560, 28 mi. NNE of Evansville. The town's economy is dependent upon coal mining and agriculture (cantaloupe, peaches, sweet potatoes, corn, soybeans). The town is the seat of Oakland City College (1885), a Baptist liberal arts institution which has an average enrollment of 550 students.

OAKTOWN, town (pop. 726), Knox County, SW Indiana, zip 47561, 14 mi. NNE of Vincennes. It is a shipping center for melons, peaches, apples, and sweet potatoes. There is a fruit packing plant in town and oil and natural gas wells are in the vicinity.

ODON, town (pop. 1,433), Daviess County, SW Indiana, zip 47562, 31 mi. ENE of Vincennes in an agricultural area (livestock, feed grains).

OGDEN DUNES, town (pop. 1,461), Porter County, NW Indiana, on Lake Michigan just E of Gary. In the early 1900s the dunes were the home of "Diana of the Dunes," a famous female hermit also known as "Dunehilda." Reputedly the daughter of a wealthy physician, Diana lived off the meager wages she earned by selling her homemade wild berry wine. She lived alone for many years studying the plants and animals of the dunes.

Ogden Dunes was founded in 1925 and laid out along 432 acres of dune country. It has always been a residential and resort town, and no commercial enterprises have been allowed there. Remnants of a 1927 Olympic-size ski jump can be seen. Excellent boating, fishing, swimming, and golfing facilities are in and around the town.

OHIO, county (pop. 4,289), SE Indiana, area 87 sq.mi., bounded on the E by Kentucky and drained by the Ohio River and Laughery Creek. Organized in January 1844, the county was named for the Ohio River. Rising Sun is the county seat.

Agriculture is the mainstay of the economy. The river valley soils are fertile and conducive to truck and tobacco farming and livestock raising. The rest of the county is very rugged and picturesque, broken by several ranges of heavily forested hills.

OHIO RIVER, 981 mi. long, formed by the confluence of the Allegheny and Monongahela rivers at Pittsburgh, Pennsylvania. In Indiana, the river forms the state's southern boundary and has long been an important means of commerce. It was discovered by La Salle in 1669 and became a major navigation center for settlers heading west and south. Improvement of navigability came with the opening of the Wabash and Erie Canal in 1827.

Chief tributaries of the Ohio River are the Muskingum, Scioto, Kanawaka, Miami, Wabash, Big Sandy, Tennessee, Green and Cumberland rivers. The total watershed encompasses 200,000 square miles.

The Indiana topography around the Ohio is particularly rugged and beautiful. High, wooded bluffs border both banks and between the north bank and Bloomington lies a vast limestone belt broken by numerous disappearing streams, mineral springs, caves, and sinkholes. The Ohio River is an important part of the extensive Mississippi River system of inland waterways. The original Ohio River Navigation Project, which was completed in 1929, has increased traffic from 20,000,000 tons to 89,000,000 tons annually.

The U.S. Army Corps of Engineers has established flood control projects all over Indiana, but mainly in the Ohio River Basin. The program deals with the problems of flood control, water supply, water quality, navigation, hydroelectric power, floodplain planning, recreation, and fish and wildlife development.

OLDENBURG, town (pop. 758), Franklin County, SE Indiana, zip 47036, ESE of Shelbyville. Oldenburg was founded in 1837 by German immigrants who worked in the town's once prosperous brick factories. Today, Oldenburg is a quiet farming community. In town is the Sisters of St. Francis Convent and Academy (1851), which operates more than 70 mission schools. A Franciscan monastery and seminary is next to the Church of the Holy Family. The Shrine of the Sorrowful Mother (1871), 1 mi. E of the town, resembles the wayside chapels in the Bavarian Alps. A fragment of a rock from Calvary, another from the temple ruins at Baalbek, and a third from the Roman Colosseum are contained within the shrine.

ONWARD, town (pop. 111), Cass County, N central Indiana, zip 46967, 10 mi. ESE of Logansport in an agricultural area (livestock, feed grain).

OOLITIC, town (pop. 1,155), Lawrence County, S Indiana, zip 47451, on Salt Creek, 4 mi. NNW of Bedford. The town was named for the oölitic (fish-egg) texture of the limestone found in the quarries that surround it. Many of the buildings are composed of the limestone, which was mined up to the peak year of 1924. Since then the industry has declined, and the town's economy is now largely based on agriculture.

ORANGE, county (pop. 16,968), S Indiana, area 405 sq.mi., drained by the Lick, Lost, and Patoka rivers. The county was organized in February 1816 and named for Orange County, North Carolina, from which many of the early settlers came. Paoli is the county seat.

Orange County is rugged, hilly, and unsuitable for most farming. Fruit growing, dairying, and stock raising are profitable activities. The greatest resources of the county, however, are its world-famous mineral waters. Health spas such as French Lick and West Baden attract thousands of visitors yearly. "Pluto Water" from Pluto Spring at French Lick is sent all over the world. There is some industry at Paoli, including the manufacture of television receivers, radios, and furniture.

ORESTES, town (pop. 519), Madison County, E central Indiana, zip 46063, 7 mi. E of Elwood. Originally called Lowry's Station, the town began as a railroad switch stop, with a grain elevator constituting the only business. The natural gas boom of 1887 brought some industry to Orestes, but the town declined with the gas supply. Orestes was almost totally destroyed in 1922 when a tornado struck without warning.

Today, Orestes is a sleepy farming community. The Madison County Historical Society dedicated a memorial plaque to a 300-

year old oak tree in town on May 6, 1973. The tree was once a landmark for a Delaware Indian trail and for Orestes.

ORLAND, town (pop. 457), Steuben County, NE Indiana, zip 46776, near the Michigan border, 55 mi. E of South Bend in an agricultural area (cattle, hogs, feed grains). Nearby is the 90-year old Collins School, a restored memorial to early education in which 19th-century school books and desks are on display.

ORLEANS, town (pop. 1,834), Orange County, S Indiana, zip 47452, near Lost River, 14 mi. S of Bedford. Founded in 1815, the town was named for New Orleans, Louisiana, and is the oldest town in the county. Orleans is a dairy center and has a large creamery. There are also several large fruit orchards. Orleans is the home of the annual spring Dogwood Festival and has been called the "Dogwood Capital of Indiana." Of note is the grave of Ann Todd Teagarden, aunt to Abraham Lincoln's wife.

OSCEOLA, town (pop. 1,572), St. Joseph County, N Indiana, zip 46561, on the St. Joseph River, 10 mi. E of South Bend in a resort and agricultural area (livestock, feed grains).

OSGOOD, town (pop. 1,346), Ripley County, SE Indiana, zip 47037, 18 mi. SE of Greensburg. A farm trading center for the surrounding area, the town is also a manufacturer of wood and cement products, polo balls, and condensed milk. Limestone quarries are nearby.

OSSIAN, town (pop. 1,538), Wells County, E Indiana, zip 46777, on Longlois Creek, 14 mi. S of Fort Wayne in an agricultural area (cattle, hogs, feed grains).

OTTERBEIN, town (pop. 899), Benton County, W Indiana, zip 47970, 13 mi. WNW of Lafayette in an agricultural area (livestock, feed grains).

OTWELL, town (pop. 550), Pike County, S Indiana, zip 47564, 12 mi. E of Petersburg in a lumbering and farming area. The town has an agricultural feed plant.

OUABACHE STATE RECREATION AREA, Wells County, E Indiana, 6 mi. E of Bluffton. Formerly known as the Wells County State Game Farm, it encompasses 1,037 acres of woods and has a small lake for fishing and boating. There are also camping, picnicking, and hiking facilities, as well as a wildlife exhibit and a lookout and fire tower.

OWEN, county (pop. 12,163), SW Indiana, area 390 sq.mi., drained by the West Fork of the White River and Mill Creek. The county was organized in January 1819 and named for Col. Abraham Owen, who was a casualty of the Battle of Tippecanoe (1811). Spencer is the county seat.

The topography of Owen County is rolling to hilly, and the heavy forest cover forms the basis of the leading lumbering industry. It is both an agricultural (grain, fruit, livestock) and manufacturing center. Industries include cement production, food processing, and the production of drugs, and typewriter ribbons. The county has a large limestone and bituminous coal output. Although the coal has been greatly depleted, its quality has been described as Indiana's best, with only a 15 percent ash content.

Prehistoric artifacts and Indian burial mounds are evident throughout the county. Points of interest are Cataract Falls on the Eel River and McCormick's Creek State Park (*q.v.*).

OWEN-PUTNAM STATE FOREST, Owen County, S Indiana, 10 mi. NW of Spencer. The forest encompasses 6,235 acres of primarily beech and maple forest and has recreational facilities for hiking, picnicking, hunting, and horseback riding.

OWENSVILLE, town (pop. 1,110), Gibson County, SW Indiana, zip 47565, 22 mi. NNW of Evansville. Owensville was settled in 1817 and incorporated in 1881. It is a flourishing farm trade and mining center in an area rich in natural resources. Some of the most fertile soils in the state surround Owensville. Orchards, truck, livestock, and grain farms are numerous and densely wooded, areas provide lumber for the town's mills. Coal mines and oil and gas wells are nearby.

OXFORD, town (pop. 1,098), Benton County, W Indiana, zip 47971, 21 mi. W of Lafayette in an agricultural area (soybeans, livestock). Oxford was the birthplace and home of the famous race horse, Dan Patch. The horse was born in December 1896 on a manure pile behind Kelly's 'Livery Stable. Dan Messner, his owner and an Oxford storekeeper, was at first disappointed in Dan Patch's appearance. Under the careful training of John Wattles, however, he became a fine pacer with great stride and grace. At age four, Dan Patch won his maiden race at Boswell by one-eighth of a mile: After that, he never lost a race. Dan Patch toured the country, changed hands many times, and was admired the world over. At his death in 1916, he had earned $2,000,000 for his owners.

PALMYRA, town (pop. 483), Harrison County, S Indiana, zip 47164, 18 mi. WNW of New Albany. Palmyra was founded in 1810 as a farming community.

PAOLI, town (pop. 3,281), seat of Orange County, S Indiana, zip 47454, on the Lick River, 22 mi. S of Bedford. Paoli was settled in 1807 and developed into a regional trade and manufacturing center. Products include furniture, wood items, canned goods, timber, dairy items, and chairs. The courthouse (1850) is a masterpiece of Greek Revival architecture; 6 fluted Doric columns accent the portico, and a cupola with a four-faced clock surmounts the roof. NW of town is a bubbling mineral spring formed where Lost River emerges from its underground limestone channel and continues above ground. Lost River Acres is a popular resort along the river. Nearby Spring Valley, Tucker, and Walton lakes provide other recreational facilities.

PARAGON, town (pop. 538), Morgan County, central Indiana, zip 46166, near the West Fork of the White River, 16 mi. N of Bloomington in an agricultural (livestock, feed grains), and lumbering area. Nearby is Tumbling Waters Cave, a small natural cavern formerly known as Porter's Cave, which has an underground stream and a 35-ft. waterfall. The cave and stream canyon are popular with hikers and tourists.

PARKE, county (pop. 14,600), W Indiana, area 451 sq.mi., bounded on the W by the Wabash River and drained by Sugar and Raccoon creeks. The county was established in 1821 and named for Benjamin Parke, first territorial delegate to the U.S.

Congress. The county seat, Rockville, is a leading manufacturing center.

Parke County is generally rolling, wooded, and traversed by creeks and streams that have cut gorges and canyons in many areas, making it one of the most scenic areas in the Midwest.

The county is noted for its many covered bridges, which were built between 1856 and 1921. The bridges, built when timber was cheaper than iron, were covered to preserve the wood. Although many other counties also have covered bridges, Parke County carried out an extensive program to preserve them. Of the original 52 bridges, 36 remain. An annual Covered Bridge Festival is sponsored in conjunction with autumn activities and maple fairs.

Parke County is noted for feed grains and livestock and includes a bituminous coal-mining area. Timber, clay and gravel pits, mineral springs, and fisheries are important to the county's economy. Leading manufacturing centers are Rockville and Montezuma. Within Parke County are Turkey Run and Raccoon Lake state parks (*q. q. v.*).

PARKER CITY, town (pop. 1,179), Randolph County, E Indiana, zip 47368, 9 mi. E of Muncie in an agricultural area (livestock, feed grains).

PATOKA, town (pop. 529), Gibson County, SW Indiana, zip 47566, on the Patoka River, 19 mi. S of Vincennes. The town was settled in 1789 and platted in 1813. Its name was derived from Indian words meaning "logs on the bottoms," that described the Patoka River.

The low hills surrounding the town has given it an air of serenity. Patoka began as a center for distilleries and saw and gristmills, but has become the center for the SW Indiana fruit and vegetable growing district. Feed grains are also an important commodity. Of note are the two 19th-century covered bridges, which are 163 ft. and 150 ft. long, respectively. Long Pond, 3 miles W, provides recreational facilities.

PATOKA STATE FISH AND WILDLIFE AREA, Pike County, S Indiana, just S of Winslow. The area covers 7,000 acres and has a 300-acre lake which is available for fishing and boating. There are also a campground, picnic area, and hiking trails.

PATRIOT, town (pop. 216), Switzerland County, SE Indiana, zip 47038, on the Ohio River, 24 mi. SW of Cincinnati, Ohio. Patriot was an active river port until a disastrous flood inundated the town in 1937. Patriot never fully recovered and is a quiet community for retired farmers and river men. Several 19th-century homes overlook the river.

PAYNETOWN STATE RECREATION AREA, Monroe County, S central Indiana, 6 mi. S of Bloomington. It is one of two recreational units located on the Monroe Dam and Reservoir, the whole of which encompasses 22,500 acres. Facilities include swimming, picnicking, boating, camping, fishing, and hunting.

PEKIN, town (pop. 912), Washington County, S Indiana, zip 47165, 7 mi. SE of Salem in an agricultural area (livestock, feed grains). The main industry in Pekin produces plastics. There are also livestock feed mills and a newspaper plant. Pekin has the longest tradition in the U.S. of celebrating the Fourth of July. The annual celebration, begun in 1830, features a parade which is famous throughout the state.

PENCE, town (pop. 100), N Indiana, Warren County, zip 47973, 19 mi. NW of Williamsport in an agricultural and dairying area. Pence is a trade center for fertilizer, seed, and feeds.

PENDLETON, town (pop. 2,243), Madison County, E central Indiana, zip 46064, 27 mi. NE of Indianapolis. Called the "Cradle of Madison County," Pendleton was originally settled by colonists from Ohio. The town was platted in 1823 by Thomas Pendleton, for whom it is named. Shortly thereafter it became the first seat of Madison County, a position it relinquished to Anderson in 1827.

Pendleton is a center for agriculture (livestock, grains, dairy products) and manufacturing (clothing, canned goods, metal products). Nearby is Falls Park, a scenic spot whose natural pool just below the waterfall was closed to swimmers because of heavy pollution. Many well-kept century-old buildings are a source of pride to the citizens of Pendleton. Among them, the Methodist Episcopal Church (1823) dates back to the original settlers. The Pendleton Town Hall, a long-time landmark, was destroyed in an accidental explosion in 1936.

PENNVILLE, town (pop. 798), Jay County, E Indiana, zip 47369, on the Salamonie River, 24 mi. NNE of Muncie in an agricultural area (livestock, feed grains). A memorial tablet to Eliza Harris, a runaway slave who was depicted in *Uncle Tom's Cabin,* is N of town.

PERRY, county (pop. 19,075), S Indiana, area 384 sq.mi., bounded S and partially E by the Ohio River, which forms the border with Kentucky. It is drained by the Anderson River, a tributary of the Ohio. The county was formed in 1814 and named for Commodore Oliver H. Perry. Cannelton was designated the county seat. Agriculture plays a leading part in Perry County's economy, as do lumbering and sandstone quarrying. Leading manufactures include radio and television tubes and furniture.

PERRYSVILLE, town (pop. 510), Vermillion County, W Indiana, zip 47974, on the Wabash River, 40 mi. N of Terre Haute in an agricultural area (livestock, feed grains). Cannel coal mines are nearby.

PERU, city (pop. 14,139), seat of Miami County, N central Indiana, zip 47970, on the Wabash River, 15 mi. E of Logansport. Peru was founded in 1826 on the site of a Miami Indian village. SE of the city is the old trading post of Francois Godfrey, the second richest Indian in America in his time.

Peru has sometimes been referred to as the "Circus City of the World." In 1883 Ben Wallace bought a defunct traveling show and set up an amateur circus. From that time on, the Wallace Circus Farm was the winter headquarters of many of America's great traveling circuses. Each year, Peru stages a 4-day festival, complete with a 3-ring circus, to commemorate those days. In 1969 the city finished roofing its remodeled lumber yard to accomodate a performing arena half as large as a football field. Pioneer, circus, and Indian relics are displayed in the Miami County Historical and Puterbaugh museums. The songwriter Cole Porter was born in Peru in 1893; his home is 7 mi. SE of town.

Peru is a transportation and trading center for agricultural products, and is a manufacturer of canned goods, heating equipment, plastics, and paper. Grissom Air Force Base and the Mississinewa Reservoir are nearby.

PETERSBURG, city (pop. 2,697), seat of Pike County, SW Indiana, zip 47567, near the White River, 19 mi. SE of Vincennes. Petersburg was founded in 1817 at a fording place on the White River. It developed during the days of the Wabash and Erie Canal; the passenger depot (now Wyatt Seed Company) and a section of the old canal can still be seen. Several 19th-century buildings have been restored. Of note is the 12-room Proffit-Morgan House. Petersburg is a shipping center for coal, oil, timber, flour, and concrete blocks. NE of town is the R.E.A. power plant with its two 300-ft. smokestacks.

PIERCETON, town (pop. 1,175), Kosciusko County, N Indiana, zip 46562, 30 mi. WNW of Fort Wayne in an agricultural area (lifestock, poultry, feed grains). There is a lumber mill in town. Nearby Robinson Lake provides recreational facilities.

PIGEON RIVER, NE Indiana and S Michigan, rises in Indiana in NE Steuben County and flows SW, NW, and W to widen into several small lakes. Also known as Pigeon Creek, it reaches a reservoir in N Lagrange County, where it runs through Pigeon River State Fish and Wildlife Area and then flows NW into Michigan. The river returns SW into Indiana to the St. Joseph River just N of Bristol, having covered a distance of approximately 65 miles.

PIGEON RIVER STATE FISH AND WILDLIFE AREA, Lagrange County, NE Indiana, near Mongo. Its 10,535 acres have facilities for water recreation in a 150-acre lake and adjacent Pigeon River. There are also facilities available for hiking, picnicking, camping, and hunting. It is a favorite spot for trout fishermen, mushroom hunters, and bird watchers.

PIGEON ROOST STATE MEMORIAL, Scott County, S Indiana, near Underwood. It commemorates the pioneers who were slain there by the Shawnee Indians in 1812. The attack has been ascribed to resentment over the Battle of Tippecanoe (1811) and the excitement of the War of 1812. A 44-ft. limestone shaft marks the site.

PIKE, county (pop. 12,281), SW Indiana, area 335 sq.mi., bounded on the N by the White River and its East Ford and drained by the Patoka River. The county was formed on February 1, 1817, and named for Gen. Z.M. Pike, who fell at the capture of York in April 1813. Petersburg is the county seat.

Pike County lies in the heart of Indiana's coal-mining country and is almost wholly underlain by fine workable veins of bituminous coal 4 to 9 ft. thick. Oil wells, clay pits, and fine stands of timber abound, and agriculture is also important. Leading crops are feed grains and tobacco. Manufactures include concrete blocks, wood products, and flour.

PIKE STATE FOREST, Pike County, S Indiana, 6 mi. E of Winslow. The forest encompasses 2,898 acres of land and has facilities for hiking, picnicking, fishing, camping, hunting, and horseback riding.

PINE VILLAGE, town (pop. 291), Warren County, W Indiana, zip 47975, on Big Pine Creek, 20 mi. W of Lafayette in an agricultural area (livestock, feed grains).

PINNACLE, THE, natural stone formation resembling a pillar, in Jug Rock Park, S Indiana, 5 mi. N of Shoals. The Pinnacle is formed of variegated rock strata and is a favorite attraction to visitors in the park. Jug Rock (*q. v.*) for which the park is named, is also located there.

PITTSBORO, town (pop. 867), Hendricks County, central Indiana, zip 46167, 18 mi. NW of Indianapolis in an agricultural area (livestock, feed grains).

PLAINFIELD, town (pop. 8,211), Hendricks County, central Indiana, zip 46168, on the Whitelick River, 14 mi. WSW of Indianapolis in an agricultural area (livestock, feed grains, dairy products). The town contains the Indiana Boys' School (1867) for the reform and education of juvenile delinquents. Two unusual monuments are on the grounds. One, a statue carved by a 15-year old inmate from a block of Bedford limestone, represents Whittier's "Barefoot Boy." The other is a monument to the memory of Thomas Pain Westendorf, a school official and composer of the song "I'll Take You Home Again Kathleen."

Recreational facilities are provided at nearby Pay Lake.

PLAINVILLE, town (pop. 538), Daviess County, SW Indiana, zip 47568, 11 mi. N of Washington in an agricultural area (feed grains, livestock). Plainville is a trade center for feeds and grain.

PLEASANT LAKE, town (pop. 600), Steuben County, NE Indiana zip 46779, 4 mi. S of Angola in a resort and farming area. Manufactures include concrete blocks and septic tanks.

PLYMOUTH, city (pop. 7,661), seat of Marshall County, N Indiana, zip 46563, on the Yellow River, 24 mi. S of South Bend. Founded in 1834, Plymouth occupies the site of a former Potawatomi Indian village. Between Pretty and Twin lakes is the Chief Menominee Monument, which honors the Potawatomi leader who unsuccessfully fought the removal of his tribe to the West. U.S. soldiers surrounded the Indians on Myers Lake in 1836, and marched them across the prairies in the summer's heat. Many died along the way, and the trek is remembered as the "Trail of Death."

Plymouth is a shipping and agricultural trading center for the surrounding area. Manufactures include grinding machines, automobile parts, stokers, batteries, and emery products. The Marshall County Historical Society and Museum has interesting local pioneer artifacts. Centennial Park and Camper's Roost provide camping and recreational facilities.

POKAGON STATE PARK, Steuben County, NE Indiana, 6 mi. N of Angola. Known as Indiana's year-round playground, this 1,175-acre park on the shore of beautiful Lake James offers a vast variety of activities for the sports enthusiast. It was named for the Potawatomi Indian chief, Simon Pokagon, who was educated at the University of Notre Dame and Oberlin College. The park is located at an altitude of 1,000 ft., one of the highest points in the state. Facilities include a saddle barn, bicycle rentals, an archery range, a bathing beach, picnic grounds, and campgrounds.

Water-skiing and sailing are popular summer pastimes and, in the winter, Pokagon's 1,700-ft. double-lane toboggan slide attracts thousands of enthusiasts.

The charming Potawatomi Inn sits on a ridge overlooking the lake and offers dining and accommodations all year.

POLAND, town (pop. 200), Clay County, central Indiana, zip 47868, 16 mi. SE of Brazil in an agricultural and farming area. Manufactures include crates, pallets, and knock-down boxes.

PONETO, town (pop. 286), Wells County, E Indiana, zip 46781, 7 mi. SSW of Bluffton in an agricultural area (livestock, feed grains).

PORTAGE, city (pop. 19,127), Porter County, NW Indiana, zip 46368, 9 mi. E of Gary. Originally located in a sparsely settled farming area, Portage, was incorporated as a town in 1958 and as a city in 1969. Its borders include Midwest Steel, Burns Ditch, and part of Bethlehem Steel. In 1966, a federal grant was made available for the construction of the state's only deep-water harbor on Lake Michigan, known as the Port of Indiana.

Portage continues to grow as a major steel-producing industrial complex. Midwest Steel, which began operations there in 1957, produces cold steel rolled products. Boat-launching facilities are located where the Little Calumet and Illinois rivers empty into Lake Michigan. Woodland Park provides picnicking, swimming, ice skating, tennis, and a nature area.

PORTER, town (pop. 3,058), Porter County, NW Indiana, zip 46304, near Lake Michigan, 13 mi. E of Gary. Porter was once a thriving rail and brick manufacturing center. The brickyards are gone, however, and most of the population is employed in Gary's steelworks. The Sander Wood Engraving Company, last of its kind, does wood block engraving for books, magazines, and catalogs.

Nearby is the Augsburg Svenska Skola (Augsburg Swedish School) built in 1880. It is in fact, not a school at all, but a white shingled church with a seating capacity of only 7. The cemetery behind it covers an Indian mound. Porter Park is 1½ mi. S of town.

PORTER, county (pop. 87,114), NW Indiana, area 425 sq.mi., bounded on the N by Lake Michigan, and S by the Kankakee River. It is drained by the Little Calumet and Grand Calumet rivers.

The county was organized in February 1836 and named for Commodore David Porter of the U.S. Navy. Valparaiso is the county seat.

Porter County is well-known for its huge stretches of wild, sparsely populated dunelands bordering Lake Michigan. Indiana Dunes State Park attracts thousands of visitors on hot summer weekends. The dunelands' unique flora and fauna comprises a natural outdoor laboratory for the serious or amateur biology student.

The rest of the county is rich farmland conducive to the raising of corn, soybeans, and dairy cattle. Industrially, it is one of the fastest growing areas in Indiana. Steel, non-ferrous castings, bearings, and magnets are among the leading manufactures.

PORTLAND city (pop. 7,115), seat of Jay County, E Indiana, zip 47371, on the Salamonie River, 28 mi. NE of Muncie. Once an important lumber-milling town, it has gradually become an agricultural center (livestock, dairying, soybeans, grain). Manufactures include work clothes, canned goods, silos, brooms, and dairy equipment. Portland is the birthplace of Hoosier automobile inventor Elwood Haynes; the site is marked at High and Commerce streets. Hickory Grove Lake, 8 mi. S of town, is a popular resort.

POSEY, county (pop. 21,740), SW Indiana, area 412 sq.mi., bounded W by the Wabash River, and S by the Ohio River, and drained by Big Creek. The county was formed in November 1814 and named for Thomas Posey, the last governor of Indiana Territory. The county seat is at Mount Vernon.

The surface of the land is level to gently rolling and ideally suited for the growing of feed grains, vegetables, and fruit. Posey County is especially noted for its watermelon and cataloupe. Mount Vernon and New Harmony have some industry (machinery, tanks, stoves, cigars, and food products).

POSEYVILLE, town (pop. 1,034, Posey County, SW Indiana, zip 47633, 18 mi. NW of Evansville in an agricultural area (cattle, calves, hogs, soybeans, wheat, corn). Poseyville has a poultry hatchery and a meat-packing plant.

PRINCETON, city (pop. 7,431), seat of Gibson County, SW Indiana, zip 47570, 27 mi. N of Evansville. The city was founded in 1814 and named for Capt. William Prince, later a representative in the U.S. Congress. The courthouse was built in 1884 and many other fine 19th-century buildings remain.

Princeton has become an important oil, coal, and agricultural center. Diversity of manufactures—among them oil-well supplies, paint brushes, electric clocks, and food products—reflect Princeton's economic prosperity. Railroad repair shops are in the city, and bituminous coal mines are nearby. King's Mine, 450 ft. deep, is Indiana's deepest coal mine shaft. Lafayette Park and South Side Park provide recreational activities.

PULASKI, county (pop. 12,534), NW Indiana, area 433 sq.mi., drained by Big Monon Creek and the Tippecanoe River. The county was formed in 1835 and named for Casimir Pulaski, a Polish officer who was killed in the American Revolution. The county seat is at Winamac.

The county's soil ranges from clay to loam and is considered among the best in the state for the cultivation of corn and soybeans. One of the world's largest game farms (5,200 acres) and Tippecanoe River State Park are located in Pulaski County.

PUTNAM, county (pop. 26,932), W central Indiana, area 49; sq.mi., drained by the Eel River and Raccoon and Mill creeks. The county was organized in April 1822 and named for Gen. Israel Putnam of the American Revolution. The county seat is Greencastle.

Agriculture and stone quarrying are the mainstay of the economy, but there is some manufacturing at Greencastle. Richard Lieber State Park, encompassing 1,500-acre Cataract Lake, is located in the southern section of Putnam County.

RACCOON LAKE STATE RECREATION AREA, Parke County, W central Indiana, 7 mi. E of Rockville. The 3,938-acre recreation area provides access to the Mansfield Flood Control Reservoir, which is operated in cooperation with the U.S. Army Corps of Engineers. Five boat-launching ramps are situated around the lake, which provides excellent boating, swimming, and fishing. There is also a campground and a picnic area.

RAMSEY, town (pop. 700), Harrison County, S Indiana, zip 47166, 11 mi. NW of Corydon in a lumbering and farming area. Ramsey is a trade center for chicks, feeds, dog food, and popcorn.

RANDOLPH, county (pop. 28,915), E Indiana, area 457 sq.mi., bounded on the E by Ohio and drained by the Mississinewa and Whitewater rivers and the West Fork of the White River. The county was formed in August 1818 and named for its sister county in North Carolina. The county seat is at Winchester.

Randolph County is in a rich agricultural area noted for livestock, feed grains, and poultry. There is also some stone quarrying and manufacturing at Union City and Winchester, including the production of glass containers, castings, foods, and truck bodies.

RED BRIDGE STATE RECREATION AREA, Miami County, E central Indiana, 7 mi. SE of Peru. It is one of two units located on the Mississinewa Dam and Reservoir. The facilities encompass a total of 14,000 acres and include the 3,300-acre Mississinewa Lake, which was developed jointly by the state of Indiana and the U.S. Army Corps of Engineers. Recreational facilities include campgrounds, picnic areas, a swimming beach, and boat ramps.

RED KEY, town (pop. 1,667), Jay County, E Indiana, zip 47373, 18 mi. NE of Muncie in an agricultural area (livestock, feed gains). Red Key has a canning food plant and a lumber mill.

REELSVILLE, village (pop. 155), Putnam County, S Indiana, zip 46171, 10 mi. SW of Greencastle in a stone quarrying and lumbering region. The local stone quarry produces crushed stone and agricultural lime.

REMINGTON, town (pop. 1,127), St. Joseph County, NW Indiana, zip 47977, 12 mi. S of Rensselaer in an agricultural area (livestock, feed grains). Remington is a manufacturer of fertilizers, soy protein concentrates, and other food products, metal alloys, and lumber.

RENSSELAER, city (pop. 4,688), seat of Jasper County, NW Indiana, zip 47978, on the Iroquois River, 45 mi. S of Gary. The city was established in 1837 and named after James Van Rensselaer, merchant and founder of the town. Rensselaer was incorporated in 1897.

The town is a prosperous trading center for agricultural products, especially flour and dairying items. Saint Joseph's College (1889) is located there; its oldest building, Drexel Hall, was once an Indian mission school. The college is a fully-accredited four-year liberal arts institution. The Halleck Student Center is named for Congressman Charles Halleck, a Rensselaer resident. In the city, Milroy Park contains a statue of Gen. Robert Milroy, a Civil War hero and member of the 1850 Indiana constitutional convention.

REYNOLDS, town (pop. 641), White County, NW central Indiana, zip 47980, 24 mi. N of Lafayette in an agricultural area (livestock, feed grains).

RICHARD LIEBER STATE PARK, Owen County, W Indiana, 15 mi. S of Greencastle. The 8,283-acre park provides access to Cataract Lake, which covers 1,500 acres and offers excellent swimming, boating, and water-skiing. The adjacent lands are all part of Cagles Mill Flood Control Reservoir. Federal authorities control the lake level.

RICHLAND, town (pop. 600), Spencer County, S Indiana, zip 47634, 10 mi. NW of Rockport in a scenic part of the "Hoosier Hills." Richland is a trade center for agricultural products, chemicals, and automobile-body masking supplies.

RICHMOND, city (pop. 43,999), seat of Wayne County, E Indiana, zip 47374, on the East Fork of the Whitewater River, 65 mi. E of Indianapolis. Richmond was founded in 1806 by soldiers who once served under George Rogers Clark. Initially, it was the fertile soils which attracted settlers to the area, and the village expanded rapidly. Richmond became a town in 1816, the year of Indiana's statehood. The Quaker community in 1847 founded the Friends' Boarding School that, in 1859, became known as Earlham College. A four-year liberal arts school, Earlham College has an enrollment of about 1,100 students annually. On campus, the Joseph Moore Museum houses a fine display of birds and mammals in their native habitats.

William Foulke, Indiana political reformer and supporter of women's suffrage, once lived in Richmond and became editor of the local newspaper. At the turn of the century, he established a precedent by hiring the city's first female stenographer.

Modern Richmond is a leading industrial community. Diversity of manufactures reflect its economic prosperity. Among many of the products manufactured there are machine tools, farm implements, automobile parts, phonograph records, lawn mowers, school buses, moving stairs, aircraft parts, clothing, pianos, refrigerators, and plastics. Richmond also has one of the largest rose-growing industries in the world. Hill Greenhouses produces roses, chrysanthemums, and grafted rose plants. The concern was founded by E. Gurney Hill (1847-1935), who was noted for his introduction of such new roses as the Richmond Rose, a beautiful hybrid produced in 1905.

The Wayne County Historical Museum is housed in the former Hicksite Friends' Meeting House, built in 1864. It has a reconstructed pioneer kitchen, general store, apothecary shop, and cobbler shop. Many historic relics are on display, including an Egyptian mummy. Three outside buildings are encompassed by the museum: the county's first log school house; an agricultural building with pioneer farm implements; and a pole barn with early farm machinery.

Glen Miller Park features rose gardens, a golf course, a zoo, summer bandstand concerts, and an archery range. "Madonna of the Trails," a monument to pioneer women, is located in the park. Other recreational facilities can be found at Clear Creek Park and the 177-acre Middlefork Reservoir.

RIDGEVILLE, town (pop. 924), Randolph County, E Indiana, zip 47380, on the Mississinewa River, 20 mi. ENE of Muncie in an agricultural area (livestock, feed grains). There is some stone quarrying. The town was settled in 1817 and incorporated in 1868.

RIPLEY, county (pop. 21,138), SE Indiana, area 442 sq.mi., drained by Laughery and Graham creeks. The county was organized in April 1818 and named for Gen. E.W. Ripley, an officer in the War of 1812. The county seat is at Versailles.

Ripley County is noted for feed grains, corn, tobacco, dairying, and livestock. The leading industries produce furniture and caskets. Versailles State Park, Indiana's second largest, is located in the county.

RISING SUN, town (pop. 2,305), seat of Ohio County, SE Indiana, zip 47040, on the Ohio River, 22 mi. SW of Cincinnati, Ohio. Rising Sun was platted in 1814 and for many years flourished as a major river port. Several old buildings remain along Front Street as relics of the riverboat era. The Ohio County Courthouse (1845) is the oldest courthouse in Indiana and is still in use today. The Speakman House (1846) is built on an Indian mound and was originally a stopover on the Underground Railway. The Ohio County Historical Society operates a museum which includes in its displays the "Hoosier Boy," record-holding speedboat of the early 1900s.

Rising Sun is a shipping point for livestock, truck, tobacco, flour, dairy products, and furniture. Arnold's Creek Embayment and Island Branch provide recreational facilities.

ROACHDALE, town (pop. 1,004), Putnam County, W central Indiana, zip 46172, 35 mi. WNW of Indianapolis in an agricultural area (dairy products, grain, soybeans).

ROANN, town (pop. 509), Wabash County, NE central Indiana, zip 46974, on the Eel River, 14 mi. NNE of Peru in an agricultural area (livestock, feed grains).

ROANOKE, town (pop. 858), Huntington County, NE central Indiana, zip 46783, on the Little River, 16 mi. SW of Fort Wayne. The town was founded in 1861 and was perhaps best known for the Roanoke Classical Seminary, which was considered "the last word in culture by Hoosier." Eventually, the school was moved to North Manchester and became Manchester College. The Home of Kilsoquah, granddaughter of the Miami Indian chief Little Turtle, is at the SE edge of town. At the time of her death in 1915, she was the only full-blooded

Indian in Huntington County. Roanoke is a center for grain and dairy products and a manufacturer of electric coils.

ROCHESTER, city (pop. 4,631), seat of Fulton County, N Indiana, zip 46975, near Lake Manitou, 24 mi. NNE of Logansport. Rochester was founded in 1831 as an Indian trading post. Four years earlier, a gristmill had been constructed there by the U.S. government to grind corn for the Potawatomi under the terms of an 1826 treaty.

Indian legends state that Lake Manitou was the home of the "Great Spirit Manitou" who, if angered, swallowed up canoes and their passengers. Stories about monsters which occasionally surface are still told today. Several popular resorts and a golf course are located along the shores of the lake. Rochester is also a trading center for soybeans and grain, and is a manufacturer of cement products, canned goods, and dairy products.

ROCKFIELD, town (pop. 300), Carroll County, N Indiana, zip 46977, 12 mi. SW of Logansport in an agricultural area (feed grains, livestock, hogs). The town is a center for farming cooperatives, the first of which was founded there in 1915.

ROCKPORT, city (pop. 2,565), seat of Spencer County, SW Indiana, zip 47635, on the Ohio River, 29 mi. ESE of Evansville. Rockport is picturesquely situated on high bluffs overlooking the river. According to tradition the family of revivalist preacher James Langford occupied a cave in the bluffs for one winter season. Subsequently, the site was settled by Daniel Grass in 1807. Abraham Lincoln settled 16 mi. north of town in 1816 and remained there for 14 years. The Lincoln Pioneer Village in the city park contains restored pioneer cabins. The entire village was designed by artist and sculptor George Honig and constructed during the Great Depression. In addition to the reproduction of Lincoln's cabin, the village includes a museum, law office, church, blockhouse, and pioneer farm implements. The Crooks-Anderson House (1859) on Walnut Street is one of only 6 octagonal houses remaining in Indiana.

Rockport is in an area rich in natural resources. Oil and natural gas wells are nearby, and the city is a manufacturing center for bricks, tiles, concrete, buttons, and flour. Recreational facilities are at Lake Alda, an artificial reservoir.

ROCKVILLE, town (pop. 2,820), seat of Parke County, W Indiana, zip 47872, 23 mi. NNE of Terre Haute. Rockville was settled in 1823 and incorporated in 1854. It is mainly a farming community, but is also involved in bituminous coal mining and lumber milling. Covered bridges stand in Rockville's town square and in the golf course, the only one in the world with that distinction. Billie Creek Village is a reconstructed turn-of-the-century community complete with a one-room school house, country store, weaver's shop, barn, livery stable, governor's hourse, and log cabin.

The annual Parke County Maple Fair is held in Rockville in March when the "sap's a' runnin'," and the Parke County Covered Bridge Festival is held in the city every October. Recreational facilities can be found at nearby Raccoon Lake State Recreation Area and at Turkey Run State Park (*q.q.v.*).

ROLLING PRAIRIE, town (pop. 700), La Porte County, NW Indiana, zip 46371, 7 mi. NE of La Porte in a resort and farming area noted for feed grains and livestock. Three Indian trails crossed the site of the present town, among them the famous Sauk Trail.

Rolling Prairie was founded in the early 1830s by Ezekiah Provolot and has thrived ever since as a farming community. The La Porte County Farm Bureau Co-op Association is located there; it deals in feeds, seeds, and grain. Manufactures include copper wire, tools, dies, and axle assemblies for mobile homes and utility trailers. Recreational facilities can be found at nearby Hog, Rolling Timbers, and Saugany lakes.

ROME CITY, village (pop. 1,354), Noble County, NE Indiana, zip 46784, on Sylvan Lake, 7 mi. NW of Kendallville. The site was settled in 1837 primarily as a base camp for French and Irish workers who built a dam across a tributary of the Elkhart River, creating Sylvan Lake. Rome City, platted in 1839 is a resort community. Several springs in and near the village have medicinal properties, but they have not been fully exploited.

ROSEDALE, town (pop. 817), Parke County, W Indiana, zip 47874, near Raccoon Creek, 14 mi. NNE of Terre Haute in an agricultural (livestock, feed grains) and coal-mining region.

ROSELAND, town (pop. 895), St. Joseph County, N Indiana, a N suburb of South Bend in an agricultural area (livestock, feed grains, peppermint).

ROSSVILLE, town (pop. 830), Clinton County, central Indiana, zip 46065, on a fork of Wildcate Creek, 16 mi. E of Lafayette in an agricultural area (feed grains, livestock).

ROYAL CENTER, town (pop. 987), Cass County, N central Indiana, zip 46978, 11 mi. NW of Logansport in an agricultural (livestock, feed grains) and lumbering area. There is a canned food plant in town.

RUSH, county (pop. 20,352), E central Indiana, area 490 sq.mi., drained by the Big Blue River and Flatrock Creek. The county was organized in December 1821 and named for Dr. Benjamin Rush, famous early American physician. The county seat is at Rushville. The soils are especially fertile and suited for feed grains, corn, apples, and livestock. The area specializes in importing and breeding of Jersey cattle. The leading industry produces furniture.

RUSHVILLE, city (pop. 6,686), seat of Rush County, E central Indiana, zip 46173, on Flatrock Creek, 40 mi. ESE of Indianapolis. The city was founded in 1822 and named for Dr. Benjamin Rush, noted physician, philanthropist, and signer of the Declaration of Independence. Rushville is centrally located in a rich farming area noted for corn and hogs. Manufacturing plays a leading part in the city's economy; products include lumber, furniture, machinery, flour, packed meat, canned goods, and gloves.
Wendell Wilkie, presidential candidate, lived there and was the owner of 7 farms. The Wendell Wilkie Grave and Memorial is in Rushville's East Hill Cemetery. The many historical sites in Rushville include the century-old blacksmith shop across from the courthouse. The Hackleman Log Cabin in Memorial Park was the birthplace of Gen. Pleasant A. Hackleman, a Civil War hero. Of note is the Rush County Historical Museum, which houses one of the finest collections of North American artifacts in the country. The museum's stable annex houses a pioneer vehicle exhibit.

The Werline and Halblieb Horse Auction is held in Rushville every week, and is the largest such auction in the U.S. Annual events include the Rush County Fair and the Festival of Arts and Crafts. Recreational facilities are available at nearby Wofal Lake.

RUSSELLVILLE, town (pop. 390), Putnam County, W central Indiana, zip 46175, 36 mi. NE of Terre Haute in an agricultural area (feed grains, livestock, poultry).

SAINT ANTHONY, town (pop. 290), Dubois County, S Indiana, zip 47575, 10 mi. S of Jasper in a lumbering and agricultural area noted for feed grains and livestock. The town is a trade center for corrugated boxes, hospital equipment, furniture, fertilizer, and poultry feeders.

SAINT BERNICE, town (pop. 900), Vermillion County, W Indiana, zip 47875, 18 mi. SW of Newport. Saint Bernice is a trade center and manufacturer of sportswear, rainwear, and fertilizer.

SAINT JOE, town (pop. 564), De Kalb County, NE Indiana, zip 46785, on the St. Joseph River, 21 mi. NE of Fort Wayne in an agricultural area (feed grains, pickles, flour).

SAINT JOHN, town (pop. 1,757), Lake County, NW Indiana, zip 46373, 12 mi. SW of Gary. A small community of Roman Catholic farmers, it was named after John Houck, the town's first German settler and builder of NW Indiana's first Roman Catholic church (1842). Saint John is noted for its horse farms, which have increased steadily in importance since the 1960s. Every summer weekend, horse shows are held in Saint John and nearby Dyer. It has been said that the area around the town has more riding horses than anywhere else in the country.

SAINT JOSEPH, county (pop. 245,045), N Indiana, area 466 sq.mi., bounded on the N by Michigan and drained by the St. Joseph, Yellow, and Kankakee rivers. The county was formed in 1830 and named for the St. Joseph River. South Bend is the county seat. The county was the first area of Indiana to be seen by a European, when Père Marquette visited the region in 1675.

Saint Joseph County is rich in fruit orchards, mint farms, and grain fields. Diversified manufacturing is prevalent in the larger cities; the leading industrial products are automobiles, automobile parts, aircraft parts, industrial machinery, rubber and plastic products, food and missiles.

SAINT JOSEPH RIVER, rises in Hillsdale, S Michigan, and flows NW and then generally W and SW past Elkhart and South Bend. It empties into Lake Michigan. The Elkhart River and Pigeon Creek are its major tributaries.

SAINT MARY'S RIVER, rises in Auglaize County, Ohio, and flows about 100 mi. NW past Saint Mary's, Medon, Rockford, and Wilshire, Ohio, into Indiana. In Indiana it passes Decatur and Fort Wayne, where it joins the Saint Joseph River to form the Maumee. The river was a key point in the development of the Wabash and Erie Canal system (1832-70).

SAINT MEINRAD, village (pop. 850), Spencer County, SW Indiana, zip 47577, on the Anderson River, 15 mi. N of Tell City. The village is a community of German Roman Catholics most of whom are employed by the Benedictine Saint Meinrad Archabbey. The abbey and seminary, which are the focus of the village, were founded in 1857 by two Benedictine monks from the Archabbey of Einsiedein, Switzerland.

The Archabbey is totally self-sufficient. Members of the order engage in a variety of agricultural and industrial activities, including those of the carpentry shop, coal mine, and rock quarry. The seminary is the second largest in the U.S. The Abbey Press, founded in 1876 when a small printing press and some type were purchased, publishes on a wide variety of subjects. Recently, an abbey chicken coop was converted into a modern plaster-casting and metal finishing studio. Visitors to Saint Meinrad are immediately impressed with the beauty of the village and the hospitality of its inhabitants.

The archabbey, which is 100 years old, is a striking sight with its Romanesque church and towers. There are 13 altars within the church; the one in the crypt is of gold. Rock gardens were built in 1936 to enhance the terrain's natural shale outcroppings. The surounding countryside is given over to the monastery vineyards, which provide the monks with their own wine. NE of Saint Meinrad is the Monte Cassino Chapel (1868), a popular shrine for the backwoods Roman Catholic families. Pilgrimages from the abbey to the shrine are held each May and October.

SAINT PAUL, town (pop. 785), on the border of Decatur and Shelby counties, SE central Indiana, zip 47272, 11 mi. SE of Shelbyville in an agricultural area (livestock, feed grains).

SALAMONIA, town (pop. 47381), Jay County, E Indiana, on the Salamonie River, 30 mi. ENE of Muncie in an agricultural area (livestock, feed grains, poultry).

SALAMONIE RIVER, E and NE central Indiana, rises near Salamonia in E Jay County and flows about 82 mi. NW past Portland and Mount Pelier to the Wabash River opposite Lagro. The river is dammed in Wabash and Huntington counties to form the Salamonie Reservoir, a joint recreational project developed by the state of Indiana and the U.S. Army Corps of Engineers.

SALAMONIE RIVER STATE FOREST, Wabash County, N Indiana, 14 mi. SE of Lagro. The northern and southern recreational units—Salamonie Forest State Recreation Area and Lost Bridge State Recreational Area (*q.v.*), respectively—are encompassed within the state forest's boundaries. Open all year, the Salamonie State Forest provides water recreation on the adjacent Salamonie River and Salamonie Reservoir. There are also facilities for camping, picnicking, hunting, and horseback riding.

SALEM, city (pop. 5,041), seat of Washington County, S Indiana, zip 47167, on the Blue River, 27 mi. SE of Bedford. Salem was founded in 1814. Its growth was severely hampered by the cholera epidemic of 1833, which virtually depopulated the town. Salem is now a trade center for the surrounding agricultural area. Its manufactures include furniture, wood products, work clothes, rock wool, and lumber.

Salem was the birthplace of John Hay (1838-1905), the statesman, author, and private secretary to Abraham Lincoln from 1861 to 1865. Hay House, which has been restored, was originally built in 1824 to house the Salem Grammar School. The school building soon became too small and was sold in 1831 by Hay's father, who was one of the county's pioneer physicians. The house was declared a National Historic Site in 1971. To the rear of Hay House is the Stevens Memorial Museum (1970), which is built of native bricks taken from old local buildings. The Historical Society of Washington County is located there. The county courthouse dates back to 1886.

SW of Salem is Beck's Mill, built in 1808. Recreational facilities can be found at Elk Creek and Salinda lakes and at the Western Hills Golf Course. Two impounding reservoirs, Lake Salinda and Lake John Hay, provide adequate supplies of water to the city and have given the area a new source of recreational activities.

SANDBORN, town (pop. 528), Knox County, SW Indiana, zip 47578, 24 mi. NE of Vincennes in an agricultural and bituminous coal-mining area.

SAN PIERRE, town (pop. 300), Starke County, S Indiana, zip 46374, 21 mi. SW of Knox in an agricultural area noted for feed grains and livestock. San Pierre is a manufacturer of fertilizer and feeds and has a printing and a die-stamping plant.

SANTA CLAUS, village (pop. 267), Spencer County, SW Indiana, zip 47579, 38 mi. ENE of Evansville. The village, founded in 1846, receives mail addressed to Santa Claus and has the only post office in the U.S. with this name. The post office is situated next to Santa Claus Land, one of the largest amusement parks in the country. It covers 45 acres and includes Santa's Headquarters, Toyland, and a petting zoo.

SARATOGA, town (pop. 406), Randolph County, E Indiana, zip 47382, 25 mi. E of Muncie in a limestone quarrying and agricultural area noted for livestock and feed grains.

SCALES LAKE STATE BEACH AND STATE PARK, Warrick County, S Indiana, near Booneville. Less well-known than other Indiana state parks, Scales Lake offers camping, boating, fishing, and swimming. Also located there is the Scales Lake Fish Hatchery.

SCHERERVILLE, town (pop. 3,663), Lake County, NW Indiana, zip 46375, 10 mi. SW of Gary. Originally a crossroads for several Indian trails, Schererville later became a stopping place for wagon trains going West. The town was named for Nicholas Scherer, its founder. His house, on Wilhelm Street, has been restored. The town is a quiet residential community, and much of the population is employed in the Gary steel works. Recreational facilities include an amusement park, a golf course, a stock-car race track, and a riding school.

SCHNEIDER, town (pop. 426), Lake County, NW Indiana, zip 46376, near the Kankakee River, 29 mi. S of Gary in an agricultural and resort area.

SCOTT, county (pop. 17,144), SE Indiana, area 193 sq.mi., bounded on the N by the Muscatatuck River and drained by its tributaries. The county was organized in January 1820 and named for Gen. Charles Scott, an officer in the American Revolutionary War. The county seat is at Scottsburg.

Although it is the state's fourth smallest county, its topography is diversified, ranging from hills to tablelands and bottomlands. An abundance of bottomlands has provided large areas planted in grain, tobacco, and truck. Livestock and poultry are also noted in the region. The main industry is canning.

SCOTTSBURG, town (pop. 4,791), seat of Scott County, SE Indiana, zip 47170, 28 mi. N of New Albany. The town was platted in 1871 as the new county seat, replacing Lexington. It is picturesquely situated in a wide valley surrounded by tumbled, wooded hills known as The Knobs. The economy is based on agriculture (grain, truck, poultry) and manufacturing (canned goods, work clothes, lumber). Limestone quarries are nearby. Raintree Lake Park resort is 4 mi. W of town.

SEELYVILLE, town (pop. 1,195), Vigo County, W Indiana, zip 47878, 8 mi. ENE of Terre Haute. Seelyville began as a prosperous coal mining town but has since declined. Farming is now the main activity.

SELLERSBURG, town (pop. 3,177), Clark County, SE Indiana, zip 47172, near Silver Creek, 8 mi. NNE of New Albany in an agricultural area noted for livestock and feed grains. Sellersburg is mainly a residential suburb of New Albany. Manufactures include special machines, asphalt paving materials, kitchen cabinets, and cement products.

SELMA, town (pop. 890), Delaware County, E Indiana, zip 47383, 6 mi. E of Muncie in an agricultural area noted for feed grains and livestock.

SELMIER STATE FOREST, Jennings County, S Indiana, 7 mi. NE of North Vernon. The forest covers 352 acres and has facilities for hiking, fishing, and hunting.

SEYMOUR, city (pop. 13,352), Jackson County, S Indiana, zip 47274, 17 mi. S of Columbus in an agricultural area noted for livestock and dairy products. The world's first train robbery occurred at Seymour on the night of Oct. 6, 1866. The Reno Gang of Jackson County took over an Ohio & Mississippi train and escaped with $15,000.
Seymour is a modern manufacturing center whose diverse products include appliances, furniture, canned goods, flour, fertilizer, cheese, drugs, printers' supplies, and lumber.·The H. Vance Swope Memorial Art Gallery has a fine collection of original paintings. A stone marker stands 1 mile N of Seymour on the site of the first blockhouse built in defense against attacking Indians. Recreational facilities can be found at nearby Cypress and Labline Bed lakes.

SHADES STATE PARK, near Waveland, Montgomery County, W central Indiana. Natural beauty is reflected in the dense stands of virgin woods and deep ravines of the 2,948-acre park. Sugar Creek abounds in game fish, and the park offers camping, picnicking, hiking, and boating. Shades is the site of the annual Sugar Creek Canoe Race.

SHAFER RESERVOIR, White County, NW Indiana, at Monticello. Shafer Reservoir, also known as Shafer Lake, was created in 1923 by the Norway Dam, which reaches 1,200 ft. across the Tippecanoe River. Lake Freeman forms a south unit, and together the two bodies of water furnish hydroelectric power and recreational facilities for hundreds of surrounding communities. The E shore of Shafer Reservoir is the site of Indiana State Beach.

SHAKAMAK STATE PARK, near Jasonville, Greene County, SW Indiana. The 1,000-acre park was established in 1929 and was named for a local stream known to the Indians as Shakamak ("river of the long fish"). Shakamak Lake, within the park, offers swimming, boating, and fishing. The park is heavily wooded and some parts of it contain reclaimed strip mines. The park has a wildlife exhibit.

SHARPSVILLE, town (pop. 672), Tipton County, central Indiana, zip 46068, 8 mi. SSE of Kokomo in an agricultural area noted for livestock and feed grains. The town is a manufacturing center for fiberglass boats, pedal boats, specialty wire, lumber, chemicals and metal farm structures.

SHELBURN, town (pop. 1,281), Sullivan County, SW Indiana, zip 47879, 21 mi. S of Terre Haute. The town was founded in 1818 in a region noted for a variety of natural resources (coal, oil, timber, fertile soils). Its real growth did not begin until 1868, when the district's first of 12 bituminous coal mines was opened. The town became incorporated in 1872 as a direct result of the mining industry's prosperity.

Agriculture, along with coal mining and lumber milling, plays an important role in Shelburn's present economic picture. Grain, livestock, and poultry farms are plentiful, and dairy products are shipped to local marketing centers.

Near Shelburn is Morrison Creek, site of the May 13 1815, massacre by Potawatomi Indians of Lt. John Morrison and four of his soldiers. The incident was the last encounter between the white man and the Indian in the region.

SHELBY, county (pop. 37,797), central Indiana, area 409 sq.mi., drained by the Big Blue River and Flatrock and Sugar creeks. Shelby County was part of a huge territory known as the New Purchase which was ceded by the Delaware Indians to the U.S. on Oct. 3, 1818. The county was officially established in 1821 and named for Isaac Shelby, twice governor of Kentucky and a resident of Indiana. The town of Shelbyville is the county seat. The county encompasses a rich farming region noted for corn, hay, grain, stock raising, and dairying.

SHELBYVILLE, city (pop. 15,094), seat of Shelby County, central Indiana, zip 46176, on the Big Blue River, 27 mi. SE of Indianapolis. The city was platted in 1822 and named for Isaac Shelby, officer of the American Revolutionary and Indian wars and the first governor of Kentucky. Shelbyville's location in the middle of Indiana's richest corn, livestock, and dairy belt has aided its growth as a leading trade and manufacturing center. Manufactures include furniture, paper products, stoves, lawn mowers, clothing, dairy products, and canned foods.

Shelbyville was the home of author Charles Major (1856-1913) and Thomas A. Hendricks (1819-1885), vice-president of the U.S. and governor of Indiana. A stone marker outside of the city commemorates the building of the first railroad in Indiana. The track was 1½ mi. long and had wooden rails and horse-drawn carts. Today, the Penn Central Railroad serves Shelbyville.

The Shelby County Historical Society maintains the Bear of the Blue River Trail, a 15-mi. nature walk along the Blue River. The trail passes over Hog Back Ridge, an ancient Indian burial ground.

SHERIDAN, town (pop. 2,173), Hamilton County, central Indiana, zip 46069, 25 mi. N of Indianapolis in an agricultural area (feed grains, livestock, dairy products). Sheridan is a commercial trade center for cement products, canned goods, condensed milk, flour, chemicals, and packed meats.

SHIPSHEWANA, town (pop. 448), Lagrange County, NE Indiana, zip 46565, 20 mi. E of Elkhart in a farming area that includes one of the largest Amish communities in the U.S. Their closed horse-drawn buggies can be seen in and around town. Nearby is Lake Shipshewana, a popular resort. Near the lake is a 12-ft. stone memorial that marks the grave of Chief Shipshewana, a Potawatomi leader.

SHIRLEY, town (pop. 958), on the border of Hancock and Henry counties, E central Indiana, zip 47384, 32 mi. ENE of Indianapolis in an agricultural area (livestock, feed grains).

SHOALS, town (pop. 1,039), seat of Martin County, SW Indiana, zip 47581, on the East Fork of the White River, 21 mi. E of Washington. The town was founded in 1816 and was named for its location at a shallow ford, or shoals, in the river. The area is very picturesque; high hills and woodlands interspersed with caves and cliffs surround the town. Jug Rock and The Pinnacle (*q.q.v.*), eroded rock formations, are out 276 ft. above the White River near Shoals. According to legend, an Indian silver treasure remains hidden in the caves around McBride's Bluff.

The townspeople are engaged in lumber milling and furniture and button production. Farming and fishing supplement their income. Near the town is the U.S. Gypsum Company plant, which employs a large portion of the population in its underground mines.

Beautiful Hindostan Falls, Martin State Forest, and Trinity Springs, popular tourist attractions, are all near Shoals.

SILVER LAKE, (pop. 588), Kosciusko County, N Indiana, 40 mi. W of Fort Wayne. Silver Lake is basically a resort town surrounded by lakes, but is also a shipping point for vegetables.

SOMERVILLE, town (pop. 313), Gibson County, SW Indiana, zip 47583, 23 mi. NNE of Evansville in an agricultural and bituminous coal-mining area.

SOUTH BEND, city (pop. 125,580), seat of St. Joseph County, N Indiana, zip 46600, on the St. Joseph River, 75 mi. ESE of Chicago, Illinois. The area around the present city was first visited by Europeans in 1675, when Père Marquette explored the region from N Illinois to the shores of Lake Michigan. Four years later, Robert Cavelier sieur de La Salle, the French explorer, made a portage between the St. Joseph and Kankakee rivers, opening up a new passage between the St. Lawrence Basin and the Mississippi River. He later succeeded in obtaining a treaty of alliance between the Miami and Illinois indians, signed under the Council Oak now in South Bend's Highland Cemetery.

In 1820, the American Fur Company appointed agents to establish fur-trading posts throughout the Northwest Territory. Two of them, Alexis Coquillard from Detroit and Pierre F. Navarre from Monroe, established a post on the St. Joseph River for all those who traded with the Indians in N Indiana and S Michigan. The post became known as Big St. Joseph Station. Settlers, however, called it "The Bend," or "South Bend," for a meander in the river. The latter name was finally adopted in 1830. South Bend was platted in 1831, and its designation as seat of newly-formed St. Joseph County followed shortly thereafter. Incorporation to town status came in 1835 and to city status in 1865.

The city's growth was slow until 1925, when Henry and Clement Studebaker opened a blacksmith and wagon shop there. The business was the foundation for the Studebaker Brothers Manufacturing Company (1852), which for many years was the mainstay of the city's economy. South Bend remains a diversified industrial center whose manufactures include automobile accessories, aircraft and parts, industrial and farm machinery, foundry products, ranges, sewing machines, paint, paper, clothing, textiles, watches, toys, asphalt insulation, beer, and sporting goods.

The city is the seat of Indiana University-South Bend campus (1933) and two Roman Catholic universities are located in the nearby suburb of Notre Dame—the University of Notre Dame (1842) and St. Mary's College (1843). Leeper Park, in the city, contains Pierre Navarre's original log cagin. The Northern Indiana Historical Society Museum is housed in the former St. Joseph Courthouse (1855) and contains more than 15,000 historical artifacts reflecting the life and times of pioneer Indiana. Entertainment and recreational facilities can be found at Storyland Zoo, in 160-acre **Rum Village Park,** and at Potawatomi Park with its conservatory and indoor swimming pool.

SOUTH MILFORD, town (pop. 200), Lagrange County, N Indiana, zip 46785, 15 mi. SE of Lagrange in an agricultural and dairying area. The town is a manufacturing center for insulated wire products, hardwood lumber, and electronic wire products.

SOUTHPORT, town (pop. 2,505), Marion County, central Indiana, zip 46227, 9 mi. S of Indianapolis in an industrial and agricultural area. Southport is a quiet residential suburb of Indianapolis.

SOUTH WHITLEY, town (pop. 1,362), Whitley County, NE Indiana, zip 46787, on the Eel River, 25 mi. W of Fort Wayne in an agricultural area noted for livestock and feed grains. It is a shipping point for railroad equipment and grain.

SPEEDWAY, town (pop. 15,056), Marion County, central Indiana, zip 46224, just W of Indianapolis. The town was laid out in 1912 and incorporated in 1926. It is the home of the Indianapolis Speedway, which stages the Indianapolis "500" race every Memorial Day. More than 250,000 fans annually arrive to see some of the greatest race-car drivers in the world compete for top honors. A museum at the track has an exhibit of race cars which date back to 1909. The rear-view mirror, the balloon tire, and ethyl gasoline are a few of the many innovations inaugurated at the track. The speedway itself embraces 433 acres, has a 2½ mi.-long rectangular track, and has a grandstand with a seating capacity of 234,000. Most of the residents of Speedway are employed by factories in town. Manufactures include storage batteries, steel castings, and electrical goods. In 1970, Speedway was one of 4 small communities that chose to remain independent of the expanded metropolitan government of Indianapolis, known as Uni-Gov.

SPENCER, town (pop. 2,423), seat of Owen County, SW central Indiana, zip 47460, on the West Fork of the White River, 45 mi. SW of Indianapolis. The town was settled in 1815 and named for Capt. Spier Spencer, killed at the Battle of Tippecanoe (1811). Several distinguished citizens—including the Hoosier poets William Vaugh Moody and William Herschell—made their homes in Spencer. It was also the home of Ban Johnson, one of the founders of the American Baseball League and of Samuel Ralston, former governor of Indiana.

Spencer is a farming community (corn, fruit, livestock) and manufacturer of food products, drugs, and typewriter ribbons. Bituminous coal mining and limestone quarrying are carried out on a lesser scale. Many of the town's older buildings are constructed of St. Genevieve limestone, which characteristically turns whiter with age.

Recreational facilities can be found at nearby McCormick's Creek State Park (*q.v.*) and at Shady Lake.

SPENCER, county (pop. 17,134), SW Indiana, area 396 sq.mi., bounded on the S by the Ohio River and drained by the Anderson River and Little Pigeon Creek. The county was formed in February 1818 and named for Capt. Spier Spencer, who was killed at the Battle of Tippecanoe (1811). The county seat is at Rockport.

The area is noted for livestock, feed grains, and poultry and is also a center for manufacturing. Leading industries produce bricks, tile, concrete blocks, buttons, flour, and lumber. The Lincoln Boyhood National Memorial and Lincoln State Park (*q.q.v.*) are located within the county.

SPENCERVILLE, town (pop. 340), DeKalb County, NE Indiana, zip 46788, 12 mi. S of Auburn in an agricultural area noted for feed grains and livestock. Spencerville is a trade center for swimming pool parts, boats, petroleum equipment, and livestock and poultry equipment.

SPICELAND, town (pop. 957), Henry County, E central Indiana, zip 47385, 8 mi. SSW of New Castle. The town was settled in 1828 by Quakers who farmed the fertile surrounding soils. Today, the main occupation is still farming. Spiceland Academy (1834), now a high school included the noted historian Charles A. Beard among its alumni.

SPRING MILL STATE PARK, Lawrence County, S Indiana, just E of Mitchell. Spring Mill, one of the best-loved parks in Indiana, contains an authentic restoration of an early pioneer village and an 1816 gristmill with an overshot waterwheel. Col. Richard Lieber (1869-1944), a former state conservation officer who was responsible for the preservation of the village, said of it: "You come down from the top of the hill 200 feet and you go back 100 years." The mill grinds corn for visitors who come to the park year round. The village includes many of the original residences and the hat shop, post office, boot shop, and apothecary. A visitor's center in memory of Virgil "Gus" Grissom, the U.S. astronaut who was killed in a launchpad fire at Cape Canaveral in 1967, has been erected in the park.

The park consists of 1,319 acres of hills, woods, and caves. Virgin woodlands covering 100 acres contain some of the largest specimens of white oak and tulip known in the area. There are many small caverns within the park, most of which can be explored on foot. Of special note are the Donaldson and Twin caves, which have unusual limestone formations, underground streams with blind fish, and daily boat excursions. Also featured at the park is the annual candlelight tour of the poineer village which takes place in September in conjunction with the Mitchell persimmon festival. Park activities include hiking, swimming, horseback riding, camping, and boating.

SPRINGPORT, town (pop. 236), Henry County, E Indiana, zip 47386, 10 mi. S of Muncie, in an agricultural area (feed grains, livestock).

SPRING VALLEY STATE FISH AND WILDLIFE AREA, Orange County, N Indiana, 8 mi. SE of French Lick in a scenic wooded and hilly region. Water recreation is available on a 127-acre lake which has a maximum depth of 37½ feet. There are also facilities for camping and picnicking. The game area encompasses 1,165 acres of land.

SPURGEON, town (pop. 285), Pike County, SW Indiana, zip 47584, 26 mi. NE of Evansville in an area noted for agriculture, oil-wells, and bituminous coal mines.

SQUIRE BOONE CAVERNS, natural limestone caves near Corydon, Harrison County, S Indiana. The caverns were discovered in 1790 by Squire Boone, a brother of Daniel Boone, while he was on a hunting trip. On one occasion he was attacked by Indians and hid in the caves. He later returned there many times, and at the mouth of the caverns built a gristmill which was powered by an underground stream. Boone died in 1815 and was buried in the cave. His grave was later desecrated, and his remains were removed to a secret place in Kentucky.

The caverns became privately owned in 1973. They contain many examples of cave formations, among them the world's largest known rimstone formation. (Rimstone, or travertine as it is most commonly called, is formed by water running over rock-pool ledges, evaporating, and leaving a drapery-like deposit.) Cave onyx, stalagtites, stalagmites, cave pearls, and a waterfall are found within the caverns. An artificial exit has been blasted out of the solid rock.

STAR CITY, town (pop. 500), Pulaski County, N Indiana, zip 46985, 7 mi. SE of Winamac in an agricultural and dairying area. The town is a manufacturing center for farm supplies, millwork, and concrete blocks.

STARKE, county (pop. 19,280), NW Indiana, area 310 sq.mi., bordered on the NW by the Kankakee River and drained by the Yellow River and tributaries of the Kankakee River. The county was organized in 1844 and named for Gen. John Starke, a war hero. Knox is the county seat.

Starke County is in a rich agricultural area especially noted for its mint and onions. There is some manufacturing at Knox. Koontz Lake, in the NE corner of the county, is famous for its excellent fishing.

STARVE HOLLOW STATE FOREST, Jackson County, S Indiana, 3 mi. SE of Vallonia. Starve Hollow encompasses 270 acres, including a 170-acre lake. Recreational facilities include picnicking, fishing, camping, boating, and swimming.

STAUNTON, town (pop. 582), Clay County, W Indiana, zip 47881, 12 mi. E of Terre Haute in an agricultural area noted for livestock and feed grains and some bituminous coal mining.

STEUBEN, county (pop. 20,159), NE Indiana, area 309 sq.mi., bounded on the N by Michigan and E by Ohio, and drained by Pigeon Creek.

The county was organized in February 1832 and named for Baron Steuben who joined the U.S. army during the American Revolution. The county seat is at Angola.

Steuben County contains numerous Indian mounds and burial grounds indicating settlement of the region by Indian tribes over the centuries. In addition to being a rich farming, timber, and dairying area, the county is also a popular resort spot with numerous lakes. The N central area encompasses Pokagon State Park (*q.v.*), with beautiful Lake James.

STILESVILLE, town (pop. 352), Hendricks County, central Indiana, zip 46180, on Mill Creek, 27 mi. WSW of Indianapolis in fertile agricultural area ideally suited for oats, wheat, soybeans, and feed corn.

STINESVILLE, town (pop. 291), Monroe County, S central Indiana, zip 47464, 11 mi. NW of Bloomington in an agricultural area (livestock, feed grains).

STRAUGHN, town (pop. 329), Henry County, E Indiana, zip 47387, 10 mi. SSE of New Castle in an agricultural area (feed grains, livestock).

SULLIVAN, city (pop. 4,683), seat of Sullivan County, SW Indiana, zip 47882, near Busseron Creek, 25 mi. S of Terre Haute. The city was platted in 1842 and named for Gen. Daniel Sullivan, an Army courier. Sullivan prospered as a coal-mining and agricultural trade center. In 1925 it was the scene of one of the state's worst mining disasters. A gas explosion at the City Coal Mine buried 55 miners under tons of rubble. Deadly after-damp impeded rescue operations and it took 2 days to reach the men. Only 4 of the 55 survived.

Sullivan was the home of William H. Hayes, movie czar and postmaster general of the U.S. who was in charge of the "Hayes Office," a 1930s censorship board.

Sullivan is a modern manufacturing city whose diverse products include machine-shop tools, cheese, fertilizer, and lumber. Oil and gas wells are nearby, and coal mining continues to be an important aspect of the city's economy.

Two popular local resort areas are at nearby Lake Paradise and Sullivan County Park.

SULLIVAN, county (pop. 19,889), SW Indiana, area 457 sq.mi., bounded on the W by the Wabash River and drained by Busseron and Maria creeks. The county was formed in January 1817 and named for Gen. Daniel Sullivan, who was killed by Indians while carrying dispatches for George Rogers Clark. The county seat is at Sullivan. The county is located in a rich coal, oil, and natural gas area. Agriculture (grain, fruit, livestock, poultry, dairy products) is also prevalent and there is diversified manufacturing in Sullivan and Farmersburg.

SULPHUR SPRINGS, town (pop. 387), Henry County, E central Indiana, zip 47388, 7 mi. NNW of New Castle in an agricultural area (livestock, feed grains).

SUMMITVILLE, town (pop. 1,104), Madison County, E central Indiana, zip 46070, 15 mi. S of Marion. Summitville was incorporated as a town in 1881. It is basically a farming community (chiefly feed grains and livestock), but has a canned foods plant. The largest drain tile business in the country was at one time located there.

SUNMAN, town (pop. 707), Ripley County, SE Indiana, zip 47041, 23 mi. ESE of Greensburg in an agricultural area (feed grains, livestock). Resort facilities can be found at nearby Bar-K Lake.

SWAYZEE, town (pop. 1,073), Grant County, E central Indiana, zip 46986, 9 mi. WSW of Marion in an agricultural area (livestock, feed grains). There is a canned foods plant in town.

SWEETSER, town (pop. 1,076), Grant County, central Indiana, zip 46987, 6 mi. W of Marion in an agricultural and dairying region. Sweetser is a trade center for ready-mix concrete, liquid and dry fertilizers, and tomatoes.

SWITZ CITY, town (pop. 301), Greene County, SW Indiana, zip 47465, 35 mi. NE of Vincennes in an agricultural area (livestock, feed grains). Many of the inhabitants are employed in the nearby bituminous coal mines.

SWITZERLAND, county (pop. 6,306), SE Indiana, area 221 sq.mi., bounded on the E and S by the Ohio River. The county was organized in October 1814 and named for the European country of Switzerland. The county seat is at Vevay.

Rivers and creeks have formed large alluvial bottomlands which are ideal for the cultivation of feed grains, tobacco, and vegetables. The major industry is the manufacture of shoes.

SYLVAN LAKE, Noble County, NE Indiana, just E of Rome City. The 1,200-acre artificial lake was built in 1827 as a feeder for the proposed Michigan and Erie Canal. The canal was never completed, and today the lake serves as Rome City's principal tourist attraction. The south shore is the site of the Gene Stratton Porter State Memorial (*q.v.*).

SYRACUSE, town (pop. 1,546), Kosciusko County, N Indiana, zip 46567, on Lake Wawasee, 32 mi. SE of South Bend. Surrounded by lakes, it is basically a resort community. There is also a cedar chest business in town which employs a large number of residents. Lake Wawasee, named for Chief Wawasee, has 21 mi. of shoreline and is the largest natural lake in Indiana. The Wawasee Fish Hatchery is at the SE corner of the lake. Syracuse also has two municipal golf courses.

T.C. STEELE STATE MEMORIAL, memorial to the famous Indiana artist, Theodore Clement Steele, near Belmont, Brown County, S central Indiana. The memorial includes the painter's home and studio, which are situated on a 211-acre tract. Steele was the originator of the Brown County Art Colony.

TELL CITY, city (pop. 7,933), Perry County, S Indiana, zip 47586, on the Ohio River, 45 mi. W of Evansville. The city was founded in 1857 by a colony of Swiss immigrants who named it for William Tell, their legendary hero. Old World craftsmanship has contributed to Tell City's renown as a leading furniture maker. Other manufactures include electronic equipment, electric motors, woolen textiles, river barges, and pleasure craft. There are also an oil refinery, distillery, coal mines, and packing plants. The Tell City Chair Company (1865) manufactured the "Jackie Kennedy" ballroom chairs ordered in 1962 for the White House by the former First Lady. Byrd's Echo Lake, 3 mi. E of Tell City, is a popular resort.

TENNYSON, town (pop. 335), Warrick County, SW Indiana, zip 47637, 27 mi. ENE of Evansville in an agricultural and bituminous coal-mining area.

TERRE HAUTE, city (pop. 70,286), seat of Vigo County, W Indiana, zip 47808, on a plateau above the Wabash River. The city was founded in 1816 on the border between the former French colonial provinces of Canada and Louisiana. It was named Terre Haute ("high land") by the French who governed the area until 1763. Fort Harrison was built in 1811 by the Americans 3 mi. to the N, and in 1818 the town was designated the county seat.

During the early 1800s Terre Haute was an important point on the National Road and the Wabash and Erie Canal. New factories were established along the canal, including a flour mill, foundry, brewery, candle factory, and blast furnace. Before long, the city was known as the "Pittsburgh of the West." After the decline of the canal in the 1860s, the railroads continued the economic expansion of the city. Large-scale mining of nearby vast bituminous coal deposits added new sources of fuel. Much of the coal was later mined to supply World War I demands. The coal-mining business increased steadily, although several miners strikes caused periodic declines.

Terre Haute was the birthplace of Paul Dresser, the composer of Indiana's state song "On the Banks of the Wabash," of his brother, the novelist Theodore Dreiser; and of Eugene V. Debs, socialist leader and founder of the American Railway Union.

Terre Haute is a leading industrial, mining, and railroad center. Manufactures are diverse, including brick, tile, glass, coke by-products, steel, paper, clothing, pharmaceuticals, liquor, and food products. Disaster struck Terre Haute in 1963 when an explosion at the Home Packing Company killed 17 people and injured 50 more. Two more explosions followed within a month, causing more injuries and damages. Leaking gas was said to be the cause, and city residents sarcastically began to refer to Terre Haute as "Boomtown, U.S.A."

Of cultural interest are the Sheldon-Swope Art Gallery, which features European, American, Oriental, and African works of art; the Historical Museum of Wabash Valley, housed in an 1868 Italianate mansion; and the Early Wheels Museum, which has a collection of antique and classic automobiles.

Terre Haute is the seat of Indiana State University (1865), a four-year fully-accredited school with an enrollment of 13,000 students. The university also has a School of Graduate Studies and the Turman Gallery of Fine Arts. Nearby are St. Mary-of-the-Woods College (1840) for women and Rose Polytecnic Institute (1874), the first private and independent engineering school west of the Alleghenies. Of note is the J.W. Davis Company, the largest greenhouse in the world, with 35 acres cultivated under glass.

Many recreational and resort spots can be found in and around Terre Haute. They include Deming Park, 160 acres in town; Raccoon Lake State Recreation Area; Fowler Park; Hartman, North, South, and Walton lakes; the Rea Park Golf Course; and Indiana State University Stadium Golf Course.

THORNTOWN, town (pop. 1,399), Boone County, central Indiana, zip 46071, on Sugar Creek, 18 mi. ENE of Crawfordsville. On the site of an 18th-century Indian village, called Keewaskee ("place of thorns"), the town was an early trading post and Jesuit mission. From 1818 until the Indians were removed in 1828, Thorntown was an Indian reservation. The land tract was sold in 1829 to Cornelius Westfall, who platted the present town. Modern Thorntown is a trade center for livestock and feed grains and has poultry hatcheries and a livestock serum plant.

TIPPECANOE, town (pop. 350), Marshall County, N Indiana, žip 46570, 18 mi. SE of Plymouth. The town is a manufacturing center for mill equipment, iron castings, plastic parts, tools, dies, metal siding, building components, scout hats, and pallets.

TIPPECANOE, county (pop. 109,378), W central Indiana, area 500 sq.mi., crossed by the Wabash River and drained by the Tippecanoe River and Wildcat Creek. The county was organized in March 1826 and named for the Tippecanoe River. It was in Tippecanoe County that Gen. William Henry Harrison defeated the Indians led by Tenskwatawa, the Shawnee Prophet and brother of Tecumseh, in 1811. The county seat is at Lafayette.

Although most of its surface is level, sections of Tippecanoe County along the Wabash River are broken into rugged hills ranging from 50 to 200 ft. in height. Agriculture, coal mining, and manufacturing are the mainstays of the economy. Diversified manufacturing includes the production of aluminum extrusions, prefabricated homes, automotive gears, and fabricated metals.

TIPPECANOE BATTLEFIELD STATE MEMORIAL, Battle Ground, Tippecanoe County, W central Indiana, 7 mi. N of Lafayette. The memorial marks the site of the Battle of Tippecanoe, Nov. 7, 1811, in which soldiers of the 4th Regiment under the leadership of Gen. William Henry Harison were victorious over Indian forces led by Tenskwatawa, The Shawnee Prophet. Tenskwatawa, who was Tecumseh's brother, led 700 warriors into battle in an attempt to win back Indian lands and drive the white settlers south of the Ohio River. The Indian losses were reportedly greater than those of Harrison's men, 37 of whom were killed, 29 fatally wounded, and 150 others wounded. A 100-ft. shaft marks the site and smaller stones indicate where officers fell. The soldiers were buried in a mass grave.

TIPPECANOE RIVER, Indiana, rises in NW Whitley County, flows 166 mi. NW to W past Monterey and then SW to the Wabash River, of which it is a major tributary. The river was the site of the 1811 Battle of Tippecanoe (at Battle Ground) in which Gen. William Henry Harrison defeated the Indians led by Tenskwatawa, The Shawnee Prophet.

The Tippecanoe River is the site of Indiana's largest hydroelectric power plant. The Oakdale Plant has a producing capacity of 11,000 kilowatts. Tippecanoe River State Park is located near Winamac in Pulaski County.

TIPPECANOE RIVER STATE PARK, Pulaski County, NW Indiana, just N of Winamac. The park, which encompasses 2,761 acres of land, stretches for 8 mi. along the Tippecanoe River. The scenic woods have winding roads and hiking trails and there are facilities for group camps and family camping. There are also areas for swimming, fishing, and picnicking.

TIPTON, city (pop. 5,176), seat of Tipton County, central Indiana, zip 46072, on Cicero Creek, 15 mi. SSE of Kokomo. Originally known as Canton, the city was platted in 1845. It has become a leading agricultural trade and manufacturing center. Products include machinery, furniture, piston rings, canned goods, cigars, chemicals, and brooms. Library park contains a memorial erected to celebrate the state's 100th anniversary. A museum containing pioneer relics is in the county courthouse.

TIPTON, county (pop. 16,650), central Indiana, area 261 sq.mi., drained by Cicero, Turkey, and Wildcat creeks. The county was organized in May 1844 and named for Gen. John Tipton, a U.S. senator (1832-39). The city of Tipton (formerly Canton) is the county seat.

Much of the county, which is level, was once covered by water, but the many marshlands have been drained and turned over to farming. The extremely fertile soils produce vegetables and grains of all kinds. Food canning is the leading industry.

TIPTON TILL PLAIN, vast glacial morainic deposit covering central Indiana. During the Pleistocene Epoch, glaciers covered most of Indiana and laid down what came to be known as the Tipton Till Plain. The ice, at times 2,000 ft. thick, leveled the entire area. The glacial subsoil of the plain is many feet deep and composed of finely ground rock flour, clay, sand, and gravel. The area has been traditionally noted for its fine farm and pasture lands.

TOPEKA, town (pop. 677), Lagrange County, NE Indiana, zip 46571, 24 mi. ESE of Elkhart in an agricultural area (cattle, sheep, poultry, feed grains). Emma Lake and the L.C.C. Association Golf Course offer recreational facilities.

TRAFALGAR, town (pop. 457), Johnson County, central Indiana, zip 46181, 25 mi. S of Indianapolis in an area noted for some of the best corn production in the world.

TRAIL CREEK, town (pop. 2,697), La Porte County, NE Indiana, just E of Michigan City in the sand dune region of the state. The area is noted for fruit orchards specializing in apples, cherries, pears, cider, honey, and grapes.

TRI-COUNTY FISH AND WILDLIFE AREA, Kosciusko County, N Indiana, 2 mi. NE of North Webster in a gently rolling area of prairie lands. Its 3,437 acres include a 500-acre lake which has excellent fishing and boating.

TRINITY SPRINGS, Martin County, S Indiana, about 8 mi. N of Loogootee. The springs, together with nearby Indian Springs, were popular health and recreation spas in the early 20th century. Eleven hotels, a dance hall, bowling alley, swimming pool, and restaurant were part of the facilities. Today, only crumbling buildings remain, and the springs are overgrown by brush.

TROY, town (pop. 575), Perry County, S Indiana, zip 47588, at the confluence of the Ohio and Anderson rivers, 3 mi. NNW of Tell City. Troy was one of the first settlements downstream from the falls of the Ohio. Many of the early houses were built of sandstone quarried from the hill around which the town is situated. Early settlers from Virginia turned Troy into an important river shipping point, and it was the county seat until 1818.

Above the Ohio River on a bluff is the "Christ of the Ohio," a statue erected by Dr. James, a Tell City physician, to inspire riverboat travelers. Today, Troy is a quiet farming community. Many of the residents are employed at the nearby bituminous coal mines.

TURKEY RUN STATE PARK, Parke County, W Indiana, near Marshall. The park derives its name from the thousands of wild turkeys that once sought shelter in the area. Turkey Run is 2,181 acres of rugged gorges, steep canyons, glens, bathing beaches, and waterfalls. Formed by the erosive action of Sugar Creek, a tributary of the Wabash River, the park is a haven for thousands of tourists who visit it annually. Sugar Creek abounds in black bass, crappie, and rock bass. Miles of foot trails lead through a virgin forest of black walnut, oak, and poplar. There is a new campground and the remodeled Turkey Run Inn.

TWIN CAVES, Spring Mill State Park (*q. v.*), Lawrence County, S Indiana, near Mitchell. Twin Caves are part of a vast system of limestone caverns which traverse the park and are available for exploration. The caves are unique in that they contain a small lake; boat rides are frequently taken into them. The boats usually go in for 475 ft., but Upper Twin Cave has been explored by this means for 4,674 ft. Both have typical cave animals and limestone formations.

ULEN, town (pop. 138), Boone County, central Indiana, just N of Lebanon in an agricultural area (livestock, feed grains).

UNION, county (pop. 6,582), E Indiana, area 168 sq.mi., bounded on the E by the Ohio and drained by the East Fork of the Whitewater River. The county was organized in February 1821 and derived its name from the hope that it would harmonize the difficulties that existed in relation to Wayne and Fayette counties, which border it N and W, respectively. Liberty is the county seat.

The eastern part of the county is level and composed of deep fertile soils. Farming in the region produces quality corn, wheat, hay, and tobacco. There is also livestock and hog raising on the less fertile areas. The western part has an abundance of limestone hills which produce high-quality building stone. There are also several bituminous coal mines and sand and gravel pits. There is manufacturing at Uniontown, Sturgis, and Morganfield. Whitewater State Park (*q.v.*) is nearby.

UNION CITY, city (pop. 3,995), Randolph County, E Indiana, zip 47390, 30 mi. E of Muncie. Union City straddles the state line between Indiana and Ohio, although 3/4 of it is in Indiana. It also sits astride the Quaker Trace, a favorite route for runaway slaves which linked Richmond and Fort Wayne. The trace was also the first road through Randolph County.

Union City is a manufacturing center for bus bodies, automobile parts, furniture, luggage, canned goods, and dairy equipment. It is also a shipping point for agricultural products and livestock. A memorial to the Greenville Treaty Line (1794), which led to the peaceful settlement of E Indiana and half of Ohio, lies 13 mi. NW.

UNIONDALE, town (pop. 349), Wells County, E Indiana, zip 46791, 19 mi. SSW of Fort Wayne in an agricultural area (livestock, feed grains).

UNION MILLS, town (pop. 600), La Porte County, N Indiana, zip 46382, 11 mi. S of La Porte in an agricultural area noted for feed grains and livestock. Union Mills has a cluster of 11 Indian mounds from which have been excavated human skeletons, clay pipes, hatchets, and other artifacts. The artifacts are on display in local museums. The town is otherwise a quiet farming community with a farm cooperative that stocks grains, fencing, coal, farm supplies, and fertilizer.

UNIVERSAL, town (pop. 462), Vermillion County, W Indiana, zip 47884, 12 mi. NNW of Terre Haute in an agricultural area noted for livestock and feed grains. Bituminous coal mining is an important activity.

UPLAND, town (pop. 3,202), Grant County, E central Indiana, zip 46989, 11 mi. ESE of Marion. Upland was platted in 1867 in conjunction with the coming of the railroads. It thrived for a time as a sawmill center, but with the natural gas boom of 1887, Upland mushroomed into a self-sufficient manufacturing center (window glass, gloves, canned goods, lumber).

Upland is the seat of Taylor University (1893), a United Brethren coeducational college of liberal arts. Of note is the Ayres Memorial Library.

Recreational facilities can be found at nearby Kilgore and Pine lakes.

URBANA, town (pop. 350), Wabash County, N Indiana, zip 46990, 7 mi. N of Wabash in an agricultural area noted for feed grains and livestock. Urbana is a manufacturer of farm equipment, metal stampings, seed sowers and spreaders, and poultry equipment.

VALLONIA, town (pop. 500), Jackson County, S Indiana, zip 47281, 4 mi. SW of Brownstown in an agricultural and timbering area. Vallonia is a trade center for lumber and feeds. It was founded in 1812 on the site of Fort Vallonia, a French outpost. The location was once considered for the state capitol.

VALPARAISO, city (pop. 20,020), seat of Porter County, NW Indiana, zip 46383, 18 mi. ESE of Gary. The site of Valparaiso was originally purchased from the Potawatomi Indians by the U.S. government in 1832. The first white settlers arrived in 1834. Valparaiso became the county seat in 1837 and obtained city status in 1865. It is popularly known as "Valpo" in the vicinity.

The city has become ⌐ major industrial and manufacturing center, and the majority of Valparaiso residents are employed in local industries. Major enterprises include Coca-Cola, Owens-Corning Fiberglass Corporation, and McGill Manufacturing Company. Principal manufactures include bakelite products, magnets, ball bearings, electric lamp guards, automobile parts, refined metals, fiberglass tanks, steel rollers, and automatic sprinkler systems.

Higher educational opportunities are plentiful in Valparaiso. Located there is Valparaiso University (1859), originally owned by citizens of the city and by the Methodist Church. It was purchased in 1925 by the newly-formed Lutheran University Association, and has since remained under Lutheran administration. The university is a fully-accredited four-year college offering 57 fields of study. Average enrollment is 4,000 students. Of note is the Chapel of the Resurrection (1956), the world's largest college chapel with a seating capacity of 3,000. Architectually, the chapel resembles the Church of the Nativity in Bethlehem, Israel. The Brandt Campanile, 140 ft. high, plays morning and evening hymns and marks the class hours. Also in Valparaiso is the Valparaiso Technical Insititute (1874), known nationally for its excellent electronics and communications progams.

Porter Memorial Hospital and Porter County Municipal Airport serve the surrounding area. Recreational facilities can be found at nearby Indiana Dunes State Park (*q.v.*).

Valparaiso is situated on the Valparaiso Glacial Moraine, and is surrounded by rolling hills and glacial lakes that provide unlimited recreational facilities. The Porter County Historical Society Museum, in the County Building, has pioneer relics and dresses from the Lincoln inaugural ball.

Annual events include the Porter County Fair, which features agricultural displays.

VAN BUREN, town (pop. 1,057), Grant County, E central Indiana, zip 46991, 11 mi. ENE of Marion in an agricultural area (livestock, feed grains).

VANDERBURGH, county (pop. 168,772), SW Indiana, area 241 sq. mi., bounded on the S by the Ohio River and drained by Pigeon Creek. The county was organized in February 1818 and named for Capt. Henry Vanderburgh of the American Revolutionary War. Evansville is the county seat.

Farming and manufacturing go hand in hand in Vanderburgh County. Fertile soils are used for the cultivation of winter wheat, soybeans, and corn. Hog raising is also a leading activity. The county is a major manufacturing and market center for refrigerators, meat, flour, beer, fabricated metals, construction machinery, air conditioners, and pharmaceuticals.

Prehistoric Indians lives in the area and their artifacts can be found throughout the county. Angel Mounds near Evansville is the site of an ancient city of Mound Builders from the Mississippian culture.

VEEDERSBURG, town (pop. 1,837), Fountain County, W Indiana, zip 47987, near the Wabash River, 21 mi. WNW of Crawfordsville. Veedersburg developed rapidly as a manufacturing and shipping center because of its location near excellent railroad facilities. Chief industries include a brick factory and a condensed milk plant. Bituminous coal mines are nearby. Rogers Lake, 2 mi. SE of town, is a popular recreational area.

VERMILLION, county (pop. 16,793), W Indiana, area 263 sq.mi., bounded on the W by Illinois, E by the Wabash River, and drained by the Vermillion River. The county was formed in January 1824 and named for the Vermillion River. Newport has been the county seat since it was organized.

Vermillion is sometimes called the "Shoe String County" because of its long, narrow shape, averaging only 6 mi. in width. The land surface is high and generally level, except near the streams. Seams of cannel (block) coal underlie the land. The beds average 5 to 7 ft. in thickness and are interstratified with fine-quality fire clay. Coal mining is a major activity. Feed grains and fruit are grown on the bottomlands, and there is some manufacturing at Cayuga and Clinton.

VERNON, town (pop. 440), seat of Jennings County, SE Indiana, zip 47282, on Vernon Creek, 20 mi. NW of Madison. The provisions of the land grant of 1815 included a clause which stipulated that Vernon remain the county seat forever.

During the Civil War 400 men gathered in Vernon to ward off Confederate Gen. John Hunt Morgan and his 2,200 cavalrymen.

It was the only town in Indiana not conquered by Morgan's Raiders.

The North American House, across from the courthouse, contains the Jennings County Historical Society Museum. The house, built in the 1820s, was a former stagecoach stop and inn. The Milhouse Home is the birthplace of former Pres. Richard Nixon's mother. Vernon remains a quiet farming community given over to livestock raising and feed grains. Wipporwill Lake provides recreational facilities.

VERSAILLES, town (pop. 1,020) seat of Ripley County, SE Indiana, zip 47042, 40 mi. SE of Shelbyville. The town, founded in 1818, has always served as a farm center.

The Ripley County Historical Museum has many Civil War relics. Outside the city is Versailles State Park, second largest in the state, with its 176-ft. covered bridge built in 1885.

VERSAILLES STATE PARK, Ripley County, SE Indiana, near the town of Versailles. The park, which encompasses 5,897 acres, was founded in 1818 and is one of the most popular parks in Indiana. It is unexcelled for its field trial running grounds. Flowing through it are Laughery and Fallen Timber creeks, which are noted for good fishing. Recreational facilities provide areas for camping, picnicking, horseback riding, swimming, and boating. There is also a lookout fire tower within the park, and near its entrance is a 176-ft. covered bridge which was built in 1885.

VEVAY, town (pop. 1,463), seat of Switzerland County, SE Indiana, zip 47043, on the Ohio River, 15 mi. E of Madison. The town was founded in 1801 by a group of Swiss immigrants who settled there to establish vineyards. The resultant wine industry became nationally famous, but eventually gave way to agriculture. Today the town is a center for dairy products, flour, grain, livestock, vegetables, and tobacco.

Vevay was the birthplace of Edward Eggleston, the 19th-century author, who is best known for his novel *The Hoosier Schoolmaster* (1871). His home stands near the courthouse.

The "Martha A. Graham," last of the side-wheel ferries on the Ohio River, continued to operate between Vevay and Ghent,

Kentucky, in the mid-1970s. The Switzerland County Historical Society Museum contains riverboat artifacts and memorabilia of the life of Edward Eggleston. Vevay was the setting for the 1975 television movie, *A Girl Named Sooner,* starring Lee Remick.

The annual Swiss Wine Festival at Vevay features a cheese garden, whole hog sausage, and Swiss-Bavarian entertainment.

VIGO, county (pop. 114,528), W Indiana, area 415 sq.mi., bounded on the W by Illinois, and drained by the Wabash River and Honey Creek. The county was formed in January 1818 and named for Col. Francis Vigo, an Italian merchant who came to Vincennes in 1777. Terre Haute is the county seat.

The land surface throughout the county is level and unbroken and most of it is underlain with bituminous coal seams. The coal has been mined since the 1800s and the county is still a leader in its production. The soils are especially good for raising wheat, and stock-raising is prominent in all sections of Vigo County. There is diversified manufacturing at Terre Haute; leading industries produce foods, plastic film, chemicals, drugs, fabricated metals, castings, and extrusions. There are also printing and publishing firms.

VINCENNES, city (pop. 19,867), seat of Knox County, SW Indiana, zip 47591, on the east bank of the Wabash River, 55 mi. S of Terre Haute. Vincennes is the oldest city in Indiana and the third oldest in the territorial expanse known as the Northwest Territory. The first permanent white settlement was the French mission-fort built in 1732 by Francois Morgan de Vincennes, for whom the town is named. It was established on the Buffalo Trace, an old trail beaten out by thousands of buffalo as they forded streams there. The land around the early settlement was parceled off by lots, and deeds were sold to anyone who wished to settle there.

Vincennes was ceded to Great Britain in 1763 by the Treaty of Paris and continued a peaceful pastoral existence under British control until February 1779, when the fort, then known as Sackville, was captured by Virginia troops under the leadership of George Rogers Clark. Upon surrender, the state of Virginia claimed all the lands northwest of the Ohio River, and Illinois County was organized. Virginia was unable to govern this huge expanse of land and ceded it to the U.S. in 1784. The Northwest

Territory consequently was organized in 1787, and on March 5, 1791, 5,000 acres were given by Congress to all the inhabitants of Vincennes for use as pasture lands.

The year 1800 saw the formation of Indiana Territory. Vincennes became the first territorial capital and began to take on a new character. Until then Vincennes had been a rough-and-tumble prairie town with little law and order, but with the arrival of influential government officials, lawyers, and other professionals, it began to take on a more distinguished air.

The capitol building, a two-story frame house, was erected in 1800. It has been restored and commemorated as a state memorial (*see* Territorial Capitol State Memorial). Vincennes remained the territorial seat of government until 1813, when the capital was removed to Corydon.

Historical landmarks are profuse in Vincennes. The Old Cathedral (1826) and the adjoining Old French Cemetery are noted landmarks, as are the William Henry Harrison mansion of Grouseland (1803) (*q.v.*), the first mansion in Indiana; the George Rogers Clark National Historic Park, a 20-acre plaza at the site of Fort Sackville; and the Old State Bank (1836), now an art gallery with exhibits of the Northwest Territory.

Vincennes depends heavily on the tourist trade, but is also a leading rail-shipping and manufacturing center. It is noted for its peach and apple orchards and its truck farming and dairy complexes. The Tip-Top Creamery is the second largest creamery in Indiana. Manufactures include structural steel, glass, ice, boxes, canned vegetables, paper products, and flour. Power is supplied to many of the industries by coal mined at the Standard Coal Company; 1,500,000 tons of coal are produced annually in and around Vincennes.

The town is the seat of Vincennes University (1801), which was the first land-grant college of the Northwest Territory and the oldest junior college in the U.S. Sigma Pi fraternity was organized here, and Indian youths from neighboring tribes were given a free education. On campus is the Territorial Capitol, the Dunseth Planeterium and Museum, and the Maurice Thompson Birthplace (1842). Thompson was the author of *Alice of Old Vincennes,* a popular novel. The replica frame building of the first newspaper printing shop is here; Elihu Stout the publisher, issued the *Indiana Gazette* in 1804.

Kimmell Park, a favorite local camp and fishing site, is

located 1¼ mi. NW of Vincennes. The Trailblazer Railroad offers tourists a historic sightseeing tour of the city.

VIRGIL I. GRISSOM STATE MEMORIAL, Spring Mill State Park (*q.v.*), Lawrence County, S Indiana, near Mitchell. Indiana's newest memorial was dedicated on July 21 (Apollo Day), 1971, and serves as the visitor's center for the park. It is dedicated to Virgil "Gus" Grissom, the Hoosier astronaut who was killed in a fire on Jan. 27, 1967. The building houses a display of America's space age achievements, including the original space capsule in which Grissom and John Young made their 81,000-mi. Gemini flight on March 23, 1965. Memorabilia of Grissom's life are placed throughout the building. Some of the exhibits are on loan from the Smithsonian Insitution and will be rotated periodically as new material becomes available. Within the memorial, the Universe Room includes a 6-ft. diameter illuminated globe of the Earth in bas relief.

WABASH, city (pop. 13,379), seat of Wabash County, NE central Indiana, zip 46992, on the Wabash River, 40 mi. WSW of Fort Wayne. The territory surrounding the city site became available for white settlement with the signing of the Treaty of Paradise Springs in October 1826. A bronze plaque on a boulder near the courthouse in Wabash marks the treaty site. The city was founded in 1835 at a former gathering place for the Indians known as Oubache ("water over white stones"). It was located on the Wabash and Erie Canal, which was completed from Ohio, through Wabash, to Evansville in 1853. The canal, however, was soon to be overshadowed by the railroads. Wabash was the first electrically lighted city in the world. Four electric arc "Brush Lights" invented by Charles F. Brush, were installed on the courthouse tower and tested at twilight on March 31, 1880.

Wabash is an agricultural and manufacturing center noted for electronic equipment, furniture, automobile parts, asbestos, clothing, baking powder, lime, and rubber products. Livestock and dairy farming are also important.

The Wabash County Historical Museum houses pioneer artifacts. Of note are the Honeywell Auditorium and the Honeywell Gardens, resplendent with flowers and landscaped shrubbery. Nearby are several excellent recreational spots, among them the Frances Slocum State Recreation Area, Salamonie River State Forest, Salamonie Dam and Reservoir, and the Mississinewa Dam and Reservoir (*q.v.*).

WABASH, county (pop. 35,553), NE central Indiana, area 398 sq.mi., drained by the Wabash, Eel, Salamonie, and Mississinewa rivers. The county was organized in March 1835 and named for the Wabash River. The city of Wabash is the county seat.

The land surface is level to gently rolling, and a good part of the county is covered by river bottomlands which are extremely fertile and conducive to growing soybeans, wheat, and corn. The drier sections are turned over to pasture for horses, cattle, hogs, and sheep. Wabash County is distinguished for its horse markets and is a leader in horse breeding. Manufacturing is an important part of the county's economy, especially the production of furniture, store fixtures, wood products, electronic equipment, and rubber goods.

The Mississinewa Dam and Reservoir, which was dedicated in 1969, is located almost entirely in Wabash County.

WABASH AND ERIE CANAL, federal waterways project begun in 1832. The canal stretched for 468 mi. from Evansville, Indiana, to Toledo, Ohio—380 mi. in Indiana alone. It was one of the worst financial disasters in transportation history. The longest canal in the U.S., it failed through mismanagement, floods, and the coming of the railroads, and cost Indiana $25,000,000, too much for so young and poor a state.

Only two boats ever traveled the entire route from Lake Erie to the Ohio River. Descendants of the early canal workers, most of whom were Irish, still live along the canal route in Indiana. Remnants of the bed and old canal locks can be seen in many places.

WABASH LOWLAND, physiographic region of SW Indiana, the northern two-thirds of which is covered with glacial drift. The Wabash Lowland is also an alluvial plain through which the Wabash River and its tributaries meander to the Ohio River. Alluvial and glacial deposits are everywhere underlaid with limestones, shales, and thin coals which in many places are mined.

WABASH RIVER, rises in Grand Lake, Ohio, enters Indiana in Jay County, and flows W and SW past Logansport and Lafayette. It then turns S and SW past Terre Haute and Vincennes, forming 200 mi. of the Indiana-Illinois border to finally flow into the Ohio River at the SW corner of Indiana. In all, the Wabash is 475 mi. long and drains two-thirds of the state. Its principal tributary is the White River.

WAKARUSA, town (pop. 1,160), Elkhart County, N Indiana, zip 46573, 10 mi. S of Elkhart in an agricultural area noted for feed grains and livestock. Wakarusa is a manufacturing center for ladders, dairy products, concrete vaults, truck caps, travel trailers, polyurethane foam, farm supplies, and camping equipment.

WALDRON, town (pop. 700), Shelby County, central Indiana, zip 46182, 8 mi. SE of Shelbyville in an agricultural area noted for feed grains and livestock. Waldron is a manufacturing center for wire enameling dies, dune buggies, boats, and fiberglass products.

WALKERTON, town (pop. 2,006), St. Joseph County, N Indiana, zip 46374, 19 mi. SW of South Bend. Walkerton is a shipping point for peppermint, onions, and feed grains. The area is one of the largest mint-growing centers in the U.S., its peaty soils being conducive to the cultivation of the crop. Recreational facilities can be found at nearby Indiana Dunes State Park (*q.v.*).

WALLACE, town (pop. 126), Fountain County, W Indiana, zip 47988, 14 mi. WSW of Crawfordsville in an area noted for feed grains, livestock, and bituminous coal mining.

WALTON, town (pop. 1,054), Cass County, N central Indiana, zip 46994, 10 mi. SE of Logansport in an agricultural area (feed grains, livestock).

WANATAH, town (pop. 773), LaPorte County, N Indiana, zip 46390, 20 mi. SW of LaPorte in an agricultural and manufacturing area. Wanatah is a trade center for conveyors, aluminum products, lumber, and building supplies. It was settled in 1865 and thrived briefly as a railroad hub. The name comes from an Indian phrase meaning "knee-deep-in-mud", referring to Hog Creek which to this day periodically overflows its banks.

WARREN, county (pop. 8,705), W Indiana, area 368 sq.mi., bounded on the W by Illinois and on the SE by the Wabash River.

The county was formed in March 1827, and was named for Gen. Joseph Warren who served in the Revolutionary War. The county seat is at Williamsport.

The surface ranges from level to hilly, and the NW corner is covered by fertile, black loam soils which yield large crops of corn, oats, hay, and soybeans. Lumber milling is still prevalent although many of the well-wooded hills have been depleted of trees. The manufacture of cellophane is the county's chief industry.

WARREN, town (pop. 1,229), Huntington County, NE central Indiana, zip 46792, on the Salamonie River, 14 mi. SSE of Huntington. Warren is located midway between the Huntington and Salamonie reservoirs, which are dam projects developed jointly by the State of Indiana and the U.S. Army Corps of Engineers. Both are popular recreational spots. The town is a center for poultry, livestock, soybeans, grain, dairy products, and canned tomatoes.

WARRICK, county (pop. 29,972), SW Indiana, area 391 sq.mi., bounded on the S by the Ohio River and drained by Pigeon and Little Pigeon creeks.

The county was formed in March 1813, and was named for Capt. Jacob Warrick who was a casualty of the Battle of Tippecanoe in 1811. The county seat is at Boonville. The old Wabash and Erie Canal traversed the NW part of Warrick County, and the canal bed can still be seen in several places.

Coal is the county's chief resource, and coal-mining its principal industry. The rich bottomlands produce large crops of corn, fruit, and vegetables. Several upland sections yield good quality tobacco.

WARSAW, city (pop. 7,506), seat of Kosciusko County, N Indiana, zip 46580, on the Tippecanoe River, 40 mi. WNW of Fort Wayne. Warsaw, founded in 1836, is in the center of Indiana's lake region, and is a popular resort city. Over 100 lakes are in the vicinity, including those in the Chain O'Lakes State Park (*q.v.*). Warsaw is a leading manufacturing center whose diverse products include automobile and aircraft equipment, castings, furniture, vacuum cleaners, and cut glass. There is also a lumber mill. Recreational facilities include the Rozella Golf Course.

WASHINGTON, city (pop. 11,358), seat of Daviess County, SW Indiana, zip 47501, 19 mi. E of Vincennes. The city had its beginnings in 1805 when Fort Flora was erected on the site to protect the white population from Indian attacks. It possesses many century-old buildings. Amish farmers, with their horse-drawn buggies and austere garb, are often seen on the streets on their way to market. A large colony of Amish is located in Daviess County. Washington is a leading manufacturing center for wood products, clothing, flour, canned goods, toys, railroad supplies, and electric signs. The fertile soils in the vicinity yield feed grains and fruit. Oil and gas wells are nearby. Recreational facilities can be found at Dogwood Lake in the Glendale Fish and Wildlife Area, and at the Washington Country Club.

WASHINGTON, county (pop. 19,278), S Indiana, area 516 sq.mi., bounded on the N by the Muscatatuck River and the East Fork of the White River. It is drained by the Blue and Lost rivers and by Twin Creek. Washington County was organized in 1813 and Salem became the county seat the following year. The county is rich in natural resources and is a noted grain producing, lumbering, and stone quarrying center. Major industries include cabinet making and furniture manufacturing.

WATERLOO, town (pop. 1,876), DeKalb County, NE Indiana, zip 46793, on Cedar Creek, and 26 mi. NNE of Fort Wayne in an agricultural area noted for livestock and feed grains, especially soybeans. Commodities such as canned goods, wood products, and flour are shipped to other communities in NE Indiana.

WAVELAND, town (pop. 557), Montgomery County, W Indiana, zip 47989, 34 mi. SW of Lafayette in an agricultural area noted for livestock and feed grains. Shades State Park (*q.v.*) lies north of the town.

WAWAKA, town (pop. 300), Noble County, N Indiana, zip 46794, 4 mi. N of Albion, in an agricultural and dairying region. Wawaka is a manufacturing center for camper and truck caps, sit-down bath units, and reinforced plastics.

WAWASEE, LAKE, N Indiana, at Syracuse. The lake, largest in Indiana, is 4 mi. long and is an important tourist attraction. The Wawasee State Fish Hatchery and Fishing Area are located here. The lake covers an area of 3,060 acres and is noted for its excellent fishing. Some of the fish have been stocked from the hatchery, which is the oldest in the state. Its ponds are fed by the artificial Papakeechee Lake. Lake Wawasee derives its name from an Indian chief, also called Old Flat Belly.

WAYNE, county (pop. 79,109), E Indiana, area 405 sq.mi., bounded on the E by Ohio, and drained by the Whitewater River, as well as its East Fork and other tributaries.

The county was organized in November 1810, and was named in honor of Gen. "Mad Anthony" Wayne. Richmond is the county seat. Wayne County was a center for abolitionist movements even before the Civil War, and became an important stopover on the Underground Railroad which took runaway slaves to freedom in the North and Canada.

In early days the National Road, which crosses through Wayne County, was a pioneer gateway for emigrants travelling to Indiana and the great West. Wayne is mainly a farming county, and its rich soils yield feed grains, flowers, and apples. It is famous for poultry, livestock, and horses, and contains some large animal farms. Wayne County has diversified its manufacturing, and leading products include piston rings, agricultural machinery, fabricated metals, insulated wire, bus and truck bodies, and missile parts.

WAYNETOWN, town (pop. 993), Montgomery County, W Indiana, zip 47990, 10 mi. WNW of Crawfordsville. Waynetown is a leading manufacturer of tile and brick, a result of its location in an excellent fire clay area. There are also lumber, feed, and flour mills in town.

WEED PATCH HILL, (elevation 1,085 ft.), Brown County, S Indiana, in Brown County State Park. The scenic beauty that surrounds Weed Patch Hill made it a popular visitor's attraction long before the state park was opened in 1929. At its summit is a 100-ft. watch tower. The entire region was formed by melt-waters from the Illinois Glacier which stopped just north of the Bean Blossom Overlook. The resultant streams carved valleys in the uplands, leaving a system of ridges (of which Weed Patch Hill is a part), that has been called the "Little Smokies". There are three mineral springs near the summit and the remnants of two old bear wallows. The hill was named by a group of Kentucky hunters who found rank weeks growing on the top.

WELLS, county (pop. 23,821), E Indiana, area 368 sq.mi., drained by the Wabash and Salamonie rivers, and by Longlois Creek. The county was formed in February 1837, and was named after Capt. William H. Wells, who was killed by Indians in 1812 while attempting to escort the garrison of Fort Dearborn (in what is now Chicago, Illinois) to Fort Wayne. Bluffton is the county seat.

Wells County is located in a rich agricultural area noted for livestock, dairy products, soybeans, and feed grains. There is also some limestone quarrying. Manufacturing is prevalent in the larger towns, and industries include canning, food processing, and the production of motors.

The 1,000-acre Ouabache State Recreation Area is located in Wells County, as also are the peat bogs immortalized by Gene Stratton Porter in her novel *A Girl of the Limberlost.*

WEST BADEN SPRINGS, town (pop. 930), Orange County, S Indiana, zip 47469, on the Lost River and 22 mi. SSW of Bedford. West Baden is picturesquely located in the wooded hills of southern Indiana. It grew up to become an important resort town as a direct consequence of its location near seven medicinal springs. Long before the coming of the white men, the Indians had declared it a neutral area designed for hunting the wild animals which came to lick the minerals deposited by the springs on nearby rocks.

The West Baden Springs Hotel, "eighth wonder of the world", was built in 1901 and thrived as a fashionable resort until the Great Depression of the 1930s. Its casinos were sometimes frequented by the Chicago gangster Al Capone. The hotel contains 708 rooms, the world's widest unsupported dome (208 ft.), and a mosaic tile floor in the atrium. The floor has since been damaged by settling. The hotel is now the headquarters for the Northwood Institute, a coeducational liberal arts and vocational college.

WEST COLLEGE CORNER, town (pop. 709), Union County, E Indiana, 17 mi. S of Richmond. It is the sister town of College Corner, Ohio across the state line.

WEST HARRISON, town (pop. 395), Dearborn County, SE Indiana, on the Whitewater River, and 32 mi. SSE of Connersville. West Harrison was founded in 1813 and was the event. Many Indian mounds are found in the vicinity.

WESTFIELD, town (pop. 1,837), Hamilton County, central Indiana, zip 46074, 19 mi. N of Indianapolis in an agricultural area noted for livestock and feed grains. There are many gravel pits nearby. Westfield was founded in 1834 by Quakers and was a stop on the Underground Railroad, the secret network by means of which slaves from the southern states escaped northward to gain their freedom before the Civil War.

WEST LAFAYETTE, city (pop. 19,157), Tippecanoe County, W central Indiana, zip 57906, on the Wabash River opposite Lafayette. West Lafayette was incorporated in 1924 and is the home of Purdue University (1869), one of the first land grant colleges. The school was named after John Purdue, its first benefactor, and is a leading technical college with an enrollment of 25,000 students. It has excellent agricultural and engineering programs. Outside of the city is the State Soldiers' Home, and Tecumseh Trail Rest Park which is on the site of a famous Indian trail.

WEST LEBANON, town (pop. 899), Warren County, W Indiana, zip 47991, 29 mi. WSW of Lafayette in an agricultural area noted for livestock and feed grains.

WESTPORT, town (pop. 1,170), Decatur County, SE central Indiana, zip 47283, 27 mi. SSE of Shelbyville in an agricultural area noted for livestock and feed grains.

WEST TERRE HAUTE, city (pop. 2,704), Vigo County, W Indiana, zip 46885, just W of Terre Haute. West Terre Haute was incorporated as a city in 1933. The city is a manufacturing center for steel products, lumber products, and commercial printing.

WESTVILLE, town (pop. 2,614), La Porte County, NW Indiana, 10 mi. WSW of La Porte in an agricultural area noted for livestock, feed grains, and horses. Westville is situated on the old Sauk Trail. Within the town are located Beatty Memorial Hospital for the mentally ill, and Purdue-North Central campus. Recreational facilities can be found at Red Rock Ranch (horseback riding), and at Clear Lake, just north of town. An historical marker records a stop of President Lincoln's funeral train.

WHEATFIELD, town (pop. 679), Jasper County, NW Indiana, zip 46392, 32 mi. SSE of Gary in an agricultural area noted for livestock and feed grains.

WHEATLAND, town (pop. 713), Knox County, SW Indiana, zip 47597, 11 mi. E of Vincennes in an agricultural area noted for feed grains and livestock. Wheatland is a leading shipping center for the surrounding fruit growing area. Recreational facilities can be found at nearby Thompson Bed Lake.

WHETZEL TRACE, a wilderness road through central Indiana terminating at Waverly, a former pioneer village located 19 mi. S of Indianapolis. The trace, cut through 60 mi. of wilderness by Jacob Whetzel in the early 1800s became the route for the majority of the early settlers entering central Indiana.

WHITE, county (pop. 20,995), NW central Indiana, area 497 sq.mi., bounded on the E by the Tippecanoe River (which also drains it), and by Big Monon and Little Monon creeks. The county was organized in April 1834, and was named after Col. Isaac White who died in the Battle of Tippecanoe in 1811. Monticello is the county seat. The land surface is almost wholly covered by rich, loamy soils which yield abundant crops of corn, oats, wheat, and soybeans. Manufactures include dairy and food products, furniture, bricks, electrical wire assemblies, and TV cabinets.

WHITELAND, town (pop. 562), Johnson County, central Indiana, zip 46184, 16 mi. SSE of Indianapolis in an agricultural area noted for feed grains and livestock.

WHITE RIVER, principal tributary of the Wabash River. The White River, Indiana, is formed by the confluence of the East Fork and West Fork rivers. The West Fork rises in Randolph County, E Indiana and the East Fork is formed by the confluences of tributaries near Columbus, Indiana. The East and West Fork rivers merge to form the White River in their journey S and SW. The U.S. Corps of Engineers has three flood control reservoirs in the White River Basin:—Cagles Mill on Mill Creek, Mansfield on Raccoon Creek, and Monroe on Salt Creek.

WHITESTOWN, town (pop. 569), Boone County, central Indiana, zip 46075, 15 mi. NW of Indianapolis in an agricultural area noted for feed grains and livestock.

WHITEWATER CANAL STATE MEMORIAL, Franklin County, E central Indiana, 2 mi. W of Metamora. The Whitewater Canal, part of a vast and ambitious government waterways project, was built between 1836 and 1845. It cost Indiana $1,165,000 to build a total length of 76 mi. of canal between Hagerstown, Indiana, and Elizabethtown, Ohio. Along the way were seven feeder dams and 56 canal locks, with a total fall of 490 feet. As with other canal projects in the area at this time, the Whitewater Canal suffered great financial losses due to mismanagement, floods, and the coming of the railroads. The Whitewater Valley area was an early crossroads for pioneer settlements in Indiana which followed centuries of Indian occupation as evidenced by the Indian mounds which can be found throughout the valley. The Whitewater Canal Memorial preserves a 14-mi. segment of the canal, extending from the Laurel Feeder Dam to Brookville. An operating gristmill at Metamora houses a museum which overlooks the sluiceway, and the canal boat "Valley Belle" provides rides through the Millville Lock and the shed aqueduct.

WHITEWATER RIVER. in Indiana and Ohio, formed by the headstreams N of Connersville, Indiana. It flows generally in a S and SE direction past Brookville and on to the Great Miami River in Hamilton, Ohio. The total length is 70 mi. Along its course are remnants of the old Whitewater Canal (*q.v.*), which has been preserved for 14 mi. near Metamora.

WHITEWATER STATE PARK, Union County, S central Indiana, 2 mi. S of Liberty. The park covers 1,515 acres of woods and water. It is dedicated to those men and women who served in World War II. A 200-acre lake provides boating, fishing, and swimming. Other recreational facilities include a modern campground and a riding stable.

WHITING, city (pop. 7,247), Lake County, NW Indiana, zip 46394, on Lake Michigan near Chicago, Illinois. Whiting was founded in 1885 and for many years remained a predominantly German settlement. It incorporated in 1903 but remained economically stagnant until 1934 when the Carbide and Carbon Chemicals Corporation built its plant right across from that of Standard Oil, the town's only enterprise at the time. Today, Whiting remains an industrial community, part of the vast Calumet district which includes Gary, Hammond, and East Chicago. Large chemical plants and oil refineries can be seen for miles.

Of note is the Memorial Community House (1938), built with funds contributed by John D. Rockefeller and Standard Oil. Recreational facilities can be found at Whiting Park on Lake Michigan. The park offers tennis, picnicking, and fishing.

WHITLEY, county (pop. 23,395), NE Indiana, area 336 sq.mi., drained by the Blue and Eel rivers. The first white settlers arrived in the early 1820s to find a fertile land of woods and lakes inhabited mainly by Miami and Potawatomi Indians. The land was ceded to the white settlers by treaties with the Indians.

For many years lumbering was the county's main source of occupation, but as the timber was exhausted, agriculture began to predominate. Livestock, grain, truck, poultry, and soybeans are the main products. Manufacturing is prevalent in Columbia City, the county seat, and South Whitley. The leading industries make electrical wire assemblies and electronic components.

WILBUR WRIGHT STATE MEMORIAL, Henry County, E central Indiana, 2 mi. N of Millville. The memorial marks the site of the birthplace of Wilbur Wright (Aug. 16, 1867) co-inventor, with his brother Orville, of the airplane. The farmhouse was destroyed by fire in 1884. The monument is in the shape of a propeller mounted on a stone base.

WILBUR WRIGHT STATE RECREATION AREA, Henry County, E central Indiana, 2 mi. N of New Castle and near the Wilbur Wright birthplace (*q.v.*). Covering 850 acres, the recreation area provides water sports on the adjacent stream and has facilities for camping, picnicking, and hiking.

WILKINSON, town (pop. 480), Hancock County, central Indiana, zip 46186, 31 mi. ENE of Indianapolis in an agricultural area noted for livestock and feed grains.

WILLIAMS DAM STATE FISHING AREA, Lawrence County, S Indiana, 10 mi. SW of Bedford in a scenic hilly and wooded area. 21 acres of land facilitate fishing on the adjacent White River, as well as camping and boating.

WILLIAMSPORT, town (pop. 1,661), seat of Warren County, W Indiana, zip 47993, on the Wabash River, and 24 mi. WSW of Lafayette. The town was settled in 1829, and was named after Gen. William Henry Harrison, who owned the land on and around the present site. A spur of the Erie Canal was built to the town, bringing business to local merchants. In 1856, the Wabash Railroad arrived and consequently diverted traffic from the river and canal. The town boasts a lumber mill and poultry hatchery. Near the business district, the waters of Fall Creek drop over a 75 ft. sandstone ledge to form the Williamsport Falls.

WILLOW SLOUGH STATE RECREATION AREA, Newton County, NW Indiana, 4 mi. NW of Morocco. The recreation area centers on the 1,500-acre Willow Slough which has a maximum depth of 8 ft. The entire state land area covers 9,280 acres and has an abundance of woods, water, and wildlife. There is open hunting during the fall season, at which time the lake is closed to water recreation. Recreational facilities include a campground, picnic area, boat rental, beach, and licensed fishing.

WINAMAC, town (pop. 2,341), seat of Pulaski County, NW Indiana, zip 46996, on the Tippecanoe River, and 45 mi. NNE of Lafayette. Winamac was founded in 1835 and was named for Chief Winamac, a Potawatomi Indian who made a stand against white soldiers in the Battle of Tippecanoe. The site of the present town was once a Miami village, but the land was later ceded to the Potawatomis.

Winamac is a trade center for livestock, poultry, grain, and soybeans, and manufactures canned goods, clothing, and lumber. The Tippecanoe River flows through the town with the Tippecanoe River State Park (*q.v.*) on its northern bank. Five mi. SW of town is the Moss Creek Country Club.

WINCHESTER, city (pop. 5,493), seat of Randolph County, E Indiana, zip 47394, on the West Fork of the White River, and 20 mi. E of Muncie. Winchester was founded in 1812 and has become a leading grain and livestock shipping center for the area. Manufactures include glass, machine-shop products, furniture, and gloves. Northwest of the city are the Fudge Indian Mounds which were excavated in 1931 and found to be contemporaneous with the Adena culture of AD 400-800. Artifacts include skeletons, copper bracelets, and spear points.

Recreational facilities can be found at nearby Mont Longnecker Lake. The city is also the site of the Winchester Speedway, "The World's Fastest Half Mile High Bank Asphalt Track."

WINDFALL, town (pop. 946), Tipton County, central Indiana, zip 46076, 12 mi. SE of Kokomo in an agricultural area noted for livestock and feed grains.

WINGATE, town (pop. 437), Montgomery County, W Indiana, zip 47994, 14 mi. NW of Crawfordsville in an agricultural area noted for livestock and feed grains.

WINONA LAKE, resort town (pop. 2,811), Kosciusko County, N Indiana, zip 46590, on Winona Lake, just SE of Warsaw. The town holds an annual Chautauqua Bible conference and is the scene of many summer religious activities. Evangelist Billy Sunday and singer Homer Rodeheaver were among the town's noted citizens. The Billy Sunday Tabernacle, with a seating capacity of 7,500 people was built by the evangelist.

WINSLOW, mining town (pop. 1,030), Pike County, SW Indiana, zip 47598, on the Patoka River, and 26 mi. SE of Vincennes in an agricultural and coal mining region.

WOLCOTT, town (pop. 894), White County, NW central Indiana, zip 47995, 26 mi. W of Logansport in an agricultural area noted for livestock and feed grains. The town is a manufacturing center for tile and bricks.

WOLCOTTVILLE, town (pop. 915), on the Noble and La Grange county lines, NE Indiana, zip 46795, 34 mi. NNW of Fort Wayne in a lake resort and agricultural area noted for feed grains and livestock. Wolcottville was settled in the early 1800s and grew up around a gristmill, sawmill, tan yard, and distillery. Chain O'Lakes State Park (*q.v.*) is nearby.

WOLF LAKE, town (pop. 400), Noble County, N Indiana, zip 46796, 7 mi. S of Albion in an agricultural and dairying area. The town is a manufacturing and trade center for pallets, lumber, wood products, tubular heaters for the refrigeration industry, automobile parts, and tires.

WOODBURN, town (pop. 688), Allen County, NE Indiana, zip 46797, 17 mi. E of Fort Wayne in an agricultural and dairying area. The town is a manufacturing center for tires, crushed stone, agricultural lime, light production machinery, wire-drawing dies, and petroleum products.

WORTHINGTON, town (pop. 1,691), Greene County, SW Indiana, zip 47471, on the West Fork of the White River, and 33 mi. SE of Terre Haute. The town owes its existence to the Wabash and Erie Canal, but declined after the canal project was abandoned. Worthington is an agricultural trade center for feed grains and livestock.

WYANDOTTE, town (pop. 50), Crawford County, SE Indiana, zip 47179, 12 mi. W of Corydon. Wyandotte became known for its two large limestone caverns, Little and Big Wyandotte. Big Wyandotte Cave is the second largest cave in the U.S. and was named for the Wyandotte Indians who used it for shelter and for the mining of alabaster deposits. There are 23 mi. of explored passageways in Big Wyandotte Cave, but Little Wyandotte, although an entity in itself, is believed to be an extension of the larger cave. Big Wyandotte has five levels and the largest underground room of any cavern in the world. Its circumference reaches 1/4 mile and it has a height of 200 feet.

Scientists feel that the cave was used by Indians as far back as 7000 BC, primarily for shelter. The War of 1812 saw it being used as a source of saltpeter which was used in the manufacturing of gunpowder. A new entrance was found in 1850, and visitors began flocking to it in order to view its varied formations which included stalagmites, stalagtites, helictites, gypsum flowers, and epsom salt crystals. Both Little and Big Wyandotte caves are dry, maintain a year-round temperature of 52°F, and have been modernized with electric lighting by the Indiana Department of Natural Resources which purchased the caves and surrounding forest lands in 1966.

YELLOWWOOD STATE FOREST, Brown County, S Indiana, just N of Belmont. Yellowwood State Forest encompasses 22,451 acres of forest and is located in one of the most scenic parts of Indiana. Fall colors bring thousands of visitors to the area, which is also a favorite with artists. Excellent facilities for camping, hiking, picnicking, fishing, and hunting are available. There is a 135-acre lake which is used for water recreation.

YEOMAN, town (pop. 145), Carroll County, NW central Indiana, zip 47997, 20 mi. NNE of Lafayette, near Freeman Lake and in an agricultural area noted for livestock and feed grains.

YORKTOWN, town (pop. 1,673), Delaware County, E central Indiana, zip 47396, on the West Fork of the White River and 6 mi. W of Muncie in an agricultural area noted for livestock and feed grains.

ZIONSVILLE, town (pop. 1,875), Boone County, central Indiana, zip 46077, on small Eagle Creek, and 14 mi. NNW of Indianapolis. Zionsville is a farming community in a rich dairy and livestock area. Its main business enterprise is the manufacturing of pharmaceuticals. At the Lions Club Memorial is a stone marker which indicates where Abraham Lincoln spoke from the back of a train platform on Feb. 11, 1861 on a stop enroute to his inauguration. The town was recently remodeled into a colonial village complete with gas lights and fancy trimmings.

* * *

Limberlost State Memorial, a tribute to Hoosier authoress Gene Stratton Porter.

Visitor's center of the Lincoln Memorial at Lincoln City.

476 The Delta Queen, one of the last remaining stern-wheelers, makes a regular stop at Madison.

Ingrid Eklov Jonsson

Business district of Logansport, the seat of Cass County.

Indiana Department of Commerce

International Friendship Gardens, with flower displays
from around the world, are located near Michigan City.

478

The Culbertson Mansion (1868), one of the many historic buildings of New Albany's riverboat era.

Flood tower of the Mississinewa Dam and Reservoir.

Indiana Department of Commerce
The Roofless Church, New Harmony.

Indiana Department of Commerce
The Cannelton Locks on the Ohio River.

The Mecca Covered Bridge (1873) in Parke County.

Barge traffic on the Ohio River.

Ingrid Eklov Jonsson

The Potawatomi Inn, Pokagon State Park.

Indiana Department of Commerce

The double-lane toboggan slide in northern Indiana's Pokagon State Park.

482

Maple syrup tapping is popular in Spring.

Cataract Falls in Richard Lieber State Park.

grid Eklov Jonsson

Atop the Salamonie Dam in Jay County.

grid Eklov Jonsson

Billie Creek Village, a restored turn-of-the century community, Rockville.

The archabbey at Saint Meinrad's Benedictine monastery.

Aerial view of Salem with Washington County
Courthouse in the center foreground.

Cool ravines along Sugar Creek in Shades State Park.   485

486   The Rimstone Cascade in Squire Boone Caverns near Corydon.

The Rock of Ages Column in Squire Boone Caverns near Corydon. 487

The main library, Notre Dame University, South Bend.

Athletic and Convocation Center, Notre Dame University, South Bend.

The "Indy 500" race at the Indianapolis Speedway.

Lower Hamer House at the restored pioneer
village in Spring Mill State Park.

Ingrid Eklöv Jonsson

Vigo County Courthouse, Terre Haute.

The 1816 grist mill in Spring Mill State Park.

Tipton County Courthouse, Tipton.   491

STRICKEN DOWN IN THE
PERFORMANCE OF DUTY

In tribute to
Major Joseph Hamilton Daviess,
Grand Master of Masons in Kentucky,
who fell in battle here, and
to the many Freemasons
of General Harrison's command
whose valor is held
in grateful remembrance.

Indiana Department of Commerce

The 100-foot shaft erected in memory of the slain
soldiers of the Battle of Tippecanoe in 1811.

Shaded ravine in Turkey Run State Park.

Boat trips are frequently taken into Twin Caves in Spring Mill State Park.

494   Prehistoric Indian mounds near Vincennes.

Wabash County Courthouse, Wabash.   495

496

Ingrid Eklov Jonsson

The Virgil I. Grissom State Memorial and Visitor's Center in Spring Mill State Park.

Ingrid Eklov Jonsson

Seal of Wabash, the world's first electrically lighted city.

Rural setting in agricultural Wells County.

Memorial Center of Purdue University in West Lafayette. 497

Canal boat rides are still given through the locks and the shed aqueduct, Metamora and Whitewater Canal.

498   Limestone formations in Wyandotte Cave.

Bibliography

GENERAL

1. Ade, George, *Hoosier Handbook,* Indiana Society of Chicago (1911)
2. Alsberg, Henry, *The American Guide,* Hastings House, New York, N.Y. (1949)
3. Carmony, Donald F., Indiana, *A Self-Appraisal*, Indiana University Press, Bloomington, Ind. (1966)
4. Leary, Edward A., *Indiana Almanac and Fact Book,* Ed Leary and Associates, Indianapolis, Ind. (1969)
5. Liebowitz, Irving, *My Indiana,* Prentice-Hall, Englewood Cliffs, N.J. (1964)
6. McLaughlin, Robert, *The Heartland,* Time-Life Books, New York, N.Y. (1967)
7. Nolan, Jeanette C., *Indiana,* Coward-McCann-Geoghegan, Inc. New York, N.Y. (1971)
8. Writers' Program of the Work Projects Administration, *Indiana, A Guide to the Hoosier State,* reprint, Somerset Publishers, St. Clair Shores, Mich. (1973)

DESCRIPTION AND TRAVEL

1. American Automobile Association, *Northeastern Camping,* AAA, Falls Church, Va. (1974)
2. American Automobile Association, *Tour Guide-Great Lakes,* AAA, Falls Church, Va. (1975-1976)
3. Cook, William and Gayle, *A Guide to Southern Indiana,* William and Gayle Cook, Bloomington, Ind. (1974)
4. Division of Tourism, "Calendar of Events" Department of Commerce booklet, Indianapolis (1973, 1974, 1975, 1976)
5. Hill, Herbert R., "Grissom Memorial is State's Newest", *Outdoor Indiana,* vol. 36, no. 9, Indiana Department of Natural Resources (Nov. 1971)

6. Kingsbury, Robert C., *An Atlas of Indiana,* Department of Geography, Indiana University Press, Bloomington, Ind. (1970)
7. Mobil Travel Guide, *Great Lakes Area,* Rand McNally, Chicago, Ill. (1974)
8. Reader's Digest *America the Beautiful,* Pleasantville, N.Y. (1970)

GEOLOGY

1. Agricultural Experiment Station, *The Story of Indiana Soils,* Purdue University Special Circular no. 1, Lafayette (1944)
2. Dunbar, Carl O., *Historical Geology,* John Wiley & Sons, Inc. New York, N.Y. (1960)
3. Fowke, Gerard, *The Evolution of the Ohio River,* Hollenbeck Press, Indianapolis, Ind. (1933)
4. Greenberg, Seymour, et al., *Guide to Some Minerals and Rocks in Indiana,* Geological Survey, Bloomington, Ind. (1958)
5. Leet, Don L., and Judson, Sheldon, *Physical Geology,* Prentice-Hall Inc., Englewood Cliff, N.J. (1959)
6. Powell, Richard, *Caves of Indiana,* Geological Survey, Bloomington, Inc. (1961)
7. Schultz, Gwen, *Glaciers and the Ice Age,* Holt, Rinehart, and Winston, Inc., New York, N.Y. (1963)

PREHISTORY AND INDIANS

1. Barce, Elmore, *The Land of the Miamis,* Benton Review Shop, Fowler, Inc. (1922)
2. Black, Glenn A., "Angel Site", Indiana Historical Society, Indianapolis, Ind. (1967)
3. Dorwin, John T., *Fluted Points and Late Pleistocene Geochronology in Indiana,* vol. IV, no. 3, Prehistory Research, Series (out of print)
4. Hodge, Frederick Webb, ed., *Handbook of American Indians North of Mexico,* Government Printing Office, 2 vols. Washington, D.C. (1912)
5. Indiana Historical Bureau, "Little Turtle" (publ. unknown)
6. Lilly, Eli, *Prehistoric Antiquities of Indiana,* Indiana Historical Society, Indianapolis, Ind. (1937)

7. Oskinson, John M., *Tecumseh and His Times,* C.P. Putnam's Sons, new York, N.Y. (1938)
8. Peckham, Howard H., *Pontiac and the Indian Uprising,* 1947

HISTORY

1. Carmony, Donald F., ed., *Handbook on Indiana History,* Indiana Sesquicentennial Commission, Indianapolis, Ind. (1966)
2. Cauthorn, George S., *A History of the City of Vincennes,* Margaret Cauthorn, Publishers, Terre Haute, Inc. (Oct. 15, 1901)
3. Clark, George Rogers, *The Capture of Old Vincennes,* (reprint), Bobbs-Merrill (1927)
4. Cottman, George S., *Centennial History and Handbook of Indiana,* Max R. Hyman, Publishers, Indianapolis, Ind. (1915)
5. Funk, Arville L., *Squire Boone in Indiana,* Adams Press, Chicago, Ill. (1974)
6. Henricks, Sylvia, "The Story of Acton Camp Ground", *Indiana Magazine of History,* vol. LXVI, no. 4, Indiana Historical Society, Indianapolis, Ind. (Dec. 1970)
7. Indiana Department of Conservation, "Tippecanoe Battlefield" Memorial Publication no. 8, (date unknown)
8. Peat, Wilbur D., *Indiana Houses of the Nineteenth Century,* Indiana Historical Society, Indianapolis, Ind. (1962)
9. Smith, William Henry, *History of the State of Indiana,* vol. 1, vol. 2, Western Publishing Company, Indianapolis, Ind. (1903)
10. Wilson, William E., *Indiana, A History,* Indiana University Press, Bloomington, Ind. (1966)
11. Woschitz, Frank, ed., *Madison County Sesquicentennial,* Anderson Chamber of Commerce (1973)

NATURAL RESOURCES AND THE ECONOMY

1. Indiana State Chamber of Commerce, *The Indiana Industrial Directory,* Indianapolis, Ind. (1974, 1975)
2. Montogomery, Robert, ed., *The Hoosier Annual,* vol. 3, Finance Advisory Commitee (1965, 1966)
3. Udall, Stewart L., *Natural Resources of Indiana,* U.S. Department of the Interior

TRANSPORTATION

1. Burns, Lee, *The National Road in Indiana,* Indiana Historical Society, vol. 13, no. 1, Indianapolis, Ind. (1938)
2. Cain, Mary Helen, *Travel in Indiana Long Ago,* Indiana Historical Bureau, no. 4
3. Garman, Harry O., *Whitewater Canal,* Indianapolis, Ind. (1944)
4. State Highway Commission, Indiana, *Official Highway Map,* (1976) published annually
5. State Highway Commission, *Status of Interstate Highways in Indiana,* Indianapolis, Ind. (1969)
6. Vernon, Edward, *Travelers' Official Railway Guide for the United States and Canada,* National Railway Publication, New York, N.Y. (1969)
7. Wilkinson, Norman B., *The Conestoga Wagon,* Indiana Historical Bureau, no. 5

PEOPLE AND POPULATION

1. Barnhart, John D., and Carmony, Donald F. *Indiana from Frontier to Industrial Commonwealth,* Lewis Historical Publishing Company Ind., New York, 1954, vol. 2
2. Barnhart, John D., and Riker, Dorothy L., *Indiana to 1816: THE Colonial Period,* Indiana Historical Bureau & Indiana Historical Society, Indianapolis, 1971
3. Bureau of the Census, *1970 Population Reports,* Government Printing Office, Washington, D.C.
4. Carmony, Donald F., *A Brief History of Indiana,* Indiana Historical Bureau, (1966)
5. Davidson, Mabel E., *Legend and Lore from America's Crossroads,* Publishers Printing House, Berne, Indiana, (1971)
6. Leary, Edward A., *The Nineteenth State, Indiana,* Ed Leary & Associates, Indianapolis, (1966)
7. Lockridge, Ross F., *The Story of Indiana,* Harlow Publishing Company, Oklahoma City and Chattanooga, 1958 (Third Edition)
8. Nicholson, Meredith, *The Hoosiers,* MacMillan Co., New York, N.Y. (1900)
9. Phillips, Clifton J., *Indiana in Transition, The Emergence of an Industrial Commonwealth,* Indiana Historical Bureau & Indiana Historical Society, Indianapolis, (1968)

10. Thomas, Bill, "Amishville", *Indiana History Bulletin,* Indiana Historical Bureau (Sept. 1969)
11. Thornburgh, Emma Lou, *Indiana in the Civil War Era,* 1850-1880, Indiana Historical Bureau & Indiana Historical Society, (1965)

ADMINISTRATION

1. Indiana Department of Commerce, *Indiana State Government Guide.* Indianapolis, Ind. (1973)
2. Indiana Sesquicentennial Commission, *A Guide,* Indianapolis, Ind. (1967)
3. Sikes, Pressly Spinks, *The State Government of Indiana,* Principia Press, Bloomington, Ind. (1937)

THE SOCIAL MILIEU

1. Barnhart, John D., & Carmony, Donald F., *Indiana from Frontier to Industrial Commonwealth,* Lewis Historical Publishing Company Inc., New York, vol. II (1954)
2. Leary, Edward A., *The Nineteenth State, Indiana,* Ed Leary & Associates, Indianapolis (1966)
3. Lockridge, Ross F., *The Story of Indiana,* Harlow Publishing Corporation, Oklahoma City and Chattanooga, (1958) (Third Edition)
4. Thornburgh, Emma Lou, *Indiana in the Civil War Era,* 1850-1880, *The History of Indiana,* vol. 3, Indiana Historical Bureau & Indiana Historical Society, Indianapolis (1965)

BIOGRAPHY

1. Coleman, McAlister, *Eugene V. Debs, A Man Unafraid,* Greenberg, New York, N.Y. (1930)
2. Dickey, Marcus, *The Maturity of James Whitcomb Riley,* Bobbs-Merrill, Indianapolis, Ind. (1919)
3. Indiana Historical Bureau, *George Rogers Clark,* Indiana Heroes for Young Hoosiers, no. 1
4. Indiana Historical Bureau, *William Henry Harrison,* Indiana Heroes for Young Hoosiers, no. 3
5. Thompson, Charles N., *Sons of the Wilderness, John and William Conner,* Indianapolis, Ind. (1937)

Index

Page numbers in italic indicate photograph locations.

"Abe Martin," 251
abrasives, 82
Academy of Music, 157
Acton, 262
Adams, Thomas H., 178
Adams County, 18, 28, 32, 262,
    263, 270, 298, 322, 378, 394
Ade, George, 60, 184, 251, 252,
    276, 367, 382
Adena culture, 34, 36
Administration of Indiana, 129-40
administrative agencies
    state, 141-53
    local, 153
Administrative Building Council,
    147
administrative officers, of state
    government, 131-32
admission to Union, 240
Advance, 262
aeronautics, 152, 215
Aeronautics Commission of
    Indiana, 152
age, median, 25
agencies, administrative
    local, 153
    state, 141-53
agriculture, 91-93, 179
    cattle, 92
    and climate, 87
    crops, 91-92
    Evansville/area, 309
    farm employment, 93
    Grange movement, 248
    growing season, 20
    Indian, 39,63
    poultry, 91, 92
Air Force bases, 151
Air National Guard, 150-51

airlines, 126-27
airports, 127
alabaster deposits, 473
Albany, 262
Albion, 262
Alcoa, 309
Alcoholic Beverage Commission,
    152
Akron, 262
Alexander, 251
Alexandria, 262
Alfordsville, 263
Algonquian language, 39
Alice Adams, 209
Alice of Old Vincennes, 59
Allegheny Airlines, 126, 127
Allen, John, 263
Allen County, 18, 28, 32, 72, 263,
    304, 313, 325, 331, 357, 359,
    378, 395, 405, 472
    courthouse, 346
Allison, 252
Altona, 263
Ambia, 263
Amboy, 263
amendments
    process for, 130
    14th, 248
    15th, 248
    25th, 185
    26th, 185
American Airlines, 126, 127
American Athletic Union, 170
American Baptist Convention, 68
American Basketball Association,
    170
American Circus Company, 254
American Federation of Labor,
    162, 249

American Fletcher National Bank, 159

American Fur Company, 438

American Legion, 201, 253, 256

American Railway Union, 109, 162, 191, 250

American Revolution, 189, 213, 236, 237

American Tragedy, An, 254

Amish, 335, 339
  customs and language, 70, 263, 270
  settlements in north-east Indiana, 5, 25, 402, 437

Amish Acres, 25

Amishville, 263, 270, 335

Amo, 263

Amtrak, 125

Anchor Industries, 104

Ancient Order of United Workmen, 249

Anderson, Chief, 263

Anderson, 37, 69, 73, 78, 125, 241, 251, 263, 304, 336
  population, 32

Anderson College, 264

Andrews, 264

Angel Mounds, 62

Angel Mounds State Memorial, 7, 265, 307, *335*

Angola, 265

animals, 21, 22, 83, 86

Apollo, 187, 194

apples, 91

Appleseed, Johnny, 189, 314
  gravesite, *347*

Aquifers, 89

Arcadia, 265

Arch, Alexander D., 252

archaeology, 34-40, 62, 264, 265, 298, 307

Archaic Stage, 34

Architects Registration Board, 152

architecture
  building stone, 81
  Beverly Shores, 271
  Columbus, 8, 290-91
  of courthouses, 5
  Evansville, 309
  Grouseland, 46, 458
  Indianapolis, 6, 158, 159-60
  Madison, 383
  New Albany, 403
  post World War II, 183
  See also names of houses

area, 1, 9

Argos, 266

Arkla Air Conditioning, 309

Arlington, 266

Army Finance Center, 256

Army National Guard, 150-51

Art Association of Indianapolis, 249

artesian springs, 89, 387

Article IX of Constitution, 50

artifacts, Indian, 34-38, 265

artists' colony, 8

arts
  Indian, 35, 37
  in Indianapolis, 6
  see also cultural activities; cultural institutions

Arts Commission, The, 147

ash, 94

Ashley, 266

astronaut, 187, 194

Atheneum, 6, 157, 167

"Athens of the Prairie," 290

Athletic Commission, 147

Atlanta, 266

Atlatl, 35

Atterbury State Fish and Game Area, 304

Attica, 266

Attorney General, term and duties of, 132

Atwood, 266
Auburn, 5, 267, 299
auditor
    county, 133
    state, term and duties of, 132
Aurora, 8, 267
Austin, 267
Australian ballot, 250
authors, 57, 59-60, 71-72, 167
auto racing, 5, 59, 79, 123, 257,
        259, 440, 489
    see also Indianapolis Motor
        Speedway
Avilla, 267
Avoca, 267
automobile industry
    in Anderson, 264
    in Auburn, 5, 267
    automobile design by Elwood
        Haynes, 58, 199-200
    classic names in, 5, 58-59, 99,
        267
    in Connersville, 292
    in Indianapolis, 58, 161
    in Kokomo, 58, 99, 199, 251
    in South Bend, 5, 99, 244, 439
Avoco State Fish Hatchery, 267

Badollet, John, 50
Baer Field, 151
Bainbridge, 268
Ball Brothers, 250, 252, 400
Ball STate Teachers College, 253
Ball State University, 145, 253,
        401
banking, 100, 161, 240, 242, 244,
        245
Baptists, 68
Bargersville, 268
Bartholomew County, 28, 268,
        288, 290, 304, 305, 332, 358,
        366
Barton, John J., 259

baseball, 59
basketball, 59
Bass, 86, 267
Bass Lake, 268
Bass Lake Hatchery, 268
Bass Lake State Beach, 268
Batesville, 268
Battle of Brandywine, 213
Battle of Buena Vista, 55
Battle of Corydon, 293
Battle of Fallen Timbers, 39, 45,
        46, 213, 214, 238, 314
Battle Ground, 268
Battle of Mississinewa, 384
Battle of Pogue's Run, 247
Battle of the Thames, 47, 211
Battle of Tippecanoe, 5, 47, 197,
        210, 239, 269, 441, 448, 449,
        471, *492*
Bayh, Birch, Jr., 185-86, 257
Bear Creek Canyon, 266
Beatles, 258
Beaver Dam, 69
Beck, George, 269
Beckner-Nelson house, 266
Beck's Mills, 269
Bedford, 81, 95, 269, *337, 338*
Beech, 94, 287, 293, 298; 303, 311
Beech Grove, 162, 269
Beecher, Henry Ward, 68, 243
beef cattle, 91, 92
Bell Creek, 299
Belleville, 269
Ben Hur, 55, 59, 167, 212, 249
Ben Hur Museum, 294
Benedictine Saint Meinrad
        Archabbey, 431
Benjamin Harrison Memorial
        Home, 269-70
Benton, Thomas H., 270, 272
Benton County, 28, 263, 270, 274,
        302, 316, 411, 412
Bentonville, 270

Berne, 270, 339
Berry, John, 264
Bethany Assembly, 69
Bethlehem Steel, 257, 420
Beveridge, Albert J., 60, 253, 254
Beverly Shores, 270-71
Bicknell, 271
Biddle, Judge Horace, 271
Biddle's Island, 271
Bierce, Ambrose, 306
Big Bayou River, 328
Big Blue River, 271
Big Fisherman, The, 192
Big Sandy River, 409
Big Wyandotte Cave, 473, *498*
Bigger, Samuel, 53
Billie Creek Village, *483*
bills, in General Assembly, 132
biographees, 184-215
Birch, 94
Birch Creek, 274, 287
birds
  game, 86
  state, 2
Birdseye, 271
Black, Charles, 251
Black, Glenn, A., 265
black gum tree, 21
Black Hawk War, 242
Black Horse Troop, 296
Black River, 323, 328
Blackford, Judge Isaac, 271
Blackford County, 28, 271, 301,
  332, 396
Blacks
  in Gary, 113
  and Indiana Colonization
    Society, 241
  location of, 27
  number of, 25, 65, 73,
  population growth rate of, 74
  rights of, 247
  and school segregation, 142

bladderwort, 21
blast furnace, 277
bloc voting, 259
Bloomfield, 272, 326
Bloomingdale, 272
Bloomington, 72, 81, 95, 114,
  125, 127, 241, 272
Blue Jacket, 45, 210
Blue Lake, 286
blue laws, 245
Blue River, 272, 294
blueberries, 21, 91
bluegill, 267, 268
Bluffton, 272-73, *339*
Board of County Commissioners,
  133, 135
Board of Town Trustees, 135
boating, *see* state parks, state
  recreation areas
"Boatload of Knowledge," 52,
  176, 241
Bobbs-Merrill Co., Inc., 168, 249
bog willow, 21
Boggstown, 273
bogs, 10, 82
Boiler and Pressure Vessel
  Inspection Board, 152
Bolton, Sarah, 244
Bonesteel, Luke, 290
Bonneyville Mill, 275
Boone, Daniel, 186, 273, 274
Boone, Squire, 186-87, 442
Boone County, 23, 28, 33, 68, 99,
  262, 273, 304, 363, 377, 448,
  452, 468, 474
Boone Grove, 273
Boone's Pond State Fishing Area,
  273
Boonville, 273
Booth Tarkington Civic Theatre,
  167
Borden, 274
Borman, Frank, 187, *217*

Boston, 274
Boswell, 274
boundaries, 1, 9
Bourbon, 274
bow-and-arrow hunting, 85
Bowen, Otis R., 149, 187-88, *218*, 259
Bowles, William A., 55, 56
Bowling Green, 274
Boys' School, at Plainfield, 148
Brandywine, Battle of, 213
Brandywine Creek, 326-27
Branigin, Roger D., 61, 259
Brazil, 274-75, 287
Bremen, 275
Bridgeport, 275
bridges, 6, 59, 280, *356*, 395, 414, *480*
Bridgeton, 275
bridle paths, 85
Bright, Jessie D., 53
Brimfield, 275
Bringhurst, 275
Bristol, 275
Bristow, 275
British in Indiana, 41, 43, 63, 67
Broadview, 275
Bronson Cave, 276
Brook, 276
Brooklyn, 276
Brookstone, 276
Brookville, 49, 71, 239, 276
Brookville Reservoir, 277
Brown, Jacob, 277
Brown, Mordecai, 59
Brown, O. V., home of 296
Brown County, 8, 13, 28, 93, 277, 333, 402, 446, 465, 473
Brown County Art Gallery, 402
Brown County Artists' Colony, 4o2
Brown County State Park, 85, 272, 280

Brownsburg, 278
Brownstone Hills, 13
Brownstown, 47, 71, 278
Brownstown State Fishing Area, 278
Bruceville, 278
Bryan, William Jennings, 389
Bryant, 279
Buck Creek, 279, 299
Buena Vista, Battle of, 55
Buffalo Trace, 269, 279
buffalofish, 94
building industry, 81
building stone, 81
Bunker Hill, 279
Burch Plow, 309
Bureau of Motor Vehicles, 149
burial mounds, Indian, *see* Indian burial mounds
Burket, 279
Burlington, Chief, 279
Burlington, 279
Burnettsville, 279
Burney, 280
Burns Ditch, 257
Burns Harbor, 4, 102, 105, 280
Burns Waterway Harbor, 127
buses, 123, 256
Bush Creek State Fish and Wildlife Area, 280
busing, 166
Butler, Amos, 276
Butler, 280
Butler Theatron, 167
Butler University, 57, 161, 165, 167, 245
Butlerville, 278

cabbage, 91
Cabin Creek, 242
Calhoun, John C., 53
Calumet district, 98, 280, 303, 321, 330, 469
Calumet Extension Center of

Indiana University, 303
Cambrian Period, 16
Cambridge City, 4, 280
Camby, 281
Camden, 281
Camp Atterbury, 151
camp meetings, religious, 67, 69, 70
Camp Morton, 246
Campbell, John B., 239
Campbellsburg, 281
canals, 54, 118-20, 156, 241, 243, 245, 277, 308, 314, 383-84, 468-69, *498*
Cannelburg, 281
Cannelton, 242, 281-82
Cannelton Locks, *479*
canning industry, 267
canoeing, 6
Canterbury College, 297
Capehart, Homer, 257
capital
  territorial, 46, 49, 71
  state, 1, 25, 50, 239, 240, 241
Carbide and Carbon Chemicals Corporation, 469
carbon, 282
cardinal, 2
Carlisle, 282
Carlos, 282
Carmel, 25, 282
Carmichael, Hoagy, 188, 253
carp, 94
Carpenters Union, 162
Carroll County, 28, 258, 275, 279, 281, 282, 299, 312, 427, 474
  courthouse, *343*
carrots, 91
Carswell, G. Harrold, 185-86
Carthage, 283
Cass, Lewis, 283
Cass County, 28, 283, 320, 380, 410, 429, 461

Castleton, 283
Cataract Lake, 289
catfish, 86, 94
Cat's Cradle, 211
cattle, 91, 92
Cave River Valley, 281
caves
  location of, 13
  Marengo, 11, 294
  Spring Mill State Park, 278, 451, *494*
  Squire Boone Caverns, 332, 442, *486, 487*
  Wyandotte, 11, 294, 473, *498*
Cayuga, 283
Cedar Creek, 299
Cedar Grove, 284
Cedar Lake, 283
celery, 91
centennial year, 252
Center Township, 25
Centerpoint, 284
Centerville, 4, 284
central agricultural plain, 17, 18
Central Canal, 54
Central Indiana, 5-6
Central Normal College, 297
Central Public Library, Indianapolis, *353*
ceramics
  manufacture, 82
  see also pottery
Chaffee, Roger B., 258
Chain O'Lakes States Park, 262, 284
Chalmers, 284
Chandler, 284
Chapman, George, 53
Chapman, J. Wilbur, 68
Chapman, John, 189, 314
Charlestown, 71, 239, 285
Charlottesville, 285
Chautauqua, 389

Chesterfield, 70, 285
Chesterton, 285
Chicago, 4, 5
Chicago, Indianapolis, and
    Louisville Railroad, 125
Chicago-Gary-—Hammong-East
    Chicago area, 303
Children's Museum,
    Indianapolis, 167
Chinook salmon, 94
Chippewa Indians, 45
Chrisney, 286
Christ Church Cathedral, 159
Christian Church, 68
Christian Science, 70
Christian Theological Seminary,
    166
Christian Theological Seminary
    Repertory Theater, 167
Chronology, of Indiana, 235-60
Church of Christ, 68
Church of God, 69, 264
church membership, 68
churches, *see* names of
    denominations
Churubusco, 286
Cicero, 286
Cincinnati, population of Indiana
    portion, 32, 73
Cincinnati Arch, 16
circuit courts, 137
circuit-riders, 67
circuses, 416
cities, 1, 26
    population of, 25, 32-33, 71, 72
Citizens Gas & Coke Utility, 164
city charters, 73
city council, 134, 135
city government, 134-35
City Hall, 167
City Market, Indianapolis, 6, 157
City-County Building, 157, 159
civil defense, 151, 256

civil rights, 152, 185, 198
Civil War, 212, 246-47
    Corydon, Battle of, 293
    impact on Hoosier society, 180
    loss of life in, 65
    period, in Indiana, 55-57
    in Vernon, 455-56
Clark, Daniel, 296
Clark, George Rogers, 7, 41-42,
    189-90, 236, 286, 287, 323,
    457, *frontispiece*
    memorial, *347*
Clark, William, 46
Clark County, 11, 23, 33, 81, 238,
    274, 285, 286, 287, 297, 365,
    434
Clark Maritime Center, 102
Clark State Forest, 286-87
Clarks Hill, 286
Clarksburg, 286
Clarksville, 42, 71, 190, 237, 287
Clay, Henry, 53, 67, 287
clay, 15, 81-82, 96
Clay City, 287
Clay County, 14-15, 28, 33, 76,
    81, 274, 282, 284, 287, 304,
    369, 420, 443
Claypool, 287
Clayton, 288
Cleary Creek, 288
Clerk, of circuit court, 133, 134,
    136
Clerk, of Supreme Court, 139
Clermont, 148, 288
Cleveland, Grover, 196
Clifford, 288
Clifty Creek, 288, 298
Clifty Falls State Park, 288
climate, 19-20
Clinton, DeWitt, 288, 289
Clinton, 289, *340*
Clinton County, 28, 288-89, 313,
    317, 368, 391, 400, 429

Cloverdale, 289
Clowes Hall, 6, 167
coal
  bituminous, 14, 76
  cannel, 281, 455
  consumption, 78
  location of, 14-15, 76-77, 95
  mining problems, 76-77
  number of mines, 94
  production, 94
  strip mining, 15, 76-78, 94-95
  uses of, 14, 78, 99
Coal City, 289
Coal Creek, 315
Coatesville, 289
Coca-Cola, 309, 454
Coffin, Levi, 316
Coffin, Tristram, 167
Coho salmon, 5, 94
coke production, 78
Cold Water Spring, 267
Colfax, Schuyler, 54
Colfax, 289
Colgate-Palmolive plant, 287
College Park, 161
colleges, *see* names of colleges
Collegeville, 289
Columbia, 290
Columbia City, 289-90, *341, 342*
Columbus, 8, 72, 98, 268, 290,
  341
Columbus Chamber of
  Commerce, 291
commerce, development of, 54
Commission of Aging and the
  Aged, 147
Common Council, 134, 135
Communist Party, 192
communities, loan fund for, 104-5
community living, 172-77
compulsory school attendance
  law, 250, 251
Concordia College, 70, 243, 315

congressmen, 48, 49
Conner, John, 292
Conner, William, 168, 264, 291
Conner Prairie Farm, 6, 168, 291,
  340
Connersville, 79, 291-92, 311
conservation, 10, 21, 77-78, 86,
  89-90, 200
conservatism, of Hoosiers, 179
consolidated schools, 256
constitution, state
  amendments, 60, 129, 130
  of 1816, 129, 144, 240, 292
  of 1851 (present) 129-40, 142,
    179-80, 244
  and judicial system, 137-40
Constitution, U.S., 248
constitutional conventions, state
  of 1816, 49-50, 174
  of 1850, 53, 244
"Constitutional Elm," 50, 292
Conteiental Trailways, 123
Converse, 292
copperheads, 55, 56
Coquillard, Alexis, 241
corn, 91, 92, 161, 262, 275
Corn Island, 287
coroner, 133, 134
corporations, 99
  and state income taxes, 108
Cortland, 292
Corunna, 292
Corydon, 49, 71, 155, 174, 239,
  292-93, *342, 486, 487*
Corydon, Battle of, 293
Corydon Capitol State Memorial,
  293
Cottonwood, 94
counties
  map, 26
  population distribution, 23
  population tables, 28-33
  see also names of counties

County Council, 133
county government
    financial powers of, 133
    officers, 133-34
County Superintendent of
    Schools, 249
Court of Appeals, 137, 138-39
courthouses, 5
Covington, 293, 315
cranberries, 21
Crandall, 293
crappies, 267
Crawford, William, 294
Crawford County, 11, 28, 294,
    303, 307, 377, 384, 392, 473
Crawford Upland, 11-13, 294-95
Crawfordsville, 54, 125, 241, 242,
    246, 262, 294, *344*
creeks, 18
crime rates, 149
Criminal Justice Planning
    Agency, 152
Criterion, 169
Cromwell, 295
crops, 39, 91-92
Crosley Fish and Wildlife Area,
    295
Crothersville, 295
Crown Point, 295
crude petroleum, 80
Cubberley, Ellwood Patterson, 265
cucumbers, 91
Culbertson Mansion, *478*
cultural activities, 167-68, 309,
    315, 447
cultural areas, 4
cultural heritage, 4-8
Culver, 296
Culver Bird Sanctuary, 296
Culver Military Academy, 296
Cumberland River, 409
Cumberland Turnpike, 117
Cummins Diesel Engine

Company, 291
Curtis Publishing Company, 169
Cynthiana, 296
cypress, southern, 21

Daily Art Collection, 272
dairy cattle, 91
dairy farming center, 266
Dale, 296
Daleville, 296
dams, 18-19, 88
Dan Patch, 59
Dana, 296
Danville, 296-97
Darlington, 297
Daviess, Joseph Hamilton, 297
Daviess County, 28, 68, 263,
    281, 297, 306, 396, 408, 419,
    463
Davis, Elmer, 60
Deam, Charles C., 21-22, *219*
Dearborn, Henry, 298
Dearborn County, 14, 23, 28, 32,
    48, 62, 267, 298, 300, 326,
    376, 397, 466
Dearborn Upland, 12, 14
death ceremonialism, Indian, 35
Debs, Eugene V., 4, 57, 109, 161,
    190-91, *220,* 245, 250, 251,
    253, 254
Decatur, Stephen, 298
Decatur, 262, 298
Decatur County, 28, 280, 286,
    298, 327, 391, 392, 406, 432,
    467
Decker, 298
deer, 86
DeKalb, Baron, 299
De Kalb County, 28, 32, 263, 267,
    280, 292, 299, 320, 430, 441,
    463
DeKalb Memorial Hospital, 267
Delaware County, 28, 33, 262,

299, 303, 322, 398, 401, 435, 474
Delaware Indian village, 263
Delaware Indians, 38, 39-40, 45, 62, 64
Delco Battery, 400
Delco Electronics plant, Kokomo, *356*
Delphi, 282, 299, *343*
Delta Airlines, 127
Delta Queen, *476*
Democratic convention, first, 241
Democratic machine, in Gary, 199
Democratic Party. *see* political party
Demotte, 300
Denver, 300
Department of Administration, 141
Department of Corrections, 148-49
Department of Defense, U.S., 151
Department of Financial Institutions, 151
Department of Insurance, 151
Department of Mental Health, 146-47
Department of Public Welfare, 146
Department of Traffic Safety and Vehicle Inspection, 150-51
DePauw, John, 50
DePauw, Washington C., 50
DePauw University, 50, 57, 242, 325-26
deputy, 300
derby, 300
desegregation, in housing, 152
Devil's Backbone, 300
Devonian Period, 16
Diamond Mineral Spring Resort, 387
Dietz Lake, 284

Dillinger, John, 154, 255, 295
Dillsboro, 300
dimension stone, 81
director of public printing, 136
Disciples of Christ, 68, 166
Distinguished Service Award, 258
Division of Labor, 147
Divisions of Probation and Adult Parole, 148
divorce laws, 181
Dixie Highway, 194
dog, domesticated by Indians, 35
Don Pierro, 236
Dorland, Annie B., 70
Douglas, Lloyd C., 60, 192, 290
drainage, 18, 87-88
effect of glaciers, 17
Drake, James P., 55
Dream Lake State Recreation Area, 297-98
Dreiser, Theodore, 4, 57, 60, *221,* 248, 254, 266
Dresser, Paul, 4, 192, 266
drift areas, 10-11, 89
droughts, 20, 87
Dubin, 300
Dubois, Toussaint, 301
Dubois, 300
Dubois County, 28, 271, 300, 301, 311, 357, 359, 362, 363, 430
courthouse, *355*
ducks, 86
Dugger, 301
Dune Acres, 301
dunelands, plants of, 21
dunes, 4-5, 10, 21, 85-86, 285, 351, 361, 390, 421
Dunkards, 69-70
Dunkirk, 301
Dunlap, 301
Dunn, Jacob Platt, 51, 64
Dunning, Paris, 53
Dunreith, 302

Dupont, 302
Du Pont, E. I., and Company, 285
Duvall, John L., 178
Dyer, 302

Eagle Creek Park, 169
Eagle Creek Reservoir, 164, 169
Earl Park, 302
Earlham, 302
Earlham College, 168, 244, 302
Earthworks, Indian, 7, 37-38
East Chicago, 73, 82, 98, 101,
    127, 302-3, *345*
  population, 33
East Gary, 303
Eastern Airlines, 126
Eaton, 250, 303
Eckerty, 303
economic legislation, 104-5
economy, 91-102, 103-14, 304
  fluctuations in, 111-12
  of Indianapolis, 156, 160-62
  policies for, 111
  regional differences in, 114
  and rural areas, 114
Edgerton, 302
Edgewood, 304
Edinburg, 304
education, 67, 142-46, 244, 252
  attainment level of population,
    143
  in 1850s, 180
  in New Harmony, 176-77
  opening of Indiana Seminary,
    241
  in state constitution, 130
  state's responsibility for, 50
Education Center, 159
Edwardsport, 304
Eel River, 18, 237
Egbert, Sherwood H., 258
Eggleston, Edward, 59, 248
eggs, 91, 92

Elberfeld, 305
election boards, 136-37
Electra Memorial, 282
electric power, 78, 99
electricity, early uses of, 57
Eli Lilly Company, 160, 168, *348*
Elizabeth, 305
Elizabethtown, 305
Elk Creek State Fish and Game
    Area, 305
Elkhart, 98, 124, 305-6
Elkhart County, 29, 70, 72, 275,
    301, 305, 306, 324, 391, 402,
    406, 461
Elkhart County River Preserve,
    306
Elkhart Institute of Technology,
    306
Elkhart River, 306
Elkhart River Hydroelectric
    Canals, 306
Ellettsville, 306
elm, 94
Elnora, 306
Elwood, 306, *344*
emigration, 65
Empire State Building, 269
employment
  farm, 93
  in industry, 98, 103, 104,
    111-12
Enabling Act, 49
energy, 99-100
English. *see* British in Indiana
Englishtown, 294, 307
environment
  forest exploitation, 83
  preserving, 77-78, 112
Environmental Protection
    Agency, 112
Equal Rights Amendment, 185
Erie Canal, 470
erosion, 13, 90

ethnic groups, 5, 25
  in Indianapolis, 156-57
Etna Green, 307
European immigrants, 25
evangelism, 68-69
Evans, Robert M., 308
Evansville, 1, 7, 49, 62, 73, 76,
    94, 119, 145, 147, 265,
    307-10, *335*
  airline service, 127
  as financial center, 101
  industry in, 58, 89, 104, 309
  population, 25, 32, 72
  port city, 128
Evansville Economic Develop-
    ment Commission, 104
Evansville and Ohio Valley
    Company, 58
explorers, 63, 186
export products, 101

Fables in Slang, 60, 184, 251,
    280
facilities for foreign trade, 102
Fairbanks, Charles, W., 54, 163
Fairfax State Recreation Area,
    310, 394
Fairland, 310
Fairmount, 310
Fairview Park, 310
Fall Creek, 117, 164, 240
Fallen Timbers, Battle of, 39, 45,
    46, 213, 214, 238, 314
farms
  employment, 93
  income, 91
  migration from, 114
  see also agriculture
Farmersburg, 311
Farmland, 311
Fauntleroy, Jane Dale Owen, 52
Fayette County, 29, 79, 270, 290,
    291, 311, 324

federal conservation agencies, 90
Federal Courts Building, 159
federal funds, 106, 199
Federation of German Societies,
    157
Female Social Society, 176
Ferdinand, 311
Ferdinand State Fish Hatchery,
    311-12
Ferdinand State Forest, 311-12
fertilizer, 263
"Fifty-Four Forty or Fight," 293
Fillmore, 312
financial agencies, 151
financial services, 100-104
fireclay, 82
firemen, 153, 164
Fish and Game Division, 86
fish hatcheries, 86, 90, 265, 268,
    311-12, 433, 464
Fisher, Carl, 168, 193, 253
Fishers, 312
Fishers Station, 312
fishing
  commercial, 87, 94
  recreational 5, 86-87
  see also state fish and wildlife
    areas; state fishing areas
500-Mile Race, 257, 440, *489*
flag, state, 2
Flat Rock, 312
"Flats," 11
flood control system, 19
floods, 87, 255
Flora, 312
flouride, 258
flowers, state, 1
Floyd, Davis, 313
Floyd, John, 312
Floyd County, 13, 29, 33, 312,
    320, 323, 328, 369, 402
Floyds Knobs, 312-13
folk music, 4

football, 59, 207
foreign trade, 101-2
foreign-born, percentage of, 65, 73
forests, 2, 10, 15, 75, 89
  afforestation, 77
  area, 83-84
  commercial, 93-94
  forestation, 90
  preservation of, 83, 84
  use of, 84
  see also national forest; state forests
forestry management program, 83
Fort Ancient variant, 37-38, 235
Fort Azatlan, 38, 62
Fort Branch, 313
Fort Defiance, 45
Fort Benjamin Harrison, 151, 162, 239, 252, 256, 313
Fort Miami, 70, 236, 313

Fort Ouiatenon, 5, 235, 236
Fort Recovery, 45
Fort Sackville, 41, 189
Fort Wayne, 1, 5, 18, 25, 38, 40, 48, 116, 119, 127, 239, 243, 258, 263, 313-15, *346, 347*
  building of, 238
  city charter, 73
  early industrial city, 58
  financial center, 101
  foundation of, 45
  French settlers in, 63, 70
  industry in, 98, 124
  population, 25, 32, 72
  railroads to, 125
  school system in, 142
  unemployment in, 112
Fort Wayne Bible School, 315
Fort Wayne School of Fine Arts, 315

Fortville, 313
Fountain City, 56, 316
Fountain County, 29, 266, 315, 334, 368, 389, 407, 455, 461
Fowler, 270, 316
Fowlertown, 316
Foyt, A. J., 259
France, 235
Frances Slocum State Forest, 316
Francesville, 317
Francisco, 317
Frankfort, 288, 317
Franklin, 317-18, 243
Franklin College, 243, 317-18
Franklin County, 29, 80, 276, 277, 284, 293, 318, 376, 409, 468
Frankton, 318
Fredericksburg, 319
Free Soil Democrat, 245
Freelandville, 318
Freeman Reservoir, 318
Freetown, 319
Freie Presse, 245
freighters, 127
Fremont, 319
French and Indian War, 7, 41, 67, 236, 313
French in Indiana
  cession to British, 41
  forts, 235, 236
  habitants, 46
  settlements, 5, 6-7, 40-41, 63, 70
  before World War I
    French Lick, 11, 89, 319
French Lick Springs, 55
Fretageot, Marie Duclos, 52
frosts, 20
fruit, 91
fuel, shortages of, 78
Fulton, Robert, 320
Fulton, 319
Fulton County, 28, 262, 319, 367, 377, 427

fundamentalist gospel, 68-69
fur trade, 41, 241, 314, 438

Galena, 320
Gallatin, Albert, 50
Galvaston, 320
game birds, 86
game preserves, 90
Gamelin, Antoine, 44
Garrett, 320
Gary, 1, 101, 251, 258, 320-21
    black population in, 27, 73
    industrial employment in, 98
    lime production near, 82
    population, 25, 72, 33
    public housing in, 148
    school system in, 142
    socio-economic problems of,
        112-13
    steel industry in, 4, 58, 113, 127
gas, natural, 15, 78-79, 96-97,
    250
    boom, 264, 299, 303, 322, 384,
        396, 400
Gas City, 96, 250, 322
gasoline engine, 58
Gaston, 322
Gatling, Richard, 99, 246
geese, 86
"Gem City," 266
Gemini, 187, 194
Gene Stratton Porter State
    Memorial, 322
General Assembly, 130, 132-33,
    240, 241, 259
General Motors, 255, 264
Geneva, 322
Gentes, Indian, 39, 40
Gentleman from Indiana, The,
    209, 251
Gentryville, 322-23
geographical configureation, 9-22
geological formation, 15-17

George Rogers Clark National
    Historic Park and Memorial,
    323
George W. Julian House, 284
Georgetown, 323
Germans in Indiana, 51, 180, 268,
    311, 409, 431, 469
    in Indianapolis, 157
    language, 66
    percentage of, 64, 65
    the Rappites, 171-74, 240
    religious groups, 69-70
Gibson, John, 46, 48, 239, 279
Gibson County, 11, 14, 25, 29, 32,
    52, 79, 95, 313, 317, 323, 333,
    408, 412, 414, 421, 438
Girl of the Limberlost, A, 60, 204,
    273
girls' School, 148
glacial drift, 267
Glacial Kame culture, 34-35, 235
glaciers, 9, 10, 89, 450, 460, 465
    effects of, 17
    and soils, 19, 269
glass manufacturing, 81
Glendale, 256
Glendale State Fish and Wildlife
    Area, 323-24
Glenwood, 324
glider, 215
Gold Creek, 276
gold mining, 279
goldsmith, 324
Gompers, Samuel, 162
Goodland, 324
Goodyear Tire and Rubber
    Company, 285
"Gore, The," 48
Goshen, 25, 324
Goshen College, 324
Gosport, 241, 324
government
    municipal, 73, 134-35, 162-63

reform, 60, 73
state, 49-51, 60, 129-33
territorial, 43-44
governor
duties of, 131
reelection, 60
term of, 131
Governors of Indiana
Bigger, Samuel, 53
Bowen, Otis R., 149, 187-88, *218*, 259
Branigin, Roger D., 61, 259
Dunning, Paris, 53
Harrison, William Henry (territorial), 45-48, 197-98
Hendricks, Thomas A., 54, 163, 437
Jackson, Ed, 177, 178-79
Jennings, Jonathan, 47-48, 49, 50-51, 240, 285
Lane, Henry S., 55, 246
McCray, Warren T., 178
McNutt, Paul V., 60, 182-83, 201-2, *224*, 254, 255
Marshall, Thomas R., 54, 163, 205, 289
Morton, Oliver P., 56, 60, 245, 246, 247
Noble, Noah, 53
Ralston, Samuel, 205-6, *228*
Ray, James, 53
Schricker, Henry F., 255, 256
Wallace, David, 53
Whitcomb, James, 53, 55
Grabill, 325
grain, 91
Grand Army of the Republic, 248
Grand Canyon, 126
Grand Calumet River, 303
Grandview, 325
Grange Movement, 248
Granger, 325
Grant County, 29, 310, 316, 322,

325, 357, 366, 384, 387, 445, 453, 454
Grassy Fork Fish Hatchery, 387
Graustark, 60
grave goods, 35, 36
gravel, 15, 81, 96
gravel pit, *350*
Great Depression, 141, 182, 201, 254, 271, 283
Great Lakes, 102
Great Plains, point of origin, 5
Green, William, 162
Green Forks, 327-28
Green River, 409
Greenback Party, 249
Greencastle, 125, 242, 325-26
Greendale, 326
Greene County, 29, 76, 79, 272, 326, 363, 379, 382, 403, 436, 445, 473
Greene-Sullivan State Forest, 15, 326
Greenfield, 326, *348*
Greensboro, 327
Greensburg, 298, 327
Greensburg Reservoir State Fishing Area, 327
Greentown, 328
Greenville, 328
Greenville, Treaty of, 214
Greenwood, 328
Greyhound, 123
Griffin, John, 46
Griffin, 328
Griffith, 328
Grissom, Virgil "Gus," 194, 258, 393
memorial, *496*
ground water, 89
grouse, 86
Grouseland, 46, 328, *348, 349*
gypsum, 81, 82, 96

Habitants, French, 46
Hagerstown, 329
Halleck, Charles A., 195, *222*
Hamer House, *489*
Hamilton, Alexander, 329
Hamilton, Francis, 253
Hamilton, Henry, 41-42, 236
Hamilton, 329
Hamilton County, 23, 25, 29, 33, 62, 81, 265, 266, 282, 286, 291, 312, 329, 437, 466
Hamlet, 329-30
Hammond, 6, 25, 73, 98, 101, 248, 330
  population, 3
Hancock, John, 331
Hancock County, 23, 29, 33, 285, 313, 326, 331, 387, 388, 406, 437, 470
Hanover, 331
Hanover College, 241, 331
Hanna, Robert, 53
Hanna, 330
Hannegan, Edward A., 53, 293
Happy Birthday, Wanda June, 211
Hardinsburg, 331
Hardwoods, 75, 82, 84, 93-94
Hardy Lake State Recreation Area, 331
Harlan, 331
Harmonie, 6, 7, 51, 71, 171-75
Harmonie State Recreation Area, 331
Harrison, Benjamin, 54, 158, 195-96, 250, 270
  home of, 269,70, *338*
Harrison, Thomas, 68
Harrison, William Henry, 5, 45-48, 50, 53, 54, 195, 197-98, 238, 239, 243, 268, 279, 292, 324, 328-29, 332, 448, 470

  home of, *348, 349*
Harrison County, 13, 29, 48, 93, 239, 292, 293, 305, 332, 371, 374, 387, 392, 406, 407, 413, 423, 442
Harrison Land Law, 238
Harrison-Crawford State Forest, 332
Harroun, Ray, 168
Hartford Bakery, 104
Hartford City, 272, 332
Hartke, R. Vance, 257
Hartsville, 332-33
Harvester, The, 204
Hatcher, Richard, 198-99, 258
hatcheries, 86, 90, 265, 268, 311-12, 433, 464
Haubstadt, 333
Hay, John, 432-33
hay, 91
Hayes, Joseph, 60, 167
Hayes, William H., 444
Haynes, Elwood, 58, 99, 199-200, 250, 251
Haynes-Apperson Automobile Company, 200
Haynsworth, W. Clement, 185
Hazelton, 33
health facilities, in Indianapolis, 164-65
health and welfare, 146-47
heart transplant surgery, 259
heat, 78
Hebron, 333
Helmer, 333
Helmsburg, 333
Heltonville, 333
Hemlock, 333
Henderson, Charles R., 69
Hendricks, Thomas A., 54, 163, 437
Hendricks, William, 50, 51, 240
Hendricks County, 23, 29, 33,

263, 278, 288, 289, 296, 333, 380, 418, 443
Hennepin, Father, 66
Henry County, 29, 271, 302, 327, 334, 367, 368, 378, 391, 397, 399, 404, 437, 441, 442, 444, 470
Henryville, 334
hickory, 94
highest point, 9
Highland, 334
highway programs, 257
highways, 4, 83, 94, 112, 122-23, 161, 194
hiking, 2, 6, 85
Hillsboro, 334
Hindostan Falls State Fishing Area, 334
Hinkle, Paul D. "Tony," 165
Hinkle Fieldhouse, 165
historic sites, 56, 168, 309, *338, 383, 340, 342,* 344, *347, 348, 349, 351, 352,* 403, 432-33, 458, *478, 489, 491, 492*
history, 6-7, 115-21, 235-60
    French period, 40-42
    Indian period, 38-40
    prehistory, 34-38, 62
    religious groups, 66-70
    from statehood to present, 51-61, 63-65
    territorial period, 43-49
Hoagland, 357
Hobart, 357
Hodges, Gil, 59
hogs, 91, 92
Holcomb Institute, 165
Holcomb Planetarium, 165
Holcomb Research Institute, 161
holiday, 169
Holiness Sects, 69
Holland, 357
Holliday James, 248

Holton, 357
Home Corner, 357
honey, 91
"Hoosier," origin of, 3-4, 63-64
Hoosier conservatism, 179
Hoosier Hills, 286
Hoosier National Forest, 2, 269, 357
Hoosier School-Master, The, 59, 248
Hoosier social environment, 171-83
Hoosiers, The, 251, 202
Hope, *349,* 358
Hopewell culture, 34, 36-37
horses, 464
    auction, 430
    racing, 59
    riding, 85
hospitals, 147
    in Indianapolis, 164-65
House of a Thousand Candles, The, 203
housing developments, 86
Hovey Lake, 358
Hovey Lake State Fish and Game Area, 358
Howard County, 29, 328, 333, 358-59, 370
Howard Shipyards, 287
Howard Steamboat Museum, 287
Howe, 359
Hubbard, Frank McKinney "Kin," 251
Hudson, Thomas B., 105
Hudson, 359
Hulman, Anton, "Tony," 4, 168
Hulman Field, 151
hunters, 235
Huntertown, 359
hunting, 85, 86
hunting and gathering cultures, 35, 36, 62

Huntingburg, 359
Huntington, Samuel, 359
Huntington, 119, 359-60
   Huntington County, 29, 264,
      350, 359, 360, 385, 426, 462
   Huntington Grain Company, *350*
   Huntington Reservoir, 360
Huntley Creek, 301
Huntsville, 360
Huron Indians, 38
Hutchenson, Big Bill, 162
hydroelectric resources, 88-89
Hymera, 361

Ice Age, 17, 89
ice sheet, Pleistocene, 34
Idaville, 361
Illinoian Drift Area, 10-11
Illinois Basin, 15
Illinois Glacier, 465
Illinois Oil Basin, 309
Illinois River, 88, 420
illiteracy rate, 248
immigrants,
   European, 25, 64, 65, 73
   from other states, 25, 44, 63,
      64, 65, 70
Imperialism, 60
income taxes, 107-8
Indians
   aesthetic activities, 35, 37
   agriculture, 62
   archaeological stages, 34-36
   cultures, 34
   death ceremonialism, 35
   historic period, 38-40, 62
   place-names, 2,40
   prehistoric 4, 7, 34-38, 62, 235
   relationship to British, 41
   relationship to settlers, 43-45
   settlement patterns, 35,36, 37,
      39, 70
   social structure, 39, 40

   technology, 35
   wars, 5, 41, 44-45, 48-49
   westward migration, 40
Indian burial mounds, 36-38, 62,
   254, 264, 265, 283, 284, 285,
   291, 307, 389, 412, 443, 452,
   469, 471, *494*
Indian Creek, 293
Indian Knoll culture, 34, 35, 235
Indian treaties, 39, 40, 41, 42, 45,
   46, 47, 64, 197, 201, 210, 214,
   236, 237, 238, 239, 240, 241,
   266, 276, 457
Indian tribes
   Chippewa, 45
   Delaware, 38, 39-40, 45, 62, 64,
     304
   Huron, 38
   Illinois, 438
   Kickapoo, 62
   Mascontin, 38
   Miami, 201, 242, 273, 235, 282,
     313, 316, 380, 438, 470, 471
   Ojibwa, 45
   Ottawa, 41
   Piankashaw, 62
   Potawatomi, 38, 40, 45, 62,
     241, 243, 304, 313, 380, 419,
     470, 471
   Shawnee, 45, 62, 210, 282, 448,
     449
   Wea, 62
   Winnebago, 38
   Wyandotte, 62, 277, 473
Indiana, University of, 57, 59,
   144, 165, 243, 248, 265, 272
   Calumet Extension, 303
   South Bend Campus, 439
   Southeast branch, 403
Indiana Academy of Science, 246
Indiana America, 245
Indiana Asbury College, 242
Indiana Association of

Spiritualists, 70
Indiana Baptist Manual Labor
    Institute, 243
Indiana Bell Telephone Company,
    164
Indiana Central College, 269
Indiana Central University, 166
Indiana Civil Liberties Union, 259
Indiana Civil Rights Commission,
    152
Indiana Coal Association, 77
Indiana Colonization Society, 241
Indiana Convention-Exposition
    Center, 159
Indiana Department of
    Commerce, 105, 107, 109
Indiana Department of Natural
    Resources, 84, 90, 473
Indiana Divide, 4, 5
Indiana Dunes National
    Lakeshore, 4, 10, 21, 271,
    390
Indiana Dunes State Park, 5, 10,
    21, 86, *351,* 361
Indiana Economic Development
    Authority Act, 103, 104
Indiana Forestry Association, 83
Indiana Gazette, 48, 238
Indiana governors. *see* Governors
    of Indiana
Indiana Harbor, 127, 303
Indiana Historical Bureau, 252
Indiana Historical Society, 242,
    265
Indiana Institute of Technology,
    315
Indiana Limestone Corporation,
    269
Indiana Motor Vehicles
    Department, 256
Indiana National Bank, 159
Indiana Pacers, 170
"Indiana Plan," 255

Indiana Port Commission, 257
Indiana Repertory Theatre, 6, 167
Indiana School of Art, 208
Indiana Seminary, 241, 243
Indiana State Chamber of
    Commerce, 103, 107
Indiana State Fairgrounds
    Coliseum, 258
Indiana State Library, 241
Indiana State Museum, 259
Indiana State Teachers College,
    248
Indiana State University, 144,
    145, 310, 447
Indiana Steel and Wire Company,
    400
Indiana Territory, 197, 238, 458
Indiana Territory State Memorial,
    351, 361
Indiana Toll Road, 122, 256
Indiana Tube Corporation, 104
Indiana University Medical
    Center, 165
Indiana University School of
    Medicine, 252
Indiana Vocational and Technical
    College, 143, 310
Indiana War Memorial, 259
Indiana World Trade Center, 102
Indiana's Women's Prison, 154
Indianapolis, 54, 57, 70, 71, 78,
    109, 117, 120, 121, 122, 124,
    125, 147, 148, 154-70, 167,
    174, 240, 241, 242, 244, 245,
    247, 249, 250, 255, 256, 257,
    259, 338, 352, 353, 354, 355
    airline flights to and from, 126
    architecture, 95, 158, 159-60
    blacks in, 27
    as center of industry, 98
    character of, 72-73, 154-55
    city plan, 155
    communications media, 169

cultural life, 166-68
demography, 156
economy, 156, 160-62
educational institutions, 165-66
elevation, 9
environment, 156
ethnic groups, 156-57
financial services, 100, 161
500-Mile Race, 168-69
government, 162-63
history, 155-56
incomes in, 114
libraries, 166
manufacturing in, 160-61
museums, 6
Northside, 157
Plymouth Church, 69
political life, 163-64
population, 25, 33, 73
public services, 164-65
recreational facilities, 169-70
research in, 161
school enrollment in, 142
slum clearance in, 148
streets in, 122
as trade center, 161
and transport, 161
as trucking center, 123
urban transition, 158-60
Indianapolis Athletic Club, 157
Indianapolis Center for Advanced Research, 161
Indianapolis Fire Department, 164
Indianapolis 500-Mile Race, 259.
  see also Indianapolis Motor Speedway
Indianapolis Indians, 170
Indianapolis Metropolitan Area, 262
Indianapolis Motor Speedway, 59, 79, 117, 123, 162, 168,

193, 252, 253, 254, 259, 440, *489*
Indianapolis Museum of Art, 6, 167
Indianapolis News, 169, 178, 248
Indianapolis Parks and Recreation Department, 169
Indianapolis Police Department, 164
Indianapolis Power & Light Company, 164
Indianapolis Races of the World Hockey Association, 170
Indianapolis-Scarborough Peace Games, 170
Indianapolis Saenger-Chor, 157
Indianapolis Star, 169
Indianapolis Symphony Orchestra, 154, 167, 256
Indianapolis Times, 178, 254, 258
Indianapolis Water Company, 164
Indianapolis Zoo, 168
Industrial Development Fund, 103, 104, 105
Industrial Workers of the World, 191
industry, 58, 72, 78, 81, 83, 86, 87, 93-94, 97-99, 103
  mortgages for, 104
  pollution by, 112
  products of, 97
  safety in, 252
  see also names of industries
Ingalls, 362
Inland Steel Company, 302-3, 250, *345*
Institute for Sex Research, 144
insurance industry, 100, 105, 108, 161
International Friendship Gardens, *477*
interstate highways, 4, 112, 194,
Interstate 90, 112

Interurban railways, 57-58, 126, 250, 251, 252, 255, 275
Interurban Terminal, 126
Ireland, Merritt W., 290
Ireland, 362
Irish in Indiana, 64, 65, 180
"Iron Brigade," 57
iron industry, 78, 82. *see also* steel industry
Iroquois River, 362
Irvington, 158
Irwin Union Bank, 291
ITT Business and Technical Institutes, 310

Jackson, Andrew, 53
Jackson, Ed, 177, 178-79
Jackson County, 13, 29, 278, 292, 295, 319, 362, 388, 435, 443, 453
Jacksonian democracy, 129
Jackson-Washington State Forest, 278
jails, 149
James Lake, 363
Jamestown, 363
Jasonville, 363
Jasper, 301, *355,* 363
Jasper County, 23, 29, 289, 300, 364, 424, 467
Jasper-Pulaski Fish and Wildlife Area, 364
Jay County, 29, 279, 301, 364, 416, 421, 423, 432, *483*
Jefferson County, 11, 23, 29, 288, 300, 302, 331, 364, 374, 383
Jefferson Proving Ground, 280, 357
Jeffersonville, 49, 54, 71, 72, 102, 238, 365
Jennings, Jonathan, 47-48, 49, 50-41, 240, 285
Jennings County, 11, 29, 280,

295, 365, 401, 435, 455
Jesuits, French, 40
Jewish Post, 169
John Birch Society, 154, 163, 257
Johnson, Douglas W., 68
Johnson, John, 48, 366
Johnson County, 23, 29, 33, 268, 304, 317, 328, 366, 450, 468
Jones, James W., 308
Jonesboro, 366
Jonesville, 366
Jordan, David Starr, 144
Judicial Nominating Commission, 138, 139
judicial system, 137-40
Judson, 366
Jug Rock, 295, 366, 418, 438
Julian, George W., 181
  house, 284

Kanawaka River, 409
Kankakee River, 88, 366
Kankakee State Recreation Area, 367
karst, 13
Kaskaskia, 236
Kekionga, 40, 41, 238
Kempton, 367
Kendallville, 367
Kennard, 367
Kennedy, Robert F., 61
Kentland, 367
kerogens, 15
Kethippecanunk, 237
Kewanna, 367
Keystone, 250
Kickapoo Indians, 38, 62
Kilbuck Creek, 299
Kimmell, 368
King Oliver's Creole Jazz Band, 253
Kingman, 368
Kingsbury, 368

Kingsbury State Fish and
  Wildlife Area, 368
Kingsford Heights, 368
Kinsey, Alfred, 60, 144
Kirklin, 368
Kitty Hawk, 215
Knights of the Golden Circle, 56,
  247
Knights of Labor, 249
Knightstown, 4, 368
Knightsville, 369
Knobs, The, 312, 369, 434
Knobstone Escarpment, 13, 402
Knox, 369
Knox County, 29, 38, 48, 72, 79,
  145, 237, 238, 271, 278, 279,
  298, 304, 318, 323, 361, 369,
  394, 408, 433, 457, 467
Kokomo, 16, 40, 58, 79, 98, 125,
  127, 243, 250, *356,* 358, 370
Kosciusko County, 18, 29, 69,
  266, 279, 287, 307, 370, 377,
  389, 417, 438, 446, 450, 463,
  472
Kouts, 371
Ku Klux Klan, 60, 154, 163, 164,
  171, 177-79, 253, 254, 256

labor unions, 109-10, 161-62, 191,
  249
Laconia, 187, 371
La Crosse, 371
Ladoga, 371
Lafayette, 5, 18, 40, 63, 70, 73,
  98, 101, 119, 121, 127, 235,
  237, 241, 246, 248, 250, 371-
  72, 448,
  population, 33
LaFayette, Marquis de, 371, 372
Lafayette Springs, 282
La Fontaine, 372
LaGrange, 242, 372
Lagrange County, 29, 70, 359,

372-73, 393, 417, 437, 439,
  450, 472
Lagro, 373
Lain Technical Institute, 310
Lake County, 10, 23, 27, 29, 33,
  72, 82, 98, 112, 283, 295, 302,
  303, 320, 328, 330, 334, 357,
  361, 373, 382, 389, 401, 404,
  430, 434, 469
Lake Dilldear, 300
Lake Erie, 119
Lake Freeman, 318
Lake Jewell, 278
Lake Maxinkuckee, 265, 296
Lake Michigan, 4, 9, 18, 19, 54,
  85, 87, 88, 90, 102, 105, 115,
  118, 127, 285, 390
lake plain, northern, 9-10, 12
Lake Village, 374
Lake Wawasee, 18
lakes, 4, 5, 9, 10, 15, 17, 19, 21,
  77, 85, 86, 87, 358.
  see also names of lakes
Laketon, 374
Lakeville, 374
lambs, 92
land area, 9
land reclamation, 15, 77-78, 90
land surveys, origin, 46-47
landscape, natural, 9-22
Lane, Henry S., 55, 246
Lane, James H., 55
Lane, Joseph, 55
Lanesville, 374
languages
  Algonquian, 39
  spoken in Indiana, 66, 70
Lanier, James F.D., 374
Lanier State Memorial, 374
Laotto, 374
Lapaz, 374
Lapel, 374
La Porte, 242, 243, 375

La Porte County, 23, 25, 29, 72, 82, 330, 368, 371, 375, 381, 390, 428, 450, 452, 461, 467
Larwill, 376
La Salle, Robert Cavelier, Sieur de, 40, 63, 235, 438
Lash, Don, 59
Late Prehistoric Stage, 34, 37-38
Laughery Creek, 298
Laurel, 240, 376
Law Enforcement Training Board, 153
Lawrence, 162, 376
Lawrence County, 14, 18, 29, 80, 81, 85, 95, 267, 269, 276, 300, 333, 376, 410, 441, 451, 459, 470
Lawrence County Historical Museum, 269
Lawrenceburg, 49, 71, 123, 238, 298, 376, 437
laws, territorial, 239
Leavenworth, 377
Lebanon, 273, 377
Leesburg, 377
Legislative Act, 245
Legislative Council, 132
legislature, 132-33
  territorial, 238
Leiters Ford, 377
L'Enfant, Pierre Charles, 155
Leo, 378
Lesueur, Charles-Alexandre, 52
Levi Coffin House, 56
Lewis, John L., 162
Lewisville, 378
Lexington, 378
Liberty, 378
Liberty Mills, 378
libraries
  first circulating, 239
  public, provision for, 50
Lieber, Richard, 200

Lieber State Park, 289
lieutenant governor, duties of, 131, 133
Life of Abraham Lincoln, 254
life-span, increased, 74
Ligonier, 378
Lilly, J.K., 167
Lilly Company, 160, 168, *348*
Lilly Endowment, 157, 160
Limberlost State Memorial, 378, *475*
lime, 81, 82
limestone, 11, 13, 14, 19, 75, 80-81, 95-96, 269, *498*
Lincoln, Abraham, 7, 54, 55, 240, 242, 246, 247
Lincoln Boyhood National Memorial, 7, 379, *475*
Lincoln Heritage Trail, 379
Lincoln Highway, 193
Lincoln Library and Museum, 315
Lincoln Memorial, Lincoln City, *475*
Lincoln State Park, 379
Lindbergh, Charles A., 254
Linden, 379
Lindsay, John, 290
Linton, 379-80
literature, 57, 59-60
Little Calumet River, 420
Little Cedar Grove Baptist Church, 279
Little Clifty Creek, 288
Little Italy Festival, *340*
Little Pigeon Creek, 7, 11, 240, 301
Little River, 359, 360
Little Theater Society, 252
Little Turtle, Chief, 38, 39, 45, 201, 237, 290, 314
Little Wyandotte Cave, 473
Little York, 380

livestock, 91, 92
Livonia, 380
Lizton, 380
Lockefield Gardens, 148
Lockerbie Square, 158
Lockridge, Ross, 66, 178
locks, *479, 498*
Lockycar College of Business, 310
Logansport, 16, 18, 119, 125, 147, 241, 264, 283, 380, *477*
Long Beach, 381
Longlois Creek, 262
Loogootee, 381
Losantville, 381
Lost Bridge State Recreation Area, 381-82, 432
Lost River, 381
Louisville, Indiana portion, population, 33, 73
Lowell, 382
Lower Wabash Valley, 11
lowest point, 9
lowlands, plants of, 21
Lugar, Richard G., 163
lumbering, 83-84
Lutherans, 68, 70, 243
Lydick, 382
lynching, 181-82
Lynd, Helen Merrell, 400-401
Lynd, Robert, 400-401
Lynn, 382
Lynnville, 382
Lyons, 382

McCarthy, Eugene J., 61
Macedonian Tribune, 169
McCordsville, 388
McCormick's Creek State Park, 85, 388
McCray, Warren T., 178
McCulloch, Oscar O., 69
McCutcheon, George Barr, 60
McFadden's Landing, 399

McGary, Hugh, 308
McGill Manufacturing Company, 454
machine gun, invention of, 99
McKinley Site, 62
McKinley Tariff Act, 196
MacLean, J. Arthur, 254
Maclure, William, 52, 176
McNutt, Paul V., 60, 182-83, 201-2, *224,* 254, 255
Macy, 382
Madison, James, 240
Madison, 8, 49, 54, 71, 120, 147, 239, 240, 241, 242, 383, *476*
Madison County, 29, 32, 81, 262, 285, 296, 303, 304, 306, 318, 360, 362, 374, 383-84, 385, 399, 410, 415, 445
Madison-Indianapolis Railroad, 120, 244
Magnificent Ambersons, The, 209
Magnificent Obsession, The 192
mail, air-delivered, 246
Main Chance, The, 202
"Main Street of the Midwest," 122
Major, Charles, 59, 167
Mammoth Internal Improvement Bill of 1836, 54, 242
manufacturing, 81, 82, 97-99, 103, 111, 160-61, 173-74, 250, 308-9
maple, 82, 94, 287, 293, 298, 311
maple syrup tapping, *482*
Marengo, 384
Marengo Cave, 11, 294, 295
Marian College, 255
Marion, 78, 79, 96, 242, 250, 325, 384-85
Marion County, 23, 24, 25, 27, 29, 33, 81, 162, 256, 259, 262,

269, 275, 281, 283, 288, 376, 385, 403, 439, 440
Marion County General Hospital, 147, 165
Marion County Jail, 149, 159
Marion County Police Department, 164
marital status of population, 74
Market Square Arena, 159, 170
Market Street, 157
Markle, 385
Markleville, 385-86
marl, 81
Marquette, Jacques, 63, 321, 438
Marshall, Thomas R., 54, 163, 205, 289
Marshall, 386
Marshall County, 29, 33, 68, 265, 274, 275, 296, 374, 386, 387, 419, 448
marshes, 9, 10, 17, 18, 21
marshlands, plants of, 21
Martin, John Barlow, 167
Martin County, 29, 82, 295, 366, 381, 386, 437, 450
Martin State Forests, 386
Martinsville, 11, 387
Mary Gray Bird Sanctuary, 290
Mascontin Indians, 38
mason jars, 250
Masonic lodge, 239
Matthews, 387
Matyr, Gilbert de la, 69
Mauckport, 387
Maumee River, 18, 88, 119, 263, 313, 387
Maumee-Wabash route, 235
Maxinkuckee, Lake, 387
Maxwell, David, 50
Maxwell, 387-88
mayor, 134
Mayor's Breakfast, 168
Mays, 388

Mead Johnson and Company, 309
Mecca Covered Bridge, *480*
Medaryville, 388
Medicaid, 146
medical school, first, 243
medical society, first, 240
Medicare, 146
Medora, 388-89
Mellott, 389
melons, 91
Memorial Day Race, 59, 168
Mennonite Book Concern, 270
Mennonites, 25, 70, 270, 324
mentally retarded, 249
Mentone, 389
Merchants National Bank, 159
Mercury, 194
Meredith, Solomon, 280-81
Merom, 38, 62, 389
Merrillville, 389
Mesker Zoo, 309
Mesozoic Era, rock formations, 17
Methodist Church, first in Indiana, 285
Methodist Foundation for Social Services, 69
Methodist Hospital, 165
Methodists, 67, 68, 69
metropolitan areas, 26
population, 32-33
Mexican War, 54-55, 244
Mexicans in Indiana, 65, 66
Mexico, 389
Miami Beach, 193, 253
Miami confederacy, 238
Miami County, 29, 263, 292, 300, 382, 389, 390, 393, 416, 423
Miami Indians, 38-39, 40, 41, 44, 45, 62, 64
Miami River, 409
Miami State Recreation Area, 390
Michigan, Lake. *see* Lake Michigan

Michigan Central Railroad, 10
Michigan City, 53, 54, 148, 198,
    242, 245, 390-91, *477*
Michigan Road, 117, 242
Michigantown, 391
Middlebury, 25, 391
Middletown, 391, *401*
Middletown in Transition, 401
Midwest Steel, 420
migrant workers, 93
Milan, 391
Miles Laboratories, 305
milfoil, water, 21
Milford, 391
milk, 91
Mill Creek, 263
millennarianism, 51
Millennium, 172
Millersburg, 391
Millhousen, 392
Mills, Caleb, *223,* 244
Milltown, 392
Milroy, Samuel, 299
Milroy, 392
Milton, 392
mine inspection, 249
mineral springs, 11, 319
minerals, 11, 14-15, 89, 75-82
Minerva Society, 52, 246
mining, 14, 15, 76-78, 94-95
Mishawaka, 392
missions, 39-40, 66
Mississinewa, Battle of, 384
Mississinewa Dam and Reservoir,
    393, *478*
Mississinewa River, 18, 393
Mississippi culture, 34, 37-38,
    265, 285
Mississippi River, 18, 88, 128,
    438
Mississippian Period, 16, 235
    upper, 19
Mitchell, 85, 258, 393

Mitchell Plain, 12, 13, 293
mobile homes, 271, 305, 306
Modern Maid Food Products, 104
Modoc, 393
Moieties, Indian, 40
Monon, 125, 393-94
Monon Railroad, 120, 245, 259,
    283, 393
Monroe, James, 394
Monroe, 394
Monroe City, 394
Monroe County, 14, 18, 29, 72,
    80, 81, 93, 95, 272, 275, 288,
    306, 310, 394, 397, 415, 444
Monroe Dam and Reservoir, 18,
    394
Monroeville, 395
Monrovia, 395
Mont Longnecker Lake, 471
Monterey, 395
Montezuma, 47, 395
Montgomery, 396
Montgomery County, 29, 294,
    297, 371, 379, 395, 406, 407,
    464, 472
Monticello, 396, 468
Montpelier, 396
Monument Circle, 156, 159
Moody Bible Institute, 284
Mooreland, 397
Moores Hill, 397
Mooresville, 397
moraines, 10, 17
Moravian Church, Hope, *349*
Moravian missionaries, 263
Moravians, 39-40, 358
Morgan, John Hunt, 55, 247
Morgan County, 23, 29, 33, 81,
    276, 387, 395, 397, 398, 413
Morgan-Monroe State Forest,
    397-98
Morgantown, 398
Morningside, 398

Morocco, 398
Morris-Butler House, 168
Morristown, 398-99
Morton, Oliver P., 56, 60, 245, 246, 247
Motor Vehicle Certificate of Title Act, 150
motto, state, 1
mound builders, 235
    legend of, 36
mounds, Indian. *see* Indian burial mounds
Mounds State Park, 37, 264, 277 399
Mount Ayr, 399
Mount Summit, 399
Mount Tom, 10
Mount Vernon, 102, 128, 182, 239, 399
Muhler, Joseph C., 258
Mulberry, 400
Muncie, 33, 73, 78, 79, 96, 98, 101, 112, 125, 145, 241, 250, 252, 299, 303, 400-401
Muncie Normal Institute, 252
municipal bonds, 104, 105
Municipal Economic Development Act, 103, 104
municipal government, 73, 134-35, 162-63
Munster, 401
Muscatatuck Regional Slope, 12, 13-14
Muscatatuck State Park, 401
Museum of Art, Indianapolis, 154, *355*
Museum of Indian Heritage, 6, 168
museums, 6, 154, 168, 265
music, folk, 4
Muskingum River, 409

name of state, origin, 2, 62

Napoleon, 401
Nappanee, 25, 402
Nashville, 13, 277, 402
National Clay Courts tennis tournament, 170
National Drag Races, 170
national forest, 84, 357
National Guard, 150-51
National League of Cities, 163
National Park Service, 7
National Railroad Passenger Corporation, 125
National Road, 117, 241, 242, 300, 447, 464
natural gas. *see* gas, natural
natural resources, 75-90
Navy, 258
Negroes. *see* Blacks
Nering, Theodore, 199
New Albany, 8, 54, 71, 72, 121, 243, 245, 312, 402-3, *478*
New Augusta, 403
New Carlisle, 403-4
New Castle, 147, 404
New Chicago, 404
New Deal, 254
New Harmony, 6, 7, 51-53, 171-77, 241, 246, 404-5, *479*
New Haven, 405-6
New Market, 406
New Middletown, 406
New Palestine, 406
New Paris, 406
New Point, 406
New Richmond, 406
New Ross, 407
New Salisbury, 407
Newberry, 403
Newburgh, 403
Newport, 406
newspapers, 53, 169, 238
    anti-slavery, 245
    first, 48

Newton County, 23, 30, 276, 324, 367, 374, 398, 399, 407
Newtown, 407
New York Central, 125
New York Century, 124
Nicholson, Meredith, 71-72, 167, 202-3, *225,* 251, 294
Nicholson File Company, *336*
nickname, origin of, 3-4, 63-64
Noble, James, 51, 240
Noble, Noah, 53
Noble County, 30, 262, 267, 275, 284, 295, 322, 367, 374, 378, 407-8, 428, 445, 464, 472
Noble County Historical Society, 262
Noblesville, 241, 329, *340*
No'Kamena, 271
Nolen, Jeannette Covert, 167
nominating convention, 135, 136
normal school, first, 279
Norman Upland, 12, 13
North Central Airlines, 126
North Christian Church, Columbus, 291, *341*
Northern Indiana, 4-5
northern lake country, 17, 18
northern lake plain, 9-10, 12
Northwest Territory, 2, 42, 43, 45-46, 190, 197, 237, 457-58
Northwestern Christian University, 245
Notre Dame University, 5, 59, *488*
Nowlin Mound, 62

oak, 94
Oak Tree Council, 235
Oakland City, 408
Oaktown, 408
oats, 91
Odon, 408
Ogden Dunes, 408

Ohio, 125
Ohio County, 23, 30, 408-9, 426
Ohio River, 8, 9, 11, 14, 17, 19, 21, 37, 63, 87, 88, 89, 99, 102, 105, 115, 118, 119, 120, 127, 128, 409, *479, 480*
oil, 15, 75, 78, 79-80, 95, 247, 250, 309, 373, 469
oil, vegetable, 92
oil shale, 15
Ojibwa Indians, 45
"Old Buffalo Trail," 83
Old Goshen Church, 187
"Old Jail" museum, 262
Old Swimmin' Hole and 'Leven More Poems, The, 206, 249
Old Tunnel Mill, 285
"Old Vesuvius," 264
Oldenburg, 409-10
Oldfields, 167
Oliver, James, *226,* 248
"On the Banks of the Wabash," 192, 266
onions, 91
Onward, 410
Oolitic, 81, 410
Opinion, 169
Orange County, 30, 82, 319, 410, 411, 413, 442, 465
orchards, planting, 77
Ordinance of 1787, 43-44, 49, 122, 197
Ordovician Period, 16
Orestes, 410
organized labor, 109-10, 161-62, 191, 249
Orland, 411
Orleans, 411
Osceola, 411
Osgood, 411
Ossian, 411
Ottawa Indians, 41, 45
Otterbein, 411

Otwell, 411
Ouabache, State Recreation Area, 273, 412
Ouiatenon, 40, 63, 70
overburden, 76, 77
Owen, David Dale, 52
Owen, Richard Dale, 52
Owen, Robert, 7, 51-52, 53, *227*, 241, 404, 174, 175
Owen, Robert Dale, 52-53, 296
Owen County, 14, 30, 85, 289, 324, 388, 412, 424, 440
Owen-Putnam State Forest, 412
Owens- Corning Fiberglass Corporation, 454
Owen's Creek, 238
Owensville, 412
Oxford, 59, 412-13
Ozark Airlines, 126

"Paddle Your Own Canoe," 244
Paleo-Indians, 34, 235
Paleozoic Era, 15-17
Palmyra, 513
Pan-American Union, 196
Panic of 1837, 119
Paoli, 46, 413
Paoli Road, 54
Paoli Turnpike, 117
Paragon, 413
Parke County, 30, 81, 85, 272, 275, 295, 366, 386, 395, 413-14, 422, 428, 451, *480*
Parker City, 414
parks, 85-86, 90, 169. *see also* state parks, state recreation areas
parochial schools, German, 66, 70
Patoka, 414
Patoka River, 11
Patoka State Fish and Wildlife Area, 414
Patriot, 415

Paxon, Frederick L., 72
Paynetown State Recreation Area, 394, 415
Peace Monument, 298
peaches, 91
peat, 15, 82, 96-97
Pei, I. M., 8, 290
Pekin, 415
Pence, 415
Pendleton, 148, 415
Pennsylvania Railroad, 124, 125
Pennsylvanian Period, 16
Pennville, 416
Penrod, 209
People's Party, 245
peppermint, 21, 91
per capita income, 101, 114, 160
perch, 94
Permian Period, 16
Perry County, 13, 30, 93, 275, 281, 300, 416, 446, 451
Perrysville, 416
persimmon, 21
Peru, 125, 254, 257, 263, 416
Petersburg, 59, 417
petroleum, 15, 75, 78, 79-80, 95, 247, 250, 309, 373, 469
pheasant, 86
Phiquepal, Guillaume, 52
physiographic zones, 9-11
Piankashaw Indians, 38, 62
Picard, Paul R., 68
pickerel, 86
Pierceton, 417
Pigeon River, 417
Pigeon River State Fish and Wildlife Area, 372, 417
Pigeon Roost Massacre, 48, 239
Pigeon Roost State Memorial, 417
pike, 86
Pike County, 14, 30, 76, 79, 411, 414, 417-18, 442, 472

Pike State Forest, 418
Pine Lake Assembly, 69
Pine Village, 418
Pinnacle, The, 418, 438
pitcher plant, 21
Pittsboro, 418
Pittsburg Screw and Bolt
     Company, 321
place-names, Indian, 2, 40
Plainfield, 148, 418
plains, 9-13, 17, 18
Plainville, 419
plank roads, 244
planning and development
     regions, 23, 24
plants
   carnivorous, 21
   of dunes, 85-86
   domesticated by Indians, 36
   indigenous, 21-22
platform pipes, stone, 37
Pleasant Lake, 419
Pleistocene Epoch, 17, 34, 450
Plymouth, 242, 419
Plymouth Church, Indianapolis,
     69
"Pocket," 11
Poet, The, 203
point system, 256
Point Township, 9
Pokagon State Park, 265, 419, *481*
Pokeberry Creek, 31
Poland, 420
pole-timber, 83
police, 153, 164
polio vaccine, 256
Polish in Indiana, 65, 66
political parties, 53, 57, 135-36,
     137, 180
politics, 57
   in Indianapolis, 163-64
   pre-Civil War period, 53-55
   twentieth-century, 60-61

pondweeds, 21
Poneto, 420
Pontiac, Chief, 41
Pontiac's Rebellion, 236
popcorn, 91
poplar, yellow, 1
population
   black, location of, 27, 65, 73, 74
   breakdown, 73
   of cities, 25, 32-33
   of counties, 28-31
   distribution, 72
   growth, 27
   of Indiana Territory, 63
   marital status of, 74
   median age of, 25
   mobility, 27
   in nineteenth century, 71
   race distribution, 25
   regional distribution, 23, 24
   requirement for statehood, 44,
      49
   rural, 71, 72
   sex ratio, 25, 74
   total, 1
   of townships, 23, 25
   in twentieth century, 65
   United States, center, 72
   urban, 71-73
population, census figures
   1814, 240
   1840, 243
   1850, 244
   1860, 246
   1870, 248
   1880, 249
   1890, 250
   1900, 251
   1910, 252
   1920, 253
   1930, 254
   1940, 255
Portage, 420

Porter, Cole, 203-4
Porter, Gene Stratton, 60, 204,
    273, 298, 322, 379, 465
    memorial, *475*
Porter, 420
Porter County, 10, 23, 30, 33, 98,
    112, 257, 270, 273, 280, 285,
    301, 333, 371, 408, 420-21,
    453
Portland, 421
portland cement, 82
ports, 4, 105, 127, 128, 257, 420
Posey, John, 239
Posey, Thomas, 48, 51
Posey County, 9, 11, 30, 32, 38,
    51, 79, 171, 182, 240, 296,
    328, 331, 358, 399, 404, 421
Poseyville, 421
potatoes, 91
Potawatomi Indians, 38, 40, 45,
    62, 64, 241, 243, 304, 313,
    380, 419, 437, 470, 471
Potawatomi Inn, Pokagon State
    Park, *481*
Potawatomi village, 266
pottery, 82, 287, 288, 359
    Fort Ancient, 37-38
    Hopewell, 37
poultry, 91, 92
prairies, 10, 11
precipitation, 20, 87
prehistory, 34-40, 62
Presbyterians, 68, 241
presidents, Hoosier, 53-54
primary elections, 135-36
Princeton, 71, 323, 421-22
Prohibition, 245, 252
property tax, 106-7, 142, 259
prosecuting attorneys, 140
Protestantism in Indiana, 66-70
public defender, 139-40, 153
public education, 142-46. *see also*
    education

public housing, 147-48
public school system, 67, 142-43,
    244, 252
Public Service Commission, 152
Public Utility Holding Company
    Act, 255
Pulaski County, 23, 30, 317, 364,
    388, 395, 422, 443, 449, 471
Pulliam, Eugene S., 169
Pullman Car Company, 109, 191
Pumpkin Vine Pike, 58, 250
Purdue, John, 248
Purdue University, 5, 57, 59, 145
    248, 253, 258, 372, 466-67,
    497
    at Indianapolis, 165
Pure Food and Drug Act, 252
Putnam County, 30, 268, 289,
    312, 325, 422, 423, 426, 430
Putnamville, 148
Pyle, Ernie, 205-6, 296

quail, 86
Quakers, 67, 244, 246, 304, 310,
    316, 424, 466
quarrying industry, 14, 80-81,
    269, 272, 276, 281, 301, *338,*
    392, 423. *see also* limestone
quarrying products, 96. *see also*
    limestone
"Queen City of the Gas Belt,"
    264
Quinn, Bernard, 68

rabbits, 86
Raccoon Lake State Recreation
    Area, 422
Radigan, Joseph, 199
radio stations, 169
race, distribution by, 25
racial unrest, 259
railroads, 10, 54, 57, 97, 119-21,

124-26, 156, 242, 244, 245, 246, 249, 437, 458
rain, 87
Rain Tree County, 334
Ralson, Alexander, 155
Ralston, Samuel, 205-6, *228*
Ralston Purina, 104
Ramp Bridge, 278
Ramsey, 423
Randolph, Thomas, 48
Randolph County, 9, 18, 30, 242, 282, 311, 381, 382, 393, 414, 423, 425, 433, 452, 471
Rapp, Frederick, 51, 170, 173, 241
Rapp, George, 51, 171-73, 240, 404
Rappites, 171-75, 240, 404
Ratliff Boon, 273
Ray, James, 53
Reapportionment Act of 1971, 60, 259
recession, 111-12
reclamation, land, 15
Recorder, 169
recorder, county, 133
recreation areas, 18, 77, 84-87, 169-70, *see also* state parks; state recreation areas
Red Bridge State Recreation Area, 423
Red Key, 423
redear, 267
Reed, Myron W., 69
Reelsville, 423
Reeves Octauto, 291
reforestation, 83
Regency Hyatt Hotel, Indianapolis, 159
Regenstrief Institute for Health Care, 161
relief, 13, 14
religion, decline in, 68

religious groups, 5, 25, 27, 66-70, 263
 Moravians, 39-40
 Rappites, 51
religious leaders, 68-70
Remington, 423
Rensselaer, 424
reporter of Supreme Court, 139
representatives, 132
Republic Steel, 321
Republican Party. *see* political parties
research, 161
reservoirs, man-made, 18-19
revivals, 68
Revolutionary War. *see* American Revolution
Reynolds, 424
Richard Lieber State Park, 424, *482*
Richardson Wildlife Foundation, 301
Richland, 424
Richmond, 4, 16, 71, 98, 147, 239, 244, 424-25, 464
Rickenbacker, Eddie B., 168, 254
Ridgeville, 425
right-to-work law, 110, 257
Riley, James Whitcomb, 3, 60, 64, 158, 167, 203, 206-7, *230,* 249, 252
Riley Hospital for Children, 165
Rimestone, 442, *486*
Ringling Bros. & Barnum & Bailey Circus, 254
Ripley County, 11, 14, 23, 30, 268, 357, 391, 401, 411, 426, 445, 456
Rising Sun, 240, 408, 426
riverboat era, 399, 402, 403, 426, *476, 478*
rivers, 6, 8, 9, 10, 11, 14, 17, 18, 37, 38, 53, 63, 76, 83, 87-88

Roachdale, 426
roads, 54
    building, 80, 81
    early, 116-18
    modern, 121-23
Roann, 426
Roanoke, 426-27
Robe, The, 192
Robertson, Oscar "Big," 154
Robinson, Solon, 295
Roche, Kevin, 290
Rochester, 320, 427
rock strata, 15-16
Rockfield, 427
Rockne, Knute, 59, 207, *229*
Rockport, 427
Rockville, 428, *483*
Rodehever, Homer, 472
Rogers Memorial Library,
    Columbus, 291
Rolling Prairie, 428
Roman Catholics, 68, 242
    missions, 40, 66
Romantic Music Festival, 167
Rome City, 428
Roofless Church, 405, *479*
Roosevelt, Franklin D., 60, 254
    255
Roosevelt, Theodore, 60
Rooster, Democrats' symbol, 53
Rose, Chauncey, 249
Rose-Hulman Institute of
    Technology, 249
Rosedale, 428-9
Roseland, 429
Rossville, 429
round-leafed sundew, 21
Route 40, 4, 6
Royal Center, 429
Runyon Damon, 207
rural areas
    population, 72
    religion in, 68

settlement patterns, 70-71
Rush, Benjamin, 429
Rush County, 30, 266, 283, 324,
    388, 392, 429
Rushville, 429-30
Russell, Louis, 259
Russellville, 430
Rutherford, Johnny, 168
rye, 91

Saarinen, Eero, 8, 290
Saarinen, Eliel, 8, 290, 291
Saint Anthony, 430
St. Benedict's College, 315
Saint Bernice, 430
St. Clair, Arthur, 44-45, 214, 237
St. Francis College, 315
Saint Joe, 430
Saint John, 430
St. John's Catholic Church, 159
St. Joseph County, 30, 33, 72, 81,
    325, 374, 382, 392, 403, 411,
    423, 429, 430-31, 438, 461
St. Joseph River, 18, 88, 431
St. Joseph's College, 289, 424
St. Lawrence Basin, 438
St. Lawrence drainage system, 18
St. Lawrence Seaway, 102, 105,
    127
St. Mary-of-the-Woods College,
    243
St. Mary's College, 439
St. Mary's River, 18, 88, 262, 431
St. Maur's Theological Seminary,
    166
Saint Meinrad, 431-32
Saint Meinrad Seminary, 245,
    431-32, *484*
Saint Paul, 432
Salamonia, 432
Salamonie Dam, *483*
Salamonie River, 18, 432
Salamonie River State Forest, 432

Salem, 49, 71, 240, 432-33, 463, *484*
Salem Limestone, 11, 14
sales tax, 106, 107, 108, 258, 259
salmon, 5, 94
San Pierre, 433
sand, 15, 81, 96
sand dunes, 4-5, 10, 21, 85-86, 285, *351*, 361, 390, 421
Sandborn, 433
sandstones, 13, 19, 81, 281, 416
Santa Claus, 7, 433
Saratoga, 433
Sargent, Winthrop, 44, 237
Saturday Evening Post, 169
savings and loan associations, 100, 161
sawmills, 83, 94
sawtimber, 75, 83, 84, 94
Say, Thomas, 52
Scales Lake State Beach and State Park, 433
Scales Lake State Forest, 274
Schererville, 434
Schneider, 434
schools, 44, 67, 142-43, 244, 252
   constitutional provision for, 50
   integration, 166, 256
   parochial, 66, 70
   segregation, 248
Schricker, Henry F., 255, 256
Schwartz, Rudolph, 399
Scott, Caroline Lavinia, 270
Scott County, 13, 30, 48, 239, 267, 286, 331, 378, 417, 434
Scottish Rite Cathedral, Indianapolis, 159
Scottsburg, 434
Scottsburg Lowland, 12, 13
Scoville, Charles R., 68
Second Bank of Indiana, 245
secretary of state, duties of, 131
sedimentary rocks, 15

Seelyville, 434
Sellersburg, 434-35
Selma, 435
Selmier State Forest, 435
senators, 132
Seventeen, 209
Seventh-Day Adventists, 286
Sevitzy, Fabian, 256
Sewall, May Wright, 249
sex ratio of population, 25, 74
sexuality, research in, 144
Seymour, 435
Shades State Park, 294, 435, *485*
Shafer Reservoir, 435-36
Shakamak State Park, 436
Shale, 13, 15, 96
Sharpsville, 436
Shawnee Indians, 45, 62, 210, 282, 448, 449
sheep, 92
Shelburn, 436
Shelby County, 23, 30, 33, 273, 310, 312, 398, 432, 436, 437, 461
Shelbyville, 242, 437
Sheridan, 437
sheriff, county, 133, 134
Sherman Anti-Trust Law, 196
Sherman Silver Purchase Act, 196
shipping, 4, 101-2
Shipshewana, 437
Shirley, 437
shoals, 96, 295, 437-38
shopping centers, 256
Shore Line, 58
Shortridge, Abram C., 145
Sierra Club, 77
silt, 19
Silurian Period, 16
Silver Lake, 265, 438
sinks, 13
Sissle, Noble, 253
Skelton, Red, 207-8

Sky Hawk, 126
Skyline Drive, 278
Slaughterhouse-Five, 211
Slavery
  Henry Clay on, 67
  in early Indiana, 49
  prohibition of, 44, 64, 237
  Underground Railroad, 56, 242,
    245-46, 272, 316, 426, 464,
    466
Slocum, Frances, 242, 316
smelt, 94
Smith, Oliver H., 53
Smithsonian Institution, 53
snowfall, 20
Social Democratic Party, 251
social gospel, 69
Socialist Party, 109, 162, 190,
  191, 251
soils, 92
  formation, 17
  parent materials, 19
  types of, 19
Soldiers Home, 246
Soldiers Monument, Dephi, *343*
Soldiers and Pioneers Monument,
  Bedford, *337*
Soldiers and Sailors Monument,
  Indianapolis, 155, 251, *353*
Solomon, Izler, 256
Somerville, 438
sorghum, 91
South Bend, 1, 18, 101, 125, 127,
  438-39, *488*
  automobile manufacture in, 5,
    99, 244
  city charter, 73
  electric streetcars in, 57, 249
  founding of University of Notre
    Dame, 243
  industry in, 58, 98
  population, 25, 33, 72
  racial unrest in, 259

South Milford, 439
South Shore Line, 125
South Whitley, 440
southern hills and lowlands,
    10-11, 12, 17, 18
Southern Indiana, 6-8, 18
Southport, 162, 439
Southwind Maritime Center, 102
soybeans, 91, 92
Spanish-American War, 250
Spanish language, 66
Sparks, Elijah, 48
spearmint, 91
Speedway. *see* Indianapolis
    Motor Speedway
Spencer, 85, 440
Spencer County, 30, 240, 245,
    286, 296, 322, 325, 379, 424,
    427, 431, 433, 441
Spencerville, 441
Spiceland, 441
spiritualism, 70
"spoils system," 53
sports, 5, 6, 85-86, 59, 169-70
Spring Mill State Park, 85, 272,
    276, 441-42, 451, *489, 491,
    494, 496*
Spring Valley State Fish and
    Wildlife Area, 442
Springport, 442
Spurgeon, 442
Squire Boone Caverns, 186, 442,
    486, 487
squirrels, 86
stagecoach, 241
stainless steel, 200
Standard Oil, 250, 469
Standard Steel Spring Company,
    321
Star City, 443
Starke County, 23, 31, 268, 329,
    367, 369, 433, 443
Starve Hollow State Forest, 443

state beaches, 268, 433
state bird, 2
State Board of Agriculture, 244
State Board of Education, 142
State Board of Health, 146, 249
State Board of Tax
    Commissioners, 153
State Budget Agency, 141
state capitol, Indianapolis, *352*
state capitol, Corydon, *342*
State Commission for Higher
    Education, 144
State Department of Commerce,
    111
State Department of Geology,
    248
State Election Board, 152
State Fair, 245
State Farm, 148
state fish and wildlife areas, 276,
    295, 305, 323, 358, 364, 368,
    375, 414, 417, 442, 450
state fishing areas, 273, 276, 327,
    334, 470
state flag, 2
state flower, 1
state forests, 286, 311, 316, 326,
    332, 362-63, 386, 397, 412,
    418, 432, 435, 443, 473
state government
    branches of, 129-30, 131-33
    establishment of, 49-51
    reforms in, 60
state highway scandals, 257
State Hospital for the insane, 244
state income tax, 106
State Library, 167
State Museum, 167
State Office Building, 159, 257,
    354
state parks, 21, 37, 85, 90, 280,
    284, 288, 361, 379, 388, 435,
    399, 401, 419, 424, 433, 435,
436, 441, 449, 451, 456, 469,
    481, 482, 485, 489, 493, 496
state police department, 150
State Prison, 148
state recreation areas, 297, 310,
    331, 367, 381, 390, 412, 415,
    422, 423, 470, 471
State Reformatory, 148
State Sanitary Commission, 247
State Scholarship Commission,
    147
State School for the Blind, 244
State School for the Deaf, 244
state seal, 2
State Soldier's and Sailors'
    Orphans Home, 248
state song, 266
State Spiritualist Association, 285
State Supreme Court, 130
state tree, 1
state universities, 144-46
State Welfare Department, 254
statehood, 48-49, 240
Staunton, 443
steel industry, 58, 72, 78, 82, 97,
    98, 113, 251, 257, 277, 302-3,
    320-21, 373
Steele, Theodore Clement, 208-9
    state memorial, 446
Stellite, 200
Stephenson, David Curtis, 60,
    163, 177, 178, 253, 256
Steuben County, 31, 265, 319,
    333, 359, 363, 411, 419, 443
Stilesville, 443
Stinesville, 444
stockades, 70
Stout, Elihu, 48, 51, 238
    print shop of, *352*
Stout, Rex, 60
Straughn, 444
strawberries, 91
Strawberry Festival, 159, 281

streams, 14, 18
streetcars, 247, 249, 250, 256
strikes, 253
strip mining, 15, 76-78
Studebaker, 5, 123, 244, 258, 439
"Sturbridge Village of the
    Midwest," 168
suffrage
  Negro, 180
  women's, 181
Sugar Creek, 451, *485*
Sullivan, 94, 444
Sullivan County, 14, 31, 33, 38,
    76, 77, 254, 282, 301, 311,
    361, 389, 436, 444
Sulphur Springs, 444
Summitville, 445
Sun Pacer, 126
Sunday, Billy, 69, 389, 472
sunfish, 86, 267
Sunman, 445
superintendent of public
    instruction, 132, 142-43
Supreme Court, 137-39
surveyor, county, 133, 134
surveys, origin, 46-47
swamps, 9
  plants of, 21
Swayzee, 445
Sweetser, 445
Swiss settlements, 71, 238, 270
Switz City, 445
Switzerland County, 23, 31, 81,
    238, 415, 445, 456
Sylvan Lake, 445
Syracuse, 446, 464

Taggart, Thomas, 55
tamarack, 21
tariffs, 196
Tarkington, Booth, 60, 157, 167,
    209-10, *231*, 251
TAT-Maddux Transcontinental

Airline, 254
  tax reform, 103, 107, 188
taxation, 105-9, 257
Taylor, Waller, 48, 51, 240
Taylor University, 453
technology, of prehistoric
    Indians, 35
Tecumseh, Chief, 2, 45, 47, 197,
    210-11, 239, 266, 449
television, 169, 208, 256
Television and Radio Service
    Examiners Board, 153
Tell City, 257, 446
temperance crusade, 181
temperature, 19
  average annual, 20
"Ten O'Clock Line," 47
Tennessee River, 409
Tennessee-Cumberland
    variant, 38, 235
Tennyson, 446
Tenskwatawa, 5, 47, 197, 210,
    268, 448, 449
Terre Haute, 4, 5, 73, 76, 151,
    243, 248, 249, 257, 446-48,*490*
  as financial center, 101
  founding of, 240
  as industrial city, 58, 98
  petroleum discovered in, 247
  population, 33
  as railroad center, 57
Territorial Period, 43-49, 63
Thames, Battle of the, 47, 211
Thomas, Jesse Brooks, 276
Thompson, Maurice, 59, 294
Thornton, 241, 448
till, 10
timber, 83, 84, 93-94
Times, The, 179
Tippecanoe, 448
Tippecanoe, Battle of, 5, 47, 197,
    210, 239, 269, 441, 448, 449,
    471, *492*

Tippecanoe Battlefield State Memorial, 273, 448-49, *492*
Tippecanoe County, 31, 81, 145, 268, 279, 286, 371, 448, 466
population, 33
Tippecanoe River, 18, 449
Tippecanoe River State Park, 449
"Tippecanoe and Tyler too," 53, 198, 269
Tippy, Worth M., 69
Tipton, John, 53, 290
Tipton, 449, 491
Tipton County, 31, 324, 367, 436, 449, 450, 472
courthouse, *491*
Tipton Knoll, 291
Tipton Till Plain, 10, 12, 269, 450
tobacco, 91
Tobin, Dan, 162
tomatoes, 91, 93
Topeka, 450
topsoil, formation, 17
tornadoes, 258, 288, 331
tourism, 85
towns, 42, 133, 135
Townsend, Clifford, 255
township and range system, 122
townships, 23, 25, 42, 133, 135, 237
trade in Indianapolis, 161
Trafalgar, 450
traffic safety, 151
Trail Creek, 450
"Trail of Death," 243
Trans World Airlines, 126
transition
to cosmopolitanism, 179, 183
from frontier to industrial state, 179
urban, 158-60
transportation, 54, 57, 115-28
centered in Indianapolis, 161
historic development of, 115-21

reasons for density of, 115
travel, early, 118
Travertine, 442
treasurer, county, 133-34
treasurer, state, 132
treaties
of Fort Greenville, 45, 47, 214, 238, 266
of Fort Wayne, 239
of Paris, 41, 42, 236, 457
of Wabash, 241
see also Indian treaties
Treaty Elm, 282
trees
planting, 77
species of, 21-22
state, 1
Trenton's Field, 78, 296, 299, 303
Tri-County Fish and Wildlife Area, 450
Trinity Springs, 450-51
Tri-State College, 265
trolley cars, 57-58. *see also* Interurban railways; streetcars
Troy, 451
trucking industry, 113
tulip tree, 1
Turkey Run State Park, 85, 451, *493*
turkeys, 86
turnpikes, 54, 117
Twin Caves, 451, *494*
"Two Per Cent Club," 202, 255, 259
Tyler, John, 198

Ulen, 452
Underground Railroad, 56, 242, 245-46, 272, 316, 426, 464, 466
unemployment, 111-12
compensation, 109
Uni-Gov, 141, 162-63, 164, 259

Union City, 452
Union County, 31, 277, 378, 452, 466, 469
Union Mills, 452-53
Union Station, Indianapolis, 16, 124, 159, 245, 247
Uniondale, 452
Unions, 109-10, 161-62, 191, 249
United Methodist Church, 68, 166
United Mine Workers Union, 162, 250
United Presbyterian Church, 68
Universal, 453
universities, 5, 50, 57, 59, 144-46, 161, 165-66, 239, 242, 243, 245, 253. *see also* names of universities
University of Evansville, 310
University of Notre Dame, 207, 243, 459
University Square, 159
Upland, 453
Upper Mississippian culture, 37-38
Urbana, 453
U.S. Gypsum Company, 438
U.S. highways
 40, 117
 50, 83
 150, 117
 31, 123
U.S. mail, 241
U.S. Steel Corporation, 58, 72, 113, 251, 320, 321

Vaile, Rawson, *232*
Vallonia, 453
Valparaiso, 453-54
Valparaiso University, 454
Van Buren, Martin, 53, 198
Van Buren, 454
Van Slyke, Peter, 272
Vanderburgh, Henry, 46

Vanderburgh County, 11, 31, 32, 38, 72, 79, 265, 307, 308, 454-55
Veedersburg, 455
vegetable oil, 92
vegetables, 91
veneer, 93
Vermillion County, 15, 31, 33, 76, 283, 289, 296, 310, 406, 416, 430, 453, 455
Vernon, 49, 455-56
Versailles, 456
Versailles State Park, 456
Veterans Administration Hospital, 256
Vevay, 8, 71, 238, 456-57
vice presidents, 54
Vigo, Francis, 279
Vigo County, 11, 31, 33, 434, 446, 457, 467
 courthouse, *490*
Viking Mine, 257
villages, Indian, 35, 36, 37, 39, 70
Vincennes, 6-7, 42, 48, 54, 70, 123, 239, 240, *347, 348, 349, 351, 352,* 457-58, *494*
 capital of Indiana Territory, 46
 fort at, 236
 French settlement at, 40-41, 63, 66
 state capital, 71, 238
 Vincennes University founded, 145
Vincennes Commercial, 178
"Vincennes Junta," 48, 49
Vincennes Trace, 46
Vincennes University, 145, 239, 458
vineyards, 71, 238
Virgil I. Grissom State Memorial, 459
Vonnegut, Kurt, Jr., 60, 154, 167, 211, *233*

Wabash, 6, 57, 125, 459-60, *495, 496*

Wabash College, 242, 294, *344*

Wabash County, 31, 316, 372, 373, 375, 378, 426, 432, 453, 459, 460

courthouse, *495*

Wabash and Erie Canal, 54, 117, 118, 119, 241, 243, 245, 266

Wabash Enquirer, 53

Wabash Lowland, 12, 460

Wabash Railroad, 470

Wabash River, 6, 9, 11, 18, 76, 89, 172, *339*

and canal building, 118, 119

coal mine under, 95

commercial fishing in, 87-88

flood control system, 19

generating facilities on, 99

rampage, 257

upper, 17

Wabash Township, 25

Wabash University, 57

Wabash Valley, lower, 11, 37

Wakarusa, 461

Wakefield, Dan, 167

Waldron, 461

Walkerton, 461

wall-eyed, 268

Wallace, David, 53

Wallace, Lew, 55, 59, 167, 212-13, 249, 252, 293, 294

Wallace, 461

Wallace Circus Farm, 416

walnut, 93-94

Walton, 461

Wanatah, 461-62

War of 1812, 48, 197, 239, 473

War Memorial, Indianapolis, 159, 253

Warnecke, John Carl, 290

Warner, Daniel S., 69

Warren, 462

Warren County, 31, 415, 418, 462, 467, 470

Warrick County, 11, 31, 32, 76, 273, 284, 305, 308, 382, 403, 433, 446, 462

Warsaw, 463

Washington, 297, 463

Washington County, 13, 14, 31, 269, 272, 281, 319, 331, 380, 415, 432, 463

courthouse, *484*

Washington Elementary School, Elwood, *344*

Washington Park, Indianapolis, 168

Watergate scandal, 163

water

quality, 89

resources, 87-89

sub-surface supplies, 89

supply, 18

water milfoil, 21

Waterloo, 463

watershed, St. Lawrence and mississippi, 18

waterways, 88, 118-20, 127-28

Waveland, 464

Waverly, 467

Wawaka, 464

Wawasee, Lake, 464

Wawasee State Fish Hatchery, 464

Way, Amanda, 300

Wayne, Anthony, 39, 45, 46, 213-14, 237, 238

Wayne County, 31, 274, 280, 284, 300, 302, 304, 316, 327, 329, 392, 424, 464

Waynetown, 464-65

Wea Indians, 62

Webster, Daniel, 53

Weedpatch Hill, 13, 278, 465

Weese, Harry, 8, 290

Weir Cook Municipal Airport, 102, 161

Welch, Robert, 163, 257

Wells County, 31, 32, 250, 272, 368, 385, 411, 412, 420, 452, 465, *497*

Wells County Historical Museum, 273

West, Jessamyn, 60

West Baden Springs, 11, 465-66

West College Corner, 466

West Harrison, 466

West Lafayette, 33, 372, 466-67, *497*

West Lebanon, 467

West Terre Haute, 467

Western Presage, 245

Western Sun, 48, 238, 352

Westfield, 466

Westport, 467

Westville, 25, 147, 467

WFBM, 256

wheat, 91

Wheatfield, 467

Wheatland, 467

When Knighthood Was in Flower, 59

Whetzel, Jacob, 240

Whetzel Trace, 467

Whig Party, 53-54

Whirlpool Corporation, 309

Whitcomb, James, 53, 55

White, Albert S., 53

White, Edward, II, 258

White County, 31, 276, 279, 284, 361, 393, 396, 424, 435, 468, 472

White River, 11, 18, 37, 87, 88, 99, 117, 155, 164, 167, 240, 264, 278

Whiteland, 468

Whitestown, 468

Whitewater Canal, 54, 277, 292, 468-69

Whitewater Canal State Memorial, 468-69

Whitewater River, 14, 280, 291, 298, 304, 311, 318, 329, 469

Whitewater State Park, 277, 469

Whiting, 73, 250, 469

Whitley County, 31, 286, 289, 376, 440, 469-70

courthouse, *342*

Whitley County Jail, *341*

Wickard, Claude, R., 258

Wilbur Wright State Memorial, 470

Wilbur Wright State Recreation Area, 470

wildlife, 86, 89. *see also* state wildlife areas

Wiley, Harvey W., *234*

Wilkinson, James, 44

Wilkinson, 470

Williams Dam State Fishing Area, 470

Williamsport, 241, 470-71

Willkie, Herman F., 307

Willkie, Wendell L., 60, 195, 255, 307, 429

Willow Slough State Recreation Area, 471

Winamac, Chief, 471

Winchester, 471

Windfall, 472

Wingate, 472

Winnebago Indians, 38

Winona Bible Conference, 69

Winona Lake, 472

Winslow, 472

winter, temperature in, 19-20

Wolcott, 5, 472

Wolcottville, 472

Wolflake, 472

woman's club, first, 52

women's movement, 176

Women's Prison, 148, 249
women's rights, 53
women's suffrage, 181
Woodburn, 472-73
Woodland Stage, 34, 36
Woodruff Place, 158-159
Workmen's Compensation Act,
    252
World War I, 182, 252
World War II, 183, 205, 211, 255
Worthington, 473
Wright, Frances, 176
Wright, Orville, 214, 470
Wright, Wilbur, 214-15, 470
WRTV, 256
WTTV, 256
Wyandotte, 473

Wyandotte Cave, 11, 294, 295, *498*
Wyandotte Indians, 62, 473

Yamasaki, Minoru, 165
yellow perch, 268
yellow poplar, 1
Yellowwood State Forest, 473
Yoeman, 474
Yorktown, 474
Youngstown Sheet and Tube
    Company, 302-3
Youth Center, Plainfield, 148
Youth Rehabilitation Facility, 148

Zelda Dameron, 202-3
Zionsville, 474
zoning, 153

* * *